LLOYD G. REYNOLDS

Sterling Professor of Economics
Yale University

LABOR ECONOMICS
AND LABOR RELATIONS

fourth edition

Prentice-Hall, Inc., Englewood Cliffs, New Jersey

for ANNE, PENNY, and BRUCE

© 1949, 1954, 1956, 1959, 1964 by Prentice-Hall, Inc., Englewood Cliffs, N.J.

Library of Congress Catalog Card No.: 64-22311

Printed in the United States of America
C-51775

Current printing (last digit):
14   13   12   11   10   9   8   7   6   5

PRENTICE-HALL INTERNATIONAL, INC., *London*
PRENTICE-HALL OF AUSTRALIA, PTY., LTD., *Sydney*
PRENTICE-HALL OF CANADA, LTD., *Toronto*
PRENTICE-HALL OF JAPAN, INC., *Tokyo*
PRENTICE-HALL DE MEXICO, S.A., *Mexico City*
PRENTICE-HALL OF INDIA (PRIVATE) LTD.. *New Delhi*

Preface

*In this edition, as in earlier ones, I have found that re-*vision requires a great deal of rethinking and rewriting. There have been important historical changes in recent years, many new research findings, some developments in analysis, and shifts of priority among policy issues. So while the sequence of chapters is virtually unchanged from the previous edition, the reader will find substantial changes in approach and coverage within many of the chapters.

In Part I it has been necessary to give special attention to the stagnation of union membership in recent years and the question of what this portends for the future; the attempt by the federal government to regulate internal union affairs under the Landrum-Griffin Act; the revival of management initiative and significant changes in management organization for collective bargaining; and the development of important new bargaining issues and techniques, such as protection of workers against displacement through technical change, long-term agreements with automatic wage adjustments, and standing committees for study and negotiation of especially complex issues during the period between contract settlements.

Developments in labor economics which have required increased space in Part II include the gradual upcreep of unemployment rates over the past decade, and the question of how far this is due to deficient aggregate demand as against structural characteristics of the unemployed; the need for retraining programs and improved labor market machinery to move people from labor surplus points to labor shortage points in the economy; the increased attention to investment in "human capital" through education, and the problem of equal educational opportunity; the dynamics of the money wage level and the continuing controversy over cost inflation; the reasons for continuing islands of poverty in a sea of affluence, and the broad strategy of an attack on poverty.

I have tried to eliminate as many pages as I have added, in order to retain the brevity which many users of the book have found advantageous. Some readers may accordingly feel that topics in which they are particularly interested are not discussed at adequate length. It is not possible, however, to combine compactness with encyclopedic treatment, and I have opted deliberately for the former.

It continues to be an open question whether the discussion of unionism and collective bargaining in Part I comes most logically before or after the economic analysis of Part II. There are advantages and disadvantages in either course. I have tried to meet the problem by making each Part a self-contained unit, which does not depend on the other as a prerequisite, making it feasible for users of the book to follow whichever sequence they prefer.

I have profited by advice and help from many quarters: Susan Foster and Joanne Clifford helped with statistical compilations and other background research; Mrs. Olive Higgins bore the brunt of the typing and editing; Mrs. Rudolph Zallinger drew the diagrams; Professor William G. Bowen of Princeton University and Professor David G. Brown of the University of North Carolina made many helpful suggestions for this edition, and Professor George Delehanty of Northwestern University commented in detail on the revised manuscript. I accepted some of their suggestions and resisted others, and am alone responsible for the final outcome.

In addition to those whom I can thank by name, I should like to express appreciation to the many teachers of labor courses throughout the country whose suggestions have contributed so materially to improvement of this book.

L. G. R.

Contents

INTRODUCTION

1 Labor In Industrial Society, 3

*Two Meanings of Labor Problems, 8   Labor Problems of an
Industrial Society, 10   Mechanisms of Adjustment: Institutions and the Market, 15*

PART ONE   TRADE UNIONISM AND COLLECTIVE BARGAINING

2 The Growth Of American Unionism, 25

*Reasons for the Development of Unions, 25   Union Growth
in Modern Times, 28   The Evolution of Union Structure, 31
The Dominance of the National Union, 32   Peak Federations: The American Federation of Labor, 35   The Rise of
Industrial Unionism, 39   Rivalry and Reunion, 1935 to
1955, 40   The Trade Union World Today, 45   Membership
Stagnation and the Future Outlook, 48*

3 Trade Union Philosophy And Objectives, 54

*Trade Unionism and Left-Wing Politics, 55   Trade Union
Participation in Management, 62   Union Objectives in Col-
lective Bargaining, 65   Political Objectives and Tactics, 68
Some General Conclusions, 75*

4 The Government Of Trade Unions, 79

*Managing a National Union, 79   Problems of Union Struc-
ture and Administration, 88   Regulation of Internal Union
Affairs, 97*

v

5   The Legal Framework Of Collective Bargaining, 109

*Judicial Regulation of Union Activities, 110   The Emergence
of a Statute Law of Labor Relations, 117   The Framework
of Collective Bargaining Today, 125   Applying the Law: Unfair Labor Practices, 129   Continuing Issues of Public
Policy, 136*

6   Management's Approach To Collective Bargaining, 141

*The Function and Outlook of Management, 141   Manage-
ment and the Unions: Some Sources of Tension, 148   Organization for Industrial Relations, 153*

7   Bargaining Procedures And Tactics, 159

*The Area of the Collective Agreement, 160   Bargaining Rep-
resentatives and Bargaining Demands, 167   Adjustment of
Grievances, 176   Some Peculiarities of American Collective
Bargaining, 182*

8   Issues In Bargaining: Job Tenure And Job Security, 186

*Control of Hiring: Apprenticeship; the Closed Shop, 188
Compulsory Membership: the Union Shop, 194   Job Tenure:
Security and Opportunity, 198*

9   Issues In Bargaining: Work Schedules, Work Speeds,
And Production Methods, 210

*Hours of Work, 210   Work Speeds and Work Assignments,
216   Production Methods and Employment Opportunities,
224   Physical Conditions of Work, 234*

10   Issues In Bargaining: Wages And Income, 238

*The Market Context: the Firm, 238   The Market Context:
the Industry, 240   Bargaining over the Industry Wage Level,
243   Wage Structure: Inter-Firm Differences in an Industry,
254   Wage Structure: Occupational Wage Relationships, 258
Supplementary Income Payments, 260*

11   Strikes, Strike Tactics, And Strike Prevention, 266

Why Strikes Occur, 266   The Legality of Strikes and Strike

Tactics, 271   What Else Should Government Do? 278   Adjustment of Disputes in Essential Industries, 285

12   The Balance Sheet Of Trade Unionism, 295

Structure of Labor and Product Markets, 296   Money Wages and the Price Level, 299   Real Wages and the Distribution of National Income, 300   Unionism and Relative Wage Rates, 304   Non-Wage Benefits and Their Cost, 305   Social Structure of the Shop, 308   Status of the Individual Worker, 310   Balance of Political Power in the Community, 312   Is Unionism a Good Idea? 313

PART TWO   ECONOMICS OF THE LABOR MARKET

13   Dynamics Of Labor Supply, Employment, And Unemployment, 317

Some Questions About Labor Supply and the Labor Market, 318   Participation in the Labor Force, 320   Level and Composition of Employment, 328   Volume and Characteristics of Unemployment, 338

14   Reduction And Control Of Unemployment, 345

Sources of Unemployment, 345   Lines of Action: Seasonal and Casual Unemployment, 349   Lines of Action: Frictional Unemployment, 351   Lines of Action: Demand Unemployment, 354   Financing Unavoidable Unemployment: Unemployment Compensation Systems, 356   Continuing Problems of Unemployment Compensation, 364

15   Labor Mobility And Labor Market Policy, 371

Movement Within an Area, 374   Geographical Movement, 386   Movement Up the Occupational Ladder, 390

16   Money Wages And The Price Level, 405

The Meaning of Wages, 406   A Century of Rising Wages, 413   Money Wages and the Price Level, 420   Issues of Wage-Price Policy, 428   Money Wages and Employment, 432

17   Productivity, Real Wages, And Labor's Share Of
     National Income, 438

         *Inputs, Output, and Productivity, 438   Distribution of Na-
         tional Output, 446*

18   The National Wage Structure, 462

         *Influence of Occupational Level on Earnings, 463   Explana-
         tion of Occupational Wage Differences, 469   Wage Differ-
         ences within an Occupation, 476   Concluding Comments,
         485*

19   Wage Determination At The Plant Level, 488

         *General Wage Level of the Plant, 488   The Nature of Wage
         Policy, 495   The Impact of Collective Bargaining, 501   De-
         termination of Occupational Wage Rates, 503*

20   Family Income, Inequality, And Poverty, 510

         *Distribution of Family Incomes, 511   Trends in Inequality,
         513   The Extent of Poverty, 519   Strategy of an Attack on
         Poverty, 523   Eliminating Substandard Wages: Minimum
         Wage Legislation, 525   Income Security: Role of Social In-
         surance Systems, 531   Low-Cost Provision of Social Necessi-
         ties, 535*

EPILOGUE

21   Issues For This Generation, 541

         *A High Level of Employment, 542   Improved Labor Market-
         ing, 546   Equal Job Opportunities Through Education, 548
         Equal Opportunities for Negro Workers, 552   Eliminating
         Pockets of Poverty, 553   Improving the Framework of Col-
         lective Bargaining, 555*

     Index, 558

INTRODUCTION

1

Labor in Industrial Society

The problems with which this book is concerned are historically rare. Throughout human history most of the world's population has worked the land. The town dwellers were in earlier times largely slaves, in more recent times independent traders and artisans. Situations in which many people work for wages in large production units have arisen only within the past two centuries.

Even today most of the world's population remains in the pre-industrial era. In most countries of Asia, Africa, and Latin America, 60 to 80 per cent of the labor force is engaged in agriculture. The remainder are mainly petty traders, service workers, or artisans producing goods in their own small workshops. Only a tiny fraction of the population work in factories and other modern enterprises. Some countries are working hard to change this situation and to enlarge the industrial sector; but success is still uncertain, and at best will require decades of effort.

The great transformation which ushered in the industrial society began in Great Britain in the period 1750-1880. During the nineteenth century the movement spread to a dozen other countries. Accelerated industrial development can be dated, for example, from about 1830 in France, Belgium, and the United States, 1850 in Germany, 1870 in Sweden and Japan, 1890 in Canada and Russia. During the first half of this century Australia, New Zealand, South Africa, several countries of Latin America, and most of southern and eastern Europe joined the procession. The list of heavily industrialized nations will certainly be longer by the year 2000, but one cannot

3

foresee just *which* countries will succeed in breaking into the charmed circle.

Today's industrial countries differ widely in size, climate, geographic characteristics, language and cultural traditions, and form of government. Yet they also have many features in common. Similarities in the economic matrix give labor problems a family resemblance throughout the industrial world. These common features include:

1. THE PATTERN OF EMPLOYMENT. Most of the labor force is employed in manufacturing, construction, public utilities, and government. Agriculture employs only a declining minority; and while employment in trade remains substantial, trade is carried on increasingly by mass distributors rather than small shopkeepers. The economy is characterized by large production units, which employ hundreds or thousands of people and often use large amounts of capital equipment per worker. Occupations are highly specialized and diversified, with many jobs requiring substantial skill and training. Many people work in clerical, technical, and professional occupations, and this white-collar segment of the labor force grows considerably faster than the blue-collar segment. A description of the United States? Yes, but a description also of Sweden, the U.S.S.R., and Japan.

2. THE LEVEL OF OUTPUT AND INCOMES. Large, capital-intensive production units applying modern technology yield high output per worker, and this provides higher real incomes and living standards. This accounts for the mystique of industrialization throughout the underdeveloped world. One can argue over how much more the American worker produces than the Soviet worker. But there is no doubt that each produces more than the average worker in Uganda or Indonesia. A large and growing national output, of course, may produce controversy over the division of the gains. How much should go to employees as against the owners of capital? How much should go to each group of wage and salary earners? These issues are more intense under industrialism than in a static, agricultural society where incomes are assigned by tradition and paternal authority.

3. THE DEPENDENT STATUS OF EMPLOYEES. From one standpoint, the shift from self-employed farmer or artisan to employed wage earner liberates the individual. He is free to move about in search of work, to better himself, to work his way up the occupational ladder. But in other ways it reduces his independence. The wage earner must find work in order to live, while the farmer can always live after a fashion from his own output; and when he is employed

the details of his work are closely regulated. Someone else specifies the times at which work is to be done, the nature of the task, the materials and equipment to be used, the pace of work, and the expected quantity and quality of output. Above the worker stand all the layers of management, from first-line supervisor to company president.

4. ADMINISTRATION AND THE WEB OF RULES. Dependence does not stop with the worker. The supervisor is himself under higher authority, and so are the general foreman, the plant superintendent, and the vice-president in charge of production. Even the company president is responsible to a board of directors. A large enterprise is bound together by an elaborate hierarchy of authority, which specifies the powers and responsibilities of everyone from company president to laborer.

It is bound together also by a network of rules governing output and cost targets; products, equipment, and production methods; types and amount of compensation; employment, promotion, discharge; and many other things. At a particular time most of these rules are taken as fixed, and changes are occurring only at the margin; so one is apt not to realize their extent and complexity. But reading a fifty-page union contract reminds one how complicated the internal government of a large business can be. When we say that the industrial worker must learn discipline, we mean that he must know and observe this web of rules, in addition to submitting to the personal authority of the supervisor.

5. WORKER PROTEST AND LABOR ORGANIZATION. Workers new to industry often find it difficult to submit to rules which they have had no hand in creating, and which may appear harsh and arbitrary. So the early stages of industrialization are usually attended by labor unrest and spontaneous individual protest. This may show up in high absenteeism and turnover, disobedience to the foreman, and underperformance on the job. There may also be sporadic strikes and riots by large numbers of workers. This was common in early British and American industry, and is common today in the newly industrializing countries.

Eventually, however, protest is channeled into continuing organizations and takes a more effective if less violent form. Prominent among these organizations are the trade unions, whose tactics normally include both political action and defense of the workers' interests in the plant. Fitting trade unions into the social structure, and

defining their functions relative to those of industrial management
and of government, is a characteristic problem of industrial society.

6. INSECURITY AND MOBILITY. An industrial economy is by definition a changing economy. Products, methods of production, the location of industry, and the demand for specific skills are in constant
flux. Without these changes the economy cannot continue to advance
to ever-higher levels of productivity and income.

These dynamic shifts keep open the frontier of opportunity. The
new plants and industries are typically more efficient than those which
they supplant. They provide more productive jobs at higher wages.
But the opposite side of the coin is a high degree of personal insecurity. Plants fail and are shut down, products and services become
obsolete, jobs disappear through technical change, locational shifts
leave stranded populations in depressed areas. The worker has to be
quick on his feet to avoid being stranded and to seize new opportunities as they appear. Even if he is quick and lucky, this enforced job-
hopping involves anxiety and dissatisfaction, and it leads workers and
unions to be preoccupied with the problem of job security.

7. THE PERVASIVENESS OF LABOR MARKETS. Under slavery or feudalism workers can be ordered to the places where they are needed. But
in a complex industrial economy coercion is inefficient, quite apart
from its infringement on human dignity and independence. Even in
planned economies, direct allocations of workers to jobs has been
used only in periods of national emergency. The general rule is that
each worker hunts his own jobs and each plant recruits its own
workers. Employers use wages as the main magnet for attracting labor,
and income is a major consideration in workers' minds when choosing
jobs. There are markets for labor, though usually not very efficient
ones. The wage for each kind of labor is heavily influenced, if not
fully determined, by supply and demand conditions in the market.
This is what brings the study of labor into touch with the central
core of economic theory.

In stressing the resemblance among industrial economies, one should
not overlook important points of difference. There are differences, for
example, in the strength and activities of trade unions. There are
differences also in the balance of power among unions, industrial
managers, and government officials. In some countries management
still lays down the rules of industrial employment with little hin-
drance from any source. In others management is forced to negotiate
with strong unions but is largely free of government control. In still

others government participates actively in setting the terms of employment, and in some countries it has the dominant voice. This point will be elaborated in a moment.

The focus of this book is on the labor problems of *mature* industrial economies. We shall not say much in later chapters about the problems which arise during the early stages of industrialization in so-called underdeveloped countries, so a few comments are in order at this point.

New industries in a primarily agricultural economy have a problem of labor *recruitment*; but this is not very difficult. There is usually a surplus of underemployed labor in agriculture, and also in trade and service occupations in the cities. Modern industry is so productive that it can afford to offer wages well above what people have been used to receiving; and most factory work is also lighter and pleasanter than agricultural labor. This makes it easy to persuade people to transfer to industrial employment. It is sometimes harder to get them to stay steadily in the new job. In parts of Africa, for example, there is a tradition of single men migrating to the cities, working until they have accumulated a certain amount of money, and then returning to the native village. But this tradition can be broken gradually by persuading whole families to move to the city, which requires mainly provision of housing and other urban facilities.

Having recruited a labor force, the employer faces a problem of *training*. This problem is more severe than in a mature industrial country because the worker, in addition to learning job skills, must become habituated to the pace and discipline of factory work. This takes time and effort. Most managers in these countries seem to underestimate the need for training and to invest too little effort in it.

One can distinguish also a problem of labor *productivity*. Productivity depends partly on the strength, intelligence, training, and motivation of the worker. But more importantly it depends on tools and equipment, job set-up, supervision, and personnel policies. New industrial managements often fail to put enough thought and effort into developing effective foremen and supervisors. And they often follow personnel policies which assume (misguidedly) that their workers are unresponsive to economic incentives. Improvement of supervision and personnel policies can often produce remarkable gains in productivity. There is truth in the saying that "there are no labor problems—only management problems."

From a national standpoint, the newly developing countries face important problems of *wage policy*. Wages at the outset of industrialization are low, and modern factory industries, with efficient management, can earn large profits. Part of the profits may be consumed by the owners, but part is reinvested in plant expansion, and part may be taxed away to support public development expenditures. But the workers are likely to demand that profits be transferred to them in higher wages; and since they typically lack effective unions, they will work through political channels to get minimum wage legislation, social security legislation, and so on. How far government can or should resist these pressures in the interest of greater capital investment is a major issue of development policy.

Union-management relations are not a major problem area in early industrialism. Where unions exist at all, they are usually weak and impermanent, poorly financed, often led by lawyers or white-collar intellectuals without industrial experience. Influence over politics and legislation is apt to be their main objective, and unions are in fact often organized along political lines—communist unions, socialist unions, nationalist unions, and so on. They can mount impressive protest meetings and short, violent strikes; but they cannot hold workers out long enough to bargain effectively with employers. Development of stable unions with real bargaining power seems to require several decades of industrial experience.

After this brief detour, let us come back to define the problems of mature industrialism with which this book is mainly concerned.

TWO MEANINGS OF LABOR PROBLEMS

The term "labor problems" is ambiguous, because it can mean either the personal problems of the individual worker, or the general economic and social problems arising from industrial employment. At a personal level, one can ask what problems the worker encounters in his everyday life on the job and what he thinks should be done about them. It is important to understand the worker's outlook and values, because these condition his labor market behavior, his reaction to management policies, and his participation or nonparticipation in union activity.

The typical worker, like the average man, is of course a fiction. Workers may be men or women, old or young, skilled or unskilled, mobile or sedentary, of high intelligence or low intelligence. A multitude of personal characteristics, as well as the nature of the job he is doing, will influence the worker's perception of his problems.

Despite this diversity of temperament and experience, one can make a few generalizations. Most workers by the time they reach twenty-five or thirty have accepted the probability that they will remain workers and may not rise much above their present occupational level. Moreover, they usually show a strong desire to stay with the same employer. The worker's primary drive is toward security— of employment, of income, of residence. He believes that there are always more workers than jobs, that unemployment is lurking around the corner, and that the safe course is to dig firmly into his present position.

This preoccupation with security does not mean that the worker is uninterested in progress; but progress to him has a limited and concrete meaning. It does not mean anything so intangible as increased productivity and output in the economy as a whole, or even in the plant where he is employed. These things are not his responsibility. To the typical worker, progress does not even mean shifting to a better employer or to a higher job with the same employer. It means rather an improvement in the conditions of his present job—a wage increase, a reduction of hours, a more agreeable foreman, a slower pace of work, better physical conditions, and so on. He usually expects to be on his present job for as far ahead as he can see. The things which he wants, therefore, he must get on his present job; and he wants them, not at some time in the future, but here and now.

The main criteria which workers use in appraising a job as good or bad may be grouped in three categories: (1) relations with one's immediate supervisor, including protection against arbitrary treatment; (2) the nature of the work itself, including the strenuousness and speed of the work, physical working conditions, hours, and shift arrangements; (3) the level of wage rates and weekly earnings. The relative importance of these factors varies greatly from one situation to the next. In a particular plant, one condition may be so unsatisfactory that it assumes preponderant importance in workers' minds; in other plants, this factor may be of minor importance.

Though it is important to understand these characteristic worker reactions, they can scarcely be taken as a safe guide to economic policy. Some things which the worker perceives as problems may be so firmly rooted in the structure of an industrial economy that one cannot speak of solutions in any fundamental sense. Other problems which are important for the over-all functioning of the economy may not be perceived at all by the individual worker. Some of the solutions which the worker desires may be utopian or may impose excessive burdens on other members of the community.

LABOR PROBLEMS OF AN INDUSTRIAL SOCIETY

So it is necessary to probe deeper. What can we identify as "labor problems" in a general economic sense? What issues are of sufficient importance to the whole community that they must be resolved if an industrial society is to operate peaceably and efficiently? At least seven major issues can be distinguished:

1. MAINTAINING ADEQUATE TOTAL DEMAND FOR LABOR. This is a chronic problem for economies in the early stages of industrialization, which usually have a surplus of underemployed labor in agriculture. It is a recurrent problem for industrialized capitalist economies, whose growth is interrupted occasionally by general depression. Depression cuts national output and reduces the incomes of workers along with those of most other people. It usually means a sharp reduction of new investment, the major source of economic progress and higher living standards. It reduces the opportunity for people to change jobs and make occupational progress. It leads to adoption of unwise government policies, which are presented with plausible arguments as depression remedies.

For these reasons almost everyone now subscribes to "full employment" as an economic goal. But how full is "full"? Does full employment mean an average of 2 per cent of the labor force unemployed between jobs, or an average of 5 per cent? Does it mean trying to maintain about as many vacant jobs as there are unemployed workers, or an actual excess of vacancies? The higher the employment target, the more likely it is that there will be consistent upward pressure on the price level. Should one worry more about unemployment or about inflation? One can scarcely expect union leaders to give the same answer as pensioners or insurance executives.

2. DEVELOPING EFFECTIVE LABOR MARKETS. Ours is a market economy. To a greater degree than most other countries we have succeeded in establishing free choice of occupation by individuals,

free choice of goods by consumers, and free access to markets by businessmen. The market mechanism is far from ideal, however, and labor markets are less efficient than most others.

Workers presently market their labor under serious handicaps of ignorance, misinformation, and uncertainty. Employers are not much better off in their effort to locate the best workers available. Job hunting will always be something of a game of blindman's buff because of the innate complexity of the employment process. It should be possible, however, to enlarge and improve the state employment services and to find other ways of raising the plane of competition in the labor market. A better matching of individual capacities with job requirements would improve productive efficiency and increase national output.

Efficient labor marketing is needed in any economy, developed or underdeveloped, capitalist or communist. Russia has had a continuing problem of getting workers to move to the places where new industries are expanding and to stay on the job in those places. Labor turnover has remained high despite all efforts to discourage it. Compulsory controls over the movement of labor have not been enforced seriously except in wartime. For the most part each Russian plant manager has to compete for labor in the market, using a package of wage and nonwage incentives somewhat similar to that of the capitalist employer.

3. TRAINING, ORGANIZING, AND MOTIVATING THE LABOR FORCE. The labor market is supposed to achieve a distribution of the labor force among industries, plants, and localities which corresponds to the detailed pattern of demand for labor. But this is only a first step. Workers as they come through the hiring office are a conglomerate of isolated individuals, not a working team. They have to be trained, organized, supervised, and motivated to perform efficiently in the production process. They must be subjected to a new network of rules and controls, a new industrial discipline quite unlike that of an agricultural society.

The importance and generality of this problem has been well stated by Kerr and Siegel:

The process of industrialization may then be seen as involving in the productive sector the addition or the changing of a complex body of working rules . . . concerned with the recruitment of a labor force, with the training of that labor force in the myriad skills required by the advanced division of labor, with the locating of workers in some appropriate pattern of geographical, industrial, and occupational dispersion. It involves the setting of rules on times to work and not to work, on pace and quality of work, on method and amount of pay, on movement into and out of work and from one position to another. It involves rules pertaining to the maintenance of continuity in the work process (so intimately related to the maintenance of stability in the society)—the attempted minimization of individual or organized revolt, the provision of views of the world, of ideological orientations, of beliefs, the introduction of some checks on the individual insecurity inherent in an industrial order. The structuring of this web of rule must be undertaken regardless of the form of industrialization, in Russia and the United States alike.[1]

4. DETERMINING WAGE RATES AND LABOR INCOME. This set of rules has such a venerable tradition in economics that it may be singled out for special mention. The wage problem comprises at least four subproblems:

a. *Determining the general wage level.* Within the enterprise, how much of sales revenue can fairly be claimed by labor as against other operating expenses and profits? When should the company's wage level be raised, and on what grounds? Looking at the economy as a whole, what should be the level of money wages and real wages? What is a proper split-up between labor and property incomes? How fast should the national wage level be raised over the course of time, and why?

b. *Determining relative wage rates for different types of work.* How is the national wage total to be divided among the individuals comprising the labor force? Within a particular plant or industry, should the most skilled job pay 20 per cent more than the least skilled, or 50 per cent more, or 100 per cent more? Should some industries pay higher wages than others, and how much higher? Should workers earn more in some geographical regions than in others, or more in large cities than in small towns? The relationship among wages in different occupations, industries, and areas is commonly termed the problem of "wage structure" or "wage differentials."

c. *Deciding the method of wage payment.* The leading issue here is between payment on the basis of hours worked and payment on the basis of output ("piece work" or "incentive" payment). This issue arouses strong feeling among workers and is decided differently in different industries and countries. Piece rate payment is used more

---

[1] Clark Kerr and Abraham Siegel, "The Structuring of the Labor Force in Industrial Society: New Dimensions and New Questions," *Industrial and Labor Relations Review*, VIII (January 1955), p. 163.

widely in Russia than in the United States. Within the United States, some industries use piece rate payment exclusively while others do not use it at all.

d. *Deciding the form of workers' income receipts.* The national wage bill may go almost entirely into direct wage payments, or a substantial share may go into old age pensions, family allowances, medical and hospital services, unemployment compensation, and other indirect benefits. In some European countries these indirect benefits are one-third to one-half as large as direct wage payments. In the United States, where they are less fully developed, the proportion is approaching one-fifth.

5. BALANCING PRODUCER AND CONSUMER SATISFACTIONS. There is an obvious conflict of interest between the workers engaged in producing a particular product and the consumers of the product. It is to the workers' interest to work short hours, at a leisurely pace, amid pleasant surroundings, and to receive high wages plus ample fringe benefits. These things raise costs, however, and must be paid for by consumers through higher prices. How can one strike a proper balance between the interests of the two groups?

Wage earners, moreover, form close to half of the consuming public and salary earners another quarter. There is thus a conflict of interest *within* the wage and salary group. People can work longer and harder as producers in order to enjoy more goods as consumers, or they can take things easier and consume less.

Two "automatic" solutions of this problem appear in economic writings. The independent producer consuming his own product— Crusoe on his island—can presumably strike a direct balance between effort and consumption. He can judge the point at which the effort of knocking down another coconut or catching another fish would outweigh the satisfaction from eating it. Subsistence farmers, who form a large part of the world's population, are in much the same situation.

In a complex industrial society, it can be argued that the problem is still solved by the normal working of the labor market. Each worker, by choosing his employer and occupation, can get long hours or short hours, heavy work or easy work, pleasant or disagreeable conditions. Greater effort or unpleasantness will presumably have to be compensated by higher wages. The worker will choose the combination of wages and working conditions that best meets his personal preferences.

There is something to this line of argument, but one should not rely on it too heavily. The labor market is a rather blunt instrument even for determining relative wage rates. It is even less adequate for determining optimum hours, proper work speeds, and desirable working conditions. Despite our best efforts to improve the market mechanism, it will remain necessary to supplement it by institutional regulation.

6. PROTECTING AGAINST PREDICTABLE RISKS. The industrial worker depends heavily on a regular flow of money income. This dependence is increasing with the growth of credit facilities and installment buying. Anything which cuts off the weekly paycheck threatens not only the worker's dinner table but also his house, car, furniture, and household appliances.

The reasons why the stream of income may fail are well known and many of them are predictable. It is certain that everyone must grow old, and probable life spans can be predicted fairly precisely. These are good figures on the incidence of industrial accidents and on various types of disabling illness. We know that there is a certain minimum of unemployment even in good years. It seems sheerest common sense to develop ways of protecting workers' incomes against such contingencies. This not only benefits the people concerned but also increases the stability of the economy. There is room for argument over the desirable level of protection, the proper balance betwen private insurance funds and government systems, and how much of the cost should be borne by workers as against employers or consumers. The need for a comprehensive network of protective measures, however, is no longer seriously questioned.

7. ASSURING A MINIMUM LEVEL OF LIVING. There is also increasing consensus that no member of the community should be allowed to fall below some minimum level of subsistence. Social security and private insurance systems, minimum wage legislation, farm income supplements, and state and local relief systems are all expressions of this concern. Arguments are not so much over principle as over feasible support levels and detailed institutional arrangements.

This issue is usually discussed in a labor course because it touches many wage-earning families. But it is not exclusively or even mainly a problem of manual workers. The group below the poverty line also includes rural families living on inferior land, who have lower living standards than any sizeable group in the urban population; broken homes containing no wage earner, or in which the principal wage earner is disabled; and many older people drawn from all occupational levels. Inability to work and produce, rather than low wage levels, is now the main source of poverty in the United States.

MECHANISMS OF ADJUSTMENT: INSTITUTIONS AND THE MARKET

Two main mechanisms are available for resolving these issues—the competitive labor market, and institutional rules imposed by business concerns, trade unions, and government. Though these may be regarded as alternatives at a theoretical level, in practice they will always be found operating together. Even Russia, which might seem to be an extreme case of government control, has important elements of a competitive labor market. Individual establishments recruit labor as best they can, workers move about the country in search of better jobs, occupational and regional wage differentials are adjusted to lure workers to the places where labor is scarcest.

One should not assume either that market forces and institutional rules necessarily conflict. They may do so, but they may also work in the same direction and institutional regulation may simply ratify a market decision. We shall argue in Chapter 10 that this is largely true of wage determination in the United States. Both the general wage level and relative wage rates for different jobs are determined mainly by supply and demand pressures in the labor market. Unions largely take credit for wage increases that were "in the cards" on economic grounds. It is politically necessary for a union to do this, just as it is necessary for whichever party holds power in Washington to take credit for business prosperity which it may have done little to create. But the fact that under collective bargaining the union is entitled to *announce* a wage increase does not constitute evidence that it *caused* the increase.

The question of how far labor conditions are or should be determined by institutional rules as against market pressures rouses strong emotions and leads people into extreme positions. One school of thought tends to glorify the market, to assert that it does or could adequately regulate terms of employment, and that institutional "interference" is bound to be either ineffective or harmful. At the other pole, some people write off the market as ineffective and defend the necessity and beneficence of institutional controls. Reality is certainly more complicated than these extreme views would suggest.

The labor market seems to perform some functions quite effectively, while in other areas its performance is less satisfactory. Starting with as little bias as possible, we must try to discover where the market performs well and where it breaks down, to explain why the relative importance of market and institutional regulation differs from country to country and time to time, and to analyze what happens when the two mechanisms pull in opposite directions. This is the task of the whole book; but a few preliminary comments will help to set the stage.

The role of the labor market

Elementary economics texts describe the operation of a competitive labor market and the results it might be expected to yield. The broad argument is that, given free and informed competition among workers and employers, each worker must be paid the value of his contribution to production. He cannot be paid more, because the employer could not continue to operate. He will not be paid less, because the employer would be making abnormal profits and some other alert businessman would enter the industry and bid up the price of labor. There is thus little scope for controversy or bargaining over the price of labor.

This is of course a very simplified and idealized picture. It assumes many small employers competing for labor, no collusion among employers or workers, adequate channels of information, and a number of other things. It is no secret that actual labor markets depart considerably from this competitive ideal. Many employers are large and the worker's choice is often restricted to one or a few companies; employers often get together on wage rates and on policies which make it hard for workers to change employers; channels of information are poor and there is no effective central clearinghouse for labor; the exchange of a machinist's labor for a "package" of wages and working conditions is a more complicated transaction than setting a price on a loaf of bread; workers dislike changing jobs and, when forced to do so, they hunt new jobs in a haphazard and ill-informed way; during periods of heavy unemployment the worker's bargaining power—which depends basically on his power to change jobs—is seriously reduced.

Despite these deficiencies, the labor market is a reasonably effective instrument both for determining relative wage rates and for raising the general wage level as national output rises. The great increase in real wages in the United States over the past century has not been due in any large measure to collective bargaining or government decree. It has occurred mainly because employers were able and impelled to keep raising their wage offers in the market year after year: able because development of new machinery and production methods was steadily increasing output per man-hour; impelled because the labor market forces each employer to bid against others to hold his share of the labor supply. The labor market is the main mechanism by which increases in productivity have been translated into higher wages and living standards.

The market also does reasonably well in determining relative wage levels for different plants, industries, occupations, and regions. One can always find many queer or inequitable wages rates; but viewed broadly and over the long run, the national wage structure is not unreasonable. Moreover, it is evolving over the course of time in a way which is understandable on economic grounds. Wage inequalities of every sort are diminishing and this is due mainly, though not exclusively, to changing supply and demand conditions.

Finally, the labor market is the only device we have for sorting out many millions of workers with varying skills and interests among the multitude of different jobs in the economy. Any attempt to do this by administrative methods, in addition to encroaching on personal liberty, would be hopelessly cumbersome and inefficient. Even communist countries, as noted earlier, rely mainly on wage inducements in the market to secure a desirable allocation of the labor force.

Recognition that the labor market does some things well, however, should not blind us to the things which it does poorly or cannot do at all. It is not highly effective, for example, in regulating working conditions—physical conditions, safety and sanitation, work speeds, treatment by supervisors, and other personnel policies. The market still sets limits in the sense that, if plant conditions become too bad, workers have the option of leaving. But these limits may be quite wide. Working conditions are hard for the market to evaluate and control because they are intangible, qualitative, hard for the worker to discover before he is on the job, and hard to bargain about on an individual basis. Workers conclude that the effective remedy is not individual bargaining or quitting (the market solution) but group pressure through a union.

The market cannot provide security against arbitrary demotion or discharge by supervisors, nor can it establish equitable rules concerning layoff, rehiring, and promotion. These require administrative procedures within the enterprise. The market is not very good at bringing about marked changes in employment practice, such as a shift from a ten-hour to an eight-hour day. It is not good at establishing minimum standards which, in order to survive, must be enforced on all employers simultaneously. Examples are rules concerning work by women and children, safety and health standards, and minimum wage legislation. Nor is it a good device in areas where there are substantial economies in collective action. Pensions, unemployment compensation, and other income security devices could be set up entirely by individual employers and, if enough employers adopted them, the market might force others to follow. There are clear economies, however, in applying insurance principles to the entire labor force through government security programs. Finally, the labor market obviously cannot improve itself. Organized effort is required to mitigate the structural defects noted earlier and to enable the market to perform its natural functions better.

An important and irremovable source of difficulty is that most workers regard resort to the market—i.e., a change of employers— as a disaster rather than an opportunity. They typically want to continue with their present employer. Advice that they can improve their employer's behavior by leaving him they regard as academic. They prefer to change the employer's behavior without leaving him, and for this they need union organization.

The place of institutional rules

Organizational rules may be imposed to override market determinations which are displeasing to workers or employers. More importantly, however, they are a way of reaching decisions at points where the market is imprecise or ineffective. They supplement the market mechanism at least as much as they compete with it.

The main contenders for rule-making authority are the business firm, the trade union, and the state. Adherents of each of these often regard it as the normal rule-making body, entitled in principle to exclusive authority. Many businessmen still regard management as the proper group to decide on terms of employment and resent "outside interference" by unions or government. To the trade unionist, it is an article of faith that conditions of employment should be regulated by union-management agreement. Socialists tend to regard government as the logical guardian of workers' welfare.

Looking at the world as a whole, however, it is clear that no one system of rule-making can be regarded as inevitable. This point has been cogently argued by Kerr and Siegel:

Given these three contestants, there are seven general systems for distributing the essential power to make rules governing the labor force. Three of these possible rule-making relationships may be designated as monistic, in the sense that the rules . . . are set primarily by one of the contestants. . . . (1) The employer may set the rules, and . . . may follow a policy of paternalism, as in Japan before World War II, or a policy of forced worker self-dependence, as in England in the early period of industrialization. A conceivable, though much less likely actual possibility is that (2) the worker may give the directions. His "union" then becomes more or less of a producers' cooperative (as in sectors of the Israeli economy). . . . (3) The state may issue the commands, as it does in Russia and in all the nations within the Russian orbit. The "unions" there are essentially "agents of the state" with only such authority as may be granted them by the state.

Three additional systems may be called dualistic, since two of the contestants share rule-making power in the industrial sector. (4) This power may be shared, as in the United States prior to the recent rise in state interest, primarily by the employer and the unions whose relationships may range from reserved tolerance to secret collusion. (5) Or the employer and the state may divide the authority between them. The power of the state may be ranged alongside that of the employer, as in Nazi Germany, or in opposition, as in Mexico or Argentina or Guatemala in recent years; or the state may vacillate back and forth as in France and Italy. . . . (6) Or the state and the worker may participate jointly in rule-making, as in the nationalized industries in Great Britain.

Finally (7), the three contestants may share rule-making power in a pluralistic system . . . as evidenced in Scandinavia, the United States, and several of the member nations of the British Commonwealth.[2]

This last situation, where all three parties have a finger in the pie, seems to be characteristic of countries with a long history of democratic government and industrial development. This group includes the Scandinavian countries, the Netherlands, West Germany, Britain, Canada, the United States, Australia, and a few others. Taking the world as a whole, it is an exceptional rather than a typical situation, though a number of other countries—France, Italy, Mexico, Japan, India—may evolve gradually in the same direction.

Though all three groups share rule-making power in these econ-

---

[2] Kerr and Siegel, "The Structuring of Labor Force," p. 163.

omies, each has certain areas of decision within which it has a comparative advantage and therefore a preponderant voice. Even in strongly unionized economies management retains a large measure of administrative authority. It typically has exclusive control over, or at least the right to take initial action concerning, production organization, production methods, production volume and labor requirements, recruitment and hiring of labor, assignment of workers to specific jobs, appointment of supervisors, determination of work speeds, establishment of shop rules and application of penalties for violating them, layoffs, and other personnel matters. Management acts; the union protests or appeals. The union may eventually secure a reversal of the decision, but the power to act retains much of its pristine potency.

The specific function of unionism is to police in-plant decisions and actions of management. This means negotiating a general framework of rules within which management action is confined (the union contract) and insuring equitable application of these rules to individual cases (the grievance procedure). Rules concerning the conditions under which a worker may be penalized, demoted, or discharged are of prime importance, as are rules concerning layoffs, rehiring, promotion, and other matters of job tenure. Though unions also do much to influence wages and working conditions, their distinctive function is to establish a system of industrial jurisprudence through which the individual can seek redress from harmful decisions by management.

Government has a comparative advantage in establishing minimum standards which are considered sufficiently important that they should be enforced on everyone. This may mean either bringing laggards up to the market level or establishing standards in areas where the market is not very effective. Government is an efficient mechanism for devising protection against loss of income through unemployment, old age, total or partial disability, and other causes. It is now generally agreed that government has responsibility for maintaining adequate total demand for labor. Finally, only government can prescribe rules to govern union and employer conduct in collective bargaining.

Solutions or working compromises?

Labor problems, whether conceived in the sense of individual workers' problems or of over-all social objectives, cannot be "solved" as one might solve a problem in mathematics. This is partly because a dynamic industrial society is constantly changing, so that rules and institutions are always in need of repair and improvement. More fundamentally, it is because workers' perceived interests conflict at certain points with those of other groups in the economy. In such cases, controversy is natural and even healthy. One can arrive only at working compromises which the parties are willing to accept for the time being, and which are subject to continual renegotiation and revision. An honest treatment of labor, therefore cannot attempt to teach a fixed set of solutions, which may appear to work well today but which may be inappropriate a generation from now. Its purpose is rather to explain why interests and attitudes conflict, how these conflicts are compromised through market and institutional channels, how the agreed-on compromises have changed over the course of time, and what new issues are emerging for the future. If the student can learn to think in relativistic, expedient, historical terms rather than in terms of unchanging rules, the course will have served its purpose.

Discussion questions

1. What features of modern industrialism give rise to labor problems? What kinds of labor problem might arise even in a purely agricultural economy?

2. "Manning new industries in an undeveloped country requires active measures by both employers and government." Explain.

3. During the nineteenth century some writers predicted that, with the growth of industry, the population would soon consist mainly of manual workers. Why has this not happened?

4. "Development of strong trade unions usually takes a half century or more after the appearance of modern industry." Do you agree? If so, what reasons can you give for the slow development of union strength?

5. What are the main elements in the manual worker's conception of a "good job"?

6. What are the principal "labor problems" in a general social sense? Would you expect these problems to differ substantially in the United States, the U.S.S.R., Japan?

7. Why is the labor market usually supplemented by institutional rules in determining wages and conditions of employment?

8. "The operation of the labor market has done more over the past century to improve wages and working conditions in the United States than trade unions and government together." Discuss.

Selected reading

Bergson, Abram, *The Soviet Economy*. New Haven: Yale University Press, 1964.

Galenson, Walter, ed., *Labor and Economic Development*. New York: John Wiley & Sons, Inc., 1959.

————, *Labor in Developing Economies*. Berkeley: University of California Press, 1962.

International Labor Office, *Employment Objectives in Economic Development*. Geneva, 1961.

Kerr, C., J. Dunlop, C. Myers, and F. Harbison, *Industrialism and Industrial Man*. Cambridge: Harvard University Press, 1960.

Moore, Wilbert E., and Arnold S. Feldman, eds., *Labor Commitment and Social Change in Developing Areas*. New York: Social Science Research Council, 1960.

Phelps Brown, E. H., *The Economics of Labor*. New Haven: Yale University Press, 1962.

I

TRADE UNIONISM AND COLLECTIVE BARGAINING

2

The Growth of American Unionism

More than fifty years ago Sidney and Beatrice Webb
defined a trade union as "a continuous association of wage earners
for the purpose of maintaining or improving the conditions of their
working lives." This chapter is concerned with the development of
such associations in the United States since their origin around the
year 1790.

REASONS FOR THE DEVELOPMENT OF UNIONS

The history of American unionism is frequently dated from 1792,
when a local union was formed by the journeymen cordwainers (shoemakers) of Philadelphia. Within the next ten years unions of
shoemakers, carpenters, and printers were founded in Baltimore, Philadelphia, Boston, New York, and several other cities.

What accounts for the appearance of these associations? They cannot be traced to particular oppression of workers at that time. On the
contrary, most workers were better off in 1800 than they had been in
1780. It is significant also that unions did not appear at first among
the most exploited groups—the cotton mill workers, and home workers
on piece rates—but among skilled tradesmen, such as the printers, carpenters, and shoemakers. In the United States, as in most other
industrial countries, the relatively skilled and prosperous workers
organized first. The first unions in Great Britain, for example, consisted of building and printing trades workers, who were followed

shortly afterward by unions of tailors and wool combers. The prosperous condition of the wool combers is indicated by the fact that
they normally came to work in top hats and long coats. In Sweden,
the first unions were formed by the printers, the next by the carpenters, and the next by the skilled metal trades workers.

Neither can the rise of unionism be traced to the introduction of
machine production. None of the industries organized during the
period 1790 to 1830 had been significantly affected by machine methods. An important stimulus to union organization in some industries
was the broadening of the domestic market for manufactures which
resulted from the improvement of transportation facilities. This expansion meant intensified competition in the sale of goods—shoes
made in Philadelphia competed increasingly with shoes made in New
York, Baltimore, and other cities. The merchant capitalist appeared,
playing off small masters against each other and forcing them to cut
wages in order to survive. This activity threatened the journeymen's
customary standard of life and forced them into defensive organizations.

The growth of the market also fostered division of labor and
development of larger production units. Even without mechanization
of production, this meant that it took more capital to set oneself up
in business and that it was increasingly difficult for journeymen to
rise to the master class. The gulf between worker and employer
widened. For the first time there appeared a group of permanent wage
earners, who had little expectation of becoming masters in the future.
Moreover, greater specialization of tasks reduced the element of skill
in the production process. The semiskilled operative made his
appearance and the need for fully skilled craftsmen diminished. This
threat to the craftsman's skill was unpleasant in itself and also
threatened his earning power.

The extension of the market for manufactures can scarcely explain
the rise of unionism in industries such as printing and building construction, which continued to cater to purely local markets. While
product markets in these industries remained local, however, the labor
market broadened steadily as improved transportation increased the
mobility of labor. Printers, carpenters, and bricklayers began to move
about the country in considerable numbers, and were sometimes used
by employers to undercut local wage scales. Some means had to be
found for controlling this competition. Moreover, in local-market as
well as national-market industries, employers were sometimes led by

business depression or price competition to make a direct onslaught on established wage scales and working conditions. The development of local unions was a natural protective response to this pressure.

Until after the Civil War, almost all unions were local unions of workers in a particular trade or industry, and they were confined largely to a few cities along the Atlantic seaboard. These early unions were strikingly modern in objectives and methods. From the beginning, regulation of wages was the main issue and the strike was the main weapon. There was little, it is true, which could be termed "collective bargaining" during this period. In the beginning, the union simply decided on its "price" (i.e., wage rate), and the members pledged themselves not to work below this price. A little later, it became customary for a union committee to visit each employer and request his adherence to the union rate. Those who refused to agree were struck. There was still no written agreement with employers, and the procedure could scarcely be called bargaining. The wage scale was determined unilaterally by the union, and employers were given the choice of conforming or not conforming. When non-conforming employers were struck, the "walking delegate," who at first was an unpaid worker but later became a paid official, went from shop to shop to make sure that all union members were out. Strikebreakers were termed "rats," and later "scabs." The locals of the same trade in different cities exchanged lists of scabs and agreed not to admit them to membership. This activity was almost the only contact between local unions in the early days. Strikes were financed by levies on the membership. They were relatively peaceful, and, except in depression periods, most of them were successful.

Another policy of the earliest trade unions was not to work with nonunion men. The union shop, like the union wage scale, was enforced directly through a pledge by unionists "not to work for anybody who does not pay the rate nor beside anyone who does not get the rate." Nonunionists were also boycotted socially; union men would not live in the same boarding houses or eat at the same places as nonunion men. Thus the union shop, which is sometimes pictured as a new invention, actually dates from the earliest days of unionism in this country. Apprenticeship regulations were another major concern of the early unions. Their main purpose was to prevent employers from replacing journeymen with learners, runaway apprentices, and women, at wage rates below the union scale. The number of apprentices which an employer might train was usually limited to a certain proportion of the number of journeymen employed. They were required to serve a specified period of apprenticeship, and only journeymen who had completed this apprenticeship were admitted to the union and allowed to work in union shops.

These unions, though few in number, were sufficiently strong and aggressive to arouse consternation among employers. Editorial writers denounced unionism, employers' associations were formed to combat it, and conspiracy cases were launched against the unions in the courts. The antiunion arguments, like the union tactics of the day, have a surprisingly modern ring.[1] One hundred and fifty years have brought little change in the issues at stake and the arguments advanced on either side. Many of the arguments put forward today might easily have been copied from newspapers and speeches of a hundred years ago.

An important characteristic of these early unions was their inability to withstand business depression. They sprang up and flourished in good years but were nearly all wiped out during depression periods. After the Civil War, however, the situation began to change. The depression of 1873-78 reduced union membership from about 300,000 to 50,000; but it did not wipe out unionism completely, as earlier depressions had done. With this development, and with the foundation of the American Federation of Labor (AFL) in 1886, we enter a new period of trade union history.

UNION GROWTH IN MODERN TIMES

The growth of unionism in the twentieth century is shown in Figure 1 and Table 1. Figure 1 shows the estimated number of union

---

[1] The master carpenters of Boston, for example, when confronted in 1825 with a demand for a ten-hour day, replied that they could not believe "this project to have originated with any of the faithful and industrious sons of New England, but are compelled to consider it an evil of foreign growth, and one which we hope and trust will not take root in the favored soil of Massachusetts. . . . And especially that our city, the early rising and industry of whose inhabitants are universally proverbial, may not be infected with the unnatural production." John R. Commons and associates, *History of Labor in the United States*, Vol. I (New York: The Macmillan Company, 1918), p. 160. See also the antiunion statements on p. 271 of this same volume and those contained in E. W. Bakke and Clark Kerr, eds., *Unions, Management, and the Public* (New York: Harcourt, Brace & World, Inc., 1948), pp. 272-280.

members year by year since 1897.[2] Table 1 shows union membership as a percentage of nonagricultural employment for selected years since 1880.

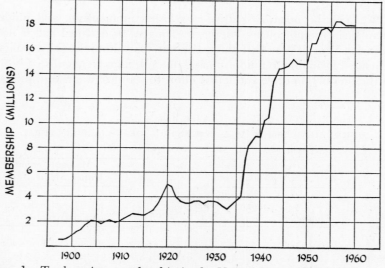

FIG. 1   *Trade union membership in the United States, 1897-1960.*

From 1880 until the early nineteen thirties union membership rose gradually and intermittently, going up in prosperity periods and falling back in depression. Unionism was confined largely to the skilled crafts and did not succeed in penetrating the basic manufacturing industries. Except for a brief spurt during and after World War I, union membership never rose above 10 per cent of nonagricultural employment. Membership declined gradually during the complacent 'twenties, and more sharply during the severe depression of 1929-33.

The New Deal era brought a great upsurge of union strength. Between 1933 and 1939 union membership tripled, and unions for the first time became firmly established in steel, automobiles, and most other branches of manufacturing. Organization spread from the skilled crafts to the semiskilled and unskilled. The reasons included a federal administration favorable to unionism, new legislation guaranteeing

---

[2] Data from 1897 through 1940 are from the Bureau of Labor Statistics, *Handbook of Labor Statistics*, 1950, p. 139. Figures for 1941 through 1960 are from the Bureau of the Census, *Statistical Abstract of the United States*, 1962.

the right to organize and improving the legal status of trade unions, a substantial recovery of employment from 1933 to 1937, and the vigorous organizing efforts of the Congress of Industrial Organizations (CIO).

By 1939 the organizing drive was losing momentum, and union membership might once more have stagnated or declined had it not been for World War II. During the war years administration policy remained favorable to unionism, and union leaders were enlisted both in the production drive and in the effort to stabilize wages and prices.

TABLE 1

UNION MEMBERSHIP AS A PERCENTAGE OF NONAGRICULTURAL
EMPLOYMENT, SELECTED YEARS, 1880-1960

	Average Annual Union Membership			Average Annual Union Membership	
Year	Thousands	Per cent of nonagricultural employment	Year	Thousands	Per cent of nonagricultural employment
1880	200.0	2.3	1933	2,857	11.5
1890	372.0	2.7	1939	8,980	28.9
1900	865.5	4.8	1945	14,796	35.8
1910	2,140.5	8.4	1956	18,477	33.7
1920	5,047.8	16.3	1960	18,117	32.1
1930	3,392.8	8.8			

Source: Through 1956, from Lloyd Ulman, "American trade unionism—past and present", in Seymour E. Harris, ed., American Economic History (New York: McGraw-Hill, 1961), p. 393 and p. 421. Figures for 1960 from Statistical Abstract of the United States, 1962. The figures slightly exaggerate American union membership, since they include Canadian members of unions with headquarters in the United States, who numbered 1,068,000 in 1960.

The sharp increase of employment in war industries was favorable to enrolling more union members. Employers were more concerned with recruiting labor and getting out production than with fighting the union, and employer resistance to organization subsided for the time being. So another five million union members were added. Unions came to include more than a third of the nonagricultural labor force and about 60 per cent of all manual workers in the economy.

In retrospect, 1945 appears as a high watermark in union penetration of the economy. Membership spurted briefly during the Korean War, but has stagnated since that time. Since the labor force has continued to grow, the percentage of nonagricultural workers who are union members has been falling. What accounts for this stagnation of membership during a period of sustained prosperity? What does it portend for the future? Is unionism over the hill, or will there be a fresh upsurge at some time in the future? We shall comment on these questions at the end of the chapter. But first we must examine the structure of union organization and how this has changed over the course of time.

THE EVOLUTION OF UNION STRUCTURE

There are four main types of organizational units in the trade union world: local unions of workers in a particular trade or industry; city-wide and state-wide federations of local unions, regardless of industry; national unions of workers in the same trade or industry; and peak federations of these national unions, such as the AFL-CIO.

The organizational structure may be visualized more readily by looking at a particular union. The printers' Local Number 6 in New York City is a branch of the International Typographical Union, and holds its charter and authority only from the international union. At the same time, Local Number 6 is a member of the New York City Federation of Labor and the New York State Federation of Labor. At the national level, the Typographical Union is affiliated with the AFL-CIO.

These organizational units did not develop overnight, nor did they develop simultaneously. They represent successive stages of development, comparable to strata in a geological formation. The first local union was the Philadelphia shoemakers' union, founded in 1792. Next in order of development came the city federations of local unions, the first of which were founded in New York, Philadelphia, and Baltimore in 1833. The first national union which has had a continuous existence up to the present day was the International Typographical Union, founded in 1850. The first federation of national unions which has had a continuous history to date was the American Federation of Labor, founded in 1886.

Numerous other forms of organization have also been tried during the past one hundred and fifty years. There have been attempts to combine people from different trades and industries into a single local union, and to combine these "mixed locals" into an all-inclusive national organization. The outstanding example of this type of organization was the Knights of Labor, which flourished briefly during the eighteen eighties. There have also been attempts to merge federations of local trade unions, local labor political clubs, and miscellaneous labor groups into a federation such as the National Labor Union, which flourished during the late eighteen sixties. The reasons for the failure of these movements will be discussed below. Briefly, they suffered from a lack of homogeneity of interest among the underlying membership. Because of diversity of the membership, a chronic shortage of funds, an absence of systematic organizing tactics, and a lack of interest in continuous bargaining with employers, they made only slight headway on the economic front. Their activities were oriented mainly toward politics, and here they tended to dissipate their energies in broad middle-class reform movements of little immediate interest to wage earners. The organizational forms which we find in existence today are the survivors, which have proved their ability to survive by the concrete functions they perform.

These different organizational units are not of equal importance in the labor world. The key unit around which all else revolves is the national union of workers in a particular trade or industry. The national union is more important than the locals of which it is composed, and it is also more important than the federation with which it is affiliated. This has not always been the case, and we need to ask how the national union has come to occupy its present key position.

THE DOMINANCE OF THE NATIONAL UNION

The beginnings of local unionism around the year 1800 have already been described. These isolated locals soon found that they were in a relatively weak position compared with that of a strong employer. Consisting of workers in only one trade, with limited funds and no outside support, they often crumbled when forced to strike against a large employer or employers' association. The need for some kind of defensive alliance with other unions was felt almost from the beginning.

Such an alliance can be formed on either of two bases. The local may join with local unions of other trades in the same *area* to form a city-wide or state-wide organization; or it may join with other local unions in the same *trade or industry* to form a national trade union. The first efforts were in the former direction. City-wide federations, called at the time "trade assemblies," sprang up in Philadelphia, New York, and Baltimore in 1833, as we have noted, and in ten other cities during the next two years. The main function of these groups was mutual aid in strikes. Funds were obtained by taxing each local so many cents per member per month, and the tax was sometimes raised to meet emergency situations. A local wishing to go on strike usually had to secure approval either by a majority or by two-thirds of the member locals in order to draw strike benefits from the common fund. The trade assemblies also functioned as boycott organizations, lobbyists, propaganda bureaus, publishers of labor newspapers; and in some cities sponsored an independent labor party. The usefulness of the city federation is proved by the fact that it has persisted, with some change of functions, to the present day.

Why did the local unions find it necessary to go beyond this and to establish national unions of their respective trades and industries? One important reason was the nationalization of the market for many goods. Hoxie has laid down the principle that union organization tends to parallel the organization of the industry. In an industry in which employers compete on a national basis, the isolated local soon finds itself competing with local unions in other plants of the industry. In this sort of competition, wages tend to be leveled down to the lowest rates prevailing anywhere in the country. In some trades, too, migration of journeymen from one city to another early became a problem. The local unions of printers, for example, began to exchange lists of scabs, to regulate the conditions under which printers from one area might secure work in another area, and to provide "tramping benefits" to support the brother in the trade during his journeys in search of employment. A permanent national organization facilitated these exchanges and made it possible to enforce uniform apprenticeship and membership rules. With the passage of time, improved transportation facilities made it easier for delegates to assemble at national conventions and for organizers from the national office to travel throughout the country.

National unions date for all practical purposes from the Civil War. Two so-called national unions of shoemakers and printers were formed in 1835-36, but they were confined to the Atlantic coast and were wiped out almost immediately by depression. Three permanent organizations appeared during the 'fifties: the printers (1850), molders (1859), and machinists and blacksmiths (1859). The first period of intensive national organization, however, was from 1863 to 1873.

During these years some twenty-six new national unions were formed, many of which have survived to the present day. The present unions of locomotive engineers, locomotive firemen, carpenters, cigar makers, bricklayers, and painters date from this period.

The national unions showed much greater resistance to depression than the earlier local unions. The depression of 1873-78 caused a great decline in union membership, but at least eleven nationals are known to have survived these years and eight new nationals were founded during the depression. The reasons for the greater permanence of a national union are not difficult to see. Even though many of its local unions are wiped out during a depression, the national headquarters can continue on a reduced scale and serve as a center for reviving the lost locals when prosperity returns. Moreover, a national union tends constantly to expand to the limits of its trade or industry. Its officers have the duty of organizing the unorganized; their prestige, and even their continuance in office, depend on successful performance of this function.

The national unions not merely survived, but gradually took over more and more functions from the local unions and the city federations. They early began to build up war chests to aid in financing strikes. To prevent dissipation of these funds, it was necessary to forbid local unions to call strikes without the sanction of the national union. The national officers thus became involved in all important disputes between local unions and employers, with a view to preventing strikes except where absolutely necessary. From this it was a natural step for national officers to begin participating in the negotiation of new contracts with employers. This action was desirable also in order to keep some reasonable relation among the wage schedules and other contract terms secured by the various locals.

It was natural also that national officers with an intimate knowledge of the trade or industry should take over the work of organizing new locals. The great majority of full-time union organizers now draw their pay from the treasuries of the national unions. The benefit functions of the unions also became centralized increasingly in the national office. Uniform rules for sickness benefits, death benefits, strike benefits, and other types of payment were established throughout the union, and funds were paid to the national treasurer and were disbursed by him.

The expanding functions of the national unions tended to transfer the loyalty of local unions from the city federations to the national union of their trade. Most workers naturally have a sense of closer kinship with others in their own trade or industry. This feeling was now reinforced by the material benefits received from the national organizations. Dues payments to the national and cash benefits received from it soon amounted to many times the amounts paid to the city federations. The national unions benefited by the truth expressed in the maxim, "where your treasure is, there will your heart be also."

The predominance of the national union was strengthened also by the turn which the labor movement took in the 'eighties away from political action and toward direct bargaining with employers on the economic front. Had the labor movement taken a strongly political turn, the outcome might well have been different. The city, state, and national federations are the natural units for political action. For reasons to be discussed below, however, political action has played a minor role in the labor movement over the past century. The state and city federations have accordingly fallen to a subordinate position. They continue to meet regularly, give a certain amount of support to member locals in strikes and organizing campaigns, approve legislative demands of member locals and lobby for them in city councils and state legislatures, conduct educational and propaganda activities, and in some cases support candidates for public office. The local union's real loyalty, however, is to the national union of its trade or industry. It is to the national union that it looks for support, and in any conflict of principles or policies it is the policies of the national union which will prevail.

The cornerstones of the trade union world today are the great national unions, which have a more lasting significance than any federation based on them. It was a question of less importance than one might think whether the old AFL and CIO survived as separate organizations, or whether they agreed to merge into a new federation, as actually happened. The important thing is the growth and development of the national unions of steelworkers, automobile workers, textile workers, machinists, teamsters, carpenters, painters, mine workers, and other key groups.

PEAK FEDERATIONS: THE AMERICAN FEDERATION OF LABOR

Federation of these national unions into an overarching labor organization dates from the 1880's. Several attempts at national federation were made in earlier years, notably by the ill-fated Knights of Labor established in 1869. This heterogeneous organization cut across industry lines and included large numbers of low-skilled workers, who joined enthusiastically but were easily discouraged and quick to drop out. The national unions of skilled craftsmen eventually concluded that they would do better to form their own federation. The American Federation of Labor, founded in 1886, quickly assumed a leading role in the trade union movement. It was a hard-hitting organization, led by Samuel Gompers and other energetic men in their thirties, who almost immediately launched the first successful strikes for the eight-hour day. The AFL also had a distinctive philosophy of unionism which appealed strongly to most organized workers.

What were the cardinal points of this trade union philosophy? The first element which may be noted is group consciousness. Before this time workers had not distinguished their interests from those of farmers and other middle-class people. They had joined in political reform movements which also drew support from these other groups. All this was changed by Gompers and his followers, most of whom had been reared as Marxian socialists. Although they later abandoned most of the tenets of Marxism, they retained a conviction that the interests of workers are distinct from those of other groups. Gompers argued that the workers must defend their own interests, and must refuse to be drawn into middle-class reform movements. He asserted also that there is little hope of the workers' climbing out of their class through producers' cooperatives, antimonopoly campaigns, or other methods.

A second principle was that of organization by trades. Gompers believed that to lump together different trades, as the Knights of Labor had done, reduced the cohesiveness of the union. Greatest solidarity was obtained when each craft had its own union. The desirability of strong national unions, buttressed by large treasuries and extensive benefit systems, was stressed from the beginning. The Cigar Makers' Union, under Gompers' leadership, showed the way in this direction in 1879 by adopting a high scale of dues and benefits, and by giving the national officers complete control over the local unions. The Cigar Makers' organization was used as a model by most other national unions during the next ten years, and its prestige contributed to the election of Gompers to the AFL presidency. The marked success of British craft unions cut on this same pattern, and the influence of British immigrants in American unions, also helped to shape AFL thinking in these formative years.

Early AFL leaders insisted also that each national union must be autonomous within its own field of operation. The Federation entered the scene only to define and enforce the jurisdictions of the member unions, and to perform certain political and educational functions. The Federation, in short, was a confederation of sovereign bodies. Its chief power was that of granting jurisdiction over particular trades or industries: jurisdiction granted to one union must be observed by others, and dual unionism must be suppressed at all costs. This attitude toward dualism sprang partly from the unfortunate experience of the national unions in competition with the Knights of Labor during the 'eighties. It sprang also from the fact that the AFL had to contend with strong and determined employer opposition. The existence of two unions in an industry gave the employer a chance to play each against the other, and the labor movement therefore has a strong practical interest in preventing dual organization. The bitterness of the rivalry between AFL and CIO from 1935 to 1955 can be understood only in terms of this long-standing taboo on dual unionism.

The third cardinal principle was that labor's objectives should be pursued mainly on the economic front through collective bargaining with employers. In spite of the socialist training of its founders, the AFL soon came to accept the main outlines of the capitalist order. Gompers believed that unions should try, not to overthrow capitalism, but to get as much as possible for the workers by collective bargaining within the confines of the existing system. When someone asked Gompers what the aims of the Federation were, he is reported to have answered, "More, more, more—now!" When another AFL leader was called before a Congressional committee in 1883 and asked about the ultimate objectives of trade unionism, he replied as follows: "We have no ultimate ends. We are going on from day to day. We are fighting only for immediate objects . . . we are opposed to theorists . . . we are all practical men."[3] There has never been a better summary of the traditional AFL position.

The device of the union contract or collective agreement, which had been used by a few unions in the 'eighties, became during the 'nineties the accepted method of dealing with employers. The AFL hammered out and wrote into union contracts a new conception of the union as a continuously operating organization, rather than a sporadic protest and strike movement. The union was to be a partner, though perhaps only a junior partner, in the conduct of industry.

---

[3] J. B. S. Hardman, *American Labor Dynamics* (New York: Harcourt, Brace & World, Inc., 1928), p. 99.

It was to be active every day in the year, representing the interests of its members on all fronts, winning small gains which would eventually mount up to an impressive total.

A corollary of the AFL's emphasis on collective bargaining was the avoidance of political organization, or at least of anything approaching an independent labor party. The labor movement had experimented with labor parties and political action since at least 1830. Gompers and his group felt that these activities had not gotten anywhere in the past and had served mainly to split the unions and divert them from their real business. They believed that the unions could get what they wanted through pressure on the established political parties—voting for candidates who had shown themselves to be "friends of labor," getting union demands written into party platforms, lobbying in Congress and the state legislatures, and so on. Along with this avoidance of labor politics went a suspicion of intellectuals and of their tendency to foist abstract programs on the workers. There has been in the United States nothing of that close connection between intellectuals and the labor movement which exists in most European countries. Union leaders have had a similar distrust of socialists and other radical groups which attempt to divert trade union energy to revolutionary ends. This point of view is well expressed in Gompers' statement to an AFL convention:

> I want to tell you Socialists, that I have studied your philosophy, read your works upon economics. . . . I have heard your orators and watched the work of your movement the world over. I have kept close watch upon your doctrines for thirty years; have been closely associated with many of you, and know what you think and what you propose. I know, too, what you have up your sleeve. And I want to say that I am entirely at variance with your philosophy. . . . Economically, you are unsound; socially, you are wrong; and industrially you are an impossibility.[4]

All in all, then, the AFL provided a model of organization well suited to the requirements of the skilled trades. It stimulated the formation of new national unions. It acted as a stabilizer of union membership during depression periods. It shook the labor movement free of an incubus of unfruitful ideas and presented a practical operating program which proved very successful in winning gains on the economic front. Except for the short-lived Industrial Workers of the World, which flourished just before the first World War, the story of American unionism for almost fifty years was the story of the AFL.

---

[4] *AFL Convention Proceedings*, 1903, pp. 188-192.

THE RISE OF INDUSTRIAL UNIONISM

While the growth of union membership from 1880 to 1930 occurred largely within the skilled trades, there was also some development of unions which included all workers in a particular industry. The most important of these were the United Mine Workers, the Amalgamated Clothing Workers, and the International Ladies' Garment Workers.

In many areas of the economy the issue of craft versus industrial organization does not arise. In some cases—barbers, musicians, teachers—craft and industry are virtually synonymous. But the issue does arise acutely in large-scale, mechanized manufacturing industries. In most of these industries, 80 to 90 per cent of the plant labor force is semiskilled or unskilled. The remaining 10 to 20 per cent of skilled workers are the plant aristocracy: the loomfixer in textile mills, the machine tender and his assistants in paper mills, the toolmaker and machinist in metalworking plants, the cutter in garment shops. Most large plants also employ considerable numbers of carpenters, electricians, pipe fitters, and other skilled tradesmen on maintenance work. The question is whether each of these skilled groups should have its own local union, affiliated with a national union of its trade, leaving the low-skilled workers as a headless remnant; or whether all workers in the plant should belong to a single local, whose bargaining strength would be enhanced by including the skilled men.

So long as organizing conditions were unfavorable, this issue was largely academic. But the favorable political and economic climate after 1933 presented the labor movement with an unprecedented opportunity to penetrate the manufacturing industries. The question of how to go about it became practical and immediate. Two points of view quickly developed within the AFL. A minority, spearheaded by the leaders of existing industrial unions, demanded an aggressive organizing drive and the chartering of industrial unions in the mass production industries. Craft union leaders, however, representing a majority of the Federation's membership, urged a more cautious policy. They were skeptical of the organizability of the low-skilled workers; and they wished to preserve the right of existing craft unions to enroll members of their trade who worked in manufacturing plants.

This difference of opinion came to a head in the national AFL conventions of 1934 and 1935. The industrial unionists were led by

Lewis of the Mine Workers, Hillman of the Clothing Workers, and Dubinsky of the Ladies' Garment Workers. After being outvoted at the 1935 convention, six unions set up a Committee for Industrial Organization devoted to organizing industrial unions in the basic manufacturing industries and then bringing these new unions into the AFL. The AFL Executive Council, however, scenting a threat of dual unionism, first suspended and then expelled the unions which had formed the CIO. These unions then banded together in 1938, along with the new unions which they had fathered in the meantime, to form a rival federation—the Congress of Industrial Organizations.

The success of the CIO organizing drives is now a matter of history. During the late 'thirties one antiunion citadel after another capitulated. The list of employers organized by the CIO between 1936 and 1941 reads like a roster of Who's Who in American industry: Ford, General Motors, Chrysler, General Electric, Westinghouse, United States Steel, Bethlehem Steel, Republic Steel, Youngstown Sheet and Tube, Goodyear, Firestone, Goodrich, the major oil companies, the larger radio and electrical equipment manufacturers, the "big four" meatpacking companies, and so on down the list.

Why was the CIO able to organize industries which had hitherto presented an impenetrable front to unionism? The most important factor was probably a favorable government attitude toward unionism throughout the Roosevelt era. Unions which formerly had to strike to win union recognition could now use the election procedures of the National Labor Relations Board, and the Board also protected them against harassing tactics by the employer, which were now forbidden as "unfair labor practices." The CIO organizing campaigns were aggressive, well financed through donations from the sponsoring unions, and led by experienced and capable organizers, many of whom had grown up in the rough school of the United Mine Workers. A final important factor was the prolonged rise in business activity after 1933. Except for the relapse of 1937-38, employment and production rose steadily from 1933 to 1945. Good times, as was noted earlier, have always provided a favorable setting for union organization.

RIVALRY AND REUNION, 1935 TO 1955

The rise of the CIO was paralleled by a great growth in AFL membership. The AFL, like its rival federation, benefited from prosperity and the favorable attitude of government, and made good use of its opportunities. The AFL pulled ahead of the CIO in total membership by 1940 and widened its lead in subsequent years. There were several reasons for this. First, the craft unions continued to enlarge their membership. There was a striking growth of such old-line unions as those of the teamsters, machinists, carpenters, electrical workers, and hod carriers. Second, the AFL went into competition with the CIO in organizing manufacturing plants on an industrial basis. It sponsored industrial unions in the automobile, textile, boot and shoe, meatpacking, pulp and paper, and men's clothing industries. The AFL Electrical Workers, formerly confined mainly to the construction industry, later recruited many workers in plants manufacturing electrical equipment, competing in this area with the International Union of Electrical, Radio and Machine Workers, CIO. The International Association of Machinists entered into competition with CIO unions in the metal and machinery industries, particularly aircraft manufacture. The marked success of the AFL unions in this rivalry is suggested by Table 2.

Third, several of the unions instrumental in forming the CIO, including the Mine Workers and the Ladies' Garment Workers, later withdrew from the CIO and rejoined the AFL. Fourth, the AFL proved more successful than the CIO in expanding into retail trade, service, and other industries. The CIO remained largely confined within basic manufacturing.

Finally, in 1949 and 1950 the CIO expelled a number of important left-wing unions following the refusal of their officers to sign the non-Communist affidavits required by the Taft-Hartley Act. The eleven unions expelled included the powerful United Electrical, Radio and Machine Workers, with a membership of 600,000. In all, nearly a million workers were involved. The CIO organized new unions to take over the jurisdictions of the ousted unions, and claimed to have recaptured 70 per cent of their former members by 1950. Nevertheless the expulsions and reorganization were a setback for the CIO in its competition with the AFL.

As a result of the growth of the CIO and the growth of industrial unions within the AFL, there was a marked increase in the percentage of all union members who are in industrial unions. Only about one-third of the AFL membership was in industrial unions in 1933. By 1952, more than two-thirds of the combined CIO and AFL membership were in industrial or semi-industrial unions.

The cleavage in the labor movement after 1935 had disadvantages

TABLE 2
MEMBERSHIP GROWTH IN SELECTED AFL AND CIO UNIONS
1940-1956

Union	Affiliation	1940	1951	1956
Boot and Shoe Workers Union	AFL	30,800	50,000	40,000
United Shoe Workers of America	CIO	53,627	60,000	60,000
United Brotherhood of Carpenters and Joiners	AFL	305,867	750,000	850,000
International Woodworkers of America	CIO	58,682	117,251	88,517
International Brotherhood of Electrical Workers of America	AFL	209,700	500,000	675,000
United Electrical, Radio, and Machine Workers of America	CIO, Ind.	206,824	*	100,000
International Union of Electrical, Radio, and Machine Workers of America	CIO	—	*	397,412
Amalgamated Meat Cutters and Butcher Workmen	AFL	70,000	195,000	310,000
United Packing House Workers of America	CIO	90,000	132,000	150,000
International Brotherhood of Paper Makers	AFL	24,300	70,000	
United Paper Workers of America	CIO	—	50,000	
Merged to United Paper Makers and Paperworkers	AFL-CIO	—	—	130,000
Seafarers International Union of North America	AFL	18,700	70,000	75,000
National Maritime Union of America	CIO	52,000	43,000	40,000
International Brotherhood of Teamsters, etc.	AFL	393,700	1,000,000	1,368,082
International Association of Machinists	AFL	190,100	699,298	949,683

* Split over Communist issue; membership unknown.

Source: Lloyd Ulman, *op. cit.*, p. 412.

on both the political and collective bargaining fronts, and leaders on the two sides worked sporadically to close the breach. Negotiations looking toward unity were conducted by joint committees in 1937, 1939, 1942-43, 1947, and 1950. For a number of reasons, however, all of these discussions bogged down. Until 1945 both groups were making good gains in membership and unity was not a primary concern. Each group continued, skeptical of the other's chances of survival, and hoped for victory in a straight competitive struggle. There was a mistaken idea that reunion must be preceded by an ironing out of all jurisdictional problems between overlapping unions in the two federations. The CIO tended to insist that its affiliates be taken into any merged federation "as is"; but the AFL typically insisted that the new unions, which in a sense were "outlaw" from their point of view, must have their jurisdictional status regularized before admission. There were substantial differences of political outlook between the two federations. Finally, personal bitterness among John L. Lewis, William Green, Philip Murray, and other leaders who had been involved in the original split was an obstacle to unity.

By the early 'fifties many of these circumstances had changed. Organizational and membership stability had been achieved on both sides. Instead of expanding into new territory, the unions found themselves engaging in intensified competition for workers already organized. Interunion "raiding" of membership increased to an uncomfortable degree. The political climate had also become increasingly unfavorable to unionism. In 1947 the Taft-Hartley Act imposed new federal restrictions on trade unions, and restrictive state laws continued to multiply. A Republican President was elected in 1952 despite both AFL and CIO opposition. Many labor leaders concluded that unity was essential to protect established positions and fight off political attacks.

In late 1952 Presidents William Green of the AFL and Philip Murray of the CIO died within a month of each other. The new presidents, George Meany and Walter Reuther, quickly reactivated the twenty-four man Joint AFL-CIO Unity Committee. Over the next two years this body succeeded in hammering out, first a "no-raiding agreement" between most of the national unions on both sides, and later the terms of a full merger. The key to the final agreement was a decision that all national unions in both groups would be taken into the new federation "as is." Mergers and other methods of eliminating overlapping jurisdiction would be encouraged, but were not made compulsory. In December 1955, the AFL and CIO held their last separate conventions and then met jointly for the first convention of the new American Federation of Labor and Congress of Industrial Organizations.

The superstructure of the AFL-CIO is complicated, since it adds together the top management structure of the two predecessor bodies. In addition to a President and Secretary-Treasurer there are twenty-seven vice-presidents, distributed on an agreed basis between former AFL and former CIO affiliates. In addition to the trade departments of the old AFL (Building and Construction Trades, Metal Trades, Union Label Trades, Maritime Employees, and Railway Employees) there is now an Industrial Union Department, open to all unions organized wholly or partly on an industrial basis. Headed by Walter Reuther, it serves to maintain something of the identity and spirit of the old CIO.

Merger of the central AFL and CIO organizations was intended to stimulate merger of subordinate bodies on both sides. In the case of national unions, merger was to be encouraged but not enforced. A few mergers have since been consummated, but there is no indication that the structure of the major unions will be seriously altered. The state and city federations of local unions, where parallel AFL and CIO organizations had grown up, were definitely ordered to merge. These mergers proceeded more slowly than was originally intended, but have now been substantially completed.

The old AFL had quite limited powers over the affiliated national unions, and this remains basically true of the AFL-CIO. Two significant differences, however, should be noted:

(a) The old AFL attached great importance to avoiding overlapping jurisdiction among the national unions, and asserted the right to draw clear jurisdictional boundary lines. This principle of exclusive jurisdiction was abandoned in 1955 for the sake of labor unity, and all national unions were taken into the new federation with the territory which they had managed to occupy by that time. Another new feature in the situation is the election procedures of the National Labor Relations Board, which give workers the ultimate right to decide whether they shall be represented by one union or another. The AFL-CIO retains the right to define the jurisdiction of new affiliates, to mediate jurisdictional disputes among its constituent unions, and if necessary to make decisions in such disputes. It has no enforcement powers, however, short of the drastic step of expelling an offending union. As a practical matter, jurisdictional controversies are now resolved mainly through NLRB elections and through a large network of bilateral agreements between unions in neighboring fields.

(b) The AFL-CIO constitution goes farther than its predecessors in prescribing standards of conduct for the national unions. No union which is controlled or dominated by communists, members of other totalitarian movements, or racketeers ("corrupt influences") may remain affiliated with the federation. The Executive Council has power to investigate situations where such control or domination is alleged, to make recommendations or give directions to the union in question, and to suspend the union from membership by a two-thirds vote. Council actions may be appealed to the biennial Convention, which has final authority to reinstate or expel the accused union. But the threat of expulsion, while it may have some effect on small unions, is ineffective against the more powerful organizations. The outstanding example is the Teamsters' union, which simply ignored federation orders to eliminate corruption, and accepted expulsion in 1957 with equanimity. Since then the union has continued to flourish on its own, while the federation had been deprived of valuable revenues and support.

The national unions, then, remain largely autonomous in managing their internal affairs and continue to be the real power centers of the labor movement. The national unions are not members of the AFL-CIO in the sense that Minnesota is part of the United States. Their position is more like that of countries within the United Nations, which by threatening to withdraw can veto actions contrary to their interests. They confer power on the federation much more than they draw power from it.

THE TRADE UNION WORLD TODAY

It is appropriate to close this survey of union development by indicating the centers of union strength at the present time. It is apparent from Table 3 that membership is highly concentrated in a few large organizations.[5] Three unions—the Teamsters, Automobile Workers, and Steelworkers—have more than a million members each.

---

[5] Bureau of Labor Statistics, *Directory of National and International Labor Unions in the United States, 1961*, Bulletin No. 1320, March 1962.

TABLE 3

UNIONS REPORTING 100,000 OR MORE MEMBERS, 1960[a]

Teamsters, Chauffeurs, Warehousemen and Helpers (ind.)	1,484,433
Steelworkers	1,152,000
Automobile, Aircraft, and Agricultural Implement Workers	1,136,140
Machinists	898,139
Carpenters and Joiners	800,000
Electrical Workers, International Brotherhood of	771,000
Mine Workers of America, United (ind.)	600,000
Garment Workers Union, International Ladies'	446,554
Hotel and Restaurant Employees and Bartenders	443,000
Hod Carriers, Building and Common Laborers	442,473
Clothing Workers, Amalgamated	377,000
Retail Clerks	342,000
Meat Cutters and Butcher Workmen	333,482
Railway and Steamship Clerks, Freight Handlers, Express and Station Employees	300,000
Engineers, Operating	291,000
Electrical, Radio and Machine Workers, International Union of	287,937
Building Service Employees	272,000
Musicians, American Federation of	266,618
Communications Workers	259,917
Plumbing and Pipe Fitting	251,273
State, County and Municipal Employees	210,000
Painters, Decorators and Paperhangers	192,568
Textile Workers Union of America	192,000
Oil, Chemical and Atomic Workers	174,000
Pulp, Sulfate, and Paper Mill Workers	170,544
Rubber, Cork, Linoleum and Plastic Workers	170,000
Maintenance of Way Employees	164,447
Electrical, Radio and Machine Workers of America, United (ind.)	160,000
Railroad Trainmen	159,384
Bricklayers, Masons and Plasterers	155,000
Iron Workers, Bridge, Structural and Ornamental	147,982
Retail, Wholesale and Department Store Union	143,300
Boilermakers, Iron Shop Builders, Blacksmiths, Forgers, and Helpers	140,000
Papermakers and Paperworkers	140,000
Letter Carriers	138,000
Transport Workers	135,000
Street, Electric Railway, and Motor Coach Employees	132,100
Railway Carmen	125,000
Printing Pressmen and Assistants	113,903
Typographical Union	105,033
Sheet Metal Workers	100,000
Mine, Mill and Smelter Workers, International Union of (ind.)	100,000

[a] Affiliated with AFL-CIO unless designated as independent (ind.)
Source: Department of Labor, Bureau of Labor Statistics, *Monthly Labor Review* (Dec. 1961).

The ten largest unions have about eight million members, or almost half of all union members in the country. At the bottom of the scale are about one hundred national unions with less than 25,000 members each. Although this group includes half of the unions in the country, it is comprised of only about 5 per cent of all union members.

The degree of union penetration varies widely among sectors of the economy. In mining, construction, and transportation the great majority of wage earners are union members. In manufacturing a substantial majority are members, though the ratio varies in different branches of manufacturing—high in steel and automobiles, low in textiles. These four sectors—manufacturing, mining, construction, and transportation—account for more than 80 per cent of total union membership. In the trade and service sectors, on the other hand, unionism has made little progress. The 1960 ratio of union members to total employment was 17.4 per cent in the service industries, 12.6 per cent in government service, 7.4 per cent in wholesale and retail trade, and 2.7 per cent in finance and insurance.

The geographical distribution of union membership reflects in part the distribution of employment. States which have many workers in construction, transportation, and manufacturing also have many union members. In 1960 five states (New York, California, Pennsylvania, Illinois, and Ohio), each with more than a million union members, accounted for about 51 per cent of total membership. They also represented 39 per cent of nonagricultural employment in the country.

In addition to the distribution of employment, however, regions differ in their susceptibility to union organization. In 1960 the highest ratio of union members to nonagricultural employment was found in the state of Washington (43 per cent), followed by Pennsylvania, Alaska, Missouri, Illinois, Ohio, New York, Massachusetts, Michigan, Montana, and Oregon (all with ratios between 30 and 40 per cent). Union organization is strongest in the Middle Atlantic, East North Central, and Pacific Coast states. The Mountain and West North Central states, the South, and the Southwest are weakly unionized. The 1960 ratio of union members to nonagricultural employment was lowest in South Carolina (6 per cent), North Carolina and New Mexico (7 per cent), Oklahoma and Virginia (9 per cent), Florida, Georgia, and Mississippi (11 per cent). In the rapidly expanding industrial state of Texas the ratio was 15 per cent.

The weakness of unionism in the South is not just a matter of the industry mix. The same industries are less unionized there than in other parts of the country. An interesting calculation, made in 1953 near the peak of union strength, showed that union membership in the Southern states was only 57 per cent of what it would be *if each industry were as strongly unionized in the South as in the nation as a whole.*[6] The reasons for this weak showing include unusually active employer resistance to unionism, a generally unfavorable attitude in state legislatures and the courts, a new industrial labor force recruited largely from agriculture, and the complicating factor of racial divisions in the work force.

MEMBERSHIP STAGNATION AND THE FUTURE OUTLOOK

The most striking feature of the past decade is the stagnation of union membership. After twenty years of rapid expansion, membership has stopped growing and the percentage of the labor force in unions has dropped. In the traditional strongholds of manufacturing, mining, and transportation, most unions have lost members since the mid-'fifties. The unions which have managed to swim against the tide and increase their membership are largely outside these areas. They include the Teamsters; Retail Clerks; Retail, Wholesale, and Department Store Employees; Letter Carriers; State, County, and Municipal Employees; Musicians; Building Service Employees; Plumbers; and Electrical Workers (IBEW).

There are several reasons for the leveling off of union membership. By the mid-'fifties the most easily unionized people—manual workers in large establishments in cities of the Northeast and Pacific Coast— had already been substantially organized. As unionism presses out into white-collar employment, smaller establishments, smaller cities and towns, and more heavily agricultural regions, it encounters increasing resistance.

The composition of employment has been changing in ways unfavorable to unionism. The number of production workers in manufacturing has been cut by technological improvements, and employment in mining and transportation has fallen sharply. The sectors with a strong uptrend of employment are trade, government, finance,

---

[6] Leo Troy, "The Growth of Union Membership in the South, 1939-1953," *Southern Economic Journal* (April 1958), pp. 407-420.

and services; but in these largely white-collar areas unionism has only a slight foothold. Geographically, industry has tended to move from the Northeast to the South and Southwest, and from metropolitan areas to smaller communities, i.e., to areas in which union organization seems inherently more difficult. For the time being, unionism seems to be confined within a shrinking area of the economy.

There has been a marked change in public attitudes and in the political climate over the past generation. The low wages, heavy unemployment, and other hardships of the nineteen thirties have receded into the past. No longer can unions count on public sympathy for the underdog. On the contrary, they now attract part of the criticism and distrust of concentrated economic power formerly reserved for big business. The Taft-Hartley Act of 1947 and the Landrum-Griffin Act of 1959, apart from their direct effect on union operations, are symbolic of a changed climate of opinion which makes organization more difficult.

In addition to these external influences, some observers assert that the labor movement itself has become bureaucratic and complacent, and that the internal pressure for expansion has slackened. While lip service is still given to the principle of organizing the unorganized, most union officers are in fact content to settle down within the area won in the past.

Future expansion of union membership, however, will have to come from moving outside existing frontiers. Geographically, the main frontier now lies in the South. If each industry in the South were unionized to the same degree as in other regions, this would add about a million and a half members to union rolls; and this figure of "hypothetical members" will grow as the southward trend of industry continues.

But the obstacles to successful organization in the South are formidable and are unlikely to be overcome in any near future. This is a surplus-labor region which is still in the early stages of industrialization. The public authorities, who have worked hard to attract industry to their communities, view unionism as a threat to their efforts. Workers recently recruited from agriculture, who are now earning much more than they did before, are concerned above all with holding on to these desirable new jobs in the face of other workers eager to replace them. This makes them reluctant to offend the employer, go out on strike, or do anything else which might threaten their job security. Manufacturing industries in the South are often small-scale, labor intensive, and highly competitive. This combination of circumstances has thus far made Southern industry very resistant to union penetration.

Union membership might increase also by a breakthrough into the trade, finance, and government sectors. The economic and social status of white-collar workers has deteriorated in ways which might conceivably make unionism attractive. Sales and clerical jobs now pay little more, on the average, than manual labor. In government agencies, insurance offices, and elsewhere, large numbers of white-collar people work together under something like factory conditions. Problems of salary levels, fringe benefits, fair treatment by supervisors, job tenure and promotion, threatened displacement by automation and technical change are presumably no less compelling for them than for manual workers.

On the other side stands the traditional middle-class orientation of white-collar workers and the feeling that unionism is beneath them. The lower ranges of white-collar employment are populated mainly by women. Young women usually expect to be married before long, and older women are usually supplementary earners rather than family heads. So while issues of employment are important for them, they are not fighting issues as they may be for men. At the supervisory, technical, and professional levels, where men preponderate, the orientation toward management is typically strong. These people do enjoy an income advantage, and they also have chances of promotion and professional advancement. So they tend to think in terms of individual progress rather than group action.

The area of white-collar employment is so vast that one should discriminate between a variety of situations. In some cases, such as retailing, insurance, or banking, the whole work force is white-collar. Here it might be possible to organize everyone in the store or office into a straightforward industrial union. The feasibility of this is suggested by the fact that half a million retail workers already are in unions. But major success in this area might require a new organizing approach, designed to convince white-collar people that their organizations are different from the present concept of a trade union. As one observer has remarked, "Unions will not secure their allegiance . . . so long as they consider white-collar employees to be simply blue-collar employees with bleached shirts."[7] Even a new central federation might prove necessary. In some of the Western European countries, where white-collar unionism is strong, these unions have their own federation distinct from that of the manual workers.

A different situation exists with office workers in a manufacturing company whose manual labor force is already organized. Here the existing union could take the initiative in stimulating white-collar organization, and some industrial unions have already done so. In these cases, however, the office workers will doubtless want to have their own local union, and sometimes even a national union distinct from that of the factory workers.

Government employment is again different for political and legal reasons. Many states and cities prohibit unionization of their employees, and almost all actively discourage it. The right to strike is universally denied, though not always successfully. Despite these restrictions, there are large unions of schoolteachers, firemen, and other employees at the state and local levels. At the federal level there are strong unions of postal workers and of manual crafts in government arsenals and navy yards. Deprived of the strike weapon, these unions operate largely through lobbying in Congress for wage and employment legislation.

Technical and professional people are perhaps least likely to unionize, though there are substantial unions of airline pilots, engineers, teachers, musicians, newspaper writers, theatrical workers, and other groups. To be successful in this area, a union probably has to take on something of the dignity of a professional association—a marriage of AMA and UAW, with the former predominating.

Prophecy is hazardous. Scarcely anyone in the nineteen twenties foresaw the unionization of mass production manufacturing in the 'thirties and 'forties. One cannot deny the possibility of a similar expansion of white-collar unionism at some time in the future. It seems likely, however, that expansion will be quite gradual, perhaps no more than sufficient to offset the decline of union membership in other areas. So total union membership is unlikely to change much in the foreseeable future, and the percentage of the labor force in unions will probably continue to fall.

[7] B. C. Roberts, *Unions in America: a British View* (Princeton: Industrial Relations Section, Princeton University, 1959), p. 13.

Discussion questions

1. To what factors can one attribute the beginnings of modern trade unionism around 1800?

2. In a depression, workers would seem to need special protection against wage cuts and loss of jobs. Why, in spite of this, has union membership usually declined in depression periods?

3. Explain why skilled workers have usually been the first to form stable trade unions.

4. What explains the dominance of the national union over other forms of trade union organization in the United States?

5. The rise of the CIO was pictured at the time as a victory of "industrial unionism" over "craft unionism." What do these terms mean? Is this a correct interpretation of CIO development?

6. The AFL in its later years forged steadily ahead of the CIO in total membership. Why was this? Did it indicate a decline of belief in industrial unionism?

7. "The formation of the AFL-CIO was a merger of two radically different organizations which had different problems, goals and philosophies." Discuss.

8. Should union strength be defined in terms of the number of union members, or the percentage of the labor force in trade unions? Using the definition you prefer, would you expect union strength in 1975 to be greater or less than today? Explain.

9. "Union organization in a newly industrialized area is always slow and difficult. This is the basic reason for the limited progress of unionism in the South." Discuss.

10. How would you appraise union prospects in the area of white-collar employment?

Selected reading

Bakke, E. Wight, and Clark Kerr, eds., *Unions, Management and the Public*, rev. ed. New York: Harcourt, Brace and Company, 1960. Section 1, "Sources of the Union Movement"; Section 2, "History of Unionism in the United States."

Barkin, S., *The Decline of the Labor Movement*. Santa Barbara: Center for the Study of Democratic Institutions, 1961.

Bernstein, Irving, "The Growth of American Unions," *American Economic Review*, XLIV (June 1954), pp. 301-318.

Commons, John R., "American Shoemakers, 1648-1895," *Quarterly Journal of Economics*, XXIV (November 1909), pp. 39-81.

————, and associates, *History of the Labor Movement in the United States* (4 vols.). New York: The Macmillan Company, 1918.

Goldberg, Arthur J., *AFL-CIO Labor United.* New York: McGraw-Hill Book Company, Inc., 1956.

Lorwin, Lewis L., *The American Federation of Labor.* Washington: Brookings Institution, 1933.

Perlman, Selig, *A History of Trade Unionism in the United States.* New York: The Macmillan Company, 1937.

Taft, Philip, *The A. F. of L. in the Time of Gompers.* New York: Harper & Row, Publishers, 1957.

Ulman, Lloyd, *The Rise of the National Trade Union.* Cambridge: Harvard University Press, 1955.

————, *American Trade Unionism Past and Present.* Berkeley: Institute of Industrial Relations, University of California, Reprint No. 157, 1961.

Webb, Sidney and Beatrice, *The History of Trade Unionism.* London: Workers Educational Association, 1919.

3

Trade Union Philosophy
And Objectives

*In the remaining chapters of Part I we shall be deal-*ing with the intricate details of union and management organization, collective bargaining procedures, and day-to-day issues of labor relations. Before plunging into this detailed examination, it is desirable to take a broad look at the scope and significance of trade unionism. What is the general outlook, drive, objective of the movement? What are the unions really after? Where is the whole movement headed over the long run?

It is surprising how many different answers have been given to these questions. Union leaders frequently deny that they have any general objectives and assert, in Strasser's words, that they are simply "going on from day to day." Many management leaders nevertheless believe that, even if there is no deliberate union policy of displacing management over the long run, this is at least the unintended consequence of union development. Leaders of political movements often regard the true purpose of unionism as the establishment of whatever political system they happen to favor—socialist, communist, or what not. Yet some students of unionism maintain that it is essentially conservative and antirevolutionary over the long run.[1]

Still other students have maintained that there are several varieties

---

[1] For a strong expression of this viewpoint, see Frank Tannenbaum, *A Philosophy of Labor* (New York: Alfred A. Knopf, Inc., 1951).

54

of unionism, each with its own ideology and objectives. Thus R. F. Hoxie distinguished between uplift unionism, business unionism, revolutionary unionism, and predatory unionism.[2] These he regarded as distinct and permanent types, which would continue to coexist indefinitely in the labor movement. Selig Perlman, on the other hand, regards business unionism as the central type which most unions tend to approach over the long run.[3] In Perlman's view, a union dominated by mutual benefit activities or revolutionary politics is simply an immature union which, if it survives, will move in the direction of business unionism.

The central issue is whether trade unionism is a revolutionary institution, which deliberately or unintentionally produces a drastic shift in the balance of social power in the community; or whether it is a conservative institution which produces gradual and mild reforms but leaves the existing economic and political order substantially intact. In an effort to arrive at some conclusion on this point we shall review the evidence concerning: (1) The relation of the trade unions to socialist and communist political parties; (2) The degree of union interest and participation in managerial functions; and (3) The specific objectives which trade unions seem to regard as most important, and which they seek to attain through political activity and collective bargaining. A listing of these objectives should help to determine how far union activity is compatible with the existing economic order.

We shall examine these matters in the light of experience both in the United States and in other industrial countries.[4] Beneath the variety of union activities in different countries there appears to be a sufficient core of common outlook and purpose to justify certain general conclusions about trade unionism.

TRADE UNIONISM AND LEFT-WING POLITICS

The tradition of left-wing politics—syndicalist, socialist, communist, or what not—is in most countries as long as the history of trade

---

[2] R. F. Hoxie, *Trade Unionism in the United States* (New York: Appleton-Century-Crofts, Inc., 1923).

[3] Selig Perlman, *A Theory of the Labor Movement* (New York: The Macmillan Company, 1928).

[4] Walter Galenson, ed., *Comparative Labor Movements* (Englewood Cliffs, N.J.: Prentice-Hall, Inc., 1952), contains an excellent account of the development and current state of trade unionism in Italy, France, Germany, Britain, Australia, and the Scandinavian countries.

unionism itself. The relationship between the political and union organizations is a complicated one, varying a good deal from one
country to the next. We must nevertheless try to summarize it as
adequately as can be done in a few pages.

Radical political ideologies have for the most part originated outside the trade union movement. Sorel in France; Marx, Engels, and
Lasalle in Germany; the Webbs, Shaw, Cole, and other Fabian socialists in Britain; Bakunin and Lenin in Russia—none of these was
from the working class. They were educated people of middle-class
background who had developed doctrines which they considered to
be strongly in labor's interest. The doctrines did not emanate from
the trade union world. They were developed elsewhere, and their
champions then set out to convert trade unionists to them.

The trade unions, on their side, have developed independently of
political theories, in response to the concrete problems of workers in
an industrial society. They have their own dynamic and sources of
strength. Their growth has never depended on general ideologies. and
they have survived many shifts of political fashion. The grow~.. of
trade unionism and of left-wing political parties over the decaaes
have been parallel, but quite distinct, developments.

There has been, to be sure, a considerable interpenetration of ideas
and personnel. Radical parties, while appealing also to middle-class
people and intellectuals, have usually made a special effort to attract
labor support. This is partly because, in most left-wing systems of
thought, the working class is regarded as playing a key rôle in ushering
in the new society. Thus, on theoretical grounds, it seems important to recruit working-class members. More important, however,
is the practical consideration that winning over union leaders and
members is the quickest way to build a mass following for a political
movement. Left-wing political leaders have therefore made special
efforts in this direction, and with considerable success. Syndicalist,
socialist, and communist philosophies have penetrated deeply into
working-class circles. Many trade unionists have risen to political
leadership through left-wing parties. Individual unions, and at times
national federations of unions, have endorsed and supported one party
or another.

At bottom, however, the purposes of the trade union and the political party remain distinct. The party is interested in capturing political
power, which requires that it build a mass following by any means

available. The trade union is regarded as an easy way of mobilizing large numbers of workers behind the party's purposes. It is a means to an end, not an end in itself. In the event of a conflict between union and party interests, the unions must be prepared to sacrifice their interests to ensure party victory. This outlook is exemplified most strongly in the case of communist parties, but it is a natural point of view for any political leader. The party is interested in unionism for the sake of the party.

The trade union, however, is interested in political parties for the sake of union objectives. It finds that certain kinds of economic objectives can be achieved most readily through legislation. It is often willing, therefore, to line up behind a political organization which promises to enact such legislation. At the same time, it has independent objectives to be achieved on the industrial front through collective bargaining; and it has an organization, leadership, and institutional life of its own. It cannot afford to become a mere appendage to some political apparatus. An additional consideration is that the union normally includes workers of differing political outlooks. Tying the union too closely to one party involves a risk of alienating some workers and reducing the union's size and strength. Union-party relations have been closest in countries where a large majority of workers were of the same political faith, as in Britain and Scandinavia during recent decades. Where this is not so, the unions either avoid any firm party alignment, as in the United States; or politics becomes a divisive influence which splits the union movement into several competing groups, as in France and Italy.

These general statements may be illustrated from the relation of trade unionism to communist and socialist political parties.

Communist parties

The function of trade unions in the communist scheme is to mobilize worker support for the communist party and to serve as an instrument of day-to-day combat with employers. The idea of an enduring union-management agreement which may be beneficial to both parties is rejected as "reformism," or "opportunism." The employer is the enemy. The duty of the union is to harry him in every way possible, to undermine his position in the plant and build up bitterness toward him among the workers, and eventually to dispossess him. The role of trade unions after the revolution is usually left conveniently vague. In actuality, Russia and other communist countries have subordinated the trade unions completely to the party and the state.

Throughout the world, the communist party in each country has worked tirelessly to capture control of as many trade unions as possible. The tactics used have varied with the circumstances. In some cases the communists have tried to build up their influence within existing unions to the point where they could capture the top union offices. In other cases they have set up new unions, under firm communist control from the outset, and then tried to win away members from the noncommunist unions in the hope of eventually destroying them.

In the United States and most other democratic countries, these tactics have had only very limited success. Communist influence in American unions reached a peak between 1935 and 1945. The rapidly expanding new unions were in desperate need of experienced organizers and officials, and welcomed recruits without much concern for their political beliefs. From 1941 to 1945 the communists, because of the military alliance between the United States and the U.S.S.R., were among the strongest advocates of maximum war production and threw their full support behind the Roosevelt administration. With the end of the wartime alliance and the adoption of opposing foreign policies by the U.S. and the U.S.S.R. after 1945, the tactics of the American communists changed. They became bitterly hostile to American foreign policy, withdrew their support from the Democratic Party, and helped to organize the new Progressive Party for the presidential campaign of 1948. At the same time American public opinion became increasingly anticommunist. Communists were belabored in the public press, persons suspected of communist sympathies were haled before Congressional committees, national leaders of the party were indicted for sedition, and a number of noncitizens were deported for illegal entry into the United States.

All this created an atmosphere in which the noncommunist majority in the CIO could mobilize to drive communist sympathizers from union office. In several important unions, strong leaders, such as Reuther in the Automobile Workers, Curran in the National Maritime Union, and Quill in the Transport Workers Union, were able to defeat communist-supported candidates for union office and establish noncommunists in firm school. The national CIO organization also undertook to expel affiliated unions which were unable or unwilling to free themselves of communist influence. During 1949 and 1950, eleven national unions[5] with some 900,000 members were expelled from the CIO. The present AFL-CIO constitution contains strong provisions against domination of unions by communists and other totalitarian groups, and communist influence has fallen to a very low level.

The trend of events in most other countries has been broadly similar. In Britain and the Scandinavian countries, communists attained considerable influence during and just after World War II. Since about 1947, however, their openly pro-Soviet and antinational policies have led trade union leaders to take countermeasures against them, and their influence has been sharply reduced. In West Germany the labor movement, while officially neutral, is in fact anticommunist as well as antifascist. Most union members are socialists and support the Social Democratic party, although there are also many Catholic unionists who favor the Christian Democrats.

In Italy and France, on the other hand, the communists continue to play a leading role in the trade union movement. The communist-dominated *Confederation Generale du Travail* (CGT) in France has a membership exceeding the total of the two rival federations—the Catholic CFTC and the generally socialist CGT-FO. In Italy, the *Confederazione Generale Italiana del Lavoro* (CGIL), which is led by communists and left-wing socialists in close alliance with them, includes the great bulk of union members, and the Catholic and right-wing socialist federations are much smaller.

Several factors help to account for communist strength in France and Italy. In both countries class lines are firmly drawn and class feeling is bitter. Employers typically look down on their workers to an extent which is difficult to imagine in the United States. They are bitterly opposed to dealing with trade unions, and collective bargaining is poorly developed. The unions are weakly organized, poorly financed, and the attachment of workers to them is so loose that one can scarcely speak of "union membership" in the American sense. A union may be able to call out a large number of workers for a short strike, but it cannot get these same workers to pay dues or participate

---

[5] These were the United Electrical, Radio and Machine Workers; the United Farm Equipment Workers; the Mine, Mill, and Smelter Workers; the United Office and Professional Workers; the United Public Workers; the Food, Tobacco, and Agricultural Workers; the American Communications Workers; the Fur and Leather Workers; the Internatioal Longshoremen's and Warehousemen's Union; the Marine Cooks and Stewards; and the Fishermen and Allied Workers.

in ordinary union activities. Seeing no way of rising through their own efforts and apparently blocked from advance through collective bargaining, not surprisingly, the workers turn to political activity. Economic and social reforms in these countries have been achieved almost entirely through legislation rather than through private collective bargaining. It is not surprising, then, that the political parties dominate the trade unions, and that the party with greatest popular appeal is the one which denounces employers in the strongest terms.

The situation is somewhat similar in many of the newly indus-trializing countries. The social gulf between employer and employee is wide, unions are weak and led largely by outsiders rather than men who have worked up from the ranks, collective bargaining is almost nonexistent, and improvements in wages and working conditions must be sought through government regulation. These conditions tend to produce a strong political orientation of the trade unions.

Socialist parties

In most industrial countries the strongest influence on the trade unions has been the movement which may be described as gradualist, nonrevolutionary, or democratic socialism. While there is some tendency in the United States to confuse the socialist and com-munist movements, the two are basically different and are in fact bitterly opposed. In many countries the socialist parties now provide the strongest bulwark against communist control, and are the only alternative movement which has any likelihood of winning majority support.

The list of democratic socialist parties includes the Labour Parties of Great Britain, Australia, and New Zealand; the Socialist parties of France and Belgium; the right-wing socialists (PSLI) in Italy; the Social Democratic parties of Denmark, Sweden, and Western Ger-many; the Labor Party of Norway; and a number of important socialist parties in Asia and Latin America. The history of these parties has been broadly similar. Most of them originated in the closing decades of the nineteenth century, drawing their intellectual inspiration from a variety of sources, including Marx and other rev-olutionary theorists, the British Fabian group, and the Christian socialist writers. Their growth since that time has been intermittent, but with a strong upward trend. By the early 1900's several of them had elected members to parliament. By the 1920's, several had formed the governments of their respective countries. They grew with particular vigor during the depression and war years of 1930-45. By 1950, in most democratic countries other than Canada and the United States the socialists either constituted the government of the country (in some cases, one element in a majority coalition), or were the leading opposition party.

The United States provides the leading exception to this general trend. The Socialist party polled its largest presidential vote in 1912, when almost a million people voted for Eugene V. Debs. The strength of the party has declined steadily since that time and is negligible at present. This is to some extent misleading, however, because certain elements of socialist philosophy have been taken over by the two major parties. The influence of socialist thought has thus been considerably greater than the voting strength of the party would suggest.

The relation of socialist parties to their trade union supporters is quite different from that of the communist parties to the communist-led unions. The communists believe that union activities must be geared strictly to the purposes of the party, and that both party and unions must be firmly controlled from the top down. The socialists conceive of the union-party relation as an association of equal partners, within which each organization performs its own functions under its own leadership. They also believe in democratic control from below over the union and party organizations. Indeed, the fact that both organizations are controlled by the mass membership at the bottom of the pyramid, and that most members of one are also members of the other, is the main thing which binds them together.

Elections are held on a geographical basis and a socialist party, like any other, must try to attract as many supporters as possible in each locality. This is done through a network of local party clubs throughout the country, which are open to anyone who is willing to join and pay dues. Trade unionists, including white-collar as well as manual workers, normally form the bulk of the membership; but the clubs also include professional people, small businessmen, and others.

In some countries, including Denmark and West Germany, individuals can join the party only by enrolling in one of these local associations. In most countries, however, there is provision for blanket affiliation of union members. In Norway and Sweden, for example, many local unions are affiliated as a group with the socialist party. About half the membership of the Norwegian Labor Party, and about two-thirds that of the Swedish Social Democratic Party, come from workers who have affiliated in this way. In some countries national unions may affiliate for their entire membership. In Great Britain, for example, some eighty national unions are affiliated with the Labour Party, and these unions provide more than four-fifths of the Party's members. Where block affiliation is practiced, there is normally a legal provision that individual union members who favor another political party may claim exemption from contributing money to support of the affiliated party.

The relationship between the two groups in Britain has been well described as follows:

> The question frequently asked in other countries is whether the trade unions control the Labour Party or the Labour Party controls the trade unions. In fact neither interpretation would be true. Naturally the trade unions have an influence on Labour Party policy, but theirs is one influence among several and it is not uniform in character. On the whole it is probably more negative than positive: It would be difficult for the Labour Party (or a Labour Government) to disregard any strong and widely held trade union opinion, but policy, except in those matters with which the trade unions are intimately concerned, is rarely initiated by the trade union wing of the Party. The trade unions for their part are usually careful not to act in such a way as to injure the Labour Party's prospects, but there is no merging of identities . . . it is not uncommon for the Trades Union Congress and the Labour Party to take a different view upon a subject, although they then endeavour to reach an agreement, or at least to avoid any violent conflict in public.[6]

Much the same statement could be made for Australia, Norway, Sweden, and other countries.

TRADE UNION PARTICIPATION IN MANAGEMENT

The discussion thus far suggests that, with the exception of communist-led unions in some countries, trade unionism is not a revolutionary political movement. Its political affiliations are with center parties or moderate socialist parties which, while breathing occasional fire for election purposes, do not in fact seek drastic reconstruction of the economic system.

It may be argued, however, that this is not conclusive. Even though labor's political intentions appear peaceable, may not its economic

---

[6] Galenson, *Comparative Labor Movements*, p. 90.

consequences be revolutionary? May not union encroachment on management functions eventually reduce the private business manager to complete impotence? Some management people suspect that union leaders are secretly aiming at this objective. Others see it as a possible unintended consequence of union operations.

This fear is expressed in such statements as the following:

> Restriction on management freedom is a big issue. This isn't breast-beating. We've got heavy responsibilities for making quick, accurate and effective decisions. Sometimes there are considerations that we can't divulge or that wouldn't be understood if we did. We're held responsible for the success of them, but the union isn't. It takes complicated maneuvering to run a business, and all the parts have to be kept working together. You have to have a good deal of free play in the rope for that. Sometimes there is a particular restriction that gets your goat, but on the whole it's the overall sense of being closed in on, and the anticipation of more of the same, that gets you. It's the cumulative effect of one area of freedom after another being reduced and the promise of still more that give us real concern, but you make adjustments and go on to every particular one. It's not impossible, but you wonder how long it can go on and leave you able to meet your responsibilities.[7]

Or consider another statement by a management spokesman:

> Union representatives are demanding, and succeeding inch by inch in obtaining the demand, that they exercise judgment before management can act . . . if the management representatives must talk to the union representatives before they can act or make a decision, then management has lost its management function. The function is then being discharged by the party with whom management must consult before acting and the party whose approval must be obtained. That is the drive that is being made.[8]

Officials of American trade unions strongly deny any such long-range program. Their outlook is represented by such statements as these:

> The union doesn't want to run the business. It doesn't want to take over management. At the same time, while we don't attempt to usurp management's prerogatives, we do attempt to mitigate them so that their exercise cannot endanger the security and well-being of the workers.
>
> If the unions are planning a drive to secure a greater voice in management, I haven't heard of it. Of course, it may work out that our program may lead into socialism, as they worry about, but it won't be because

---

[7] E. Wight Bakke, *Mutual Survival* (New York: Harper & Row, Publishers, 1946), p. 29.

[8] Neil W. Chamberlain, *The Union Challenge to Management Control* (New York: Harper & Row, Publishers, 1948), p. 3.

we planned it that way. The basic motivation is security. As long as management's decisions don't adversely affect the security of the workers or their unions, we are glad to let the management run the business—we don't want any part of that responsibility.[9]

These disclaimers, granted their sincerity, are not sufficient to dispose of the matter. They leave open the question of how far unions may eventually feel obliged to go in order to protect the security and job interests of their members. Almost any kind of business decision —about plant location, products, methods of production, pricing, marketing methods, finance—affects the company's ability to pay wages and the volume and regularity of employment which it affords. Must unions try to limit management's discretion on all these matters? May they not feel obliged, in order fully to protect the interests of their members, to assume virtual management of industry?

One approach to an answer is to examine the content of union-management agreements in the United States. The bulk of the clauses in a typical contract relate either to recognition of the union as an institution, and provision for orderly dealings between union and management representatives, or to matters of personnel administration—wage rates and supplementary benefits; hours and work schedules; hiring, promotion, layoff, and discharge; health, safety, and other aspects of working conditions; work speeds and work assignments. Some unions have also taken considerable interest in production methods, usually with a view to creating additional employment by prescribing time-consuming methods of work, or to protecting workers against displacement by new machinery.

Most aspects of management, however, have been left largely untouched by collective bargaining. Few unions have sought any voice in selection of products, determination of production volume and inventory policy, choice of market channels and sales methods, determination of prices and other terms of sales, competitive relations with rival companies, methods of financing new capital requirements, dividend policy, and other aspects of financial management. Personnel decisions have been brought squarely within the orbit of collective bargaining. Production, sales, finance, and general executive coordination of the business have been affected only tangentially.[10]

Is this only because many American unions are relatively new?

---

[9] *Ibid.*, p. 90.
[10] For a more detailed analysis, see Chamberlain, *op cit.*, chaps. 4 and 5.

May they not penetrate much more deeply into management functions as they grow older and stronger? It is instructive to look at some of the long-established unions in the United States. In industries such as building construction, printing and publishing, railroad transport, and coal mining, trade unions have been in continuous operation for a hundred years. The unions are powerful, they bargain with management on a multitude of issues, and they have tied management's hands at many points where management would have preferred to remain free. Management continues, however, to have the dominant voice in production, marketing, finance, and other matters of business strategy. It has by no means been eliminated from the scene. Nor is there any indication that the scope of collective bargaining will expand much beyond its present limits.

The evidence suggests that a union, after an initial period during which it extends its membership to the limits of the industry and gradually widens the scope of collective bargaining, settles down to keeping its fences mended and wielding established authority without seeking further expansion of that authority. The long-run result is not displacement of management by the union, but an equilibrium between the expansive power of unionism and the resistance which management never ceases to offer.

There is a strong likelihood that the newer unions in the United States will evolve in this same way and will eventually arrive at a stable balance of forces in their respective industries, a balance which will permit both strong unions and responsible private management to coexist over an indefinite future. This possibility is aptly summarized in Bakke's phrase, "mutual survival"—not destruction of the power of either party, not abandonment of conflicting objectives, but a recognition that these objectives must be reconciled through negotiation on terms which do not threaten the basic security of either group.

UNION OBJECTIVES IN COLLECTIVE BARGAINING

A third way of appraising the nature of trade unionism is to look at union activities in the short run. What kinds of demands do unions make on employers year by year? What provisions do they try to get written into collective agreements? What kinds of political program do they support and what specific pieces of legislation do they favor or oppose? Listing these immediate objectives does much to illumine the general thrust of the union movement.

Looking first at collective bargaining, unions concentrate on objec- tives which can be classified under the following headings: mainte- nance of the organization; rationing of scarce job opportunities; improvement of working conditions; and development of a judicial system for deciding disputes over rights of individual workers.

The right to maintain a union organization is basic, since without this nothing else can be accomplished. The union's right to exist is usually challenged by employers at the outset, and conflict over this issue may continue for decades before the union is finally accepted as a permanent feature of the industry. During this time the union spends much energy in fending off employer attacks, developing experienced leadership and stable organizational forms, and persuad- ing workers of the need to join the union, pay dues, and support union objectives. The right to organize is one of the few tenets which is accepted implicitly by all unionists everywhere and which will never be compromised. Even after the union's survival is no longer in doubt, much attention is still given to keeping the organi- zation intact and strong.

A second facet of union activities, so important that Perlman has found in it the key to union policy, involves the control of job opportunities. Workers old enough to have lived through a depression are deeply convinced that there is never enough work to go around. Beyond this, there is clearly a shortage of "good" jobs, and the number of people trying to get into these jobs far exceeds the number of vacancies available. This poses the problem of who is to get the good jobs and who is to be left on the street or pushed into undesira- ble kinds of work.

In economic theory, this problem would be solved through em- ployers' appraisal of workers' efficiency. The employer would select the "best man for the job" at a given time. In principle, he would be free to change his opinion from month to month—to promote or demote, to hire or discharge, on the basis of his most recent evidence concerning relative worker efficiency. It is not surprising that this solution does not commend itself to most manual workers. It implies great insecurity of job tenure, a constant threat of displacement if the employer can find someone else to do the job better. It also implies that nothing but efficiency should be taken into account in hiring and firing. Most workers would not agree. What about length of service, age, family responsibilities, membership or nonmembership in the union, and other considerations?

Faced with an assumed scarcity of jobs, and faced with the insistent demand of workers for security of job tenure, the union develops policies designed to maintain or increase the total number of jobs in its industry, to ensure that union members get first chance at these jobs, and to see that the different kinds of jobs are distributed among workers in a fair and reasonable way. The distribution of the available work is too vital to be left to the sole discretion of the employer, and steps are taken to control it by rules which the union has helped to formulate. In Perlman's words,

> *The group then asserts its collective ownership over the whole amount of opportunity*, and, having determined who are entitled to claim a share in that opportunity, undertakes to parcel it out fairly, directly or indirectly, among its recognized members. . . . Free competition becomes a sin against one's fellows, anti-social, like a self-indulgent consumption of the stores of a beleaguered city, and obviously detrimental to the individual as well. A collective disposal of opportunity, including the power to keep out undesirables, and a "common rule" in making bargains are as natural to the manual group as "laissez-faire" is to the business man.[11]

The feeling that people already engaged in an occupation have a right to protection against outside competition, that experience on a job constitutes a kind of property which deserves equal protection with other forms of property, is strongest among the skilled crafts. Almost a century ago the leaders of a British craft union put the point as follows:

> Considering that the trade by which we live is our property, bought by certain years of servitude, which gives us a vested right, and that we have a sole and exclusive claim on it, as all will have hereafter who purchase it by the same means. Such being the case, it is evident it is our duty to protect, by all fair and legal means, the property by which we live, being always equally careful not to tresspass on the rights of others.[12]

This feeling may be declining somewhat with the decreasing importance of the skilled crafts, but the tradition of "property in the job" is still strong even among low-skilled workers.

A third set of union objectives has to do with improvement of wages, hours, and other terms of employment. On this front, the

---

[11] Perlman, A *Theory of the Labor Movement*, p. 242.
[12] Sidney and Beatrice Webb, *The History of Trade Unionism* (London: Workers Educational Association, 1919), p. 564.

unions are riding a flood tide. National output per capita has been rising for many decades in most countries of the Western world, and continuing improvement in wages and working conditions has come to be taken for granted. The unions may speed up this process in some respects. At any event, they usually take credit for the improvements which occur over the course of time, even though most of these may already have been "in the cards"; and they strengthen the workers' conviction that progress is normal and right. When an economist tells him that things are bound to get better for him because of the mysterious working of economic forces, he may have doubts; but when the union tells him that things will be better next year because this is his right and the union will demand it, he is likely to believe. Thus normal economic progress takes on the aspect of a social movement, of something which is organized, planned, and inevitable.

It is above all in bargaining over terms of employment that unionism reveals its flexible and pragmatic character. There are no general principles determining how large the demands should be at a particular time, or what should be their specific character. At one time the unions will push for reductions in hours, at another time for pension plans or medical care funds, at other times for straight wage increases. In one year the wage demand may be 5 cents an hour, in another 15 cents, as circumstances seem to warrant. The only firm principle is that the movement must always be in the same direction—forward.

A fourth sphere of union activity involves the process by which the general rules stated in the union contract are interpreted and applied to individual workers. The union is concerned, not only with a voice in making the rules, but with seeing that they are equitably applied and that the rights of individual workers are fully protected. The "grievance procedure" through which this is typically done in the United States is described in Chapter 7.

POLITICAL OBJECTIVES AND TACTICS

Unions have no real choice about going into politics. They are in politics automatically because they exist under a legal and political system which has been generally critical of union activities. The conspiracy suit and the injunction judge have been a problem for unions from earliest times. A minimum of political activity is essential for unions to survive and engage in collective bargaining.

There are two other practical reasons for labor political activity. First, some things can be obtained in this way which cannot be obtained at all through collective bargaining. Good public education, unemployment compensation and other forms of social insurance, adequate housing and medical care, or effective antidepression measures cannot be negotiated separately with each employer, but must be established as matters of public policy and applied uniformly throughout the community. Second, certain objectives which might conceivably be attained through collective bargaining can be reached a good deal faster through legislation. Minimum wages, maximum hours, and elimination of child labor are illustrations of this type of objective.

In addition to such general objectives, many unions have specific problems in their respective industries. Only a few illustrations need be given. The railroad industry has been faced for decades with increasing competition from trucking, shipping, and air transport. The railroad unions have therefore advocated legislation designed to protect the competitive position of the railroads. They have supported proposals for increased taxation and regulation of trucking, opposed subsidies to shipping, and opposed the St. Lawrence waterways program. They have also tried to meet the problem of declining employment by sponsoring the train-limit laws and full-crew laws discussed in Chapter 9. They have tried to reduce the legal workday on the railroads from eight to six hours. They have taken an active interest in legislation governing industrial relations on the railroads, and played a large part in the enactment of the Railway Labor Act of 1926 and amendments to this Act in 1934 and 1951. They have promoted legislation requiring the railroads to install such safety devices as air-brakes, automatic couplers, and automatic signal systems. They have also been active in promoting state and federal employer liability laws.

The seamen's unions have been mainly responsible for legislation to improve the working and living conditions of seamen on shipboard. They have also advocated the maintenance of a large American merchant marine by shipping subsidies and other methods. The United Mine Workers has been mainly responsible for mine safety legislation. It has also been the strongest sponsor of legislation to regulate prices and output in bituminous coal, a competitive industry faced with chronic overcapacity. Unions in low-wage industries, such as textiles and certain types of clothing, have been the strongest supporters of minimum-wage legislation. Most of the unions in manufacturing have lined up with employers in support of tariff protection and other advantages for their industries. Unions of government employees work mainly through legislation, since their wages and working conditions are governed by legislative enactment. The barbers' union has promoted state legislation limiting weekly hours of work, requiring licensing of barbers in order to control entrance to the industry, and legalizing price-fixing arrangements to prevent "unfair competition."

After several abortive attempts to form a labor party, organized labor in America has concentrated its efforts on influencing the two major parties. Labor is frankly a lobby. It seeks leverage in national conventions, in state party conventions, in elections, in the legislative process, and in the making of administrative policies. Its techniques are those of the other great American lobbies: business, agriculture, veterans, and many other similarly organized groups. It is only since the 'thirties, and especially since the formation of the CIO, that labor has shown the energy and effectiveness in lobbying which characterize it today. Lobbying by other groups, including those directly opposed to labor, has increased during the same period.[13] Seen in perspective the political activities of organized labor are just one part of a kaleidoscope of pressure group operations in the Federal Government and in the states. The power of the labor lobby is greater, especially in the national government, than it has been in the past, but it is still not very great vis-à-vis other groups. This section will examine some of the sources of that power and some of the ways in which it has been used to influence governmental action.

Labor in elections

The top leaders of labor have since the time of Samuel Gompers been pragmatic and nonpartisan. Under the Gompers slogan, "Reward your friends—punish your enemies," candidates of both major parties have received labor endorsement for offices ranging from the Presidency down to counties and municipalities. City and state

---

[13] It seems to be a law of politics that a build-up of political pressure generates counterpressure. After 1932 the National Association of Manufacturers increased in size, tightened up its organization, enlarged its financing for political purposes, and after 1935 concentrated its political efforts on opposing organized labor. See V. O. Key, Jr., *Politics, Parties and Pressure Groups*, 3rd ed. (New York: Thomas Y. Crowell Company, 1952), pp. 112 *et seq.*

federations of labor have given official endorsement to selected candidates for at least fifty years. National federations have been somewhat more cautious about endorsing national candidates. They hesitate to take a public stand that would certainly not be supported by some members of the executive council and by some of the constituent unions. In 1952, however, both the AFL and CIO endorsed the Democratic candidate for President, and the AFL-CIO followed the same course in 1956 and 1960. Endorsement is a publicity device, useful in building up an impression of irresistible strength for a candidate. Voters are thus encouraged to get on the bandwagon and there is some evidence that, if the union leadership has been tactful, the union membership may be solidified.

A resolution of endorsement lays a foundation for financial support of the chosen candidate. Union contributions to election campaigns have been restricted in a series of acts culminating in the Taft-Hartley Act of 1947, which prohibited political contributions in elections, primaries, or conventions involving federal offices. Some state legislatures have enacted similar bans on union activity in state elections. This has forced the unions to operate through quasi-independent political affiliates, such as the AFL-CIO Committee on Political Education. This Committee collects donations from union members for political activity and maintains a separate treasury. Below the national COPE are state and local committees which interest themselves in elections at those levels, and which actually spend a good deal more money than the national body.

The funds collected, which in a key election in a major industrial state may amount to several hundred thousand dollars, are used in several ways. Part may be contributed directly to the candidate's campaign fund. Some may be spent on radio and television time, advertisements, pamphlet material, and other campaign publicity, thus relieving the candidate of certain expenditures. Material on campaign issues and on the voting records of various candidates may be distributed directly to union members. In some cases labor has built up its own precinct organization and used money to pay election-day workers and other workers recruited from the unions rather than from party organizations.

Contributions of unpaid time by union members are probably as important as cash contributions. Of particular importance is the systematic organization which actually gets out the vote. Door-to-door canvassing must be carried out in advance of election day.

Lists of qualified voters must be checked to see that maximum registration is achieved. On election day, more lists must be checked, telephone calls made, and automobile transportation and even babysitting provided, to be sure that all those registered either appear at the polls or vote by absentee ballot.

There is little evidence that the labor vote can be "delivered" in the sense that union members will necessarily vote as their leaders advise. Economic interest counts for something and the union member will respond to political appeals partly as a worker, but he responds also as (for example) a father, a homeowner, a Roman Catholic, a person of draft age, or a resident of a small New England town. It remains likely, however, that in a particular election the bulk of unionists will decide on their own to vote for the candidates who have been officially designated as "pro-labor." It thus pays to try for a hundred per cent turnout at the polls in the hope that most of the membership will vote the "right" way.

Labor in the legislative process

It is not enough to elect friendly candidates to executive and legislative positions. It is important also to have continuous contact with the legislature while it is in session. Thus we find the AFL-CIO and many of the larger national unions maintaining permanent legislative representatives in Washington. In most state capitals legislative representation is a part-time function of officers of the state labor federation and of individual unions.

The strategy of the labor lobbyist is more or less fixed by the nature of legislative operations. Although details vary from one session to another, a pattern can be seen. First, his staff will keep track of bills concerning labor, many of which will actually be written by the union's own lawyers. Second, the labor lobby will exert whatever influence it can on appointments to standing and special committees —controlling if possible the membership, chairmanship, and employees—and will make the best contact it can with those committees which experience has shown will be handling labor bills. Third, when bills arrive at the stage of committee hearings, the labor lobby will put into action a carefully prepared campaign to get the best press for their point of view on the bill. Fourth, they will see that the timetable for debate on each of their bills is set up to give maximum advantage to their viewpoint. Fifth, as the time for a vote arrives the staff will canvass the legislature continuously so that they can predict the voting lineup and take appropriate action—either insist on an immediate vote, or delay voting on the bill until more support can be mobilized. Every bill goes through a series of votes which make it easy to forecast the lineup and plan further parliamentary strategy before final action is taken. Sixth, they will try to use whatever influence they have with the White House (or the governor) both at the early stages of discussion of a bill and, if all else fails, after passage of an unfavorable bill to get an executive veto.

What does the lobbyist do? Close personal contact has always been the most effective method of persuasion with legislators. During the height of the session the labor lobbyist will very likely be active right around the clock. In the state legislatures especially, the heavy pressure of large numbers of bills on a tight schedule means that things happen very fast and a lobbyist's success or failure may depend on being at the elbow of the legislative leadership at one fleeting but crucial moment. Ubiquity alone carries a positive advantage. "In Congress, from my experiences," said one of the most famous lobbyists, "the fellow that makes the most noise, and the fellow that makes the most demands, that keeps his problems in front of them all the time, he gets service."[14]

The lobbyist on the spot anticipates the critical moment for mobilizing grass roots sentiment, and it is his job to bring it to bear on the individual legislators. This may take the form of a letter or telegram or a personal call from the state labor leaders or the national president of the union, or the lobbyist may call for a rank-and-file delegation to descend on the capitol. The technique of inundating the legislator's office with letters from constituents has diminished in effectiveness because of its wide use, the ease with which this tap can be turned on to produce a flood of messages, and a widespread belief that such messages do not represent genuine conviction on the part of the sender. When a representative's mail comes in by the truckload, a sampling usually shows that hundreds of messages follow identical forms furnished by the lobby. Hundreds more come from outside the constituency, sometimes in bulk from a single postoffice. The fact is that the representative's mail from home is, at most, only one factor in making up his mind.

On the surface, it looks as though the lobbyist's task is to convince

---

[14] J. R. Grundy, quoted in Key, *Politics, Parties, and Pressure Groups*, p. 174.

the representative that there is substantial local support for the action desired by the pressure group. Actually, the lobbyist often tries to reassure the representative that general interest in a bill is so slight that the requested action will do him no harm with his constituency. Old hands try to frame legislation so that a desired end may be accomplished without touching the vital interests of groups most likely to oppose it. Passage of an entirely new law stirs up widespread public interest; amendment of an existing law may go through almost unnoticed, especially if the amendments are technical. One explanation of the passage of the Taft-Hartley Act at a time when labor union strength was apparently very great is that it was framed in such a way as to avoid attacking the matters with which the unions were most directly concerned—wages, hours, and working conditions. By dealing with "the institutional privileges of the union," the Act "minimized opposition both from within and from outside the ranks of organized labor."[15]

The legislative specialist soon becomes expertly informed on the details of rules and procedure, and uses his knowledge to advance his group's interests both defensively—to protect advantages already won—and aggressively, to obtain or to exploit procedural changes which will help his group obtain some new advantage or privilege. This is a big job, a complicated job, and one that is not done inside the legislative halls. Labor's legislative operations are really public relations work. The best lobbyist does not confine himself to the relatively narrow aim of influencing legislators. He "sells" his cause simultaneously to those who control the press and other communications media, to the general public, and to other organized groups which might form a temporary alliance with him.

Labor in the administrative process

Organized labor thinks of the state and federal departments of labor as the voice of labor inside the administration. Since the creation of the U.S. Department of Labor in 1913, it has been taken for granted that the Secretary of Labor will be someone acceptable to the unions, and a certain number of ex-labor leaders will usually be found at lower levels in the Department. In many of the state governments, union leaders have regularly been appointed to head the

---

[15] Arthur M. Ross, *Trade Union Wage Policy* (Berkeley: University of California Press, 1948), p. 24.

state labor departments. One finds also an increasing number of independent regulatory agencies dealing with labor matters, notably the National Labor Relations Board and the state labor relations boards in many states. Labor is naturally concerned that both the members and the key employees of these agencies should be sympathetic to labor's interests. The attitude of administrative officials, the interpretation placed on statutory provisions, and the vigor or lack of vigor in enforcement are often of key importance.

The fact that many appointments of trade union officials and sympathizers are made to administrative posts is significant, but it is easy to overstate the importance of such appointments. Regardless of his origins, anyone who spends any length of time in public service tends increasingly to identify himself with the public interest—or at least to take a viewpoint broader than that of the pressure group that originally put him in his job. Probably the expectation of the pressure group that an administrator recruited from its own ranks will give it an inside track is about balanced by the expectation of the chief executive that such a man will be useful in persuading organized labor to swallow unpalatable policies.

SOME GENERAL CONCLUSIONS

Let us return now to the general question raised at the beginning: "What are the unions after?" To a singular degree the trade union movement is a movement without ideology. Its objectives are not deduced from broad principles of politics or economics. Union leaders have no picture in mind of an ideal future society which will remain unchanged for all time.

Change and reform are of the essence of unionism. But the direction of change is only vaguely formulated, the ends are immediate and concrete, the demands change with changing circumstances. This earthy and practical character of unionism, the despair of intellectuals who would like to see in it the vehicle for achieving some social millennium, has proved a great source of strength to the movement. Unions have shown themselves able to survive war and military defeat, prosperity and depression, economic expansion and great shifts in the structure of industry, socialization of privately owned businesses, and many other changes. The very lack of a fixed ideology, the willingness to adjust both objectives and tactics to changing circumstances, has enabled unionism to survive cataclysms which would have broken a more rigid and brittle institution.

It is clear that unionism brings important social changes. The trade union becomes a leading community institution, more central in the lives of many workers than the lodge, the company, the political party, or anything else. Other basic institutions must, so to speak, "move over" to make room for it. The union comes to play an important role in industrial management, particularly as regards wages and hours, working conditions, job tenure, and other personnel matters. Perhaps most important, unionism brings a considerable shift in the balance of political power in the community. It exerts effective pressure in the direction of what has come to be termed "the welfare state" and bars any return to the governmental policies of the nineteenth century. In a strongly unionized democracy, every political party must take account of labor's interests in order to survive.

Reform is the enemy of revolution; and one can make a good case that the conservative aspects of unionism are at least as important as its reform aspects over the long run. We have already noted that trade unionism is a powerful competitor to revolutionary political movements. The radical politician tells workers that "the system" is wholly bad, that they must reject and overturn it, that progress can come only through a drastic transformation of society. The trade union points out that workers do in fact have a stake in the existing order, which they should not risk without forethought. It assures workers that if they will support and work through the union, they will reap modest but tangible benefits year by year. As workers find that these benefits actually materialize, their belief in the need for revolutionary change diminishes.

It is no accident that in countries where union organization is strong—the United States, Britain, northern Europe, the British dominions—revolutionary political movements (anarchist, syndicalist, communist, or what not) have never attained great strength. Moreover, revolutionary politics is weaker in these countries than it was thirty or forty years ago, whereas union organization is much stronger. Conversely, where unionism is weak, as in Italy or France, revolutionary political parties are strong. There can be little doubt that stronger trade unions and development of effective bargaining procedures would reduce the appeal of the communist parties in these countries.

Within industry, the unions do not seek to dispossess management and take over all managerial functions. They do strive to limit the discretionary powers of management in a variety of ways. This again is reform, not revolution. In some countries, to be sure, the unions have supported nationalization of certain types of industry. Over the course of time, however, enthusiasm for nationalization has diminished, partly because unions have found that dealing with a public manager is not very different from dealing with a private manager.

One of the most important ways in which unionism tends to conserve and strengthen the social structure is by strengthening the worker's attachment to his job, his work group, and his employer. It provides him with a club, a fraternity, which helps to gratify the natural desire for social bonds with one's fellows. It provides a channel through which he can seek redress of grievances against supervisors or others, so that he has the feeling of living in a self-governing society rather than in an autocracy. It dramatizes the gradual improvement of wages and other conditions from year to year. It strengthens his security in his job and, through the influence of seniority rules, makes it more likely that he will stay with the same employer over the long run. In all these ways unionism gives workers a "stake in the system," a sense of belonging and participation, a feeling that the existing setup of industry is reasonably satisfactory, and an antipathy to proposals for radical change.

Some observers would disagree with this characterization of unionism as a conservative movement. In the light of the drastic changes in western capitalism over the past two hundred years, however, and in the light of the revolutionary political movements now sweeping the world, the demands and achievements of the trade unions seem modest. Certainly they appear to be well within the range of tolerance both for private capitalism and democratic government.

Discussion questions

1. "In most democratic countries, the trade unions are the strongest obstacle to communist influence over the working class. As union strength grows, communist strength seems to diminish." Discuss.

2. "The alliance in many countries between the trade union movement and a labor political party is always an uneasy one. The objectives of union leaders and labor politicians are quite different and frequently in conflict with one another." Discuss.

3. Is there a genuine danger that trade unions, while not taking responsibility for industrial management, may become so strong as to prevent existing managements from functioning effectively?

4. "The idea that the political objectives of trade unions are 'liberal' or 'reform' objectives is an illusion. The political programs of American trade unions have been precisely as selfish as those of business associations, farm groups, and other economic interests." Discuss.

5. "Trade unionism is basically a conservative institution, and does more to perpetuate private enterprise than to destroy it." Discuss.

6. Outline the principal methods by which labor unions participate in politics.

7. Discuss some of the reasons why organized labor has failed to form or join a labor party in the United States.

8. "Powerful lobbies form a 'third house' in American legislative bodies." Discuss this proposition with reference to organized labor.

Selected reading

Bakke, E. Wight, *Mutual Survival*. New York: Harper & Row, Publishers, 1946. Yale Labor and Management Center Series.

Calkins, Fay, *The CIO and the Democratic Party*. Chicago: University of Chicago Press, 1952.

Chamberlain, Neil W., *The Union Challenge to Management Control*. New York: Harper & Row, Publishers, 1948.

Galenson, Walter, ed., *Comparative Labor Movements*. Englewood Cliffs, N.J.: Prentice-Hall, Inc., 1952.

Key, V. O., Jr., *Politics, Parties and Pressure Groups*, 4th ed. New York: Thomas Y. Crowell Company, 1958.

Kornhauser, Arthur, Albert J. Mayer, and Harold L. Sheppard, *When Labor Votes*. New York: University Books, Inc., 1956.

Lester, Richard A., *As Unions Mature*. Princeton: Princeton University Press, 1958.

Perlman, Selig, *A Theory of the Labor Movement*. New York: The Macmillan Company, 1928.

Saposs, David, *Left-Wing Unionism in the United States*. New York: International Publishers, 1926.

Tannenbaum, Frank, *A Philosophy of Labor*. New York: Alfred A. Knopf, Inc., 1951.

Truman, David B., *The Governmental Process*, rev. ed. New York: Alfred A. Knopf, Inc., 1960.

Webb, Sidney and Beatrice, *Industrial Democracy*. London: Longmans, Green and Company, 1897.

4

The Government of Trade Unions

Collective bargaining is a relationship between organizations—the business firm and the trade union. The internal structure of these organizations affects the relations between them and helps mold the daily life of the worker. In this chapter we examine first the broad outlines of union government at the national and local levels. Next we shall consider some common criticisms of internal union management, and then review the efforts which have been made to correct these deficiencies through legislation.

MANAGING A NATIONAL UNION

A national trade union operates under a written constitution, which may run to forty or fifty closely printed pages. These constitutions are much more detailed than the charters of business corporations or of most other organizations. The duties and powers of union officers, the rights and duties of members, and all procedures for the conduct of union business are usually set forth at length.

The supreme governing body is usually the national convention. Most unions hold their conventions every year or every two years, though sometimes conventions are four or five years apart. The convention consists of delegates from the affiliated local unions. Each local is usually represented in proportion to its dues-paying membership, which means that the locals from the larger plants or cities have a dominant voice. The convention has a number of functions and powers. It listens to reports by the national officers on their activities since the last convention, discusses these reports, and approves or disapproves them. It elects officers to serve until the next convention. It is free to debate any question of union policy or organization, and has power also to amend the basic constitution of the union.

The national convention provides a forum in which the views of local unions throughout the country can be expressed. Most of the delegates are local union officials. Many locals pass resolutions at their local meetings for submission to the national convention, and frequently instruct their delegates on the stand which they should take. The convention provides an opportunity for leaders of a particular local to learn about the problems facing other locals and the national organization as a whole. It thus widens the viewpoint of local leaders and makes them more cognizant of the part which they play in a national institution. The convention debates also allow able local officials to display their leadership ability, thus giving them a channel into national office. Almost all national union leaders rise from lower ranks in the union, and must demonstrate their ability repeatedly before they attain high office.

The initiative in bringing business before the convention does not rest entirely, or even mainly, with the delegates. The national officials work out in advance their own policy proposals and seek support for them from the convention. The officers are also usually seeking re-election for another term. The union convention is therefore "stage-managed" in much the same way as the national convention of a political party. The top union officials appoint the key convention committees—the credentials committee, the resolutions committee, the committee on officers' reports, and so on. They determine the order of business and the time allowed for discussion of various subjects, and the union president from his position in the chair can do a good deal to influence the course of discussion. Much of the important business of the convention is done in private through individual discussions and committee meetings, and many key decisions are made in advance of any discussion on the convention floor. The delegates occasionally revolt and take decisions out of the hands of the union leaders. The leaders are usually astute enough, however, to appraise correctly the feeling of the delegates on each issue, and to shape their proposals so as to be sure in advance of a favorable vote. Their control is not arbitrary, but is based on a well-developed talent for keeping an ear to the ground.

A number of unions, primarily craft unions which have been in existence for forty or fifty years, use the referendum procedure, either alone or in conjunction with conventions. In some unions all national officers are elected by referendum vote of the membership, and all constitutional amendments must be ratified in the same way. In some cases, even though there is a national convention, all policy decisions of the convention must be submitted to a referendum vote. A few unions provide for initiation of new legislation directly by the membership. A petition signed by a certain number of union members or endorsed by a certain number of locals compels the national officers to submit the proposition in question either to the convention or to a referendum vote.

Administration of unions

Administration of the national union's affairs is entrusted to an executive board, consisting usually of a president, secretary, treasurer, and numerous vice-presidents who are responsible for particular geographical areas or segments of the industry. Subject to any constitutional limitations, the executive board has full power to act for the union during the period between conventions.

The executive board, or in some cases the president acting for the executive board, appoints the salaried staff of the union and directs its day-to-day work. In the larger unions, the salaried staff includes several hundred people. At national headquarters there are usually departments for research, legal problems, education, the union magazine, organizing, and other functions, plus a clerical staff to handle bookkeeping and correspondence. If legislation is important to the union, and if national headquarters is not located in Washington, there will be a branch office in Washington staffed by a legislative representative and frequently several assistants.

The field organization of the union usually consists of several regional or district offices, each headed by a regional director. If the union has jurisdiction over several industries, as in the case of the Textile Workers' Union, there may be a regional director for each industry. Under the regional directors are the field representatives or "organizers," who organize new local unions and assist existing locals in their dealings with employers. The field representatives are the cement that binds the locals to the national union. They move around their regions constantly, keep in close touch with grass roots sentiment, report back to national headquarters, and at the same time interpret national union policies to local officials and the rank and file.

The salaries of most union officials are modest by business standards. Two unions—the Mine Workers and the Teamsters—currently pay their presidents $50,000 per year, but this is unusual. The average for presidents of the larger unions would probably be in the neighborhood of $25,000. Most second-echelon union officials would fall in the range of $10,000 to $20,000 per year. Local officers frequently serve without pay. Salaried local officers and field representatives usually do not receive much more than they could make by working in the plant. The practical reason for this is that union members are envious of anyone appointed to a job paying more than they earn themselves, and it is therefore poor politics to let the salaries of union officials get much out of line with the members' earnings. In addition to salary, union officials usually receive allowances for travel and other necessary expenses.

Almost all of the top officials of American unions began as workers in the industry and rose to their present positions through the union's ranks. A man begins as a worker in the plant, is elected shop steward or shop committeeman, goes on to become an official of the local union, rises to international representative or district director, and finally becomes an officer of the international union.[1] A man rarely leaps from nowhere to high office in the union, just as he does not often became a candidate for President of the United States without having served his time in lesser political positions. Disappointing as it may be to college graduates who wish to contribute their talents to the labor movement, there is virtually no way of winning elective office in a trade union except by starting in the plant and coming up through the ranks.

In addition to its administrative functions, the executive board exercises supreme judicial authority during the period between con-

---

[1] See Eli Ginzberg, *The Labor Leader* (New York: The Macmillan Company, 1948), particularly chaps. 5 and 6. See also Jack Barbash, *Labor Unions in Action* (New York: Harper & Row, Publishers, 1948); C. A. Madison, *American Labor Leaders* (New York: Harper & Row, Publishers, 1950); and Florence Peterson, *American Labor Unions—What They Are and How They Work*; rev. ed. (New York: Harper and Row, Publishers, 1952).

ventions. It hears appeals of union members from actions of local officials, mediates disputes between local unions or factions within a local, and has broad authority to discipline local officials for maladministration or violation of the union constitution. Decisions of the executive board can usually be appealed to the next national convention, but there are a few cases in which this is not true. The president of the American Federation of Musicians, for example, has the right to perform any act on behalf of the union, including making amendments to the union constitution, with no appeal by the membership. There are historical reasons for this provision, connected with the unstable and migratory character of musicians' work, which created a special need for strong central authority. Instances of this sort, however, are very rare in the union world.

Union finances

The main source of union income is dues paid by the members. Most unions now have dues of three to five dollars a month, and it remains true that "in most unions the monthly dues can be earned in less than two hours of work."[2] The highest dues are usually charged by unions of skilled workers whose earning level is higher. In the craft unions, too, dues frequently include an insurance premium to cover sickness, retirement, death, and other benefits provided by the unions. Dues are collected by the local union and divided between it and the national union in some specified proportion. The commonest basis is a 50-50 division, but in some cases the national office takes as little as 25 per cent, and in a few cases it takes more than 50 per cent.

As the functions of the national union have grown, there has been a tendency for its share of dues payments to increase. The level of dues has also risen over the course of time. Wage levels have also risen greatly, however, and it is doubtful whether dues are now as large relative to earnings as they were ten or twenty years ago. It is hard for national union officials to get dues raised fast enough to keep up with rising wage levels and the growing needs of the union. Convention delegates who are tractable enough on other issues frequently kick over the traces when it comes to approving a dues increase which they know will be unpopular with the members.

A secondary source of revenue is initiation fees for new members,

[2] Philip Taft, *The Structure and Government of Trade Unions* (Cambridge: Harvard University Press, 1954), p. 81.

which are generally less than twenty-five dollars and in many cases only five dollars or so. Only seven of the eighty unions Taft studied, all seven in the building trades, had initiation fees averaging as much as seventy-five dollars. There is considerable variation among local unions, which are usually allowed to set their own initiation fees within outside limits specified by the national. Recent reports by about 39,000 local unions under the Landrum-Griffin Act showed 325 locals with fees of two hundred and fifty to five hundred dollars, and 17 with fees ranging from five hundred to a peak of fourteen hundred dollars.[3]

Where does the money go? A union economist has estimated that about one-third of national union expenditures goes for organizing purposes, with benefits to members accounting for 22 per cent, administrative expenses 15 per cent, and strike benefits 13 per cent.[4] Publications, research and legal expenses, and other minor items account for the balance. The major expense item for a local union is salaries of local officers, business agents, and clerical help.

The finances of the national union are carefully safeguarded. Officers who handle funds must be bonded, and there is usually a requirement that checks be signed by at least two officials. The union's books are normally audited at least once a year, and a statement of receipts and expenditures is usually printed either in the union magazine or in the proceedings of the national convention. Most national unions also require that the books of local unions shall be inspected periodically by a traveling auditor from the national office. Despite these precautions, embezzlement of local union funds still occurs occasionally, though it is very rare at the national level. Taft found that in any given year a certain proportion of local unions, ranging usually between 1 and 3 per cent, will report shortages in their accounts. Some of this is of course due to inexperience and poor bookkeeping rather than deliberate misappropriation. After considering amounts recovered from surety companies and other bonding agencies, net losses are a very small percentage of total dues collections.[5]

---

[3] Albert Rees, *The Economics of Trade Unions* (Chicago: University of Chicago Press, 1962), p. 127.

[4] Cited in Jack Barbash, *The Practice of Unionism* (New York: Harper & Row, Publishers, 1956), p. 79.

[5] Taft, *Structure and Government of Trade Unions*, chap. 3.

Government of local unions

The government of local unions may be described more briefly. The local union is usually a branch of a national organization, though there are a few unaffiliated locals that have chosen to go their own way. An affiliated local operates within the constitution of its parent organization, which defines what it can and cannot do. In many unions, for example, a local cannot sign a contract with an employer until the contract has been approved by the national executive board. A local is usually forbidden to call a strike without national approval. If it does so, it is entitled to no funds or other support from the national organization, and may be subject to disciplinary action.

The business of a local union is carried on in weekly or monthly meetings of the membership. Where plants are very large, as in the automobile industry, some locals are so large that it is physically impossible to have a single meeting, and a delegate system has to be used. The typical local union, however, has at most a few hundred members, who can be brought together in a single meeting and can take a direct hand in union affairs if they wish to do so.

Only a small proportion of union members actually take an active and continuous interest in union affairs. On important occasions— the election of officers for the coming year, the formulation of demands to be presented to the employer, the ratification of a new contract, or the taking of a strike vote—a large percentage of the membership will appear at the meeting. In between crises, however, attendance shrinks to perhaps 5 to 10 per cent of the membership.[6] The day-to-day work of the union is carried on by a few "wheel horses" who are willing to put in the necessary time. These are the professional politicians of the labor movement, corresponding to the ward and precinct leaders in a political machine. This active minority, however, is in close touch with the remainder of the membership. Even though only two men from a certain department of the plant show up at the meeting, they probably have a good idea of

---

[6] According to one survey the "normal" attendance in medium-sized established locals, i.e., of 200 to 4000 members, is 2 to 8 per cent. See George Strauss and Leonard Sayles, "The Local Union Meeting," *Industrial and Labor Relations Review*, VI (January 1953), pp. 206-209.

what the other men in the department are thinking. They also carry back and explain to their fellow workers the decisions which were taken at the meeting. There is thus a great deal of informal representation of the inert majority, and the government of the union is more democratic than might appear at first glance.[7]

The officers of the local union usually work in the plant along with the rest and receive no pay for their union activities. Exceptions are sometimes found in large locals, where union office may become a full-time job. The local officers carry on the day-to-day work of keeping the union running, persuading new workers to join, collecting dues, handling grievances arising in the plant, and so on. On major problems, such as the negotiation of a new contract, the handling of a strike, an important grievance, or an arbitration case, they are usually advised and assisted by a national field representative.[8]

The local and the national

Over the past fifty years there has been a general tendency toward greater centralization of authority and responsibility in the national union. The main reason is increased centralization of bargaining negotiations with employers, which stems in turn from the broadening of competition in product markets and the increasing scope of employer organization. It is significant that local union autonomy is greatest in industries where the product market remains local, as in building construction, newspaper printing, local trucking, and the like. In such industries as steel, automobiles, clothing, and coal mining, on the other hand, competition is national, bargaining is in effect national, and union organization is correspondingly centralized. Key negotiations with major companies are conducted by the national officers, national field representatives typically sit in on local negotiations, all agreements are required to conform to national standards,

[7] See George Strauss and Leonard Sayles, "What the Worker Really Thinks of His Union," *Harvard Business Review*, XXXI (May-June 1953), pp. 94-102, and "Patterns of Participation in Local Unions," *Industrial and Labor Relations Review*, VI (October 1952), pp. 31-42.

[8] See George Strauss and Leonard Sayles, "The Unpaid Local Leader," *Harvard Business Review*, XXX (May-June 1952), pp. 91-104; Joel Seidman, Jack London, and Bernard Karsch, "Leadership in a Local Union," *American Journal of Sociology*, LVI (November 1950), pp. 229-237; and Eli Chinoy, "Local Union Leadership," in A. W. Gouldner, ed., *Studies in Leadership* (New York: Harper & Row, Publishers, 1950), pp. 157-173.

and local policy decisions are closely monitored. A large national staff—a union "bureaucracy"—has been developed to service the local unions. Another significant tendency is the growth of intermediary bodies between the local union and the national office—regional or district councils on a geographical basis, conferences to deal with a major industry subdivision or a single major employer, and the like. For a million-member union operating in a variety of industries and in all parts of the country, some intermediate organization of this sort is essential.

Two aspects of local-national relations should be noted particularly, since they have given rise to considerable controversy and occasional charges of abuse. First, local union officers are subject to disciplinary action by the national officers. If the officers of a local are accused by members of violating the national constitution, mishandling union funds, or other misdeeds, they may be brought to trial before the national executive board. If the verdict is against them, they may be removed from office and the national union may appoint a trustee or receiver to manage the affairs of the local until the situation can be rectified and new officers installed.

National officers are reluctant to take such drastic action because of the possibility of local opposition and schism, and in most unions the receivership device is used very sparingly. The commonest reasons for national intervention are financial irregularity, intense factionalism in the local, failure to organize the trade or locality, failure to reopen agreements on time, strikes in violation of contract commitments, communist domination and use of the local for political purposes, and toleration of racketeering in the local.[9] National intervention, in short, is typically a method of protecting the membership against incompetence, venality, or oppression by local leaders. The receivership device can also be used, however, to suppress local union democracy, to get rid of critics of the national machine, and to loot the local treasury. This has led to government regulation of trusteeships and receiverships, which will be considered in the next section.

A second issue concerns the adequacy of present procedures for protecting the "civil rights" of the individual union member. A member may be accused of having violated some working rule of the union, such as accepting pay below the union scale, doing piece work contrary to union policy, or working overtime without permission; or of

---

[9] For detailed evidence, see Taft, *Structure and Government of Trade Unions,* chap. 4.

misbehavior on the job—fighting, drinking, failure to perform job duties, or refusing to follow reasonable instructions of the shop steward. Less frequently, but more dangerously, he may be accused of antiunion activity, defaming a union officer, and so on. There certainly is such a thing as antiunion activity and the union constitution must provide against it, but such charges can also be a way of getting at men whose only real offense is criticism of the officers in power.

Any charge against a member is heard and decided initially at the local level, either by a trial committee or by vote of the entire membership. The penalty, if guilt is established, is typically a fine appropriate to the offense. Expulsion from membership is regarded as a drastic measure and is rarely used. Either the member or his accusers may appeal the decision to the national president or the executive board, and there is usually a final right of appeal to the next national convention. Taft's study of the records of eight national unions indicates that the right of appeal is used quite frequently. The president and executive board typically review anywhere from twenty-five to one hundred appeals per year. The handling of appeals by national officers appears to be careful and conscientious. The ratio of reversals or modifications of local decisions is quite high—often between 30 and 50 per cent of all cases considered. Even when a member's guilt is reaffirmed on appeal, the size of the penalty is frequently reduced. Emotion and personal vindictiveness run higher at the local level than in the national office. Taft concludes:

> The cases that arise out of what might be termed civil rights are relatively few . . . disciplinary penalties are usually imposed for the violation of trade rules and rather infrequently over issues such as free speech or publication of unauthorized materials. It is difficult for outsiders to evaluate the reasonableness of penalties, but the information does indicate that they are seldom severe or unwarranted. . . . On the whole, there is no evidence that the appellate machinery does not function effectively, that it is vain or useless, or that it would be improved by government supervision.[10]

PROBLEMS OF UNION STRUCTURE AND ADMINISTRATION

The internal procedures of trade unions have produced a variety of criticisms and complaints. In a minority of unions, officers have used their positions for self-enrichment and have been guilty of gross

---

[10] Taft, *op. cit.*, p. 180.

breaches of trust. More generally, it is charged that the officers typically dominate union affairs, and that members who oppose the leadership have inadequate protection against retaliation and arbitrary penalties. The proven instances of corruption, and the more general accusation of autocratic government, have led to increasing public control over union affairs. Let us first consider the criticisms before proceeding to the supposed remedies.

Financial malfeasance

Direct embezzlement of union funds occurs mainly at the local rather than the national level, and is relatively rare. The most important methods of self-enrichment are more subtle. They involve use of the union officer's position of power to secure special perquisites, while at the same time damaging—or at any rate failing to advance—the interests of the membership.

The union leader may negotiate a "sweetheart contract," in which he settles for less than the union's strength would have allowed, receiving a kickback from the employer in return. Or he may own a share in the business with which he is negotiating on behalf of the union. Or he may set up a business of his own to sell supplies or services to the union at inflated prices. Or he may arrange for the union health and welfare fund to place its insurance with a company in which he has a financial interest.

Congressional investigations have turned up a wide variety of such practices. Here are a few examples:

1. Loans may be secured from the union to finance the officers' personal investments. Dave Beck, former president of the Teamsters' union, was found to have borrowed $270,110 from union sources. Vice-president Frank Brewster, operating at a lower level, confined his borrowings from the Western Conference of Teamsters to $77,660.[11]

2. Ownership of securities or other interests in a business with which the union deals in collective bargaining. In 1950 Peter Weber, business manager of Local 825 of the Operating Engineers, secured a one-eighth interest in Public Constructors, Inc., a company under contract with the union, in exchange for a loan of $2,500. By Septem-

---

[11] Hearings before the Select Committee on Improper Activities in the Labor and Management Field (*cited hereafter as "McClellan Committee"*), 85th Congress, 1st Sess., pursuant to Senate Resolution 74, part 4, pp. 1357, 1370.

ber, 1957, the book value of these shares had risen to $108,677.[12] This is one way in which a company could bribe a union official to go easy on the company in bargaining or to avoid pulling strikes on company projects.

3. A less direct form of the same thing is interest in a business selling services or supplies to, or otherwise dealing with, a company involved in bargaining with the union. Mrs. Dave Beck purchased 40 per cent of the stock of K and L Distributing Co., which distributed beer for Anheuser-Busch, Inc., a majority of whose employees are members of the Teamsters' union. The territory of K and L was enlarged and it received preferential shipments of beer as a result of Beck's influence. Later the investment was sold at a 60 per cent profit. The present Teamster president, James Hoffa (or his wife), held a substantial interest in companies which rented equipment to trucking concerns under contract with the Teamsters.[13]

4. Ownership of an interest in a business which buys from, sells to, or otherwise deals with the union itself. Dave Beck bought two lots which adjoined the Teamsters' Joint Council in Seattle for $39,000 and then sold them to the union for $139,000. He also, through a front man, had a hand in the National Mortgage Company, which handled $9,000,000 of Teamsters' funds.[14]

5. Other business transactions with employers. The McClellan Committee hearings revealed that a number of union officials had sold equipment to, received loans from, or received other special payments from employers with whom they negotiated. These payments were presumably intended to influence the officers' conduct in organizing and collective bargaining.

These practices are concentrated in certain of the conservative craft unions. Unions with a strong welfare tradition, such as the Clothing Workers, Ladies' Garment Workers, and the newer industrial unions organized by the CIO, have been almost completely free of corrupt practices.

Racketeering

"Racketeering" is not a very precise term, but may be taken to include extortion from workers or employers under threat of physical violence, typically involving alliance with gunmen and local criminal

---

[12] McClellan Committee Hearings, part 2, pp. 8134-8140.
[13] McClellan Committee Hearings, part 7, pp. 2058-2068, and 2099-2102; part 13, pp. 4933-4950, and 4966-4971; part 13, pp. 5543-5557.
[14] McClellan Committee Hearings, part 5, p. 1671; part 7, pp. 2106-2112.

syndicates. It has flourished principally in New York, Chicago, and a few other large cities, and in highly competitive industries catering to a local market, such as restaurants and other service establishments, local trucking, and building construction.[15]

The position of the union business agent in the construction industry is rather unusual. The business agent acts as an employment agency, and his control of jobs gives him power over the union membership. He also negotiates with employers, polices the terms of union contracts, and usually has the right to call an immediate strike where he believes the contract is being violated. This power enables him to make things easier or harder for the employer. An inopportune strike may prevent a contractor from finishing a building on time and subject him to a large penalty. The selling of "strike insurance" to employers has sometimes yielded incomes for union officials. The practice is by no means general in the building trades, but it has happened.

There have occasionally been large-scale combinations of union leaders and building contractors to exploit the public. The career of Robert P. Brindell, who flourished in New York from 1918 to 1920 in alliance with Tammany Hall and the local building contractors, is a case in point. Brindell, after winning control of the carpenters' union in New York, formed a building trades council, got himself elected president for life, and gathered around him a group of high-salaried associates. He then formed an agreement with a price-fixing association of building contractors. The unions agreed to work only for members of the association, so that any contractor who tried to remain outside the association was unable to obtain labor and was forced into line. The contractors agreed to employ only workers belonging to the unions which Brindell controlled. Brindell's central position in this arrangement enabled him to levy tribute on both workers and employers. In one year he collected over $500,000 in "strike insurance" alone, and must have obtained at least an equal amount from the 115,000 building trades workers under his control.[16]

Racketeering sometimes results from the invasion of a union by gangsters who turn the union to predatory purposes. Instances of this sort were especially numerous after the repeal of prohibition in 1933. Many gangsters had been employed in the bootlegging industry.

---

[15] See on this point the interesting analysis in Philip Taft, *Corruption and Racketeering in the Labor Movement*, Bulletin 38 (1958), New York School of Industrial and Labor Relations (Ithaca).

[16] This and several other cases are reported in Harold Seidman, *Labor Czars* (New York: Liveright, 1938).

When liquor became lawful, these men were left unemployed and had to find some other use for their talents. In Chicago and New York, in particular, they turned to control of local unions as a source of revenue. The main attempt was to control transport unions—drivers of milk wagons, coal trucks, oil trucks, laundry trucks, and so on. Control of transportation enables the gang to "shake down" the businesses which depend on transportation for their existence. In some cases rival gangs tried to win control of the same union, and pitched battles were fought in Chicago for control of the milk-wagon drivers and certain other locals. It was estimated that in the mid-'thirties about two-thirds of the union members in Chicago were paying tribute in one way or another to the Capone organization. It must not be forgotten, of course, that a large proportion of the businessmen of the city were also paying tribute to the same organization.

An aggravated and long-standing example of racketeering involves the longshore industry in the Port of New York. Hearings before a special Crime Commission of New York State in 1952 revealed that numerous locals of the International Longshoremen's Association had been taken over forcibly by men with criminal records; that both rival gangsters and rebels within the union had been silenced by violence and even murder; that union funds had been spent and union business conducted with no effective control by the membership; that large amounts of money had been extorted from shipowners and other businessmen in the port by threats of strike action, damage to merchandise, and other forms of violence; that longshore workers had been forced to pay for their jobs through "kickbacks," "presents," and other payments to those in control; and that the gangsters involved had good political contacts in the cities surrounding the port.

As a consequence of the inability or unwillingness of top ILA officials to correct these conditions, the AFL expelled the union from Federation membership in 1953, and chartered a new longshoremen's union in the hope of winning away members from the expelled organization. The ILA won a subsequent NLRB election by a narrow margin, however, and has continued to maintain control of the port. Perhaps a more significant development was the establishment of a joint Waterfront Commission by the states of New York and New Jersey as a result of the 1952 hearings. The Commission has endeavored to abolish the notorious "shape-up system" and to substitute hiring through Commission employment offices, to reduce the amount of surplus labor on the docks by issuing longshore licenses only to reasonably regular workers, and to weed out racketeers by refusing licenses to men with criminal records. These measures may gradual-

weaken the economic basis for racketeering and provide a climate in which honest unionism can develop and survive.

Racketeering is a law enforcement problem rather than a problem of trade union government. The practices just described are already unlawful and can continue to exist only where the law is not enforced. Racketeering in unions is usually carried on in collusion with local political organizations and often with local business interests as well. It is not specifically a union sin, but stems from a generally low level of political and business morality.

Mills concludes that racketeering has been most prevalent in small-scale industries where intense competition has prevailed and where business has not yet grown large enough to maintain its own cartel arrangements. "In the main, these have been the building trades, cleaning and dyeing, restaurants, the garment trades, furriers, trucking, theaters, produce and live poultry markets.[17]

It should be re-emphasized that racketeering is not of great quantitative importance in the labor movement. In most cases, union leaders maintain control of the organization by peaceable and lawful methods, by skillful use of the normal tactics of machine politics. This leads us to another line of complaint against trade unions—a complaint, not of wrongdoing, but of serious defects in internal structure.

Leadership domination

Union government is democratic in the sense that officers at all levels are elected from below and are formally responsible to the membership. But in union elections, unlike elections for public office, there is usually only one recognized party. The Typographical Union, which has an old and successful two-party system, is a rarity in the trade-union world. Normally all the political machinery of the union is controlled by the people in office, who naturally use it to remain in office. People who oppose them are "factionalists," "dual unionists," "union busters." The concept of a loyal opposition is not recognized.[18]

[17] C. W. Mills, *The New Men of Power* (New York: Harcourt, Brace & World, Inc., 1948), p. 129.

[18] For discussions of this problem see Will Herberg, "Bureaucracy and Democracy in Labor Unions," *Antioch Review*, III (Fall 1943), pp. 405-417; Joseph Kovner, "Union Democracy," Industrial Relations Research Association, *Interpreting the Labor Movement* (1952), pp. 83-88; Joel Seidman, "Democracy in Labor Unions," *Journal of Political Economy*, LXI (June 1953), pp. 221-231; Joel Seidman, *Union Rights and Union Duties* (New York: Harcourt Brace & World, Inc., 1943); Philip Taft, "The Constitutional Power of the Chief Officer in American Labor Unions," *Quarterly Journal of Economics*, LXII (May 1948), pp. 459-471; and Philip Taft, "Democracy in Trade Unions," *American Economic Review Supplement*, XXXVI (May 1946), pp. 359-69.

Strong leadership in a union seems unavoidable and even desirable for at least two reasons. The union is in part a fighting organization. It reaches crises in negotiating with employers which can be met only by a strike. It may have to fend off attacks my employers, government agencies, or others which threaten the very existence of the organization. Hardman has aptly said that a union is part army and part debating society;[19] but it cannot be both things at once. Debate is all right before the battle is joined; but while the battle is on, someone must have authority to issue commands. A strike may be won or lost by a single decision, which has to be made so quickly that the members cannot be consulted, and on which the members might not be able to give an informed judgment in any case.

In addition to threats from without, unions are often threatened by factional strife within their own ranks. Unions are especially susceptible to penetration by doctrinaire political groups who are more interested in establishing their idealogy than in the strength of the union. When a politically-minded minority captures control of a union, the result is frequently the atrophy and eventual disappearance of the organization. Union officials must have sufficient authority to prevent schism and to defend the union against internal as well as external enemies. This is admittedly a delicate matter. It is hard to distinguish between legitimate criticism of union officers and a movement to subvert the union's purposes. The charge of "union-wrecking" has been used to crush a minority whose only real offense was differing with the leadership. One must recognize, however, that there is such a thing as antiunion activity by those professing allegiance to the union, and that a means of defense is necessary.

A striking feature of trade union government is the long tenure of office by national union officials, particularly national presidents.[20] John L. Lewis of the Mine Workers, David B. Robertson of the Locomotive Firemen, and William Hutcheson of the Carpenters were union presidents for more than thirty years. Daniel Tobin of the Teamsters, William Mahon of the Street Railway Employees, and George Berry of the Pressmen held office for more than forty years.

Long terms of office have advantages for the union as well as dis-

---

[19] See J. B. S. Hardman, *American Labor Dynamics* (New York: Harcourt, Brace & World, Inc., 1928), particularly the articles by Hardman and Muste. See also Sylvia Kopald, "Democracy and Leadership," in E. W. Bakke and Clark Kerr, eds., *Unions, Management and the Public* (New York: Harcourt, Brace & World, Inc., 1948), pp. 180-184.

[20] Mills, *The New Men of Power*, p. 64.

advantages. A union needs skilled and experienced leadership. Running a large union requires a detailed knowledge of the economics of the industry, wide acquaintance with management people and political officials, skill in speaking and writing, administrative ability, and experience in negotiation and in the management of men. A leader who is competent and experienced in these respects is a valuable asset to the union. This is a major reason for the long tenure of office by national union leaders. It is true, of course, that many union officials are continued in office beyond the point at which their usefulness has begun to diminish. After a man has been a union official for many years, there is scarcely anything else to which he can turn for a living. The union members, recognizing this fact and appreciating the leader's past services, are usually reluctant to "turn the old horse out to grass."

On the other hand, long tenure of office presents certain problems. The viewpoint and objectives of the union leaders tend to diverge more and more from those of the rank and file. The leaders become increasingly interested in sheer perpetuation of the organization, in "union-oriented demands" rather than "membership-oriented demands." Union-shop and checkoff clauses are a case in point. The members would frequently trade such objectives for immediate benefits. The leaders also become more skeptical about the possibility of rapid progress. The union members exaggerate business profits and believe that more money can always be had for the asking. The leaders know that this is not so. They tend to become conservative in their demands, to moderate the zeal of the membership, to settle for less than the members think possible. To the rank and file, this attitude often appears as a "sell-out" to the employers; to the leaders, it means being realistic and practical.

The dilemma is this: in order to protect the long-run interests of the union, the leaders must have enough power to pursue union-oriented objectives, to make compromises with employers, and to override excessive and ill-advised demands by the membership. Given this power, however, it is difficult to prevent them from slighting the interests of the membership if they choose to do so.

Another problem is that union officers—like officeholders in industry, government, and elsewhere—become attached to their jobs and bend a good part of their energies to staying in office. The methods used are those of machine politics anywhere. The union leader makes friends with as many members of the organization as he can, performs various services for them, distributes salaried positions in the right quarters, stage-manages the union conventions, and makes full use of oratory and the other political arts. All this he does in perfectly good faith. He becomes convinced after a few years that he can run the union better than anyone else, and in many cases he is right. Indeed, unless he is able to "deliver the goods" year in and year out, no amount of political machination will suffice to keep him in office.

Where a strong leader has remained in office for twenty or thirty years, it will usually be found that he is an exceptionally able person with a profound grasp of the union's problems, and also that he has kept in close touch with membership opinion. The main function of the leader's political machine is not to suppress opposition, but rather to give an accurate report of rank-and-file sentiment which will enable the leader to develop a program commanding general approval. It will be found also that the successful and long-lived leader has achieved substantial gains for his membership in terms of wages and conditions. He is in most cases overwhelmingly popular with the rank and file. Such leaders as Lewis of the Mine Workers, Petrillo of the Musicians, Tobin of the Teamsters, and Hillman of the Clothing Workers certainly used astute political manipulation to perpetuate their control. At the same time they have been tremendously popular with union members and could easily have been re-elected at any time in the freest referendum.

The meaning of trade union democracy

In what significant sense may this structure of control be regarded as "democratic" or "undemocratic"? If one asks, "Are the forms of democracy observed?" the answer must be "Yes." Union constitutions are thoroughly democratic. The system of government is normally a one-party rather than a multiple-party system, but this is characteristic of virtually all private associations.[21]

If one asks, "Do the members determine union policy?" the answer is usually "No." Policy is determined by the national leaders and to

---

[21] The only two-party system which has operated over a long period of time is found in the International Typographical Union. This is an unusual situation which is scarcely likely to develop in other unions. For a good analysis of the ITU case, see Seymour M. Lipset, J. S. Coleman, and M. Trow, *Union Democracy in the International Typographical Union* (Glencoe, Ill.: Free Press, 1956).

a lesser extent by local leaders, within rather wide limits set by the members' interests and attitudes.

If one asks, "Are unions by and large operated in the interest of the members?" the answer is predominantly "Yes." Most union officers are honest and men of good will. They would rather do a good job for their members than not, and this is sensible also from a political point of view. It helps to keep the machine popular and re-election easy.

If one asks, "Can the members get rid of their leaders and install new ones whenever they wish?"—perhaps the most searching test of democratic control—the answer is "Yes and no." Contests over local office are frequent and the turnover of local officers is high. At the national level, it is possible to revolt against and overthrow an entrenched machine, but it is certainly not easy. It requires organization and hard work, and involves a good deal of personal risk for leaders of the insurgent faction.

The most damaging criticism of union government in the United States is that it fails to recognize the right of legitimate opposition and to provide adequate protection for the dissenting member. A salaried union official who finds himself on the losing side of an internal power struggle is almost certain to be out of a job. A member who opposes the leadership will in some unions find himself exposed to physical violence. In others he will be expelled, with possible loss of employment; and if he appeals his case through union channels, he may find the very people he has opposed sitting in judgment upon him.

REGULATION OF INTERNAL UNION AFFAIRS

Self-Regulation

The labor movement itself has taken some steps toward meeting these criticisms. The United Automobile Workers in 1957 established a Public Review Board, composed of leading lawyers, professors, and clergymen. Members can appeal decisions of the union's international executive board to this outside body, and the Review Board can take up cases on its own motion. If the Board finds that a worker's membership rights have been violated, it can revoke the penalties imposed on him, and the union is pledged to abide by the decision. As of

1963 the Board had heard several dozen cases, upholding the union's executive board in about three-quarters of these, and reversing it in the remainder. It is regrettable that only two other unions, the Upholsterers and the Packinghouse Workers, have thus far adopted this promising technique.

The AFL-CIO constitution of 1955 pledged the organization "to protect the labor movement from any and all corrupt influences." An Ethical Practices Committee was appointed, which drew up six codes of ethical practice covering issuance of local union charters; operation of health and welfare funds; barring of racketeers, criminals, communists, and fascists from union office; preventing conflicts of interest between union officers and their organizations; setting up adequate accounting and financial controls; and establishing minimum standards for union elections and disciplinary procedures. Any national union which after hearings is found guilty of violating these codes may be directed to mend its ways. If it declines to do so, the AFL-CIO Executive Council may suspend it from membership by a two-thirds vote. Suspension can be appealed to the next AFL-CIO convention, which has the ultimate right of expulsion. The Executive Council may also charter a new union to compete with the expelled organization and try to take over its membership.

This procedure has a good chance of success where there is a "clean" faction in the union which is willing to mobilize against a corrupt leadership. The Bakery Workers, whose president had been guilty of malpractice but where corruption was not deeply entrenched, was expelled at the 1957 convention and a rival union was chartered. The new union quickly took over the bulk of the membership in the industry. But where corruption is of long standing and is tolerated by the membership, as in the Teamster and Longshoremen cases, federation action can accomplish little. The Longshoremen were expelled by the AFL in 1953 and a rival union was chartered, but the new union did not succeed in winning mass support. The old union was eventually cleaned up somewhat and was readmitted to the federation in 1961; but this was due mainly to reforms instituted by the New York-New Jersey Waterfront Commission. When the powerful Teamsters Union was expelled in 1957, the federation did not even venture to charter a rival union, and the Teamsters continued to flourish as before. This case has done much to discourage AFL-CIO efforts against corruption.

Court regulation

A member who has suffered damage from some union action can always go to court and seek redress under the common law. The legal status of unionism and collective bargaining is the subject of the next chapter; but we may comment here on court attitudes toward internal union affairs.

The courts have traditionally regarded a trade union as a private association, comparable to a lodge or social club. Like any club, the union could admit people or bar people as it saw fit, and could set up any rules it liked for internal government. So long as the union observed its own constitution, the courts would not intervene; and they were disinclined to intervene in any event. Only when it came to handling of union funds did the courts become interested, for here property was involved and analogies were available from trust and corporation law.

With the growing economic power of unions, however, this view has become less and less appropriate. Most collective bargaining agreements now provide for a union shop or its equivalent, under which a worker is expected to be a union member as a condition of continued employment. All workers are bound in any event by the conditions of employment which the union negotiates. A worker excluded from the union is thus bound by the actions of an organization in which he has no voice. Rules concerning admission, discipline, and expulsion can threaten a man's livelihood. So the courts have moved toward the view that a union resembles a public utility or government agency, and that its internal procedures are a matter of public concern. The new view is well stated in a California court decision:

Where a union has, as in this case, attained a monopoly of the supply of labor by means of closed shop agreements and other forms of collective labor action, such a union occupies a quasi-public position similar to that of a public service business and it has certain corresponding obligations. It may no longer claim the same freedom from legal restraint enjoyed by golf clubs or fraternal associations. Its asserted right to choose its own members does not merely relate to social relations; it affects the fundamental right to work for a living.[22]

[22] Cited by Joseph R. Grodin, "Legal Regulation of Internal Union Affairs," in J. Shister, B. Aaron, and C. W. Summers, eds., *Public Policy and Collective Bargaining* (New York: Harper & Row, Publishers, 1962), p. 192.

Following this doctrine, the courts have become more willing to probe into union affairs and to require not merely that the union abide by its own rules, but that the rules themselves should be reasonable. Courts have held, for example, that a closed-shop union must admit Negroes to membership or else give up the closed shop; that union disciplinary procedures must meet the test of due process of law; that a union member may not be tried by people having a direct interest in the controversy; and that the union cannot prescribe support of a particular political candidate or otherwise regulate the member's private life.

An aggrieved member, then, may be able to bring a successful suit against the union under common law; but as a practical matter few people are willing to do this. Courts make most people nervous, lawyers are expensive, lawsuits are slow, and long before the worker can get redress he may be out of a job and even out of town. There has consequently been a demand for legislation to spell out standards of good union conduct, to ward off injury to members before it occurs, and to place enforcement responsibility on public officials. After exposure of serious malfeasance in the Teamsters and a number of other unions in the McClellan Committee hearings, Congress passed the Labor-Management Reporting and Disclosure Act of 1959, usually referred to as the Landrum-Griffin Act or the LMRDA. Discussion of this Act is in a sense ahead of our story. The evolution of labor law in the United States is the subject of Chapter 5. Since most of the LMRDA bears directly on internal union government, however, it seems best to discuss it here while the issues with which it deals are fresh in mind.

Statutory regulation: the Landrum-Griffin Act

The main provisions dealing with union government[23] appear in the first five Titles of the Act: *Title I*—Bill of Rights of Members of Labor Organizations; *Title II*—Reporting by Labor Organizations, Officers and Employees of Labor Organizations, and Employers; *Title III*—Trusteeships; *Title IV*—Elections; and *Title V*—Safeguards for Labor Organizations.

---

[23] There are in addition certain provisions dealing with picketing, boycotts, and other union *practices*, inserted into the LMRDA as amendments to the Taft-Hartley Act of 1947. These provisions will be considered at the appropriate point in Chapter 5.

Title I, the "bill of rights" section of the LMRDA, guarantees the right of each member, subject to reasonable rules, to attend and participate in union meetings, vote in union elections, and nominate or support candidates for union office. This would prevent unions from denying the franchise to Negro locals or "class B" locals, as has sometimes been done in the past, or from interfering in any other way with equal membership participation. Members are also assured of the right to obtain copies of collective bargaining agreements signed by the union; the right to testify, communicate with legislators, and bring suit against the union; and protection aaginst dues increases or special assessments except under specified procedures, usually involving a secret ballot of the membership.

There is little in these provisions which is controversial or which differs from established practice in most unions. The most interesting and potentially significant part of Title I deals with discipline and expulsion of union members. The importance of this issue was underlined in earlier sections. The LMRDA provides that, if a union wishes to discipline a member for reasons other than nonpayment of dues, it must serve him with written charges, give him adequate time to prepare his defense, and assure him a fair hearing, i.e., something approaching the safeguards which apply in a court of law. A member who believes his rights have been violated can bring suit against the union, provided his action is not instigated by an employer and provided he has exhausted the union's own appeal procedures. These procedures, however, cannot bar a worker from going to court if they take more than four months.

These provisions are commendable; but they will probably prove less effective in practice than they appear on paper. The aggrieved member who wishes to carry his case outside the union is still faced with a slow and costly court procedure. Few workers will actually take advantage of their right to go to court; but the possibility of their doing so may lead unions to improve their internal procedures.

A significant omission from Title I concerns the most basic right of all, the right of equal admission to union membership. A number of unions, particularly in the building and railroad trades, have customarily discriminated either by barring Negroes from membership or by segregating them into separate locals. But while the LMRDA is silent on this point, there are other statutes bearing on the matter. The Taft-Hartley Act provides that an employer under a union shop agreement cannot be obliged to discharge a worker if the worker has been expelled from or refused admission to the union on any ground other than unwillingness to pay the usual dues and initiation fees. A union could still refuse to admit a Negro to membership, but it could not compel the employer to discharge him. Federal policy is further set forth in an Executive Order of March 1961, which prohibits racial discrimination in federal employment or by contractors doing business with the federal government, and gives enforcement powers in this area to the Secretary of Labor. In addition, nineteen state legislatures have passed fair employment practice laws which prohibit employers from discrimination in hiring, firing, or promotion, and also forbid unions to discriminate by withholding membership.

Title II, on reporting and disclosure, requires every union covered by the Act to adopt a constitution and bylaws and to file a copy with the Secretary of Labor, along with specific details of procedure for the conduct of internal union affairs. Every union must also file an annual financial report "in such detail as may be necessary accurately to disclose its financial condition and operations." Union officers must report personal financial transactions with the union, or in which their interest might be in conflict with that of the union. Employers must report any payment of money or other things of value to a union, its officers, or employees; and also any payment to the company's own employees or to an outside consultant for the purpose of getting information about the union or influencing workers in the exercise of their right to collective bargaining. In plain language, if an employer wishes to engage in old-fashioned labor espionage or bribery of union officials, he must let the Secretary of Labor know what he is doing.

The reports to the Secretary are public property, and anyone may get a copy by paying a copying charge. The union must make copies of its reports available to members, and must also permit members for good cause to examine the underlying books and records. Failure to report, or falsification of reports, is a criminal offense under the Act.

The reporting requirements, which are very detailed, have worked hardship on small locals which must rely on amateur and part-time help. There is also some question whether employers should be given such easy access to the union's financial records when the union has no comparable access to the company's books. With these qualifications, the provisions of Title II seem legitimate and useful.

Title III places restrictions on the taking over of local unions under *trusteeships.* This is a device by which national union officers can correct corruption or incompetence at the local level. Trusteeships can also be used, however, to raid rich local treasuries, to eliminate opposition to the national leadership, and to control representation and voting at national conventions. This has been done on a considerable scale in the Mine Workers, Teamsters, Hod Carriers, Operating Engineers, and a number of other unions. In some cases as much as twenty per cent of the membership has been operating under national supervision, and some locals have been held in trusteeship for twenty years or more.

The LMRDA provides that a union may assume trusteeship over a subordinate body only when the purpose is to prevent corruption or financial malpractice, restore democratic procedures, assure performance of a collective bargaining agreement, or otherwise carry out the legitimate objectives of the union. It prohibits the national union from transferring local funds to itself, and prohibits the counting of votes of delegates from trusteed locals in union elections unless the delegates were elected by secret ballot of the membership. Any national union taking over a local must report to the Secretary of Labor within thirty days, and semiannually thereafter, giving the reasons for the trusteeship and a full account of the local union's finances. Provided these conditions are met, the trusteeship is presumed to be valid for a period of eighteen months, after which the burden of proof rests on the union. Almost five hundred trusteeships were reported immediately after passage of the Act, but by 1962 this had shrunk to less than two hundred.[24] This suggests that the Act stimulated termination of existing trusteeships and discouraged new ones. Of the trusteeships remaining in 1962, more than half had been established on a "caretaker" basis because of inactivity of the local union, or had resulted from local mismanagement.

Title IV regulates union election and voting procedures in considerable detail. National officers must be elected at least once every five years, local officers every three years, and officers of intermediate bodies every four years. All members must be given a fair chance, free of "improper interference" or threat of retaliation, to run for office or to nominate and support candidates of their choice. All candidates must be given reasonable opportunity to campaign, inspect membership lists, have watchers at the polls, and participate in count-

---

[24] U. S. Department of Labor, *Union Trusteeships* (Washington: Government Printing Office, 1962), p. 7.

ing ballots. Voting for local officers and for delegates to national conventions must be by secret ballot. Complaints of violation of these requirements may be filed with the Secretary of Labor who, after investigation, may petition a court to declare the election void and to order a new election under the Secretary's supervision.

These provisions, for the most part, simply embody accepted standards of good procedure; but it is doubtful that they will have much effect on union government. Election procedures in most unions were already thoroughly democratic; yet leadership domination has continued for reasons already explained. One disadvantage of writing election procedures into law is that any litigious member, of whom there are a certain number in any organization, can now throw an election into dispute by claiming that some procedural nicety was not observed. The Department of Labor and the federal courts are likely to find themselves drawn into intra-union disputes over rather minor points.

Title V specifies that union officers and agents occupy a position of trust, and endeavors to prevent abuse of this position. Larceny or embezzlement of union funds, which presumably was already illegal, is now defined as a federal offense punishable by a fine of up to $10,000 and imprisonment up to five years. If the union has property or annual income in excess of $5,000, officers in charge of these funds must be bonded. No officer or employee may borrow more than $2,000 from the union. An employer may not make any payment or loan to officers of a union which represents his employees, or which seeks to represent them, or to any committee or group of employees which seeks to influence other employees in the exercise of their right to collective bargaining.

There are restrictions also on who may serve as a union official. No one who has been convicted of certain types of criminal offense (and no one who is a member of the Communist Party) may hold union office until five years after the end of his prison sentence (or the termination of his Party membership).

Even this brief summary suggests the complicated and wide-ranging nature of the Landrum-Griffin Act. Any evaluation of it must be on a clause-by-clause basis. Some of its provisions are generally acceptable to union officials, while others continue controversial.

A further difficulty in evaluating the Act is that evidence on its practical effects is still fragmentary. There are scattered court decisions and journal articles; but no one has undertaken a general review of enforcement activities under the Act and their possible effects on union government.[25] The number of cases prosecuted under the Act has been small. Previant reports, for example, that during the first three years of the Act the Secretary of Labor charged 27 unions with violation of the election rules. Nine of these cases were settled by new elections, and none has yet come to court trial. During the same period, 74 union officers or employees were charged with embezzlement of union funds. There were 35 convictions, 5 acquittals, and the remaining cases were still pending. But the meaning of such evidence is unclear. Since there are probably more than 100,000 local and national union officials in the United States, the small number of prosecutions can be interpreted as evidence of a high level of honesty. On the other hand, it can be argued that the possibility of prosecution under the Act has a deterrent effect, and that without this the level of honesty would be lower.

One must also distinguish between the two major targets of the Act: financial malfeasance on the one hand, and machine control of union government on the other. It is possible that the Act may prove quite effective on one front but largely ineffective on the other.

As regards financial malfeasance, the practices described in earlier sections were doubtless already illegal under the common law or state legislation. But the law was not well enforced, partly because union officials were often allied with the local political machine. Landrum-Griffin makes embezzlement or larceny of union funds a federal offense, subject to investigation by federal agents and prosecution in the federal courts. This provides a new avenue of attack on flagrant cases of corruption. The cost of this gain is that Department of Labor and F.B.I. investigators have been given broad powers to comb through union records on mere suspicion of wrongdoing. One may hope that these powers will be exercised in a restrained and judicious fashion; but in view of the long record of employer and public hostility to unionism, it is not surprising that union officials are apprehensive on this score.

As regards membership participation and influence in union government, the Act could conceivably work in either direction. On one

---

[25] Bits of factual evidence, however, will be found in Robert J. Connerton, "The Practical Impact of the New Law," *Proceedings of the Thirteenth Annual Meeting of IRRA* (1960), pp. 27-39; and David Previant, "Have Titles I-VI of Landrum-Griffin Served the Stated Legislative Purpose?", *Labor Law Journal* (January 1963), pp. 28-41.

hand, it has already produced a tendency to tighten union constitutions and bylaws, spell out officers' powers in greater detail, and establish firmer bureaucratic control over the organization to safeguard it against legal attack. On the other hand, if the Act succeeds in protecting the members' right to criticize without reprisal, this could strengthen the hand of dissident groups and reduce the control of established union officials. Such gains in democracy might be purchased at some economic cost. Established officials are usually conservative in the sense of preferring to avoid strikes and to reach moderate economic settlements. Weakening the "ins" as against the "outs" might lead to more frequent strikes, more extravagant contract demands, and larger wage settlements.

The most likely prospect, however, is that Landrum-Griffin will have little effect on union government one way or the other. It does not alter the conditions which naturally give rise to one-party government and machine control; and such control will doubtless continue in most unions with the tacit consent of the membership. This prospect has been suggested by Benjamin Aaron:

> However, the . . . law is bound to fall short of its goals because most of the intended beneficiaries do not fervently believe in or ceaselessly strive to maintain the democratic rights which the statute purports to secure for them. Many of the worst situations existing in some unions today are largely the result of membership apathy—an unwillingness to participate actively and continuously in the government of their organizations so long as they operate with acceptable efficiency. This indifference is, of course, but a reflection of a similar attitude evinced by the average citizen toward his own local and national government. Law cannot create a desire for democracy; it can only help those who want it to get and maintain it.[26]

Fortunately, abuse of officers' powers is limited to a minority of organizations. Most unions are administered honestly and with a concern for members' rights. One can reasonably expect continued improvement of union government from within, partly because of the changing composition of the working population. A union of workers born in the United States, most of whom have been through high school and some through college, should operate differently from earlier unions of immigrant workers with limited education and little experience of democratic procedures. At best, however, we cannot expect workers to be more effective as citizens of a union than they

---

[26] Benjamin Aaron, "The Labor-Management Reporting and Disclosure Act of 1959," *Harvard Law Review* (March 1960), p. 905.

are as citizens of the republic. In all matters touching the quality of citizenship, the law may prevent us from being too bad. It cannot make us good.

Discussion questions

1. What are the dangers and advantages of strong control over local unions by national unions?

2. What advantage does a national union derive from affiliation with the AFL-CIO? Is expulsion of a national union from the federation an effective disciplinary measure?

3. In what ways have some union officers used their positions for personal advantage? What remedies for this situation have been attempted, and what others might be tried?

4. "Unions are democratic in form, undemocratic in substance. Policy is determined by the leaders, and membership participation is at a minimum. There is urgent need of reforms to return the unions to membership control." Discuss.

5. Draw up specifications for a perfectly democratic national union.

6. "There is an inherent conflict between maximum democracy in a union and maximum effectiveness of the union in serving membership interests." Discuss.

7. Why do national union officers usually remain in office for long periods? Is this an undesirable tendency?

8. Why has racketeering occasionally developed in trade unions, and what remedial measures can be taken?

9. In what ways may the LMRDA be expected to improve the internal government of unions?

10. What else might be done to protect union members in exercising their right to criticize and displace existing union officials?

Selected reading

Barbash, Jack, *Labor's Grass Roots*. New York: Harper & Row, Publishers, 1961.

Fisher, Lloyd H., and J. W. McConnell, "Internal Conflict and Labor Union Solidarity," in Kornhauser, Dubin, and Ross, eds., *Industrial Conflict*. New York: McGraw-Hill Book Company, Inc., 1954, pp. 132-143.

Galenson, Walter, *Trade Union Democracy in Western Europe*. Berkeley: University of California Press, 1962.

Ginzberg, Eli, *The Labor Leader*. New York: The Macmillan Company, 1948.

Kahn, Robert L., and Arnold S. Tannenbaum, *Participation in Union Locals*. New York: Harper & Row, Publishers, 1958.

Kerr, Clark, *Unions and Union Leaders of Their Own Choosing*. New York: The Fund for the Republic, 1958.

Leiserson, William, *American Trade Union Democracy*. New York: Columbia University Press, 1959.

Mills, C. Wright, *The New Men of Power*. New York: Harcourt, Brace & World, Inc., 1948.

Sayles, Leonard R., and George Strauss, *The Local Union: Its Place in the Industrial Plant*. New York: Harper & Row, Publishers, 1953.

Taft, Philip, *Corruption and Racketeering in the Labor Movement*. Ithaca, N.Y.: New York State School of Industrial and Labor Relations, Cornell University, 1958.

———, *The Structure and Government of Labor Unions*. Cambridge: Harvard University Press, 1954.

5

The Legal Framework of
Collective Bargaining

The remainder of Part I will be concerned with collective bargaining between unions and management over terms and conditions of employment. Collective bargaining necessarily operates within a framework of public control. The Constitution of the United States guarantees certain basic rights of the individual, including the right to own property and to associate with others in trade unions. The trade union and the business corporation, however, have no absolute rights of their own. The rights which they enjoy at a particular time are granted to them by government as a matter of policy, in order to achieve purposes regarded as socially desirable.

The desirability of any type of public control depends on the policies which one wishes to further. With respect to collective bargaining, for example, at least three alternative policies are possible: (1) that it is desirable to extend collective bargaining as rapidly as possible throughout all lines of industry; (2) that the effects of collective bargaining are undesirable and that its growth should be retarded; or (3) that the main objective should be to protect the individual worker's freedom of access to jobs and his freedom in deciding whether or not to join a trade union. The controls necessary to promote one of these policies will differ from those appropriate to a different policy. There is no scientific way of reconciling such differences. They rest on differing political value judgments, which must be fought out and compromised in the political arena.

The instrument of public control is law, administered through the courts and through administrative agencies. This chapter will discuss the general nature of legal rules and the main stages in the development of labor law in the United States. During the past century and a half we have passed from government hostility toward union objectives, to official neutrality, to positive support of union organization, and finally, to detailed federal regulation of union-management relations. The only certain thing is that further changes lie ahead.

JUDICIAL REGULATION OF UNION ACTIVITIES

There are two main types of legal rule: statutory rules enacted by Congress or a state legislature and common law rules based on previous court decisions. Both types of rule are administered primarily through the courts. Even where an administrative agency is authorized by statute to investigate and punish certain types of offense, as is the National Labor Relations Board, the accused party can appeal the agency's decision to the regular courts and eventually to the Supreme Court of the United States. It is the judges who say what a statute means in particular cases, and this process of judicial interpretation determines the practical effect of a law. Moreover, the judges determine whether a particular statute conflicts with the Constitution, i.e., whether the legislative body had the right to enact it. This is a broad and important power which has shaped the whole course of our labor law.

The courts really come into their own, however, with respect to issues not covered by any statute. These issues have to be decided in the light of the whole body of previous court decisions, which together make up "the common law." A dispute comes to court and the judge is faced with the practical problem of settling it. There is no statute law on the subject. The judge is obliged to fall back on previous court decisions in similar cases. If the facts of the case are novel and direct precedents do not exist, he may be forced to fall back on general principles of common law—for example, the rule that contracts in restraint of trade are not enforceable at law, or that deliberate damage to another is unlawful if done out of malice but may be lawful if incidental to the pursuit of one's own self-interest. In the light of such general rules, and on the basis of his own knowledge and beliefs, the judge makes a pioneer decision which becomes a precedent for courts in future years. This was essentially what happened in the early days of trade unionism.

Many people do not realize that trade unions have been subject to comprehensive government control through the courts from the very beginnings of union organization. Until recent years there were scarcely any statutes dealing with labor relations; but unions have always been subject to common law rules and precedents. Anyone aggrieved by the action of a trade union could take the matter to court and, if the union's action was in violation of some common law principle, the court would grant remedies to the injured party. Judicial opinion concerning what unions should be allowed to do and be forbidden from doing has shaped the growth of unionism and collective bargaining to the present day.

Legal remedies for unlawful action

What practical difference does it make whether a judge finds a particular union action lawful or unlawful? What can he do about it? Three main types of legal remedy are available. The first of these is criminal prosecution. If it can be shown that union members have broken laws concerning theft, trespass, assault and battery, arson, and other crimes, or even that they have violated local ordinances concerning loitering, obstructing traffic, disturbing the peace, and so on, they may be subject to fine and imprisonment. The number of workers who have been punished for real or alleged misdemeanors since the beginning of unionism runs into the hundreds of thousands. The second type of remedy is civil suit for damages. If union members cause damage and destruction to an employer's property, suit for damages can be brought against the workers and, under some circumstances, against the union itself. The third and perhaps the most important type of remedy is the injunction. This is a court order restraining the party against whom it is issued from doing specified acts. If the person goes ahead and does these things anyway, he may be convicted of contempt of court and punished by fine or imprisonment. The speedy and powerful character of this procedure has caused it to be widely used in labor cases. The way in which it has been used, and the repeated efforts of unions to confine its use within narrower limits, will be discussed in a moment.

The courts thus have wide authority to make law in labor matters and powerful sanctions which can be applied against offenders. Until the 1930's, indeed, public control of labor relations in this country was almost entirely court control. When trade unions first appeared around 1800, employers appealed to the courts for help. The judges of the day were forced to decide what they thought about this new type of organization and its tactics. For the most part, they concluded that unionism was an undesirable sort of activity which, if it could not be prevented altogether, should be held within narrow limits.[1]

This view was due partly to the nature of law itself and partly to personal predilections of the judges. Law is necessarily a conservative force. It exists to protect established rights. The common law of Great Britain and the United States gives especial weight to rights connected with property ownership. Unionism attacks the right of the owners of industrial enterprises to manage them as they see fit. It seeks to curb this right in order to establish new and legally unrecognized rights of workers in their jobs. The common law also regards freedom of contract and freedom of trade as desirable social objectives. The union exists to restrict competition and establish a quasi-monopolistic position for its members. Unionism thus seemed contrary to the spirit of the common law, and it was natural that judges steeped in this tradition should have greeted its appearance with suspicion.

The judges' legal training was buttressed by their political preferences. They were drawn mainly from the propertied class, mingled more frequently with employers than with workers, and tended naturally to sympathize with the propertied interests. Their political thinking was influenced also by the classical economics, which could find no useful place for joint action by wage earners.

The antipathy of most judges to trade unionism was a powerful factor throughout the nineteenth century, and has continued with diminished force to the present time. It is largely responsible for the unwillingness of unions to get involved in any sort of court proceedings. Unions dislike legal proceedings partly because they are time-consuming and expensive; the employer can usually hire more and

---

[1] On the historical development of labor law in the United States, see J. R. Commons *et al.*, *Documentary History of American Industrial Society* (Cleveland: A. H. Clark Company, 1910-11); and J. R. Commons and associates, *History of Labor in the United States* (New York: The Macmillan Company, 1918, 1935, 4 vols.) vol. I. See also C. O. Gregory, *Labor and the Law*, rev. ed. (New York: W. W. Norton and Company, 1958), and Edwin E. Witte, *The Government in Labor Disputes* (New York: McGraw-Hill Book Company, Inc., 1932).

better lawyers, and the proceedings drag on until the union's funds or patience are exhausted. The main reason for unionists' fear of court proceedings, however, is a deep-seated conviction that the law and the judges are biased against them, and there is some historical justification for this feeling.

The doctrine of criminal conspiracy

In a number of cases brought against trade unions during the early nineteenth century, any sort of union activity was held to be a criminal conspiracy punishable by fine or imprisonment. In other cases, it was held that union actions designed to raise wages or reduce hours were lawful, but that other objectives such as the closed shop were unlawful. The legality of trade unionism remained in considerable doubt until the case of *Commonwealth* v. *Hunt,* decided in 1842. In this case, the Chief Justice of Massachusetts held that union activities were not unlawful *per se,* their legality depending rather on the objectives which they were designed to attain. He held further that the closed shop was a legitimate union objective and that a strike to obtain it was not illegal.

From this time onward, the doctrine that any union is a criminal conspiracy fell increasingly out of favor. The thinking of the judges was no doubt influenced by the fact that unions continued to grow despite judicial disapproval. If "the Supreme Court follows the election returns," as Mr. Dooley avers, lower courts are also responsive to major trends in public opinion.

Trade unions "lawful for what?"

Trade unions thus came to be regarded as lawful associations in themselves. There remained the important question, "lawful for what?" What kinds of activity could a union legally pursue, and what actions were forbidden to it? In deciding this question the courts fell back on the common law principle that harm intentionally inflicted on another is actionable unless it can be shown that the harm was justifiable under the circumstances. In cases involving business concerns, the courts have usually held that pursuit of economic self-interest by normal business methods is sufficient justification for harm done incidentally and without malice to the interests of others.[2]

---

[2] On this point, see Gregory, *Labor and The Law,* chaps. 2 and 3.

A strike or boycott clearly harms the employer and frequently other groups as well. This fact provides a ground for finding such activities unlawful unless the union can justify them as necessary to promote the economic interests of the workers involved. But who is to say what tactics really further the economic interests of the workers and under what conditions the workers' interests are sufficiently strong to justify the damage inflicted on the employer and on third parties? The courts took it on themselves to d̲ union was pursuing the interests of its member simply inflicting unjustifiable damage. The door open for the judges to apply their preconceptions a union objectives and tactics.

This latitude was used somewhat differently in the The courts of New York State, for example, allowed more scope for union activities than did the courts of N or Pennsylvania. In most states, however, legitimate un was confined to peaceable strikes for improved wages, working conditions. Strikes for the closed shop, sympathe in aid of workers in related trades or industries, strikes aga employer to compel him to bring pressure on another e (secondary boycotts), and many other types of activity we unlawful in most states. Once the objective of a strike had bee unlawful, even peaceable actions in furtherance of the strike b equally unlawful. Where the object of the strike was lawful, other hand, a court might still find that the tactics used were coercive and injurious, hence unlawful in themselves. There were thus set up a great many roadblocks over which a union might stumble.

What could be done to a union whose objectives or tactics were held unlawful? Early cases usually took the form of criminal prosecution of union leaders. Beginning with the 1880's, however, employers and the courts discovered the efficacy of the injunction in controlling union activities. From 1880 to 1930 this device reigned almost supreme, and unions came to use the phrase "government by injunction" as one of the worst epithets in their vocabulary.

Government by injunction

The injunction was originally a court order designed to prevent threatened damages to property before they occurred, under circumstances in which later action would not provide an adequate remedy.

How could this procedure be used to prevent peaceable strikes involving no damage to the physical property of the employer? Legal ingenuity soon found ways around this problem. It was held that a strike, even when it did not injure the employer's physical property, was certain to injure his "justifiable expectation of profit" from continuous operation of the business. By treating this expectation of profit as a kind of intangible property, it could be shown that *any* strike was injurious to property. The employer could also allege, and the judge was free to believe, that the strikers were threatening physical damage as well, even when it later turned out that there was no basis for the claim. A sufficiently timid judge could see a bomb-throwing revolutionist even in a business agent of the carpenters' union, and could set about to restrain him by court decree.

Judges differed greatly, of course, in their use of the injunction device. Some judges issued drastic decrees at the slightest sign of trouble; others were much more careful and restrained. On the whole, however, there was much abuse of the injunction procedure, and unions rightly came to regard it as the employers' strongest weapon.

The injunction procedure operated about as follows.[3] The company would go to a judge, usually carefully chosen for the purpose, and present a written complaint against the union. The complaint usually included statements that the union was threatening imminent damage to the employer's property, and that this damage could be prevented only by issuing an injunction. The judge might then decide to issue a temporary injunction immediately; many injunctions were actually drawn up by the company attorney and simply signed by the judge. On the other hand, the judge might decide to take evidence from the union as well. In this event, the union was allowed to file an affidavit replying to the employer's charges, but could not call witnesses or present oral testimony. After considering the employer and union statements, the judge decided whether to issue a temporary injunction.

The temporary injunction, or "restraining order," was usually drawn in sweeping terms, restraining anyone from interfering with the employer's business in any way. Judges occasionally went into some detail, specifying that there must be only one picket at each plant entrance, that he must stand so many feet from the plant gate,

---

[3] For a thorough discussion of the pre-1930 use of injunctions in labor cases, see Felix Frankfurter and Nathan Greene, *The Labor Injunction* (New York: The Macmillan Company, 1930).

and so on. The general vice of injunctions, however, was their vagueness. They were drawn in such broad terms that anyone supporting the strike in any way might be held guilty of a violation. Anyone accused of violating the injunction could be tried without jury for contempt of court and, if found guilty, was punishable by fine or imprisonment.

In theory, there was a final stage of the procedure at which witnesses were heard, after which the temporary injunction was either vacated or rendered permanent. This procedure often took several months, however, and the strike was usually won or lost in the meantime. The injunction device clearly hampered unions in their conduct of strikes. Even when the injunction was not strictly enforced, it stigmatized the union before the public, tended to demoralize and intimidate the strikers, interfered with picketing and other strike activities, consumed the time of union leaders, and cost the union money for legal expenses. Where the injunction was broadly drawn and vigorously enforced by the police, it was an almost infallible method of strike-breaking.

An indirect result of the injunction procedure was to stimulate union interest in political activity. The unions concluded that if judges were going to control them, they had better try to control the judges. They began, therefore, to take a hand in the election and appointment of judges. They also appealed repeatedly to Congress and the state legislatures to pass statutes specifically legalizing trade union activities and forbidding the courts to interfere with them. These efforts were largely unsuccessful. Few laws were passed, and even these were largely nullified by court decisions.

The Clayton Act of 1914

The unions believed that they had scored a great victory in 1914, when Congress wrote into the Clayton Act a long list of normal strike activities, provided that these should not be regarded as in violation of any law, and specified that the federal courts should not issue injunctions against them *under any circumstances*. Samuel Gompers and other AFL leaders hailed this as the Magna Carta of American labor. The courts, however, had the last word as to what the Clayton Act meant. In 1921 the Supreme Court held that Congress had not said anything new at all. This section listing the legitimate strike activities of unions contained the words "peaceably" and "lawfully."

Well, said the Supreme Court, the courts have always held that workers could strike peaceably and lawfully, so the law has not been changed at all. What constitutes "peaceable" and "lawful" activity is still up to the courts to decide, as it always has been.

In 1930, then, the unions were not much better off than they had been in 1880. Public control of labor relations continued to be court control, with relatively little check on the predilections of individual judges. The record of judicial control over this period is, on the whole, a poor one. There is no evidence that labor disputes were reduced or violence minimized. There is quite clear evidence that the burden of the law was unequal. Unions were called into court and penalized in a variety of ways—through criminal prosecutions, damage suits, and injunctions backed up by proceedings for contempt of court. Little restraint was exercised, however, over the tactics of employers, who were left free to combat unionism by any and all methods.

THE EMERGENCE OF A STATUTE LAW OF LABOR RELATIONS

During the 1930's there occurred a virtual revolution in labor law. With the depression and mass unemployment, there was a marked change in the public attitude toward labor organizations. Trade unions became recognized as institutions to be encouraged, not only to give the worker some kind of job security but also to help raise the purchasing power of the workers as an aid in business revival. Congress and many of the state legislatures laid down new rules for the conduct of labor relations and curbed the discretion of the courts in many respects. Special administrative agencies were created to supervise the operation of the new laws. These actions marked a permanent break with the past. Although the laws passed during the 'thirties have now been considerably amended and will probably be so again, the basic fact is that with the passage of these laws, we passed from an era of common law control of labor relations into an era of increasing statutory control.

Norris-LaGuardia Act of 1932

The first step in the new direction was the Norris-LaGuardia Act of 1932, which was designed to prevent abuse of the injunction device in labor disputes. The Act declares that, as a matter of public policy, the individual worker should "have full freedom of association, self-organization, and designation of representatives of his own choosing, to negotiate the terms and conditions of his employment, and that he shall be free from the interference, restraint, or coercion of employers of labor, or their agents, in the designation of such representatives or in self-organization or in other concerted activities for the purpose of collective bargaining or other mutual aid or protection." The Act then lists numerous types of conduct which the courts are forbidden to enjoin when undertaken by persons "participating or interested in" a labor dispute. They cannot enjoin a concerted refusal to work, membership in or support of a labor organization, peaceable urging to others to leave work, publicizing a trade dispute by any method not involving fraud or violence, peaceable assembly, or payment of strike benefits. The Act furthermore makes "yellow-dog contracts" or any other kind of anti-union contract unenforceable in the courts.

The procedure to be used by the federal courts in issuing injunctions was also materially altered. The employer was now required to prove that the regular police force was either unwilling or unable to protect his property. He also had to be innocent of violating any labor law. The judge, before issuing a temporary injunction, had to hear witnesses from both sides instead of relying solely on affidavits. A jury trial was permitted in contempt of court proceedings arising from an injunction. These and other provisions of the Act made it much harder to secure an injunction than it was before 1932 and gave the union reasonable opportunity to present its case. The Norris-LaGuardia Act was followed by anti-injunction acts in most of the major industrial states, laying down similar rules of procedure for the state courts.

The way in which the substantive provisions of the Norris-LaGuardia Act were subsequently modified by the Taft-Hartley Act of 1947 will be discussed later in this chapter. The Norris-LaGuardia Act was a "liberal" measure in the strict sense. Its effect was to remove certain governmental restraints on trade union action and to leave the unions more nearly free to exert their full economic power against the employer. Government soon moved beyond this, however, to give positive support and protection to trade unionism and collective bargaining. This policy was set forth in the National Industrial Recovery Act of 1933 and more specifically in the National

Labor Relations Act of 1935, usually referred to as the Wagner Act, after its principal sponsor.

The Wagner Act of 1935

The philosophy of the Wagner Act was essentially as follows: it is desirable that terms and conditions of employment be regulated by collective bargaining between management and trade unions. It is also desirable, therefore, that workers should organize strong and stable unions as rapidly as possible. This objective will not be accomplished if government follows a laissez-faire policy, since employers have many effective methods of combating union organization. It is necessary, therefore, that government should restrain the use of certain types of coercion by employers during the period in which unions are being formed throughout industry. Employers have frequently argued that the Wagner Act was "one-sided," that it restricted employers without placing any comparable restrictions on unions. This one-sidedness was intended to prevent employers from fighting unionism for a sufficiently long period to allow unionism to spread throughout the economy.

Workers were not required by law to join unions, but the union organizer was given free rein in presenting his case to them, while the employer was required to remain on the side lines. The Act took the position that a worker's decision concerning union membership is none of the employer's business. Its authors assumed that, if pressure from the employer were removed, most workers would choose to join unions in the near future. The growth of union membership from about four million in 1933 to fifteen million in 1948 seems to confirm the essential accuracy of this forecast, though it must be remembered that high employment and active demand for labor after 1940 also did a great deal to promote unionization.

The principal terms of the Wagner Act were as follows: employees were to have the right to organize into trade unions, to bargain collectively through representatives of their own choosing, and to engage in other concerted activities for the purpose of mutual protection. In order to assure them the exercise of this basic right, employers were prohibited from carrying out certain anti-union practices designated as "unfair labor practices." The five unfair labor practices forbidden to employers were (1) interference with, or restraint or coercion of, employees in the exercise of their rights under the Act; (2) domination of, interference with, or financial support of a labor organization; (3) discrimination to encourage or discourage union membership except where a closed- or union-shop was established by agreement with a majority of the employees; (4) discrimination against an employee for filing charges or giving testimony under the Act; and (5) refusal to bargain with the legal representatives of the employees. The Act also provided that, where doubt existed as to the majority status of a union, the matter could be determined by a secret ballot of the workers involved or by some other suitable method. Administration of the Act was entrusted to a National Labor Relations Board, which was made responsible for prosecuting unfair labor practices by employers and deciding disputes over union representation.

The Wagner Act was the basic labor law of the land for twelve years. In the early years, before its general acceptance by the employers, there were serious difficulties in administering it. The staff was inadequate and inexperienced for handling the flood of unfair labor practice charges which came in 1937 and 1938. Nevertheless, by developing informal and increasingly effective administrative procedures and by concentrating their effort on key cases, the NLRB (National Labor Relations Board) was able by the early 'forties to bring about widespread acceptance of the Act. Over 45,000 unfair labor practice cases and over 59,000 representation cases were handled either formally or informally over the twelve years. Whatever its weaknesses or failures, the Wagner Act was an important and remarkably effective instrument in the establishment of collective bargaining as the accepted method of conducting industrial relations.[4]

Passage of the Wagner Act was soon followed by the passage of "little Wagner Acts" in many of the industrial states. State labor relations acts were enacted by Utah, Wisconsin, New York, Pennsylvania, and Massachusetts in 1937, Rhode Island in 1941, and Connecticut in 1945. These state laws are quite important. The Wagner Act and its successors cover only establishments engaged in interstate commerce. Killingsworth has estimated that about 40 per cent of all nonagricultural workers in the country are subject primarily

---

[4] See H. A. Millis and E. C. Brown, *From the Wagner Act to Taft-Hartley* (Chicago: University of Chicago Press, 1950). Chap. 7, "A Twelve Year Balance Sheet," is an excellent summary chapter.

to state regulation.[5] The bulk of these workers are employed in retail trade, building construction, utilities, amusements and recreation, hotels, garages, insurance and real estate, laundering and dry cleaning, and miscellaneous personal services.

Government protection of union organizing activities, combined with the rising level of employment after 1933, led to a rapid increase in union membership. The CIO, which was not in existence when the Wagner Act was passed, appeared on the scene and quickly unionized most workers in the mass-production industries. This was not accomplished, however, without a number of large and bitter strikes, culminating in the wave of sit-down strikes during 1937. Regardless of the reason for these strikes, middle-class opinion tended to place the blame for them on the unions. The alleged "radicalism" of the new unions, instances of violence or irresponsibility during strikes, and occasional malfeasance by union officials were publicized by newspaper editors, columnists, and commentators. Public opinion, particularly in small towns and rural areas, became increasingly critical of union objectives and tactics.

The strongest criticism of the Wagner Act, if one ignores the attacks of those who accepted no part of it, was that its treatment of unions and of management was inequitable. Employers were said to have no protection against unions' unfair use of their economic power. A further objection was that individual and minority rights were not sufficiently protected under the Act. This objection is perhaps not surprising since the purpose of the Act was to favor collective action in all cases where it had majority support.

The unfavorable reaction of public opinion to union activities did not lead to general repeal of the federal and state labor relations acts, though this was an end devoutly wished by many employers. It resulted rather in the passage of additional laws intended to control certain types of union activity. In an effort to achieve a workable balance of power between unions and employers, government was projected ever farther into the labor relations scene.

---

[5] C. C. Killingsworth, *State Labor Relations Acts: A sudy of Public Policy* (Chicago: University of Chicago Press, 1948), chap. 1. It should be noted that any estimates of this sort are necessarily approximate, because the line between intrastate and interstate industries is somewhat hazy and subject to change in the light of administrative and judicial decisions. Building construction, for example, has usually been considered an intrastate industry. The National Labor Relations Board, however, undertook to apply the Taft-Hartley Act to building construction, i.e., to treat it as an interstate industry.

The first of the new acts, which Killingsworth has termed "restrictive laws" as contrasted with "protective laws" of the Wagner Act type, were passed in the states. As early as 1939, Pennsylvania amended its state labor relations act, while Wisconsin repealed its act and passed a new one designed to impose certain controls on union activities. In the same year, Minnesota and Michigan passed new labor relations acts of a restrictive type. Kansas and Colorado followed in 1943, and Utah in 1947. In addition to these comprehensive labor relations acts, the years 1937-47 saw a multitude of state acts imposing specific restrictions on trade unions. These laws dealt, among other things, with sit-down strikes, use of force and violence in strikes, mass picketing, jurisdictional strikes, sympathy strikes, strikes in the absence of an agreement, strike votes, picketing in the absence of a labor dispute, picketing of agricultural premises, picketing by nonemployees, primary and secondary boycotts, refusal to handle nonunion materials, coercion or intimidation of workers by trade unions, prohibition of the closed or union shop and the checkoff, licensing of unions and their officers, registration and submission of information by unions to the state government, filing of financial reports, control of union membership requirements, control over expulsion of workers from membership, regulation of strikes in public utilities, and regulation of strikes in public employment. By the late 'forties, there was scarcely a state which did not have one or more union control laws on its statute books.

The Taft-Hartley Act of 1947

On the federal front, the movement to impose additional restrictions on trade unions made slower headway. Numerous amendments to the Wagner Act were introduced in every session of Congress, but none was enacted because of the opposition of President Roosevelt and the leaders of the Democratic majority in Congress. During the war years amendments were pressed less vigorously, since labor disputes were handled under special emergency provisions by the National War Labor Board.

After the war, however, the campaign to curb union power was intensified. When government control of wages ended with the war, there was no accepted plan for resolving the difficult issues of wages and hours in the reconversion period. Unions demanded higher wage rates to compensate for reduced earnings due to fewer hours and less overtime pay. Serious strikes over this issue occurred in the steel, coal, and automobile industries in 1946, and there was also a nation-wide railroad strike. Public alarm over these strikes was partly responsible for election of a Republican majority to Congress in 1946. In 1947 Congress proceeded to pass the Labor-Management Relations Act of 1947, commonly known as the Taft-Hartley Act after its two principal sponsors.

The new law was in form an amendment of the Wagner Act, and most of the Wagner Act's provisions were carried over intact. Many new provisions were added, however, embodying a different philosophy of labor relations. The Wagner Act assumed that most workers prefer to join unions, that the interests of unions and their members are identical, that restricting certain employer tactics will ensure rough equality of bargaining power between unions and management, and that once the parties have been brought to the bargaining table they should be left free to write whatever contract provisions they choose. Government should not try to shape the content of union contracts.

The contrasting outlook underlying the Taft-Hartley Act can be summarized as follows: (1) Workers may or may not wish to join unions. Their right to stay out should be protected against coercion from any quarter, including the union; and workers already in unions should be given reasonable opportunity to get out if they so desire. (2) The interests of members and of the union organization are not necessarily identical. Workers need protection against the union as well as against the employer. Government may have to regulate internal union affairs for this purpose. (3) Unions are not necessarily the weaker party in collective bargaining. In some areas of the economy the employer may be the underdog. To ensure true equality of bargaining power, the law must restrain unfair tactics of unions as well as of employers. (4) There is a public interest in the terms of union contracts. Some contract provisions may be sufficiently against the public interest that they should be prohibited. Government is entitled to scrutinize bargaining results as well as bargaining procedures. (5) The public also requires protection against crippling strikes in essential industries, and special procedures are needed to deal with such strikes.

While the emphasis of the Wagner Act was on protecting unions, the emphasis of Taft-Hartley was on protecting employers, individual workers, and the general public; and toward this end a variety of restrictions were imposed on union operations. The unions strongly opposed the Act and later worked energetically to secure its repeal. These efforts were unsuccessful, however, and the Act continues as the main federal legislation governing labor relations.

The Landrum-Griffin Act of 1959

Taft-Hartley established the principle that government might regulate internal union affairs but did not go far in that direction. A union which wished to use the facilities of the Act, including NLRB election procedures, was required to file with the Secretary of Labor a copy of its constitution and bylaws; an annual financial report; a list of its officers, including their salaries and allowances; and an affidavit by each officer that he was not a member of the Communist Party or any other subversive organization. This last provision was particularly offensive to the unions, and a number of unions, including the conservative United Mine Workers, declined to comply with it, thereby putting themselves outside the protection of the Act.

During the 'fifties there was continued complaint of corruption and undemocratic procedures in trade union government, and growing sentiment for legislative reform. The outcome was the Landrum-Griffin Act of 1959, whose main provisions were described in Chapter 4, and which has now superseded Taft-Hartley as regards control of internal union affairs. The drafters of Landrum-Griffin also took the occasion to amend Taft-Hartley in certain respects, mainly by tightening previous restrictions on organizational picketing and secondary boycotts. The thrust of the new law was restrictive and generally in the spirit of Taft-Hartley. But it also included several concessions to the unions. The offensive non-Communist affidavit was eliminated. The closed shop, prohibited by Taft-Hartley, was (in effect) relegalized in the building industry, thus softening the opposition of the powerful building trades group to the new legislation. It was also provided that the restrictions on secondary boycotts should not prevent the building and clothing workers' unions from moving to control subcontracting in their respective industries.

Before describing the present legal framework of collective bargaining, let us review briefly the zigzags of policy in this area. Before 1930 the scales were tilted against unionism and collective bargaining by the negative attitude of the courts. Norris-LaGuardia attempted to establish a laissez-faire policy by freeing unions of their existing legal disabilities, but leaving everything beyond that up to the unions and employers. But this was superseded almost immediately by the Wagner Act policy of government intervention to promote union organization. Looking backward, the Wagner Act does not seem so great a triumph for the unions as it appeared at the time. It was naïve to think that government could be drawn in only to control employer practices while leaving the unions entirely free. By the late 'forties the political pendulum had swung back toward the employer side; and conservative legislators took the opportunity to write into law a different conception of "equal bargaining power" and proper union behavior. The consequence of inviting government intervention was to fasten an increasingly complex network of controls on unions and employers alike.

The American industrial relations system, with its legalism and complexity, contrasts sharply with those of most other industrial nations. In Britain, for example, there is virtually no legislative control over how unions shall be organized or operated, how the parties shall behave in collective bargaining, or what provisions may be written into collective agreements. The reason is partly that British unions have fought shy of either government support or regulation. American unions and employers have been inclined to "call for the cops," and government intervention does not vanish as quickly as it comes.

A second impression which stands out from the historical record is the volatility of policy in this area. We have had a major new piece of industrial relations legislation about every twelve years. We have veered from anti-unionism to laissez-faire to pro-unionism and back toward neutrality plus controls. We don't seem able to make up our minds. Professor Dunlop has argued that this reflects a basic lack of consensus in the American community concerning the value of unionism and the results of collective bargaining.[6] Where there is no real consensus, legislation is apt to reflect expedient compromises and to change frequently with the shifting tides of political power.

THE FRAMEWORK OF COLLECTIVE BARGAINING TODAY

The Taft-Hartley Act is a detailed and complex piece of legislation, running to thirty closely-printed pages; and it has been elaborately footnoted by decisions of the NLRB and the courts. All that we can do in a few pages is to convey the general flavor of the present control system.

---

[6] John T. Dunlop, "Consensus and National Labor Policy," *Proceedings of Thirteenth Annual Meeting of IRRA* (1960), pp. 2-15. See also Douglass V. Brown and Charles A. Myers, "Historical Evolution," in Joseph Shister, Benjamin Aaron, and Clyde W. Summers, eds., *Public Policy Toward Collective Bargaining* (New York: Harper & Row, Publishers, 1962).

Most provisions of the Act can be related to three professed objectives:

(a) to equalize bargaining power by restraining certain tactics of both unions and employers. To this end the Act lists certain unfair practices on the part of unions, paralleling the list of unfair employer practices which was carried over intact from the Wagner Act. Unions may not interfere with the individual employee's right not to participate in collective bargaining. They may not attempt to cause employers to discriminate against nonunionists, except as may be required by a valid union shop agreement. They may not refuse to bargain collectively with an employer. They may not engage in secondary boycotts or jurisdictional strikes, nor in strikes to force recognition of one union when another has already been certified as bargaining representative. They may not extract money from an employer for work not needed or not actually performed.

(b) Second, the Act attempts to protect individual employees against the union in a variety of ways. The provisions on this front are highly controversial. Presented by the Act's sponsors as a "bill of rights" for the individual worker, they have been denounced by unionists as thinly disguised efforts to hamper normal union operations and reduce union strength.

The most striking example is a provision permitting any worker to take up his grievances directly with management "without intervention of the bargaining representative," i.e., to bypass the normal union-management grievance procedure described in Chapter 7. Most workers have shown little disposition to take advantage of this provision and most employers have also found it unworkable, so that it has had little effect in practice.

Union contracts may no longer establish a closed shop or any other system of preferential hiring, except for the special provisions already mentioned for the building industry. Under the original terms of the Act, it was not lawful even to require union membership after hiring (a "union shop") unless a majority of workers had voted in favor of such a clause in a secret ballot conducted by the Board. This provision backfired, because it turned out that workers consistently voted for the union shop by large majorities and employers then had little alternative but to concede the demand. The same employers who had favored this provision soon sought its repeal and it was repealed after a few years of experience.

A union may not charge excessive dues or initiation fees. While it remains free to discipline and expel members, it cannot cause the employer to discharge a worker under a union shop contract if the worker was denied membership or dropped from membership for any reason other than nonpayment of dues and initiation fees. In addition, employees are given a way of getting rid of a union which they no longer wish to represent them. If 30 per cent of the employees in a bargaining unit file a petition requesting decertification of the union representing them, the NLRB must conduct a secret ballot to determine the wishes of the majority. Between 1948 and 1959, about 150 decertification elections per year were held under this provision, of which the unions won about one-third and lost two-thirds.

The checkoff system of collecting union dues is regulated by a proviso that dues can be deducted from the pay check only with the written consent of the individual employee. Employer payments to union welfare funds are only permitted if certain conditions are observed, such as separation of the welfare funds from general union funds and joint union-management administration. The Act provides further, as noted in Chapter 3, that union funds may not be used for political purposes.

(c) A third professed objective is to protect innocent bystanders against the consequences of interunion or union-management strife. The innocent party may in some cases be the employer. Under the Wagner Act, an employer sometimes found himself caught in the cross fire of two rival unions, each seeking to organize his plant and each threatening to shut it down, unless granted recognition. Since the employer could not petition for an NLRB election to settle the issue, his hands were tied. The Taft-Hartley Act accordingly provides that employers as well as unions may petition the NLRB for a representation election. A similar situation often arises in jurisdictional disputes where two unions—say, the Carpenters and Machinists—each demand that the employer assign a certain type of work to its members under penalty of shutdown. The Taft-Hartley Act forbids strikes in such situations and provides that they may be decided by the NLRB unless the rival unions work out their own arrangements for settlement. This has stimulated the growth of private settlement machinery, notably as between the various building trades unions.

We have already noted the Act's restrictions on the secondary boycott, an old union device of putting pressure on one employer so that he will exert pressure on another employer whom the union is really after. The carpenters' union, for example, has jurisdiction over factories making millwork and other lumber products. These plants are numerous, small, and often difficult to organize. One way to organize them is for the union carpenters on construction jobs to refuse to install millwork from nonunion factories. This forces the building contractors to buy from union plants only. The nonunion plants find their market reduced or even destroyed, and are forced to recognize the union.

The legitimacy of such "billiard-shot" tactics has been debated for decades. Boycott activities have usually been held illegal at common law. The Taft-Hartley Act reinforced this view by making it an unfair labor practice to encourage a strike or a concerted refusal to handle a company's goods when the purpose is to force the company to stop doing business with another company. This has led to complicated litigation over who is the "primary" and who is the "secondary" employer in a particular case, whether the secondary employer is actually neutral or whether he is in effect an ally, and so on. Secondary boycotts have certainly not been eliminated by the Act, but they have probably been hampered and reduced.

Strikes often cause inconvenience to another neutral party, the consuming public. The Taft-Hartley Act contains no limitations on strikes in general, but it does provide a procedure for use in so-called "national emergency" disputes. Strikes which, in the opinion of the President, imperil the national health or safety are made subject to injunction for a maximum period of eighty days. The President is authorized to appoint a special board of inquiry, which makes a preliminary investigation prior to the time an injunction is sought, and must turn in a final report when the injunction has been in effect for sixty days. If the parties, with the aid of the Federal Mediation and Conciliation Service, have not been able to settle the dispute by this time, the NLRB is required to poll the employees as to whether they are willing to accept the employer's last offer. After this step the injunction is dissolved and the President may, if he wishes, refer the dispute to Congress and recommend a course of action concerning it. The board of inquiry is specifically prohibited from recommending terms for settlement of the dispute. These provisions do not apply to government employees, who are prohibited by the Act from striking; nor do they apply to railroad workers, for whom a special procedure is provided by the Railway Labor Act.

APPLYING THE LAW: UNFAIR LABOR PRACTICES

The National Labor Relation Board consists of five members, appointed by the President with the advice and consent of the Senate. Changes in the membership of the Board with changing administrations have sometimes produced substantial changes in general policy. Under the Board is a General Counsel, who has sole authority to investigate and prosecute complaints of unfair labor practices. He also has general supervision of the attorneys employed by the Board, as well as of the officers and employees of the regional offices. The Board members themselves have essentially judicial functions.

The volume of Board activity is impressive. Representation cases and unfair labor practice cases together total something like fifteen thousand in a typical year. About 85 per cent of these are disposed of at the regional level; but the two thousand or so cases which reach the Board each year are still a heavy burden, which has sometimes caused a serious lag in Board decisions.

Representation disputes will be examined in Chapter 7, in connection with bargaining units and bargaining procedures. This leaves for discussion here only the Board's work in connection with unfair labor practices.

Unfair practices of employers

Of the five prohibited employer practices, three have given rise to the greatest number of cases:

1. An employer may not "interfere with, restrain, or coerce" employees in the exercise of their right to self-organization and collective bargaining. It is unlawful for the employer to set up a spy system in the plant, either one maintained by the company itself or one hired from an outside detective agency. It is unlawful also to shadow union organizers and officers, to spy on union meetings, and to harass union members in other ways. The employer may not hire strong-arm men to beat up union organizers or members. He may not threaten to fire men for joining the union or promise them special privileges for not joining. He may not call workers into his office and interrogate them about their union membership or activities. He is

free to address his employees either orally or in writing, to express his
views on unionism and to advise the workers against joining a union,
but only if there is no threat of reprisal or promise of benefit. The
test is whether the employer's action gives the worker reason to fear
loss of his job or some other penalty unless he accepts the employer's
view.

It has proven difficult in practice to draw a line between legitimate
employer free speech, on the one hand, and intimidation and coercion
on the other. In early Wagner Act days the NLRB restricted employers severely, on the ground that their power over the jobs of their
employees may give even innocent-sounding words a coercive effect.
Employers complained bitterly that they were being silenced while
union organizers could villify them and their companies at will.
Congress accordingly wrote into Taft-Hartley a provision that "the
expressing of any views, argument or opinion . . . shall not constitute
. . . an unfair labor practice . . . if such expression contains no threat
of reprisal or force or promise of benefit." In recent years the NLRB
and the courts have been much more permissive as regards employer
statements. It has been held that the employer is within his rights in
calling meetings of all employees during working hours to present
the company's viewpoint, in disparaging the union and its leaders, and
in predicting dire economic consequences should the union enter the
plant, even to the point of stating that the plant may have to shut
down. It is now the unions who complain that the pendulum has
swung too far and that the Board is allowing employers to use intimidating tactics.[7]

2. An employer may not discriminate "in regard to hire or tenure
of employment or any term or condition of employment to encourage
or discourage membership in any labor organization." This makes it
unlawful to discharge a man for belonging to a union. In one case, for
example, a foreman said to the men in his department, "Are you with
the union or not? If you are with the union, you cannot work here."
Another foreman said, "You know we don't allow no union workers
on this platform." In another case, the employer discharged all
workers in the plant and then told them that they could be reinstated
if they quit the union.

These cases are quite clear. In some cases, however, the company
states that a man was fired for inefficiency or some other reason, while

---

[7] For a more extended discussion, see Benjamin Aaron, "Employer Free Speech:
the Search for a Policy," in Shister, Aaron, and Summers, eds., *op. cit.*, pp. 28-59.

the union suspects that union activity was the real reason for the discharge. The National Labor Relations Board then has to examine the employee's previous work record, his efficiency compared with that of other workers, the way in which similar cases have been handled by the company in the past, and so on. It sometimes develops that the company's reason for discharge was specious, and that the man was actually discharged for his union activities. In one case, for example, a truck driver employed by a cartage company joined the union and was elected president. Three days after his election, the secretary-treasurer of the company followed his truck in a car, detected a minor infraction of company rules, and discharged him on the spot. Testimony taken by the NLRB revealed that the worker's previous efficiency had been entirely satisfactory, and that violations of this particular rule had not been punished by the company up to this time. The Board held that the man had been discharged on account of his union activities and ordered his reinstatement.

Discharge of an unduly large proportion of union men over a period of time may provide ground for suspicion of the company's motives. Nor can the company evade this provision of the Act by shutting down its plant entirely and later taking back only nonunion workers. In one case, for example, the company shut down the plant and spread the word around town that union men would not be taken back. This rumor caused union members to delay making application for reinstatement. When they finally did apply, the company expressed regret that their places had already been filled. The Board held that this was a subterfuge designed to get rid of union members in the plant, and directed that the union members be reinstated in their previous jobs.

3. An employer may not "refuse to bargain collectively with the representatives of his employees." The original purpose of this provision was simply to effectuate the workers' right to self-organization. There would not be much point in forming a union if the employer could simply decline to have any dealings with it.

In the years after the Wagner Act, decisions of the NLRB and the courts spelled out what the employer is obliged to do under this provision. If a union has a majority in an appropriate bargaining unit, the employer must meet with their representatives. Nothing excuses him from this obligation. He may think that the leaders of the union are communists, that they are plotting to take over his business, and that unionism will ruin his enterprise. He must still meet with them and discuss their demands. This discussion must be conducted "in good faith" with the intention of reaching an agreement. The employer cannot simply say "No" to every proposal the union makes. He is not compelled to accept the union demands, but he must be willing to give reasons for his refusal and to make counter-proposals. If an agreement is finally reached, the employer must be willing to put it in written form for a specified period of time. Moreover, he cannot escape the obligation to bargain by discharging his present labor force, refusing to deal with their representatives, and filling the plant with new men. In several cases of this sort the NLRB has held that the former workers are still "employees" under the Act, and has ordered the employer to reinstate them and to bargain with their representatives.

What is the employer obliged to bargain *about?* The Act mentions "wages, hours, and other terms and conditions of employment." But what are "other terms and conditions"? In interpreting this language the Board has held that employers must bargain on a wide range of issues, including merit increases, pension and retirement plans, insurance benefits, health and welfare funds, prices of employee meals, stock-purchase and profit-sharing plans, discontinuance and removal of one department in a plant, closing a plant, relocating a plant, and contracting out work to another company.

In general, it is unions which have been seeking to expand the scope of collective bargaining and employers who have been holding back. But this is not invariably true. Employers have demanded contract clauses limiting the right of the union to discipline its members, placing liability on the international union for breach of a no-strike clause, requiring a ballot of all employees on the employer's last offer before a strike can be called, calling for posting of a performance bond by the union, requiring the union to register under state statute to make it suable in state courts, and numerous other subjects. Since Taft-Hartley requires that the union must also bargain in good faith, the NLRB has had to decide whether these demands involve "other terms and conditions of employment" and whether the union is bound to bargain about them.

It is now clear, though it was not foreseen at the outset, that the Board's power to define good faith bargaining gives it power to specify what clauses may properly be written into a union contract. Either the union or the employer may contend that a certain issue is not bargainable and carry the point to the Board for decision. The Board must then decide whether the issue is subject to mandatory bargaining under the Act, or whether bargaining is merely voluntary. The practical difference is this: on a subject of mandatory bargaining, the parties must negotiate but need not concede. Either side may stand firm to the point of provoking a strike. If the issue is ruled to be voluntary, however, the party making the demand may not insist on it as a condition for signing a contract. If he remains adamant and a strike results, he can be charged with an unfair labor practice. Examples of such issues abound. Suppose a union whose members are threatened by automation demands a contract clause providing that no displaced worker may be laid off. Can the union insist on this clause? Or suppose the employer demands that the union agree to a clause calling for a pre-strike vote of all employees (union and nonunion) on the employer's last offer. Can the company press this demand to the point of stalling negotiations and causing a strike? The power of the Board, and ultimately of the courts, to decide such questions gives government wide powers over the substance of collective bargaining.[8]

Unfair practices of unions

Three categories of "unfair labor practice" by unions have given rise to the great majority of complaints:

1. The Act prohibits strikes and picketing to compel one employer to cease dealing with another (secondary boycott), or to compel recognition otherwise than through NLRB representation procedures, or to force recognition where another union is already established as bargaining agent, or to assert jurisdiction over a particular type of work. The secondary boycott provision has proven especially tricky and difficult to handle, and the line between legal and illegal activity is still quite unclear.[9]

2. It is an unfair labor practice for any union to "restrain or coerce" workers in their decisions concerning union membership. It has of course always been unlawful for a union organizer to recruit

---

[8] See on this problem Robben W. Fleming, "The Obligation to Bargain in Good Faith," in Shister, Aaron, and Summers, eds., *op. cit.*, pp. 60-87; and Russell A. Smith, "Government Intervention in the Substantive Areas of Collective Bargaining," *Proceedings of the Fifteenth Annual Meeting of IRRA* (1962), pp. 237-247.

[9] See Donald H. Wollett, "The Weapons of Conflict: Picketing and Boycotts," in Shister, Aaron, and Summers, eds., *op. cit.*, pp. 121-151.

members by violent methods. He cannot legally hit nonunion workers over the head, wreck their automobiles, or cause them other physical harm. If he does, he can be arrested and prosecuted.

The sponsors of the Taft-Hartley Act presumably intended to go beyond this and to restrain other types of pressure against nonunion workers. They seem to have had in mind such things as threats of high initiation fees if the employee does not join the union before it gets bargaining rights, false electioneering statements, threats of violence or reprisal during an organizing campaign, threats to get a union shop and make the employee lose his job, and mass picketing to prevent nonunionists from entering a plant. The right of an employee not to take part in collective bargaining has been stretched in some cases to include his right to go to work in the face of a strike. This application of the Act has naturally caused much controversy and complaint.

3. It is an unfair labor practice for a union to "cause or attempt to cause" an employer to discriminate against any employee in terms or conditions of employment or to encourage or discourage membership in a labor organization. The only exception is that under a union-shop agreement a union may cause an employee to be discharged for failure to pay his regular dues. The NLRB has ruled that a union may not try to make an employer fire a man for nonmembership in a union, for failure to take a union oath, or for opposition to the union leaders. It is this section of the Act which prohibits any kind of preferential hiring system, since such a system would mean causing an employer to discriminate against nonunion members. The discrimination need not take the form of firing to be illegal. In one case the Board ruled against a union which requested that the company lower a union member's seniority rating in compliance with the union by-laws because he had not paid his dues on time.

Enforcement procedures

What happens when it is alleged that a union or an employer has committed an unfair labor practice? What can the NLRB do about it? Charges are submitted by the aggrieved party—an employer, a union, or an individual worker as the case may be—to the nearest of the Board's regional offices. The situation is then investigated by a field examiner to see whether the Board has jurisdiction and whether there is evidence that an unfair labor practice actually has been committed.

The great majority of complaints are disposed of informally at this stage. Many are dismissed because of flimsy evidence, and many others are settled by agreement of the parties.

If there is reasonable evidence of an unfair labor practice and if an informal settlement cannot be reached, the regional office issues a formal complaint and the case is heard before a trial examiner. His decision may be appealed by either party—the General Counsel or the defendant—to the Board itself. When an appeal is filed, the Board reviews the case, permitting the parties to present additional oral evidence if this seems advisable. The Board then either dismisses the case or, if it finds the defendant guilty of unfair labor practices, issues an order requiring him to "cease and desist" from these practices. Where an employer has discharged workers in order to discourage union membership, or where a union has caused discharge, the Board normally requires reinstatement with back pay from the date of the discharge. Apart from this, however, the Board has no power to levy financial penalties against an employer or a union. It can only tell them to stop what they have been doing.

A defendant convicted by the Board may, in fact, ignore the Board's order and continue to behave as before. The Board can then apply to a federal circuit court of appeals for a decree ordering the defendant to comply. If the case is important, it is likely to be appealed eventually to the United States Supreme Court. Final decision on what the law means, and what practices the NLRB may lawfully prohibit under it, thus remains in the hands of the courts. The courts are required, however, to accept the Board's factual conclusions if supported by "substantial evidence on the record considered as a whole." The record of the NLRB before the courts is good, the great majority of its orders having been upheld, particularly at the Supreme Court level.[10] After the courts have affirmed an order of the Board, the defendant must comply or suffer penalties for contempt of court.

It is often several years between the first filing of charges with the Board and the final settlement of a case by the courts. In the meantime, the original cause of the dispute may have disappeared. A company can often kill off a prospective union during the years in which

---

[10] Of 1,821 Board decisions appealed to the courts from 1935 to 1957, the Board was reversed in only 310 cases. These were probably, to be sure, the more sensitive and precedent-setting cases. (Hywell Evans, *Government Regulation of Industrial Relations*. New York State School of Industrial and Labor Relations, 1961, p. 58.)

the Board is trying to prevent it from doing so. This slowness is due partly to the legal requirements of fair trial for the accused. It is aggravated, however, by the fact that the Board has never had sufficient staff to keep abreast of the duties placed on it by Congress. It has always had a large backlog of cases awaiting it before current cases could be considered. As a practical matter, the extent to which unfair labor practices are prevented in the future will depend largely on the willingness of Congress to supply the Board with an adequate budget.

CONTINUING ISSUES OF PUBLIC POLICY

The Taft-Hartley Act has not had the drastic consequences predicted by either its supporters or opponents. While it may have hampered the expansion of union membership somewhat, it has not seriously disrupted the operation of established unions. On the positive side, while it accomplished some desirable reforms, it fell short of correcting all defects in union government and collective bargaining practices. Many provisions of the Act turned out to have little effect. This was true, for example, of the anti-closed-shop provisions, the requirement of an election to validate a union shop, the antifeather-bedding clause, the provisions concerning dues and initiation fees, and the restrictions on management of welfare funds. The procedure for handling of "national emergency" disputes has been invoked only rarely and with indifferent success.

Some of the failures of the Act stem from a misconception of what goes on in collective bargaining and a consequent overestimate of what can be accomplished through legislation. There is little basis for the idea that equality of bargaining power between unions and employers can be accomplished by imposing parallel lists of "unfair practices" on both sides. Relative bargaining power depends much more on the economic structure of the industry, the extensiveness of employer and union organization, the level of business activity, and other factors. Unions continue to have more power than employers in some industries and less power in others for reasons quite unconnected with Taft-Hartley. The Act also assumed that employers were eager and able to protect the individual employee against misuses of union power, provided only that they were given proper legal instruments. Most employers, however, seem to prefer peaceful relations with the union to insistence on perfect justice for the individual. Nor do many workers consider it sensible to look to the employer for "protection" against the union.

The main consequence of Taft-Hartley has been to project government ever farther into the labor relations scene. The relatively simple provisions of the original Wagner Act have been replaced by an expanding network of controls over employer and union behavior, bargaining procedure, and the content of collective agreements. As defects appear in the present structure of controls there is pressure for still further legislation.

It must be remembered, too, that Taft-Hartley does not have the field to itself. It is superimposed on a substantial body of state legislation and common law precedent. Twelve of the states have state labor relations acts applying to retail stores, service establishments, local transportation, and other intrastate industries. Twenty states have "right to work" laws prohibiting the closed shop and union shop and applying to *all* employment in the state. (The Taft-Hartley Act provides that state legislation on this matter shall take precedence over anything in federal statutes, despite the general rule that Congressional legislation supersedes state action.) These states are principally in the South and Midwest. Indiana is the only northern industrial state which has passed this type of legislation.

Beyond this lies the vast body of court decisions concerning the legality of strikes, boycotts, picketing, and other union activities. Judges have been wrestling with these matters for more than a century, as was indicated earlier in this chapter. Where an activity is specifically legalized or expressly prohibited by Taft-Hartley or by a valid state statute, the legislative view is binding. The courts still have the final word, however, as to how the wording of the statute should be interpreted and applied in particular cases. And in the large number of situations where there is no clear legislative guidance, courts continue to make the law as they always have. Workers can and do sue unions for damages suffered as a result of union activity. More frequently, employers come to court seeking injunctions and other types of redress against picketing and other union pressures. The willingness of courts to restrain union activity varies considerably from state to state, depending on the tradition of court decisions in the state, political liberalism or conservatism, and so on.

Labor relations has consequently become a lawyer's paradise. Managements and unions now spend a great deal of money in protecting and promoting their interests through legal channels. It has become increasingly difficult and unwise to make any categorical statements about what is "legal" in labor relations. The answer depends on the specific facts of the case, the state in question, and the latest turn of Supreme Court opinion. The only safe advice which can be given in most situations is, "See your lawyer."

Among the multitude of controversial issues in this area, a few stand out as a special importance.

1. More government control of labor relations or less? The trend since 1935 has been toward increasing control, and as new problems emerge the first reaction of most people is to advocate additional legislation. Some of the leading students of labor relations, however, feel that we have already gone too far and that the trend toward greater control should be reversed. They point out that for a century before 1935 unions and management survived and settled their disputes reasonably well without specific legislation. They point out also that we have much more government intervention in collective bargaining than any other democratic country with the possible exception of Australia. Clark Kerr has suggested that statutory regulation could be stripped down to four points:

  i. provision of a mediation service for industrial disputes, but without arbitration or other compulsory powers;
 ii. conduct of representation elections, as is now done by the NLRB;
iii. a law concerning union pressure on third parties to get at an employer;
 iv. a law guaranteeing certain elementary worker rights—admission to union membership, participation in union affairs, and outside review of discipline imposed by the union.[11]

This would provide some protections not now available, while at the same time reducing and streamlining our basic labor legislation. Most coercive tactics of unions and employers would be left to court control, as they were before 1935, while the content of collective agreements would be left entirely to union-management negotiation.

2. To the extent that statutory control of labor relations is desirable, should this be done through federal legislation or state legislation? Employer groups sometimes urge that Taft-Hartley be amended to give a general priority to state legislation, so that wherever state and federal rules concerning labor relations conflict, the state law would take precedence. The reason is that many state legis-

---

[11] Clark Kerr, "Industrial Relations and the Liberal Pluralist," *Proceedings of the Seventh Convention of the IRRA* (1954), pp. 14-15.

latures are more conservative than Congress in labor matters, and employers would often have better success with antiunion legislation by operating at the state level. Union leaders and supporters usually argue that federal law should prevail, because they can reasonably expect to win better treatment at the federal level. There is also the practical consideration that national unions and large interstate employers find it awkward to be bound by widely differing laws in different states.

3. In addition to these broad philosophical differences, there are several specific issues on which feeling has run particularly high in recent years: the status of the closed shop and union shop (see Chapter 8), the secondary boycott issue, prevention of abuses in internal union administration (see Chapter 4), and alternative techniques for handling "emergency strikes" threatening public health or safety (see Chapter 11). Some of these issues will be examined further as they arise in the logical development of later chapters. On each of them there are wide differences of opinion as to what types of government action are either just or feasible. Political conflict on this front seems likely to continue for as far ahead as one can see, and the law will doubtless never reach a state fully satisfactory to all parties.

Discussion questions

1. "Until recent years there were practically no statutes affecting labor relations; yet public control over labor relations is as old as trade unions themselves." Explain, giving specific examples.

2. Why have unions taken strong objection to the injunction procedure? In what ways did the Norris-LaGuardia Act alter the use of this device?

3. Explain why the Wagner Act was so helpful to union organization during the 'thirties and 'forties.

4. Compare the philosophy and objectives of the Taft-Hartley Act with those of the Wagner Act.

5. "Experience since 1933 has proved that it is impossible to legislate good labor relations. The best thing that could be done would be to repeal all federal and state statutes on the subject and turn the matter back to the regular courts of law." Discuss carefully.

6. "The Taft-Hartley Act has weakened unions and thereby restored the balance of power in union-management relations." Discuss.

7. How would you draw a line between employer statements which are a legitimate exercise of free speech and statements which should be considered intimidating and coercive?

8. How far should one stretch the concept of "other terms and

conditions of employment" in defining good faith bargaining? List some issues which you believe should be, and others which should not be, considered subjects for mandatory bargaining.

9. Where federal and state labor relations statutes contain different provisions on the same subject, which should have priority?

10. Evaluate Clark Kerr's proposal for simplification of present labor relations legislation.

Selected reading

Bernstein, Irving, *The New Deal Collective Bargaining Policy.* Berkeley: University of California Press, 1950.

Evans, H., *Government Regulation of Industrial Relations.* Ithaca: New York State School of Industrial and Labor Relations, 1961.

Frankfurter, Felix, and Nathan Greene, *The Labor Injunction,* New York: The Macmillan Company, 1930.

Gregory, Charles O., *Labor and the Law,* (new) rev. ed. New York: W. W. Norton and Company, 1958.

Killingsworth, Charles C., *State Labor Relations Acts: A Study of Public Policy.* Chicago: University of Chicago Press, 1948.

Millis, Harry A., and Emily C. Brown, *From the Wagner Act to Taft-Hartley.* Chicago: University of Chicago Press, 1950.

Shister, J., B. Aaron, and C. Summers, eds., *Public Policy and Collective Bargaining.* New York: Harper & Row, Publishers, 1962.

Slichter, Sumner H., *The Challenge of Industrial Relations.* Ithaca, N.Y.: Cornell University Press, 1947.

————, "Revision of the Taft-Hartley Act," *Quarterly Journal of Economics,* LXVII (May 1953), pp. 149-180.

Taylor, George W., *Government Regulation of Industrial Relations.* Englewood Cliffs, N.J.: Prentice-Hall, Inc., 1948.

Witte, Edwin E., *The Government in Labor Disputes.* New York: McGraw-Hill Book Company, Inc., 1932.

6

Management's Approach
To Collective Bargaining

It is frequently said that collective bargaining is a relationship between a political organization, the trade union, and a business organization. What does this business organization look like? What is the management group trying to accomplish? What attitudes and practices do they inherit from pre-union days? How do they typically react to the appearance of a trade union on the scene? These questions must be examined before we can understand what goes on in collective bargaining.

THE FUNCTION AND OUTLOOK OF MANAGEMENT

We may best begin by examining the economic function of the business firm. The central purpose of a business organization is to purchase certain inputs (labor, materials, capital equipment), transform these into saleable products, and dispose of the products on the market at a price that will at least cover costs. The complexity of this operation varies enormously with the size of the organization, type of industry, and variety of goods and services produced. Compare the corner grocery store with the complicated organization of the General Motors Corporation. Both General Motors and the corner grocery, however, meet the definition which we have given of a business organization, and the logic of their operation is basically similar.

The principle that receipts from sales must cover costs distinguishes the business organization from certain other types of organization, such as governmental agencies. There is no legal requirement that the receipts of the U.S. Post Office Department must cover the costs of operating the department. It would be impossible to "put the post office out of business" by paying too high wages to postal employees, since operating losses can be made up from tax revenues. A business organization, however, has no recourse to the taxing power. It must live on receipts from sales, and wage increases must be offset over the long run by higher prices or greater productive efficiency. It would be quite possible in a private business to establish a level of wages and prices so high that the company could not continue in operation.

The picture of the business concern which one meets in economic textbooks is considerably simplified, partly because of the emphasis which economists have placed on the theory of pure competition. Under purely competitive conditions, the prices which must be paid for all factors of production are strictly determined by the market, and the prices of the company's products are similarly determined. The only decision left to management concerns the method of production to be used. On closer investigation, however, it turns out that management has no real choice even in this respect. By the definition of pure competition, new producers are free to enter the industry at will. Unless a particular company uses the most efficient possible methods, therefore, it will not be able to keep pace with rival producers. It will find itself losing money and will eventually have to go out of business. Under purely competitive conditions, in short, the business concern is a puppet maneuvered by the general forces of supply and demand. Management discretion and judgment do not exist.

In practice, however, we know that management does do some managing. There is scope for initiative and judgment. The main reason is that actual business concerns operate under conditions of imperfect competition. They are sheltered in greater or lesser degree from the full sweep of market forces.

The price of labor, for example, is not completely determined by market forces; it can be altered within limits by management decision or union-management negotiation. Prices of purchased material and equipment are frequently open to bargaining. The types, specifications, and prices of the products which the company sells can usually be adjusted within limits. Production methods can be altered somewhat. The upshot is that competing companies in the same industry may show quite different levels of cost and profit. Every industry has its high-cost and low-cost producers. This is due partly to factors other than management; but managerial skill and ingenuity do make a difference.

The extent of management's freedom, however, should not be exaggerated. First, management is bound by the simple accounting principle that you cannot make something out of nothing. A wage increase, to take the most relevant example, has to come from somewhere. Either product prices must be raised, or the volume of sales must be expanded, or money must be saved on material costs, selling expenses, or some other non-labor item. If none of these things is done, profits will be reduced by the amount of the wage increase. Accounting logic allows no other possibilities.

Second, management is put under pressure by certain long-run tendencies which characterize our type of economy. The long-run tendency of wages is upward, for reasons which we shall discuss later in this book. Any company must count, year after year, on finding more money to pay for the labor it uses. At the same time, however, the company is subject to downward pressure on the prices it can charge, because of the existence of rival producers and products, and because of continuing technical progress which makes possible better products at lower costs. Management is caught in a scissors between a steady expansion of its costs and at least a potential shrinkage of its revenues.

The only escape from this dilemma lies in managerial efficiency and inventiveness. In order to survive in a competitive world, management must continually search for new or improved products, better methods of merchandising, improved machinery and production techniques, and more efficient administrative organization within the company. These things can be neglected for a year or two, but any company which neglects them for ten or twenty years is headed for economic extinction.

These basic characteristics of business management help to account for certain attitudes which influence the process of collective bargaining. Top management officials feel that the essence of their job lies in adjusting the conflicting pressures impinging on the company from competitors, customers, stockholders, wage earners, and others. The conflicting character of these pressures means that management cannot afford to respond fully to any one of them. It may, for example, have to resist certain union demands in order to ensure reasonable prices to consumers or reasonable returns to stockholders. Further, management people are inclined to feel that they, along with the scientists and engineers, are responsible for most of the improvement in products and production methods which constitutes economic progress and has made possible present living standards. Union demands are sometimes resented as an effort by a group which has contributed little to higher productivity to "cash in" on the fruit of management's labors.

The significance of profit

Our economy is sometimes described as a "profit system," or as being guided by "the profit motive." Economists often assume that each business concern tries to make as large a profit as possible. How much is there to this, and what is its significance for collective bargaining?

Much of our economic theory still relates to a one-man business, in which the owner directs all operations of the business and personally receives any profit which remains after costs have been met. This picture of business operations has some relevance for agriculture, small-scale retailing, and some of the service industries. In most types of industry, however, it has long since ceased to be the dominant pattern. The large business enterprises which form the core of the American economy are managed by salaried executives who typically receive little direct share in company profits. One must distinguish, therefore, between the personal motives of individual executives and the institutional objectives of the business organization as such. We are concerned here primarily with the latter subject.

Since the first objective of a business organization is survival, the first rule is that losses must be avoided. Operating losses, with the dependence on banks and other creditors which follow from them, sap the independence and maneuverability of the firm. If they continue for very long, they result in bankruptcy and economic death. Failure does not necessarily mean physical disappearance of the company's plant and facilities. It is more likely to mean a change in ownership or at least a shake-up in the top management of the business. Even this, however, is a disaster from the standpoint of the previous owners or managers. For this reason management officials are ever conscious of the danger of financial loss, and try constantly to build defenses against the uncertain economic future. The large number of business failures even in good years suggests that these are not just idle fears.

Survival is a minimum. The typical corporate management aspires to something better than that. The goal is not "maximum profit" in the economist's sense—a will-of-the-wisp so changeable and so hard to calculate that no business man could reasonably hope to keep up with it. The objective is rather to achieve a "reasonable," or "normal," or "safe," level of profits. Why is this considered necessary? First, profit provides a margin of security for the company. The higher the company's profit margin, the farther it can fall if business turns bad before encountering actual losses. Second, profit is important as a return to present and prospective investors in the company. Stockholders who find their dividends falling off seriously are likely to become discontented with the management and may try to do something about it. More important, a low rate of profit may make it difficult or impossible for the company to raise funds for expansion by floating new securities. Third, profits are themselves a source of funds for expansion of plant and purchase of new equipment. In many types of industry, "plowed-back" profits are now the main source of capital for expansion. A low rate of profits may mean that the company will have insufficient funds to finance projects which would help to increase profits. Fourth, profits are an index of management success. A management which is not able to turn in as good a profit rate as other companies in its industry, or which finds its profit rate declining from year to year, is apt to feel this as a criticism of its own performance. Even though the profit rate may have no direct bearing on executive salaries, any manager likes to feel that he is "up to par" with others in his profession.

There has been little study of what management people regard as a "satisfactory" or "reasonable" level of business profits. The figure doubtless varies with the past profit level of the industry, the special circumstances of the particular company, the general state of business, and other factors. If one could take a general canvass of business opinion, one would probably find that a net return of 5 to 10 per cent on capital investment is regarded as reasonable in most cases. Actual realized profits, averaged over industry as a whole, tend to fluctuate within this range except for very prosperous or very depressed years. The profit rates of individual companies vary greatly, of course, and many thousands of companies show a net loss even in years of good business.

Some of the difficulties of collective bargaining arise from the difference in the way profits are regarded by management and by union officials. In the eyes of management, profit is not merely a legitimate form of income but an essential element in the operation of a private enterprise system. The expectation or hope of profit is a major incentive to managerial efficiency, and serves to call forth capital investment in new enterprises. Realized profits are a major source of funds for expansion of existing businesses. A positive rate of profit is thus an essential condition for economic growth and development.

Most union leaders would not quarrel with this in principle. Their enthusiasm over profits is more restrained than that of management people, however, and their idea of a "reasonable" rate of profit is apt to be more modest. They sometimes talk as though the net income of a company were a simple surplus performing no function in the economy, a pool into which the union can dip at will without any economic consequence. Management people object strongly to this as a simplified and incorrect view of the situation.

There is also a general feeling among management people that profits are none of the union's business anyway. Management believes that the company should pay "fair wages," which usually means fair in comparison with what other employers are paying for similar work. If management can pay "fair wages" and still make large profits, this is purely management's business. Union officers and members, on the other hand, feel that high profits should be shared with workers in the enterprise through better wages. The workers have helped to produce these profits, it is argued, and hence should be entitled to a share in them. When a company is taking losses, however, the two parties usually switch sides in the argument. The union is apt to argue that the company should still pay fair wages and that its losses are of no concern to the union, while the company may now argue that losses should be taken into account.

A further source of difficulty is that the relevant profit figure in collective bargaining is the estimated profit for the year ahead. Past profits are bygones. The union and management are bargaining over the wage level which the company can afford to pay *next year*, not *last year*. This involves forecasts of future sales volume, product prices, material costs, and numerous other things. Sales volume, which depends so largely on general business conditions, is especially hard to forecast in many industries, and a small change in volume may make a large difference in the firm's profit position. Faced with these uncertainties, management typically tries to "play it safe," to leave some margin for a possible downturn in business, to make a conservative estimate of probable profits. Union leaders, on the other hand, have a strong interest in taking a rosy view of the future, estimating profits at a high level, and trying to get wages set accordingly. The union, in short, is constantly trying to get management to stick its neck out farther than management likes to do.

This is a serious complication in the path of collective bargaining. If sales and profits for the next year could be known with certainty, if management could be sure just how much it was giving away and how much it would have left after paying a specified rate of wages, negotiations would be much simpler than they actually are.

Management as transmitter of economic forces

It has been neecssary to dwell on the situation and problems of management at some length in order to correct a widespread misunderstanding of the nature of collective bargaining. The view held by many workers and members of the general public may be put in a simple and extreme form as follows: Collective bargaining is a struggle solely between management officials and the union. The union serves certain demands on management. It is within the power of management to grant these demands or to put up varying degrees of resistance to them. There is some tendency to think, on the basis of sympathy with the underdog, that demands for higher wages and other benefits are usually justified and that management resistance to these demands is an indication of stubbornness, conservatism, or greed. If only management would be liberal, broad-minded, and simply say "Yes!" This is an extreme picture, but probably not too far from the view of labor disputes which is held by many people.

The reality is much more complicated and difficult. There are doubtless cases in which wage increases or other concessions to the union can simply be taken out of company profits. On this basis, however, profits throughout American industry would long since have shrunk to zero. The margin of profit is too narrow for management simply to give away money year after year. The typical situation is one in which changes in labor costs are reflected in product prices. The money which management gives the union is the customers' money, not the company's money. Management resistance to union demands is motivated mainly by doubt that customers will pay high enough prices, or will buy enough goods at these prices, to keep the company in profitable operation. The union is not really up against management. It is up against the limitation of consumer demand in the product market, as estimated by and transmitted through management.

Management is not an all-powerful agency which can deliver anything the union may ask at a particular time. It is a transmission mechanism through which pressure from customers for lower prices is passed back to wage earners in the form of upper limits on feasible wages; and pressure from wage earners for higher wages is passed forward to customers in the form of lower limits on feasible prices. This interaction of the labor market with the product market is a two-way affair, with management in the middle trying to maintain a workable equilibrium.

Management resistance to union demands can be simply ill-informed or short-sighted. On the other hand, a proper degree of management resistance based on economic considerations may be essential for survival of the industry and equitable treatment of consumers. A management which says "yes" too easily may eventually find itself facing liquidation and its workers facing unemployment, while a management which "drags its feet" at the right times may be serving the general interest. How far the union demands in a particular situation are justified and should be granted can be learned only by careful investigation of all the circumstances.

MANAGEMENT AND THE UNIONS: SOME SOURCES OF TENSION

The general orientation of management toward maximum efficiency and minimum costs has already been explained. In the modern corporation, pursuit of efficiency requires coordination of the efforts of hundreds or thousands of individuals.

The business manager is not just an expert in production techniques. He is the leader of an organization, the captain of a team. Successful performance of his functions requires that he have wide latitude in making decisions, and that he have "cooperation" or "teamwork" from those under him. To most management people, teamwork seems to mean mainly fealty—a willing acceptance of managerial decisions and an earnest effort to execute them. It leaves room for tactful and "constructive" criticism of particular decisions, but no room for any challenge to management's right to make these decisions. The ideal situation is one in which the manager functions as a benevolent monarch. No one questions his authority, but his exercise of authority is so just and reasonable that his subordinates esteem rather than fear him. The feeling that one has been fair even when one didn't have to be is probably one of the greatest satisfactions obtainable from a management position.

Bakke has summarized management's conception of its role in the following terms.[1] First, business managers are *inventors and initiators*. "They start things, figure out new ways, take risks, take the initiative." Second, they are *leaders*. "They are decision makers, men of perspective, foresight, and balance in a troubled and confused world, the head of the business, the captains of industry, men of standing who are looked to for guidance." Third they are *organizers*. "They organize, coordinate, gear together the factors of production. They reconcile the conflicting interests of workers, stockholders, suppliers, and customers." Fourth, they are *trustees* or *stewards*—for workers and customers as well as stockholders. They are builders, creators of national wealth, public benefactors.

All this leads to a characteristic management view of satisfactory industrial relations, which has been summarized by Bakke in four major principles:

Industrial relations are primarily and basically a matter of relations between management and employees, its own employees.
The first objective of industrial relations, like that of every function of management, is the economic welfare of the particular company.
Industrial relations arrangements must leave unimpaired management's prerogatives and freedom essential to the meeting of management's responsibilities.
All parties to industrial relations should be businesslike and responsible.[2]

Trade unionism challenges these cardinal points in management's philosophy. It interposes between employer and employee the trade

---

[1] E. Wight Bakke and Clark Kerr, eds., *Unions, Management and the Public* (New York: Harcourt Brace & World, Inc., 1948), pp. 242-243.

[2] E. Wight Bakke, *Mutual Survival* (New York: Harper & Row, Publishers, 1946), pp. 2-3.

union, an organization which many managers believe is more interested in its own growth and power than in the economic welfare of either workers or the company. It refuses to accept survival and profitability of the company as the sole aim of business management. It interferes with management's effort to achieve lowest money cost of production, and with the freedom of maneuver which most managers consider essential to successful performance of their functions. At point after point the union says, "You can't do that," or, "You must consult us before doing anything." Many management people see in this a deliberate policy of union encroachment on management functions. They ask themselves where the process will end, and whether they may not be forced eventually to abdicate control of the plant to the union.

Management opposition to unionism is based partly on self-interest. Being human, managers dislike a reduction in their authority just because it is a reduction. Unionism also makes the manager's job harder by increasing the number of people whose agreement must be secured for a given decision, and by presenting the risk that agreement may not always be secured. If a lower executive of the company refuses to comply with a decision of top management, he can be removed from office; but management cannot fire the union or its officials. Unionism increases the number of conflicting pressures which converge on management. Between the insistent demands of organized workers for more money, customers for lower prices, and the Board of Directors for larger profits, the manager may be ground to pieces. In all these ways, unionism increases the amount of frustration, personal insecurity, and nervous wear and tear to which management is subjected.

It is too narrow a view, however, to regard management opposition to unionism as entirely self-interested. Most managers believe that unionism, by limiting managerial initiative and discretion, strikes directly at the roots of economic progress and rising national income. Unionism thus tends over the long run to reduce rather than raise the real income of the working class. This conviction is held just as firmly and sincerely as the conviction of union leaders that they are leading a crusade for social progress.

Another element in the differing outlook of managers and unionists is the difference in their personal background and experience. Two-thirds of the top management officials in American corporations come from business and professional families. Three-quarters of them have been to college. Only a small percentage have engaged in manual labor at any stage of their careers.[3] The day-to-day problems of the plant worker are something they have read about in business school casebooks, but have not experienced directly. Contrast this with the background of the union official, almost invariably a former worker, short on formal training but long on plant experience. It is not surprising that the two groups view the world of industry differently and have different conceptions of "proper" personnel management.

The general outlook of management toward unionism, then, is critical and even hostile. Concrete strategies, however, differ greatly from one situation to the next. They range all the way from forcible opposition and a determination to get rid of the union at one extreme, through various shades of reluctant acceptance, to positive cooperation with the union at the other pole. The commonest situation is one which might be termed "defensive endurance," a feeling that "if this is what our workers want, I guess we'll have to go along with it. But we don't understand why they want unionism. There's nothing in it for them. Perhaps they'll eventually see the light and the whole thing will go away."

Underlying this outlook are two assumptions which may be termed the "harmony of interests" assumption and the "management can do it better" assumption. The first asserts that there is no real divergence of interest between employer and employees. Prosperity for the worker depends on prosperity for the company. Management and workers have an equal interest in harmonious coordination of the enterprise and maximum productive efficiency. We shall have occasion in later chapters to examine both the element of truth in such statements and the qualifications which must be attached to them. Regardless of the truth of the matter, however, this attitude is sincerely held by large numbers of management people. It leads them to a conclusion that unions are stirring up conflict where no real conflict exists, and that they are useless or even harmful.

The second assumption flows logically from the first. It asserts that all legitimate interests of the employee can be protected adequately by management itself. The union can do nothing which

---

[3] Based on a sample survey of 8,300 top management people in 1952. See W. Lloyd Warner and James C. Abbeglen, *Occupational Mobility in American Business and Industry* (Minneapolis: University of Minnesota Press, 1955); and Mabel Newcomer, *The Big Business Executive* (New York: Columbia University Press, 1955).

management, with its greater technical skills and more reliable information, could not do even better. If the workers accept unionism, then, this must be due to some failure of management to organize itself effectively and to "put across" its story to employees. Unionism, in short, results from managerial failure and nothing else.

Managements in this frame of mind accept unionism as a punishment for their sins and because it is legally obligatory. They continue, however, to regard it as an alien growth against which management must protect itself at every turn. They try to build dikes against the advance of union influence, to restrict the area of collective bargaining, to resist union intrusion on "mangerial prerogatives."

One management technique has become known as "boulwarism," after a former vice-president of the General Electric Company. The general practice in collective bargaining is for the union and the company to take extreme positions at the outset, each concealing from the other the terms on which it would actually be willing to settle. After days or weeks of negotiation, the true terms begin to emerge and eventually a compromise solution is reached. Mr. Boulware's technique, on the contrary, was to announce the company's final position at the outset, and to refuse to budge form this position in the subsequent negotiations. Not only was this position announced to the union, but a barrage of publicity was launched at employees and the general public, designed to convince them that the company's position was reasonable, that there would be no concessions, and that the only alternative to acceptance was a strike.

The unions have attacked this technique as an effort to undermine the union and a denial of true collective bargaining. Mr. Boulware would probably have replied that it is a legitimate exercise of management initiative. It does seem to reflect a view that management is capable unilaterally of setting fair terms of employment, and that there is no constructive role for union pressure.

These attitudes, however, are not immutable over the course of time. After twenty or thirty years of collective bargaining (in some cases, only after the rise of a new generation of top executives!), a company may come round to a different view of unionism. It finds that the union, while it limits management at many points, can also be used to further the broad objective of profitable operation of the enterprise. Information about the economic situation and problems of the company, for example, may be accepted more readily by workers if funneled through the union organization than if disseminated directly by management. Union leaders who know the company's problems and have confidence in management may be able to "sell" the membership on new company policies and to elicit worker co-operation in production which could not be obtained in any other way. The grievance procedure to be described in the next chapter provides a sensitive instrument which top management can use to detect disturbances in lower levels of the organization. There are numerous ways in which a positive acceptance of the union, an effort to integrate it into the administrative structure of the enterprise instead of treating it as a thing apart, can contribute to efficient management.

Companies which take this point of view are still a decided minority. There are more of them today than there were a generation ago, however, and the number will probably continue to increase gradually in the future.

ORGANIZATION FOR INDUSTRIAL RELATIONS

Two kinds of management official are involved in handling industrial relations: "line" officials who are directly responsible for production, and "staff" officials who function mainly in an advisory capacity.

In a manufacturing company, for example, line authority runs from the company president through a vice-president in charge of production to the superintendent of a particular plant. Under the superintendent are division heads, department heads, and so on down to the foreman. If the foreman has many workers to supervise, he may be aided by one or more assistant foremen or group leaders. The number of layers of supervision in the plant depends mainly on its size. The management of forty or fifty thousand people in a single plant, as in some of the giant automobile factories, require a complicated hierarchy of production officials. This makes it difficult to get effective upward and downward communication, and to ensure uniformity of policy throughout the organization; and this gives rise to complicated problems in union-management relations.

The most important staff group involved is the industrial relations department. This group is charged with developing and recommending policies on such matters as employee recruitment and selection;

training; employee rating and promotion; transfer, downgrading, and layoff; discipline and discharge; wage policies and wage administration; hours of work and shifts; services for employees; employee health and safety; and employee participation in production problems. There may also be a separate industrial engineering department responsible for analysis of job methods, time study, determination of output standards, and application of wage incentive systems.

People in the production line of command are responsible for issuing orders about what is to be done, how it is to be done, and who is to do it. They authorize changes in production schedules, methods, and personnel. They initiate layoffs, new hirings, discharges, promotions, and transfers of workers. Members of the industrial relations staff recommend over-all company policies on these matters, check on how they are working in practice, and suggest changes as needed. But no orders can be issued until the production manager or some other line official has been sold on the policy in question. Indeed, people all the way down the chain of command must be sold on a policy to make it fully effective. Not least important is the foreman, who gives direct orders to the work force. The modern foreman has been shorn of much of the authority which he once possessed, but he still has considerable power to sabotage policies which he does not understand and accept.

In theory, then, line officials are the doers, while staff officials look over their shoulders as advisers. The actual relation, however, is more complex and variable; and it is defined through day-to-day decisions in the plant rather than by the lines which appear on the organization chart. Suppose a foreman discharges a worker. The labor relations officer assigned to the department considers the discharge unwise and so reports to his superiors. There follow further discussions, perhaps between the industrial relations director and the plant superintendent. Eventually the decision is confirmed or reversed. If line officials find that too many of their decisions are reversed at higher levels under pressure from the industrial relations staff, they will become more hesitant about making decisions; and the *de facto* authority of the industrial relations department will have increased. Personalities are also important. If the industrial relations director is capable, assertive, and able to win the support of top management on disputed issues, the authority of those working under him is increased.

Union impact on management organization

In pre-union days, most managements did not attach major importance to the industrial relations function. The director of industrial relations, in those days commonly called personnel director, was usually not an outstanding man and did not rank high in the management hierarchy. In large measure the line officials made personnel policy through their day-to-day decisions, which the personnel department had little power to influence. Many managements, either deliberately or through inadvertence, left wide latitude in decision making to lower levels of supervision. Thus actions on a particular subject might vary widely from one department to another; and top management might know little about what was actually happening at the grass roots.

The coming of a union changes the situation drastically. Personnel actions are no longer solely a matter of management discretion. They are governed by provisions of the union contract, and the union is there to police observance of the contract. It has its own information network throughout the plant, can detect discrepancies in management's actions, and is then likely to demand that the most favorable practice in any department be extended to all other departments—a tactic commonly known as "whipsawing." Moreover, unsettled grievances between the union and management are normally referred to an outside arbitrator, under procedures to be described in the next chapter. So management must try to ensure that its decisions are consistent and will stand up under outside review.

Unionism, in short, compels *management by policy* rather than by off-the-cuff decisions. A newly-unionized company usually reacts in three ways. First, it has to strengthen its industrial relations department, both because there is more work to be done and because top-flight people are needed to deal with the professional union leaders. Second, it may decide that personnel decisions should be made at higher levels of management, in order to ensure uniform interpretation of company policies and union contract provisions. Third, this normally means that industrial relations officials will have greater voice in decisions and line officials will have less. Some managements, indeed, have panicked to the point of virtually abolishing line authority over personnel actions and work standards, and turning these matters over to the industrial relations department for handling.

While greater centralization of decision making and greater staff authority are natural first reactions, they have their own disadvantages. Foremen know what is happening on the plant floor and are in closest touch with the facts on which correct personnel decisions should be based. They are also the people in charge of production. To hold them responsible for production results while depriving them of disciplinary authority over the work force is scarcely feasible over the long run. So in recent years many companies have been moving back toward decentralization, toward pushing decisions down to the plant floor, and toward reconstituting the authority of line supervisors.[4]

Both line supervisors and industrial relations people are involved in applying personnel policies to concrete situations and in handling grievances brought by the union. The problem is to work out the most effective cooperation between them. This must take account of characteristic differences of outlook arising from their differing functions in the organization. Line officials are naturally more production-oriented, while industrial relations people are more labor-relations-oriented. This does not necessarily mean that the former are "tougher" in holding the line on plant discipline and work standards. Foremen will often make special deals with a worker to secure his cooperation in getting out a rush production job, and it may be the staff people who have to insist on strict adherence to company policy. It is probably fair to say that the industrial relations people typically take a longer-range view, and are more concerned with how decisions made today will affect company relations with workers and the union next month or next year.

But foremen and supervisors can also be trained to take a long-range view and to be concerned with the policy implications of specific decisions. This is essentially an educational task, a task of inculcating understanding and acceptance of the company's over-all personnel policies. A foreman who has been trained in this way can and should be given the right to make initial decisions on all personnel matters arising in his department, which includes the right to make mistakes. It is important also that correct decisions based on established policy should be ratified and defended at higher levels

---

[4] See on this point Sumner H. Slichter, James J. Healy, and E. Robert Livernash, *The Impact of Collective Bargaining on Management* (Washington: Brookings Institution, 1960), chap. 29.

of management. A foreman who finds his decisions constantly overturned because of union pressure or second-guessing by staff officials will soon cease to make any decisions, and will pass all problems up the line. This is a common reason for "clogging up" of the grievance procedure and accumulation of problems in the front office.

Discussion questions

1. What are the central characteristics of a business organization?

2. "The profit motive no longer operates in the simple manner assumed by economic theory. The managers of a large corporation are interested in profit, to be sure, but their interest is quite different from that of the small owner-operator." Discuss.

3. What features of management's job produce a natural opposition to trade unionism?

4. "Whether the plant is already unionized, or whether it is merely liable to unionization in the future, management is forced to engage in a long-drawn-out competition with unionism for the attention and loyalty of its employees. In such a competition, the union has certain natural advantages which usually bring it out ahead over the long run." Discuss.

5. What does a management stand to gain, and to lose, by accepting the union as a permanent feature of its operations and trying to establish a cooperative relationship with it?

6. How many different groups of management people come into contact with the union? How may this complicate the problem of establishing satisfactory union-management relations?

7. "A wise industrial relations director does not try to exercise authority—only influence." Discuss.

8. How is a company's problem of managing its industrial relations altered by the appearance of a trade union?

9. A foreman considers a worker in his department guilty of behavior warranting discharge. The union asserts that the discharge is unjustified. Analyze the proper functions of the foreman, an industrial relations officer attached to the department, the plant superintendent, and the plant director of industrial relations in handling this case.

Selected reading

Baker, Helen, *Management Procedure in the Determination of Industrial Relations Policies.* Princeton: Princeton University Industrial Relations Section, 1948.

Bakke, E. Wight, *Mutual Survival.* New York: Harper & Row, Publishers, 1946.

Gardner, Burleigh B., and David G. Moore, *Human Relations in Industry*, rev. ed. Chicago: Richard D. Irwin, Inc., 1950.

Hill, Lee H., and Charles R. Hook, Jr., *Management at the Bargaining Table*. New York: McGraw-Hill Book Company, Inc., 1945.

Pigors, Paul, and Charles A. Myers, *Personnel Administration*, rev. ed. New York: McGraw-Hill Book Company, Inc., 1961.

————, *Readings in Personnel Administration*. New York: McGraw-Hill Book Company, Inc., 1956.

Slichter, S. H., J. J. Healy, and E. R. Livernash, *The Impact of Collective Bargaining on Management*. Washington: Brookings Institution, 1960.

Whyte, William F., *Pattern for Industrial Peace*. New York: Harper & Row, Publishers, 1951.

Wilcock, Richard C., "Industrial Management's Policies Toward Unionism," pp. 275-315 in Derber and Young, eds., *Labor and the New Deal*. Madison: University of Wisconsin Press, 1957.

7

Bargaining Procedures And Tactics

Trade unions try to advance the interests of their members mainly by negotiating agreements, usually termed "union contracts" or "collective agreements," with employers. The processes by which these agreements are negotiated, administered, and enforced are included in the term "collective bargaining." The word "collective" indicates that the agreement is negotiated on behalf of a *group* of workers. The workers present a united front to their employer, and the terms of the bargain apply uniformly to all members of the group. Different employers may also band themselves together for the purpose of negotiating an agreement with a union. Such an agreement is frequently said to be "collective on both sides."

From the union's standpoint, the object of collective bargaining is to prevent unilateral action by the employer. This is accomplished by requiring him to sign a contract fixing conditions of employment for a specified period and establishing a procedure for handling disputed issues arising during the period. Collective bargaining is thus an employer-regulating device, a method of guaranteeing certain rights and immunities to the workers by limiting the employer's freedom of action. The employer must now apply uniform procedures to all workers in the group; these procedures can be changed only at fixed intervals after negotiation with union officials; and any charge that the agreed procedures have been violated can be taken up through a series of appeal courts (the "grievance procedure"). There is thus created what Slichter has termed a "system of industrial jurisprudence," a body of common law rights and obligations binding on workers, union officials, and management officials alike.

Collective bargaining includes two different kinds of union-management negotiation. General negotiations are entered into at regular intervals, usually once a year, to revise the basic agreement between the parties and extend it for a further period. At this time any term of the contract—wage schedules, work assignments, rules concerning layoff and promotion, union security provisions, and all the rest—may be reopened for discussion. These negotiations are usually carried on by top union and management officials. After the agreement has been signed, there are frequent discussions between lower union and management officials throughout the plant for the purpose of clarifying particular provisions and applying them to concrete situations. The method of resolving these day-to-day disputes, usually termed the "grievance procedure," is specified in the contract itself. While the annual negotiations are more dramatic, the day-to-day negotiations may be equally important. Through them the contract is enforced, or, in the case of a new or weak union, not enforced. Through them the general provisions of the contract are given specific meaning and application.

These two aspects of collective bargaining—contract negotiations and the grievance procedure—will be discussed in turn. The present discussion is concerned with bargaining *procedures* rather than the substantive issues over which bargaining occurs. The main issues which are bargained about will be discussed in the next chapters.

THE AREA OF THE COLLECTIVE AGREEMENT

The Labor Management Relations Act requires an employer to bargain with representatives of a majority of his employees "in an appropriate bargaining unit." But what unit is "appropriate"? At one extreme, a single employer may bargain with representatives of a single skilled craft. At the opposite extreme, an employer's association may bargain with an industrial union over terms for all employees in the industry throughout the country.

The scope of bargaining units reflects mainly the interests and attitudes of the unions and managements concerned. Since 1935, however, the National Labor Relations Board has played an important part in defining the scope of new bargaining units. The normal method of securing union recognition since 1935 is to file a request with the NLRB for certification as bargaining representative. If the union's claim to represent a majority of the workers is challenged by the employer, or if more than one union is seeking to represent the same workers, the Board will conduct an election to determine the employees' wishes. The outcome is either a majority for a particular union which is then certified as bargaining representative, or a majority for "no union," in which event the case is closed. Thousands of such elections are held every year and most local unions now in existence won initial recognition in this way.

In order to conduct an election the NLRB must first decide on the "appropriate bargaining unit," i.e., the scope of the election district. Depending on his estimate of where the union has penetrated most effectively, the employer may wish to include certain departments or plants and exclude others. The union's preference may be different. If two or more unions are involved, they may differ on the proper scope of the unit. The NLRB officials, after hearing the parties and considering the pattern of bargaining elsewhere in the industry, must decide what is appropriate.

A particularly controversial issue has been that of craft versus industrial units. After 1935 the NLRB often encountered situations in which a CIO industrial union urged a single unit covering all employees while one or more AFL craft unions urged that groups of skilled workers be carved out as separate units. For some years the Board showed a marked preference for industrial units—sufficiently so to permit the major companies in steel, automobile, electrical manufacturing, and other mass production industries to be oragnized on this basis. Yielding to AFL criticism and pressure, however, the Board by the early 'forties was permitting craft groups to vote separately whenever they showed any marked inclination to do so. The Taft-Hartley Act increased the possibility of "craft severance" by providing that the NLRB may not refuse a craft group's claim to separate representation simply because of some previous Board decision concerning the bargaining unit. The general policy at present is that where there are indications that a skilled group may prefer separate representation, the Board will allow them to vote separately from the rest. If a craft union wins out, it will be certified as bargaining representative. This policy has not been applied, however, to steel, aluminum, and a few other mass-production industries where the Board has held that production processes are so highly integrated as to make craft severance impracticable.

Another controversial issue has been whether bargaining should be conducted separately by each employer or whether groups of employers should bargain together. So it is interesting to examine current practice in this respect.

There are estimated to be about 150,000 union contracts in the United States. The great majority of these cover only one company and a small number of workers. In 1961, however, there were 1,733 contracts covering 1,000 or more workers each; and these contracts together covered 8.3 million workers, or about half of all workers under union contract.[1] About half of these major agreements include more than one employer. Multiemployer bargaining is traditional in many industries, including railroading, trucking, mining, construction, maritime work, longshoring, hotels and restaurants, retail trade, and the service industries. In manufacturing it is the decided exception; but it is predominant in men's and women's clothing, printing, baking, canning and preserving, brewing, glassware, pottery, lumber, furniture, and leather goods. Multiemployer bargaining is commoner in local-market industries than in industries where companies compete in national markets; and it is commoner for small employers than for large employers who are better able to stand on their own feet.

The main pressure for multiemployer agreements stems from selling competition among employers in product markets. If different companies organized by the same union are in selling competition with one another, the bargains between the union and various companies cannot be kept separate. The union cannot raise the labor costs of some plants so much above the general level that these plants are forced out of competition. Employers paying the highest wage rates in the industry are likely to demand that the union bring low-wage plants up to their level. Union members also compare wage rates in different plants. Members of one local who find their rates below those of certain other locals will be quick to protest and to demand that they be brought up to levels prevailing elsewhere. Apart from this political pressure, it seems natural to union officials that wages and conditions should be standardized for competing plants. The concept of "the standard rate," of "equal pay for equal work," is deeply engrained in union thinking. For all these reasons, unions seek some measure of uniformity, though not necessarily complete uniformity, among employers in the same competitive area.

---

[1] U. S. Bureau of Labor Statistics, *Monthly Labor Review* (October 1962).

The area of the collective agreement is thus strongly influenced by the area over which employers compete in the sale of their products. If competition is limited to the immediate locality, city-wide agreements are likely to develop. This is the typical situation in building construction, hotel and restaurant work, newspaper and job printing, milk and bread delivery, local trucking and warehousing, retail trade, laundry and dry cleaning, and other local industries.

The individual employer in these industries is typically small and is in a weak position to negotiate separately with the union. So after a little experience, employers often decide to pool their strength in a bargaining association. The result is a single agreement, reached by bargaining between representatives of the employer association and representatives of the union.

After the master agreement has been concluded, its administration and enforcement are usually left to the union and individual employers. In areas which have gone farthest in the direction of master agreements, however, such as San Francisco, the employers' association sometimes takes a continuing interest in the administration of the agreement. Several of the San Francisco associations maintain expert staffs to assist their members in processing grievances and handling other problems which arise during the life of the contract. A few have even gone so far as to forbid members to settle grievances without association approval. The purpose of this policy is to prevent the union from "whipsawing" the employers, i.e., securing more favorable treatment on a certain point in some plants than in others, and then using this as an argument to bring all plants up to the most favorable settlement achieved anywhere.[2]

A master agreement with the union has several advantages from the employers' standpoint. It enables employers to meet the union on more equal terms. It also places employers on an equal competitive footing as regards wage rates and other items in labor cost; the "chiseler" can no longer undercut the employer who pays a "decent" wage. Moreover, the agreement with the union can often be used to police price-fixing and other monopolistic practices within the industry. Union and employers, instead of fighting each other, can unite with mutual benefit to levy tribute from consumers.

This situation has been particularly common in building construction. The building contractors' association generally agrees to employ

[2] Clark Kerr and L. H. Fisher, "Multiple-Employer Bargaining: The San Francisco Experience," in R. A. Lester and Joseph Shister, eds., *Insights into Labor Issues* (New York: The Macmillan Company, 1948).

only union men, thereby strengthening the building trades unions. The unions on their side agree to work only for members of the association. This agreement enables the established contractors to "freeze out" newcomers to the industry by refusing them membership in the association and thus shutting off their labor supply. The unions have also frequently agreed not to work for any contractor found guilty of departing from the established methods of figuring bids in the industry, i.e., of cutting prices. The two main channels of competition—free price-setting and free entrance of new firms to the industry—are thus effectively blocked.

Industries such as laundering and dry cleaning have frequently achieved the same result by allying themselves with the deliverymen, who usually belong to a local of the Teamsters' Union. Firms which cut prices or engage in other "unethical" practices forbidden by the association are brought into line by strikes or threatened strikes. It has not been unknown for "accidents" to happen to the property of uncooperative employers; clothes get lost or misdelivered, acid gets spilled in the wrong places, or delivery trucks break down mysteriously.[3] In agreements between the Barbers' Union and the master barbers' association of a city, the price which must be charged for haircuts, shaves, and other services is frequently included in the agreement, so that any price-cutter is guilty of a violation of contract and is struck automatically.

It should not be inferred that unions are mainly responsible for local price-fixing arrangements. In many cases, price agreements existed long before the union made its appearance. The union does, however, strengthen such agreements by providing an additional method of disciplining price-cutters. It also siphons off part of the profits derived from price-fixing for the benefit of workers in the industry.

While there is strong pressure in local market industries to standardize terms of employment *within* each locality, there is no similar pressure for equalization *among* localities. Bricklaying in Pittsburgh does not compete with bricklaying in Minneapolis, and there is no reason why the union scale should be the same. Union scales in

---

[3] See in particular: C. L. Christenson, "Chicago Service Trades," in Twentieth Century Fund, *How Collective Bargaining Works*, chap. 15; and C. L. Christenson, *Collective Bargaining in Chicago* (Chicago: University of Chicago Press, 1933).

building, printing, and similar industries vary a good deal throughout the country, and national union control over local settlements is quite loose.

Quite different is the situation in those industries, including the bulk of manufacturing, in which competition is regional or national in scope. Here the national union must take an interest in securing similar contract terms from competing employers. This does not necessarily lead to multiemployer bargaining. Most frequently the union tries to impose its program unilaterally through separate negotiations with individual employers. A common technique is to single out one leading employer as the initial target in a particular year. After negotiations have been completed and certain concessions extracted, the union insists that all other employers in the industry sign up on the same terms under penalty of a strike.

This technique, often termed "pattern bargaining," may be illustrated by the procedure in the basic steel industry. The contract terms to be presented to employers for the coming year are worked out first by the Executive Board of the United Steelworkers. They are then presented for discussion to a Policy Committee, consisting of some 250 delegates from all parts of the country. After the program has been ratified by the Policy Committee, negotiations for a new contract are begun with the United States Steel Corporation. Since U.S. Steel has long been the wage leader in the industry, it is generally understood that any wage changes negotiated between it and the union will apply to the entire basic steel industry. After a settlement is reached with U.S. Steel, the union proceeds to sign contracts with the other basic steel companies. While these resemble the U.S. Steel contract in most major respects, there are differences in detail, some of which are rather important.

Negotiations with the hundreds of smaller companies engaged in steel fabricating are left mainly to district and local officials of the union. International headquarters, however, distributes to local officials a mimeographed list of the demands which are to be made on all employers. With respect to many contract terms, these instructions specify minimum as well as maximum terms of settlement. They tell local officials not only what they should demand to begin with, but also the minimum which they must get in order to have the agreement approved by the international office. The union's objective here is to prevent "whipsawing" by employers. If the union accepts a poor settlement in one plant, word will spread rapidly throughout the industry, and the case may rise to plague the union in another plant a thousand miles away.

In spite of this effort toward uniformity, the contracts signed with the fabricators show considerably more variation than the contracts with the basic steel companies. The wage settlements made with the smaller companies appear to be consistently lower than those made with U.S. Steel, and to vary a good deal from one company to the next. The union takes care not to push a particular company beyond the maximum which it is able to pay, because it has no wish to cause plant shutdowns and unemployment for its members.[4]

This general approach is common in manufacturing industries. The Pulp, Sulphate, and Paper Mill Workers traditionally open negotiations first with the Great Northern Paper Company. The International Electrical, Radio, and Machine Workers attempt to establish a pattern by dealing first with General Electric or Westinghouse. The United Automobile Workers direct their main pressure at Ford in some years and at General Motors in others. After a settlement has been reached with one of these giants, the union goes on to other automobile manufacturers and to the multitude of smaller auto parts companies. The major unions also watch each other's patterns carefully, and if one makes a good settlement this tends to be taken as a target by others. One reason is that unions such as the Steelworkers, Machinists, Auto Workers, and Electrical Workers are multi-industry unions with overlapping jurisdictions which often bring them into direct rivalry with each other. No one can afford to be left much behind the others in a particular year. Through this complex network of relationships a few key bargains with major corporations have an influence out of proportion to the numbers of workers directly involved.

An interesting question is why employers do not more frequently stand together to resist the union's demands. This has now become common practice in local market industries. Why has it not become the general practice in national industries as well? Why will the other automobile companies, for example, allow the union to single out General Motors for a threatened shutdown to enforce concessions which they must know will then be demanded of everyone? No outsider can say. Traditional intercompany rivalry in product markets,

---

[4] On this point, see George Seltzer, "Pattern Bargaining and the United Steelworkers," *Journal of Political Economy*, LIX (August 1951), pp. 319-331.

fear that any concerted action may fall foul of the antitrust laws, and emotional resistance to "industry-wide bargaining" may all play some part. These attitudes may change over the course of time and one may find more consultation among employers. The large manufacturing unions are obviously not eager to encourage such a development. While they often argue that industry-wide bargaining is a desirable principle, they have found as a practical matter that they can do better by picking off employers one at a time.

Multiemployer bargaining on a regional or national basis exists at present mainly in the industries longest unionized, including railroading, anthracite and bituminous coal, hosiery, men's and women's clothing, pottery, lumbering, canning, glass and glassware, longshoring, merchant shipping, and over-the-road trucking. In most of these industries employers are numerous and relatively small. This makes it difficult for the union to find any firm prominent enough to establish an industry "pattern." On the other side, small employers cannot feel much confidence in their own strength and tend to band together for mutual protection and support. Both employers and the union find a master agreement convenient in enforcing minimum labor standards —"putting a floor under competition"—in highly competitive industries. One can perhaps conclude that employers who feel powerful enough to "go it alone" will hold out for single-company bargaining. Employers who feel weak will federate. In some cases special circumstances favor regional or national bargaining. Thus the extensive federal control of the railroad industry under the Railway Labor Act and the Interstate Commerce Commission Act has been a major force making for centralization of bargaining negotiations.

BARGAINING REPRESENTATIVES AND BARGAINING DEMANDS

Who represents labor and management in collective bargaining negotiations? How are demands formulated on the two sides? What authority do the negotiators have to make concessions and arrive at a settlement?

On the union side, it will be simplest to begin with the situation of a local union negotiating with one or more employers in its area. As the expiration date of the old contract approaches (most contracts at present run for either two or three years), the demands to be served on the employer will probably be discussed at a general membership meeting. A committee will then be appointed to put the demands into better shape and to draft proposed terms for a new contract. In doing this they must weigh and balance numerous considerations: what they know about the financial situation of the company and the business outlook; instructions or advice from national union head-quarters; what has been happening to wages in other companies in the locality, and also in other companies in the same industry; the wishes and expectations of union members; differences of interest among different groups within the membership; and how far the members appear willing to back up their demands by strike action. Union leaders must demand and win enough to keep the members reasonably content; yet they must not set their sights so high that the organization is forced into a strike which members are reluctant to support. Strikes are rarely popular with the rank and file, and a local cannot strike more than once every few years without a decline in morale and effectiveness.

After the drafting committee has done its best, the proposed contract terms are taken back to another membership meeting. There they are discussed at length, perhaps revised, and eventually approved. A negotiating committee is then selected to meet with management. This will normally include the chief officers of the local, but may include other members as well. The national union representative for the area normally sits in on the negotiations and frequently plays a leading role. At some point prior to or during negotiations a strike vote of the membership will usually be taken. This does not necessarily mean that a strike is going to occur. The purpose is to strengthen the union representatives' hand by advance authorization to call a strike if negotiations with the employer break down.

The actual conduct of negotiating sessions will be described in the next section. Meanwhile, we may note that after the union negotiators feel they have got as much as they can from management, they must come back to the membership for approval of the new contract before it becomes valid. In many unions the contract must also be approved by the national office. Participation by a national union representative is designed partly to ensure that the terms will be in conformity with national policy.

Preparation for regional or national negotiations, or for bargaining with a major pattern-setting employer, is considerably more complicated. National union officers normally take a leading role in such negotiations. Proposed union demands are hammered out by the national executive board, and then submitted for discussion to a conference of delegates from the local unions and district organizations. Depending on bargaining practices, this conference may cover the entire industry throughout the country, or all local unions dealing with a particular employer, or some other grouping. After revision and ratification of demands by the conference, the union negotiators begin discussions with management representatives. At the end of the process, the proposed contract terms must usually be reported back to the conference for further discussion and approval. Membership participation in national negotiations is typically indirect and vicarious. In local negotiations, local officers bear the brunt of the discussions with national representatives serving as advisers. In national negotiations, national officers play the leading role, with local representatives serving as critics and advisers.

On the management side, contract negotiations are usually conducted by a small group of top management officials. In a small or medium-sized company, the president may serve as chief management negotiator. In large organizations, this responsibility is more likely to fall on the executive vice-president or some other line official. The chief counsel and the treasurer frequently participate and several top production officials normally sit in on the negotiations. The industrial relations director and members of his staff take part as expert advisers. Where the industrial relations director is a forceful individual with high status in the company, he may even serve as chief company spokesman.

The management representatives, like the union negotiating committee, begin to formulate their position well in advance of the start of negotiations. An effort is made to anticipate the main union demands and to determine a position on them. Management may itself want to take the initiative on certain points. Management initiative in presenting demands, instead of simply responding to union demands, is commoner today than it was ten or twenty years ago. Anything which requires a major change in company policy, such as agreement to a union shop, must normally be ratified in advance by the board of directors or the executive committee. Proposals involving money also require advance ratification. The management representatives go into negotiations with instructions that they may not raise the company's labor costs by more than a certain figure. If they are unable to reach agreement with the union within the specified limits, they must go back to the board for further discussion.[5]

Where there is multiemployer bargaining, representatives of the various companies involved will be called together for a preliminary conference. If there is a formal association, members of the association staff may take a prominent part in working out proposals to the union. Important conflicts of interest may have to be faced and resolved. Some companies, for example, may be in a comfortable profit position and able to afford substantial wage increases. Other companies closer to the margin may feel obliged to fight any increase in costs. These and other differences must be compromised in order to present a united front to the union. After policy has been determined, the actual conduct of negotiations is usually delegated to a small committee of the most experienced and influential company representatives.

Negotiations typically begin with a general assembly of all the union and management representatives involved. In the case of a large regional or national agreement, this may include several hundred people and fill a hotel ballroom. The chief union spokesman goes through the list of union demands and explains the considerations behind them. The leader of the management group presents and justifies the counterproposals of management.

These opening statements usually reveal a wide gap between the official positions of the parties. The union presents a long list of demands which would cost perhaps fifty cents per man-hour and cut heavily into managerial autonomy. Management may insist that no wage increase is possible and take a generally "stand pat" position. It is apparent from the outset that these are "shadow demands," intended to mask rather than reveal the true position of each side.

In a minority of cases, the initial statements of the parties are close to their final positions. This may be true, for example, in the case of a "pattern following" company, where the union demands and is prepared to insist on acceptance of terms already conceded by a

---

[5] In one case that came to the author's attention, the management negotiators were instructed by the board of directors that they could not concede more than five cents an hour. Agreement on this basis appeared impossible, so the vice-president conducting the negotiations came back to the board with an earnest plea that he be allowed to go up to eight cents. After he had made an eloquent statement of his case, the president burst out laughing and said, "Why, that's fine! We were willing to go to ten cents all along!"

leading company. A strong company in a protected competitive situation may also be able to lay down a position and adhere firmly to it, even at the cost of a strike.

In general, however, both sides follow the technique of "the big demand." Why is this? One reason is the process by which demands are formulated. On the union side, every member is entitled to put forward proposals. The list of proposals is bound to be long and some of them are bound to be impracticable. Rather than take responsibility for weeding out the list and convincing the members that certain things are unfeasible, union officials find it politic to shift this unpleasant task to the employer. They put as many of the members' demands as possible into their initial program, knowing full well that many of them will be shot down by management or traded off in the course of negotiations.

A long and ambitious list of demands has other advantages. It conceals one's true minimum demands and "keeps the other fellow guessing," which is an important element in bargaining strategy. It provides ample room for negotiation and maneuver, for trading elimination of some items against concession on others. It serves as protection against a marked change in economic conditions during the course of negotiations. Some negotiations go on for months, during which prosperity may change to recession or vice versa. If one's initial demand turns out to be less than would be feasible several months later, one is bound to be criticized for ineptitude or worse. Finally, some demands are put in with no expectation of immediate gain, but with a view to a genuine push on the matter in subsequent years. The Automobile Workers and Steelworkers unions, began talking about a "guaranteed" annual wage in the mid-'forties, and were met with complete and outraged opposition by employers. In 1955, this demand finally bore fruit in both industries in the form of "supplementary unemployment benefit" programs. Pensions, health and welfare funds, and numerous other union proposals have had a similar history.

Presentation of long and "impossible" lists of initial demands, then, should not be taken as an indication of greed or unreasonableness on either side. It is the normal opening gambit in the annual chess game.

The course of the subsequent negotiations is never the same in any two situations. One can nevertheless distinguish certain typical stages in the collective bargaining process. These stages may overlap somewhat in practice, but can be separated out for analytical precision.

First comes a period of probing, in which each side questions the other's demands at some length. Clause by clause questioning of the other party produces various kinds of information: the detailed content of a particular proposal, the reasons it is considered necessary, the kinds of factual data which have been assembled to support it, sometimes a preliminary indication of the firmness with which the demand is held.

Next the negotiating group is usually scaled down to more manageable size—a few key people on each side who have authority to make concessions and decisions. Discussion can move more rapidly in such a group, and can also be more frank and informal. Each side contines to probe the other's position while trying to protect its own freedom of maneuver. There may be indications of willingness to make concessions on certain items. Some of the less controversial issues may be resolved and set aside, subject to the general rule that no one subject is regarded as settled until all items in dispute have been settled. For the key issues in dispute, each side may eventually indicate one or more "packages"—combinations of terms—which it would consider acceptable. In constructing such packages, monetary items are treated as interchangeable—an addition of fifteen cents an hour to payroll costs may be distributed in a variety of ways—and monetary items may also be traded against non-monetary items. The union official who said, "Every year I sell the union shop for a nickel," was describing a central feature of collective bargaining.

The content of these package proposals is significant in indicating which demands the parties are really serious about. The packages put forward by the two sides, however, are likely still to be some distance apart. The thing which forces further concessions and final compromise is the approach of the deadline date after which a strike will occur. It is no accident that many contract settlements are reached after all-night conferences on the eve of a strike. The imminence of a strike, with the attendant costs and uncertainties for both sides, forces each party to re-examine its position realistically and to ask, "Is it really worth it?" This usually leads to a lowering of union demands and a raising of management offers to the point where they overlap and settlement becomes possible.

Between 98 and 99 per cent of the contract negotiations carried out in the United States each year result in agreement without a strike. The possibility of a strike, however, is a central feature of the bargaining process and the main force making for ultimate agreement.

Where a strike does occur, this usually means either (1) that the true minimum terms of the parties failed to overlap even under the pressure imposed by a strike threat, or (2) that one or both parties miscalculated the true position of the other side. One party, firmly convinced that the other will improve its final offer, may refuse concessions which it would have been willing to make had it accurately estimated the other's intentions. Thus there may occur "a strike which nobody wants."

A strike exerts continuing pressure on the parties to reach agreement. Bargaining negotiations usually continue, though perhaps only intermittently, while the strike is in progress. As the strike lengthens and cost mount on both sides, the greater will become the willingness of one or both parties to make concessions in order to end it. In this sense a strike, instead of being considered an alternative to agreement, should be considered a different route toward agreement.

Why do the terms of the eventual settlement come out as they do? Why do they sometimes lie closer to the initial position of the union, and in other cases closer to management's position? Numerous efforts have been made to answer this in terms of the "bargaining power" of the parties, but the definition of bargaining power usually turns out to be circular. Power is what power does. A union has high bargaining power if it is able to achieve a "good" settlement. One must conclude that, despite a number of interesting contributions, there is still no acceptable theory of bargaining or negotiation.[6]

A different kind of question can be answered with greater confidence: to what extent are the terms of agreement influenced by objective economic circumstances, to what extent by the forcefulness, shrewdness, the tactical skill of individual negotiations? There can be little doubt that objective factors are of dominant importance. They include the comprehensiveness of union organization in the industry; the economic structure of the industry—small or large units, competitive or monopolistic characteristics, geographical dispersion, and the like; elasticity of product demand and rate of secular increase or decrease in demand; significance of labor costs as a proportion of total costs; and whether the year in question is one of general business expansion or contraction. A skillful negotiator can marshal favorable background circumstances to maximum effect; but most union and

---

[6] For a good review of the available literature, see papers by Carl Stevens and Myron L. Joseph in *Proceedings of Thirteenth Annual Meeting of IRRA* (1960), pp. 122-165.

management negotiators are skillful in this sense, otherwise they do not survive. While an occasional coup can be traced to a particular individual, over the long run personalities are much less important than one would judge from newspaper headlines.

The technique of continuous negotiation

A prominent feature of contract negotiations in the United States is their crisis atmosphere. Discussion usually begins only a few weeks before the contract expiration date, and not until a few days before the deadline do the negotiators begin to reveal their basic positions. Hence the familiar sight of weary negotiators working right down to the deadline in day-and-night sessions, and finally signing an agreement the last possible moment. This may not work too badly for wage issues, where the positions of the parties can be stated and compromised in quantitative terms. But it is not a good way of resolving more intricate problems, such as rewriting the company's seniority rules, or compromising management's desire for flexibility in production methods with the union's desire to protect the job security of its members.

There has been a growing tendency, therefore, to refer such problems to special committees, whose mission is to work on them continuously between contract negotiations, and to have agreed proposals ready in advance of the next contract deadline. These are sometimes tripartite bodies, including neutrals as well as union and management representatives. In other cases they include labor and management representatives only. In either event they have leisure to undertake thorough exploration of the issues, to commission special studies and expert reports, to test the acceptability of various possible solutions, and to draft clauses for inclusion in the next contract.

After the long and bitter steel strike of 1959, the parties agreed to set up two special committees. The controversy over management's right to change established working methods was referred to a tripartite study group, the labor and management members of which were to agree on a single neutral member to serve as chairman. It proved impossible to agree on a chairman, and this venture came to nothing. More successful was a "Human Relations Research Committee," which included union and management representatives only and which was assigned to look into matters touching on job security, particularly "seniority, including maximum practicable protection for long-service employees against layoffs and for recalls after layoffs." This committee worked continuously from 1960 to 1962, and both parties give it much of the credit for the fact that the 1962 negotiations were concluded three months before the old contracts expired. The 1962 agreement provided that the committee should be continued and should work on additional problems of job security, such as subcontracting of work by the steel mills to outside contractors.

During the 1959 steel strike the Kaiser Steel Company broke away from the rest of the industry and reached a separate agreement with the union. This provided among other things for a tripartite nine-member committee, charged with designing a plan to protect workers against displacement by technical change, and to ensure equitable sharing of the gains from technical change among workers, stockholders, and the public. The public members of the group were George W. Taylor, John T. Dunlop, and David L. Cole. An agreed program, the content of which is described in Chapter 9, was announced in late 1962 and came into effect in 1963. It has been widely hailed as a pioneer effort to resolve one of the thorniest issues in industrial relations.

In mid-1959 the Armour Company decided to close six of its meatpacking plants, raising the issue of what would happen to the 5,000 production workers involved. The company and the two principal unions in the industry agreed to set up what became known as the Automation Committee, including four management members, four union members, and Clark Kerr as neutral chairman. A distinctive feature of this committee's work was the commissioning of numerous economic studies, mainly by faculty members of the University of Illinois and the University of Chicago. While in the nature of the case unemployment could not be entirely prevented, the committee's recommendations eased the hardships resulting from displacement and probably averted major strikes in the industry.

In West Coast longshoring, the union and the employers association agreed in 1957 to re-examine union work rules, which had seriously reduced efficiency and had embittered union-management relations for a generation. Negotiations continued over a period of three years and were finally concluded in late 1960. The outcome was a complicated trade, which each party considered to its advantage, and which could certainly not have been agreed on in a few weeks of hasty negotiation.

It is not surprising that the technique of continuous negotiation should have been used most frequently to deal with problems arising from technical change. Here basic interests of both parties are deeply involved. Management feels that without freedom to close and open plants, to introduce new machinery, and to make other changes in production methods it cannot control costs and maintain the company's competitive position. The union wants to protect workers' rights in their jobs, which it considers akin to property rights, and to hold displacement or downgrading of workers to a minimum. Compromise of these interests is possible, but workable compromises require inventiveness and the drafting of intricate contract provisions. The substantive problems of technical change, and the lines of compromise which seem gradually to be emerging, are examined in Chapter 9. We are concerned at this stage with procedure only, with the advantages of handling complicated problems through leisurely and thorough analysis rather than hurried improvisation.

These advantages are sufficiently clear that many companies and industries are now considering some system for negotiation between contract deadlines. In late 1963 the major building trades unions and contractors' associations were reported to be moving in this direction. Many smaller companies, which cannot afford outside, blue-ribbon neutrals, are considering committees of union and management representatives. One may expect a considerable spread of this technique over the years ahead.

ADJUSTMENT OF GRIEVANCES

Collective bargaining does not end with the signing of an agreement. Union and management officials must live under the agreement during the ensuing year, and the agreement must be applied to concrete situations arising in the plant. Contract provisions must at best be rather general. They are often unduly vague, even self-contradictory, because of unwillingness of the parties to face and resolve an underlying difference of opinion. It is easier to compromise on a vaguely worded clause which each party may interpret differently. The necessities of plant administration, however, compel specific decisions in particular cases. For this reason virtually all collective agreements contain a "grievance procedure" providing for adjustment of disputes arising during the life of the contract.

The grievance procedure serves a variety of functions in a collective bargaining relationship.[7]

(1) The most obvious function is that of interpreting the terms of the agreement and applying them to particular cases. Two or more sections of the agreement may be in conflict. Which is to govern? The contract may be silent on a particular problem, so that grievance adjustment involves closing a gap in the agreement. The language of a particular section may be unclear. What does the section actually mean? Even where the wording is clear, its application to a particular case frequently involves a finding of fact. The agreement may say that smoking on duty is a valid reason for discharge. A foreman discharges a man on this ground. The man says that the foreman's charge is incorrect. Was the man smoking or wasn't he? Shall he be discharged or not?

(2) The grievance procedure is also a means of *agreement making* in two senses. To the extent that it reveals problems which are not covered clearly enough or not covered at all in the existing agreement, it helps to build up an agenda of issues for the next contract negotiation. Further, the body of decisions on past grievances itself froms part of the agreement in the broadest sense. There gradually develops, case by case and precedent by precedent, an impressive body of shop law. In old unionized industries such as railroading and coal mining, this body of precedents is much larger than the formal union agreement, and is understood by both sides to be in effect incorporated in the agreement.

(3) The grievance procedure can be a sensitive device for locating "sore spots" in the plant organization and for pointing up inadequacies of particular foremen or union committeemen. The fact that an unusual number of grievances is filed in a particular department or on a particular issue may be more significant than the intrinsic merit of the grievances. Several leading students of industrial relations have urged the wisdom of taking a clinical rather than a legalistic view of the grievance procedure, of seeking to remove sources of conflict rather than to score points or win cases.

(4) Where relations between the parties are good, the grievance procedure may be used to adjust virtually all day-to-day difficulties

---

[7] For a good discussion of this matter, see Van Dusen Kennedy, "Grievance Procedure," in Arthur Kornhauser, Robert Dubin, and Arthur M. Ross, eds., *Industrial Conflict* (New York: McGraw-Hill Book Company, 1954), chap. 21. See also Slichter, Healy, and Livernash, *op. cit.*, chaps. 22-26.

between workers and supervisors, whether covered explicitly by the agreement or not. It can become an orderly and systematic way of examining any disputed personnel action.

(5) Conversely, where relations are poor, the procedure may become an instrument of conflict. It may be used ". . . not to settle problems between worker and supervisor or union and management but to promote the interests of either or both parties in connection with a future test of strength. . . . In unusually incompatible relationships the grievance process may operate as a sort of guerilla warfare during which the parties keep sniping at each other and endeavor to keep their forces at a martial pitch in preparation for the open conflict which will follow expiration of the contract." [8]

Most grievances relate to rights and duties of individual employees. Discharges, or even less severe disciplinary penalties, are frequently appealed. The application of complicated seniority rules to a particular worker may be questioned. Any choice by a supervisor which involves giving preference to one worker over another—distribution of overtime work, assignment to day work rather than night work, assignment to a preferred type of work or work location—may become a subject of grievance. Classification of a worker or his job for wage purposes—whether a job should be rated as Machinist A rather than Machinist B—may be disputed. On occasion, considerable numbers of workers may become involved in a grievance case: it is alleged that the assembly line is being run too fast, or that a foreman is speeding up those under him, or that work loads throughout a department are too heavy, or that piece rates on a certain operation have been set too low. A multitude of such issues, each of them minor from a top management standpoint but important and emotionally explosive to the workers concerned, get worked out peaceably through the grievance process.

The procedure for handling grievances varies with the nature of the industry. In building construction, for example, the work sites are scattered, jobs are often of short duration, and disputes have to be adjusted quickly or not at all. Each union normally has a *business agent* who makes frequent visits to building sites in his area to check that only union men are employed, to ensure that other contract terms are being complied with, and to hear any complaints by the members. The business agent goes over any grievances with the

---

[8] Kennedy, "Grievance Procedure," p. 282.

employer then and there. If no agreement is reached, the men simply leave the job. This is quite different from the long drawn out grievances procedures in manufacturing or railroading.

In most manufacturing industries, the basic union official concerned with grievances is the *shop steward* or *grievance committeeman.* He is usually elected by the union members in his department, and is normally a plant employee; but he is allowed time off from his job to handle grievances, which in a large department can become almost a full-time job. The time spent in handling grievances is often paid for by the company, but in some cases the union bears the cost.

The normal first step in a manufacturing plant is for the worker who is "grieving" to consult his shop steward, who discusses the matter informally with the foreman. The great bulk of grievances is and must be disposed of at this level. If this is not done, higher union and management officials face a hopeless burden of cases, settlements are long delayed, and the procedure becomes a source of annoyance rather than relief. An experienced foreman eventually learns the wisdom of bargaining things out informally with the union, trading concessions which he can afford for offsetting concessions from the union when he really needs them.

A grievance which is not adjusted between the steward and the foreman is generally reduced to writing and then goes to the shop committee on one side and the plant superintendent on the other. The next appeal stage may be discussion between a national field representative and the labor relations director of the company. The final step before arbitration may be discussion between a vice-president of the company and a national union representative. The number of stages in the grievance procedure varies somewhat with the size of the company, and the complexity of its organization. Where the procedure is working properly, the case load is gradually whittled down at successive levels, leaving only a small percentage of "hard core" cases for the final arbitration stage.

The arbitration of grievances

Unions generally favor arbitration as the final step in disposing of unsettled grievances. Many newly-unionized companies in the 'thirties and 'forties opposed it because it allowed outsiders to intervene in personnel decisions. Experience has gradually convinced most managements of the value of the procedure and its use has increased steadily. Today between 90 and 95 per cent of union contracts provide for arbitration as the final step in the grievance procedure.

Both management and the union take a risk under arbitration that they may lose decisions on matters which they consider important. Arbitration has the decisive advantage, however, of making possible a final settlement of grievances without a stoppage of work. Arbitration is also in some cases a convenient face-saving device, particularly for the union. Union officials sometimes have to push a case up through the grievance procedure to satisfy a group in their membership, even though they know that the members' demands are unreasonable. If such a case goes to arbitration and is decided against the union, the blame can be put on the arbitrator. Part of the arbitrator's function is to serve as a "shock absorber" for decisions which are unavoidable, but for which one side or the other is reluctant to take responsibility.

It should be noted that we are talking here about voluntary arbitration, agreed to in advance by the parties and limited to interpreting an existing agreement. Compulsory arbitration, in which the parties are required to submit their differences to a public tribunal, will be discussed in Chapter 11. The arbitrator under a grievance procedure is there solely to say what the existing agreement means. He has no authority to change the terms of the agreement or to rule on issues not covered by the agreement.

There are several types of voluntary arbitration clause. The commonest practice is for the parties to appoint an arbitrator each time the occasion arises. It is frequently provided that, where the parties cannot agree, the arbitrator shall be designated by the American Arbitration Association, the head of the Federal Mediation and Conciliation Service, the head of the state Department of Labor, or some other public official. In some industries it is customary to use three-man or five-man arbitration boards; each party appoints one or two members to the board, and these members select a neutral chairman. In large companies, or in agreements between a union and employers' association, there may be enough arbitration work to justify hiring a permanent arbitrator on a full-time or part-time basis. Such an official is frequently termed an "umpire" or "impartial chairman." This arrangement exists, for example, in the agreements between the Ford Motor Company and the UAW, the General Motors Corporation and the UAW, United States Steel Corporation and the United

Steelworkers, the hosiery workers' union and the association of full-fashioned hosiery manufacturers, the International Ladies' Garment Workers' Union and the several ladies' garment manufacturers' associations, and the Pacific Coast longshore employers and the Longshoremen's Union.

A properly constructed grievance procedure capped by arbitration should in principle render work stoppages unnecessary during the life of the agreement. In recognition of this fact, most contracts contain clauses denying or limiting the right to strike during the contract year. For example, "Under no circumstances shall there be any strike, sympathy strike, walkout, cessation of work, sit down, slow down, picketing, boycott, refusal to perform any part of duty, or other interference with or interruption of the normal conduct of the company's business during the term of this agreement." [9] What happens if a worker engages in a "wildcat" or "outlaw" strike during the term of the agreement? Some contracts do not contain any penalty provisions. Many contracts, however, provide that instigators of an outlaw strike may be subject to discharge, and that participants may be fined or suspended from work for a time. If there is disagreement over whether a man did instigate a work stoppage, this is taken up through the grievance procedure in the usual way.

Twenty years ago wildcat strikes were a serious problem in many manufacturing companies. Newly-organized workers were still enjoying the excitement of being able to talk back to the boss. Finding that the grievance procedure operated slowly, they often tried to get quick settlement of a disputed issue by direct action. In some plants the slowdown and the "quickie" strike virtually replaced the official grievance procedure. Managements inexperienced in labor relations got into the habit of yielding on disputed issues to avoid interruptions of production; and this success of wildcat tactics encouraged their continued use.

By the late 'fifties, however, increased experience and a different economic climate had brought a change in management attitudes. Companies found that constant yielding on work speeds, output standards, and shop discipline had raised production costs to a dangerous extent. With the ending of the postwar boom in the mid-'fifties, costs once more became a matter of concern. Many employers, therefore, decided to stand up to the situation. They began to penal-

---

[9] Agreement between the Turbo Engineering Corporation, Trenton, New Jersey, and Local No. 731, U.A.W.

ize participants in outlaw strikes; and they refused to settle disputed issues while such a strike was in progress, insisting that work be resumed first and the normal grievance procedure followed thereafter. Once management resistance was apparent, most of the unions accepted it in good spirit. The national unions had never sanctioned the unofficial tactics of their more exuberant local members, and now took steps to tighten internal union discipline. The problem of outlaw strikes receded to minor proportions.

SOME PECULIARITIES OF AMERICAN COLLECTIVE BARGAINING

It should be emphasized in conclusion that collective bargaining is not the same in all times and places. Current practice in the United States differs substantially from that in other democratic industrial countries such as Britain, Sweden, or Germany. We may use the British system to point up some instructive contrasts.

First, collective agreements in the United States are typically local agreements, covering one employer or a group of employers in the same area; and they are for a fixed period, at the end of which new negotiations are necessary. British agreements are usually national, covering all unionized employers in a particular industry, and they have no time limit. The agreement remains unchanged until economic conditions have changed sufficiently for one party or the other to request new negotiations. The absence of a fixed expiration date after which a strike must occur puts less pressure on union and management negotiators, and the frantic last-minute bargaining sessions so characteristic of the American system are rare in Britain.

Second, American collective agreements are detailed and complex documents. They contain elaborate provisions on the union shop, management prerogatives, prevention of strikes during the life of the agreement, grievance procedure and arbitration, work schedules, determination of work speeds, layoff and recall, promotion and transfer, discipline and discharge, holidays, vacations, health and welfare funds, and many other matters. They restrict the employer at many more points than is true in most other countries. The British agreements are much simpler and are basically wage agreements. They set minimum wage rates for key jobs in the industry, sometimes distinguishing between time workers and incentive workers, and sometimes setting different rates for different regions of the country. They specify the standard workweek and the method of computing overtime pay; and that is about all.

How, then, are wages and working conditions determined at the plant level? Mainly by the employer, subject to worker pressure and to informal discussion with local union officials. As a result, wage levels and shop practices often differ substantially within the same industry. Under the full-employment conditions prevailing in Britain since World War II, employers have been competing actively for labor and typically pay well above the union scale. The collective agreement simply sets a national minimum below which no one may fall. This may be partly because British unions grew up in an era of frequent depressions, when their main concern was to build defenses against wage cuts. They have not yet gotten used to chasing the employer up the wage ladder during a period of sustained boom. Their agreements are more like a minimum wage law than like an American union contract, in which wages are geared closely to each employer's ability to pay.

Third, British collective agreements contain none of the elaborate procedure for grievance handling which exists in the United States. Many plants have a works council, which consults with management on matters of joint concern; and the worker representatives on this council may well be union members. But they are not selected by or responsible to the union, and the works council system is not integrated into the local union organization. One consequence is that British local unions, which are not responsible either for collective bargaining or for grievance handling, are left rather functionless. This may be one reason why many union members in Britain seem to be apathetic and uninterested in union affairs.[10]

This sort of international comparison suggests that there is no "normal" or "best" system of industrial relations. Each country's system reflects the circumstances under which it has developed, including length of industrial experience, firmness of informal factory traditions, degree of employer association, extent of social cleavage between employers and workers, degree of past employer antagonism to unions, and legal and political traditions in the country.

---

[10] See Arthur M. Ross, "Prosperity and British Industrial Relations," *Industrial Relations* (Feb. 1963), pp. 63-94, and the same author's "The New Industrial Relations in Britain," *Labor Law Journal* (July 1962), pp. 492-501.

1. What is the meaning of the term "collective bargaining"?
   (a) What procedures and activities does it cover?
   (b) Do you think it adequately describes these procedures and activities?
2. What are the main determinants of the area of collective agreements?
3. Give an illustration of each of the following types of collective bargaining:
   (a) multiemployer bargaining
   (b) "union-wide" bargaining
   (c) industry-wide bargaining
   (d) region-wide bargaining
4. What are the techniques by which national unions sometimes control the bargaining relationships of their local unions with individual companies?
5. Why is it that unions and management prefer industry-wide bargaining in some industries but not in others?
6. "Inflation of initial demands may make for better bargaining than a frank statement of each side's true position at the outset." Discuss.
7. What are the main functions of the grievance procedure in collective bargaining? What are some of the characteristics of a satisfactory grievance procedure?
8. "Without the strike threat in the background, real collective bargaining cannot exist." Discuss.
9. What reasons can you think of for the main differences between the British and American systems of industrial relations?

Selected reading

Chamberlain, Neil W., *Collective Bargaining*. New York: McGraw-Hill Book Company, Inc., 1951.

Dunlop, John T., *Collective Bargaining: Principles and Cases*. Homewood, Ill.: Richard D. Irwin, Inc., 1955.

———, *Industrial Relations Systems*. New York: Holt, Rinehart & Winston, Inc., 1958.

Golden, C. S., and V. D. Parker, *Causes of Industrial Peace under Collective Bargaining*. New York: Harper & Row, Publishers, 1955.

Harbison, Frederick H., and Robert Dubin, *Patterns of Union-Management Relations*. Chicago: Science Research Associates, 1947.

Kornhauser, Arthur, Robert Dubin, and Arthur M. Ross, eds., *Industrial Conflict*. New York: McGraw-Hill Book Company, Inc., 1954.

Kuhn, James W., *Bargaining in Grievance Settlement*. New York: Columbia University Press, 1961.

Lester, Richard A., *Labor and Industrial Relations—A General Analysis*. New York: The Macmillan Company, 1951.

Selekman, B. M., S. K. Selekman, and S. H. Fuller, *Problems in Labor Relations*, 2nd ed. New York: McGraw-Hill Book Company, Inc., 1958.

Slichter, S. H., J. J. Healy, and E. R. Livernash, *The Impact of Collective Bargaining on Management*. Washington: Brookings Institution, 1960.

In addition, there are numerous studies of collective bargaining in particular industries. There are two important recent series of studies. The "Industry-Wide Collective Bargaining Series" of the Wharton School of Finance and Commerce at the University of Pennsylvania is edited by George W. Taylor. There are about fifteen separate pamphlets on many aspects of industry-wide and multiemployer bargaining. The other important series is that of the National Planning Association's Committee on the Causes of Industrial Peace under Collective Bargaining. These are case studies of collective bargaining relationships in particular companies.

8

Issues In Bargaining:
Job Tenure And Job Security

The matters regulated by the collective agreement or "union contract" vary greatly from one situation to the next, depending on the age of the agreement, the nature of the industry, the structure and policies of the union, and the attitudes and objectives of management. Speaking generally, unions attempt to regulate every kind of managerial action which directly affects the welfare of the membership or the strength and security of the union itself. Almost every aspect of personnel administration, and many aspects of production management, eventually become matters of collective bargaining. A list of the subjects covered in the more than one hundred thousand union contracts in the United States would include hundreds of items; and with respect to each of these, many different contract provisions have been worked out to meet differing circumstances.

To do justice to this wealth of issues and variety of solutions would require a separate book.[1] In the limited space available here it is necessary to concentrate on a few key issues and, with respect to each issue, to discuss the general objectives and attitudes of the parties rather than detailed differences in contract arrangements. The student

---

[1] For a survey of the detailed issues that arise in collective bargaining and the alternative methods of handling them, see Neil W. Chamberlain, *Collective Bargaining* (New York: McGraw-Hill Book Company, 1955); John T. Dunlop and J. J. Healey, *Collective Bargaining: Principles and Cases*, rev. ed. (Homewood, Ill.: Richard D. Irwin Inc., 1953); and H. W. Davey, *Contemporary Collective Bargaining* (Englewood Cliffs, N.J.: Prentice-Hall, Inc., 1951).

who wishes to examine the variety of contract provisions currently existing on any subject can find this information in a number of convenient sources.[2]

Union contracts normally contain a number of procedural provisions, designed to set the general framework of relations between the parties. These include provisions concerning recognition and status of the union, rights and prerogatives of management, duration of the agreement and method of extending or renewing it, prevention of strikes and lockouts during the life of the agreement, and handling of grievances arising under the contract.

The substantive provisions of the contract may be organized into three broad groups:

1. JOB TENURE AND JOB SECURITY. This includes all provisions concerning hiring, training, assignment to work, promotion and transfer, layoff and recall, and discharge. Since length of service (seniority) is an important criterion in some of these decisions, the contract must specify how seniority is to be calculated and applied.

2. WORK SCHEDULES, WORK SPEEDS, AND PRODUCTION METHODS. This includes determination of the standard workday and workweek, and payment for work in excess of the standard schedule. It covers also the determination of proper work speeds—size of machine assignments, proper speed of assembly lines, time standards and work quotas under incentive systems, and similar matters. Working conditions of every sort including health, safety, sanitation, heating and lighting, and ventilation are included. Finally, the agreement may touch on certain aspects of production methods—methods of work which may be used, number of workers to be used on a particular job, and introduction of new machinery and production processes.

3. AMOUNT AND METHOD OF COMPENSATION. This includes provisions concerning the basic wage schedule and general changes in this schedule; the method of wage payment and, if a piece rate or incentive system is used, the extent of union participation in the administration of the system; setting of wage rates on new or changed jobs; wage increases for individual workers on a seniority or merit basis; and a wide variety of indirect or supplementary wage payments to workers, including pension funds, health and welfare funds, and supplementary unemployment benefit plans.

---

[2] Notably the file of current union contracts maintained by the Bureau of Labor Statistics of the Department of Labor; and the current labor services issued by Prentice-Hall, Inc., and others.

In this and the next two chapters, we shall examine these three groups in turn. Note that they are increasingly economic, in the sense of affecting labor costs per unit of output. Methods of hiring, promotion, and layoff doubtless affect costs, but the effect is indirect and hard to estimate. Work speeds and production methods have a clearer effect, since they determine how much output the worker delivers in exchange for his wage. The wage itself, including supplementary or "fringe" benefits, bears directly on costs. So all three groups are of concern to the employer; and for different reasons, each is important to the worker as well. The first affects his employment opportunities and job security, the second affects the pleasantness of his daily life on the job, while the third sets limits to his standard of living.

CONTROL OF HIRING: APPRENTICESHIP; THE CLOSED SHOP

Economic reasoning suggests that it is natural for unions to take an interest in the supply of labor. Reducing the supply of a particular kind of labor is one way of raising its price. Or, if the union simply demands and wins a wage above the market equilibrium of demand and supply, the result will be more workers seeking jobs at that wage than employers are willing to hire. The union is then likely to take an interest in *which* workers get hired for the available jobs.

Control over labor supply might be exercised at various levels. A union might try to control the number who secure training for a particular occupation. If it cannot do this, it might restrict the number admitted to the union and make membership in the union a prerequisite for employment. Or it might admit to the union everyone who applies and still control the distribution of work among the members.

Training is important mainly for a limited number of skilled trades. Semiskilled jobs can be learned quickly and are normally learned on the job. The skilled crafts require longer training and experience, and are often learned in advance of employment either through vocational school courses or apprentice training programs. Control of the number admitted to such programs could conceivably be used to restrict the supply of labor.

This has not happened in practice, partly because there are so many other ways in which one can learn a skilled trade. Many men learn trades during service in the armed forces. Semiskilled workers are often trained and upgraded to skilled jobs within the plant. Many people simply pick up a trade by getting a smattering of it, finding someone willing to hire them, and improving their competence as they go along. Every farm boy naturally becomes something of a carpenter, painter, and auto mechanic. It has been estimated that the American economy needs about half a million new skilled craftsmen each year—about 400,000 to replace retiring workers, and 100,000 to meet growing demand. The total number of young people enrolled in apprenticeship programs, however, has in recent years been of the order of 175,000. The number entering the labor force each year via apprenticeship programs is estimated at 70,000 to 80,000.[3] Since apprenticeship provides only a small part of the supply of new craftsmen, it can scarcely form an effective method of restricting labor supply.

Unions have nevertheless taken an active interest in apprenticeship programs for several reasons. Skilled workers have pride in their craft and would like to see the next generation get a thorough training. They want to make employers pay high enough wages to apprentices so that they do not become a source of cheap labor which could undercut the union scale. There is usually a contract provision that the apprentice shall start out at, say, 40 per cent of the journeyman's rate, and work up to this rate by steps over his period of training. Craftsmen also want adequate opportunity for their sons to gain admission as apprentices. It is as customary for a plumber's son to become a plumber as for a doctor's son to become a doctor.

The Machinists, Electrical Workers, Typographical Union, Plumbers, and Boilermakers have been particularly active in developing apprenticeship programs in cooperation with employers in their respective industries. The Bureau of Apprenticeship and Training in the U.S. Department of Labor has national responsibility for fostering such programs and setting minimum standards for their operation. The main problem is not union reluctance to permit more apprentices to be trained, but rather employer reluctance to take on as many apprentices as union regulations allow. The employer puts considerable investment into each apprentice, but has no assurance that the boy will stay with him beyond the apprenticeship period. So it is to

---

[3] Slichter, Healy, and Livernash, *op. cit.*, pp. 67-69.

each employer's interest to persuade *other* employers in his industry to train apprentices whom he will later be able to hire away from them. Heavier investment in training, with each employer bearing his proper share of the cost, might well benefit employers as a group; but to sell this idea and work out an acceptable program is often difficult.

Granted that a union can rarely control the number who learn a particular trade, it might still control the number admitted to the union. Then if it could get employers to hire only people who are already union members (a *closed shop* arrangement), it would have effective control of labor supply. Admission to the union could be regulated either by closing the books when the number of union members equals the number demanded by employers at the union wage rate, or by charging an initiation fee high enough to reduce applications to the desired level.

Suppose the demand and supply curves for a particular craft are shown by the solid lines in Figure 2. The wage rate in a competitive labor market would be OW. The number seeking employment just equals the number desired by employers, and the market is cleared. The union is strong enough, however, to secure a wage of OW_1 and to insist on a closed shop rule. At this wage, the number seeking work in the trade exceeds the number employers will hire by the distance AB. The union might do one of two things. It might say: "We will admit only W_1A people to the union, and the rest must remain outside." This requires some way of selecting the lucky people to be admitted, which might be politically awkward. Alternatively, it might charge a stiff initiation fee for admission to the union. A charge for admission, by reducing the net returns from the occupation, will reduce the number seeking employment at a given wage, i.e., it will shift the labor supply curve to the left. The union could discover by experiment an initiation fee just high enough to shift labor supply from SS to S_1S_1. Then the number spontaneously seeking employment would once more equal the number desired by employers. This self-selection through the market mechanism would remove any political embarrassment to the union, while at the same time enabling it to turn a tidy profit.

Unions actually do not make much use of either method. That they do not use the second method is shown by the moderate level of union initiation fees. Out of 39,000 local unions filing reports under the Landrum-Griffin Act, only 342 reported initiation fees of more than $250, and the highest fee reported by any local was $1,400.

WAGE RATE

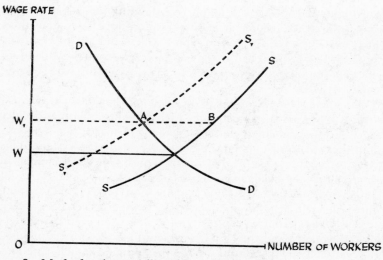

FIG. 2 *Methods of controlling labor supply.*

This must be well below the value of union membership in many cases. "Becker reports that New York City taxicab medallions have sold for about $17,000 in recent years, and San Francisco papers in 1959 reported a figure of $16,000 for the transfer of licenses to operate a taxicab in that city. The value of entry to a union with a 20 per cent effect on relative earnings would be of this order of magnitude even at fairly high interest rates."[4] One reason for not using high fees as a job rationing device is doubtless that it would outrage public opinion and publicize the monopolistic level of the union wage.

One finds occasional cases of arbitrary closing of the union books to exclude labor and buttress a high wage scale.[5] But these cases are exceptional. To leave a surplus of eager applicants (shown by

---

[4] Albert Rees, *The Economics of Trade Unions* (Chicago: University of Chicago Press, 1962), p. 128. Professor Rees adds in a footnote: "Membership in a union with an effect of 20 per cent on annual earnings would increase earnings $1,000 a year for a man whose alternative earnings were $5,000. The present value of an annuity of $1,000 a year for 40 years is over $15,000 at an interest rate of 6 per cent."

[5] "An example of a closed union is the Newspaper and Mail Deliverers Union of New York, which for years has maintained an illegal closed shop in violation of the Taft-Hartley Act. Memberships in it are reported to have sold for as much as $5,000, although about $500 is said to be the usual price." Slichter, Healy, and Livernash, *op. cit.*, p. 41.

AB in Figure 2) outside the union is a standing invitation for employers to hire these people at less than union wage rates. It is safer to take into the union everyone who applies, and this also brings in more dues revenue. Then if there is less than enough work to go around, the union can devise rules for allocating this work among the membership.

Where there is an exceptional rise in labor demand which is expected to subside in the near future, a local union sometimes decides to meet this, not by enlarging its regular membership, but by allowing outsiders to work temporarily under a *permit card* system. This is a legitimate way of covering seasonal peaks of employment in irregular industries such as food processing or construction, or of meeting labor needs on a large construction project in a remote locality where the regular labor force is small. Some locals, however, have abused the permit system by refusing admission even to regularly employed workers, and then charging them high fees for the right to work. National unions almost invariably discourage such practices, and they are also regulated by legislation. Landrum-Griffin requires local unions to report on their permit fees, and Taft-Hartley prohibits the charging of fees higher than the union's normal dues.

The main examples of labor supply restriction occur in certain occupations covered by state licensing regulations. A law is passed providing that barbers, say, can be admitted to the trade only after passing an examination set by a state licensing board. (For "barbers" read also plumbers or electricians, or, for that matter, accountants, lawyers, or doctors!) To no one's surprise, the licensing board turns out to consist of representatives of the barbers' union and the master barbers' (employers) association. The number of candidates who "pass" is held down to a level which does not endanger the jobs or wage scale of those already employed in the industry. This is typically part of a broader pattern of monopolistic control over prices, wages, and admission of new employers as well as new workers.

If the closed shop is ordinarily not used to control the number admitted to an occupation, what is the point of the closed shop? First, it is traditional in many of the skilled trades. In Britain, the principle that a union craftsman will not work alongside a nonunion man is so well established that no formal closed shop rules are necessary. Second, it strengthens the union organization. If nonunion men cannot even get hired, the employer has no opportunity to undermine and weaken the union. In addition to this defensive function, the closed shop enables the union to ration job opportunities among members of the craft on some equitable basis; and it often furnishes employers with a central employment agency.

The closed shop is typically accompanied by an arrangement under which the union acts as an employment agency for the industry and provides workers to individual employers on request. This is convenient where employers are small, as in clothing manufacture or job printing; or where jobs are of short duration and each employer's needs fluctuate widely, as in building construction. Central hiring is useful also in industries where there is a good deal of seasonal or casual unemployment, such as longshoring and merchant shipping. Where there is regular year-round employment, as in most manufacturing industries, the unions have taken little interest in closed shop clauses or central hiring facilities.

In 1946, just before passage of the Taft-Hartley Act, the closed shop appeared in about one-third of all union contracts. Taft-Hartley forbade the closed shop, and so it has almost vanished from union contracts; but this is not to say that the practice has disappeared. In building construction, the closed shop continued in open defiance of Taft-Hartley and was eventually (in effect) relegalized by Landrum-Griffin. In other cases the former contract provisions have been replaced by new clauses intended to have the same effect. For example, the contract may provide that the union shall have first opportunity to fill job vacancies, and that only if the union cannot provide workers within a certain period will the employer look elsewhere; or that preference in employment will be given to workers employed in the industry before a certain date, i.e., during the closed shop period, hence necessarily union members; or that preference will be given to graduates of a training program operated by the union; or simply that preference will be given to "experienced" or "qualified" workers. There are additional cases in which a bootleg closed shop has continued by tacit agreement between the union and employer with no contract provision. Where there is a long tradition that union members will not work alongside nonunion men, it is simpler for the employer to accept this tradition than to assert his rights and lose his labor.

The main practical problem associated with the closed shop is that of union admission requirements. Where there is a tacit closed shop, and where the union declines to admit certain kinds of workers —women, Negroes, Puerto Ricans, or whatever—these people are barred from employment in the industry. This has not been an important problem in industrial unions, since they rarely have the closed shop and rarely discriminate in membership. Some of the craft unions have followed discriminatory policies, however, and this has made it hard particularly for Negroes to get into the building trades, railroad trades, and some other areas of employment. The situation is all the more difficult because employers and the union are usually in full agreement on this policy.

COMPULSORY MEMBERSHIP: THE UNION SHOP

More than four-fifths of all union contracts contain some provision for union security. Much the commonest provision is a straight *union shop*. This leaves the employer free to hire at will; but after the worker has served his probationary period and becomes a regular member of the plant labor force, he is required to join the union. If he declines to do so, or if he drops out of the union, the employer must discharge him. A variant of the union shop is the *maintenance-of-membership* clause. This does not compel any worker to join; but if he chooses to join, he must then remain in for the duration of the contract as a condition of employment. Another rather rare variant is the *agency shop*, under which a worker who declines to join is obliged to pay the union a fee—usually set at the level of the monthly dues—in return for the collective bargaining service which it is rendering him.

In earlier times the union shop gave union leaders a powerful disciplinary weapon over recalcitrant members. Anyone who fell foul of the existing leadership could be expelled from the union, and would then be out of a job. This doubtless contributed to the growth of oppressive and corrupt practices in some unions. To correct this Taft-Hartley provided that the employer is not obliged to discharge a worker who has been expelled from, or denied admission to, the union on any ground other than failure to tender the regular dues and initiation fees.

The union shop itself is legal under Taft-Hartley. But the Act contains a curious provision that, where any state has passed a law forbidding the union shop, the state law shall take precedence. This reverses the normal rule that federal law has precedence as regards workers in interstate commerce. Twenty states have laws (often wrongly labeled "right to work laws") which prohibit both the closed and union shop. These states are almost all in the South and West (Indiana is the only major industrial state with such a statute), and include only about 15 per cent of industrial employment in the country. Unions have fought these laws vigorously on the ground that they will destroy trade unionism, while employer and farm groups have hailed them as the Magna Carta of the working man. It is doubtful that either claim could be substantiated. Research studies suggest that the practical effect of these laws has been small.[6] Employers who want good relations with their unions have usually winked at the law, just as employers in traditional closed shop industries have winked at Taft-Hartley. Where relations are bad, however, and where the employer wants to mount a drive against the union, an anti-union shop law may give him an additional club.

Some pros and cons of the union shop

The legitimacy of the union shop has been argued for generations, and the issue arouses strong emotion on both sides. Unionists argue that, since everyone in the bargaining unit benefits from the contract terms established by the union, everyone should be required to contribute to the union's support. If this is not the case, some workers will receive a "free ride" at the expense of their fellow workers. This situation is as unfair as one in which citizens of a community could decide whether or not they wish to pay taxes.

A more powerful argument for the union shop is that only if the union's existence is secure can it afford to cooperate with management and play a constructive role in the operation of the enterprise. The union interprets management's denial of the union shop as a lack of complete acceptance of collective bargaining, an indication that management does not consider the union a permanent part of the enterprise and hopes in time to be rid of it. The union must, therefore, devote much of its energy to keeping its fences mended against employer attack. It must try to hem in the employer by contract restrictions at any point where he might try to discriminate against union men; it must limit his power to select, promote, transfer, lay off, and discharge. It must manufacture enough grievances to keep the workers convinced that the employer is a tricky fellow and

---

[6] See, for example, Frederic Myers, *"Right to Work" in Practice* (New York: Fund for the Republic, 1959).

that the union is essential for their protection. It must give good service or grievances to its members, and poor service or no service to non-members, in order to emphasize the practical advantages of union membership; this discrimination makes for unequal treatment and ill-feeling within the labor force.

Employer acceptance of the union shop, it is argued, would make all this unnecessary. The time of union officials could be put to constructive use in ironing out personnel problems and production difficulties, giving prompt attention to genuine grievances, performing educational functions, and cooperating with management in other ways. Freed of any necessity to stir up antagonism to the employer in order to hold their members in line, union leaders could afford to take a reasonable position on disputed issues.

This general point of view is supported by a number of careful students of the subject. Slichter, for example, concludes that the union shop is desirable for the contribution it can make to stable industrial relations. He points out that a union whose security is beyond question can afford to be more reasonable on other matters —notably promotions, layoffs, and other points at which discrimination might be practiced against union members. A union which fears for its life must necessarily try to restrict the employer at all these points. Slichter concludes, therefore, that the employer can secure a generally more favorable contract by conceding the union-shop issue at the outset.[7]

On the other hand, many management officials argue that the union shop is coercive and involves an undue encroachment on the liberty of the individual worker. In a free society, a worker should be able to seek and accept employment with any employer who is willing to hire him, without paying tribute to a third party. The union shop forces him to join an organization of which he may not approve, and forces him to pay for the right to work, a right which he should enjoy as a citizen.

This argument that the union shop coerces workers into unionism against their will appears to have been overdone. Few workers seem to have any conscientious objection to unionism. Most of those who stay out of the union do so simply out of inertia or to avoid dues payments. The coercion involved in requiring them to join the union is mainly financial, and is no greater than that involved in levying

---

[7] See Slichter, *Union Policies and Industrial Management*, chap. 3.

payroll taxes on them for social security or other purposes. There is abundant evidence that where the union shop has been in effect in the past, the great majority of workers favor its continuance. The Taft-Hartley Act originally provided that a union-shop clause could not be included in a union contract unless a majority of the employees in the bargaining unit voted in favor of it in a secret ballot conducted by the NLRB. During the first year of the Act's operation, some twenty thousand elections were held under this section. The union shop was upheld in more than 98 per cent of these cases and secured more than 95 per cent of all ballots cast. It soon became clear, in fact, that these union shop referenda were simply an unnecessary expense to the government, and the Act was subsequently amended to eliminate the referendum requirement.

Beneath the arguments over the union-shop issue lies the hard fact of a power struggle. A union security clause strengthens the union's position in the shop, renders it less vulnerable to attack by the employer or rival unions, and helps to make it a permanent institution. It also makes the position of union officials more secure and less arduous. Management opposition to the union shop is based mainly on a recognition of these facts. Most managements see no reason to go out of their way in helping the union to become a permanent fixture. This does not necessarily mean that they have any hope of breaking the union. Their strategy may be merely to fight an effective delaying action. If the union can be kept busy holding its membership together, it will be in a weaker position to press fresh demands on the employer.

One's attitude toward the union shop is bound to depend on how one answers the following question: Is it desirable to maintain strong, stable, and permanent unions in American industry? If one answers no to this question, the open-shop position follows automatically. If one answers yes, a strong case can be made for a union-shop clause. There seems little doubt that a union is better able to function in a peaceful and constructive way if it embraces most or all of the labor force. It is unreasonable to demand that unions be "responsible" while at the same time denying union officers the control over their membership which would make group responsibility effective.

An issue related to the union shop should be noted in conclusion. Union demands for a union- or closed-shop clause have usually been accompanied by a demand for the "checkoff." This is an arrangement by which the regular weekly or monthly dues of union members are deducted from their paychecks by the employer and transmitted in a lump sum to the union. Under the Taft-Hartley Act of 1947, the checkoff became possible only with the written consent of each employee. Automatic checkoffs are thus no longer possible. Most unions prefer the checkoff, partly because it saves them a good deal of effort and unpleasantness in collecting dues from delinquent members, and partly because it still further regulates and entrenches the position of the union in the plant. Most managements oppose the checkoff because it involves the company in effort and expense for the primary benefit of the union.

In general, where one finds a closed-shop, union-shop, or maintenance-of-membership provision, one is likely to find the checkoff as well. Sixty-seven per cent of the contracts surveyed by the B.L.S. in 1952 contained this provision. There are many detailed variations in checkoff clauses. Under some contracts, dues are checked off automatically for all union members; under others, they are checked off unless the worker asks the company in writing not to deduct his dues; in still other cases, the dues are deducted only if the worker makes a positive request in writing that this be done. The whole issue, while presenting many possibilities for technical arguments, is subsidiary to the broader argument over the union shop. The outcome of that argument usually determines the outcome of the checkoff argument as well.

JOB TENURE: SECURITY AND OPPORTUNITY

An important group of provisions in union contracts concerns the conditions under which individual workers shall have access to vacant jobs, the rules governing their tenure of the job, and the conditions under which they may be separated from employment. So important is this matter that Perlman and others have found in it the key to the growth and persistence of trade unionism. Workers are continually faced with a scarcity of available jobs, and consciousness of this scarcity molds union philosophy and tactics. The union is a method of controlling the job opportunities in a craft or industry and of distributing these opportunities among union members according to some equitable principle.

The union tries to introduce into industry a "civil service system" of job tenure. The worker ceases to be so many units of productive power, which can be shifted about in the plant or dispensed with altogether at the pleasure of the employer. He becomes an individual with a system of rights, which the employer is bound to observe and which can be defended through the grievance procedure. The different matters regulated by this system of rights will be examined briefly in this section.

The seniority principle

Over the past twenty years there has been increasing acceptance of the principle that a worker's job rights should be related to his length of service. Common-sense ideas of equity suggests that a man who has devoted more years to the company deserves more of the company in return. Seniority is objective, relatively easy to measure and apply, and easy to defend before workers and outside arbitrators.

Seniority appears in the union contract in two main ways. First, it usually governs eligibility for "fringe benefits": vacations, paid holidays, pensions, severance pay, sick-leave provisions, insurance and health services, profit sharing, supplementary unemployment benefits, and the rest. In bargaining over these issues employers have usually insisted, and unions have accepted, that a man's entitlement to benefits should vary with length of service. The 20-year man gets more paid holidays, longer paid vacations, larger pension rights, more sick leave, and so on, than the 2-year-man. Slichter, Healy, and Livernash call this *benefit seniority*.

The second area they term *competitive status seniority*. Here the problem is one of ranking workers relative to each other. Several workers are in competition to get a promotion or avoid a layoff, and the seniority principle is used to resolve the competition. The most obvious applications are to layoff, transfer, and promotion; but there are also many others. The senior worker may be given first choice in picking vacation periods. He may be given first chance to earn more money through overtime work. He may lay claim to the newest of a group of machines, or to the machine in the pleasantest location. Spaces in the company parking lot may be located on a seniority basis. In one company the senior men are allowed to punch out first on the time clock at the end of the day, which has advantages in reducing the wild scramble which occurred previously.

Benefit seniority is almost always calculated from the date of first employment with the company; but competitive status seniority is harder to calculate and apply. Suppose Bill Jones has been with the company 15 years, working 5 years in department A, 5 years in department B, and 5 years in his present job in department C. Layoffs now become necessary in department C, and it is agreed that they should be in order of seniority. What is Bill Jones' seniority in department C? Is it 15 years, or only 5 years? If he is laid off from department C, can he go back to his previous job in department B and displace ("bump") some less senior worker? And how much seniority does he have in department B? The rules have to be spelled out in the contract; and the rules may be different for different problems—one principle for promotion, another for layoff, and so on. These fine details have important effects on employee security and on management's freedom to deploy its work force to greatest effect.

SHARING OF WORK OPPORTUNITIES; IRREGULAR INDUSTRIES.   In some industries, continuous attachment to a single employer is impossible by the nature of the industry. Seamen are often paid off at the end of each voyage and, after a shorter or longer period "on the beach," sign on with another vessel for a new voyage. In longshoring, the amount of work coming into a particular pier is irregular, depending on what ships happen to arrive on a particular day. When a cargo comes in and has to be unloaded, it is necessary to hire a gang of longshoremen on the spot; when the vessel is unloaded, their job ends. In other industries, production is highly seasonal. Building construction tapers off in the late fall and revives in the early spring. Each worker naturally wants to be the last man laid off in the fall and the first man hired in the spring. The men's and women's clothing industries have two production seasons during the year, one for the spring trade, the other for the fall trade. During each of these seasons activity begins slowly, mounts to a peak of production and employment, and then declines. Again, each worker in the industry wants to be the first hired and the last laid off.

In the absence of contract rules concerning hiring, the bulk of the work in such industries would go to men who were of superior efficiency or who had special "pull" with foremen and hiring officials. Workers who got relatively little work would feel that the union was not serving them effectively, and would be tempted to drop out. Partly to preserve the organization, partly out of considerations of equity, the union attempts to ensure that the available work is shared more or less equally among the membership.

Where employers are numerous and small, this attempt may require union control over the referral of workers to jobs. It is no accident that the union office has been used as an employment agency in the building, printing, and clothing industries, or that the union "hiring hall" has developed in longshoring and merchant shipping.

The devices used to ensure something like equal division of work vary from one industry to the next. In the shipping industry, the man who has been longest "on the beach" gets the first opportunity to sign up for a new voyage; all job vacancies and referrals to work are cleared through the union hiring hall. In longshoring work in Pacific Coast ports, a regular list of "gangs" (work teams) is maintained at union headquarters, and gangs are dispatched to work in the order in which they appear on this list. When a gang comes off the job it must go to the bottom of the list and wait until its number comes up again before being dispatched to a new job.

The hiring hall arrangement has traditionally been a closed-shop arrangement as well, and was therefore rendered unlawful by the Taft-Hartley Act. The maritime unions, however, have succeeded in developing formulas which have maintained the hiring hall relatively unchanged. In merchant shipping, preference in hiring is no longer given to union members as such, but is given to men who have sailed previously on the ships of members of the employers' association. Since the great majority of seamen had been unionized in the past, this amounts to almost the same thing. The new arrangement appears to have had little effect on hiring hall practices.[8] Taft-Hartley requires that, if nonunion workers do come to the hiring hall, they must be given the same service as union members and referred to work on a non-discriminatory basis.

In the clothing industries, the unions have favored reduction in working hours rather than layoffs as work tapers off toward the end of a season. In this way all workers in a shop get an equal amount of work so long as work is available. In building construction, there has been some experimentation with "first off, first on" rules, under which the first man laid off in the fall would be dispatched to the first job opening in the spring. This sort of rule, however, presents certain difficulties. The first men laid off in the fall may be chronic drunkards or undesirable for other reasons. Experience has shown that, where the first employer who starts building work in the spring is forced to hire those undesirables, there is a good deal of jockeying

---

[8] E. P. Hohman, "Merchant Seamen in the U.S., 1937-1952," *International Labour Review*, LXVII (January 1953), p. 26.

among employers to avoid this unpleasant necessity. Whether for this or other reasons, the building trades have done less than most other unions to enforce formal work-sharing rules.

SHARING OF WORK OPPORTUNITIES: REDUCTIONS IN PRODUCTION SCHEDULES. Even in stable industries the labor requirements of a firm may vary somewhat from month to month. It may fail to secure a large order on which it has been counting, the sales of a new product line may be disappointing, or a general business recession may develop. This situation causes a reduction in production schedules and man-hours worked. Almost all companies experience such reductions during depression periods; in many industries output falls during depression to 50 per cent or less of normal operations. The question then arises of who is to bear the brunt of the reduction in employment. How shall the work which is left be distributed among those who want it?

A reduction in production schedules can be met either by laying off workers, by reducing the number of hours worked per week, or by a combination of these methods. One possibility is to keep everyone on the payroll but to work the plant fewer hours per week. This policy is beneficial to the short-service employees, since it gives them some work, whereas layoffs based on length of service would put them out of work completely. Even the long-service workers are likely to consider it equitable that work opportunities be shared among the entire labor force. A policy of work-sharing also has certain advantages to management, since it enables the plant labor force to be held together and eases the problem of increasing production when demand revives.

It is necessary, however, to set some limit to a work-sharing policy. If hours fall below thirty per week, most workers will feel that they are sharing poverty rather than opportunity. They will in fact be earning little more than the unemployment compensation they would receive if totally unemployed. If the drop in demand is severe and prolonged, therefore, it will be necessary to go beyond hours reduction to layoff of workers. Many union contracts provide for something like the following combination of procedures to meet a decline in production: first, lay off all temporary and probationary employees; second, reduce hours of work as required down to some minimum—say 32 hours per week; third, if these measures are insufficient, begin to lay off members of the regular work force.

Where layoffs have to be made, unions typically and successfully insist that they should be made on a seniority basis. They argue that the workers with greater length of service will, in general, be more efficient at their jobs and more valuable to the company. In addition, the long-service workers will usually be men with family responsibilities, whose incomes should be protected on social grounds. Primarily, however, unions like the simplicity and definiteness of a seniority system, which makes it impossible for the employer or the foreman to use layoffs as an occasion for "taking it out" on certain workers. In some industries, such as the railroads, the older men are dominant in union affairs, and this may have something to do with union adherence to the seniority principle. By the same token, a straight seniority rule runs the risk of alienating the younger men by forcing them to bear the brunt of cyclical unemployment. This situation may cause serious factional conflict between younger and older men in the union, as has happened more than once in the railroad trades.

It is easier to defend the senority principle than it is to work out detailed regulations for applying it. A central issue here is the size of the "seniority district." Should seniority be considered as the man's length of service in a particular occupation, or in a particular department of the plant, or in the plant as a whole, or in all plants of a multi-plant company? Under plant-wide seniority a man laid off in one department may be able to shift over and bump a worker in an entirely different department whose seniority is less than his own, who in turn may bump someone in a third department. A single layoff may thus set off a chain of displacements throughout the plant. The more narrowly the seniority unit is defined, the smaller is the possibility of bumping and consequently the smaller the protection afforded to long-service employees. The union will typically argue for broad seniority units in order to achieve maximum employee protection, while management will argue for narrower units in order to minimize the disruption of work teams and the added training time which may result from excessive bumping. Arguments over the drafting of seniority clauses and their application to individual workers consume a good proportion of union and management time in collective bargaining.

Whatever procedure is chosen for layoffs normally applies also to rehiring. Workers are recalled to work in reverse order from that in which they were laid off—"last off, first in." The brunt of unemployment is thus borne by those with the shortest period of service.

Some agreements provide that "key men" may be exempted from the operation of the seniority rule. These men are designated by management, and it is usually provided that they may not exceed a certain percentage of the total labor force. The argument of management for this provision is that it is desirable during depression to hold together a skeleton force of men trained for strategic positions in the plant. If this force is broken up through strict application of a seniority rule, it may be difficult and costly to rebuild it. The union sometimes makes a similar argument that, if key union officials are laid off during depression, smooth administration of the union contract will be seriously hampered. On this ground they urge "super-seniority" for shop stewards and other union officials, i.e., that these men be placed automatically at the top of the seniority lists in their respective departments. Management frequently objects to this provision on the ground that it creates a privileged class and places too high a premium on running for union office. Despite the objections, super-seniority clauses appear in an increasing percentage of union agreements.

PROMOTIONS AND TRANSFERS. It is increasingly the practice in modern industry to fill "good" vacancies in the plant by promoting members of the present work force. New workers usually enter the plant in the least desirable jobs and work their way up as vacancies arise. The concept of "promotion" has more dimensions than might occur to an outside observer. Most obvious is movement to a job involving greater skill and a higher wage. But movement from the night shift to the day shift on the same job would also be considered a promotion by most workers, as would transfer to a lighter but equally well-paid job, or even movement to the newest machine or the pleasantest location in a particular work group.

The nonunion employer is free to decide whether to fill a vacancy from the outside or from within and, in the latter case, to decide who should be promoted. Decisions are made unilaterally and without advance notice. A union typically insists, as a minimum, that notice of vacancies shall be posted and that present employees shall have opportunity to apply. This enables each worker to know about vacancies as they arise, to decide whether a particular job would be a promotion *for him,* and to make his bid for it if he wants to.

Most unions try to make length of service the dominant consideration in promotion as well as in layoffs. Employers naturally resist this demand, which they feel would hamper them in rewarding merit and in selecting the most efficient man available for each job. Few contracts outside the railroad industry specify seniority as the *sole* criterion for promotion. The usual outcome is a compromise providing that where ability is relatively equal the senior man shall be promoted, or that the senior man shall be promoted if competent to do the job, or simply that both ability and length of service shall be considered in making promotion decisions. The meaning of these general statements is then worked out through the grievance procedure in individual cases. The practical outcome is usually that seniority governs in the absence of marked differences of ability among the candidates, and that where management believes there is a marked difference of ability it must be prepared to prove its case. Emphasis on the seniority factor is increasing over the course of time.

THE ECONOMIC IMPACT OF SENIORITY. Increasing emphasis on seniority in both layoffs and promotions has caused some apprehension concerning the long-run economic consequence.

We rely heavily on free worker choice in the labor market both to get the right man to the right job and to correct serious discrepancies in the terms offered by different employers. Anything which reduces workers' ability to make a free choice among alternative employers hampers the market in performing these functions. Heavy emphasis on seniority, it is argued, ties the worker increasingly to his present employer, reduces actual and potential labor mobility, and thus interferes with the market mechanism. If new employees are hired only for the least attractive positions while "good" vacancies are filled from within, the worker who seeks to change employers runs a serious risk. He may have to step down to the bottom of the occupational ladder and work his way up again slowly and painfully, meanwhile being subject to the risk of layoff as a short-service employee. The obvious moral is to stay where you are and accumulate as much seniority as possible, thus insuring yourself against layoff and strengthening your chances of promotion.

Seniority, however, is only one of numerous factors making for strong attachment of workers to their present jobs. Most people prefer stability to change in any event. Accumulated pension rights and other company benefits make it increasingly worthwhile to stay on with the same employer. Long service typically confers certain privileges even where strict seniority does not govern. It is questionable whether seniority does much more to reduce labor mobility.

Moreover, labor mobility can be too high as well as too low. It is not desirable that everyone in the labor force shuttle about constantly from job to job. Efficient operation of the market requires only a mobile minority, which may be made up largely of new entrants to the labor force plus the unemployed. For the bulk of the labor force, stability has advantages in terms of productive efficiency as well as personal satisfaction. Thus, even if it could be shown that seniority reduces labor mobility, one could not conclude that this result is necessarily harmful.

Seniority in promotions is often criticized on efficiency grounds. If capable young men find that promotion comes only through serving time and bears no relation to effort, they may decide to exert less effort and initiative. The efficiency of the economy will suffer also through failure to assign the most productive worker to each job.

There is a problem here, but it may not be as serious in practice as it may appear on paper. Many low-skilled, machine-paced jobs leave little scope for differences of ability or effort. There is likely also to be some positive correlation between length of service in a plant and ability to perform successively higher jobs. On many production operations one finds a natural promotion ladder within a work team, and it is reasonable for men to work up from one rung to the next as vacancies occur. The fifth hand on a large paper machine becomes a fourth hand, then a third hand, and finally a machine tender in charge of the crew. Promotions to foremanships and other supervisory jobs are almost always at the sole discretion of management and are made on a merit basis.

As regards seniority in layoffs, it is argued that to give a long-service employee complete job security may cause him to work less diligently than he would with the possibility of layoff hanging constantly over his head. This argument implies that fear, or at least uncertainty about the future, will stimulate maximum effort. On the other hand, it is argued that people work best when they feel secure about their future and that seniority protection will therefore increase efficiency instead of reducing it. This whole question reduces to a difference of opinion over why men work well, a matter on which there is little reliable evidence.

Seniority rules prevent employers from following the traditional practice of "weeding out" the labor force during depression periods. They may even compel an employer to keep relatively inefficient people on his payroll indefinitely. The union replies to this, however, that the employer had ample opportunity to weed out these people during their probationary period in the plant. If he chose to keep them on, he made a mistake and must abide by the consequences. Supporters of seniority argue further that inability of the employer to correct his hiring mistakes in later years will in time lead him to be more careful and make fewer mistakes, with benefit to all concerned.

It should be noted also that the employer retains the right, even after the probationary period, to discharge an employee for gross inefficiency, insubordination, or violation of plant rules. This is normally sufficient to prevent workers from abusing their seniority protection.

Even if it were decided that seniority rules make it more difficult for the individual employer to run his plant at minimum cost, this would not settle the matter from a social standpoint. The workers whom one employer "weeds out" in his search for efficiency must be hired by someone else or must become public charges. Seniority systems may be regarded as a method of distributing the less efficient workers more or less equitably among employers. Slichter points out that if employers were allowed to make layoffs on a strict efficiency basis, men over 45 or 50 would be laid off in large numbers and would have great difficulty in finding new jobs.[9] Seniority rules may prolong their working lives to the age of 60 or 65, with benefit both to themselves and to the economy. Apart from this, the peace of mind engendered by seniority rules must be counted as a positive benefit, albeit one which cannot be measured in monetary terms. Even if seniority did lead to a reduction in total physical output, which is doubtful, this reduction might be more than offset by psychic gain to the workers.

With respect to seniority in layoff and rehiring, then, one may conclude that the positive advantages probably outweigh any adverse effects. One cannot speak so confidently about seniority in promotions, and employers are probably wise in resisting this principle as regards skilled jobs where unusual ability can really show itself.

Discipline and discharge

One of the most delicate areas of day-to-day administration is the application of discipline, including use of the ultimate weapon of discharge. Because seniority now carries so many accumulated rights, discharge is a drastic economic penalty which requires careful con-

---

[9] Slichter, *Union Policies and Industrial Management*, pp. 160-161.

sideration. The union is forced to defend its members against discharge except in the most flagrant circumstances. Yet management must retain reasonable latitude to apply discipline and to enforce minimum standards of efficiency.

The union contract normally recognizes management's right to discipline the work force and to take the initiative in applying penalties "for just cause." What constitutes just cause may be spelled out in the contract itself or in supplementary rules issued by the company. Standard grounds for discipline include continued failure to meet production standards, disobeying instructions of the foreman, persistent absence from work without excuse, participating in wildcat strikes or slowdown, fighting, gambling, drinking, smoking in prohibited areas, and other personal misdemeanors. For each kind of offense there is usually a graduated series of penalties, which may begin with an oral reprimand by the foreman for the first offense, and then go on to written reprimand, a brief suspension from work without pay, a longer suspension from work, and finally discharge. The worker has thus usually had a number of warnings before incurring the ultimate penalty. Some offenses, however, may be considered so serious that suspension or discharge follows immediately.

If a worker contends that he is not guilty of the offense with which he is charged, or that the penalty imposed was too severe, the case is taken up through the grievance procedure. Discharges, because of their serious consequences for the worker, are invariably appealed and a large percentage of them are carried all the way to arbitration. Arbitrators have been reluctant to uphold discharges, especially for long-service workers, unless the offense is serious and the evidence quite clear. The box score of discharge arbitrations shows that in a substantial majority of cases the arbitrator has either reversed management's decision or scaled down the penalty to a temporary suspension from work.[10]

The union check on management's unfettered right of discipline has doubtless improved plant administration in addition to benefiting employees. In pre-union days the right of discharge was often grossly abused. The foreman could take out his temper on those under him without recourse, and favoritism and bribery were common. This produced much injustice without necessarily promoting efficiency. Protection against arbitrary discipline and discharge is probably the most

---

[10] For a detailed analysis, see Orme W. Phelps, *Discipline and Discharge in the Unionized Firm* (Berkeley: University of California Press, 1959).

important single benefit which the worker derives from trade unionism. More than anything else, this serves to make him a free citizen in the plant.

Discussion questions

1. Explain the main ways in which a union might try to restrict the supply of labor. Why is there little use of these methods in practice?

2. What are the advantages and disadvantages of a closed shop to the worker? the employer? the union?

3. "The Taft-Hartley prohibition of the closed shop has had little practical effect and has simply encouraged law violation. It would be better to repeal this section of the Act." Discuss.

4. What are the main arguments for and against the union shop?

5. Is there a conflict between the goal of stable collective bargaining, which is furthered by union-shop agreements, and the goal of maximum freedom for the individual worker? If so, how do you think the conflict might best be resolved?

6. What is the difference between *benefit seniority* and *competitive status seniority?* What are some of the difficulties in measuring seniority for the latter purpose?

7. What are the advantages and limitations of the seniority principle in making (a) temporary layoffs? (b) permanent layoffs? (c) promotions?

Selected reading

Phelps, Orme W., *Discipline and Discharge in the Unionized Firm.* Berkeley: University of California Press, 1959.

Rees, Albert, *The Economics of Trade Unions.* Chicago: University of Chicago Press, 1962.

Slichter, S. H., J. J. Healy, and E. R. Livernash, *The Impact of Collective Bargaining on Management.* Washington: Brookings Institution, 1960.

Slichter, Sumner H., *Union Policies and Industrial Management.* Washington: Brookings Institution, 1941.

Sultan, Paul, *Right-to-work Laws.* Los Angeles: Institute of Industrial Relations, U.C.L.A., 1958.

See also the general references cited at the end of Chapter 7.

9

Issues In Bargaining:
Work Schedules, Work Speeds,
And Production Methods

Unions are less directly concerned with production management than with personnel management. Their concern is limited to points at which production decisions affect the security or satisfaction of workers on their jobs. Unions are concerned that hours of work should be reasonable, that work speeds and work loads should be moderate, and that physical working conditions should be safe and comfortable. They are interested in avoiding sudden and large-scale displacement of labor as a result of technological change. They have sometimes encouraged the use of relatively expensive production methods in order to create additional employment.

The points at which union objectives impinge on production management are the subject of this chapter. The issues discussed have only one thing in common: all involve some aspect of production management, and all have a direct effect on production costs.

HOURS OF WORK

In the early days of American industry the workweek was very long—almost certainly too long to yield highest output per worker. The twelve-hour day and the seventy-two-hour week were the general rule. Employers resisted any reduction in these standards, and pressure for hours reduction came mainly from the trade unions.

There was agitation for the ten-hour day as early as the 1820's. Not until the 1860's, however, did a large proportion of the skilled trades win the ten-hour day, and even then the twelve-hour day remained entrenched in manufacturing. By 1900 the ten-hour day had spread to most manufacturing industries also, but in the strategic steel industry the twelve-hour day continued until the 1920's.

While the struggle for the ten-hour day was still continuing, agitation for the eight-hour day was begun during the 1860's by the National Labor Union and several of the national trade unions. In 1872, near the peak of the post-Civil War boom, a large number of building trades workers, mainly in New York City, struck for and secured the eight-hour day. The strugle was carried on by the AFL after its formation in 1886, the eight-hour day being perhaps the most prominent single objective of the Federation in its early years. The first substantial successes came in the 1890's, and by 1900 the eight-hour day was rather general in the skilled trades. The ten-hour day continued to be the general rule in manufacturing, however, until around 1920. The general adoption of the eight-hour day at this time was due mainly to the increased strength of the trade unions during and just after World War I.

The trade union gains up to this time were achieved largely through bargaining rather than through legislation. The trade unions continually advocated legislation, first for the ten-hour day and later for the eight-hour day, and many state laws were passed on the subject. These laws were usually so weakly drawn as to be ineffectual, however, and they were also rejected repeatedly by the United States Supreme Court as unconstitutional. Until the 1930's, the unions were thrown back on their own economic strength to achieve their objectives.

The next step, reduction of the standard workweek from forty-eight to forty hours, occurred during the 1930's. While the unions continued to be the driving force behind the movement, the new standard week was for the first time imposed by legal regulation—first by the codes promulgated under the National Recovery Administration in 1933-34, and later by the Fair Labor Standards Act of 1938. When this Act was upheld by the Supreme Court, the principle of federal regulations of wages and hours in industries engaged in interstate commerce was firmly established.

The Fair Labor Standards Act, in addition to setting minimum wage rates, provides that workers employed for more than forty hours in any week must be paid one and one-half times their regular rate for the hours beyond forty. The employer is free to work a man fifty or sixty hours if the man is willing, but he has a strong incentive to restrict the man's hours to forty in order to avoid paying overtime. With the exception of the war years 1941-45, most plants have worked a straight forty-hour week since the Act was passed. The Act makes exceptions for plants in food processing and certain other industries so that they can, within limits, average out their weekly hours over a period of months; this enables them to work more than forty hours in the busy season and offset this by a shorter week in the slack season, thereby avoiding overtime payments. The Act does not apply to workers in local industries, which fall outside the definition of interstate commerce, but these are covered by state laws in some thirty of the states and territories. The federal act and most of the state wage-hour laws exclude farm workers, domestic servants, and employees of educational, religious, and other nonprofit institutions.

These laws set only minimum standards, and higher standards may be imposed by union contract. Some unions have now established a standard workweek of thirty-five or thirty-six hours, and require

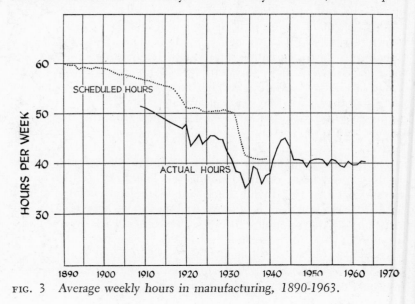

FIG. 3   Average weekly hours in manufacturing, 1890-1963.

overtime payment beyond this point. Some unions require double time for work on Saturdays, Sundays, and holidays. Most contracts also regulate the times of the day and week during which the standard hours are to be worked. One finds clauses concerning the starting and stopping time of each shift, lunch times and rest periods, payment of travel time and waiting time, and numerous other matters.

When hours were very long, unions argued that the workweek should be shortened to reduce the physical and mental strain on workers and to give them more time for recreation, education, and civic activities. Now that hours are quite short, there is more emphasis on hours reduction as a method of spreading work and reducing unemployment. Since World War II mechanization has reduced the need for production workers in a number of major industries and many steelworkers, auto workers, coal miners, and others, have been left unemployed. Some union leaders argue that this unemployment can best be absorbed by shortening the workweek and sharing the available work among more people. The fact that the economy has been sluggish and has not approached full employment since the mid-'fifties lends additional appeal to this line of argument. Since this will probably be an important issue in the next decade, it is worth a little analysis.

The economics of hours reduction

The central issues appear most clearly if we look, not at a single industry, but at the economy as a whole. There is little doubt that a cut in hours can force employers to add more people to their payrolls. Suppose that 10 per cent of the labor force is unemployed; and suppose that to offset this the standard workweek is cut by 10 per cent, from forty to thirty-six hours a week. Then if we assume that the total demand for goods in the economy has remained unchanged, so that employers want to hire *as many man-hours of labor as before,* they can accomplish this by hiring the unemployed. This overlooks any practical difficulties in working out new shift arrangements and the fact that there may not be enough unemployed workers in each industry and locality throughout the country.

What has happened? Total national output remains unchanged.[1]

---

[1] This assumes that the change in the workweek makes no difference to output per man-hour. At present work schedules in the United States this is a reasonable assumption. When hours are very long, however, a cut in the week may raise man-hour output substantially.

Those who were previously unemployed are better off, since they are getting more in wages than they were receiving in unemployment compensation or relief payments. Those who previously had jobs, however, are worse off. If hourly wage rates remain unchanged, their weekly incomes will fall because they are working fewer hours. The unions may insist that weekly paychecks be maintained by raising hourly wages to offset the cut in hours. (A little pencil work will show that it would take an increase of a bit more than 11 per cent in hourly rates to offset a 10 per cent cut in hours.) But if this is tried on a national scale, it will not work. A *general* increase in hourly wage rates will be approximately offset by a rise in the price level; so workers still come out with lower *real* incomes than before. This can be demonstrated also by considering that, if total national output remains unchanged as we have assumed, and if the formerly unemployed workers now get more of this output than before, the remainder of the population must get less.

Moreover, there has been no real increase of employment in the sense of man-hours worked. What has happened is that the man-hours of work available have been spread over a greater number of individuals. To look at it in reverse, unemployment has been spread thinly over the entire labor force instead of being concentrated on a minority of full-time unemployed.

Unemployment represents a gap between the actual and potential output of the economy. A general reduction of hours closes this gap by reducing potential output rather than by raising actual output. It lowers the definition of "full employment" and establishes a permanently lower output ceiling. It is a defeatist solution to the unemployment problem. It would be more constructive to leave the output ceiling unchanged and to raise actual output toward it by energetic use of monetary and fiscal policy.

Suppose now that the economy is operating at full employment. How does the issue of hours reduction appear under these circumstances? A general reduction in the workweek means a reduction in national output, and almost certainly a cut in workers' consumption levels.[2] This does not mean that hours should never be cut from their present level. Against a reduction in consumption must be set a gain

---

[2] This assumes, as before, that a cut of, say, 10 per cent in the workweek means a drop of 10 per cent in each worker's weekly output, i.e., that output per man-hour remains unchanged. The effect on output might not actually be this severe, but it would certainly be in this direction. Nor could workers hope to escape taking some share of this cut by juggling the hourly wage level.

in leisure and a reduction of fatigue and unpleasantness from work. The underlying issue is how workers themselves balance these considerations and what length of week they would prefer if given free choice.

There is reason to think that most workers, if faced clearly with the alternatives, would favor continuing something like the present workweek. The widespread practice of "moonlighting" (holding a second job) suggests that many workers find the hours on their primary job too short to provide the desired balance between leisure and income. Workers are generally eager to work overtime, and insistent that opportunities for overtime be allocated in an equitable way. Pressure for a shorter official week sometimes means, not a desire actually to work fewer hours, but a desire to work as much as before and get additional overtime pay for doing so.[3]

One experienced and perceptive union official put the matter as follows:

Aside from the workers' desire for their paid holidays and paid vacations there is no evidence in recent experience that workers want shorter daily or weekly hours. The evidence is all on the other side. Hundreds of local and International officers have testified that the most numerous and persistent grievances are disputes over the sharing of overtime work. The issue is usually not that someone has been made to work, but that he has been deprived of a chance to make overtime pay. Workers are eager to increase their income, not to work shorter hours.[4]

It seems likely that the workweek will nevertheless continue to decline in future, and to decline faster than workers would spontaneously prefer. The remedy-for-unemployment argument, while superficial, is appealing. The long history of union agitation for shorter hours produces strong institutional momentum in this direction; and

---

[3] In 1962 the I. B. E. W. in New York struck for and won a basic 25-hour week on New York construction jobs. This presumably does not mean electricians will sit idle the rest of the week. Some of them will continue to work longer hours on their regular job, drawing time and a half for the hours beyond twenty-five. Others doubtless do private electrical repair work or have other sideline activities. This appears to have been an income-raising maneuver as well as a work-spreading one.

It is worth noting that employers often prefer to cover production peaks by offering overtime to the existing work force rather than face the expense of hiring additional workers for short periods. See in this connection L. Moses, "Income, Leisure, and Wage Pressure," *Economic Journal* (June 1962), pp. 320-334 and W. Oi, "Labor as a Quasi-fixed Factor," *Journal of Political Economy* (December 1962), pp. 538-555.

[4] George Brooks, formerly Research Director of the Pulp and Sulphite Workers' Union, cited in Melvin W. Reder, "The Cost of a Shorter Work Week," *Proceedings of Ninth Annual Meeting of IRRA* (1956), pp. 207-221.

so does the desire of union officers to take care of unemployed members and to maintain the size of their union. The employed members, who may stand to lose by hours reduction, are apt not to see the issues clearly or to put up effective opposition. There is the further consideration that a union which succeeds in reducing its hours *faster* than other unions can gain a relative advantage, just as a union which raises its wages faster than other unions may win gains for its members. Since each union naturally thinks of the welfare of its own members rather than of broad economic consequences, there may well be a competitive race on the hours front as there has always been on the wage front.

Annual hours of work: vacations and holidays

While scheduled weekly hours of work have remained rather stable since the 'thirties, the number of hours worked *per year* has continued to decline through the spread of paid vacations and holidays. This is largely a post-1940 development. In 1940, only about one-quarter of all union contracts contained vacation provisions. Today more than 95 per cent include vacation plans and the terms of these plans have been steadily liberalized. Vacation periods typically range from one week for workers with one year of service up to three weeks for workers with ten or fifteen years of service. Some unions have won even more favorable terms, and vacations of a month for long-service workers will probably be common before many years.

About three-quarters of union contracts also include a list of holidays, usually numbering from six to eight but ranging as high as twelve in some cases, on which the plant does not operate but workers receive their regular rate of pay. If a worker is required to work on a holiday to maintain continuity of production, he is paid at a premium rate, ranging from time and a half to as much as triple time.

The rapid spread of paid vacations and holidays must be attributed largely to union pressure. It seems unlikely that company policies would have been liberalized at anything like this rate on a voluntary basis.

WORK SPEEDS AND WORK ASSIGNMENTS

Workers have an interest in how much they must produce in return for their wage. In addition to the desire to avoid "working themselves out of a job," workers enjoy a moderate work speed for its own sake.

Too rapid a pace not only robs the worker of any pleasure during the day but leaves him drained of energy and incapable of enjoyment after working hours. But what is a "moderate" pace of work in a particular situation? The workers may have one conception, while supervisors and top management may have quite another. Where there is disagreement over proper work speeds, the union is bound to get involved in bargaining over the issue.

Speed under piecework

The problem of work speeds takes a somewhat different form depending on whether the worker is paid solely on a time basis or whether his earnings are related to the amount produced. Suppose that a plant is operating under the simplest type of piecework system, in which a worker's earnings vary directly and proportionately with his output. Suppose also that it has been decided that a worker of average proficiency on a certain job should earn two dollars per hour. This is a wage decision, the basis for which will be examined in the next chapter. It is necessary next to make a work-speed decision. How many units of output should the worker be required to produce per hour in order to receive two dollars? If twenty pieces is a reasonable amount to require in an hour, the piece rate will be ten cents; if the worker should turn out twenty-five, the piece rate will be eight cents. Thus, this question amounts to asking how many seconds or minutes should reasonably be allowed for the worker to produce a unit of output. At this point the time-study man and the stop watch enter the picture.

Ideal time-study procedure, not always adhered to in practice, is about as follows. The first step is to standardize conditions on the job and to determine the best way of doing it through a methods analysis, including a study of workers' motions on the job. Operators on the job are then trained to use the proper methods until they do so naturally and automatically. This first step is essential to accurate time study, and can often by itself yield large increases in productivity. The next step is to select an operator who appears to be of average speed and ability, and to time his production over a long enough period so that variations in his speed of work can be averaged out. The worker will hardly ever take exactly the same time for two successive units of output. The only way to eliminate these irregular fluctuations in work speed is to time a considerable number of units and take an average. The actual work of timing jobs is a good deal more complex than this brief statement suggests. The timer does not simply measure the time required for the whole process of turning out a unit of output. He breaks the production process down into each separate movement of the worker's hands and body. The time required for each of these movements is recorded separately. This enables the observer to determine whether the worker is using the proper methods, whether he is using them consistently, whether certain motions are taking more time than they should normally take, and even whether the worker is deliberately "holding back" during the time study.

After the time-study man has determined the average time required to turn out a unit of product, certain adjustments must be made in this result. If it seems that the operator was above or below "normal" ability, or that he was working above or below "normal" speed during the study, an adjustment must be made on this account. In addition, allowances are usually added for fatigue, unavoidable delays, necessary personal time, and other possible interruptions to production. At the end of the process one obtains a total of, say, three minutes per unit. This indicates a normal hourly output or "task" of twenty units. If expected earnings on the job are $2.00, the piece rate must be 10 cents.

It is clear that this process is not mathematically precise and that it involves numerous judgments by the time-study observer. Was the man timed actually of average ability? was he using the best methods available? was he working at the right rate of speed? There is an almost unavoidable tendency for workers to slow down while being timed, even when they do not mean to do so, and the time-study man must correct for this as best he can. Again, what allowance should reasonably be made in the circumstances for fatigue, personal time, unavoidable stoppages of production, and other factors?

The greatest difficulty is that the question of what constitutes a proper speed of work is incapable of any strictly scientific answer. Industrial engineers tend to think of the proper or "normal" work speed as the highest rate which a man can maintain week after week without physical deterioration. This is a mechanistic concept which takes account only of physical wear and tear on the worker, analogous to the wear and tear on a machine due to the speed at which it is operated. A worker may well ask, however, "Why should I work that fast? The job will be pleasanter for me if I work at a slower rate. Why isn't my interest in a pleasant job as important as the employer's interest in greater output?" These are pertinent questions. Who is to say just how fast a man should work for the benefit of the employer or the consumer? It seems unavoidable that there will be differences of opinion between production and engineering officials on the one hand, and workers and their union representatives on the other hand, and that actual work speeds must be a matter of bargaining and compromise rather than of scientific measurement.

Unions naturally insist that work speeds cannot be left to the sole judgment of management, and that the union must have a voice in the setting of time standards and piece rates on individual jobs. The procedure under most union contracts is that management has the right to make the initial time study of a job and to set a temporary piece rate on it. The temporary rate automatically becomes permanent unless protested by the union within a certain length of time. If the rate is protested by the union, the job is usually retimed, and the dispute can be carried up through the regular grievance procedure. Some union contracts provide that a piece rate cannot be put into effect at all until it has been approved by the union, but such provisions are rather rare.

In a few industries, the union sets the piece rate and management has the right to protest rates which it believes are unfair. This is the usual procedure in the men's and women's clothing industries, and is due to the special characteristics of those industries. Employers in the clothing industries are usually small, and many of them are transient. They could scarcely afford the engineering staff necessary to determine new piece rates on a great variety of styles and types of clothing. The union, being much the largest organization in the industry, can afford to maintain a staff of rate-setting experts. Piece-rate determinations are made in the first instance by the union rate-setters, with the employer having the right to appeal any decision within a certain period of time.

Piece-rate changes

The other main problem in the administration of an incentive system is to determine the conditions under which management shall be entitled to retime a job and alter the piece rate. The generally accepted principle, written into most union contracts, is "no change in the rate without a change in the job." It is not easy, however, to get agreement on the application of this principle to specific cases. Where management has the upper hand, it will frequently try to take away from the workers the benefit even of their own greater effort or increased skill. A strong union, on the other hand, will often take the untenable position that piece rates cannot be changed unless there is a complete re-engineering of the job. This stand produces inequities in the wage structure because of differing rates of technical progress on different jobs. A job on which management has made many minor improvements or the workers have discovered numerous short cuts may gradually come to yield earnings twice as high as those on another job which requires the same skill and effort but which has undergone no changes in method. When these discrepancies have become sufficiently glaring, even the union will frequently agree to a general overhaul of piece rates. It is politically difficult, however, for a union to subscribe to a step which reduces the earnings of any of its members. The rank-and-file worker regards anything which reduces his earnings as a "rate cut," and he holds the union leaders responsible. In order to feel safe in taking such a step, the leaders must be solidly entrenched in their positions, and the union must be securely established in the plant.

The difficulty of getting agreement on piece-rate changes leads to a good deal of tactical maneuvering by workers and management. Management tries to "sneak up" on jobs where it believes earnings have got too high, and to make just enough changes in the job to justify a new time study. Workers try to hold down their rate of production while a time study is in progress. The time-study man tries to guess how much they are holding back and to correct this in his results. Determination of time standards thus becomes to some extent a battle of wits between the worker and the engineer, in which the latter does not always come out victorious.

There is also a strong tendency for incentive workers to hold down their production at all times, and for different workers on a job to maintain about the same rate of output. Workers who rise much above the accepted rate are called "speed artists," "company men," and other uncomplimentary names. Unless they desist from their high rate of production, they are likely to find that things happen to their machines, that wrenches fall accidentally on their heads, and that they are ostracized by their fellows. The result is that incentive systems usually fail to obtain maximum effort from the faster workers. Their rate of production is limited by social pressures exerted by their fellow workers, while an incentive system requires completely in-dividualistic behavior to produce its full effects.

The agreed rate of output on a job is usually set slightly below the level which the workers think would cause management to retime the job and cut the piece rate. Workers with long experience under incentive systems develop a keen sense of what is a "safe" amount to earn on a particular job, and are careful not to exceed this amount. If too much work is done one day, part of it is hidden overnight and turned in the next day, during which the worker takes it easy. Some workers prefer to work rapidly for several hours, produce their "quota," and then take it easy for the rest of the day. The most serious aspect of these output standards is that they become fixed by custom and persist even after improved methods have made a higher level of output appropriate. Where this happens, the main effect of improve-ments in methods is to increase the amount of leisure which workers have on the job rather than to increase their output.

Restriction of output by incentive workers is not due specifically to union organization, and seems to be as prevalent in nonunion as in union plants. It is not at all certain, therefore, that unionism results in slower work than would prevail without it.

Speed under timework

The oldest form of wage payment, and still a very common one, is at a flat rate of so much per hour. It has often been pointed out that under timework the employment contract is incomplete. There is an understanding as to how much the worker shall be paid, but no understanding as to how much he must produce. It is left to the foreman to get as much work out of him as he can after the wage agreement has been made. Where the job is essentially a hand opera-tion, the foreman has to rely on instruction, admonition, example, cajolery, sarcasm, and the ultimate threat of discharge. In a unionized shop, however, the foreman must stay within limits generally ac-ceptable to the workers under him. Anything which the workers regard as undue "driving" or "pushing" by the foreman is likely to be raised as a grievance by the union.

Where the work is machine-paced, and the worker is mainly a machine-tender, the problem becomes: how fast should the machin-ery run, or how many machines should one worker be expected to tend? Two examples may be cited. In preunion days, automobile assembly lines were run at a speed determined solely by management and which many workers regarded as too fast. When the United Automobile Workers was organized, one of its first actions was to seek determination of assembly-line speeds by the company and the union together. The companies first contended that determination of these speeds was a "management prerogative" which should not be made subject to collective bargaining. The matter was of such great importance to the workers, however, that the union kept pressing the issue and gradually succeeded in bringing assembly-line speeds under joint control in most plants.

Another illustration is the size of machine assignments in the cotton textile industry. A weaver, for example, usually tends a considerable number of looms. As looms have become more nearly automatic, and as improved production methods have been developed, textile companies have tended to increase the number of looms assigned to each worker—sometimes on the basis of systematic engineering studies, sometimes without such studies. The workers usually object on principle to any "stretch-out" of their work assignment, and many spontaneous strikes have occurred over the issue even in nonunion plants. Management usually contends that machine assignments should be made and altered in the sole discretion of management. The unions in the textile industry have never conceded this right, and the size of work assignments has become a major issue in collective bargaining.

The problem of work speeds is intrinsically difficult, because there is no way of determining the proper pace of work with anything like mathematical precision. A faster pace of work means more discomfort to the worker, but lower unit production costs and lower prices to consumers. At some point there must be a proper balance between the interest of workers in a pleasant job and the interest of consumers in high production at low prices. Determination of this optimum, however, seems inevitably to be a matter of judgment. It is neither given by immutable market forces nor is it capable of scientific measurement. Unions may press for a pace of work below the socially desirable optimum, just as management is likely to set a work pace above the optimum point. The outcome in a particular case depends on the relative strength and bargaining skill of the parties, and actual achievement of the optimum work speed would appear to be only a lucky accident.

Incentive work versus time work

Because of these difficulties the basic question of whether workers are to be paid on an hourly or an incentive basis is an important feature of the union contract. Union policy on this point is variable. A few unions, which have experienced employer abuse of incentive systems or have found them unsuited to the conditions of their industries, have refused to work under any sort of incentive plan. The outstanding example among the older unions is the International Association of Machinists, which has long had a constitutional provision against introduction of an incentive system in any shop where it has not previously been used. The building trades unions have also refused flatly to work under piece rates. Among the newer industrial unions, opposition to incentive payment has probably been strongest in the United Automobile Workers, which has succeeded in abolishing this type of payment throughout most of the automobile industry. Some unions which at one time opposed piece rate payment, such as the International Ladies' Garment Workers' Union, later reversed themselves and now favor this type of payment. The reversal occurred when the union became strong enough to control the employers' administration of wage incentives, so that its members could enjoy the benefit of higher incentive earnings without risking a "speed-up" of their work.

Unions have frequently opposed the use of particular incentive formulas, such as the original Bedaux system and other plans under which the amount paid for extra units of output decreases as the worker's output rises. In addition to being inequitable from the workers' point of view, these plans have often been remarkably complicated. It is hard to see how a worker can be motivated to greater output by a system which makes it impossible for him to understand the basis of his paycheck.

Employer preferences also vary considerably. In the heyday of "scientific management" many companies were enthusiastic about the potential output gains from incentive payment. It was not fully understood that realization of these gains depends on careful day-to-day administration of the incentive system, and that without this the company may quickly find itself in a difficult position. Time standards which were set correctly in the first instance become looser over time as a result of technical progress, and this happens at differing rates on different jobs. The general level of earnings is inflated, and relative earnings on different jobs get seriously out of line. Yet workers resist re-timing of jobs, and a strong union may succeed in blocking it for long periods.

From 1940 until about 1955 most manufacturing companies were operating in a sellers' market, in which the main thing was to get out production, and costs were a secondary consideration. Rather than arouse union opposition, many companies allowed their incentive systems to deteriorate. In the tougher economic climate of the late 'fifties and 'sixties, these loose standards and high costs could no longer be afforded. Some companies underwent long strikes to regain control over production standards. And some decided that the gains from incentive payment are not worth the difficulties it creates, and tried to shift back to hourly payment.

PRODUCTION METHODS AND EMPLOYMENT OPPORTUNITIES

An important reason for union interest in production methods is their effect on employment opportunities. Most workers are convinced that jobs are always scarce; it is important, therefore, to protect existing jobs and to create new ones if possible. This belief leads unions to combat technical changes which threaten to displace labor and to seek opportunities for the employment of additional workers.

These practices are particularly likely to develop in industries in which the total number of jobs is declining, such as railroading and "live" musical performances. In such industries, rising unemployment leads the union to seek desperate means of providing a livelihood for its members. Industries with rapidly increasing employment opportunities are less likely to suffer from restrictive practices. Craft unions are also more likely than industrial unions to resist technical change and to adopt make-work rules and policies. Skilled workers stand in particular danger of having their skill undermined, their job opportunities reduced, and the very basis of their craft whittled away by new production methods. An industrial union is less likely to be concerned over whether a particular operation is done by skilled men in one way or semiskilled men in a different way, since in any event the work will be done by members of the same union.

Make-work rules and policies

The effort to create employment, or to prevent a shrinkage of employment, takes many forms. The practices described in this section, however, all have the intent of increasing the number of man-hours of labor which employers must hire. For this reason they are often termed *make-work policies*.

(*a*) Limiting daily or weekly output per worker. This is a widespread practice in both nonunion and union shops, particularly where the workers are paid on a piecework or incentive basis. The motive for limitation of output is partly to make work, partly to avoid rate-cutting and speeding-up by the employer.

The output limitations are frequently quite reasonable at the time they are set, but tend rapidly to become obsolete. It is natural for the output of a work group to rise gradually over the course of time, as a result of improvements in machinery, materials, and methods. If workers continue to produce at a rate determined years in the past, the gap between actual and potential output becomes larger and larger with the passage of time. The consequence is an ever greater volume of unnecessary labor and a progressive inflating of production costs.

(*b*) Limiting output indirectly by controlling the quality of work or requiring time-consuming methods. These techniques are best illustrated in the building trades. While the unions have done a useful service in combating shoddy construction by the less reputable contractors, they have frequently insisted on needlessly high quality in order to justify spending more time on the job. The gradual decline in the number of bricks laid per hour by bricklayers, for example, is usually justified by the union in terms of the care which must be taken to ensure perfect accuracy and soundness in the product. It would seem, however, that this argument has been overworked. Plastering, lathing, painting, and other processes are often done more thoroughly than necessary in order to create additional work.

Another frequent device of the building trades is to require that work be done on the construction site rather than in the factory. Painters often require that all window frames and screens be primed, painted, and glazed on the job. Plumbers in many cities prohibit the cutting and threading of pipe in the factory, and refuse to install toilets and other fixtures that have been assembled at the factory. There has recently been a growing movement toward prefabrication of plumbing fixtures, kitchen cabinets, and even whole kitchen units as a means of reducing production costs. This movement has been resisted by the organized construction workers. The prefabrication of the whole house structure has been resisted even more vigorously.

The restrictiveness of union policies in the building trades, however, should not be exaggerated. Haber and Levinson point out that many new techniques and materials have been introduced into the industry over the past generation. Union opposition to new methods was not nearly so strong during the high-employment 'fifties as it was during the depressed 'thirties. The trades in which restrictive practices are mainly concentrated—painting, plumbing, electrical work, and sheet metal work—represent only about 20 per cent of on-site labor costs on a typical house. Haber and Levinson estimate that the total effect of opposition to new techniques, make-work rules, and other restrictive practices is to raise on-site labor costs by from 8 per cent under favorable conditions to as much as 24 per cent in areas where all union regulations are severely applied. Since labor costs form approximately 30 per cent of the selling price of a house, this means that house prices are raised by from 2 to 7 per cent.[5] These estimates are very rough, but may serve as some indication of the quantitative impact of union policies.

(c) Requiring that unnecessary work be done, or that work be done more than once. Switchboards and other types of electrical apparatus, for example, were in the earlier days always wired on the job. The recent tendency has been to have this equipment wired in the factory, where the work can be done at considerably lower cost. The New York City local and certain other locals of the International Brotherhood of Electrical Workers have refused to install switchboards and other apparatus unless the wiring done in the factory was torn out and the apparatus rewired by union members.

Another example is the "bogus" rule of the International Typographical Union. This provides that when a newspaper uses readymade plates or matrices, as is often done when the same advertisement is run in several papers, the copy must nevertheless be

---

[5] William Haber and Harold M. Levinson, *Labor Relations and Productivity in the Building Trades* (Ann Arbor: University of Michigan Bureau of Industrial Relations, 1956), particularly chaps. VII-IX.

reset, read, and corrected in each paper's composing room. The reset copy is known as "bogus." Although this is mainly a make-work rule, it is sometimes used for bargaining purposes. A publisher may be exempted from the bogus rule in exchange for an outsize wage increase or a guarantee of a certain number of jobs.

(*d*) Requiring stand-by crews or other unnecessary men. This practice is often termed *featherbedding*. The Musicians' Union, for example, attempted to enforce a rule that radio stations which broadcast recorded music or which rebroadcast programs originating elsewhere must employ a stand-by orchestra to be paid for doing nothing. This led eventually to passage of the Lea Act of 1946, which made it unlawful to compel a licensee under the Federal Communications Act to employ unnecessary people, or to refrain from using unpaid performers for noncommercial programs, or to limit production or use of records.

The theater is especially vulnerable to featherbedding because picketing can so easily interfere with attendance. The stagehands' union requires a minimum crew to be hired for any theatrical performance, regardless of whether their services are actually needed, and so does the musicians' union, the electricians', and other groups. The resulting inflation of production costs and ticket prices has contributed to the disappearance of commercial theaters in many cities.

The Motion Picture Projectors' Union has tried for years to require two operators for each projection machine, and has succeeded in some cities. The Operating Engineers asserts jurisdiction over all machines and engines used in building construction, regardless of their source of power. Even if the power is purchased from an electric company, a union member must be there to push the button or turn the switch, which may constitute his whole day's work.

(*e*) Requiring crews of excessive size. This is a common practice among the printing pressmen, longshoremen, musicians, and a number of other unions. By far the most ambitious and successful efforts, however, have been made by the railroad-running trades. They have worked through the state legislatures to get full-crew laws and train-limit laws. The full-crew laws usually provide that the crew shall consist of an engineer, fireman, conductor, and a number of brakemen varying with the length of the train. Seventeen states had such laws in 1960. The train-limit laws limit the number of cars per train,

and are intended to make more jobs for engineers and firemen. The
Arizona train-limit law, however, was invalidated by the U.S. Supreme
Court as having no reasonable relation to safety;[6] and while several
states have train-limit laws on the books, they are not enforced.

The most recent controversy in this area, which is still continuing,
concerns the use of firemen on diesel locomotives. On high-speed
passenger trains, one can make a case for having a fireman in the
cab with the engineer at all times. But the unions have been inclined
to insist also on use of firemen in local passenger, freight, and yard
service. The railroads contend that many of these jobs are unnecessary
and should be eliminated. This and other issues of train manning
were at the heart of the 1963 rail dispute, which came to the point
of a strike and led Congress to pass an act sending the dispute to
compulsory arbitration.

(f) Requiring that work be done by members of a particular occupational group. The object is to enlarge the job territory of the group,
so that there will be the maximum amount of work available to be
divided among its members. Pursuit of this objective takes various
forms. A common rule is that prohibiting employers or foremen from
working at the trade. This prevents supervisors from reducing the
amount of work available to employees by doing it themselves, and
from acting as pace-setters by working alongside the men. Another
common rule requires that skilled men be used for semiskilled or
unskilled work. The Typographical Union frequently requires that
proof be read and revised by union members before going to anyone
outside the composing room. The building trades often require that
material handling be done by craftsmen rather than laborers.

Some Teamsters locals, on the other hand, prohibit drivers from
assisting helpers in unloading their trucks. This does not make more
work for drivers, but creates more jobs for helpers, so that total employment is increased. Longshoremen in some ports refuse to shift
from ship to dock work, or even from one ship to another of the
same company, thus compelling use of multiple crews. In this, as in
other respects, the railroad unions "have gone to unbelievable extremes in restricting duties, taking the position that every item of
work *belongs* to some employee. If that employee is deprived of the
opportunity to do the work, he is entitled to compensation first. In
addition, the one who does the work is entitled to compensation.
In many instances the amount of compensation given to both is a

---

[6] *Southern Pacific Company* v. *Arizona,* 325 US 761.

day's pay. The result is that two days' pay may be given as compensation for a trivial amount of work." [7]

What can one say about the economic effects of make-work rules and policies? Pressure for them arises mainly from the threat of unemployment, but they are clearly not a desirable method of coping with unemployment. Seasonal and intermittent unemployment can best be dealt with through efforts to regularize production, supported by adequate public employment services and unemployment compensation systems. Cyclical fluctuations must be countered by fiscal policy and other types of governmental action. A long-run decline in the demand for a product requires that workers be transferred out of the declining industry.

It may be said that this is a harsh view. Why not cushion a drop in the demand for labor by creating additional jobs? Why not have everyone in an industry somewhat underemployed, instead of some workers totally unemployed? If the expedients adopted were temporary, and were used only until more basic remedies could be devised, one might make out a case for their use. The difficulty is that restrictive work rules and practices are scarcely ever discarded. They persist even during periods of full employment, when they are clearly inappropriate. They tend to freeze in each industry the maximum number of people ever employed there in the past. Over the long run, therefore, they create all sorts of anomalies in the structure of employment and production.

It is by no means clear that make-work policies are beneficial even to the group imposing them. There is a limit to the costs which a union can impose on an industry, set by the demand curve for the industry's products. If the union adds to the industry's costs through excessive employment, it must accept a lower level of wages. If restrictive practices were abandoned and excess employment eliminated, employers could be obliged to pay higher wages to the workers remaining in the industry.

It is easier to point out the undesirability of make-work rules than it is to do anything effective about them, particularly since the issue is often not as clear-cut as it seems at first glance. As Slichter points out:

It is not always easy to determine when a union is "making work." There are some clear cases, such as those in which the union requires that the work be done twice; but the mere fact that the union limits the out-

---

[7] Slichter, Healy, and Livernash, *op. cit.*, p. 319.

put of men or controls the quality of the work (with effects upon output), regulates the size of crew or the number of machines per man, or prohibits the use of labor-saving devices, does not in itself mean that the union is "making work." In such cases it is necessary to apply a rule of reason and to determine whether the limits are unreasonable. Opinions as to what is reasonable are bound to differ, but failure to apply a rule of reason would be to accept the employer's requirement, no matter how harsh and extreme, as the proper standard.[8]

The industrial unions and technical change

The quickened pace of mechanization and automation[9] since World War II has reduced employment opportunities in coal mining, basic steel, automobiles, and numerous other industries, and has caused unions in these industries to be concerned for the job security of their members. In general, their reaction has not taken the form of trying to block technical change, a policy which would have had little chance of success. The new equipment in these industries is so labor-saving and cost-reducing that employers have a powerful incentive to install it, and the unions could at most fight a delaying action for a limited period. So they have concentrated instead on ways of cushioning the impact on their members.

In bituminous coal mining, mechanization proceeded very rapidly between 1945 and 1960, both through mechanization of underground mines and acceleration of strip mining. The amount of mechanical equipment per worker doubled and output per man-hour also doubled. Since demand for coal was declining over this period, employment dropped by about 60 per cent. The United Mine Workers did not oppose the mechanization movement. Indeed, the union encouraged mechanization by raising wages rapidly even in the face of severe unemployment. It also secured substantial employer contributions for medical and hospital care, insurance, and pensions. But coal miners did not retire nearly fast enough to keep pace with the shrinkage of employment opportunities; and in the early 'sixties many coal fields had unemployment rates of 15 to 20 per cent.[10]

---

[8] Slichter, *Union Policies and Industrial Management*, pp. 165-166.

[9] The meaning of "automation" is discussed in Chapter 13, in connection with trends in labor demand and employment. The writer is inclined to regard it as complex mechanization, differing in degree, but not in kind, from mechanization in earlier decades.

[10] For a thorough analysis of mechanization in this industry, see C. L. Christenson, *Economic Redevelopment and Bituminous Coal* (Cambridge: Harvard University Press, 1962).

In automobile production, too, technical change has not been a disputed issue. The industry has a tradition of annual model changes, rapid technical innovation, and wide management flexibility in production methods. The fact that the industry operates on time payment rather than incentive payment eliminates the need for bargaining over new time standards as production methods change. Disagreements are focused on the speed of the assembly line, which has been subjected to joint control.

The record of certain other industries is less tranquil. The rubber industry operates mainly on incentive payment. During the 'forties and 'fifties this industry developed traditions of considerable autonomy by work gangs in the plant, loose incentive standards protected by deliberate restriction of output, and resistance through slowdowns and quickie strikes to management pressure for greater efficiency. As Killingsworth points out, "the syndrome of loose incentive standards, informal limitation of output, some excessive manning, and slowdowns and wildcat strikes may be considered a subterranean approach to job security." [11] In this industry there has often been a question whether, if new equipment were introduced, the workers would allow it to operate at anything like full capacity. In some cases the companies have had to threaten to build, or actually build, a new plant in a new location to break through restrictive practices and secure maximum benefit from new equipment.

The basic steel industry has a contract provision (clause 2B in the agreement with U.S. Steel and other major companies) which restricts the right of management to change established local work rules. This is an old and conservative industry, and many of these practices are of long standing. They relate to such things as crew size on various machines, seniority, distribution of overtime, work assignments, shift scheduling, contracting-out, layoffs, wash-up time, and lunch periods. The clause does not interfere with automation or other forms of technical change. Indeed, since change in equipment is a recognized basis for changing work practices, the clause may serve to encourage technical change. But it does contribute in some cases to overmanning and other forms of inefficiency. A company demand in 1959 for elimination of this clause was taken by the union as a

---

[11] Charles C. Killingsworth, "Cooperative Approaches to Problems of Technological Change," in G. G. Somers, E. L. Cushman, and N. Weinberg, eds., *Adjusting to Technological Change* (New York: Harper & Row, Publishers, 1963), pp. 61-94.

prelude to wholesale elimination of jobs and displacement of workers, and led to a record 115-day steel strike. The strike ended inconclusively, and the issue is not really resolved. In 1962, however, the union won substantially increased provisions for job security, which will probably make it more willing to accept reasonable changes in work methods.

The Kaiser Steel Company of California broke away from the other companies during the 1959 strike and reached its own agreement with the union. Among other things the agreement established a nine-man tripartite committee, including three eminent neutrals, to recommend "a long-range plan for equitable sharing between the stockholders, the employees, and the public of the fruits of the Company's progress." The plan recommended by the committee and put into effect by the Company early in 1963, is quite complicated [12] but has two essential features. First, it provides that no worker shall be laid off as a result of technical change. Displaced workers go into a work reserve, pending reassignment to another job in the company. Workers may be laid off on the usual seniority basis in the event of a drop in production. But shrinkage in the number of workers required for a given production volume as a result of technical progress will be taken care of through normal attrition of the labor force.

Second, savings in labor and materials costs per unit of product over the levels prevailing in 1961 are to be shared between workers and the company in agreed proportions. The employee share is set at 32.5 per cent, this being the average relation between labor cost and total cost which has prevailed in the past. Wage and benefit increases given by other major companies in the industry are offset against this fund, and the balance is distributed each month as a cash bonus. If the gain-sharing fund falls below the increases given by other companies, Kaiser undertakes to make up the difference, so that its employees cannot lose under the formula. One object of the plan is to get rid of incentive payment, which covers about 40 per cent of plant employees and has led to inflated and inequitable earnings on many jobs. Incentive workers can choose to remain on incentive or to go over to hourly payment. In the latter case they receive a lump-sum cash bonus equal to about 2½ years incentive

---

[12] For a detailed description, see *The Kaiser-Steel Union Sharing Plan* (New York: National Industrial Conference Board, 1963), [Studies in Personnel Policy, No. 187].

earnings, and they also come under the gain-sharing formula. If they remain on incentive, they do not participate in gain-sharing, and management has the right to re-time the jobs. No new incentive jobs are to be created in future.

In the mass production industries, then, things seem to be moving in the direction of a trade, in which management gets reasonable flexibility in changing production methods while the union gets provisions to cushion the impact on its members' jobs. The cushioning devices include pension plans, with emphasis in some cases on early retirement; severance pay for workers released permanently; supplementary unemployment benefits, beyond those provided by the social security system, for workers laid off for shorter periods; elaborate in-plant seniority and work-sharing systems; and arrangements under which workers in a plant which is closed down permanently can "follow the work" to other plants of the same company, with preferential hiring rights. The assumption is that the number of production jobs in these industries will continue to decline; and the object is to ensure that the shrinkage of employment will be orderly and will do minimum damage to the present labor force.

While this sort of trade involves costs for the employer, these may be much more than repaid by the opportunity to introduce productivity-raising improvements. A dramatic case in point is the West Coast longshore industry. From the recognition of the union in 1934 until the late 'fifties this industry was marked by poor union-employer relations, chronic guerilla warfare, and a host of inefficient work practices designed to use as much labor as possible. These included overmanning, dual handling of cargo, limitation of sling loads, and resistance to containerization and bulk cargo-handling methods. Eventually, however, union leaders became convinced that this delaying action could not succeed indefinitely, and that they would do better to make a trade. In 1960 they negotiated an agreement which gave employers virtually a free hand in overhauling work rules, installing labor-saving devices, and increasing efficiency generally. The quid pro quo for the union was a promise that no registered longshoreman would be laid off as a result of the changes, a guaranteed annual wage, and a pension fund permitting voluntary retirement at sixty-two. These guarantees are underwritten by a fund to which employers will contribute 4 to 5 per cent of longshore payrolls. "But their savings are considerably greater. During negotiations, an estimate was presented showing that the elimination of *only* the multiple-handling rules, in Los Angeles *alone*, would save the employers more than their total fund contributions." [13]

This was a special arrangement to meet an aggravated problem and is not necessarily repeatable elsewhere. But it illustrates the possibilities of peaceable accommodation and mutual gain.

PHYSICAL CONDITIONS OF WORK

Union officials spend much time negotiating with management over various aspects of physical working conditions—heating, lighting, ventilation, and cleanliness of the plant; safety arrangements; sanitary facilities; dangerous or objectionable features of particular jobs; provision of adequate cafeterias and restrooms; and many other matters. Most of these matters are discussed informally in the plant from day to day, since they are usually too small to arise as issues in contract negotiations. Taken as a whole, these matters are quite important to the workers; but they are so varied and heterogeneous that it is difficult to find any way of generalizing about them.

The nearest one can come to generalizing is to distinguish three kinds of improvement in working conditions. The first involves plant improvements which produce an increase in labor productivity more than sufficient to cover the cost of making the improvements. It is usually assumed that management will be alert to such opportunities and will seize them of its own accord, but this is not always the case. Unions can do valuable work by pointing out improvements which perhaps should have been obvious to management but were not, and which once discovered can be installed with a net gain to the company as well as the workers.

Second, one may distinguish improvements which are a matter of *degree*, and where beyond a certain point the additional cost outweighs the gain in labor productivity. Consider a plant using very hot processes, the natural temperature of which would be 130 degrees Fahrenheit. By installing an air-cooling system the plant can be cooled to any desired temperature. The lower the temperature, however, the

---

[13] C. C. Killingsworth, *op. cit.*, p. 83.

greater the cost of the system. Suppose also that worker productivity increases steadily as the temperature falls. It will pay the employer to reduce the temperature of the plant down to the point at which the additional cost of cooling just equals the additional revenue obtained from increased output. If this point turns out to be 95 degrees, this is the optimum plant temperature from the employer's standpoint.

The workers, however, might feel happiest at a temperature of 70 degrees. There is a divergence here between the interests of workers and management. In a perfectly competitive labor market, management would presumably have to pay a higher wage rate to compensate for the unpleasant working conditions. In practice, however, competitive forces work poorly in improving working conditions for the same reasons that they work poorly in reducing hours of work. One cannot be at all sure, therefore, that unpleasant conditions will actually be offset by a wage premium.

Suppose now that a union comes on the scene and compels the employer to reduce the temperature of the plant from 95 degrees to 80 degrees. Depending on the circumstances of the case, the added cost of doing this might or might not be absorbed out of existing profit margins. For the sake of argument, however, suppose that the cost is entirely transferred to buyers of the product through higher prices. The union, in effect, has taxed consumers a certain amount in order to improve the daily lives of its members in the plant. Is this action economically beneficial or harmful?

The problem appears even more clearly in a third type of case, where there is no effect on productivity, and the only consequence of the improvement is pleasanter "plant living conditions" for the workers concerned. The money cost of the improvement is felt initially by the employer, later by buyers of the product. The social cost consists in the economic resources which were used in making the improvement. How can one say whether, in a particular case, the benefit to the workers was worth the expenditure of resources? How far should consumers be taxed in order to pay for improved working conditions? How far should the satisfaction of man as consumer be reduced in order to increase that of man as producer?

There seems no way of giving any general answer to these questions. One is certainly not entitled to assume that all plant improvements of this type are economically harmful, or that all are beneficial. A separate decision must be made in each case on the basis of informed judgment and without the benefit of much quantitative evidence.

Discussion questions

1. What would be the main consequences of reducing the standard workweek in manufacturing from forty hours to thirty hours (a) during a period of heavy unemployment, and (b) at a time of full employment?

2. Unions usually argue that, when hours are reduced, workers' weekly earnings can be maintained by an offsetting increase in hourly wage rates. Discuss the feasibility of this program (a) for a single industry, and (b) for the economy as a whole.

3. How might the length of the workweek be determined in a purely competitive labor market? What are the practical difficulties in the way of such a determination? Is there any objective way of discovering what length of workweek workers prefer at a particular time?

4. How much would you estimate that make-work rules and policies reduce the potential output of the economy? Can anything be done to reduce the frequency and impact of such rules?

5. Why is it difficult for unions to resist technical changes in mass production manufacturing? What provisions have unions negotiated with employers to cushion the labor-displacing impact of such changes?

6. "Work speeds and work assignments are a matter for management decision. Union interference in these matters is fatal to productive efficiency and harmful to the public interest." Discuss.

7. "Time study is a scientific procedure which leaves no possible room for argument or bargaining over work speeds." Discuss.

Selected reading

Barnett, George, *Chapters on Machinery and Labor*. Cambridge: Harvard University Press, 1926.

Christenson, C. L., *Economic Redevelopment in Bituminous Coal*. Cambridge: Harvard University Press, 1962.

Florence, P. Sargant, *Economics of Fatigue and Unrest*. New York: Holt, Rinehart & Winston, Inc., 1924.

Gomberg, William A., *A Trade Union Analysis of Time Study*, 2nd ed. Englewood Cliffs, N.J.: Prentice-Hall, Inc., 1955.

Kennedy, Van Dusen, *Union Policy and Incentive Wage Methods*. New York: Columbia University Press, 1945.

Mathewson, Stanley B., *Restriction of Output among Unorganized Workers*. New York: Viking Press, 1931.

Palmer, Gladys L., *Union Tactics and Economic Change*. Philadelphia: University of Pennsylvania Press, 1932.

Presgrave, Ralph, *The Dynamics of Time Study*, 2nd ed. New York: McGraw-Hill Book Company, Inc., 1945.

Slichter, S. H., J. J. Healy, and E. R. Livernash, *The Impact of Collective Bargaining on Management*. Washington: Brookings Institution, 1960.

Somers, G. G., E. L. Cushman, and N. Weinberg, eds., *Adjusting to Technological Change*. New York: Harper & Row, Publishers, 1963.

10

Issues In Bargaining: Wages And Income

There has been more research and writing on wage issues in collective bargaining than on nonwage issues. This does not necessarily mean that the wage issues are more important; but they tie in more clearly with the main body of economics, and so economists feel more at home with them.

A difficulty in discussing wage bargaining at this stage of the book is that we have not yet analyzed the operation of labor markets and the economic forces bearing on wages. This is the task of Chapters 16-19. The union is in a sense intruding into pre-existing market arrangements; and the interesting question is how much difference unionism really makes. The best we can do here is to review some of the essential background concepts as we go along.

THE MARKET CONTEXT: THE FIRM

We may begin by recalling the notion of a purely competitive labor market. Concretely, this would be a town or city and the surrounding area from which people can conveniently drive to work—a radius of perhaps twenty or thirty miles in this automobile age. For the market to be purely competitive, employment in each firm must be small, relative to the number of workers available. There must be no collusion among employers in recruiting labor or setting wages. A certain proportion of the workers, at least, must be well informed about job vacancies and willing to move to better jobs; and there must be no cultural or institutional obstacles to free movement of labor. Finally, the level of total demand for labor must be high enough so that there is no problem of involuntary unemployment.

Under these conditions the market would establish a wage rate for each kind of labor, and each employer would have to pay very close to this rate. Paying a little more would get him all the labor he might need for expansion, and paying a little less would cause his labor force to melt away to other places. The individual worker's bargaining power, which consists in his ability to quit the job with impunity, would be adequate to protect him against substandard wages.

Quite commonly, however, one or more of the conditions of pure competition is missing. One employer may be large, relative to the size of the market. In the limiting case of the company town, the worker cannot change jobs without leaving the community. Or there may be substantial unemployment in the area, so that workers hesitate to change jobs for security reasons. Or the benefits which accrue with increasing seniority may tie each worker closely to his present employer. Thus the worker's bargaining power, which derives from his freedom to quit, may be seriously reduced; and an employer may be able to pay less than the competitive wage, while retaining most of his labor. Technically, the employer is a monopsonist in buying labor.

Even a monopsonistic employer will rarely find it feasible to *cut* wages. But in a world where wages are always moving upward, this does not matter. Simply by lagging behind the upward movement, he can open up a gap between his wage and what other employers are paying for similar labor. The substantial variation in rates paid by different employers for the same kind of work, one of the most familiar facts of labor markets, will be documented in Chapter 19.

A union coming into this situation can bargain the employer up to the market wage level. Assuming that the firm is of average efficiency, there need be little effect on employment,[1] and the main

---

[1] One cannot say that there will be no effect. Companies do not like having their profits reduced, even where profits are above normal; and they are likely to react by trying to raise efficiency, which may mean dispensing with some labor. This is presumably beneficial from an over-all economic standpoint, and it need not be upsetting to the work group concerned. A moderate shrinkage of employment through efficiency improvements can usually be taken care of through normal attrition of the labor force—retirements, voluntary quits, etc.—with no need for layoffs.

I am familiar, of course, with the argument that forcing up the wage rate of a monopsonistic employer will, up to a certain point, cause him to increase employment instead of reducing it. But I do not believe that this supposed reaction is of much practical importance, for reasons which will be explained in Chapter 19.

effect will be a transfer from profits to wages. Note, however, that this is a once-for-all shift. Once the low-wage employer has been brought up to the market wage level, this possibility of gain from union organization disappears.

THE MARKET CONTEXT: THE INDUSTRY

But how is the market level itself determined? What decides the prevailing level of wages in an industry? And how may the industry wage level be affected by the appearance of a union?

The market forces affecting industry wage levels may be grouped under the customary headings of supply and demand. For any industry one can construct a demand curve for labor (*DD* in Figure 4), which will slope downward from left to right in the usual way. The higher the relative wages of (say) bituminous coal miners, the fewer miners will be employed. The elasticity of the labor demand curve is of great practical importance. If demand is reasonably elastic, as it has been drawn in Figure 4, a substantial increase in relative wage rates will mean a substantial loss in employment. If on the other hand the demand curve is highly inelastic, the industry wage level can be

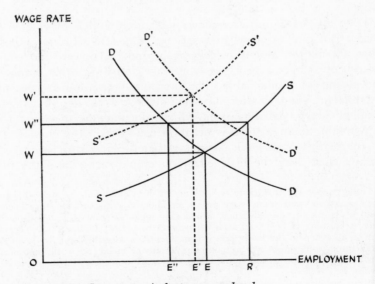

FIG. 4 *Union influence on industry wage level.*

pushed up with only a slight drop in employment. The union leader faced with an inelastic labor demand curve is a happy man indeed.

What determines the elasticity of demand for labor in a particular industry? The simplest approach to an answer is to inquire what will happen as the industry's wage level is raised, everything else remaining unchanged. First, the employer will have an added incentive to replace labor by machinery, but the feasibility of this varies greatly from industry to industry. Second, the increase in wage costs will eventually produce a price increase for the industry's products. The price increase needed to cover a given wage increase depends on whether labor costs are a large or a small proportion of total production costs. Third, the price increase will cause some reduction in sales and consequently in output and employment. The size of this drop depends on the elasticity of demand for the industry's products. Thus the labor demand curve will be least elastic, and conditions for wage-raising will be most favorable, where product demand is inelastic, labor cost is a small proportion of total cost, and further mechanization is difficult.

Each industry also has a supply curve of labor (SS in Figure 4), sloping upward from left to right. The higher the wages of coal miners relative to wages in other industries, the more workers will seek mining employment. The steepness of the labor supply curve depends on several things: whether the work requires native abilities found in only a limited number of people, whether some people find this kind of work much more attractive than others, earnings in other occupations from which additional workers for this industry would have to be withdrawn, whether the jobs are located in large population centers or isolated areas, and whether appreciable learning time and training costs are involved.

Elasticity of labor demand and supply depend on the length of time considered. Both curves are likely to be very inelastic in the short run, because reactions on both sides of the market take time to accomplish; but elasticity may be much higher if one looks a few years ahead. The degree of foresight exercised by union and management officials will thus affect their reasoning about the consequences of a certain wage level.

One must remember also that Figure 4, like any supply-demand diagram for a single industry, is constructed on the assumption of fixed conditions in other parts of the economy. Specifically, wage rates in all other industries are taken as given. When we speak of an increase in miners' wage rates, we mean an increase *relative to the wage rates of other workers.* An increase for miners which simply parallels increases for everyone else is no increase at all for present purposes. It is differential rates of increase—one industry moving ahead more rapidly than others—which are under discussion here.

If the demand and supply curves are as shown in Figure 4, the equilibrium wage for the industry will be OW. But suppose the union does not like this wage level. What can it do about it? First, it might try to manipulate the supply-demand situation, to shift DD or SS or both, so as to raise the equilibrium wage level. If the curves were shifted to D'D' and S'S', the equilibrium wage would rise from OW to OW'. A rightward shift (increase) of demand or a leftward shift (decrease) of supply will always produce a higher wage. The new employment level may be either higher or lower, however, depending on the shapes of the curves and which has been shifted the most. In the situation shown in Figure 4, employment would drop slightly from OE to OE'.

While union action along these lines is conceivable, it is not very important in practice. Some unions, to be sure, have tried to increase demand for the products of their labor. New York locals of the Ladies' Garment Workers' union have contributed substantial amounts to publicizing their city as the style capital of the world. The Hatters' union has struggled valiantly against the bareheaded trend among American men. Unions have often lined up with employers to demand tariff protection against foreign competition. The total effect of these demand-raising activities is not large. Nor have unions worked very hard to restrict labor supply to particular trades or industries, for reasons explained in Chapter 8.

There is a second and much more direct route to higher wages. Simply ask for them. Without attempting to alter DD or SS, the union may demand a higher wage, say OW''', and threaten to shut down the industry indefinitely if the demand is not granted. If the union is strong and determined, employers may have to agree and adjust to the new wage level. Product prices will typically be raised, sales and output will be reduced, and employment will drop to OE''. The new situation is one of disequilibrium, since the number of workers (OE'') whom the industry is willing to employ at the higher wage rate is considerably less than the number of workers (OR) who would like to work in the industry at that wage rate.

In a small-scale, competitive, and partially-unionized industry the existence of an excess labor supply $(E''R)$ will probably encourage the establishment of nonunion shops, which will undercut the union scale and may compel the union to retreat from OW'' to some lower level. This has been a chronic situation in textiles, clothing, shoes, and other light manufacturing industries. In a large-scale, highly concentrated industry under firm union control, however, the surplus workers may have no recourse. If they are sensible and business conditions are good, they will gradually shift to other lines of work (SS will drift upward to the left) and the visible labor surplus in the industry will disappear. Thus after a time maintenance of an industry wage level which is "too high," in the sense of being above the market equilibrium, will leave no visible trace in the form of unemployment. The long-run effect is simply that fewer workers are employed in the industry than would be employed under competitive conditions, and more workers must therefore find employment elsewhere. This will tend to increase labor supply and depress relative wage levels in nonunion sectors of the economy.

BARGAINING OVER THE INDUSTRY WAGE LEVEL

So much for the market context. Within this context, the union sets about driving a wage bargain. How do union leaders decide what wage level to push for? What determines the strength of employer resistance to union demands? What is the typical outcome? Is the relative wage level of a strongly unionized industry a good deal higher than it would be under nonunion conditions?

Theorizing on these matters has not gotten very far. One's first thought is to draw analogies with business monopoly. A monopolistic seller of a product is usually assumed to maximize profit. So perhaps the union is trying to maximize something. But what? It will scarcely try to maximize the *wage rate*, which would mean moving up the demand curve to the left, until only a few workers remain in the industry earning fantastically high wages. There is no particular reason why it should try to maximize the industry's *wage bill* (the wage rate × employment), since the wage bill goes to the workers rather than the union. It will be interested in *employment*, but to maximize employment it would have to set wages at just the competitive level—not a very ambitious objective, and one which workers could attain without the union. So most writers, in the end, fall back on rather vague formulations: a union will try to maintain wages above the competitive level (how much above?), but at the same time it will take some interest in employment (how much interest?).

Factors affecting union wage decisions

Unions and employers do not live in a static world, and do not conceive of their problem as finding the best location on a diagram such as Figure 4. The economy is in constant motion. Demand curves for most products are normally shifting upward, labor supply curves are also shifting upward, and wages are rising. The practical question confronting union and management negotiators is *how much* the industry's wage level should rise in a particular year. How much should the union demand? How much can employers afford to concede?

Union leaders do not approach this question with fixed principles of wage policy. Their thinking, like that of businessmen, is pragmatic rather than theoretical; intuition and judgment play a greater role than formal logic. One can say only that several factors will usually have some influence on the leaders' thinking. The most important of these are rank-and-file sentiment, the wage increases currently being won by other unions, the economic situation of the industry, and (if the industry is not completely organized) the problem of nonunion competition.[2] Each of these factors deserves a few words of comment.

The attitudes of rank-and-file workers on wage matters were described in Chapter 1, and this discussion need not be repeated here. During prosperity periods in which the cost of living is rising, workers generally feel that their money wages should also rise. During depression, however, they are unwilling to concede that wages should be reduced. They are not impressed by the argument that, since the cost of living has fallen, they can take a money wage cut and still be well off as regards real wages. The principle of "no wage reductions" is thus firmly grounded in membership sentiment. It is true that unions have accepted wage reductions in dire circumstances. This

---

[2] For a general discussion of the factors influencing union wage policies, see John T. Dunlop, *Wage Determination Under Trade Unions* (New York: The Macmillan Company, 1944); Albert Rees, "Union Wage Policies," Industrial Relations Research Association, *Interpreting the Labor Movement* (1952), pp. 130-148; and Arthur M. Ross, *Trade Union Wage Policy* (Berkeley: University of California Press, 1948).

acceptance is always regarded, however, as a failure on the part of union leaders, and too many such failures will spell the end of their leadership.

The *second* important factor in the thinking of union leaders is the wage increases currently being won by other unions. Union members, by reading the papers and talking to workers from other plants in the city, get a feeling of what is happening to wages in other industries. Unless their own leaders are able to keep up with the general pace, the prestige of the leaders is likely to suffer. On the other hand, a leader who consistently does better than the average strengthens his standing both in his own union and in the general labor movement.

This factor is particularly important where unions are competing for membership in the same industry. The wage gains made by one group can be used as a campaign argument to win members away from the other, and neither group can afford to be outdone in wage increases. Several interesting cases of this sort have been reported by Ross.[3]

A *third* factor which the union leader must consider is the economic situation of the industry at the time. If profits are high and the business outlook is good, he can afford to make large demands. If business is declining and profits are falling, he may have to be content with holding the present wage level. Most union presidents have a shrewd knowledge of the structure and financial prospects of their industry. This knowledge is derived from frequent discussions with employers throughout the country and long experience in negotiating with them, supplemented by the work of the union's research department and by governmental and trade reports. In many cases the union president knows more about the industry and has a broader view of its problems than does any single employer. The late Sidney Hillman was the most profound student of the men's clothing industry in the country, and John L. Lewis probably had a more acute understanding of the coal mining industry than anyone in management or elsewhere.

Although union leaders realize that there is an upper limit to what a company or industry can pay at a particular time, they do not necessarily take employers' statements about ability to pay at their face value. They believe that ability to pay is somewhat flexible; within limits, a company can pay more if it has to pay more. Any experienced union leader has had numerous experiences of wage

---

[3] Ross, *op. cit.*, chap. 3.

increases which it was claimed during negotiations would bankrupt the company, but which the company later managed to bear. Employers have cried "Wolf!" so often that the union hesitates to believe them even when their plight is really desperate.

A *fourth* consideration is that, if there are nonunion plants in the industry, the union's ability to push up wage rates in the unionized plants will be limited by the probable reaction of nonunion employers. A good illustration of this is found in the cotton textile industry. Although almost all cotton textile workers in New England are union members, only about 25 per cent of the southern cotton-mill workers are in the union. Since the industry is highly competitive, the union cannot push the wage level of union mills in the South much above the wage level of the nonunion mills. When the union is considering a wage demand, therefore, the key problem is what the nonunion mills will do. It is safe to demand eight cents per hour from the union mills only if the nonunion mills will come close to matching this increase. Similarly, since the New England mills are in competition with the southern mills, the union cannot demand much more in New England than it can get in the South. The nonunion mills in the South thus occupy a strategic position in the wage structure of the industry. A similar situation exists in other branches of the textile industry, in seamless and full-fashioned hosiery, and in some clothing lines, such as work clothes, shirts, underwear, and cotton dresses.

The existence of nonunion plants in an industry limits the union's ability to get wage increases during periods of prosperity; and during depression, wage cuts in the nonunion plants are likely to compel wage reductions in the union plants as well. Most of the cases in which unions have been forced to take substantial wage cuts during depression are to be found in industries which are highly competitive and which contain a considerable proportion of nonunion plants. An attempt by the union to hold up the wage rates of union plants during depression while nonunion plants are cutting wages and prices will mean that the union plants will lose more and more business and may eventually be forced out of existence. Unless the union knows when and how far to give way, it may find itself with no members at all.

The strength of employer resistance

Union policies are thus shaped partly by the economic situation and partly by "political" or organizational considerations—membership sentiment, interunion rivalry, and union coverage of the industry. Employer reasoning about wages is more heavily economic in character. The employer starts from a rough estimate of conditions during the year ahead. What is likely to happen to product prices? Prices may be largely determined for the company by leaders of the industry or by market competition, or they may be to some extent within the company's own control. How much will the company be able to sell at the expected prices? This estimate is a crucial and very difficult one, for it involves a forecast of general business conditions, of demand for the products of a particular industry, and of the firm's competitive position within the industry. From the sales forecast one can derive a production plan, an estimate of labor and material purchases, and a financial budget showing expected profit or loss for the year. Note that it is expected *future* profits, not past profits, which the company considers important for wage bargaining. Past profits are bygones, important only to the extent that they provide some clue to possible profits in the months ahead.

Management is now in a position to visualize the budget consequences of an increase in wages. What would an increase of five cents or ten cents per man-hour do to labor costs and estimated profits? At what point would it become necessary to raise prices in order to cover higher wage costs? Would other companies in the industry go along with a price increase? What effect would a price increase have on the physical quantity sold and on income from sales? During a period of high employment labor supply may also be a major consideration. How large a wage increase is necessary to keep pace with other employers in the local labor market, and to attract and retain an adequate labor force?

After making these calculations, management comes up with the wage change—usually an increase but conceivably a decrease or no change—which would be preferable from its point of view. The size of this figure, and the degree of resistance which management will offer to union demands for a larger increase, depends on several factors:

(1) The proportion which labor costs form of total production costs. In the petroleum refining industry, where labor costs average 5 per cent of total costs, a 10 per cent increase in wages will raise total costs only by half of one per cent. In the high-grade pottery industry, where labor costs form about 70 per cent of the total, a similar wage increase will raise total costs by 7 per cent. The impact

on company budgets and profit prospects is clearly more drastic in the latter case, and management resistance will be correspondingly stiffer.

(2) Competitive and demand conditions in product markets. If prices in the industry are controlled by tacit agreement among the leading producers, so that cost increases can be converted quickly and smoothly into price increases, management has less incentive to resist wage demands than it would in a small-scale competitive industry with wide-open pricing. Further, if price increases are expected to lead to a small drop in sales (low elasticity of product demand), management has less incentive to resist than if price increases would cause a substantial drop in sales.

(3) In addition to management's incentive to resist, one must consider its ability to resist. This is a function of the size and financial strength of employers and usually works in the opposite direction from the preceding point. A small hosiery company has greater incentive than U.S. Steel to resist union demands, but it has much less ability to do so.

(4) Of dominant importance in a particular year is the stage of the business cycle. If the economy is going into a recession most companies will be reluctant to grant any wage increase and may even demand reductions. This is not merely because profits are declining but also because of uncertainty over how fast and far the recession will go. During a period of rising business, on the other hand, most companies find their profit estimates and their wage-paying ability rising quite rapidly. Moreover, as unemployment shrinks many companies find it necessary to raise wages in order to attract and hold labor. For both reasons management will take it for granted that some increase is "in the cards" and will argue only over the size of the increase. The relatively weak resistance of most employers throughout the 'forties and 'fifties was due mainly to the fact that there were only three brief and mild recessions during this period.

(5) The employer's position on wages is related also to his general strategy toward the union and its leaders. He may take a firm stand on wages at a particular time in an effort to weaken the union, or to weaken one faction in the union as against another. On the other hand, he may make wage concessions in order to strengthen "reasonable" union officials with whom he has good relations against insurgents from the rank and file. Moreover, wages are only one of perhaps twenty or thirty issues involved in the contract negotiations.

The employer may make concessions on wages in order to hold firm against the union shop; or he may stand firm on wages and offer adjustments in the pension program or vacation rules. Wage bargaining cannot be divorced from bargaining over other terms of the contract.

Long-term agreements and wage formulas

With management and union positions thus established, the wage issue is bargained out through the procedures described in Chapter 7. Depending on the severity of the pressures impinging on the two parties, on their relative economic strength and staying power, on the stage of the business cycle, and on the tactical skill of negotiators, the bargain may come out closer to the union's or to the employer's figure.

Until recently wages and other issues were fought out every year in annual contract negotiations. Since 1950, however, there has been a marked trend toward longer agreements. Most of the major agreements [4] in the United States now run for three years or longer, and only about 10 per cent are still on an annual basis. The reasons include growing employer acceptance of unionism as a permanent institution; the fact that on many non-wage issues—union security, seniority rules, grievance procedures and arbitration—standard practices have been developed which both parties are willing to live with and which do not need to be renegotiated frequently; and the desire of employers to avoid the turmoil, expense, and uncertainty of annual negotiations. A major negotiation can tie up most of top management's time for an extended period. More and more companies have become convinced that this is not necessary, and have tried to stabilize their contract arrangements on a longer-term basis.

Most workers, however, have come to expect that their wages will rise at least once a year. For a long-term contract to be feasible, therefore, it must contain provisions for adjusting wages during the life of the contract. One possibility is a *wage reopening clause*. This permits wages to be renegotiated, normally once a year, during the life of a multi-year contract, but other issues cannot be reopened until the contract expires. About one-quarter of the workers under

---

[4] A major agreement is defined by the Bureau of Labor Statistics as one covering 1,000 or more workers. In 1961 there were 1,733 such agreements in the country, with a total coverage of 8.3 million. ("Major Union Contracts in the United States, 1961," *Monthly Labor Review*, October 1962).

major agreements in 1961 were covered by wage reopening clause.

Another common provision is the *cost-of-living escalator clause*. This provides that wages shall be reviewed frequently, usually every three months or every six months, and shall be adjusted if the B.L.S. Consumers' Price Index has changed by a certain amount. The G.M.— U.A.W. agreement, for example, provides that wages shall be reviewed quarterly and shall rise 1 cent per hour for each 0.5 point change in the C.P.I. Wages also escalate downward with price declines, though the agreement usually sets a floor to downward escalation. Escalator clauses were especially popular during the rapid price inflation of the Korean War, and have since declined somewhat in popularity. They are still common in mass production manufacturing, however, and about a quarter of all workers under major agreements are covered by this sort of provision.

A third common provision is the *deferred wage increase*, under which subsequent wage increases are built into the contract at the time it is signed. The first instance of this was the "annual improvement factor" negotiated by General Motors with the United Automobile Workers in 1948 as part of the price of a three-year agreement. This has been continued in subsequent agreements. The 1961 agreement, for example, provided that each year during the contract the rate for each job would rise by 2½ per cent or six cents per hour, whichever was greater. The intent of the percentage formula is to preserve the relative position of different jobs in the company wage structure.

Similar agreements were negotiated by the other major automobile companies in 1950. Beginning in 1955, the practice spread to basic steel, electrical equipment, rubber, meat packing, trucking, railroading, and numerous other industries. By 1961 about half the workers under major agreements had this sort of provision, either standing alone or in conjunction with a cost-of-living escalator clause. Unlike the auto agreements, however, most other industries provide a flat annual increase of so many cents per hour instead of using a percentage formula.

It is an interesting question whether these preplanned increases cause an industry's wage level to advance more rapidly over a span of years than it would have done through annual negotiations. This might happen for at least two reasons. First, annual negotiation would probably lead to low wage increases in recession years. A long-term contract with prearranged increases may wash out the effect of recession. It is doubtful, for example, that the steel industry would have given a nine-cent an hour increase at the bottom of the 1958 recession had it not already undertaken to do so in the boom year of 1956. Second, since the union can count on the wage increases assured by the annual improvement factor and by the cost-of-living escalator, it can concentrate its bargaining strength behind other demands, such as larger fringe benefits. The total cost to the employer may be enhanced.

There is no conclusive evidence on this point, and experience has doubtless varied from industry to industry. The most thorough investigation of the subject concludes that "on balance . . . the wage formula and its by-product contracts probably raised the rate of wage increase during the years 1955-60, particularly during the 1958 recession." [5]

Unionism and the industry wage level

How does all this bargaining over wages work itself out? Do unions succeed in pushing up the wage levels of their industries relative to nonunion industries, and relative to the rates which would prevail in the absence of unionism?

These questions are difficult to answer from statistical evidence. There are two main approaches to the problem. The *cross-section method* may be illustrated as follows: take a large number of cities, in some of which the carpenters are fully organized, in others partly organized, in others unorganized. Divide the carpenters' wage in each area by the wage of some base group which is entirely unorganized, say retail clerks. Then if one finds that where carpenters are fully organized their wages are 50 per cent above those of clerks, while in unorganized cities they are only 25 per cent higher, the difference can be taken as a rough measure of union influence. But this method is not foolproof. It assumes that carpenters are comparable from area to area, that retail clerks are also fully comparable, that the earnings of clerks are a good index of the area wage level, and that unionism is the only factor operating to produce the observed variation in wage ratios. None of these things is likely to be entirely true.

The *time-series approach* works with rates of increase in industry

[5] Joseph W. Garbarino, *Wage Policy and Long-Term Contracts* (Washington: Brookings Institution, 1962), p. 111.

wage levels over the course of time, and tries to correlate the rate of wage increase with the degree of union organization. Here again there are difficult logical problems. Should we compare *percentage* increases in wages or *cents-per-hour* increases? This makes a difference, because the same number of cents per hour will be a larger percentage increase for a low-wage industry than a high-wage one. From what year should the comparison start—1929, or 1940, or 1950? Different base years will yield different results. How do we know that wage relations among industries were "right" in the base year? Is the percentage of workers in an industry who are union members a good indicator of union strength? How take account of the fact that many forces other than unionism are constantly at work to change relative industry wage levels?

The evidence assembled to date suggests that some unions at some times have been able to raise their relative wages, while other unions at other times have not.[6] Such craft groups as the building trades, printing trades, and railroad operating trades seem to have been able to raise their wages on the order of 15 to 25 per cent. Among industrial unions, the Amalgamated Clothing Workers is estimated to have had about a 20 per cent effect on wages in the 1920's, and the United Mine Workers an effect of about this size in the 1950's. There has been little study of the Teamsters' Union, but one would surmise that it has had some wage-raising effect. The unions in mass production manufacturing have also been little studied, but Professor Rees ventures the judgment that "in the light of what we know about other unions, an effect of 10 to 15 per cent for the strong unions in this group, such as the steelworkers, does not seem unreasonable." [7]

Other unions, such as the Textile Workers and Hosiery Workers, have had little influence on wages because of inability to organize their respective industries and control nonunion competition. And some well-organized unions, including the Amalgamated Clothing Workers and the Street Railway Workers, have had little wage-raising influence in the years since World War II, perhaps because they are operating in declining sectors of the economy. The situation varies also as between boom and depression periods. Union influence

---

[6] The basic studies in this area are summarized in Albert Rees, *The Economics of Trade Unions* (Chicago: University of Chicago Press, 1962), chap. IV; and in H. Gregg Lewis, "The Effects of Unions on Industrial Wage Differentials," in the N.B.E.R. conference volume *Aspects of Labor Economics* (Princeton: Princeton University Press, 1962).

[7] *Op. cit.*, p. 79.

is felt most strongly in depression, when unions maintain wages or even keep them moving upward, while nonunion wages stagnate or decline. During an inflationary period such as 1940-48, on the other hand, nonunion wages are pulled up rapidly by demand forces, while the fact that union wages are set by contract for a fixed period may actually retard their advance.

Even for successful unions during successful periods, the estimates of union influence are mostly of the order of 10 to 20 per cent. This seems surprisingly low. Considering that elasticity of demand for labor varies widely among industries, and that some industries are much more expansive and profitable than others, one might expect some unions to have done substantially better than this. Why haven't they? One reason may be that many union officials function as "lazy monopolists" rather than aggressive monopolists. The politics of unionism compels them to keep up with the wage procession, but not necessarily to forge much ahead of it. They would prefer to keep out of trouble both with employers and with their members, and this dictates a certain conservatism in wage demands.

Second, even in an organized economy ideas of equity and reasonable wage relationships retain considerable force. If wages for a particular group, instead of being 20 per cent above the competitive level, came to be 50 or 75 per cent above it, other groups of workers might be resentful. Employers would feel on strong ground in resisting such demands, and would have public support in so doing.

Finally, during periods of high employment the labor market limits the wage differences which can exist among industries for similar types of work. If certain industries fall too far below the level of the highest-wage industries, they will no longer be able to recruit and hold an adequate labor force. When this limit has been reached, the unions in the high-wage industries, while they may continue to push up their absolute wage rates, will no longer be able to improve their relative positions. Instead, they will simply pull up the wage levels of the low-wage industries at the same rate at which their own wages are rising. It is as though one had two men tied together by a rope in which there is at the moment a certain amount of slack. If one of the men decides that he wants to go in a certain direction, he can walk forward until the rope is pulled taut. After that he can go no farther unless the man on the other end of the rope moves in the same direction at the same rate.

Because of these various checks, the tendency toward wage distortion under collective bargaining may not be so serious as some have feared. Only time and experience, however, will provide definite evidence on this point.

WAGE STRUCTURE: INTER-FIRM DIFFERENCES IN AN INDUSTRY

It was pointed out in Chapter 7 that there is pressure on a union to equalize the wage levels of different firms selling in the same market. In local industries there is a tendency toward wage equalization within the city, though there may be considerable variation in wage levels from one city to the next. In manufacturing industries where employers compete on a regional or national basis, there is a tendency toward leveling up of wages throughout the country. We shall be concerned in this section mainly with the economic effects of national wage equalization in manufacturing industries.[8]

It should be noted at the outset that "wage equalization" has several possible meanings: equality of the *lowest wage rate* in each plant, often termed the "common labor rate"; equality of all *job rates* in each plant; equality of *piece rates* in each plant; and equality of *labor cost per unit of output*. Each of these objectives has been pursued by one or another union at various times. Equalizing wages in one of these senses, however, will not produce equality in the other senses; and pursuit of these differing objectives will clearly have different economic consequences. Imposition of uniform hourly rates, for example, may work serious hardship on a plant with relatively inefficient workers, equipment, or management; its lower output per man-hour means that its unit labor costs are above the remainder of the industry. Uniform piece rates work no such hardship; if the workers in a particular plant produce little, by the same token they are paid little. This does not mean that the latter arrangement is necessarily preferable, but it is quite different.

Since it is not possible to discuss each type of wage equalization in the space available here, we limit ourselves to a few remarks on

[8] See the chapter on "The Standard Rate" in Sidney and Beatrice Webb, *Industrial Democracy* (London: Longmans, 1902); D. A. McCabe, *The Standard Rate in American Trade Unions* (Baltimore: Johns Hopkins Press, 1912); R. A. Lester and E. A. Robie, *Wages under National and Regional Collective Bargaining* (Princeton: Princeton University Industrial Relations Section, 1946); and Thomas Kennedy, *Significance of Wage Uniformity*, Industry-wide Collective Bargaining Series (Philadelphia: University of Pennsylvania Press, 1948).

the effects of installing a uniform scale of hourly job rates throughout an industry. This is in some ways the clearest case, and is probably the most important in practice.

Effects of wage leveling

The effects of wage leveling will depend on why wage rates formerly differed in different plants of the industry. The reasons are usually complex and vary from one industry to the next.[9] Two factors, however, are of outstanding importance:

1. The wage-paying ability of plants may differ because of variations in technical efficiency. Some plants may be newer, closer to optimum size, better designed, better located relative to materials and markets, or have other advantages. Managerial capacity also varies, and two managements may get different results from very similar plants.

2. Plants may be located in different areas with different local wage levels. Large cities typically have higher wage levels than smaller cities in the same region, the northeastern states have higher wages than the southeastern states, and so on.

The first effect of union pressure for wage equality is to test whether the low-wage firms are actually paying as much as they are able to pay. Allegations of inability to pay are not always well founded, and the union requires convincing evidence. Second, union pressure frequently forces management to step up efficiency and increase the firm's ability to pay. It may be objected that this "shock effect" works only the first few times it is applied, but a few times may be sufficient to raise the firm's efficiency substantially.

But what happens when everying possible has been done in this direction and the union comes up against irremovable differences in plant efficiency? Continued pressure for wage equalization will then tend to eliminate some of the less efficient plants from the industry. Elimination of these plants will make more business available for the more efficient plants and encourage them to expand their operations. In the end, there may be little change in total output and

---

[9] For a more thorough analysis than can be given here, see Lloyd G. Reynolds and Cynthia H. Taft, *The Evolution of Wage Structure* (New Haven: Yale University Press, 1956), chap. 7.

employment in the industry, but there will be considerable redistribution of employment. Jobs will disappear at some places and new jobs will open up at other places, possibly far distant from the first. The long-run effects may be economically beneficial; the immediate effects will be disturbing to the employers who are shut down and to their workers. Indeed, if union members in a particular plant become convinced that to bring their wages up to the national level will cost them their jobs, they will usually vote to accept a lower wage and keep the plant in operation. This is particularly true where the plant is geographically isolated and the members would have to travel some distance to find new employment. In such cases even the national union officers may be willing to tolerate some departure from wage equality.

This is one reason why, even in a strongly organized industry, one rarely finds complete uniformity of wage scales. Most plants will cluster closely around a single wage level, but one will usually find that the union has left a few plants at lower levels because these plants are unable to pay the standard rate and yet it seems expedient to keep them in operation. One may also find that in some of the most efficient plants the union has yielded to the temptation to extract a little more than the prevailing scale. In general, however, unions hew closer to the principle of "the standard rate" than to the principle of "ability to pay."

Where plants are located in different communities with different wage levels, wage equalization may have some effect on the geographical location of industry. The fact that some communities have lower wage levels than others acts as an inducement to new plants to establish themselves in those communities. Specifically, there is an inducement for new plants to spring up in small towns rather than large cities, and in the southern states rather than in the North. The effect of wage leveling is to remove this inducement. If the union insists on the same wage level in all parts of the country, there is no longer any reason for employers to prefer one locality *on grounds of labor cost*, though they may still have preferences based on access to raw materials or markets. The effect is to reduce, if not eliminate, movement of industry from North to South and from large cities to small towns. Whether this effect is desirable is certainly debatable, and the factors to be considered are not all economic.

The most celebrated issue is that of the "North-South wage differential." The reasons for the development of this differential have not been studied as thoroughly as would be desirable. There is good reason to think, however, that it is not due mainly to differences in the intrinsic efficiency of labor in the various states.[10] There is no clear evidence that workers performing under identical plant conditions are less efficient in Georgia than in New York. The main reason for the wage differential, as will be argued in Chapter 18, seems to be the fact that the supply of labor, relative to the number of job opportunities available, is considerably greater in the South than in the North. The existence of the differential has induced migration of industry from North to South and migration of labor from South to North, and this migration has tended over the past several decades to narrow the difference in wages between the two regions.

Suppose now that unionism should become sufficiently strong in the South to eliminate the differential entirely—at least as regards manufacturing industries operating in a national market. What will be the consequences? The incentive for workers to move North and industry to move South will certainly be reduced, but it will not be entirely eliminated. The pressure of population growth in the South will still force many people to move North in search of job openings. Many industries will still find better natural resources and other locational advantages in the South. This is true, for example, of the pulp and paper industry, which is learning to make efficient use of the quick-growing southern pine.

If labor should turn out to be less efficient in the South than in the North under identical conditions, wage equalization would work a hardship on southern industry. There is no clear evidence, however, that this is the case. In industries where substantial equality of wages has already been established, such as the paper and cotton textile industries, there is no indication that the southern plants are less profitable than the northern, or that they are losing out in the competitive struggle.

The effects of a wage equalization program thus depend a great deal on the factors responsible for the previous wage differentials. They depend also on what it is that the union is trying to equalize—

---

[10] Richard A. Lester, "Trends in Southern Wage Differentials Since 1890," *Southern Economic Journal*, XI (April 1945); "Diversity in North-South Wage Differentials and in Wage Rates within the South," *Southern Economic Journal*, XII (January 1946); and "Southern Wage Differentials: Developments, Analysis, and Implications," *Southern Economic Journal*, XIII (April 1947), pp. 386-394.

plant minima, hourly base rates, piece rates, or labor costs. For reasons explained earlier, equalization of piece rates places less of a burden on the less efficient employers than does equalization of hourly base rates. The effects of wage equalization also depend on how the program is put into effect—how rapidly the leveling is carried out, how high the level is set, how many exceptions are permitted, and whether the program is undertaken during a period of prosperity or depression. The fact that the marked equalization of wages in many industries during the 'forties and 'fifties has not had very serious economic repercussions may be due partly to the high level of employment and business profits during this period.

WAGE STRUCTURE: OCCUPATIONAL WAGE RELATIONSHIPS

A major issue in any plant is the relative wage rates which should be paid to men at different occupational levels. Should the top craftsman be paid 30 per cent more than the common laborer, or 50 per cent more, or 100 per cent more? And where should intermediate jobs be located within this range? Wage differences which appear microscopic to higher management may be significant to workers in terms of status as well as income.

The top and bottom of the plant wage structure are somewhat constrained by market pressures. There is something like a general market for common labor in an area and also for machinists, toolmakers, electricians, and other skilled occupations. Many semiskilled jobs are unique to a particular industry, however, and even jobs which carry the same title may differ considerably in content and skill requirements from plant to plant. For these jobs the labor market provides no clear guidance. A hierarchy of wage rates grows up in the plant, based on observation of wage schedules in other companies, on supervisors' estimates of job worth, and on informal pressures from the workers themselves. Once established, these occupational wage schedules tend to persist through custom. When asked to explain why their wage schedule looks as it does, many plant managers will say, "We have always done it that way," or, "It just grew up that way."

Reliance on custom alone, however, is not always satisfactory. It is particularly unsatisfactory as an answer to workers or union officials who complain that a particular rate is too low and should be raised. During the past twenty years or so, therefore, management has turned increasingly to systems of "job rating" or "job evaluation" which purport to provide a scientific basis for determining the relative worth of different jobs. The operation of job evaluation is described in some detail in Chapter 19. Briefly, it involves selection of a set of criteria by which the value of a job is to be judged —physical effort required, skill and education required, degree of responsibility for materials and products, and so on. Each factor is assigned a range of possible values, say from one to ten. Each job in the plant is then analyzed and given a point rating with respect to each factor. Totaling these points gives the total rating of the job. Finally, the point ratings are converted into cents per hour to yield a schedule of wage rates. Management likes the definite standards provided by a job evaluation because they make for administrative uniformity and simplicity in handling wage matters. Job evaluation also provides a yardstick by which management can appraise and answer complaints by workers or the union.

Unions have tended to be critical of job evaluation. A job evaluation system, the union argues, logically precludes bargaining over rates for particular jobs. It thus prevents the union from giving service to its members on wage grievances. It freezes the wage structure into a form which is more difficult to criticize and attack. Union objections to a particular rate can be met simply by bringing out the formula and showing that the rate is in line with the point score for the job. Job evaluation, in short, tends to take determination of job rates out from under collective bargaining and place it within the sole discretion of management.

Most union officials believe that the only test of a sound wage rate is whether both union and management agree to it. They believe that the workers in the plant have a better idea than anyone else of the relative worth of different jobs, and that the wage scale should reflect workers' opinions. Wherever union members feel that a particular job is underpaid, the union should be free to bargain with management for a rate revision. For these reasons a union will usually object to job evaluation unless it has an opportunity to negotiate over the structure of the system and to participate in the work of rating individual jobs.

Over a long period of time, the occupational wage structure may be greatly altered by the way in which *general* wage increases are made. The union may bargain for so many *cents per hour* "across the board," or it may bargain for an increase of so many *per cent* in existing wage rates. Increases on a percentage basis will keep the percentage relationship between different occupations unchanged. Increases which give an equal number of cents per hour to all jobs will gradually narrow the percentage spread between the top and bottom of the wage structure.

Many unions, and particularly industrial unions including all workers in the plant, prefer equal cents-per-hour increases. They prefer, that is, a gradual leveling-up of skilled and unskilled rates over the course of time. An important reason for this policy is that most of the members of an industrial union are in the lower wage brackets. A wage-leveling policy is therefore popular with the members and politically advantageous to union leaders.

There are limits to such a policy, however, and in recent years some unions have reversed themselves in order to prevent disaffection in the skilled segment of their membership. The United Automobile Workers has sought several special increases for the skilled tool and die makers, partly because of the danger that they might secede to a rival craft union. The United Steelworkers, after a decade of securing uniform cents-per-hour increases, shifted in 1947 to increases which raised the higher-rated workers more than the lower-rated workers. Subsequent increases have also been made on this basis, and the percentage relation among different job classes has remained almost unchanged.

Viewed in the broad, it is hard to find any marked influence of unionism on the spread between skilled and unskilled wage rates in the United States. To the extent that unionism has had any effect, this has been in the direction of narrowing the spread. There are many other reasons, however, for the declining gap between the skilled and unskilled over the past thirty years, as will be explained in Chapter 18. Unionism seems to have had only a minor influence when compared with these other factors.

SUPPLEMENTARY INCOME PAYMENTS

The modern union agreement has been described as "a contract with a fringe on top." But the term "fringe benefits," coined during World War II when such provisions were minor, is no longer appropriate. These items now constitute a large and growing proportion of workers' incomes and employers' payroll costs.

Quantitatively most important is payment for time not worked. This includes the vacation and paid holiday provisions noted in the last chapter. It includes also a great variety of provisions relating to travel time, wash-up time, paid lunch periods, pay for being called in when no work is available, pay for idle time because of machine breakdowns, and similar matters.

A second major category is "private social security" programs designed to protect the worker and his family against loss of income due to death, retirement, disability, illness, and unemployment. Employer contributions to these private plans are now comparable in size to their payroll taxes under the public Social Security system.

In many industries there is a continuing threat of labor displacement through technical change, which has led to a variety of provisions for cushioning the shock. About one-sixth of union contracts now provide severance pay for permanently laid-off workers, and these provisions are certain to grow in number and generosity. Other automation-related clauses include provision for early retirement, guarantees of being kept on the payroll until a new job assignment can be found, guarantees of some minimum number of hours work per week, retraining allowances, and payment of family moving costs to some other plant of the same company.

The private social security programs deserve additional comment. They have grown up because the public Social Security system leaves many risks uncovered, and provides rather low benefits even for covered risks; and because they have definite advantages for workers, management, and the union. Workers gain greater security, and largely in a nontaxable form, whereas a direct wage increase of the same amount would be taxed. Employers feel that these programs are helpful in holding labor, since benefit rights are usually related to length of service. Union officials also have an incentive to innovate in this area. A wage increase of 5 cents an hour is undramatic; but a new medical plan costing the same amount may win the leaders much kudos.

At one stage employers contended that pensions, insurance, health programs, and similar matters were within the sole discretion of the company, and that the union was not entitled to bargain about them. But the NLRB and the courts held otherwise, and they are now firmly established as proper subjects for collective bargaining. Union pressure has doubtless caused them to be extended further and faster than they otherwise would have been.

A substantial majority of union members are now covered by collectively bargained *pension plans*. Pension rights normally increase with length of service up to some specified maximum. The intent is usually to bring a long-service worker out with a retirement income, including Social Security as well as the private pension, equal to about half of his regular pay. One-quarter of the present plans, however, provide more than half pay, and bargaining pressure will obviously be in the direction of further liberalization.

A second major area is *health and welfare plans*. These almost always include life insurance and death benefits, hospital care, and surgical care. In addition, a majority of plans include general medical care, cash indemnity for accidental death or dismemberment, and compensation for wage loss due to illness or accident. Health and welfare funds, like pension funds, are supported mainly through payments by the employer, though about one-third of the covered workers also contribute. The funds are normally administered by a joint committee of union and management trustees—indeed, Taft-Hartley provides that the employer *must* participate in fund management. Congressional investigations in the late 'fifties, however, uncovered numerous cases in which union officials had managed to "milk" the fund—by paying themselves large salaries as fund administrators, by throwing business to a favored insurance broker and receiving a "kickback," by setting up relatives or friends as insurance agents, or even by forming a new insurance company to handle the business. The Welfare and Pension Plans Disclosure Act, passed in 1958 and strengthened in 1962, provides for full reporting of fund operations to the Secretary of Labor, requires bonding of fund administrators and employees, and sets criminal penalties for false reports, embezzling, kickbacks, and other malpractices.

A less common but growing type of program provides for *supplementary unemployment benefits*. The first SUB agreement was negotiated in 1955 between the United Automobile Workers and the major automobile companies, representing a compromise of the union's long-standing demand for a "guaranteed annual wage." A similar plan was negotiated in basic steel in 1956, and the idea has since spread to flat glass, can manufacturing, merchant shipping, and a number of other industries. Under the commonest arrangement the employer contributes so many cents per man-hour to a trust fund, from which workers who become unemployed can draw benefits for a specified number of weeks. The intent is to supplement the benefits provided by the state unemployment compensation systems, which usually amount to less than half of the worker's normal weekly earnings, and to bring him out with something like two-thirds of his normal earnings. Experience during the 1957-58 and 1960-61 recessions indicates that these plans can contribute substantially to alleviating hardship and stabilizing consumer purchasing power.

All categories of wage supplement together amount to a substantial part of employers' payroll costs. A U.S. Chamber of Commerce survey of ninety-one identical companies shows that the cost of wage supplements rose from 14.6 per cent of total payrolls in 1947 to 26.4 per cent in 1961. The largest items in 1961 were payment for time not worked, including rest periods and lunch periods (11.3 per cent of payrolls); contributions to pension, health, and other private security programs (8.7 per cent of payrolls); and legally required payments under public programs (4.5 per cent of payrolls). The total 1961 cost of wage supplements was about seventy cents per payroll hour, or over $1,400 per year per employee.[11]

The Chamber of Commerce survey includes mainly the larger companies, and its results are doubtless high for the economy as a whole. A U.S. Bureau of Labor Statistics survey, which shows that average expenditure for selected wage supplements by manufacturing industries in 1959 was thirty-eight cents per hour or 16 per cent of gross payroll, may be more representative.[12] All sources agree, however, that wage supplements have increased rapidly since 1945, and that this increase is still continuing.

Most of the money going into supplements would probably have gone otherwise into direct wage payments. If so, union pressure has served mainly to alter the form in which workers receive their remuneration rather than to increase the total amount of remuneration. But one cannot rule out the possibility that unions, by attacking on two fronts rather than one, have achieved some increase in total worker income and in employers' payroll costs.

This suggests the question whether union leaders have gone further in shifting income from direct wage payments to fringe benefits than union members would have chosen of their own accord. There are

---

[11] U.S. Chamber of Commerce, *Fringe Benefits 1961* (Washington, D.C., 1962). This survey is conducted and published every two years.

[12] U.S. Bureau of Labor Statistics, *Employer Expenditures for Selected Supplementary Remuneration Practices for Production Workers in Manufacturing Industries, 1959*, Bulletin No. 1308 (Washington, D. C. 1961).

some indications that this may have happened. In one interesting case, employees of the Ford Motor Company were given an opportunity to vote on two alternative contract proposals. One contained a pension program and seven cents per hour general wage increase, the other a fifteen-cent wage increase and no pension. The workers voted three to one for the larger wage increase.[13] This does not demonstrate, of course, that the workers' judgment is correct. They may be shortsighted, and union officials may be protecting their long-run interests by winning protection against economic risks.

Discussion questions

1. What is the significance of the *elasticity* of an industry's demand curve for labor? On what factors does elasticity depend?

2. "The proper wage level for an industry is determined by intersection of its labor demand and labor supply curves. Union efforts to alter this level are bound to be either futile or harmful." Discuss.

3. What are the main methods which a union may use to shift an industry's labor demand curve or labor supply curve?

4. Describe the process by which union leaders typically formulate their wage demands. What are the main considerations which they must take into account?

5. What are some of the factors influencing the degree of management resistance to union wage demands?

6. How would you try to determine statistically whether some unions have raised the wage level of their industries relative to other industries? Would you expect to reach conclusive results? Why, or why not?

7. What would be the main consequences of an effort by a national union to establish uniform schedules of hourly wage rates in all companies in an industry?

8. What are the most important types of supplementary income payment now being made in American industry? Should these payments be considered "wages" in the same sense as direct wage payments?

Selected reading

Dunlop, John T., *Wage Determination Under Trade Unions.* New York: The Macmillan Company, 1944.

Garbarino, Joseph W., *Wage Policy and Long-term Contracts.* Washington: Brookings Institution, 1962.

---

[13] See B. M. Selekman, S. K. Selekman, and S. H. Fuller, *Problems in Labor Relations,* 2nd ed. (New York: McGraw-Hill Book Company, 1958), pp. 370-380.

Kennedy, Thomas, *Significance of Wage Uniformity.* Philadelphia: University of Pennsylvania Press, 1949.

Kennedy, Van Dusen, *Union Policy and Incentive Wage Methods.* New York: Columbia University Press, 1945.

Lewis, H. Gregg, ed., *Aspects of Labor Economics.* Princeton: Princeton University Press, 1962.

Phelps Brown, E. H., *The Economics of Labor.* New Haven: Yale University Press, 1962.

Rees, Albert, *The Economics of Trade Unions.* Chicago: University of Chicago Press, 1962.

Reynolds, Lloyd G., and Cynthia H. Taft, *The Evolution of Wage Structure.* New Haven: Yale University Press, 1956.

Ross, Arthur M., *Trade Union Wage Policies.* Berkeley: University of California Press, 1948.

Schultz, George P., *Pressures on Wage Decisions.* New York: John Wiley & Sons., Inc., 1951.

Simmler, Norman J., *The Impact of Unionism on Wage-Income Ratios in Manufacturing.* Minneapolis: University of Minnesota Press, 1961.

Slichter, S. H., J. J. Healy, and E. R. Livernash, *The Impact of Collective Bargaining on Management.* Washington: Brookings Institution, 1960.

Slichter, Sumner H., *Basic Criteria Used in Wage Negotiations.* Chicago: Association of Commerce and Industry, 1947.

Stieber, Jack, *The Steel Industry Wage Structure.* Cambridge: Harvard University Press, 1959.

Wright, David McC., ed., *The Impact of the Union.* New York: Harcourt, Brace & World, Inc., 1951.

11

Strikes, Strike Tactics,

And Strike Prevention

It has been said that war is a continuation of diplomacy by other methods. Similarly, the strike is a continuation of bargaining by other methods. The possibility of a strike is a prerequisite of free collective bargaining, just as the possibility of war is indispensable to national sovereignty. This is not to say that either wars or strikes are desirable, but simply that they are harder to eliminate than appears at first glance and that any effort to eliminate them requires some alternative way of settling disputes.

Why do strikes happen? How much harm do they do? Under what circumstances, if any, should unions and managements be prohibited from "slugging it out"? What methods might be developed for settling disputes in essential industries without a stoppage of production?

WHY STRIKES OCCUR

In an average year of the nineteen-fifties, about one-eighth of union members in the United States were involved in strikes. The average length of these strikes was fifteen days. Thus the amount of time lost through strikes averaged about two days per union member per year.[1]

---

[1] Arthur M. Ross, "The Prospects for Industrial Conflict," *Industrial Relations* (October 1961), pp. 57-74.

Strike activity was considerably less intense from 1954-60 than it had been from 1946-54, and this reduced level of strikes has continued during the 'sixties.

Why did these strikes occur? It is customary to classify strikes according to the leading issue in a particular dispute—so many strikes over wages, so many over working conditions, and so on. This is not a meaningful classification. The issues involved in a dispute are always interrelated, and to single out one as the primary issue is an arbitrary procedure. Moreover, the important thing is not what the issue was, but why the parties were unable to reach agreement on it. In order to discover the "causes" of strikes, one must discover the kinds of circumstance in which agreement between the parties becomes impossible.

Several types of situation can be distinguished. First, there are cases in which one of the parties wants a strike. An employer may regard a strike as a good way of breaking a weak union and freeing himself from the necessity of collective bargaining. On the other side, a radical union leader may regard a strike as desirable to build up revolutionary fervor and hatred of "the capitalists," even when there is no chance that the strike will win any immediate benefits.

Second, a strike may occur because of inability of the parties to compromise their positions. A demand which the union considers vital to its security may conflict with a position which management considers essential to its own survival. The union may insist on a wage higher than the company can pay, or on a union-shop clause which management feels—rightly or wrongly—would mean the end of its authority in the plant.

Even where the negotiators themselves would be willing to compromise, they may be prevented from doing so by the fact that they are not free agents. An absentee corporation president or board of directors, sitting in the head office and looking at the balance sheet, may order a plant manager to take a position which leads inevitably to a strike. On the other side, pressure from the membership may force union negotiators to maintain a position which they know the company cannot accept. Union leaders may know that their demands are impossible; but to retreat would jeopardize their own positions and perhaps split the union. A classic example is the strike in the Naumkeag Steam Cotton Company, which brought to an end that company's brief experiment in union-management cooperation. In this case, union leaders were prepared to accept increased workloads in some departments to enable the plant to compete with nonunion mills. The union members, however, rejected the settlement recommended by the leaders and forced a strike. The strike soon came under the control of a left-wing faction in the union, the previous leaders of the union were forced out of office, the strike was lost, and the union was wrecked.[2]

When inability to compromise is due to external compulsions on one or both groups of negotiators, an outside mediator or conciliator can frequently be helpful. He can keep the parties together until they have taxed their ingenuity to the utmost; he can act as a go-between within each organization as well as between them; he may be able to produce a face-saving formula which enables one or both parties to retreat gracefully from their previous demands; and he can sometimes bring to bear on the parties the pressure of public opinion.

Third, even where compromise is possible, one side may be unwilling to compromise because it has a low opinion of the other's strength and thinks it can win its point easily and quickly. The employer may underestimate the membership, solidarity, and financial strength of the union; the union may underestimate the determination of the employer to resist further concessions. One frequently finds an employer who, by conceding wage increases and restrictive working rules year after year, has got his production costs seriously out of line with those of competing companies. He may finally decide to hold the line and prevent further cost increases. Union leaders, however, have got in the habit of securing easy concessions from him and will not take him seriously. When they find out too late that he is serious, they are confronted with a strike. Many strikes result from misjudgment of the opposing position, from calling a bluff which turns out not to have been a bluff after all.

From the mere fact of a strike it is impossible to tell which side was mainly responsible for its occurrence. The union is forced to make the first overt move, and the public therefore tends to regard the union as the aggressor. The employer may actually have precipitated the strike, however, by insisting on unreasonable demands or simply by denying all the union's proposals. The employer can cause a strike by doing nothing; the union has to take the positive step of calling out the workers. All one can conclude from the fact of a strike is that there was a failure to reach agreement. Which

---

[2] See R. C. Nyman, *Union-Management Cooperation in the "Stretch-Out"* (New Haven: Yale University Press, 1934).

party was mainly responsible for failure to reach agreement can be learned only from an "inside" knowledge of the people and issues involved.

The number of strikes fluctuates with the movements of the business cycle. Strikes fall off during depression and the percentage of strikes won by the union also declines. Rees concludes from this that union strategy rather than company strategy dominates the scene and that strikes behave as one might expect on economic grounds— they are more frequent when the chances of success are high, and *vice versa*.[3] If employers could choose when to have strikes, the number would presumably rise during depression when employers are relatively strong.

There are also marked differences in the strike-proneness of individual industries. Kerr and Siegel, on the basis of strike statistics from eleven countries for varying periods of time between 1919 and 1950, found a consistently high propensity to strike in mining, shipping, longshoring, lumber, and textiles. The lowest strike propensities were found in clothing, public utilities, hotel and restaurant service, trade, railroad transportation, and agriculture.[4] They attribute the high incidence of strikes in the first group of industries to:

1. An isolated position of the worker in society. Workers in these industries typically form an "isolated mass," living apart from other people in company towns, at sea, in the woods, and so on. All do the same work, have the same grievances, and mingle only with each other. There is little or no opportunity to rise to higher occupational levels. The employer is often landlord and governor as well. Under these circumstances, all grievances focus on the (usually absentee) employer. The union becomes a kind of working-class party or even a sub-government. "The strike for this isolated mass is a kind of colonial revolt against far-removed authority, an outlet for accumulated tensions, and a substitute for occupational and social mobility."

Workers in the low-strike industries are in an opposite situation in these respects and are integrated successfully into the larger community.

2. A subsidiary but important factor is the nature of the work

---

[3] Albert Rees, "Industrial Conflict and Business Fluctuations," in A. Kornhauser, R. Dubin, and A. M. Ross, eds., *Industrial Conflict* (New York: McGraw-Hill Book Company, Inc., 1954), chap. 15.

[4] Clark Kerr and Abraham Siegel, "The Interindustry Propensity to Strike—an International Comparison," *op. cit.*, chap. 14.

and the workers. "If the job is physically difficult and unpleasant, unskilled or semiskilled, and casual or seasonal, and fosters an independent spirit (as in the logger in the woods), it will draw tough, inconstant, combative, and virile workers, and they will be inclined to strike."

Is there any tendency for strike activity to increase or decrease over the course of time? Are some countries more strike prone than others? These questions have been investigated by Ross and Hartman,[5] and some of their results are summarized in Table 4. Looking at the period since World War II, one notes sizeable differences in the level of strike activity. Britain, Germany, and the Scandinavian countries have had very low strike rates. This is not an indication of union weakness, but rather the reverse. As Ross and Hartman point out:

> The distinction between the ability to strike and the need to strike must be strongly emphasized. We are not suggesting that Swedish or Norwegian unions, for example, are unable to strike or that they have disowned the principle of the strike. On the contrary, resort to strikes may be least necessary where threats are most effective.[6]

Italy, France, and India, where unions are relatively weak, have had high proportions of union members involved in strikes. But in some countries which have many strikes (France, Italy, Australia), the average strike lasts only two to three days, so that time lost is not great. Canada and the United States have had moderately high rates of strike activity in the postwar period, the American rate being typically about double the Canadian one.

In most countries the level of strike activity today is well below the level in earlier decades; and in some of the most strongly-unionized countries resort to strikes is approaching the vanishing point. Ross and Hartman suggest three main reasons for this "withering away of the strike":

> First, employers have developed more sophisticated policies and more effective organizations. Second, the state has become more prominent as an employer of labor, economic planner, provider of benefits, and supervisor of industrial relations. Third, in many countries (although not in the United States) the labor movement has been forsaking the use of the strike in favor of broad political endeavors.[7]

---

[5] Arthur M. Ross and Paul J. Hartman, *Changing Patterns of Industrial Conflict* (New York: John Wiley Sons, Inc., 1960).

[6] *Op. cit.*, p. 19.

[7] *Op. cit.*, p. 42.

TABLE 4

MEASURES OF STRIKE ACTIVITY IN SELECTED COUNTIES

Country	Per Cent of Union Members Involved in Strikes (Annual average)		Days of Work Lost Through Strikes per Union Member (Annual average)	
	1900-29	*1948-56*	*1900-29*	*1948-56*
Denmark	6.3	1.4	2.0	0.2
Netherlands	7.0	1.3	2.1	0.1
United Kingdom	16.1	5.9	4.3	0.2
Germany	14.2	2.6	2.2	0.2
Norway	27.0	1.2	9.4	0.2
Sweden	22.7	0.3	8.9	0.1
France	27.1	62.4	4.2	1.7
Italy	—	35.2	—	0.9
Japan	30.3	21.5	—	1.1
India	—	37.2	—	3.2
United States	33.2	15.4	—	2.4
Canada	14.7	6.3	4.4	1.3
Australia	18.2	25.2	2.6	0.9
Finland	24.5	13.9	8.1	5.8
South Africa	24.4	1.4	3.2	0.1

In the United States, however, strikes have not yet withered to the point where their effects can be ignored. They pose a variety of policy issues, which it is the task of this chapter to examine.

THE LEGALITY OF STRIKES AND STRIKE TACTICS

Each time a major strike occurs in automobiles, steel, coal, or some other key industry there is a public outcry to the effect that "something should be done." What can or should be done through legislation to reduce the number and severity of strikes? Before trying to answer this question it will be well to look briefly at the rules of the game as applied by the courts at the present time.

The "right to strike"

Although this right is often confused with the right of a worker to quit his job, the two things are quite different. A worker quits his job when he wishes permanently to sever his connection with the employer. A strike is a concerted but temporary refusal to work, not for the purpose of terminating the striker's employment, but for the purpose of resuming this employment on more favorable terms. It is possible for this concerted activity to be unlawful even though each worker *as an individual* has the right to stop work whenever he wishes.

What practical difference does it make whether the courts hold a strike lawful or unlawful? The court cannot prevent men from leaving work; nor can it, under our Constitution, compel them to return to work against their will. If a strike is held unlawful, however, all concerted activities in support of it also become unlawful. The court may issue an injunction forbidding union officers to direct or encourage the strike in any way, prohibiting picketing, preventing the payment of strike benefits from union funds, and banning other normal strike activities. The injunction, as we have seen, is a powerful weapon, enforceable by trial for contempt of court. The workers, acting as individuals, may still choose to stay away from work; but it is hard to maintain an effective strike for very long without central organization and financing. As a practical matter, then, a decision that a strike is unlawful reduces the union's ability to carry it on. It also usually frees the employer of any legal obligation to re-employ the striking workers, and the threat of discharge may be quite effective in getting men back to work.

Whether a strike is lawful or unlawful turns partly on its objectives. The courts have held that a strike is lawful only if its objectives are legitimate. How can one decide what are legitimate objectives? The main test suggested by common law reasoning, as Gregory points out, is whether or not the strike serves to promote some economic interest of the union. This test, however, has not always been clearly or consistently applied by the courts. Courts have sometimes held that a union had no economic interest in such objectives as the closed shop, a victory for a sister union in the same industry, or even the organization of a nonunion plant, whereas economic reasoning would suggest a strong and direct union interest in these matters. In other cases, the test does not seem to have been applied at all. The court has condemned certain union objectives with little more explanation than "it's wrong because it's wrong."

It is normally lawful at common law for workers to strike against their immediate employer in order to improve their wages, hours, or working conditions. Beyond this, however, one runs into doubtful ground. With exceptions in a few of the more liberal states, the courts have generally condemned strikes for the closed shop, sympathy strikes called to support a strike by another union, jurisdictional strikes called to force the employer to assign work to members of one union rather than another, and strikes called in violation of a collective agreement. Almost all courts have treated as unlawful any strike against one employer to force him to exert pressure on another employer who is the real object of the union's attack, i.e., a secondary boycott.

Court reasoning based on common-law precedents has recently been supplemented by a flood of statutory legislation. Beginning in the late 'thirties and reaching a peak during the 'forties, many states passed laws specifically outlawing the closed shop and in some states the union shop as well, sympathy strikes, jurisdictional strikes, strikes in violation of contract, and secondary boycotts. At the federal level, the Taft-Hartley Act defines as an unfair labor practice any jurisdictional strike, secondary boycott, sympathetic strike, strike to secure "featherbedding" provisions in a union contract, or strike to force an employer or self-employed person to join a union or an employer organization.

Closing the plant

The objective of a strike is to close down the plant and keep it closed, thus exerting maximum economic pressure on the employer. Circumstances frequently compel the employer to accept a shutdown. If the plant employs thousands of specially trained workers, and if they all walk out at once, it is clearly impossible to keep the plant in operation. In few of the larger strikes of recent years has there been any attempt to reopen the plant before the strike was settled. Where the employer accepts the shutdown, picketing becomes a formality and the strike settles down to a test of relative staying power.

If one wanted simply to prevent violence in labor disputes, the most effective method would be a legal requirement that, when a lawful strike has been called by a properly certified majority union, the plant must remain closed for the duration of the dispute. This is the custom in most other countries where collective bargaining exists. Such a law would doubtless be opposed by employers, since it would tend to weaken their bargaining position in labor disputes.

Position of strikers under the Taft-Hartley Act

At the present time, the employer is legally free to keep the plant in operation during a strike if he can find workers. He can try to persuade his present employees to stay at work, and he can try to hire new workers from the outside. Anyone whom he can get to work for him is entitled to free access to the plant. If the plant remains in operation, even on a skeleton basis, this fact strengthens the employer's hand in bargaining with the strikers over the terms on which they are to return to work. Recruitment of enough strikebreakers may enable the employer to dispense with the strikers altogether.

In earlier times, this was a normal method of eliminating a union when the employer wished to do so. If the union would not strike of its own accord, the employer could always bring on a strike by discharging union leaders or taking some other aggressive action. During the strike, the plant could be filled with new workers, and the strikers simply informed that they were no longer employees of the company.

Employer tactics such as these have now been curbed by NLRB decisions under the Wagner Act and the Taft-Hartley Act. The Board has held that if a strike is due to unfair labor practices by the employer—refusal to bargain, intimidation or coercion of employees, discrimination against union members, and so on—the strikers retain full right as employees and on request must be reinstated in their jobs without discrimination. An employer can no longer break a union by refusing to bargain, locking out the union members, and filling their places with nonunion workers.

If, on the other hand, the strike results from an ordinary dispute over wages and conditions of employment, and if the employer is innocent of unfair labor practices, he may hire new workers during the strike and continue to employ them after the end of the strike. Such replacements must be permanent replacements, however, if the strikers are to be refused the jobs. In one case, the courts ruled against an employer who refused a job to a striker, when his former job was open because the replacement had left after a short time. The employer may not discriminate against a former employee because of his participation in a strike or because of his union membership, once the strike is over.

If a representation election is called to determine the majority status of a union during a strike, the strikers as well as their replacements are entitled to vote, provided the election is held within one year from the start of the strike. Beyond that time the strikers lose voting rights.

Workers who go on strike are gambling with their jobs. If the employer is able to replace them during the strike, they may be permanently out of employment with the company, with all that this implies in loss of income, seniority, and customary skills. It is not surprising that strikers feel very bitterly about strikebreakers, stigmatize them as "rats" or "scabs," and take steps to keep them from working.

The right to picket peaceably

The device which unions have developed to keep workers out of a struck plant is the picket line. Strikers patrol back and forth in front of the plant entrance, advertising the existence of a strike by placards and word of mouth. Workers entering the plant are greeted with pleas not to go to work. As a worker leaves the plant at the end of the shift, a picket may walk alongside him for a few steps and urge him not to come to work next day. Under experienced direction, picketing is an effective method of peaceable persuasion, though it can also degenerate into physical conflict.

For many years the courts of most states held that all picketing was coercive and therefore unlawful. By the 1920's, however, most courts had adopted the position that peaceable persuasion by a limited number of pickets was not necessarily unlawful at common law. These courts held that the legality of peaceable picketing depended on whether the picketers were serving their legitimate economic interest. They considered that peacable picketing by strikers of their own plant was legal, but picketing by outsiders or "strangers" was not. Toward the end of the 'twenties some liberal courts even took the view that picketing by outsiders was legal where there was a common economic interest to be served, such as elimination of competition between union and nonunion labor standards. Throughout this period, however, picketing was considered as an activity which could be regulated or limited at the discretion of the courts and legislature.

Peaceable picketing won increased legal support in the 'forties with the enunciation of the *Thornhill* doctrine by the Supreme

Court. In the case of *Thornhill* v. *Alabama*, one Byron Thornhill was convicted of misdemeanor under an Alabama statute which made picketing of any sort illegal. On appeal, the Supreme Court held that peaceful picketing was a form of free speech protected by the Fourteenth Amendment of the Constitution, and which could not be prohibited by either the states or the federal government. This decision assumed picketing to be identical with other methods of disseminating information protected by the Constitution. Under such a view all peaceful picketing, no matter how unreasonable its object, would have to be permitted. The Supreme Court was obliged later to qualify this so-called free speech doctrine and to recognize picketing as a method of carrying on economic conflict between workers and others, which made it once more subject to the common law rule that economic interest must be served if harm is to be inflicted on others.

At present the law of picketing is far from clear. It appears that there may be no blanket prohibition of picketing by the states or the federal government, but it may be confined to situations in which there is a close economic relationship between the picketer and the picketed. If the picketing is in support of unlawful objectives, moreover, it may be banned. The government may also enact reasonable regulations for the conduct of peaceable picketing.[8] A number of states have passed laws limiting the number of pickets who may be stationed at a plant, requiring that they must not block access to the plant, and regulating other details of picketing procedure.

Current restrictions on peaceable picketing

Although in general the right to peaceable picketing is established, there are important restrictions on even peaceable picketing, arising from court interpretations of "peaceable," on the one hand, and from legislation defining certain objects for which it is illegal to carry on any concerted activities. In the first place, the courts still have to determine whether the conduct of a particular group of pickets is peaceable or not. Words like "intimidation," "threats," and "coercion" require interpretation in particular cases. What are the pickets allowed to say? Can they call strikebreakers "scabs"

---

[8] See J. Tannenhaus, "Picketing—Free Speech: The Growth of the New Law of Picketing from 1940 to 1952," *Cornell Law Quarterly*, XXXVIII (Fall 1952), pp. 1-50.

and use other malodorous terms? What about jeers and catcalls, "accidental" jostling as the worker goes through the picket lines, following workers for a "quiet talk" as they leave the plant? Some judges have been very liberal and others very strict in defining permissible conduct by pickets.

The heart of the problem is that picketing necessarily involves moral pressure if it is to be fully effective. It is not merely a method of reasoning with the would-be strikebreaker, but is intended also to shame him and perhaps even alarm him. The issue is how much moral pressure strikers should be allowed to exert in their struggle to protect their jobs. The judge who agrees with unionists that strikebreakers are a low form of life will naturally take a different view from a judge who regards them as the last hope of a free economy.

The second and currently more important type of restriction on picketing has to do with picketing which, however peaceable in its nature, is carried on for an illegal object. These restrictions derive from the provisions in the Taft-Hartley Act on unfair labor practices of labor organizations and the rights of workers to refrain from collective bargaining. Picketing itself is at no point forbidden; but if a union encourages picketing in connection with an illegal secondary boycott, a jurisdictional dispute, or a sympathy strike, the picketing becomes illegal and the General Counsel of the NLRB may seek an injunction against it. Furthermore, if the picketing is of a nature to prevent workers from crossing a picket line, it becomes an illegal infringement on the right of the individual worker *not* to participate in concerted activities of unions. It is sometimes difficult to know whether picketing will be legal or not in a certain situation without a court decision on the legality of the strike itself.

Violence in labor disputes

Physical violence of any sort is unlawful. The pickets may not beat up strikebreakers, injure their cars, or cause them other physical harm. By the same token, strikebreakers and company police are not supposed to assault the strikers, spray them with tear gas, or cause them physical damage. In earlier years, violence in labor disputes was quite common in spite of legal prohibitions of it. Outbreaks of violence have become less common since the mid-'thirties, however, owing partly to the National Labor Relations Act. Even the widespread strikes of 1945 and 1946 were almost entirely peaceful.

The use of violent methods by an employer to break a strike, in addition to being a criminal offense, would clearly be an unfair labor practice.

Prevention of violence in labor disputes is largely a matter of good police work, and this is not easy to obtain. The police forces of many communities are poorly paid, poorly selected, and poorly trained. They usually have no special training in the handling of labor disputes. In the past, where the regular police were unable to cope with the situation, it was a common practice to swear in company police and even strikebreakers as deputy sheriffs, with power to carry arms and arrest strikers. These practices have now virtually disappeared, however, and serious or widespread violence is in all probability a thing of the past.

WHAT ELSE SHOULD GOVERNMENT DO?

These legal restrictions leave plenty of room for "normal" strikes resulting from failure of union and management officials to agree on the terms of a new contract. There occur each year several thousand work stoppages, usually involving something like thirty million man-days of idleness, or close to 1 per cent of total working time in the industries involved. How serious a problem is this, and what might be done about it?

The loss from strikes

The economic loss from strikes is a good deal less than is sometimes assumed in popular discussion. The loss is not to be judged by how much a strike reduces the wage income of the workers or the profits of the company immediately involved. The test is rather how much the strike reduces the total national production of goods and services.

It is quite possible for a large and dramatic strike to involve no loss at all in national output. In a seasonal industry, a strike may simply change the location of the "slack season." A strike in men's clothing factories early in the spring season means only that the factories will have to work longer at the end of the season to make up for lost time. Again, the bituminous coal mines normally operate much less than a full year. A six-week strike at one point in the year may mean only that the mines will operate six weeks longer at some other point. There is reason to think that some of the strikes in this industry have been called, not because of serious union-management disagreement, but because inventories of coal above ground had reached a dangerously high level. In such situations it may be to the interest of both the union and the companies to cut off production for a time in order to reduce inventories and prevent downward pressure on coal prices.

Where a strike involves only one company in an industry, as frequently happens, this usually means that some business which would normally have gone to that company will go to its competitors instead. If General Motors is shut down, Ford, Chrysler, and others will sell more cars. The company on strike and its workers have less income, but other companies and their workers have more income. This assumes, of course, that other companies have unused capacity and are able to absorb the additional business. In the case of an industry in which all plants are operating at full capacity throughout the year, a strike anywhere in the industry will involve a reduction in national output.

The impact of a strike depends somewhat on its timing, and this can be an important factor in strike strategy. If a strike seems to be in the offing, the union will time it for the busy season rather than the slack season. The automobile workers will not strike in the spring toward the end of a model year, but rather in the fall when production is under way on new models. The 1962 New York City newspaper strike was timed for early December, when the newspapers would lose most revenue from Christmas advertising.

In industries producing services for immediate consumption, production lost today is lost forever. If I do not buy a newspaper or a subway ride today, I am not going to buy two tomorrow to catch up. There are also industries, such as electric power production and rail transportation, whose continuous operation is essential to steady production in other industries. A strike in such an industry may, by halting production in a wide variety of other industries, cause a disproportionately large drop in national output. For this reason it is tacitly recognized that strikes in such industries cannot continue for long, and they never do continue for long. Unions in such industries have the right to strike, but on the unwritten condition that they will not exercise it too forcefully.

Compulsory arbitration versus collective bargaining

It may seem that the government could simply pass a law prohibiting strikes. It is not possible, however, to prohibit differences of economic interest between unions and employers, or the disputes to which they lead. If disputes occur, and if they cannot be resolved by the test of economic power known as a strike, they will have to be resolved in some other way. The only feasible way is to set up a government board as the ultimate arbiter of industrial disputes, i.e., to impose compulsory arbitration. The important thing about compulsory arbitration is not that it prohibits strikes, but rather that it sets up a new procedure for resolving union-management disputes.

It must next be noticed that, if a government board is given power finally to determine all disputes, genuine collective bargaining over terms of employment will soon cease. Rather than make concessions on a disputed issue, one party or the other will usually prefer to "pass the buck" to the board in the hope of a favorable decision. Even if union officials know that the decision on a certain point will go against them, they will incur less disfavor with their members by forcing the board to make the decision and then exercising their democratic privilege of denouncing the board.

This is about what happened under the National War Labor Board during World War II. Union and management officials knew that by simply "sitting tight" on an issue so that a strike was threatened they could force the Board to take jurisdiction over the dispute. Why, then, should anyone make important concessions without having a try at the Board? The result was that most major disputes, especially those involving novel issues, came before the Board for settlement. The important terms of the contract—wage schedules, union security clauses, fringe wage payments, grievance procedures, and so on—were written in Washington instead of being negotiated by the parties themselves. It is true that thousands of agreements were renewed peaceably during the war years without coming to the Board; but this happened only when neither party wanted important changes in the agreement, or when both parties preferred to accept established Board policies on a certain point without going through the motions of a Board hearing. There is little doubt that the existence of the Board greatly reduced the amount of genuine collective bargaining, and that this happened increasingly as the war went on.

The policy issue, then, is who should have final authority to determine wages and other terms of employment. Under free collective bargaining, final authority rests with union and management officials. Their freedom includes freedom to disagree, with the consequent risk of strikes. The possibility of a strike or lockout hangs over every bargaining conference, and without it bargaining could have little meaning. The alternative is to vest final authority in a government board by requiring that all unsettled disputes be referred to the board for settlement. This procedure leads, as we have seen, to a withering away of collective bargaining and the assumption of full governmental control over wages and conditions of employment.

What is there to be said for and against compulsory arbitration of labor disputes? In behalf of compulsory arbitration, it is usually argued that it is a more civilized method of settling industrial disputes than the use of strikes or lockouts. It substitutes trial by jury for trial by combat. It might reduce the amount of time lost through strikes, though Austrialian experience (see below) suggests that this is rather doubtful. It may also be argued that comprehensive government control of wage settlements would produce a better national wage structure than one is likely to get from separate union-employer bargains in each plant and industry. The possibility of serious wage distortion under collective bargaining, which is discussed in Chapter 12, might be largely avoided under public control. It may also be desirable to have greater uniformity in union security provisions and other types of contract clause, and this uniformity would certainly be gained more rapidly under government control.

What can be said, on the other hand, in favor of free collective bargaining? The strength of collective bargaining is that it is primarily a process of persuasion. Resort to economic force is the exception, not the rule; nor is the threat of force the main reason for agreement. Under "mature collective bargaining," where the parties have dealt with each other for twenty or thirty years, a contract renewal usually involves genuine agreement that certain terms will work out best for both parties during the coming year. There are many plants which have had no work stoppage for decades, and in which a strike would be almost inconceivable. Compulsory arbitration is a legal procedure, a special type of court trial. The outcome of a trial is a victory. The outcome of bargaining is an agreement. There is strong reason to believe that terms which have been agreed to voluntarily, rather than forced on the parties by government decision, will be accepted with better grace and complied with more completely. In addition, the process of mutual persuasion is highly educational to both parties.

Most of this educational value would be lost if the two sides could simply turn a dispute over to their attorneys for trial before a government board.

Collective bargaining also has the merit of extreme flexibility to meet different circumstances. On any issue in dispute, the parties are free to exercise their ingenuity and to devise a contract provision different from any existing elsewhere in the country. This exercise of initiative at the grass roots of collective bargaining would be largely stultified under compulsory arbitration, which would tend to follow established precedents and to place a premium on conformity with uniform national policies. Another consideration is that compulsory arbitration would be a long step toward centralized control of the economy by the federal government. It may be possible in theory for government to control wages without controlling prices and profits, but it would be very difficult for government to do this in practice. Anyone is entitled to argue that greater central control and planning of the economy is desirable for its own sake; but the argument should be made openly on this basis. We should not introduce central economic controls by the back door under the guise of preventing strikes.

A practical consideration is that both union and management officials in this country are strongly opposed to compulsory arbitration of labor disputes in peacetime. It is hard to see, therefore, how compulsory arbitration could become a matter of practical politics within the visible future.

Australia has had a compulsory arbitration statute since 1904. Strikes affecting interstate commerce are prohibited, and the issues in dispute must be submitted to the Commonwealth Court of Arbitration. Most of the Australian states have similar legislation governing intrastate disputes. The figures in Table 4, however, indicate that Australia continues to have a high rate of strike activity. Many of these strikes are clearly illegal, but in few cases are penalties imposed on the strikers. An important factor has been the strength of the Australian Labor Party, which makes punishment of strikers politically inexpedient.[9]

---

[9] For a discussion of compulsory arbitration in Australia see W. R. Maclaurin, "Recent Experience with Compulsory Arbitration in Australia," *American Economic Review*, XXVIII (March 1938), pp. 65-81; O. de R. Foenander, *Towards Industrial Peace in Australia* (Melbourne: Melbourne University Press, 1937); George Anderson, *Fixation of Wages in Australia* (New York: The Macmillan Company, 1929). For a more general treatment of alternative government policies, see Kurt Braun, *The Settlement of Industrial Disputes* (Philadelphia: Blakiston, 1944).

In a democratic country, government regulation is never a one-way process. While in principle a government arbitration board may be exercising authority over unions and managements, in practice both labor and management will be doing their best to control the policies of the board. The history of the National War Labor Board provides abundant evidence of this tendency. Government decision of the terms of employment, then, is bound to mean decision based on political pressures and expediency rather than on ideal standards worked out by university professors. One should discard any notion that compulsory arbitration would lead to perfect justice or complete industrial peace. Where labor is politically powerful, it is not feasible simply to "crack down" on strikes, even though they may violate an established arbitration procedure.

The verdict of public opinion in this country has thus far been in favor of collective bargaining.[10] If one agrees with this verdict, one must be prepared to take the bitter with the sweet. If collective bargaining is desirable, one must accept the occasional inconvenience caused by work stoppages. The possibility of a work stoppage, as was pointed out in Chapter 7, also plays a positive role in the bargaining process.

Conciliation and mediation

While there would be widespread agreement that government should not undertake to prohibit all strikes, this does not mean that government must be an idle bystander. Government can frequently prevent the occurrence of a strike by helping the parties to reach a settlement of their dispute. This is the objective of the Federal Mediation and Conciliation Service and of the mediation services which now exist in most of the larger industrial states.

The work of mediation is difficult to describe, since it is probable that no two mediators operate in the same way. The first task of the mediator is to win the confidence of both parties and to establish himself as a benevolent, experienced, and non-partisan participant in the negotiations. The next step is to narrow the issues on which disagreement exists and to define the essence of the dispute as clearly as possible. Beyond this, tactics vary with the circumstances. A frequent procedure is for the mediator to keep the parties in separate

---

[10] For a strong presentation of the case for free collective bargaining, see G. W. Taylor, *Government Regulation of Industrial Relations* (Englewood Cliffs, N.J.: Prentice-Hall, Inc., 1948), especially chap. 1.

rooms and carry proposals and counter-proposals back and forth between them. The parties will often tell the mediator more about their true minimum demands than they will tell each other. Each fears that, if it tells the other side directly that it is willing to compromise, this will be interpreted as a sign of weakness and will cause the other side to take a stiffer position. They may be willing, however, to reveal to the mediator the extent of their willingness to compromise. When he discovers that the potential compromises overlap sufficiently to permit of an agreement, he may call the parties together and propose a settlement which each has privately indicated would be acceptable to it.

An experienced and ingenious mediator can sometimes think of compromise proposals which have not occurred to either of the parties and "sell" these proposals to them. He can make some use of the threat of adverse public opinion. Pressure must be applied with caution, however, and the mediator must generally eschew any suggestion of authority or dictation. He is there on sufferance, and if he makes himself a nuisance he may be ejected from the case by the parties.

The mediator may also serve some of the purposes, described in Chapter 7, of an umpire or arbitrator under a grievance procedure. He may act as the "goat" who, by taking direct responsibility for a decision, saves face for one or both of the parties. The union officials may be able to go back to their members and say, "We were holding out fine, but that unmentionable mediator made us give in."

The Federal Mediation and Conciliation Service and the state services are able to adjust the great majority of the disputes in which they intervene without stoppage of production. Many of these disputes would probably have been settled in any event, but some would not have been, and there is little doubt that the benefits from mediation work are worth many times its cost. There is general agreement among students of industrial relations that the number of mediators should be increased at both the federal and state levels, and that salary levels for mediators should be raised considerably. Mediation is a skilled and responsible undertaking, and people capable of performing it command a high price in private practice. If the government is to secure men who will command the respect of unions and managements, it will need to pay salaries approaching those in private industry.

An important recent development is the tendency of the Secretary of Labor to undertake mediation of major disputes. Secretary (now Supreme Court Justice) Arthur Goldberg and Secretary Willard Wirtz spent a good deal of time in this way. The status as well as the personal skills of these Cabinet members undoubtedly helped to settle some disputes in which lower-level intervention would have been ineffective.

ADJUSTMENT OF DISPUTES IN ESSENTIAL INDUSTRIES

We argued in the previous section that strikes, as an unavoidable accompaniment of free collective bargaining, are a lesser evil than government regulation of all terms of employment. In certain industries, however, continuous operation is so essential to the community that strikes cannot as a practical matter be allowed to continue for very long. At the national level, a railroad strike immediately has a severe disruptive effect on the economy. A prolonged strike in basic steel can interfere seriously with production in steel-using industries. At the state and local levels, strikes in the production or distribution of food, fuel, water, electric light and power, gas, and hospital and medical services can imperil public health and safety. Stoppages in local transportation might also be included, though these typically involve inconvenience rather than real emergency. Most "emergency strikes" occur in local industries and are a problem for state rather than federal regulation.

The objective of public policy is not just to prevent strikes in essential industries. The objective is rather to prevent strikes by methods which are orderly and uniform in their application, which involve a minimum of direct compulsion, which do not impose greater hardship on one party than on the other, and which leave maximum scope for settlements to be reached through direct negotiation between the parties. It is these subsidiary requirements which make the problem by all odds the most difficult in the field of industrial relations. After a century of thought and experimentation, we have not yet produced a generally accepted solution.

A good deal can be accomplished through the mediation methods discussed in the last section. This approach has been used with marked success, for example, by the Labor Relations Division of the New York City government. The staff of the Division, aided on occasion by the mayor and other city officials, has mediated numerous disputes in local transportation, trucking, shipping, longshoring, building service, and other industries. Although there is no legal compulsion on the parties to reach agreement, most disputes have been settled without a work stoppage or with only a brief interruption of service.

Mediation alone, however, cannot always be counted on to produce an agreement. What additional steps can government take? A number of devices have been developed, none really satisfactory in itself, but together providing an arsenal of weapons which can be used in varying combinations to meet particular emergencies as they arise. The commonest of these devices deserve brief mention.

Compulsory waiting period

Government may require both parties to maintain the status quo for a specified period before strike action can be taken. The Railway Labor Act, passed in 1926 and amended in 1934 and 1951, provides among other things for a three-man National Mediation Board to handle major disputes over new contract terms. If the Board is unable to settle a dispute through mediation or to persuade the parties to submit the issue to private arbitration, it notifies the President of the United States, who may then appoint an emergency board to investigate the dispute. During the thirty days which the emergency board is allowed for its investigation, and for another thirty days after the board's report is filed. neither party may make any change in the conditions out of which the dispute arose. The parties are not obliged to accept the recommendations of the emergency board, however, and a strike at the end of the waiting period is entirely legal.

The Taft-Hartley Act also provides a special procedure for cases in which "in the opinion of the President of the United States, a threatened or actual strike or lockout affecting an entire industry or a substantial portion thereof . . . will, if permitted to occur or to continue, imperil the national health or safety." In such cases the President, after preliminary investigation by a board of inquiry, may ask the Attorney General to seek an injunction against the strike. If the injunction is granted, strike action becomes unlawful for an eighty-day period, during which the parties may continue to negotiate. If no agreement is reached by the end of the period the injunction is dissolved and the strike may proceed. This procedure was used several times in 1948, immediately after its enactment, but has been used very sparingly since, partly because the injunction procedure is distasteful to unions and partly because the compulsory waiting period has not proven particularly effective.[11]

The compulsory waiting period is sometimes inaccurately described as a "cooling-off period," on the assumption that an industrial dispute resembles a fist fight, that strikes result from hot tempers, and that time for further reflection will produce a settlement. There is little evidence, however, that sheer postponement of the issue has any beneficial effect. Once the parties have dug in for a struggle, they may simply sit out the prescribed period with no serious effort at negotiation. A waiting period will be effective only if during the period additional steps are taken to work out possible terms of settlement.

A board of inquiry

It may be provided that during the waiting period a specially appointed board shall hold hearings on the issues in dispute, report on the merits of the case, and perhaps propose terms of settlement. The hope is that the report will focus public opinion and generate pressure on both parties to accept the recommended terms. Experience suggests, however, that public opinion is not very effective in resolving complicated and technical issues. The upshot is that if the recommended terms are seriously objectionable to one or both parties they will be rejected and the dispute will continue.

The longest experience with emergency board procedures has been under the Railway Labor Act, whose terms were described above. Before World War II labor disputes on the railroads seem to have been settled quite successfully within the framework of the Act. Between 1926 and 1941 only sixteen emergency boards were appointed, most of these disputes were settled along the lines of board recommendations, and only two minor strikes occurred. Since 1941, however, few major disputes in the industry have been settled successfully through the procedures of the Railway Labor Act. In most cases the President has had to intervene to avoid a crisis. In 1941, for instance, the unions were dissatisfied with the recommendations of an emergency board and appealed to President Roosevelt, who negotiated a settlement which gave the unions more than the emergency

---

[11] Sumner H. Slichter, "Revision of the Taft-Hartley Act," *Quarterly Journal of Economics*, LXVII (May 1953), p. 170. See also the appraisal by Frank Pierson in Irving Bernstein, Harold L. Enarson, and Robben W. Fleming, eds., *Emergency Disputes and National Policy* (New York: Harper & Row, Publishers, 1955), pp. 124-146.

board had proposed. In three cases, one in 1942-43, one in 1947, and one in 1951, both the emergency board recommendations and the terms proposed by the President were repudiated by one of the parties, and service was maintained only by government seizure of the railroads under the President's emergency powers.

The Act has been criticized not only for failing to solve major disputes but for actually hampering collective bargaining and voluntary arbitration as well.[12] It is said that the parties refuse to bargain in good faith in hopes of getting better terms out of an emergency board. The emergency boards are being used more and more to "pass the buck" to the government in minor disputes. Since there is no obligation to accept the recommendations of the emergency boards, real emergencies have to be dealt with entirely outside the framework of the Act, typically by using two further unofficial steps—Presidential conciliation or arbitration, and government seizure.

A more successful experience has been that of the Atomic Energy Labor-Management Relations Panel, a continuing board of public members charged with adjusting disputes on construction of new facilities for the AEC and on production of atomic materials. The Panel has authority both to mediate and to make recommendations for settlement of a dispute, the latter procedure having become increasingly common over the course of time. Despite the fact that there is no compulsion on the parties to accept these recommendations, they have been accepted in a large majority of cases. It is questionable, however, whether experience in this industry provides a pattern which could usefully be applied in any other industry. AEC facilities operate in virtually a wartime atmosphere, in which unions and employers might be expected to make unusual efforts to avoid work stoppages.[13]

Compulsory arbitration

If the parties to a dispute in an essential industry will not accept the recommendations of a public board voluntarily, why not provide

---

[12] Herbert R. Northrup, "Emergency Disputes under the Railway Labor Act," *Proceedings of the First Annual Meeting* (Industrial Relations Research Association, 1948). See also Herbert R. Northrup, "The Railways Labor Act and Railway Labor Disputes," *American Economic Review*, XXXVI (June 1946), pp. 324-343.

[13] For further analysis of this case, see the article by J. Keith Mann in Bernstein, Enarson, and Fleming, *Emergency Disputes and National Policy.*

that they *must* accept them and that any work stoppage shall be illegal? This approach undercuts collective bargaining in ways already suggested; and it is unpopular with both unions and employers. It was nevertheless invoked in 1963 as a last-ditch method of averting a nationwide rail strike. In this dispute the railroads contended that declining revenues compelled them to save labor by modifying work rules on the roads, and announced that new rules would be put into effect on a certain date. The train-operating unions, estimating that as many as 50,000 jobs might be involved, opposed the changes and announced that they would strike if they were put into effect. The Railway Labor Act procedures were employed, and there was intensive mediation by the Secretary of Labor and other federal officials, but no settlement was reached. A few days before the strike deadline Congress passed emergency legislation providing for binding arbitration of the key issues by a blue-ribbon board appointed by the President. The award was to be issued within a specified period. Meanwhile, strike action was prohibited for a period of 180 days. The legislation was opposed strongly but unsuccessfully by the railroad unions and by AFL-CIO leaders.

The award of the arbitration board was issued late in 1963. The board concluded that most of the disputed jobs were unnecessary and that the railroads were entitled to eliminate them. The workers currently employed on these jobs, however, were given various degrees of layoff protection, depending on their length of service. The intent was that the shrinkage of employment should occur gradually, and mainly through normal labor force attrition rather than layoff. The train-operating unions immediately announced their rejection of the award and their intention of challenging it in the courts. When the special legislation expires, there will doubtless be a renewed threat of strike action. So while a showdown has been postponed, the dispute remains unsettled.

One can no longer say that compulsory arbitration is unthinkable in the United States, since it was invoked in this case with the approval of large majorities in both houses of Congress. Unions remain strongly opposed to it, however, and most management officials would probably regard it as a last resort. Nor does it seem desirable to request special Congressional intervention in every dispute of national importance. Some orderly and accepted procedure for handling these disputes remains desirable.

Plant seizure

The federal government made considerable use of plant seizure during World War II to enforce compliance with decisions of the National War Labor Board. The "success" of the seizure device, however, depended on a wartime atmosphere in which maintenance of collective bargaining and other private rights was regarded as secondary to continuous war production. In the immediate postwar years seizure was used in three major disputes involving the railroad, bituminous coal, and steel industries, but there is considerable doubt of the legal basis for plant seizure in peacetime. In 1952 the steel companies appealed successfully to the Supreme Court against a seizure order, issued by President Truman, and there has been no federal use of the procedure since that time. There is also considerable uncertainty over the legal consequences of seizure. May the government actually install new managers, change terms of employment, and make other operating decisions? Or is seizure to be construed (as it normally has been) as a mere formality, the private management continuing to operate the enterprise and to maintain the status quo on wages and conditions? Is the government entitled to any share of profits earned during the period of seizure and must it (as the courts have ruled in one case) make up to the company any losses suffered under government operation?

At the state level, Virginia and New Jersey have laws providing for plant seizure and compulsory arbitration of public utility disputes. (Several other states have compulsory arbitration laws which do not include provision for plant seizure.) In New Jersey, a sixty-day strike notice must be given to the State Board of Mediation. If a strike actually occurs, the Governor is authorized to seize and operate the utility. This is simply a nominal seizure to keep the utility in operation. A statutory board of five members (one union member, one employer member and three public members) is then appointed to arbitrate. When the dispute is settled, the governor is required to return the plant to its owners.[14]

The New Jersey Act has accomplished its purpose of maintaining

---

[14] See Lois MacDonald, *Compulsory Arbitration in New Jersey* (New York: New York University Institute of Labor Relations and Social Security, 1949); R. R. France and R. A. Lester, *Compulsory Arbitration of Utility Disputes in New Jersey and Pennsylvania* (Princeton: Princeton University Industrial Relations Section, 1951).

reasonable continuity of service for a period of years in the public utilities. There have been only two minor gas strikes and two telephone strikes. At the same time, the New Jersey experience has indicated certain pitfalls. The penalties for striking in defiance of the Act have not been enforced, and it is questionable whether they could be without arousing bitter union opposition to the whole procedure. Seizure has posed difficult problems, since it usually lasts several months and in one case lasted over eighteen months. There is no provision for the maintenance of status quo under seizure, and it is never very clear whether the regular employer or the government is in charge of operations.

The most serious practical defect of plant seizure is that it does not settle the original dispute. There is still a problem of working out terms agreeable to both parties. Unless responsibility for doing this is clearly fixed, and unless there is some compulsion on the parties to accept the prescribed terms, government operation may have to continue more or less indefinitely. Government seizure has sometimes lasted for several years before a final settlement was reached.

It is difficult to disagree with Archibald Cox's evaluation:

> Seizure alone would seldom be an effective solution for national emergency disputes. As an available alternative, or in conjunction with other measures, it appears to have considerable psychological value both in emphasizing to employees the public need for continued work and in making it difficult for both parties to calculate the cost of disagreement. But seizure is a wasting asset because experience and the development of legal principles would tend to dissipate the peculiar risks involved. . . . Accordingly, sound policy would seem to dictate resort to seizure only in those rare crises where executive action may be justified without an established legal policy.[15]

Massachusetts "choice-of-procedures" approach

The most original state law pertaining to emergency disputes is that of Massachusetts, enacted in 1947 on the basis of a unanimous report by a tripartite committee headed by Professor Sumner Slichter, hence generally known as the Slichter Law.[16] The distinguishing feature of the law is that it provides a variety of procedures which

---

[15] In Bernstein, Enarson, and Fleming, *Emergency Disputes and National Policy*, p. 242.

[16] For an analysis of experience under the law see George P. Shultz, "The Massachusetts Choice-of-Procedures Approach to Emergency Disputes," *Industrial and Labor Relations Review* (April 1957).

the Governor may use singly or in combination to meet the needs of a particular case. This has the merit of flexibility and of "keeping the parties guessing," thus generating maximum pressure on them to settle their own disputes rather than become involved in unpredictable public procedures.

The law applies to production and distribution of food, fuel, water, electric light and power, gas, hospital care, and medical services. It does not cover local transportation or telephone service. When the Governor finds that a dispute in these industries threatens public health and safety, he may take any or all of the following steps:

1. Require the parties to appear before a moderator to show cause why they should not submit the dispute to arbitration. The moderator may also perform mediation functions. If he fails to get a settlement or a submission to arbitration, he makes a public report on responsibility for the failure but may not comment on the merits of the case.

2. Request the parties voluntarily to submit the dispute to a tripartite emergency board empowered to recommend terms of settlement. If a submission is arranged, the board must submit its findings and recommendations to the Governor within thirty days.

3. If the Governor finds these procedures inappropriate or if the dispute remains unsettled after using them, he may declare an emergency and arrange with either or both parties for continuing production to the degree necessary for public health and safety.

4. He may also seize and operate the plant or facilities. During the seizure period he may at his discretion put into effect the recommendations of the emergency board if there has been one, or he may appoint a special commission to recommend terms of employment and may put these into effect at his discretion. Seizure ends when the parties notify the Governor that the dispute has been settled, or he may terminate it when he considers it no longer necessary even though the dispute remains unsettled.

The law was invoked six times during its first decade of operation and seems to have yielded broadly satisfactory results. In no case has the law been defied. Four of the six disputes were eventually settled by collective bargaining, the other two by voluntary private arbitration. The settlements do not appear to have been consistently biased in favor of labor or management. The disruptive effects on collective bargaining do not seem to have been serious, partly because the Governor has wisely refrained from intervening automatically in every situation. The restrained use which has been made of the law is doubtless partly responsible for its generally good reputation in the state.

A summary word

The nature of sound policy concerning emergency disputes has been well stated by Cox: ". . . ideal legislation dealing with national emergency disputes would avoid any built-in bias affecting the relative bargaining power of the parties, but would nevertheless allow the administration to preserve neutrality or exert limited pressure in either direction according to economic conditions and the merits of the issue, while at the same time securing an essentially private voluntary settlement." [17]

It is easier to specify objectives than to embody them in effective legislation. The approaches described above are steps toward a comprehensive policy for handling emergency disputes, but they do not yet constitute such a policy. This will doubtless continue to be one of the most controversial and difficult areas in industrial relations.

Discussion questions

1. Why does the United States have a higher level of strike activity than Britain, Germany, or the Scandinavian countries?

2. Would you expect the severity of strikes in the United States to increase or decrease over the next twenty years? Why?

3. What factors determine whether a particular strike involves a reduction of national output?

4. What are the principal arguments for and against compulsory arbitration? What is your own appraisal of these arguments?

5. In what ways can a mediator contribute to adjustment of an industrial dispute?

6. "The Railway Labor Act has fulfilled its main objective of maintaining the continuity of railway service." Discuss in the light of the experience under the Act.

7. Evaluate the following methods of dispute settlement: (a) plant seizure, (b) an injunction, (c) a "cooling-off" period, (d) board of inquiry with power of recommendation, and (e) compulsory arbitration.

[17] Bernstein, Enarson, and Fleming, *Emergency Disputes and National Policy*, p. 233.

Selected reading

Bernstein, Irving, *Arbitration of Wages*. Los Angeles: University of California Press, 1954.

——, Harold L. Enarson, and R. W. Fleming, *Emergency Disputes and National Policy*. New York: Harper & Row, Publishers, 1955.

Kaufman, Jacob J., *Collective Bargaining in the Railroad Industry*. New York: Columbia University Press, 1954.

Knowles, K.G.J.C., *Strikes—A Study in Industrial Conflict*. Oxford: Blackwell, 1952.

Ross, Arthur M., and Paul T. Hartman, *Changing Patterns of Industrial Conflict*. New York: John Wiley & Sons, Inc., 1960.

Sharp, Ian G., *Industrial Conciliation and Arbitration in Great Britain*. London: George Allen and Unwin, Ltd., 1951.

Shister, J., B. Aaron, and C. W. Summers, eds., *Public Policy and Collective Bargaining*. New York: Harper & Row, Publishers, 1962.

Shultz, George P., "The Massachusetts Choice-of-Procedures Approach to Emergency Disputes," *Industrial and Labor Relations Review* (April 1957), pp. 359-374.

Taylor, George W., *Government Regulation of Industrial Relations*. Englewood Cliffs, N.J.: Prentice-Hall, Inc., 1948.

Walker, Kenneth, *Industrial Relations in Australia*. Cambridge: Harvard University Press, 1956.

Witte, Edwin E., "Wartime Handling of Labor Disputes," *Harvard Business Review*, XXV (Winter 1947), pp. 169-189.

12

The Balance Sheet
Of Trade Unionism

We have had much to say in earlier chapters about the effects of particular union policies. It is now time to put the pieces together into an over-all evaluation. The effects of union activity may be classified conveniently under eight headings: (1) the structure of labor and product markets; (2) the level of money wages and prices; (3) the level of real wages; (4) relative wage rates for different industries and occupations; (5) nonmonetary terms of employment; (6) the social structure of the plant; (7) the status of the individual worker; and (8) the balance of political power in the community.

In discussing items (2) and (3) we shall have to rely on some conclusions about wage determination which are not fully developed and explained until Chapters 16 and 17. The reader who is skeptical of these conclusions should suspend judgment and come back to them after examining the reasoning on which they are based.

The picture to be painted here is an intricate one. Some union gains have been achieved through political channels, others through collective bargaining. An adequate appraisal must include both. Some effects of unionism are reasonably certain, others are quite conjectural. Some of the effects may be rated as beneficial, others as harmful from a public standpoint. Whether a particular effect is considered beneficial, and whether the pros are regarded as outweighing the cons, depends partly on one's political outlook and beliefs. Any sweeping judgment of unionism, whether favorable or unfavorable, is certain to be wrong.

STRUCTURE OF LABOR AND PRODUCT MARKETS

Perhaps the commonest statement about trade unions is that they are "monopolies." In both economic theorizing and popular writing this is usually meant as a term of reproach. What precise meaning can be given to this term? In what sense do unions exert monopoly power? Are the effects necessarily and automatically harmful?

It is necessary here to distinguish between product markets and labor markets and, as regards labor markets, to distinguish between wage determination and the processes of job choice and labor mobility. Wage determination and labor mobility are obviously related but they are not the same thing, and unionism affects the former considerably more than the latter.

Job choices and labor mobility

Unionism seems to have had little direct effect on the *number of workers* admitted to particular industries and occupations. Most unions have not worked very hard to restrict entrance, and where they have tried they have not been very successful.

Union contract provisions have greater effect on *which* workers shall be employed in a particular industry or occupation. The general use of seniority in rehiring laid-off workers, plus frequent use of the closed shop, means that workers previously attached to an industry have first chance at employment opportunities. Newcomers can break into the industry only when experienced workers are fully employed, whereas in the absence of union restrictions employers might often prefer to substitute a highly competent newcomer for a less competent former employee.

Unionism probably tends in several ways to reduce interplant movement of labor. The grievance procedure makes it possible for workers to correct unsatisfactory conditions without resorting to the old expedient of quitting the job. Seniority protection, pension rights, and other benefits which accrue with length of service place a substantial premium on staying with the same employer for a long period.

Emphasis on internal promotion based on length of service increases the height of the walls around each employing unit and makes it harder for workers to make an advantageous shift between employers.

It is questionable, however, whether collective bargaining has produced any major change in the pattern of labor turnover. Laboi market studies ranging from 1900 to the present agree that the great bulk of voluntary quits occur during the first year of employment, indicating either that the worker was poorly selected and did not work out on the job, or that the job did not live up to the expectations which the worker held when he took it. Quitting is an intrinsic part of the process of job shopping in an imperfect labor market. Voluntary quit rates are also highly correlated with the business cycle, that is, with objective opportunities to change jobs. Quits rise sharply during boom years when jobs are plentiful and fall sharply during depression.

In addition to these cyclical swings, there has been a tendency for voluntary quit rates to decline gradually over the long run. Quit rates in American manufacturing were markedly lower in the nineteen-twenties than in the nineteen-tens, and were again lower in the 'fifties than in the 'twenties. Unionism, seniority rules, and pension plans have probably had something to do with this. But other factors have also been at work, including more careful selection of new employees and better personnel management in general, tapering off of the rate of increase in total manufacturing employment and consequent stabilization of the manufacturing work force, and aging of the labor force in the nation as a whole. It appears premature to attribute the decline in mobility solely or even primarily to collective bargaining.[1]

Wage determination

Unions can and do influence the wage levels of particular occupational groups, companies, and industries. This is often expressed by saying that unionism substitutes "monopoly" for "competition" in wage determination. It is questionable, however, whether this terminology clarifies the issues more than it confuses them. The market for manual labor is notoriously imperfect, as will appear more clearly in Chapter 15. There is no effective central clearinghouse, there is much ignorance and misinformation on both sides of the market, job

---

[1] On this range of issues see Arthur M. Ross, "Do We Have a New Industrial Feudalism?" *American Economic Review*, XLIX (December 1958).

hunting is haphazard, and most workers do not really have a "market outlook." Many employers are large relative to the local labor market in which they operate, and can alter wage rates rather than taking them as given by the market. They have some degree of monopsony power in buying labor.

Trade unions do not intrude into a situation in which wage rates have been perfectly aligned by competitive forces. They come into a situation in which relative wage rates have already been distorted by various types of market imperfection. Trade unions may thus *either* correct previous distortions of the wage structure or perpetuate and accentuate these distortions. How far unions actually do either or both of these things is a factual question about which we shall have more to say in a moment.

The disadvantage of the "monopoly" terminology is that it prejudges the issue before the evidence has been examined, and condemns any bargained wage rate by applying to it a term of ill repute. It would be more neutral and more accurate to say that unionism *strengthens* the workers' bargaining position. Unionism does not necessarily *equalize* the bargaining position of the parties. In some cases union strength remains inferior to employer strength under collective bargaining, while in other cases it is markedly superior. In all cases, however, one can say that the workers' relative position is stronger than before.

Competition in product markets

It is probably safe to conclude that unionism strengthens monopoly tendencies in product markets. Most unions are firm believers in "orderly" or quasi-collusive price determination, and will line up with established producers against new competition from at home or abroad. In industries with a few large companies who are able to control competition effectively, unions simply insist on a share of the proceeds. In industries with many producers where control of competition is difficult, unions may take the lead in forming and policing restrictive agreements. Unionism also makes it harder for new firms to break into an industry by preventing them from operating even temporarily at a lower level of labor costs while getting established. Unions are unenthusiastic about antitrust and other pro-competitive policies, and fall in naturally with legalized cartel arrangements, such as those established by the NRA codes in New Deal days.

As between any one industry and the remainder of the economy, the union lines up with employers and strengthens their hand against outside competition and against the consuming public. Unions are just as interested as employers in maximizing the industry's total "take" from the public,[2] and come to blows with them only over the division of the proceeds. Unionism thus tends toward what Simons and others have termed a "syndicalist" economic structure, in which organized industry groups try to extract maximum gains from the economy under a regime of fixed prices, fixed wages, and controlled entrance.

MONEY WAGES AND THE PRICE LEVEL

Does unionism cause the level of money wages and prices to rise faster over the course of time than would happen under nonunion conditions? Does it produce or strengthen an "inflationary bias" in the economic mechanism? If so, what are the economic consequences? Do workers gain anything in real purchasing power through a more rapid advance of money wages, or are the wage increases simply cancelled out by price increases? These are "iffy" questions, in the sense that it is hard to get any answers by looking at statistics and one is forced back to theoretical reasoning. They are examined at length in Chapter 16 and the reader must wait until that point for a full explanation of the conclusions suggested here.

There are several reasons for believing that unionism does strengthen inflationary tendencies in the economy. Perhaps most important is its influence on government's monetary and fiscal policies. Belief in full employment is now as firmly established as belief in motherhood and the home. But how full is "full"? Should one be content with 5 per cent unemployment or should one insist on no more than 3 per cent, or even 2 per cent? Unions tend to set the employment target high and the unavoidable minimum of unemployment low. Whenever unemployment rises above this level they insist that the federal government leap into aggressive action on all fronts—lower interest rates, easier credit, increases in government spending, reductions in

---

[2] An occasional exception be noted. During the 1958 bargaining negotiations President Reuther of the Automobile Workers proposed that automobile company profits should be reduced by lowering prices to consumers as well as raising wages to employees. This may have been merely a public relations gesture or may have been intended more seriously. In any event it was treated as a utopian idea, both by the companies and by most outside commentators, and nothing came of it.

taxes. Too aggressive action, however, may raise total money demand at a rate which will pull up prices along with production. The objectives of maximum employment and stable prices are somewhat in conflict. Unions give heavy weight to employment objectives and do not worry much about increases in the price level. To the extent that they have political influence, this outlook will be reflected in government policy.

Union pressure on the collective bargaining front also alters the behavior of money wages in several respects. Unions can usually prevent wage cuts during recession, even in industries where prices and profits are falling. Wage cuts are unpopular and rare even under nonunion conditions, but unionism strengthens the downward rigidity of wages. During expansion periods when employment and prices are rising, unionism probably reduces the lag of wages behind prices through automatic escalator clauses, through frequent wage reopenings, and through aggressive bargaining. A short price-wage lag adds to the momentum of an inflationary movement. It is possible also for unions, by pushing up wages, to produce an increase in the price level which would not have occurred otherwise, an effect usually termed "cost-push inflation." How far this possibility is actually realized is a warmly debated issue which we shall examine further in Chapter 16. Even without this, however, there are adequate grounds for concluding that unionism accentuates the long-term uptrend of wages and prices.

Does a more rapid increase in the price level add to workers' real wages or to their share of real national income? This is a large and complicated problem, full discussion of which must also be deferred until Chapter 16. The broad conclusion will be that wage earners can make some gains out of inflation at the expense of salaried groups, interest and rent recipients, pensioners, and others with fixed or sluggish incomes; but these gains are small relative to those which arise from gradual growth of productivity and per capita output over the long run.

REAL WAGES AND THE DISTRIBUTION OF NATIONAL INCOME

The level of real wages in an economy is limited by the level of labor productivity in the economy, and over long periods real wages rise at about the same rate that productivity rises. These relationships, including a definition of the slippery term "productivity," will be examined more fully in Chapter 17; but they are almost self-evident on an intuitive basis and the student should have a dim memory of them from his elementary economics course.

Productivity depends on a variety of factors, of which the following are probably most important: (1) the "industry-mix" of the economy, and particularly the proportions of the population engaged in agriculture. A major reason for rising output per man in a developing economy is transference of labor out of agriculture, where output per man is relatively low, into manufacturing and other industries which use more mechanical equipment and have higher output per man; (2) richness and location of natural resources; (3) size of the economy—greater size makes possible fuller specialization and fuller use of the economies of mass production; (4) quantity of buildings, machinery, and other capital goods available, which depends on the percentage of national income saved and invested in previous years; (5) rate of progress in science and technology, which is the source of new products and improved production methods. This depends partly on the amount of resources which the economy devotes to scientific research—one cannot be sure that putting a lot of scientists to work will produce major inventions, but it should help; (6) efficiency of managerial organization; (7) quality of the labor force, including physical stamina, training and skill, and willingness to exert a high rate of effort; (8) size of the labor force. This works in the reverse direction from the preceding factors. Given the level of factors (1) to (7), the greater the quantity of labor available the lower will be output per man and the level of real wages. Abundant labor is cheap labor, while labor scarcity makes for high wages.

How is the spread of unionism and collective bargaining likely to affect each of these factors? Several of them—(1), (2), (3), and (5) —are probably affected little if any. As regards (4), unionism probably makes for a slower rate of capital accumulation, which would mean less capital per worker and lower productivity. The collective bargaining and political policies of trade unions are critical or even hostile toward business profits, which provide both the incentive and much of the funds for new investment in plant and equipment.

The effect of unionism on factor (6)—managerial enterprise and efficiency—is conjectural. On one hand it can be argued that union pressure for higher wages provides a continuing stimulus to managerial efficiency and inventiveness. This can be supported by numerous cases in which the sudden necessity of meeting a higher wage bill has startled management into making economies which might otherwise have been postponed indefinitely. On the other hand it can be argued that if the union stands always ready to take away higher profits through wage demands, management is likely to lose interest in setting up targets at which the union can shoot. It will no longer have an incentive to raise profits by improving methods and expanding the enterprise. The tendency of unionism to strengthen monopolistic arrangements in product markets may also react adversely on managerial efficiency.

Unionism probably has significant effects on factor (7)—worker effort and efficiency—but again the effects run in both directions. Union emphasis on public education, trade training, reasonable hours, and other conditions may increase the quality and efficiency of the labor force. On the other hand, make-work rules, restrictions on work speeds, and other union policies may reduce output per man. An important effect of collective bargaining is to protect workers against arbitrary discipline and make them feel more secure in their jobs. On an armchair basis, one can reason either that this will make men work better or that it will lead to a slackening of effort. In this as in so many other matters of industrial relations, the only course at present is an honest confession of ignorance.

Concerning the final factor, the supply of labor, we can speak with greater confidence. It is almost certain that unionism in the United States has produced a considerable reduction in labor supply. The labor movement was influential in the enactment of restrictive immigration laws in the nineteen-twenties, which reduced immigration from a flood to a trickle. Trade unions have also been in the forefront of movements to raise the school-leaving age, to limit the occupations in which young people and women may engage, and to encourage earlier retirement through private and public pension systems. These things all make for a smaller supply of labor from a given population. While the great reduction in weekly hours of work over the past century cannot be attributed entirely to union activity, the unions have played a prominent role. More recently, they have secured sizeable reductions in annual hours of work through provision for longer vacations and more paid holidays. It is impossible to measure the total effect of these policies, but it would not be surprising to find that the present labor supply of the United States is 20 per cent lower than it would have been in the absence of union activity

Where does this bring us out as regards the total impact of unionism on real wages? The evidence is unclear, and one must speak of possibilities rather than probabilities. It is possible that the net effect on productivity through factors (1) to (7) has been adverse. For any given size of labor force, output per man-hour may be lower than it would be under nonunion conditions. But this effect, if it exists, may well have been outweighed by an increase in output per man-hour due to the reduction in labor supply. (For the geometrically minded, this would mean that the economy had been shifted leftward to a *higher* point on a *lower* labor productivity curve, with the former effect outweighing the latter.) One could thus argue that unionism has on balance raised real wages; but it should be repeated that the factual foundation for this or any other conclusion is very shaky.

It may be objected that the analysis to this point has proceeded on the basis of rather rigid theoretical reasoning, under which there must be definite rates of return to capital and labor, and the national income is divided neatly between the two groups. But is the real world as determinate as our theoretical diagrams? What about bargaining power? May not unions have raised labor's share of national income simply by demanding more and forcing employers to get along with less?

If we may anticipate here the findings of Chapter 17, there is no indication that unions have been able to encroach materially on profits by the collective bargaining route. The relative size of the wage and profit shares in national income has remained remarkably stable over the past fifty or sixty years. In the United States as well as in other countries, both wages and profits have gained at the expense of rent and interest payments; but this is mainly a result of wartime price inflation for which unions have little responsibility.

This does not mean that unionism has no effect whatever on the distribution of national income. There is now a substantial redistribution of income from higher to lower income brackets through government channels. Money raised through income taxation is used to provide free or subsidized public services for all citizens, and to make cash payments to the aged, the unemployable, and other dependent groups. The distribution of income after taking account of taxes and subsidies is substantially more equal than the pre-tax distribution. This is in some degree a transfer from the propertied to the wage-earning group, and unions provide a large part of the political support for it.

UNIONISM AND RELATIVE WAGE RATES

Whatever the effect of unionism on the average level of wages, it clearly can and does alter the relative earnings of particular groups of workers. Since Chapter 10 was devoted primarily to this matter, we need do little more than restate the conclusions reached there.

1. In some industries unions have succeeded in reducing labor supply, or increasing labor demand, or both, thus raising the "natural" market level of wages.

2. Both by these methods and by direct wage pressure, some unions have probably raised the wage level of their industries relative to other industries. This is even more true if one takes into account fringe benefits, which are typically higher in the unionized industries. The wage advantage of the unionized industries is difficult to assess statistically, however, and seems to be less than one might expect from armchair reasoning.

3. Unionism tends to equalize the wage levels of companies competing in the same product market. In the case of manufacturing and other industries competing on a national basis, this typically means some reduction of geographical wage differences. Southern plants are raised relative to Northern ones, and small-town plants are brought closer to the level of the large cities.

4. At the plant level, unionism tends to reduce differences between people doing the same kind of work by establishing standard job rates or rate ranges. Wage standardization is most complete under time payment, less so under incentive payment.

5. The fact that collective bargaining establishes standard rates for each job means that unions are necessarily concerned with the spread between the top and bottom of the plant wage structure, between the laborer's wage and the craftsman's wage. Experience in this respect varies widely from industry to industry. In some industries unionism has apparently tended to reduce the skilled-unskilled differential, but in others this has not happened. In few cases does unionism seem to have had a major impact on occupational differentials.

Though these effects are important, the total impact of unionism on relative wage rates should not be exaggerated. We shall see in

Chapter 18 that there are strong economic forces working toward a narrowing of most types of wage difference—between men on the same job, between occupational levels, between geographical areas, and so on. Wage equalization is in the nature of things in an advanced industrial economy. Unionism works in the same general direction and has speeded up the wage levelling process in certain respects. It does not seem, however, to have materially changed the broad contours of the national wage structure. To a considerable extent unions have been given credit (or blame) for developments which were "in the cards" on economic grounds.

NON-WAGE BENEFITS AND THEIR COST

Unions try to win for their members a wide array of benefits in addition to wages. Some of these involve little cost or may even reduce costs and add to productive efficiency. Others, however, do involve costs which must be weighed against the benefits provided.

In some cases the costs are borne mainly by the workers themselves. Shorter hours of work and supplementary income payments are two leading examples. Here it is pertinent to ask whether the benefits are worth the cost from the workers' standpoint. Would they be willing to "buy" the benefits included in the union contract through the necessary sacrifice in wages? Or may the terms worked out by the union differ considerably from what workers would have chosen on an individual basis? An answer to this question does not necessarily tell which set of terms is preferable from a welfare standpoint. Economists usually take individual preferences as the most reliable guide, on the ground that each person knows his own interests better than anyone else. Many terms of employment, however, have to be defined by organizational rules set either by management or through collective bargaining; and workers may not always be the best judge of their own interests over the long run.

Support of the union organization itself involves costs, typically amounting to something less than one per cent of members' weekly earnings. This may be regarded as a service charge for the union's efforts in policing working conditions, processing grievances, and pressing contract demands. Many workers doubtless undervalue these services and would be reluctant to pay for them on a fully voluntary basis, just as most citizens undervalue the protective services of government and grumble over the necessary tax levies. Union dues may nevertheless be a "good buy" in terms of workers' long-run interests.

A substantial part of employers' total payroll cost now goes into insurance payments and reserve funds to protect workers against retirement, illness and disability, medical expenses, unemployment, and other risks. Union pressure has been a major factor in the spread of these "private social security" systems, as well as improvement of benefits under government programs. Union members welcome these types of benefit heartily, not altogether realizing that they are partly an alternative to higher basic wage rates. If an employer is willing to concede a ten cent an hour increase in labor costs in a particular year, and if the union asks him to put five cents of this into enlarging supplementary benefits, only five cents remains for direct wage increases. There is reason to think that if workers were aware of the alternatives and could conduct referendum votes on them, they would typically prefer higher wage rates and smaller benefits than those urged by union leaders. This does not mean, however, that the workers' evaluation is correct. One can make a strong case that workers should be adequately protected against the income risks of modern industry, and that they should be obliged to "buy" this protection even though many would be too shortsighted to do so on an individual basis.

Reduction of working hours below a certain level, as was argued in Chapter 9, means a reduction of national output, and part of this will fall on workers in the form of lower real incomes and consumption levels. Here one encounters the problem of workers' valuation of income *versus* leisure. Up to the present there has probably been no serious discrepancy between union-established working hours and those which workers would have chosen voluntarily; but the problem of conflicting objectives may become more serious in the future.

The workweek and workyear will probably continue to decline gradually in unionized industries. Workers will go along with a policy of hours reduction, partly because they do not understand the income costs involved, partly because shorter hours are plausibly urged as an unemployment remedy. Actually, hours reduction is not a suitable remedy either for general unemployment or for overstaffing of a particular industry. There is also reason to doubt whether a further substantial shortening of hours would be in accord with workers' preferences. Several million people are now holding more than one job, indicating that for them the standard workweek was already too short. The eagerness of many workers to put in overtime whenever possible testifies in the same direction. It is quite possible, therefore, that unions may force down hours faster than most workers prefer, and that what used to be counted a major benefit of unionism may turn into a disadvantage.

The cost of some union benefits falls partly or mainly on consumers, among whom workers are of course included. The cost of supplementary or fringe benefits may be shifted partly to consumers. A union may be able to impose heavier labor costs on an industry by a combination of direct wages and supplementary benefits than it could through wage demands alone, leading to higher total costs and higher prices. Part of the cost of hours reduction is also shifted to the general consuming public, as was explained in Chapter 9. Union efforts to control work speeds increase production costs by increasing the amount of labor time required per unit of product. Improvements in physical working conditions usually cost money. Resistance to technical improvements, insistence that promotions be made strictly on a seniority basis, and insistence that the union's consent must be given before certain management decisions can be carried out—these and other things tend to reduce production efficiency and raise costs.

Critics of unionism sometimes imply that any union policy which reduces man-hour output or increases unit production costs is economically harmful. This is not a tenable position. The question which must be asked in each case is this: Do the benefits which workers obtain from a particular union policy outweigh the additional costs imposed on consumers of the product? This question can be answered only with respect to a particular situation; and the answer will usually depend, not on the kind of policy involved, but on the degree to which it has been carried. Down to a certain point, for example, a reduction in work speeds does more good than harm; beyond that point it becomes undesirable. The problem in each case is to strike a proper balance between the interests of a particular producer group and of society at large.

There is strong reason to think that, in the absence of trade union organization, the balance is tilted too far in the direction of minimizing money costs of production, i.e., of sacrificing the interests of workers to those of employers and consumers. There is equally little doubt that unions, in attempting to redress the balance, sometimes overshoot the mark and saddle industry with unduly high costs. On the whole, however, it seems likely that one comes closer to a proper balancing of producer and consumer interests with collective bargaining than without it.

It should be recognized also that collective bargaining yields important benefits involving little or no addition to production costs. Many improvements in working conditions and personnel methods can be accomplished with little expense; yet unless workers point out the possibilities and are in a position to insist on them, the changes may not be made. The greatest single benefit which unionism brings the worker is protection against arbitrary discharge. This involves little direct cost and seems as likely to raise worker efficiency as to lower it. Seniority rules concerning layoff and retiring are also much appreciated by workers and may well have a neutral or even favorable effect on efficiency. Where benefits accrue to the worker at little or no social cost, they would seem to be advantageous from every point of view.

SOCIAL STRUCTURE OF THE SHOP

A major consequence of collective bargaining is to change the foreman from an absolute to a constitutional monarch, who must operate within the framework of the union agreement and whose decisions can be appealed to higher authority. To the worker, this appears as an unmitigated gain. To the foreman, it appears as an increase in the difficulty and a reduction in the attractiveness of his job. It is one thing to maintain production standards when the men under you are fully subject to your authority. It is quite another when your every decision, large or small, may be taken up as a grievance by the union and you may be forced into ignominious retreat. The foreman is part of management, yet he must live with the workers and with the union. Nor can he be sure that higher management will back him up in a grievance proceeding. Management must save its powder for crucial issues and must view each case in the light of over-all strategy vis-à-vis the union. The individual foreman is expendable. The trying nature of the foreman's job under union conditions has created a real problem of persuading qualified men to accept promotion to foremanships. Many workers understandably reason, "Why should I have everybody hating me for an extra ten cents an hour?"

The degree of personal harmony and productive efficiency in the shop depends a good deal on the relations which the foreman is able to work out with the union steward in his department. A skillful foreman can use the steward as an aid to management, an informal consultant and go-between in dealing with the workers. Foreman and steward may work out flexible interpretations of personnel rules and may trade enforcement on some points for concessions on others. Carried too far, of course, this may lead to erosion of the foreman's authority. One finds situations in which the union steward is the *de facto* head of the shop and the foreman's position is secondary. The foreman's central problem is to maintain effective control while winning consent and cooperation.

Whatever difficulties the grievance procedure may pose for the individual foreman, it has important advantages from an over-all management standpoint. It provides a channel through which complaints and problems arising in the plant can be transmitted rapidly up the line to top management. In theory, the regular management chain of command already provides a means for upward communication of information and problems as well as downward communication of directives and instructions. It was pointed out in Chapter 6, however, that upward communication is apt to be heavily censored with a view to passing on only favorable news to one's superiors. Top management may thus get the impression that everything is running smoothly in the plant, when in fact discontent may have risen almost to the point of explosion.

Under collective bargaining, pressures accumulating in the plant which do not find expression through regular management channels can travel up the line through the grievance procedure. This procedure provides a supplementary, and frequently more rapid, line of communication from the bottom to the top of the management structure. Selekman has advocated that management make full use of this method of keeping its finger on the pulse of the labor force.[3] Management, he contends, should adopt a clinical rather than a legalistic approach to the grievance procedure. The first question to be asked about a grievance should not be, "Is it a valid grievance under the contract and does the worker have a legal case for adjustment?" The question should be rather, "What does the filing of this grievance, whether valid or invalid, indicate about the state of human relations in the shop? What can be done to improve the situation?"

---

[3] Benjamin Selekman, *Labor Relations and Human Relations* (New York: McGraw-Hill Book Company, Inc., 1947).

Finally, collective bargaining makes a fundamental difference in the determination and administration of personnel policies. Under nonunion conditions these can be regarded as analogous to any other group of management functions—marketing, finance, engineering, and so on. They are subject to unilateral management control, and the only question which arises is whether a particular procedure will contribute to greater efficiency of the business. Under collective bargaining, this is drastically changed. A few functions—notably the selection and training of new employees, and certain welfare activities —remain under primary control of management. With respect to the great majority of personnel functions, however, both the determination and execution of policy become a bipartisan matter. With respect to any policy, management must ask not only, "Does it contribute to efficiency?" but also, "Can it be sold to the union?" Skill in negotiation and personal contacts, rather than skill in engineering and other managerial techniques, becomes the primary requirement for an industrial relations officer. An incidental effect is usually to raise the status of the industrial relations group in the management hierarchy, and to bring about the hiring of better industrial relations personnel.

We have dwelt a good deal in earlier sections on wage rates and other economic consequences of collective bargaining. One should never lose sight, however, of the effects just described. It is these which most directly affect the daily lives of everyone in industry, from laborers to corporation presidents. These effects must consequently bulk large in any over-all appraisal of trade unionism.

STATUS OF THE INDIVIDUAL WORKER

Over the long run, one of the most important effects of unionism is that it produces a different kind of man. The worker under a union contract is freed from the danger of arbitrary and unpredictable treatment by the employer, from the necessity of flattering or bribing the foreman to hold his job, from the fear of offending the employer by his political opinions or personal conduct. To this extent he comes closer to being a completely free man.

Unionism increases the worker's sense of participation in economic and political affairs. He is no longer an isolated individual, subject to forces which he can neither understand nor control. He is a member of a powerful movement, which can influence events not only in the plant but in the economy at large. The top officers of his union are courted by political leaders and sit in the high councils of the nation. The worker's union membership gives him a more direct sense of participation than he enjoys as consumer, voter, stockholder, or in any of his other capacities. It gives him "a stake in the system" and renders him less susceptible to proposals for revolutionary change.

Unionism also opens up to the worker additional possibilities of personal progress. Workers of unusual ability can rise to salaried positions in the union hierarchy. A few go all the way to the top and become national figures. Many more rise to lower positions in which they enjoy a modest but assured income, influence over considerable numbers of workers and employers, and prominence in state and local affairs. In addition to the direct satisfactions afforded by union office, it is frequently a steppingstone to positions in industry or government. Workers can demonstrate their abilities in union affairs, rise vertically through the union hierarchy, and then move laterally to prominent positions in other types of organization.

In all these ways—by liberating the worker from arbitrary employer discipline, by increasing his feeling of participation and influence in civic affairs, and by opening up to him new channels of vertical mobility—unionism tends to create greater freedom and opportunity. At the same time it imposes a new network of union regulations with penalties for violating them. This raises a problem of guaranteeing citizenship rights in the union, of ensuring that the worker's gains in freedom as against the employer are not too heavily offset by a loss of freedom as against union officials. Clark Kerr has argued cogently for the need to protect the individual against domination by every type of private association as well as by the political state:

In the area of liberty, there are probably four imperatives. First, freedom of access of the worker, without discrimination, to corporation and union alike. Second, an opportunity for him to participate in setting the most important relationships between employer and employee on the one hand and union and member on the other—in the first case through the right to select bargaining representation and in the second through the right to vote freely in elections. Third, a right to judicial review of disciplinary action whether by employer or union.

Fourth, and this is a much neglected consideration, freedom from control or even dominant influence by the corporation or union in the non-job phases of life. . . . This means a rejection of both the all-embracing corporation of Mayo and the all-embracing union of Tannenbaum. The separation of power over job, politics, consumption patterns and so forth, has as much to recommend it as the separation of governmental power into the legislative, the executive, and the judicial.[4]

BALANCE OF POLITICAL POWER IN THE COMMUNITY

The political problem in an industrial society is exceedingly intricate. It involves preventing the individual from being overshadowed by corporations, unions, and other private associations as well as by government. It also involves some reasonable balance among private power groups seeking to influence the conduct of government. Unionism, by organizing a powerful new pressure group, produces a different balance of forces in the political arena. Union pressure, while frequently aligned with business pressure on narrow issues of industry interests, typically runs counter to it on broader issues. The range of conflict is suggested by such labor objectives as improvement of the legal status of trade unions, minimum wages and maximum hours of work, social insurance and other protective labor legislation, progressive income and inheritance taxation, full employment policies, and government subsidization of housing construction, medical care, and education.

The advance of social legislation is so remorseless that it seems on the surface to result from some sort of natural law. It is doubtful, however, whether the progress of social legislation results mainly from greater general enlightenment and greater middle-class sympathy with labor's objectives. It is more influenced by the growing membership and increasing political awareness of trade unions, and by the efforts of each political party to win enough labor votes to secure control of the government. A political party which can be labeled as hostile to labor's main objectives has no chance of survival. Since survival and power are the aims of a political organization, one can be sure that both of our major parties will try in future to look like "friends of labor"—even between elections!

It is no longer possible to have governmental policies of the sort followed by conservative administrations in Britain and the United States before 1930. This may be good or bad, depending on one's

---

[4] Clark Kerr, "Industrial Relations and the Liberal Pluralist," *Proceedings of Seventh Annual Meeting of IRRA* (1954), pp. 2-16.

outlook. It is certainly a development of major importance. Unions have a large share of the responsibility for barring the door to the past.

IS UNIONISM A GOOD IDEA?

The reader should by now have plenty of facts, ideas, and arguments on which to base his own evaluation of trade unionism. For the author to lay down the law would be wrong and would serve no educational purpose. He may perhaps be permitted, however, to sound one word of warning.

This warning is that one's evaluation of unionism should not be too narrowly economic in character. It is a curious fact that both the critics and defenders of unionism have based their arguments mainly on the wage-employment effects outlined in the first few sections of this chapter. The prevalent opinion among economic theorists has been that unions can make only limited income gains for their members, and that these gains are likely to be outweighed by the harmful effects of "artificial" interference with economic forces. Defenders of unionism have pointed to gaps in the assumptions of economic theory, have argued that unions have a substantial positive effect on productivity, wages, and employment, and have asserted that these gains benefit society at large as well as union members. Much of their reasoning, however, rests on dubious economics—for example, the familiar union dogma that a general increase in the money wage level always raises employment, in good times or bad.

Actually, there is little evidence that unionism has any striking effects on productivity, money wage levels, real wage levels, or the distribution of industry's receipts between wages and profits. These subjects bulk large in textbook discussion mainly because we have theories of a sort about wages and employment while we have no accepted theoretical framework for analyzing working conditions, social relations in the plant, personal freedom, or political power. But the fact that we have conceptual difficulty in grappling with these problems does not mean that they are less important than wage issues.

It is doubtful whether either the defenders or critics of unionism can hope for much more than a draw on the wage-employment front. The situations in which union manipulation of labor supply and wage rates has favorable effects can always be matched by others in which the effects are unfavorable. A positive case for unionism probably has to be made mainly under the last four headings listed above—nonwage benefits, the social structure of the plant, the status of the individual worker, and the balance of political power in the community. Negative points can be made here also, but they have less force, and the general case for unionism and collective bargaining appears quite strong. But there is no reason to support a good case with bad economics, as is done by many who seek to justify unionism on a narrow income basis.

Discussion questions

1. Discuss the effects of labor unions on the mobility of labor. Would the absence of unions significantly alter hiring and job seeking?

2. "Unionism substitutes 'monopoly' for 'competition' in wage determination." Discuss.

3. What are the effects of unions on competition in product markets?

4. What are the determinants of productivity? Do labor unions, on balance, raise or lower labor productivity?

5. What are the main noneconomic consequences of collective bargaining in terms of the plant and the individual worker?

6. "When all is said and done, the chief sufferer from union economic activity is the consumer." Discuss.

Selected reading

See readings for previous chapters.

II

ECONOMICS OF THE LABOR MARKET

13

Dynamics Of Labor Supply, Employment, And Unemployment

Economics is concerned with the way in which the productive services of land, labor, and capital equipment are brought together to produce a national output of a certain size and composition; and with the way in which this output is distributed among the participants. Labor economics focuses on the supply, use, and remuneration of labor as a factor of production. The labor aspects of production, however, are integrally related to the process as a whole. Labor economics is not a separate study. It is an aspect of general economics, involving within its special sphere a greater attention to factual detail and to practical applications of economic analysis than one ordinarily finds in a general treatise.

The terms "labor" or "employment" are often used as a shorthand expression for economic activity in general. When we speak of the total demand for labor, we really mean the general level of business activity or national output. A central problem in economics, usually explored in courses on macroeconomic theory and economic fluctuations, is to explain what determines the level of economic activity at a particular time. While we cannot retrace this ground in detail, it will be necessary to say something about total demand for labor in connection with the discussion of unemployment in Chapter 14.

It is necessary also to explain what determines the quantity of labor demanded by particular firms and industries. Here we rely mainly on production theory. Particular demands for labor reflect demands for the products that labor is used to produce, plus the supplies of cooperating factors and the known techniques of production. The other major concerns of this part are the supply of labor services— total supply in the nation, and supply to particular firms, industries, and occupations—and the determination of wage rates—both wage rates for particular jobs, and the average wage level for the economy.

These matters are obviously interrelated. Wages help to call forth labor supply and to determine where particular workers will seek work. Wage rates also, given particular demand curves for labor, determine how much labor each employer will be willing to hire. Labor demand and supply curves in turn are the major forces bearing on wage rates, though market determinations may be altered on occasion by collective bargaining or legal wage regulation. All the problems to be considered in Part Two, therefore, form an integrated whole.

Since it is impossible to discuss everything at once, it will be convenient to divide the subject matter into two main parts: (1) The determinants of total labor supply, the processes of employment and the structural features of labor markets. These matters are considered in Chapters 13 through 15. (2) The determination of wage rates for particular jobs, the general level of money wages and real wages, the reasons for inadequate family incomes in the United States, and the problem of establishing a minimum standard of living for all. These matters form the substance of Chapters 16 through 20.

SOME QUESTIONS ABOUT LABOR SUPPLY
AND THE LABOR MARKET

In order to reduce this general introduction to concrete terms, let us look briefly at the key issues with which we shall be concerned in the next three chapters:

1. What determines the number of people who will enter the labor force and perform gainful work in a particular society? This is a matter of great importance. A larger percentage of the population in the labor force will presumably make for greater national output and higher living standards. Does the percentage of the population in the labor force fluctuate widely, or does it remain relatively stable

over the course of time? How does it respond to changes in the level of wage rates, and to changes in the number of jobs available?

2. The number of people in the labor force is far from being the whole story. The physical efficiency of these people, the number of hours they work in a year, the intensity of effort they are willing to put forth, and the training and experience they bring to their jobs, will all have an important effect on national output. It is necessary to examine these aspects of labor supply as well as the more obvious aspect of numbers.

3. Everyone in the labor force is not necessarily employed. How do we define and measure employment? How has total employment fluctuated over the course of time? How has the detailed make-up of employment, the numbers engaged in each occupation and industry, changed over the last century or so?

4. The difference between the size of the labor force and the volume of employment is unemployment. How much unemployment have we had over the period for which measurements exist? Does unemployment seem to be increasing or decreasing? What are the main reasons for it? General depression is one important reason, but there are others. Who are the unemployed? Which groups in the labor force are hit hard by unemployment, and which groups are relatively immune? The questions listed under these first four headings will be considered in the present chapter.

5. What can be done about unemployment? This divides into two sub-questions. First, what can be done to prevent general economic depression? We must say something about this, although we obviously cannot undertake a full treatment of economic fluctuations. Second, what can be done about unemployment resulting from other causes —irregularity of operations in particular plants, seasonal fluctuations, and faulty organization of the labor market? To the extent that unemployment cannot be completely prevented, how can the hardship resulting from unemployment be reduced? The main measure which has been developed for this purpose is unemployment compensation, and we shall need to look carefully into the principles of this system. These questions will provide more than enough material for Chapter 14.

6. Even if there were always enough jobs available, there would still be a problem of the right man getting to the right job as quickly as possible. This may be termed the problem of "labor marketing," or the problem of distributing individual workers among particular

jobs. This is a serious problem for both workers and employers, and the public interest is also importantly involved. How do workers choose jobs at the present time? How does the labor market function? How can its operation be improved? The answers to these questions will occupy us in Chapter 15.

PARTICIPATION IN THE LABOR FORCE

Definition and measurement

The important thing about the labor force is not size per se. If one finds that a country with a population of one hundred million has twice as large a labor force as a country with a population of fifty million, this is not very surprising or significant. It is significant, however, to find that in one country only 40 per cent of the population are in the labor force while in another country 55 per cent are in; or to find that the percentage in a particular country has changed considerably over the course of time. The percentage of a population which is in the labor force at a particular time is termed the *labor force participation rate* of that population. We shall use this term from now on, sometimes shortening it for convenience to "participation rate." The purpose of this section is to examine what determines labor force participation rates, with particular reference to the United States.

Measurement of the labor force involves complicated problems which can only be suggested here.[1] In the United States, a complete enumeration is made every ten years in connection with the decennial census.[2] Between censuses the Bureau of the Census conducts a monthly survey of a small sample of households carefully selected to represent different sections of the country. On the basis of information obtained from these households, estimates are made of the

---

[1] The reader interested in these problems and the efforts of statisticians to overcome them should consult Clarence D. Long, *Labor Force, Income and Employment* (New York: National Bureau of Economic Research, 1950); John D. Durand, *The Labor Force in the United States, 1890–1960* (New York: Social Science Research Council, 1948); and A. J. Jaffe and Charles D. Stewart, *Manpower Resources and Utilization: Principles of Working Force Analysis* (New York: John Wiley and Sons, Inc., 1951).

[2] The census is rightly regarded as one of the most accurate of statistical sources. A July 1953 issue of the *New York Herald Tribune*, however, reported that a Chicago census enumerator had added several thousand nonexistent names to his lists during the 1950 census, and made up fictitious characteristics for these nonexistent people. When asked the reason for this, he replied, " I thought we had a quota to meet."

total labor force, employment, and unemployment in the country as a whole. This *Monthly Report on the Labor Force* is the standard source for current labor force information, though it is not quite as accurate as a complete census count.

An individual is counted as being in the labor force if he is able to work and either has a job or is "actively seeking" work. This apparently simple definition leaves considerable room for doubt in many cases. What about a man who says he is able to work, but whom employers judge to be so incapable that they are unwilling to hire him? What about a man who is not "actively" seeking work because he believes there are no jobs available in his area, but who would accept a job if offered? What about a coal miner in a depressed mining area, who is willing to take a mining job but no other kind of work? Added to these logical problems is the fact that the census interviewer usually sees only the housewife, and has to take her word about the status of other people in the household. This leaves room for a good deal of misunderstanding and faulty reporting. Another problem is that millions of workers in the United States go into and out of the labor force quite frequently. This is true particularly of students and housewives, who may work part-time or work for a few months of the year and then drop out for a considerable period.

As a result of these and other difficulties, there is a considerable range of error in published reports on the size of the labor force. While we shall follow the convention of using a single labor force figure, it would be better to think in terms of a zone around the reported figure, which in a country as large as the United States may number several million people. The complexity of the measurement problem is well illustrated in a diagram constructed by W. S. Woytinsky, and reproduced here as Figure 5.[3]

Participation rates in the United States and elsewhere

What are the facts about labor force participation rates in the United States? A good introduction to this subject is Table 5, which shows the situation for various sub-groups in the population in 1890, 1947, and 1962, with estimates for 1975.[4]

---

[3] Figure 5 is reproduced from W. S. Woytinsky and associates, *Employment and Wages in the United States* (New York: Twentieth Century Fund, 1953), p. 315.

[4] Data for 1890 from Long, *op. cit.*, Appendix A; data for 1947 and 1962, and Bureau of Labor Statistics projection for 1975, are from U. S. Department of Labor, *Manpower Report of the President* (Washington: Government Printing Office, 1963), cited hereafter as *Manpower Report, 1963*.

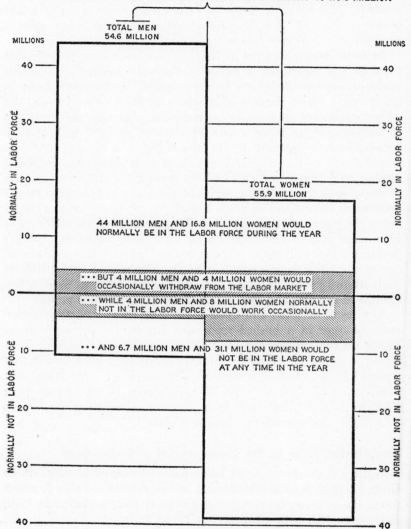

IN 1950, POPULATION OF 14 YEARS AND OVER WOULD AMOUNT TO 110.5 MILLION

TOTAL MEN
54.6 MILLION

MILLIONS

MILLIONS

TOTAL WOMEN
55.9 MILLION

44 MILLION MEN AND 16.8 MILLION WOMEN WOULD
NORMALLY BE IN THE LABOR FORCE DURING THE YEAR

••• BUT 4 MILLION MEN AND 4 MILLION WOMEN WOULD
OCCASIONALLY WITHDRAW FROM THE LABOR MARKET

••• WHILE 4 MILLION MEN AND 8 MILLION WOMEN NORMALLY
NOT IN THE LABOR FORCE WOULD WORK OCCASIONALLY

••• AND 6.7 MILLION MEN AND 31.1 MILLION WOMEN WOULD
NOT BE IN THE LABOR FORCE
AT ANY TIME IN THE YEAR

NORMALLY IN LABOR FORCE

NORMALLY NOT IN LABOR FORCE

FIG. 5 *Hypothetical distribution of population aged 14 years and over,
by work status, 1950.*

322

TABLE 5

LABOR FORCE PARTICIPATION RATES BY AGE AND SEX,
UNITED STATES, 1890, 1947, 1962, AND PROJECTIONS FOR 1975

Age Group	1890	1947	1962	Projected 1975
Male 14+				
Total	89.3	84.4	79.3	76.9
14–19	61.5	54.2	43.6	44.6
20–24	90.8	84.8	89.1	85.7
25–34 ⎫	99.0	95.8	97.4	96.2
35–44 ⎭		98.0	97.7	96.7
45–54 ⎫	98.2	95.5	95.6	94.8
55–64 ⎭		89.6	86.2	84.8
65+	74.1	47.8	30.3	25.4
Female 14+				
Total	21.0	31.0	36.7	38.2
14–19	26.9	31.6	29.0	30.0
20–24	32.1	44.9	47.4	46.5
25–34 ⎫	18.0	32.0	36.4	38.0
35–44 ⎭		36.3	44.1	47.9
45–54 ⎫	15.7	32.7	50.0	56.0
55–64 ⎭		24.3	38.7	42.5
65+	10.7	8.1	9.9	10.5
Total 14+				
Total	56.1	57.3	57.4	57.0

If one looks down the column for a recent year, such as 1962, the general shape of the figures seems reasonable. A higher proportion of men than of women is in the labor force. People in the prime of life are more likely to be in the labor force than are the very young or the very old.

Reading across the Table, we see the marked changes which have occurred over the years. Labor force participation by men has dropped sharply in both the youngest and oldest age groups. In 1890, three-fifths of boys aged 14-19 were in the labor force. Today the proportion is only a little over two-fifths. The reason is that many more young people are now completing high school, and an increasing proportion is going on to college. On the surface, we can trace this to stricter laws about school attendance and a higher social evaluation of education. More fundamentally, however, the increasing length of customary school attendance can be traced to rising national productivity and income levels. Continuation in high school to age 18 could become the normal thing only when most families felt able to get along without the child's earnings and also to finance higher educational costs through tax payments.

The drop in participation rates for men 45 to 64, and the great decline for men 65 and over, suggests that retirements are now occurring at a considerably earlier age. This reflects partly the decline of self-employment and the increase of paid employment in the economy. A farmer, grocer, or small business man can keep on working as long as he wants to, an employee only as long as the employer is willing. Many companies require compulsory retirement at ages somewhere between 60 and 65. There is also increasing reluctance to hire new employees over 45 or even over 35, partly because of (frequently mistaken) notions about the reduced efficiency of older workers, partly because of the pension and other liabilities incurred by hiring older men. Studies of the effect of public and private pension programs, which have increased greatly in scope since 1930, suggest that these are not an important factor making for earlier retirement.[5] They normally provide an income much below what could be earned by working and often inadequate for minimum living costs. Apart from this, many older people prefer to keep working as long as they can to avoid the feeling of uselessness which so often accompanies retirement.

In the United States, it is customary for adult men to engage in some productive occupation; and the great majority of them do. Even among men aged 25 to 55, however, labor force participation rates have fallen by several percentage points since 1890. The main reason is the steady increase in the real income level of the American population. As wage rates and incomes rise, more people choose not to work at all or to work for a shorter span of years. This inverse relationship between income level and labor supply has been tested by Long in a variety of ways: through cross-section comparison of income levels and labor force participation rates in a sample of American cities in the same census year; cross-section comparison

---

[5] These studies are reviewed in the most thorough monograph available on the American labor force, Clarence D. Long's *The Labor Force Under Changing Income and Employment* (Princeton: Princeton University Press, 1958).

of income level and labor force in different countries at the same time; and examination of time trends in the United States and other countries over several generations. The results of these studies are remarkably consistent with each other. In almost all cases a higher income level is associated with reduced labor supply. For the United States over the period 1890-1950, each one per cent increase in real per capita income was associated with a decrease of about one-sixth of one per cent in the male labor force participation rate.[6]

This does not mean that the increase in incomes *caused* the reduced labor supply in any simple or direct way. The cause-effect sequence is undoubtedly complex. One can say, however, that the increase in incomes gave greater latitude for choice as to whether and how much to work, and for men at all age levels the preponderant choice was less work.

The most striking feature of Table 5 is the sharp increase in the proportion of women in the labor force. In 1890, only one-fifth of the women aged 14 and over were at work. Today the proportion is approaching two-fifths. Most girls work from school leaving until marriage, and even a few years beyond. The proportion at work drops in the age bracket 25-35 because of child care responsibilities. But many women now re-enter the labor force after the children are in school. Even in the short time since 1947, the participation rate of women aged 45-54 has risen from 33 to 50 per cent; and it is expected to increase to 56 per cent by 1975. Girls in college now may well think about what kind of career they will be pursuing thirty years from now.

How can one explain the increase in women's labor force participation since 1890? The fact that wage levels have risen for women as well as for men might have worked in either direction. A higher wage level means that an hour of leisure costs more than before. This *substitution effect* inclines people to do more work. But a higher wage also means a larger income, which permits people to buy more of anything they desire, including leisure. This *income effect* makes for less work. Which effect will preponderate cannot be determined in advance. In this case, the substitution effect has clearly pre-

---

[6] Long, *The Labor Force under Changing Income and Employment*, chap. 7. Calculated for a labor force standardized for age composition and rural-urban composition on the basis of population of the United States in 1940.

ponderated, and higher wage levels have increased women's willingness to enter the labor market.[7]

There is the further consideration that a woman's choice is usually a three-way choice among paid employment, leisure, *and household production* of goods and services. The easier it is to substitute purchased goods and services for household production, the greater the likelihood of the wife working. Over the past several decades the burden of housework has been much reduced by outside purchase of food, clothing, and services formerly produced and consumed in the household. Mechanization of household operations has also contributed, though in lesser measure.

Several developments in the outside community have also speeded the entrance of women into the labor force:

1. A rising educational level has increased the employability of women even more markedly than that of men. Labor force participation by women rises sharply with degree of education. Among urban white women aged 25 to 29, the participation rate of those with four years of schooling is less than half the rate for college graduates.[8]

2. The occupations and industries that have been expanding most rapidly in recent decades—trade, service, professional occupations, government—are those in which women are particularly effective. In 1962 women constituted 69 per cent of all clerical workers, 54 per cent of service workers outside the home, 39 per cent of sales people, 36 per cent of professional and technical workers, and 28 per cent of semiskilled workers in manufacturing. Entrance of women into industry has been facilitated by mechanization and reduction in the degree of physical effort required. It was accelerated also by the wartime shortages of male labor in 1917-18 and 1941-45. During World War II, women riveted ship plates and aircraft frames, and engaged in all but the heaviest types of factory labor. Myths that "women can't do this kind of work" were dispelled and, while women withdrew

---

[7] Although the income effect has been overridden, it is nonetheless real. It is well established, for example, that the higher *the husband's income,* the smaller the likelihood of the wife working. This has been demonstrated by Long (*op. cit.,* chap. 6), using cross-section analysis at a point of time, and taking account of age of wife and number and age of children. A similar conclusion is reached in Jacob Mincer, "Labor Force Participation of Married Women," in *Aspects of Labor Economics* (Princeton: Princeton University Press, 1962), pp. 63-106.

[8] Long, *op. cit.,* chap. 6. Other categories of women in the population show the same positive relation between education and employment.

from some of these jobs after the war, there was a permanent enlarge-ment in the range of occupations open to women.

3. The reduction in the normal workweek has made it easier for women to take employment. A wife who must prepare meals and do other household tasks can work seven or eight hours a day five days a week when she could not work ten hours a day for six days. The growing custom of part-time work has also been helpful in this respect. Of the 23 million women at work in 1962, about 5 million were on voluntary part-time schedules.

4. The fact that women can usually be hired at lower wage rates than men for the same type of work has encouraged employers to substitute female for male labor wherever possible. This situation, the reasons for which will be explored in Chapter 18, may from one point of view be regarded as unjust and undesirable; but from another standpoint it gives women a competitive advantage which has speeded their entrance into more and more occupations.

It is a curious coincidence that the greater labor force participation of some groups in the population and the reduced participation of others have almost exactly offset each other. The percentage of *all* people aged 14 and over who are in the labor force is almost the same today as it was in 1890. The American labor force shows a massive stability over the long run.

There has been considerable discussion of whether the labor force fluctuates with short-run changes in the availability of jobs. Long and some other scholars consider that such fluctuations are negligible.[9] But there are bits of evidence which suggest that the labor force may expand when jobs are easy to get, and conversely that scarcity of jobs may produce a shrinkage of the labor force. In 1940, which was a year of heavy unemployment, the Census labor force totals were somewhat lower than would have been expected on the basis of long-run trends. During the prosperous years 1955-56, on the other hand, the labor force rose a good deal more than would have been expected. This evidence is confirmed by local labor market studies. Sobel and Wilcock found that establishment of new factories in four small Illinois and Missouri towns produced a permanent enlargement of the labor force, mainly through employment of housewives from the town and surrounding farm areas who had not sought work pre-

---

[9] See Long, *op. cit.*, and W. L. Hansen, "The Cyclical Sensitivity of the Labor Supply," *American Economic Review* (June 1961).

viously.[10] Conversely, a plant shutdown by the major industry in a Southern Illinois town caused about 10 per cent of the plant's employees to drop out of the labor force.[11] This suggests that the labor force fluctuates somewhat with job opportunities, the two rising and falling together.

The only thing which seems to have a large impact on participation rates is mobilization for a major war. During World War II, the percentage of the total U.S. population that was in the labor force rose from 43.1 in 1941 to a peak of 47.7 in 1944, and fell back promptly to 43.1 in 1946. At the wartime peak, there were about six million more people in the labor force than one would have expected under normal conditions. About three and one-half million of these were women who would normally have been engaged in household duties, but who were available for work because of the absence of over ten million men in the armed forces. There were also about two and one-half million additional male workers—older men who postponed their retirement because of the need for labor, young men who left school or college early, and some people not normally employable whom employers were willing to hire under war conditions.

These six million people, plus the nine million who were unemployed in 1940, gave us a wartime manpower reserve of some fifteen million people. This is the main reason why we were able to put more than ten million people into uniform, produce vast quantities of war material, and at the same time *increase* the level of civilian production.

LEVEL AND COMPOSITION OF EMPLOYMENT

Having examined the sources of labor supply, we proceed to note the obvious fact that labor supply may be employed or unemployed. One cannot take it for granted that the available supply will be fully used at all times. On the contrary, the number employed always falls somewhat short of the labor force, and sometimes falls a long way below it.

---

[10] Irvin Sobel and Richard C. Wilcock, "Labor Market Behavior in Small Towns," *Industrial and Labor Relations Review*, IX (October 1955), pp. 54-76.

[11] Richard C. Wilcock, "Employment Effects of a Plant Shutdown in a Depressed Area," *Monthly Labor Review* (September 1957), pp. 1047-1052.

The course of employment in the United States in recent years is shown in Figure 6.[12] Several things stand out clearly from this chart. The long-run trend of employment is upward, matching the trend of the labor force. In a country whose population and labor force are increasing, the number of jobs must also increase if idleness and suffering are to be avoided. The target of "full employment" rises year after year. The objective is not just a stable economy, but rather a smoothly expanding economy, which is much more difficult to achieve.

The advance of employment has not occurred at a smooth rate. There have been peaks and valleys, periods of substantial unemployment, and times when unemployment was almost eliminated. The unemployment problem seems to have increased somewhat since the mid-'fifties. We shall have more to say about this in the next chapter.

The most interesting thing about employment is something which is not revealed by the total employment figure. This is the enormous

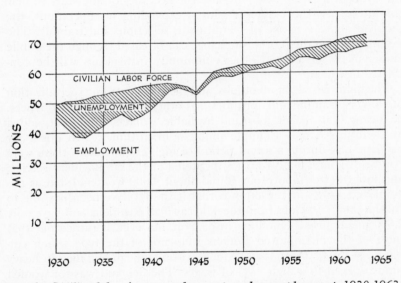

FIG. 6   *Civilian labor force, employment, and unemployment, 1930-1963.*

---

[12] The data for Figure 6 are from the Bureau of Labor Statistics, *Handbook of Labor Statistics, 1950,* and from *Manpower Report, 1963.*

variety of jobs in which people are employed. Members of the labor force work in thousands of occupations for millions of employers (and many, of course, work for themselves), scattered over the length and breadth of the United States. Moreover, the pattern of employment is undergoing continuous change. Old industries and occupations decline and disappear, while new ones spring up and expand. Thousands of businesses fail and go out of existence each year, while other thousands of new businesses are founded. Jobs disappear in one part of the country and reappear two thousand miles away. Constant change, continuous movement of labor and capital, is the essence of a growing economy.

Although rapid economic change is a hopeful thing, it also creates serious problems. Each year millions of workers are forced out of jobs through no fault of their own, and have to find new jobs at the growth points of the economy. From a broad point of view this represents progress. To the workers involved it means unemployment, the effort of locating new jobs, and the necessity of adjusting to new conditions. To the employer who is expanding his operations, the problem appears as one of recruitment, selection, and training. The extent to which the process of change can be eased through the public employment service and other community institutions will be considered in Chapter 15.

The high specialization of jobs, and the corresponding specialization of workers' training and aptitudes, has other important consequences. It means that vacant jobs and available workers cannot be added and subtracted like a simple problem in arithmetic. In one New England city during a recent period of high employment, there were typically about 1,500 vacancies registered at the employment service; and month after month one found about 4,000 workers listed as unemployed. One's first reaction is that it should have been possible to subtract the 1,500 jobs from the 4,000 available workers and have only 2,500 unemployed. On closer inspection, however, it turned out that most of the unemployed workers were not of the type which employers wanted. The unemployment was mainly among men in heavy industry used to a high level of wages. The demand was for women to do light machine-tending at a considerably lower wage level. It is quite possible for local surpluses of some kinds of labor to exist alongside shortages of other kinds—indeed, this is the typical situation in local labor markets.

The changing pattern of employment

Over the course of decades and generations, economic necessity gradually refashions labor supply to fit the changing pattern of labor demand. Workers have to take the jobs that are offered, not the jobs they might like to have. The pattern of labor demand depends on growth trends in the economy—on which industries and occupations are growing and which declining in importance.

A study of many countries over long periods reveals certain general principles of growth. As a country increases in per capita income and wealth, the relative importance of different sectors of the economy shifts in a systematic way. These shifts are confirmed also by cross-section comparisons of countries at different levels of economic development at the same time. [13]

The clearest and strongest tendency is a long-run decline in the relative importance of agriculture. The proportion of the labor force engaged in agriculture falls from 70 per cent or more in the least developed countries to between 10 and 20 per cent in the most advanced. This does not, of course, mean any decrease in agricultural output. It means rather such a great rise in agricultural productivity that the population can be fed by a much smaller segment of the labor force. One farm family, instead of feeding little more than itself, can now feed five to ten other families as well.

Industries engaged in commodity production—manufacturing, mining, construction—increase sharply in importance as economic growth proceeds, but this increase does not continue indefinitely. After a certain point, the proportion of the labor force engaged in these industries levels off and moves along on a plateau. In most advanced industrial countries this plateau level is between 30 and 40 per cent of the labor force, though in a few countries (Britain, Sweden, West Germany) it approaches 50 per cent.

With agriculture continuing to decline in relative importance as development proceeds, and with commodity production levelling off, what takes up the slack in the labor force? The answer is found in

---

[13] See particularly Simon Kuznets, "Quantitative Aspects of the Economic Growth of Nations, II: Industrial Distribution of National Product and Labor Force," *Economic Development and Cultural Change*, Supplement (July 1957). For an earlier and still classic analysis, see Colin Clark, *The Conditions of Economic Progress*, 3rd ed. (New York: St. Martin's Press, 1957).

industries producing services of every sort—trade, transportation and communication, public utilities, repair services, recreation and entertainment, professional and other personal services, and government. Except for domestic service, which declines over the long run, the proportion of the labor force employed in service activities rises steadily as national income rises. In the wealthiest countries, half or more of the labor force is employed in the service industries.

These principles are well illustrated by the case of the United States. Changes in the distribution of workers among different kinds of industry since 1870 are shown in Tables 6 and 7.[14] The trends just described are clearly evident. Agriculture, which in 1870 still employed more than half the labor force, today employs less than 10 per cent. The commodity-producing sector—manufacturing, mining, construction—increased in relative importance until about 1910, and then leveled off at a bit over 30 per cent of the labor force. This percentage has remained remarkably stable over the past half-century. The industries producing services have gained steadily in importance and now employ more than half the national labor force. In terms of rate of increase of employment, the fastest-growing areas have been business repair services, government service, finance and insurance, recreation and entertainment. In sheer numbers, the greatest increase has been in wholesale and retail trade, where employment has risen from four million in 1910 to almost twelve million at the present time.

A different classification of the labor force is in terms of the kind of work done—skilled, semiskilled, clerical, professional, and so on. Trends in the occupational distribution of the labor force stem basically from the industry shifts just described. If industries employing large numbers of clerks, typists, and salespeople are increasing in relative importance, one would expect these groups to form a growing proportion of the labor force. A second important factor, however, is changes in work methods within particular industries. Even though the relative importance of manufacturing has varied little since 1910,

---

[14] The industrial classification used by the Census was reasonably comparable from 1870 through 1930, and the changes over this period are shown in Table 6. A markedly different classification was adopted in 1940, and the 1940, 1950, and 1960 figures are accordingly shown in a separate table. The source of Table 6 is the *Sixteenth Census of the United States, 1940, Population, Comparative Occupational Statistics for the United States, 1870-1940*, p. 101. Table 7 is derived from Bureau of the Census, *Census of Population, 1960, General Social and Economic Characteristics*. United States Summary, Final Report PC(1)-1C.

changing production methods have altered the ratios of different skill groups within manufacturing and will continue to do so in the future.

Changes in the occupational distribution of the United States labor

TABLE 6

INDUSTRIAL COMPOSITION OF THE LABOR FORCE,*

1870–1930

General Division of Occupations	Percentage Distribution						
	1930	1920	1910	1900	1890	1880	1870
Agriculture	21.4	27.0	31.0	37.5	42.6	49.4	53.0
Forestry and fishing	0.5	0.6	0.6	0.7	0.8	0.6	0.5
Extraction of minerals	2.0	2.6	2.6	2.4	1.9	1.7	1.4
Manufacture and mechanical industries	28.9	30.3	28.5	24.8	23.7	22.1	20.5
Transportation and communication	7.9	7.3	7.1	6.7	6.0	4.8	4.2
Trade	12.5	10.0	9.7	10.6	8.8	7.9	6.8
Public service, not elsewhere classified	1.8	1.7	1.2	1.0	0.9	0.8	0.7
Professional service	6.7	5.1	4.6	4.1	3.8	3.2	2.6
Domestic and personal service	10.1	8.0	10.1	9.7	9.6	8.8	9.7
Clerical occupations	8.2	7.3	4.6	2.5	2.0	0.9	0.6

* Gainful workers ten years old and over by general distribution of occupations.

force since 1910, and Bureau of Labor Statistics projections for 1975, are shown in Table 8.[15] The most striking feature of Table 8 is the growing predominance of white-collar employment. Considering only the non-farm labor force, and setting aside service workers as difficult to classify, one can designate craftsmen, operatives, and laborers as "blue-collar," and professional, managerial, clerical, and sales workers as "white-collar." The proportion of blue-collar workers in the labor force has been declining gradually, from 37 per cent in 1940 to 36 per cent in 1962 to an estimated 34 per cent in 1975. At the same time

[15] 1910 and 1940 data from Gladys L. Palmer and Ann R. Miller, "The Occupational and Industrial Distribution of Employment, 1910-50," in William Haber and associates, *Manpower in the United States* (New York: Harper & Row, Publishers, 1954), p. 87. 1962 data are from *Monthly Labor Review* (July 1963), and the 1975 projections are from *Monthly Labor Review* (March 1963).

TABLE 7

MAJOR INDUSTRY GROUP OF EMPLOYED PERSONS,
1940–1960

Major Industry Group	Percentage Distribution		
	1940	1950	1960
Agriculture	19.0	12.5	6.7
Mining	2.0	1.6	1.0
Construction	4.6	6.1	5.9
Manufacturing	23.7	26.0	27.1
Transportation, communications, and other public utilities	7.0	7.9	6.9
Wholesale and retail trade	16.6	18.6	18.2
Finance, insurance, and real estate	3.3	3.4	4.2
Public administration	3.1	4.5	5.0
Professional and related services:			
Education	3.5	3.6	5.2
Other	4.0	4.9	6.5
Other service industries	11.6	9.3	9.3
Industry not reported	1.6	1.5	4.0

Source: United States Bureau of the Census, *United States Census of Population,*
1960. General School and Economic Characteristics. United States Summary,
Final Report PC (1)-1C, pp. 1-223.

there has been a sharp uptrend in white-collar employment, from 32
per cent of the labor force in 1940 to 44 per cent in 1962 to an
estimated 48 per cent in 1975.

These long-run trends in labor demand call for corresponding adjustments in labor supply. They account for part of the unemployment which persists even in good years. Many of the unemployed
have been forced out of unskilled and low-skilled manual jobs. The
demand for labor is expanding most rapidly in white-collar occupations requiring a higher level of education and technical training. It
takes time and effort to retrain people for these new opportunities.
For many of the older workers, indeed, the job of "retreading" will
never be completed. This makes it all the more urgent that young
people receive the education and vocational advice which will help
them to fit into expanding occupations and avoid declining ones.

There has been an especially sharp increase in the demand for
professional and technical skills. Professional, semiprofessional, and
technical workers have quadrupled in numbers and more than

doubled in relative importance over the past half-century. This is due mainly to a great rise in consumer incomes and living standards, which has permitted consumers to spend much more on education, health, entertainment, and other professional services. A high proportion of national income spent on professional and personal services is, in fact, almost a definition of a high standard of living. Another factor is the increasingly complex and scientific character of industrial operations, which requires large numbers of research scientists, engineers, and technical assistants. It is estimated that there were 7,000 engineers in the United States in 1870. Today there are more than half a million, and the number is still increasing.

TABLE 8

OCCUPATIONAL COMPOSITION OF THE UNITED STATES LABOR FORCE, 1910, 1940, 1962, AND PROJECTION FOR 1975

Occupational Group	1910	1940	1962	Projected 1975
Total employed	100.0	100.0	100.0	100.0
Professional, technical, and kindred workers	4.6	7.9	11.8	14.2
Farmers and farm managers	17.3	11.4	3.9	*
Managers, officials, and proprietors except farm	7.2	8.1	10.9	10.7
Clerical and kindred workers	5.5	9.7	14.9	16.2
Sales workers	5.0	6.8	6.4	6.7
Craftsmen, foremen, and kindred workers	11.7	11.5	12.8	12.8
Operatives and kindred workers	14.1	18.9	17.8	16.3
Service workers	9.6	11.8	12.9	14.3
Farm laborers and foremen	13.4	6.9	3.4	*
Laborers, except farm and mine	11.6	7.0	5.3	4.5

* Farmers, farm managers, and farm laborers are combined in the 1975 projections. It is estimated that they will together form 4.5 per cent of the labor force at that time.

Clerical and kindred workers have increased from two million in 1910 to over ten million at present. Almost two-thirds of these workers are women, and this is the main point at which women have increased their participation in employment. The rapid growth of clerical employment reflects partly the expansion of service industries in which clerical workers are especially important—government, finance and insurance, trade, communications, and the rest. It reflects also the growing size, complexity, and mechanization of industrial operations, which require more and more people to distribute and keep records on the goods produced, and relatively fewer people to produce them.

Until recently semiskilled factory operatives formed an increasing proportion of the labor force because of the growing importance of manufacturing in the economy and the accompanying mechanization of production. Increased use of hand-operated machinery created a great array of jobs which required a short period of specialized training but did not require the craftsman's all-round knowledge and experience. One should perhaps term this *incomplete or partial mechanization.* The more complete automation of many production processes since the late 'forties has reduced the need for semiskilled operatives, and their importance in the labor force has begun to decline.

Interestingly enough, the proportion of skilled workers in the economy has remained roughly constant over the past half-century instead of declining as might have been expected. The proportion of skilled men on production work in manufacturing has indeed fallen as production processes have been subdivided, mechanized, and downgraded. This has been offset, however, by a great increase in repair and service jobs—maintenance mechanics needed in factories to keep the more complicated machinery in good repair; automobile and airplane mechanics and repairmen; telephone, telegraph, and power linemen and servicemen; and a wide variety of other groups. Skilled building trades workers have increased in relative importance with the high level of construction activity since 1940; and foremen and sub-foremen, whom the Census classifies with craftsmen, have also increased in number.

Farmers and farm laborers have diminished in importance with the relative decline of agriculture. Domestic service has declined sharply as high labor demand has enabled domestics to shift to better-paid jobs in manufacturing and elsewhere. There has also been a sharp decline in the proportion of the labor force engaged in urban unskilled labor, which has been more than cut in half since 1910. There is much less "back work" in industry today than there was fifty years ago, owing partly to the development of mechanical lifting and moving devices—conveyor systems, gravity feeds, mechanized hand trucks, overhead cranes, and so on. Much of the work which used to be done by people with strong muscles is now done by a machine operated by a man who needs less strength but more intelligence and experience. In this respect, then, industrial employment has become more skilled and more pleasant.

Dynamic shifts in the composition of employment are certain to continue in the future as some industries grow relative to others and as production techniques change. Automation will have a continuing impact over the next several decades. In popular usage, automation is a loose term covering a variety of different things. Baldwin and Shultz have distinguished (1) "continuous automatic production" or "Detroit automation"—the linking together of separate production operations along a continuous line through which the product moves unaided by human hands; (2) "feedback technology"—use of built-in automatic devices (servomechanisms) for comparing the way in which work is actually being done with the way in which it is supposed to be done and then making automatic adjustments in the work process; (3) "computer technology"—use of computing machines for recording and storing information and for performing both simple and complex mathematical operations upon it.[16]

These devices can be used separately or in combination. The hypothetical "automatic factory" of the future would employ all three in various proportions. Computer technology is farthest developed at present and nearest to the point of large-scale application. Its main impact will be in the office, where it will displace a large amount of clerical labor and possibly even junior management personnel. Information technology may structure many management jobs in the future, just as Taylorism structured hourly rated production jobs in the past.

The other two types of automation are less fully developed, but have a large potential impact on factory production over the next two or three decades. Broadly speaking, these processes operate to reverse the labor force trends produced by the partial mechanization of earlier times. Old-style mechanization, as we have seen, made for a rapid multiplication of semiskilled machine tenders at the expense of skilled craftsmen. But once materials handling and machine operations have been sufficiently subdivided and routinized, they can be taken over completely by automation and the need for the semiskilled man disappears. In some industries, then, the semiskilled operative may turn

---

[16] George B. Baldwin and George P. Shultz, "Automation: A New Dimension to Old Problems," *Proceedings of the Seventh Annual Meeting of the IRRA* (1954), pp. 114-128.

out to have played a temporary and transitional role on the way from old-style handicraft production to fully automatic production.

On the positive side, automation may be expected to increase the need for skilled workers in the machine-building industries, for skilled maintenance men to keep the automatic equipment in steady operation, for design engineers and operating engineers, and for computer programmers and other technicians. The net effect seems likely to be an upgrading rather than a downgrading of average skill requirements in the labor force.[17]

VOLUME AND CHARACTERISTICS OF UNEMPLOYMENT

Unemployment is a negative or residual concept—the difference between the amount of labor power available and the amount in use at a particular time. More precisely, *involuntary* unemployment, with which we are concerned here, is the difference between the amount of labor offered *at present levels of wages and working conditions* and the amount of labor hired at these levels. The most obvious aspect of the problem is full-time unemployment—people willing and able to work who have no jobs at all. Precise determination of the size of this group is not quite so easy as may appear at first glance. How does one judge whether a worker has the necessary ability to hold a job? What about a man of sixty, or a physically handicapped person, who wants a job but may never be able to get one? What is meant by "willingness to work"? Under what terms and conditions must one be willing? What about people who are not seeking work because there is no work in their line in the area where they live? Despite these and other problems of measurement, however, the concept of full-time unemployment is reasonably clear.

A second major component of unemployment is part-time idleness. In many industries, production schedules are reduced when necessary by working the entire labor force part-time rather than by layoffs. In 1962, for example, the full-time unemployed averaged about 4 million. But in addition an average of 1¼ million were reported as "on part-time for economic reasons." These people would have preferred to work longer hours had the work been available. There were also 6½

---

[17] See George P. Shultz and Arnold Wilber, "Technological Change and Industrial Relations," in an IRRA symposium on *Employment Relations Research* (New York: Harper & Row, Publishers, 1960); and the March 1962 issue of the *Annals of the American Academy*, which is devoted to automation.

million workers, of whom two-thirds were women, on voluntary part-time schedules.[18] These people cannot be considered underemployed, since their work schedule corresponds with their own preferences.

A more elusive aspect of the problem is "disguised unemployment" —the employment of people on jobs which do not utilize their full capacity, or on which their productivity is lower than it would be in some other occupation. During a depression many skilled workers are demoted to semiskilled jobs, foremen are put back on production work, and so on. This general downgrading of the labor force means that even those workers who continue in employment are not used so effectively during depression as during prosperity.

In some industries, notably agriculture, there is a chronic tendency toward disguised unemployment even in good years. The rural areas of the country have a relatively high rate of population growth, while the labor requirements of agriculture are declining. The result is an accumulation of surplus labor in agriculture, where it earns low wage rates and has relatively low productivity. During prosperity, the situation is alleviated by large-scale migration from rural to urban areas. During depression, however, this movement is checked or even reversed, and underemployment in agriculture is aggravated.

All these forms of unemployment increase during a general decline of business activity. Many people are added to the full-time unemployed, the amount of part-time work increases, and there is an increase in disguised unemployment. Most statistics of unemployment relate only to the full-time unemployed, since this is the easiest thing to measure. It is important to realize, however, that these figures understate the amount of unemployment existing at any time and also the size of cyclical fluctuations over the course of time.

Information even on full-time unemployment is fragmentary until about 1940.[19] It appears, however, that from 1890 until 1929 unemployment fluctuated usually between 5 and 10 per cent of the labor force. There does not seem to have been any long-run tendency for the unemployment rate to increase or decrease. The Great Depression, of course, brought catastrophic unemployment. Full-time unemployment reached a peak of about 30 per cent of the labor force in early 1933, and averaged 20 per cent for the 'thirties as a whole. During

---

[18] *Manpower Report*, 1963, pp. 148-149.

[19] See, however, Paul H. Douglas, *Real Wages in the United States* (Boston: Houghton Mifflin Company, 1930), and an NBER conference volume on *Measurement and Behavior of Unemployment* (Princeton: Princeton University Press, 1956).

the early 'forties, unemployment virtually disappeared as a result of wartime industrial activity. At the peak of war production in 1944 unemployment fell to little more than 1 per cent of the labor force.

For recent years we have relatively reliable information from the Census Bureau's Monthly Report on the Labor Force. This Report is based on monthly interviews with a sample of households in representative counties throughout the United States. Questions are asked about the employment status of each person in these households— whether he is in or out of the labor force, whether he has a job, and if so, how many hours he worked at the job during a certain week. The results obtained from the sample are then expanded into estimates of the labor force, employment, and unemployment for the country as a whole. Although these estimates are subject to sampling error, they are closely comparable from month to month and give a reliable indication of the direction of changes in employment.

American unemployment rates since World War II (Figure 7) have been low by historic standards, fluctuating mainly between 3 and 6 per cent. And this has been true throughout the industrial world. Unemployment rates in Britain, Western Europe, and elsewhere were much lower in the 'fifties than in the 'twenties. They have also been considerably lower than in the United States. In 1962, for example, full-time unemployment in the United States averaged 5.6 per cent

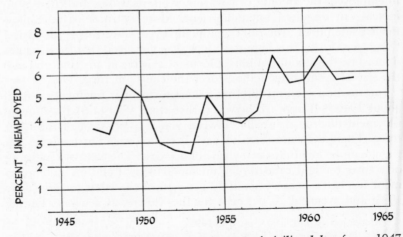

FIG. 7   *Full-time unemployed as percentage of civilian labor force, 1947-1963.*

of the labor force. The percentage rates for certain other industrial countries, calculated on the basis of the U.S. definitions, were as follows: Canada 6.0, France 1.8, West Germany 0.5, Great Britain 2.8, Italy 3.2, Japan 1.0, Sweden 1.5.[20] This suggests the question of why other countries have been able to do better in this respect than the United States and Canada.

Figure 7 shows a gradual upcreep of the U.S. unemployment rate over the past decade. Each economic upswing has left the unemployment rate higher than the one before it. At the 1953 cycle peak, unemployment was below 3 per cent, at the 1957 peak it was about 4 per cent, at the 1960 peak it was above 5 per cent. In late 1963, after almost three years of marked economic expansion, the unemployment rate remained stuck at a little under 6 per cent. The reasons for this gradual rise of unemployment, and the question of what can be done about it, will concern us in the next chapter.

In discussing unemployment, just as in discussing employment, it is important to look underneath the total figures. When one reads that 5 per cent of the labor force is unemployed, one tends to think of this 5 per cent as spread evenly over all parts of the country, every type of industry, and every kind of worker. Nothing could be farther from the truth. During depression periods many more people are laid off in iron and steel, machinery, automobiles, and other heavy industries than are laid off in food processing or clothing manufacture. Unskilled workers, who can be dispensed with most readily, are hit harder than skilled workers. States which have a heavy concentration of durable goods manufacturing suffer more unemployment than agricultural states or states in which new industries are expanding rapidly.

Whether in good years or bad, the incidence of unemployment is uneven by *industry, occupation, region,* and *personal characteristics* of the worker. In 1962, for example, the average rate of unemployment was 5.6 per cent. The rate was 12.0 per cent in construction and 8.6 in mining, however, while it was only 3.1 per cent in finance and 2.2 per cent in government service. By occupation, 12.4 per cent of laborers and 7.5 per cent of semiskilled workers were unemployed, but only 3.9 per cent of clerical workers and 1.7 per cent of professional and technical workers. The unemployment rate was 10.9 per

---

[20] *Measuring Employment and Unemployment;* hearings before the Joint Economic Committee (Washington: Government Printing Office, 1963), p. 85.

cent in West Virginia and 7.9 per cent in Pennsylvania, largely because of stranded coal-mining populations, but it was below 4 per cent
in Colorado, Iowa, Kansas, and Virginia.

It is well known that Negroes suffer much more unemployment
than white workers. The rates in 1962 were 11.0 per cent for Negroes,
4.9 per cent for whites. Young people who have recently entered, or
are just trying to enter, the labor force are also particularly vulnerable
to unemployment. The average rate in 1962 was about 16 per cent
for those aged 16 and 17, 14 per cent for those 18 and 19, and 9 per
cent for those 20 to 24.[21]

There are several reasons for these differences in unemployment
rates. Production in some industries is much more unstable than in
others. This instability may be *irregular,* as in dock work, *seasonal,* as
in building construction, or *cyclical,* as in metals and machinery.
When production in an industry drops, it has been customary to
make sharper cuts in the manual labor force than in the office staff,
though this difference is now decreasing because of union pressure
and for other reasons. Some industries are highly localized in particular regions. A production drop in such an industry will be reflected in
a high unemployment rate in the areas where it is important. The
heavy unemployment in the New England textile towns and the
Appalachian coal-mining areas are well-known examples.

Other differences in unemployment rates arise from employers'
hiring preferences based on age, sex, race, training and experience,
and other personal characteristics. When demand for labor is very
high, these preferences tend to be set aside and employers hire whom-
ever they can find. But when recession sets in and labor demand
declines, employers are able to make their preferences effective.
They hire or retain workers with preferred characteristics, and decline
to employ others. Thus the burden of underemployment falls most
heavily on the less preferred groups—inexperienced young people,
older people, Negroes, those with little education or skill, marginal
workers of low productivity. The main remedy for heavy unemployment among these groups does not lie in *changing the people,* since
most of these personal characteristics are immutable. It lies rather in
raising the general level of demand for labor to the point at which
employers revise their hiring standards.

It should be emphasized that the unemployed group is far from
stationary. The fact that the Census Bureau may report four million

---

[21] All data from *Manpower Report*, 1963.

unemployed month after month does not mean that this is the same four million people. The unemployed group resembles rather the population of a subway train. Some get on at each stop and others get off. The number in the train may stay about the same, yet those who arrive at the end of the line may be a completely different group from those who started out at the beginning.

At a time when four million are unemployed, a million or more people are likely to be finding jobs each month, and another half-million or so will be leaving the labor force. At the same time, about the same numbers will be coming into the unemployed pool because they have lost their jobs or are entering the labor force. There are two consequences of this substantial turnover. First, the number of people who experience unemployment at some time during the year is much larger than the number unemployed at any one time. In 1961 the average unemployment at any one time was 4.8 million. But 15 million people, or almost 20 per cent of the labor force, experienced one or more spells of unemployment during the year. The fact that most workers have experienced unemployment at one time or another accounts for their strong interest in job security.

A second result is that, at least in prosperous years, the bulk of the unemployed have been unemployed for only a short time. In a typical month of 1962, for example, more than 40 per cent had been unemployed for less than 5 weeks, and another 20 per cent for 5 to 10 weeks. Another 20 per cent, however, had been unemployed for 11 to 26 weeks, and about 15 per cent (585,000 people) for more than 26 weeks. It is these long-term unemployed who give cause for special concern. They are likely to be the least employable people in the population in terms of geographic location, work skills, and personal characteristics. Moreover, the longer a worker remains unemployed the smaller become his chances of finding a new job. His skills become rusty, he loses the habit of regular work, his morale declines, and employers view him with increasing suspicion. The problem of reabsorbing this "hard core" group into productive employment is another issue which will concern us in Chapter 14.

Discussion questions

1. Draw a supply curve of labor for the United States as a whole. Why does the curve look as you have drawn it?

2. What is meant by the "labor force participation rate"? Why is this rate almost the same in the United States today as it was in 1890?

3. How can one account for the large increase in labor force participation by women in recent decades?

4. What have been the major trends in the occupational distribution of the United States labor force over the past fifty years? Can these trends be expected to continue in future?

5. How is increasing automation likely to affect the composition of employment in the United States?

6. Why is the rate of full-time unemployment in most other industrial countries less than half as high as in the United States?

7. If there are three million unemployed workers in the United States at a particular time, while at the same time there are three million vacant jobs, why do these not cancel out and leave us with zero unemployment?

8. "The fact that there are at least two million unemployed in the United States even in boom years proves that we have two million workers too many. If this surplus could be removed, all would be well." Discuss.

Selected reading

Bancroft, Gertrude, *The American Labor Force*. New York: John Wiley & Sons, Inc., 1958.

Durand, John D., *The Labor Force in the United States, 1890-1960*. New York: Social Science Research Council, 1948.

Florence, P. Sargant, *Labour*. London: Hutchinson's University Library, 1950.

Industrial Relations Research Association, *Manpower in the United States*. New York: Harper & Row, Publishers, 1954.

Jaffe, A. J., and Charles D. Stewart, *Manpower Resources and Utilization: Principles of Working Force Analysis*. New York: John Wiley & Sons, Inc., 1951.

Killingsworth, C. C., ed., *Automation*, Annals of the American Academy of Political and Social Sciences, March 1962.

Long, Clarence D., *The Labor Force under Changing Income and Employment*. Princeton: Princeton University Press, 1958.

N.B.E.R., *Measurement and Behavior of Unemployment*. Princeton: Princeton University Press, 1956.

U. S. Department of Labor, *Manpower Report of the President*. Washington: Government Printing Office, 1963 and annually thereafter.

Woytinsky, W. S., and associates, *Employment and Wages in the United States*. New York: Twentieth Century Fund, 1953, Part III.

14

Reduction And
Control Of Unemployment

In order to suggest remedies for unemployment, we must first know why it exists. People are always falling out of work for one reason or another. Consumers decide to buy less coal and some coal miners lose their jobs. A new automatic process in an auto assembly plant eliminates certain operations and the men on those jobs are out of work. This by itself does not explain unemployment. People displaced from certain jobs might be reabsorbed immediately into other jobs. But in actuality displaced workers, and new entrants to the labor market, often spend considerable time looking for work. The problem is to explain this *unemployment between jobs,* and why it is longer at some times and places than at others.

SOURCES OF UNEMPLOYMENT

The explanation breaks down logically into three parts: seasonal and irregular fluctuations of labor demand in certain industries ("seasonal unemployment"); immobility of labor and imperfect organization of the labor market ("frictional unemployment"); and insufficient aggregate demand for labor ("demand unemployment"). A word of explanation about each of these.

345

Seasonal and casual unemployment

This is a familiar phenomenon, especially in agriculture and building construction. In the colder regions of the country, building activity tapers off during the winter months. In crop raising there is a peak of activity during the harvest season. The men's and women's clothing industries work hard while getting out the spring and fall styles, but slacken off in between. Seasonal industries tend to attract enough labor to meet their peak requirements during the rush season, which means that some of these people are necessarily unemployed in the slack season. It has been estimated that about 20 per cent of our unemployment in prosperous years arises from seasonal variations in demand.[1] Seasonal unemployment, in other words, accounts for close to 1 percentage point in the national unemployment rate.

There are also irregular fluctuations in labor requirements in such industries as merchant shipping and longshoring. The number of ships coming into a particular port to be unloaded varies from day to day, and workers are hired each morning for that day only. Hourly wage rates are attractive. So longshoring tends to attract, not merely the maximum number who might be employed on the busiest days, but an even larger number. All these men hang about, somewhat on the lottery principle, in the hope of getting a day's work from time to time. The result is that many workers in the industry get much less than a full year's employment.

Frictional unemployment

Each month many thousands of workers are entering the labor force, or being displaced from their jobs through layoff or discharge, or quitting their jobs in hope of finding something better. If there is no deficiency of aggregate demand for labor, however, there should be an equivalent number of jobs opening up somewhere else in the economy. Why can't the available workers be fitted into the vacant jobs so rapidly that they leave virtually no trace in the unemployment statistics?

The reason is partly that the labor market is poorly organized.

---

[1] Study Paper No. 6, *The Extent and Nature of Frictional Unemployment*, prepared by the Bureau of Labor Statistics, U. S. Department of Labor, for the Joint Economic Committee. (Washington: Government Printing Office, 1959).

There is no grain exchange for labor; and jobs and workers are not as standardized as bushels of wheat. The state employment service offices could conceivably serve as a central clearinghouse; but most of the labor market traffic bypasses the employment service. Most workers in search of a job look about on their own, following up leads from relatives and friends, or simply applying at the best-known companies in the area. Even if vacancies are available, it takes time for the worker to locate the kind of job he wants; and it takes time for the company to interview applicants, administer pre-employment tests, and decide whom to hire. The longer the time, the higher the unemployment rate.

A second difficulty is that labor demand is highly differentiated and localized. Vacant jobs require particular kinds of people, at a particular location, with certain work skills and experience. The people displaced from old jobs or entering the market for the first time may live in a different part of the country and have quite different skills. The most rapid expansion of demand may be for engineers and secretaries in San Francisco. The largest pools of unemployed may be ex-coal miners in the southern Appalachians and ex-auto workers in Detroit.

How much frictional unemployment should be taken as normal or unavoidable in the American economy? One per cent, or two per cent, or three per cent? This question is bound to be asked, but it cannot really be answered. The only reasonable answer is "it depends." It depends on the effectiveness of the public employment service, the adequacy of other sources of labor market information, the speed of long-term shifts in the composition of labor demand, and the adequacy of government retraining and mobility programs. Moreover, *it depends on the level of aggregate demand for labor.* Workers will find acceptable jobs faster if there are many vacancies than if there are few vacancies. They will also be more interested in retraining programs and in moving to other areas if there is a clear prospect of employment. People flowed out of the hills at a surprising rate in response to the high labor demand of World War II.

For these reasons one cannot draw a clear line between frictional unemployment and unemployment arising from insufficient aggregate demand. As aggregate demand rises, the level of frictional unemployment drops, though of course not indefinitely. What level of frictional unemployment can be regarded as acceptable is really a *target* rather than a *datum.*

Demand unemployment

This type of unemployment appears in clearest form during a business cycle downswing, when many industries lay off workers or shorten their workweek. Even the mild downswings of 1953-54 and 1957-58 added about two million workers to the unemployed, while the 1960-61 downswing displaced a million and a half.

But demand unemployment is not just a cyclical phenomenon. It would be so if each upswing carried all the way to full employment before toppling over into the next recession. But this need not happen, and it has not happened in the American economy during the past decade. Since 1957 the rate of full-time unemployment has never fallen below 5 per cent at cycle peaks. The upswing which began in mid-1961 was unusually large and prolonged. Yet all through 1962 and 1963 the unemployment needle remained stuck near 5½ per cent of the labor force. Many have concluded from this that we face a demand problem which is more than cyclical in character, a problem of long-run economic sluggishness; and that vigorous measures are needed to raise the level of aggregate demand.

An alternative explanation of recent high unemployment levels, offered by some economists, is that the level of normal or frictional unemployment is higher today than it was a decade ago.[2] To support this view one would have to show that shifts in the composition of labor demand (by industries, occupations, regions) have been faster since, say, 1955 than they were before 1955; or that workers' propensity to learn new skills or move to other areas has declined; or that the organization of the labor market has deteriorated. There is no clear evidence that these things have happened. The writer leans rather to the hypothesis that inadequate demand is responsible. If

[2] It has been fashionable recently to refer to unemployment among certain groups—coal miners, steel and auto workers, young people without job experience, Negro workers of low education and job training—as constituting "structural unemployment." This terminology adds little to the discussion, and it seems better to stick to the familiar concepts of frictional and demand unemployment.

For a variety of views on the explanation of high unemployment rates since 1957, see Joint Economic Committee, *Higher Unemployment Rates, 1957-60: Structural Transformation or Inadequate Demand* (Washington: Government Printing Office, 1961); Council of Economic Advisers, *The American Economy in 1961: Problems and Policies*, statement before the Joint Economic Committee, March 1961; Richard C. Wilcock and Walter H. Franke, "Will Economic Growth Solve the Problem of Long-term Unemployment?", *Proceedings of Fourteenth Annual Meeting of IRRA* (1961), pp. 37-49.

aggregate demand could be raised substantially, it seems likely that much of what now appears as frictional, or structural, or hard-core unemployment would melt away.

LINES OF ACTION: SEASONAL AND CASUAL UNEMPLOYMENT

A certain amount of seasonal unemployment is unavoidable because of climatic and other circumstances. Wheat crops can be harvested only when they are ripe, house building is not practicable in some regions during the winter, the salmon catch must be made while the salmon are running.

There are many industries, however, in which seasonal and irregular fluctuations of production could be reduced or even eliminated. In some industries, such as clothing and automobiles, the way in which new styles are introduced leads to a marked seasonality of production which might be reduced by changing the customs of the industry. Firms which buy parts and subassemblies often impose production fluctuations on their suppliers by refusing to order much in advance of delivery and by changing their orders at the last minute. In some industries, manufacturing production fluctuates unnecessarily because of inventory speculation by raw material dealers, wholesalers, and retailers. In other cases, irregularity of production and employment is due simply to lack of adequate forward planning and production scheduling within the company.

These things can never be entirely eliminated, but irregularity of employment can often be reduced by deliberate effort. The methods which can be used to stabilize employment in a firm have been discussed by many writers and need not be described here.[3] In some cases, greater care in forecasting demand and an effort to develop systematic production plans may be sufficient. Where the product is standardized and durable, it may be possible to produce for stock during periods of slack demand and to sell from stock during peak periods. Some companies have been able to stabilize their production by direct sales to retailers or by establishing their own retail outlets. Some have found it useful to offer customers lower prices and other

---

[3] See: Paul H. Douglas and Aaron Director, *The Problem of Unemployment* (New York: The Macmillan Company, 1931); and Herman Feldman, *Stabilizing Jobs and Wages through Better Business Management* (New York: Harper & Row, Publishers, 1940).

inducements to place orders in the slack season. Others have developed "fill-in lines," peak production on which comes during the slack season for the main product.

Stabilization of production is obviously beneficial to both the company and the worker. Steady production results in greater output and lower unit overhead costs, and also helps to maintain a more satisfied and efficient labor force. In addition to providing an incentive for capable workers to stay with the company, stabilization eliminates the wastes arising from frequent shifts of men to new jobs and continual hiring of new workers. It also reduces the employer's tax liability under state unemployment compensation systems and the cost of supplementary unemployment benefit programs in industries where these have been established.

It is possible also to do something about the casual unemployment which arises where labor requirements vary unpredictably from day to day. Longshoring is the classic example. The number of workers needed at a particular pier on a particular day varies widely, though the number needed in the port as a whole fluctuates much less. Under the traditional "shape-up" method of hiring, a mass of workers descended on each pier at starting time each morning in the hope that the pier boss would hire some or all of them. If a man was not hired at one pier, it was too late for him to apply elsewhere. In addition to the possibilities of bribery and racketeering created by this system, it led to a large surplus of workers in the industry and a very uneven distribution of work among them. Work was so irregular that most longshoremen had low annual incomes despite high hourly wage rates.

For this reason the shape-up has been replaced increasingly by central hiring halls under union or government auspices. The New York Waterfront Commission, for example, now requires that all longshoremen in the port of New York be licensed and that they be dispatched to work from central employment offices operated by the Commission. The licensing system is designed partly to exclude from the industry men with known criminal records. In addition, however, the system enables the Commission to squeeze out the labor surplus gradually by reducing the number of licenses as workers retire or leave the industry, and by requiring that a man work a minimum number of days per year in order to keep his license.

In 1952, just before the licensing system came into effect, some

44,000 men worked as longshoremen at one time or another during the year. Daily employment in the port, however, rarely reached 20,000 and averaged only about 15,000. The result was irregular work and low earnings for a large proportion of the labor force. Only 33 per cent of the longshoremen worked as much as 1,200 hours per year, while 39 per cent worked less than 100 hours. Almost half the labor force earned less than $500 per year from longshore employment. By 1957, the number of licensed longshoremen had been cut by about 40 per cent to 27,000, and this smaller number was able to work much more regularly. About 61 per cent worked more than 1,200 hours in 1957, while only 15 per cent worked less than 100 hours. Almost 60 per cent of longshoremen earned $4,000 or more during the year.[4]

From a narrow viewpoint such a decasualization program may seem to *create* unemployment by reducing the number of people who can find jobs in the industry in question. From a general economic standpoint, however, it is clearly efficient to concentrate the available employment on fewer people, thereby enabling them to earn adequate incomes, and to make surplus labor available to other industries which can use it more effectively.

LINES OF ACTION: FRICTIONAL UNEMPLOYMENT

It would be helpful to have in each area a "stock exchange for labor," a central point at which workers in the area could register their qualifications and to which employers could report job vacancies. This could save considerable time for both employers and workers, and bring about a better matching of individual qualifications against job requirements. It would also economize labor by enabling the community to get along with a smaller "reserve" or "float" of unemployed. If each employer must rely solely on his own resources to meet sudden demands for additional labor, the safest policy is to keep excess workers attached to the company through the hope of occasional employment—the traditional longshore policy. The result is a substantial unemployed reserve. If, on the other hand, all plants can draw on a single labor reserve through the mechanism of a

---

[4] Vernon H. Jensen, "Decasualization of Employment on the New York Waterfront," *Industrial and Labor Relations Review* (July 1958), pp. 534-50.

central employment service, fewer unemployed will be needed to provide an adequate margin of safety for everyone. The principle involved is identical with that of insurance or central banking.

This is such an obviously useful idea that it is surprising that so little has been done about it. The reason may be partly that the American economy rarely operates at full capacity except in wartime. So long as employers find labor readily available, they take little interest in central hiring facilities. Another reason is that there are difficult practical problems in operating a satisfactory employment service. What workers want from the service is not the same as what employers want from it, and the desires of both groups may conflict with community objectives. In the next chapter we shall examine the present state employment services, the reasons why they do not occupy a central position in the labor market, and the question of whether they are capable of evolving in this direction.

An efficient central clearinghouse would be the only thing needed, *provided* the skills of the workers becoming unemployed matched precisely with those required by employers. But this cannot be the case in practice. It is in the nature of economic change that employment opportunities will be shrinking permanently in some occupations and industries, and that workers displaced from these occupations must acquire the skills needed in expanding sectors of the economy. Much of this necessary retraining goes on within industry itself. Employers are accustomed to hiring inexperienced people and training them on the job. But this is easier for factory occupations than for service or clerical work; and it is easier for young, mobile people in large cities than for a middle-aged coal miner in a Kentucky valley.

There is need, therefore, for public programs to retrain people who are unlikely ever to be re-employed in their customary occupations, and to speed their entry into expanding areas of employment. A beginning in this direction was made by the Manpower Development and Training Act of 1962, which authorized a three-year program under the general direction of the Secretary of Labor. The Secretary is required to "provide a program for testing, counseling, and selecting for occupational training . . . those unemployed or underemployed persons who cannot reasonably be expected to secure appropriate full-time employment without training." This includes on-the-job training programs worked out in cooperation with employers, vocational school programs, and other types of classroom instruction.

Family heads with three years or more of employment experience who are selected for training may be paid a weekly training allowance, which will normally be no larger than they would have received from state unemployment compensation, but can continue for as long as 52 weeks. Younger people aged 19 to 22 may receive a training allowance not to exceed $20 per week. Those aged 16 to 18 may also be tested, counseled, and trained, but with no special support allowance. The Act appropriated $100 million for the fiscal year 1963, and $165 million for each of fiscal 1964 and 1965, to carry out these purposes. The federal government will bear all costs of the program through fiscal 1964. After that the states are expected to cover half the cost of training provided through the state vocational school system or other classroom facilities.

The intent of this program is wholly commendable. It is more constructive to use public funds to retool the unemployed for productive work than to support them in idleness. It is too early, however, to judge the practical success of the program. The test will be, not just how many people are put through training programs, but how many are actually employed in the jobs for which they have been trained. This requires accurate forecasting of trends in labor demand, a close gearing of training programs to these trends, and good placement work at the end of the training period. It also requires an adequate level of aggregate demand in the economy, so that enough jobs are available.

Related to the training problem is the problem of geographic mobility. There are whole communities in which labor demand is stationary or declining, while in other areas demand is rising rapidly. Thus reabsorption of the unemployed requires that large numbers of people move from the first kind of area to the second. There has always been a great deal of such movement in the United States, facilitated by cheap second-hand cars and good highways; and most of the necessary movement will doubtless continue to occur without government aid or stimulus. But there are also cases in which movement could be accelerated and made less painful by a cash grant or loan. The country which has gone farthest in this direction is Sweden. Where a worker seems unlikely to be re-employed in his home community, but where the employment service locates an acceptable job in some other area, several types of assistance are available to him: moving costs for himself and his family, an allowance for separate maintenance if the family has to stay behind until he locates housing in the new area, and even a loan to tide him over until he receives his first paycheck on the new job. This involves cost to the government, but the money is spent for a constructive purpose. Both the money and real costs are lower than if the worker had continued to sit idle in his home community.

By vigorous use of these devices—an efficient public employment service, retraining the unemployed in new skills, encouragement of geographic movement—it might be possible to reduce the unavoidable minimum level of unemployment from, say, 4 per cent to 3 per cent of the labor force. This would mean a considerable increase in the output capacity of the economy. But there is little point in doing this without reasonable assurance that the increased capacity will be used. Labor market measures must be accompanied by measures to raise the total demand for labor. Even the best employment service cannot produce jobs out of thin air; and if there aren't enough jobs to go around, workers will graduate from training programs into renewed unemployment.

LINES OF ACTION: DEMAND UNEMPLOYMENT

A generation ago this section of our discussion would probably have been headed, "Stabilizing the Business Cycle." The key problem, it was thought, was to detect a downswing of business as quickly as possible, and then to take steps to cushion and reverse the decline. Considerable progress has been made on this front, not because policy makers are so much wiser than before, but because the economy itself contains a larger number of "built-in stabilizers." A built-in stabilizer is something which operates automatically to put brakes on a recession, without requiring any specific decisions or action. Unemployment compensation systems are a good illustration. As the level of unemployment rises, payments to workers out of the unemployment compensation fund increase. This helps to sustain consumer income and consumer purchases of goods and services.

A more important stabilizing factor is the structure of graduated personal income taxes. As incomes fall during depression, assuming that tax rates remain unchanged, tax payments by individuals will fall more than proportionately to the drop in their incomes. Consumers thus have a larger *percentage* of their incomes left in their own hands and available for spending. This also tends to sustain consumer purchases and to break the force of the depression. (If this sounds mysterious to the reader, a little arithmetic applied to an income tax table will convince him that it does work out.)

This is all very well on the downswing; but the stabilizers operate also on the upswing. As national income rises, an ever-larger proportion of income is drained off in taxes, which has a braking effect on the expansion. This is one reason why an expansion may stop before the economy is operating at full capacity; and this seems to have been happening in the United States since the mid-'fifties.

The modern tendency, then, is to state the policy objective as capacity output or "full employment." This is easy to say, but not so easy to define. How full is "full"? Suppose there are 75 million people in the labor force. Do we want to have 71 million actually at work, or 72, or 73? If there are 72 million at work and 3 million seeking work, do we want to have 3 million vacant jobs available, or more or less than this? The higher the ratio of vacancies to unemployed workers, the tighter is the labor market, the easier it is for workers to find new jobs and win wage increases, and the stronger the upward pressure on the price level.

There is thus no single figure for "full employment." Choice of an employment target involves balancing the advantages of higher employment against the disadvantages of more rapid price increases. Just where the balance should be struck is a matter of political judgment.[5]

There are complications also in translating the *employment target* into an *output target*. Suppose that unemployment is running at 6 per cent of the labor force, and there is agreement that 4 per cent is a proper target figure. One might think that to reduce unemployment by 2 per cent requires raising the level of output by the same 2 per cent. But this is wrong, and would set the output target a good deal too low. Okun has estimated that "in the postwar period, on the average, each extra percentage point in the unemployment rate above 4 per cent has been associated with about a 3 per cent decrement in real GNP." [6] Thus cutting unemployment from 6 to 4 per cent would require raising real GNP about 6 per cent, or about $35 billion a year at present GNP levels.

---

[5] This issue is discussed at greater length in Chapter 16 below.

[6] Arthur M. Okun, "Potential GNP: Its Measurement and Significance," *1962 Proceedings, Business and Economic Statistics Section, American Statistical Association* (reprinted as Cowles Foundation Paper 190, Yale University, 1963).

Why does GNP rise, proportionately, so much faster than unemployment falls? The reasons are not entirely clear, but they include: an increase in the average length of workweek and a drop in part-time unemployment, which is not counted in conventional unemployment figures; probably, though this is disputed, some increase in labor force participation rates as the demand for labor rises; and a substantial rise in output per man-hour with rising aggregate demand. "The record clearly shows that man-hour productivity is depressed by low levels of utilization, and that periods of movement toward full employment yield considerably above average productivity gains." [7] This is partly because clerical, sales, and managerial employees are typically not laid off when business slackens, and even plant employees may not be laid off in a short recession. Instead of open unemployment, one has "on-the-job underemployment," which shows up as a drop in man-hour output. Conversely, on the upswing, output per man-hour rises as the same work force is more fully utilized.

Once the "capacity gap" has been determined and the output target established, there remains the problem of how to get there. What are the most effective and prudent measures for raising the level of national output? Here the discussion moves beyond labor economics into monetary economics and public finance. There would be considerable agreement that monetary policy is useful mainly in curbing an unduly strong upswing, a boom which threatens to go through the output ceiling and produce substantial inflation. If the problem is undue slack in the economy, low interest rates and easy money will be favorable to economic expansion but may not be sufficient to ensure it. In these circumstances fiscal policy—some combination of tax cuts, or expenditure increases, or both—will have a more direct and predictable effect. This conclusion leaves much room for argument over just what "fiscal package" is appropriate in a particular case.

FINANCING UNAVOIDABLE UNEMPLOYMENT: UNEMPLOYMENT COMPENSATION SYSTEMS

Even with maximum effort along all these lines, a good deal of unemployment will remain. Frictional unemployment will be with us at all times; and occasionally there will be a sharp rise in demand

---

[7] Okun, *op. cit.*

unemployment on the downswing of a business cycle. Moreover, the magnitude of unemployment arising from these causes is somewhat predictable. One cannot know *which* workers will be out of work during the coming year, but one can be sure that a certain proportion of the labor force will be unemployed at any given time.

This suggests that the principle of insurance can be applied. Insurance involves the spreading over a large number of people of a risk which is uncertain as to any one of them, but which is predictable for the group as a whole. Suppose, for example, that there are a thousand farmers in a certain county who wish to protect themselves against loss through burning of their barns. No one knows which barns will burn in a particular year, but statistical records show that an average of twenty burn every year. If the barns are worth $5,000 each, it is necessary to levy an annual premium of $100 on each farmer. Out of this $100,000 fund, the twenty farmers who lose their barns each year can be compensated.

The principle of unemployment compensation is very similar. A central insurance fund is built up by regular payments from workers or their employers and, in some countries, the government as well. From this fund, those workers who happen to be out of work during the year receive payments of so much per week up to some maximum number of weeks.

The limitations of unemployment compensation are inherent in the insurance principle. The fire insurance fund just described would go bankrupt if there were an outbreak of arson lasting for several years. Similarly, unemployment compensation funds cannot bear the burden of mass unemployment resulting from a major depression. Again, a farmer whose barn burned every year would have to be excluded from the insurance system. Similarly, people of low employability who work very irregularly cannot be covered effectively by unemployment compensation. The purpose of unemployment compensation is to carry regularly employed workers through relatively brief periods of unemployment.[8]

Unemployment compensation systems are now in operation in each of the states and in the District of Columbia. Establishment of these systems was due primarily to the Social Security Act of

---

[8] See Eveline M. Burns, *The American Social Security System* (Boston: Houghton Mifflin Company, 1949); William Haber and W. J. Cohen, *Readings in Social Security* (Englewood Cliffs, N.J.: Prentice-Hall, Inc., 1948); Federal Security Agency, *Annual Reports*.

1935. This Act levied a payroll tax of 3 per cent on employers in most industries but permitted them to offset against this tax any amount, up to a maximum of 2.7 per cent of payrolls, which they contributed to a state unemployment compensation system. While the Act did not require the states to set up unemployment compensation systems, this was its obvious intent. Any state could now set up a system of unemployment compensation, and levy taxes up to 2.7 per cent of payrolls, without imposing any additional burden on employers in the state. All of the states, therefore, created unemployment compensation systems before the end of 1937.

The remaining 0.3 per cent of the employer's payroll must be paid to the federal government and goes into a fund which is used to cover the costs of administering unemployment compensation and employment service activities in the various states. The amount granted to each state for administrative expenses is not necessarily equal to the amount collected from employers in that state. The grants depend on estimates, prepared by state officials and checked by the Social Security Board, of how much money will actually be needed in view of salary scales, prospective work loads, and personnel requirements in each state. The system of having administrative expenses collected by the Federal Government and then turned back to the states enables the Social Security Board to impose minimum operating standards on the state systems. Administrative personnel must be selected on a merit basis, minimum standards must be observed in the payment of benefits, alterations in the taxes levied on employers must have federal approval, and certain types of report must be submitted to the Social Security Board.

The main operating features of the state unemployment compensation systems may be described under the headings of coverage, costs, benefits provided, and disqualifications from benefits.

COVERAGE. Most of the state systems exclude farm laborers, domestic servants, state and local government employees, and employees of educational, charitable, and other nonprofit institutions. Most states also exclude establishments with less than four employees, though in twenty states even one employee brings an employer under the program. Irregular workers are usually excluded by a requirement that they must have earned a certain amount of money during the previous year or two in order to be eligible for benefit payments. The remaining covered workers, about 40 million in all, represent 60 per cent of the labor force and about 80 per cent of all wage and salary earners. The great bulk of unemployment occurs within the area covered by unemployment compensation. A strong case can be made that some of the groups now excluded, notably farm workers, employees of nonprofit institutions, and employees in small establishments, should be brought into the system by raising federal standards.

COSTS. The revenue for the unemployment compensation funds comes almost entirely from payroll taxes levied on the employer. Only four states levy taxes on employees, and these amount to only 1 per cent of wages. The tax rate on employers was set at the beginning of the program at 3 per cent of the first $3,000 of wages earned by an employee in a year. The actual cost to employers has been much reduced over the years, however, through application of the principle of "experience rating." Under experience rating, a separate account is kept for each employer, and the tax rate paid by the employer is adjusted in accordance with the amount of benefit payments charged against his account. The logic of experience rating is that the individual employer "causes" layoffs from his plant and should be required to pay for these layoffs through the size of his contributions to the insurance fund. Employers who make few layoffs should be rewarded by a lower tax rate, while employers who cause more unemployment should be penalized by higher taxes.[9]

The validity of this argument is quite questionable. Most cyclical and seasonal unemployment is beyond the control of the individual employer. The plants which have large fluctuations in employment are usually those in irregular types of industry. They are unlucky rather than inefficient, and there seems no reason why they should be taxed more heavily than other employers. Empirical studies show that some employers actually have made progress toward stabilization of employment in response to the tax incentive. On the other hand, a forceful argument against experience rating is that it unduly stimulates employers' interest in taking advantage of technicalities to oppose workers' benefit claims, and also leads them to suggest restrictive amendments to the state acts.

As experience rating has actually worked out, it has become mainly

---

[9] For opposing points of view on experience rating, see Herman Feldman and D. M. Smith, *The Case for Experience Rating in Unemployment Compensation and a Proposed Method* (New York: Industrial Relations Counselors, 1939); and Richard A. Lester and C. V. Kidd, *The Case against Experience Rating in Unemployment Compensation* (New York: Industrial Relations Counselors, 1939).

a way of reducing the level of payroll taxes on all employers. The tax level has fallen, first, because in all but six states the tax is still applicable only to earnings up to the limit of $3,000 per worker per year that was established in 1939. Meanwhile actual earnings levels have increased greatly. Thus while in 1939 practically all wages in covered employment were taxable, by 1960 wages subject to tax were only about 60 per cent of total payrolls. Second, the low level of unemployment during the 'forties and 'fifties combined with experience rating has operated to reduce the tax rate itself far below the original 3 per cent. By 1960 the effective tax rate averaged only about 1 per cent of total payrolls, and about one-third of covered employers had tax rates of 0.5 per cent or less. In some states present tax rates are quite inadequate to provide a proper level of benefit payments for the amount of unemployment which may be expected in years to come.

BENEFIT RIGHTS UNDER UNEMPLOYMENT COMPENSATION. The outlays of an unemployment compensation system are determined by the conditions governing eligibility for benefits, the size of the weekly benefit payment, the number of weeks for which benefit payments are available, and the length of the "waiting period" between the beginning of unemployment and the beginning of benefit payments.

The eligibility requirements have a great effect on the cost of the program. If anyone who has ever worked in a covered industry is eligible to receive benefits, there will be a heavy drain on the fund for payments to irregular workers and to workers who normally work outside covered industries but who happen to have spent a few weeks or months in them at some time. This problem is met in most of the state systems by requiring that a worker must have earned a certain minimum amount in covered employment during some recent period, usually termed the "base period." The amount of earnings required is usually only two or three hundred dollars during the past year, and it may seem that this would include many irregular workers who would be quite expensive to the system. People who had earned this little, however, would be eligible to receive benefits for only a few weeks, since the length of benefit payments is normally related to the worker's earnings during the base period.

The size of the weekly benefit payment is calculated as a percentage, usually 50 per cent, of the worker's average weekly earnings during the base period. This arrangement, which differs from the flat-rate benefits provided by the British system and most other unemployment compensation systems, reflects a belief that workers should be maintained during unemployment in somewhat the manner to which they were accustomed while at work. It is argued that workers with high earnings will thereby have developed a higher standard of living and should not be forced to reduce this standard too much. People with lower earnings will have a lower standard of living and can get along with less money during unemployment.

The 50 per cent principle has been increasingly nullified in practice, however, by another feature of the state systems—establishment of a flat maximum above which benefit payments may not rise in any event. This was not seriously restrictive when it was first established in 1939, because the weekly maxima were set high enough relative to prevailing wage rates that few workers found their benefits "cut off" below the 50 per cent level. Since that time, however, average weekly earnings have more than tripled while the benefit ceilings under unemployment compensation have no more than doubled. In 1960 only eleven states had benefit ceilings as high as 50 per cent of the state's average weekly wage in covered employment. In thirty states, with about three-fifths of all covered employees, the ceiling was between 40 and 50 per cent of the state's average weekly wage; and in ten states it was below 40 per cent.

The result is that most workers now draw benefits at the ceiling rate, and even so are unable to approach half of their normal earnings. The average weekly benefit payment in July 1963 was $34.43, whereas average weekly earnings in manufacturing were $99.23. This may impose only moderate hardship on single workers, but it can impose serious hardship on family heads. One sample survey found that the amount received by unemployed heads of families, calculated as a percentage of their previous weekly take-home, averaged only 35 per cent in Oregon, 34 per cent in New York, 32 per cent in Missouri, and 23 per cent in Florida. How did these families manage to get by under these circumstances? By cutting family expenditure by from 10 to 25 per cent, getting help from relatives and friends, using up savings and other cash reserves, and running up substantial debts.[10]

The number of weeks for which a worker may draw benefits is related in most states to his earnings during the base period, though

---

[10] See Joseph M. Becker, S. J., *The Adequacy of the Benefit Amount in Unemployment Insurance* (Kalamazoo, Mich.: Upjohn Institute for Employment Research, 1961).

fourteen states pay the same number of weeks to any eligible worker. There is an upper limit to the number of weeks for which benefits may be drawn in any one year; and after using up his benefit rights, a worker must work long enough to earn additional benefit rights should he become unemployed once more. The commonest maximum, prevailing in about two-thirds of the states, is 26 weeks. But nine states have maxima ranging from 28 to 39 weeks; and in six additional states the benefit period is automatically extended, usually to 39 weeks, when unemployment in the state reaches a specified level.

It is clearly necessary to set some maximum, otherwise unemployment compensation becomes a general relief system and its insurance character is destroyed. This means, however, that the system cannot provide for the "hard core" of long-term unemployed. It means also that about six months after the start of each recession there is a sharp rise in the number of people who have exhausted their benefit rights and need some other source of support. During the 1960-61 recession, for example, benefit exhaustions reached a peak of 260 thousand in May, 1961. Over the year October 1, 1960–October 1, 1961, about 2½ million individuals exhausted their benefit rights. This naturally produces strong pressure for extension of benefits for a longer period, which in 1958 and again in 1961 was done through emergency federal legislation.

Because many wage and salary earners are still not covered by the system, because of the ceilings on benefit rates, and because the benefit period is limited, unemployment compensation falls far short of replacing the earnings lost through unemployment. Lester has estimated that over the years 1948-59 compensation payments amounted to about 20 per cent of total wage losses.[11] Because of its limited objectives and its actuarial character, an unemployment compensation system can never make up the major part of wage losses; but the American system should be able to do considerably better than it has done to this point.

DISQUALIFICATION FROM BENEFITS. A difficult problem in the day-to-day administration of unemployment compensation is to determine when a worker shall be disqualified for benefit payments. The practical importance of disqualification is that the worker may lose all benefit rights. In the original state acts, disqualification usually

[11] Richard A. Lester, "The Economic Significance of Unemployment Compensation, 1948-1959," *Review of Economics and Statistics* (November 1960).

meant only that the waiting period was extended for several weeks. There has been a tendency, however, to replace this provision by an outright cancellation of benefit rights. Moreover, this cancellation sometimes carries on into the future, so that a worker who quit one job and was disqualified for so doing, but later was laid off from a second job, would still not be entitled to benefit payments.

All of the state systems disqualify a worker who quits his job without good cause or is discharged for misconduct. This rule is based on a belief that unemployment compensation should be provided only for workers laid off through no fault of their own. Many difficulties, however, arise in interpreting the words "good cause." In many states this phrase has been held to include only causes connected with the behavior of the employer or with conditions on the job. In these states a worker who is obliged to leave a job for personal reasons is not entitled to benefit payments.

In states with experience rating clauses, employers usually wish to prevent workers who have left them from drawing unemployment compensation, since benefit payments charged against an employer reduce his reserve and may subject him to heavier taxes. This fact leads to many disputed claims for compensation. The first step in handling these claims is usually for the local representative of the unemployment compensation system to talk with the worker and the employer and try to settle the case informally. If this does not succeed, the case is passed up to the state level and is usually heard by an examiner working under the state unemployment compensation commission. If the matter is not settled at this stage, appeal may be taken to the commission itself and ultimately to the courts.

Most states deny benefits to workers idle because of a strike, unless it can be shown that they had no part in supporting or financing the strike. Some states, on the other hand, simply extend the waiting period. All states provide that workers drawing benefits must be registered for employment and are disqualified if they refuse to accept suitable work. This provision raises the question of what is "suitable work." The Committee on Economic Security suggested the following definition: "employment at a reasonable distance, which will not endanger the individual's health, safety, or morals, at wages and working conditions prevailing in the locality, and in situations not vacant through a trade dispute."

These terms require a good deal of interpretation in particular cases. What are the prevailing wages and working conditions in a particular locality and occupation? What is a reasonable distance for people to travel to work? The reasonable distance may vary with the occupation, the locality, and the marital status of the worker. In Britain, thirty miles is usually held to be an unreasonable distance, but it might be held reasonable under some circumstances in this country. The dilemma is this: too severe administration of the "suitable work" rule will weaken the workers' bargaining position and force them to take jobs at unduly low standards. Too lenient administration, on the other hand, will make it unduly difficult for employers to recruit workers and will increase the immobility of labor.

It is difficult to generalize about the actual administration of the "suitable work" rule. Thousands of decisions have been made in each state since unemployment compensation was established, and there has been little analysis of these decisions. There is undoubtedly much variation in practice from state to state. The strength of labor and employer organizations in the state is probably an important factor. Where the unions are strong, they can help their members to appeal adverse local decisions to the state authorities, and if necessary bear the costs of an appeal to the courts. The unions can also press for revisions in the unemployment compensation act, and for the appointment of administrators who will interpret it in a way favorable to labor. Where unions are weak, on the other hand, administration of unemployment compensation is likely to lean in the direction of employer preferences.

CONTINUING PROBLEMS OF UNEMPLOYMENT COMPENSATION

Adequacy of benefits

We have already noted the tendency for ceilings on weekly benefits to be made obsolete by rising wage levels, and for benefit payments to fall farther and farther behind workers' previous earnings. Workers are now compensated on the average for less than one-third of their previous earnings instead of the one-half intended by the original legislation. The 1957-58 and 1960-61 recessions stimulated states to raise their benefit ceilings, but in most states the maximum weekly benefit needs to be further increased. To guard against future obsolescence it would be best to specify the ceiling, not as a fixed dollar amount, but as a fixed percentage of average weekly earnings in the state so that it would rise automatically with rising wage levels. Most authorities recommend a ceiling of between 60 and 70 per cent of average state-wide earnings. A few states are already using this approach.

A second issue, brought to the fore by the 1958 and 1961 recessions, is the number of weeks for which benefit payments should continue. The present maximum in most states is 26 weeks. Even in good years a quarter or so of the workers drawing unemployment compensation use up their rights and are cut off benefits before they have found new jobs, and in recession years the ratio rises sharply. Since the only alternative is general relief, which in most areas is very inadequate, there is strong pressure to spin out unemployment compensation for a longer period.

In 1958 Congress voted a fund from which the state unemployment compensation systems could borrow to extend benefit payments up to a maximum of 39 weeks. But since these loans were repayable, only seventeen states took advantage of the provision, and the amount paid out under it was only $445 million. In 1961 a different approach was adopted. The federal government took responsibility for financing the extended benefit payments, and Congress voted to recover the costs by a flat payroll tax of 0.4 per cent on all covered employers during the years 1962 and 1963. All states thus participated, and the benefits paid out between April 1961 and October 1962 were about $800 million, roughly equal to the yield of the special tax. An incidental result, however, was some redistribution of income among the states. States with heavy unemployment, such as Michigan, Ohio, and Pennsylvania, received considerably more in extended benefits than they paid in taxes. Some of the other major industrial states, including New York, Texas, Illinois, and Indiana, paid in a good deal more than they got back.[12]

This suggests two questions. First, is it a good idea to extend compensation payments, say to 39 weeks, during periods of heavy unemployment? The advantages in relieving distress and sustaining consumer purchasing power are obvious. The danger is that if the benefit period is unduly prolonged, unemployment compensation tends to lose its insurance character and slip over into a system of general relief. Second, if a system of extended benefits is desirable,

---

[12] Harry Malisoff, *The Financing of Extended Unemployment Insurance Benefits in the United States* (Kalamazoo, Michigan: Upjohn Institute for Employment Research, 1963).

should it be organized by the states or by the federal government? Federal action is probably the only way to get full participation in such a program throughout the country. It does involve some transfer of income from states with light unemployment to states with heavy unemployment. The writer would regard such transfers as reasonable, but this view is open to debate.

Costs and solvency

The drafters of the Social Security Act estimated that 3 per cent of payrolls would be needed on an average of good and bad years to cover unemployment compensation payments at the original levels. Employers nevertheless pushed energetically for lower tax rates, and with such success that by the late 'fifties tax collections had fallen to about 1 per cent of payrolls. This was feasible only because from 1942 to 1957 unemployment remained at very low levels; and because state legislatures allowed benefit levels to drop considerably below the original 50 per cent target. The reserves in the state unemployment compensation funds were also allowed to drop gradually, from about $7 billion in 1950 to $3 billion in 1960.

Unless we are able to do considerably better in reducing unemployment than we have done since 1957, the present tax level will not support the state systems over the long run. In the mild recession years 1958 and 1961, benefit payments amounted to about 3 per cent of taxable payrolls. A severe recession would mean a considerably heavier drain on the funds. Moreover, benefit payments need to be increased substantially in amount and perhaps also in duration. It seems unlikely that the cost of an adequate system over the next ten to twenty years will be less than 2 per cent of covered payrolls. If so, we shall need to raise a good deal more from payroll taxes than we have been raising during the past decade.

The three main possibilities, which are not mutually exclusive, are: (1) To increase the size of the tax base. The amount of annual earnings subject to tax might well be raised from the now obsolete level of $3,000 to something approaching $5,000, as has already happened under the federal old age insurance program. (2) The tendency toward steady reduction of the tax rate through experience rating should be checked and reversed. It would be reasonable to provide that no employer's tax obligation be reduced below 1 per cent or some other specified level regardless of his stability of employment. (3) One can make a reasonably good case that employees as well as employers should contribute to support of unemployment compensation. One reason why employers tend to have a dominant voice in unemployment compensation legislation and administration at present is that they pay the full cost of the system. Unions would be on stronger moral and political ground in fighting for higher benefits if workers were contributing part of the costs. Through some combination of these three approaches it should be possible to provide revenues to cover any likely level of unemployment over the decades ahead.

The most perplexing problem of solvency arises from the fact that some states experience much more unemployment than others. States with a heavy concentration of durable goods manufacturing, states with a high proportion of seasonal and casual industries, and states whose economy is stationary or expanding only slowly suffer more unemployment than states where opposite conditions prevail. Thus to provide equivalent insurance protection some states would have to levy much heavier payroll taxes than others. It is difficult to get state legislatures to do this because of the argument that high taxes will discourage industry from locating in the state. In states with heavy unemployment, then, one generally finds skimpier benefit provisions and less adequate reserves against depression. In Michigan, Ohio, and Pennsylvania, the reserves in the state funds now amount to less than a year of normal benefit payments. Some of the states with lighter unemployment, on the other hand, have two to three years' reserves.

One way of meeting this problem would be through a national fund to which all states would contribute and which could be drawn on to finance part of the compensation costs in states with unusually heavy unemployment. This was one feature of a comprehensive Employment Security Act amendment recommended to Congress by President Kennedy in 1961 and again in 1962. This amendment was not acted on by Congress, but may foreshadow some directions of future reform. It would have: (1) applied the federal unemployment tax to employers of one or more workers instead of four or more workers; (2) increased the base of the payroll tax from $3,000 to $4,800; (3) required the states by 1968, on penalty of employer tax-credit reduction, to escalate weekly benefit amounts to at least one-half of the

claimants' previous weekly wage, up to a ceiling of two-thirds of the
state average wage; (4) provided equalization grants to states meeting
these federal standards, amounting to two-thirds of a state's benefit
costs in excess of either 2.7 per cent of state taxable wages, or the
percentage that benefit costs in all states make up of taxable wages
in all states, whichever is greater; and (5) established a regular
federal program of 13-week extended benefits for workers who have
exhausted their state benefit rights, to be triggered off automatically
whenever either the national unemployment rate or the rate of benefit
exhaustions rises above specified levels. This program and the state
equalization grants were to be financed by a permanent increase of
0.5 per cent in the federal payroll tax.[13]

Relations of private to public programs

We noted in Chapter 10 that private unemployment benefit plans
covering some two million workers have been established through
collective bargaining in the automobile, steel, and glass industries.
This idea may spread gradually to a number of other industries,
though it is unlikely to become as widespread as union-sponsored
pension and health plans. The Supplementary Unemployment Benefit
(SUB) programs raised in the first instance a legal question of
whether private compensation payments could be combined with
state unemployment compensation payments, or whether they must
be subtracted as any earnings are subtracted in calculating the worker's benefit rights. The latter decision would destroy the point of the
SUB program, since private benefits would replace an equivalent
amount of public funds and the worker would receive no more than
before. This issue has now been resolved favorably to the SUB payments in most states. A few states, however, have not granted permission to add private payments on top of public ones, forcing unions
and managements to devise special methods for overcoming this
difficulty. One technique, found in agreements between the United
Steelworkers and the can industry and between the United Automobile Workers and Allis-Chalmers, permits the supplementary benefits
to be paid as a lump sum if and when state benefits are exhausted.

[13] For a somewhat different set of reform proposals, see Richard A. Lester,
The Economics of Unemployment Compensation (Princeton: Industrial Relations
Section, 1962), chap. 9. See also Harry Malisoff, *op. cit.*, pp. 33-35; and papers
by Norman Barcus, Philip Booth, and Fred Slavick in *Proceedings of the
Fourteenth Annual Meeting of IRRA* (1961).

Another is the system of personal accounts provided for in union agreements with Libby-Owens-Ford and Pittsburgh Plate Glass.

A more important issue over the long run is whether the spread of SUB provisions is likely to strengthen or weaken the state unemployment compensation systems. It can be argued that SUB plans, by making the covered workers less dependent on state benefits, may weaken union and worker interest in fighting for liberalization of benefits under the state systems. On the other hand, the fact that workers in the few industries covered by SUB draw considerably larger benefit payments than workers in general may cause unions and workers in most industries to push aggressively for higher state benefits. Over the long run it seems likely that the relationship between the public and private systems will be mainly complementary rather than competitive. Only a minority of the forty million workers covered by the state systems will ever be covered by SUB plans, and even for these workers SUB provides only marginal payments while the state system underwrites most of the income lost through unemployment. On the other hand, the state systems can probably not be liberalized to provide more than 50 per cent of lost earnings, and for the highest-paid workers will provide considerably less than this. The SUB program that is able to raise this to 65 or 70 per cent of lost earnings brings added protection to the covered workers and does not interfere materially with operation of the state systems.

These problems and others will attend the operation of unemployment compensation for as far ahead as one can see. There will never be a state system which is fully satisfactory to unions, management, social insurance experts, and everyone else. Few would deny, however, that these systems are now a permanent and valuable part of our general strategy against unemployment. In addition to their desirable protection of the individual worker and his family, they play an important role in reducing cyclical fluctuations in purchasing power. During the 1957-58 recession, and again in 1960-61, the state systems paid out in benefits almost a billion dollars more than they collected in payroll taxes. This was an important contribution to the stability of personal income payments which has characterized all recessions of the postwar period. The deeper the recession, moreover, the greater the stabilizing effect of unemployment compensation, pensions, and other transfer payments. Their existence is an important reason for believing that future depressions are unlikely to be as deep or as long as they were before 1940.

Discussion questions

1. Why is there always a certain amount of frictional unemployment in the economy? On what does the amount depend?

2. Is there any point in trying to reduce frictional unemployment when total labor demand is inadequate?

3. "The New York Waterfront Commission actually created unemployment between 1954 and 1957 by expelling some 18,000 men from longshore employment." Discuss.

4. What unemployment rate would you select as representing "full employment" for the United States? On what grounds?

5. If the unemployment rate is 4 per cent higher than it should be, does this mean that the output of the economy is 4 per cent below capacity output? Explain.

6. What are the main differences between, and what is the proper relation between, unemployment compensation benefits and relief payments?

7. What are the main provisions of the unemployment compensation law in your state? If you were asked to advise the Governor on revision of the law, what recommendations would you make?

8. What improvements in the unemployment compensation system may require action at the federal level?

Selected reading

Beveridge, Sir William H., *Full Employment in a Free Society*. New York: W. W. Norton and Company, 1945.

————, *Unemployment: A Problem of Industry (1909 and 1930)*, new ed. New York: Longmans, Green and Company, 1930.

Burns, Eveline M., *Social Security and Public Policy*. New York: McGraw-Hill Book Company, Inc., 1956.

Lester, Richard A., *The Economics of Unemployment Compensation*. Princeton: Industrial Relations Section, 1962.

Turnbull, John G., C. Arthur Williams, Jr., and Earl F. Cheit, *Economic and Social Security: Public and Private Measures Against Insecurity*. New York: Ronald Press, 1957.

U.S. Department of Labor, *The Labor Market* and *Employment Security Review*. Monthly issues contain current operating statistics.

Woytinsky, W. S., *Wages and Employment in the United States*. New York: Twentieth Century Fund, 1953, Part III.

15

Labor Mobility And
Labor Market Policy

*It may seem that if unemployment could be con-*trolled in the ways suggested in the last chapter, all would be well in the labor market. Employment, it may be thought, presents no problems. Any employer unable to locate the kinds of labor he needs, any worker stuck in an unsatisfactory job, any director of an employment service office could testify that this is far from being the case. The jobs available in the American economy differ greatly in the capacities they require and the rewards they offer. This creates the problem, which will be our main concern in this chapter, of getting the right man to the right job efficiently and quickly. The problem is complicated by the fact that the pattern of labor demand is constantly shifting. Growth, change, movement are of the essence of the American economy, and they compel large-scale movement of workers from one job to another.

The dimensions of this movement are suggested by Figure 8, which shows average monthly turnover rates in manufacturing industries over the years 1947-62.[1] The chart shows average monthly hirings (accessions) by all manufacturing plants, calculated as a percentage of the workers already employed. It also shows people leaving manufacturing plants, subdivided into those leaving of their own accord (voluntary quits) and workers laid off or discharged by the employer

---

[1] These figures are published currently in the U. S. Department of Labor's *Monthly Labor Review*.

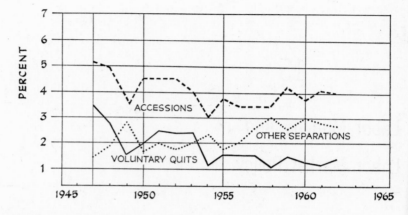

FIG. 8 *Monthly turnover rates (per 100 employees) in manufacturing industries, 1947-1962.*

(other separations). The bulk of the other separations are layoffs, since discharges never form more than a small percentage of employment.

Note first the substantial turnover shown by this chart. Average hirings and separations by manufacturing plants typically run about 4 per cent per month, or close to 50 per cent per year. This does not mean that half of all manufacturing workers change jobs every year. A good part of the movement consists of temporary layoffs followed by recall to the same job. Moreover, some very mobile workers change jobs frequently during a year and hence are counted several times in the turnover figures. The number of *movers* is less than the amount of *movement*.

The Department of Labor has recently begun to publish statistics of job changes for the labor force as a whole. In 1961 about eight million people, or 10 per cent of those who worked at any time during the year, changed their jobs. About one-third of these people changed jobs more than once, so that the total number of moves was upwards of ten million.[2] Each of these moves was a major event in the life of the person making it. Ten million job changes connote an enormous amount of human drama—experiment, risk, progress, and

---

[2] *Manpower Report, 1963,* p. 189.

disappointment. Women workers are slightly less prone to change jobs than are men; but the most striking mobility differences are related to age. In 1961, 24 per cent of male workers aged 18 to 24 changed jobs. But for men aged 25 to 54 the rate falls to 11 per cent, and for those 55 to 64 it is only 4 per cent. Mobility is high in the early stages of one's working life and declines thereafter.

In some years the volume of separations rises above the volume of new hirings. This indicates a period of recession and falling employment. Note that separations exceeded hirings during the recessions of 1948-49, 1953-54, 1957-58, and 1960-61. But there is a substantial volume of layoffs even during periods of peak prosperity; and there is a large amount of new hiring even in depression. One reason is that depression and prosperity are never uniform throughout the economy. Some companies and industries are flourishing and expanding while others are encountering rough weather.

Another interesting fact which appears from Figure 8 is that layoffs and voluntary quits fluctuate in opposite directions from each other. When times are bad, workers cling to whatever job they have rather than face the risk of unemployment. When times are good and there are plenty of job vacancies, the quit rate rises because workers feel safer in leaving an unsatisfactory job and trying their luck somewhere else. Layoffs, of course, run in the opposite direction—highest in bad years, considerably lower in years of peak prosperity.

The significance of these two types of separation is basically different. From the workers' point of view, layoff or discharge is a negative, involuntary, unpleasant kind of movement. If the problems described in the last chapter could be solved, and if employment opportunities could be stabilized to a greater degree, involuntary movement would be much lower than it is. Voluntary movement, on the other hand, is a hopeful thing from the worker's standpoint. It is the door to greater opportunity, the way in which the worker seeks to better his position. Even though he may fail, and land in a job no better than the one he left, it is important that he have the chance to try. This is one of the most important benefits from maintaining a high level of employment in the economy. Full employment assures the workers not only of a job and a means of livelihood, but it provides greater opportunity to advance to a still better job.

The focus of this chapter will be on voluntary movement. We shall examine three different aspects of labor mobility: (1) Movement from employer to employer within the same town or city. This is the commonest and simplest type of movement. (2) Migration from one geographical area to another. (3) Movement up and down the occupational ladder. These three categories overlap considerably. Movement from one area to another almost always means a change of employer, and frequently involves a change of occupational level. It is convenient to analyze each type of movement separately, however, partly because they raise different kinds of practical problems.

With respect to each type, we shall ask the following questions: how much movement is there at present, and why? To what extent is this movement desirable, in the interests of those concerned and of the community? What practical steps, what measures of labor market engineering, could be taken to change the amount and direction of movement in the public interest?

MOVEMENT WITHIN AN AREA

When people speak of a "labor market" they usually mean a particular town or city. The employers who furnish the demand for labor are tied to a particular location. The great majority of workers also prefer to stay in the same city, particularly if they have been there for many years and perhaps own their own homes. This preference is so strong that it takes unusual circumstances—prolonged unemployment or an extremely attractive job offer—to uproot people from their homes and community. If a man is out of work, his first thought is usually to look for a new job as close to home as possible. The upshot is that most movement occurs within an area rather than across area lines.

We now know a good deal about local labor mobility from case studies of particular areas.[3] It is clear that some workers do much more shifting about than others. Workers under 25 move a good deal more frequently than older workers. A youngster entering the labor

---

[3] See, for example, Lloyd G. Reynolds, *The Structure of Labor Markets* (New York: Harper & Row, Publishers, 1951); Charles A. Myers and George P. Shultz, *The Dynamics of a Labor Market* (Englewood Cliffs, N.J.: Prentice-Hall, Inc., 1951); and Gladys L. Palmer, *The Mobility of Workers in Six Cities, 1940-1949* (New York: Social Science Research Council, 1954).

market typically experiments with several jobs before settling into some steady line of work. Unskilled and low-skilled workers shift around considerably more than skilled workers. Short-service workers move more readily than long-service workers. A man who has been in a plant for only six months or a year is much more willing to pull up stakes and try again than is a man who has been there five or ten years. Most workers place a high value on security, and, if they have long seniority with one employer, are reluctant to sacrifice this and take their chances on the outside. Some workers, finally, seem to be "rolling stones" by temperament. The real source of their dissatisfaction lies within themselves, but they blame their troubles on the job or the foreman and never stay long with any employer. Other workers of opposite temperament may spend a lifetime with one company.

Recent studies have also underlined the rather haphazard character of labor mobility and the serious structural defects in labor markets. One can say, indeed, that labor markets are less adequate than any other type of factor or product market in the economy. If one thinks of degrees of perfection in competition measured along some sort of rating scale, the organized stock or commodity exchange would come closest to one end of the scale while labor markets would stand at the opposite pole. But could we not with sufficient effort create highly competitive labor markets? Could we not organize something like a stock exchange for labor?

In order to discover how far this is a practical objective for public policy, we must examine the obstacles which now impede a free flow of labor in the market. What is the nature of these "labor market imperfections"? To what extent are they removable by deliberate effort? It is convenient to divide them into factors external to the worker and factors within the psychology of the worker himself. We must first ask whether, in view of employer practices and other external features of the labor market, the worker would be able to behave economically if he wished to do so. Second, we must ask whether he actually tries to behave economically—whether he shops systematically for jobs, prefers plants with higher wage rates to those with lower wage rates, and so on. It should be remembered that we are speaking of movement of labor within a city or metropolitan area. Movement between cities and regions involves additional obstacles not discussed here.

Obstacles to labor mobility

There are at least eight external obstacles to free movement of workers among employers.[4]

1. A worker can move to another plant only when a vacancy exists in that plant. An employer might conceivably keep comparing his present employees with workers available in the outside market; and whenever an outside worker appeared superior to an inside worker, he might hire him and discharge the present employee. But employers do not actually behave in this way. So even under nonunion conditions it is not feasible for potential employees to compete with and displace existing employees—for example, by offering to work for less money. Only when the employer needs additional labor do outsiders receive serious consideration. This means that opportunities for movement occur mainly toward the peaks of business cycles and are much reduced during recession.

2. The extreme occupational specialization of modern industry means that many jobs in a plant may have no counterpart elsewhere in the area. In this event, the worker cannot change employers without also changing his occupation.

3. Partly because of this occupational specialization, many employers fill a large proportion of their vacancies by promotion from within the present labor force. In manufacturing plants, one frequently finds that hiring from the outside is confined mainly to skilled maintenance jobs and to unskilled labor, i.e., to jobs which

---

[4] There is a large literature on the nature of labor mobility under nonunion conditions. See in particular: P. E. Davidson and H. D. Anderson, *Occupational Mobility in an American Community* (California: Stanford University Press, 1937); Charles A. Myers and W. R. Maclaurin, *The Movement of Factory Labor* (New York: John Wiley and Sons, Inc., 1943); Gladys L. Palmer, "The Mobility of Weavers in Three Textile Centers," *Quarterly Journal of Economics*, LV (May 1941), 460-87, and *Ten Years of Work Experience of Philadelphia Weavers and Loom Fixers* (Philadelphia: WPA National Research Project in cooperation with University of Pennsylvania Industrial Research Department, Report No. P-4, July, 1938); Gladys L. Palmer and Constance Williams, *Reemployment of Philadelphia Hosiery Workers after Shut-Downs in 1933-34* (Philadelphia: WPA National Research Project in cooperation with University of Pennsylvania Industrial Research Department, Report No. P-6, January, 1939); Lloyd G. Reynolds and Joseph Shister, *Job Horizons* (New York: Harper & Row, Publishers, 1949); Sumner H. Slichter, *The Turnover of Factory Labor* (New York: Appleton-Century-Crofts, Mc., 1921); W. S. Woytinsky, *Three Aspects of Labor Dynamics* (Washington: Social Science Research Council, 1942).

are interchangeable among different plants. Semiskilled production jobs may be filled entirely through promotion and may never come into the outside market.

4. When employers do hire from the outside, their selection of workers is guided by an elaborate system of hiring requirements and preferences. Workers are far from being interchangeable in the employer's eyes. He is likely to give first preference to previous employees of the company whose past performance was satisfactory. Next will come people recommended by present employees of the company; having friends already in the plant usually gives one an inside track in hiring. Next will come unemployed workers, provided they have not been unemployed too long. The man who has been unemployed for a long time will have less chance of employment than anyone else, because employers tend to take long periods of unemployment as an indication that the man is not worth hiring.

5. In addition to these general preferences, employers usually have more specific hiring requirements for particular jobs. These requirements run in terms of age, sex, color, national origin, education, experience, physical qualifications, character, personality traits, and so on. Because of these numerous screening factors, only a few of the thousands of workers in an area may actually be eligible for a particular job.

6. A serious obstacle to movement, particularly in small towns and cities, is the existence of a tacit understanding among employers that they will not hire away one another's workers. These understandings, often referred to as "anti-pirating agreements," operate in the following way. An applicant for work at Plant A is asked what he is doing now, and replies that he is currently employed at Plant B but wants to move. The employment manager of Plant A then calls up the employment manager of Plant B and asks him whether his company is willing to release the worker in question. If the employment manager of Plant B says that his company still needs the worker and does not wish him to leave, Plant A will usually refuse to employ him. Where this practice exists, a worker is almost forced to cut his ties with his present employer before seeking a new one. This necessity increases the risk of movement and makes more workers unwilling to take the risk.

7. It is difficult for workers to learn about wages, conditions, and job openings in other plants. There are certain exceptions, such as printing and building construction, where the union serves as a chan-

nel of information and even as a placement agency. In most industries, however, there is no place in the area where one can find a complete listing of vacancies with the wages and terms of employment relating to each. The nearest thing to such a listing is the file of employer orders at the local office of the state employment service. Employers are under no compulsion to list jobs at the state employment service, however, and usually do so only if they have not been able to fill the job from direct application at the plant. There is thus a tendency for the worst jobs to be listed at the employment service; the better jobs are filled by people who have heard about them "on the grapevine" or who just happen to walk into the personnel office at the right moment.

Even when a worker has located a job, he cannot learn much about it until he has worked on it. He can learn in advance the general nature of the tasks and the starting wage rate, but he cannot learn how the foreman will treat him, how he will get along with the gang, how rapidly he will be able to secure merit wage increases and promotions, and many other things. The fact that some of the most important things about a job cannot be learned from the outside makes "window-shopping" for jobs difficult and hazardous.

8. Another obstacle to mobility is the fact that additional years of service in a company usually bring the worker rights and perquisites which attach him more firmly to the company. Seniority protection is the most obvious of these, but there are many others. The long-service worker may be eligible for longer vacation periods; he may have life insurance and pension rights which would be lost by leaving the company; he may have worked some distance up the occupational ladder in the plant and might have to start over again at the bottom if he moved. These things make a worker think several times before leaving his present job.

Worker attitudes to mobility

Let us turn now to the subjective aspect of labor mobility—the motives and attitudes of the workers themselves. Within the limitations just indicated, do they react to alternative job opportunities in an economic way? The answer is both yes and no. If an unemployed worker has before him two or more job opportunities, which offer different wage rates but are reasonably comparable in other respects, he can usually be counted on to choose the higher-paying job. To this extent, worker behavior is economic. The crux of the matter, however, is that workers are rarely in a position to make the kind of choice just described. The reasons for this deserve brief examination.

Most workers in an area at any time have a job, and most of them are satisfied with the jobs they have. The conditions which have greatest influence on job satisfaction were discussed in Chapter 1. If the whole constellation of job conditions is satisfactory, the worker is not likely to become concerned over his wage rate or to be interested in new job opportunities. He takes it for granted that he will continue on where he is. If it comes to his attention that higher wages are being earned elsewhere, he will probably find some good reason why his own job is better anyway, or why it would not be practical for him to move. The bulk of the workers in an area, then, are not in the labor market in any realistic sense. It does not occur to them that they should keep their eyes constantly roving around the area for the best job available. If they have a "good job," the fact that there may be a "best job" somewhere else in the area is of little practical importance.

Workers are coming into the market all the time, however, from a variety of sources—workers who have been laid off or discharged, dissatisfied workers who have quit their jobs voluntarily, people who have moved from other areas, and young people beginning work for the first time. If these people chose jobs in an economic way, the immobility of the others might not matter. Even the people who need jobs, however, do not go about finding them in a very systematic way. The commonest method is to get in touch with former employers, relatives, friends, or even casual acquaintances, in the hope of hearing about a job and getting some inside help in securing it. The next commonest method is to drop into the employment office of a plant which is near the worker's home, or which is in his usual line of industry, or which is large and well known in the area. The worker usually takes the first job which meets his minimum standards of acceptability, and very often the first job which he hears about. Few workers take the trouble to shop around for a number of jobs and then select the most promising.

Because of workers' unsystematic search for work plus employers' custom of hiring mainly at the bottom of the skill ladder, a large proportion of job shifts involve a loss rather than a gain in wages. This is particularly true of laid-off workers, of whom a large majority end up in lower-paid jobs. More surprising is the fact that, even among workers who quit their jobs in order to better themselves, a substantial proportion fail to better themselves in terms of wages. It is of course true that the starting wage may be a poor indication of the long-run potentialities of a job, and that wages are only one of numerous factors in job attractiveness. But the evidence suggests that a good deal of labor mobility is toward poorer jobs—backward or sideways movement rather than forward movement.

Improvement of labor markets

Labor market imperfections are deeply rooted in worker and employer behavior. Creation of a highly competitive labor market would require drastic changes in attitudes and institutions. Employers' hiring practices would have to be altered in basic respects; workers would have to begin thinking in market terms and to prefer opportunity to security; continuous full employment, or something close to it, would have to be assured; certain union contract rules which reduce mobility would have to be modified; an effective central labor exchange would have to be developed, and workers and employers would have to be induced to use it rather than bypass it. As a practical matter, such drastic institutional changes are not going to be undertaken solely to satisfy economists' dreams of a perfect labor market.

The fact that we cannot have perfection should not deter us from doing anything at all. Much could be done to make labor markets function better even if still imperfectly. First, however, it is necessary to ask just what we are trying to do: What are the economic objectives of labor market policy?

From a general economic standpoint, there are several shortcomings in the present movement of labor. First, there is probably too much movement—more quitting of jobs and shifting about than there would need to be if things were better organized. Unnecessary movement is a hardship to the worker and involves recruitment and training costs to the employer. Second, workers take more time to locate a new job than would be necessary in a better-organized market. Again, this is both a hardship to the individual worker and a loss of labor power to the economy. Third, a great deal of movement is in the wrong direction. After all his efforts, the worker frequently ends up in a lower-paid job. If one takes the wage paid on a job as a rough measure of the productive contribution of the worker on that job, then the worker has moved from a job in which his value was greater to a job in which his value is less. This involves a loss in general welfare as well as a loss to the individual worker.

Readers trained in economic theory will recognize that the situation is a bit more complicated than this. To define an ideal distribution of all workers in the economy among all the jobs in the economy requires that one take into account, not only each worker's productivity on each job, but also his liking for each type of work. A balance must be struck between workers' productivity and workers' job preferences, between demand and supply considerations. On this basis, which can be shown diagrammatically by using indifference curve analysis, it is possible to define an optimum distribution of workers among jobs throughout the economy at a given time. This provides a clear criterion for deciding whether a move by Mr. A. from Job 1 to Job 2 is a good or bad move from a social point of view. The object of public policy should be to ensure that as much as possible of the voluntary movement of labor will be good movement in this sense— toward a better distribution of labor rather than away from it.

There are two main lines of attack on the problem: providing workers with better job information, and strengthening the public employment service. The process of providing good job information might well begin in the public school. Toward the end of high school, or even earlier, students might be told about the range of occupations available in the community, the wages and other terms of employment in each occupation, the training and other qualifications required for admission to them, the estimated level of future demand in each, the general hiring procedures and specifications of employers, the work of the public employment service and other placement agencies in the community, and so on. Guest speakers representing various types of industry might be invited to speak at the school, and students might be taken on tours of factories, stores, and offices. These things take little time and are one of the most practical ways in which the school can contribute to satisfactory vocational adjustment in later life. An effective job in the school might reduce the amount of fumbling around by young people during their first few years in the labor market, keep youngsters out of blind-alley jobs, and encourage some to undertake the specialized training necessary for managerial and professional occupations.

What can be done to provide better job information for workers generally? Considering the importance of this matter, it is surprising that there is no place where a worker can get an accurate picture of the full range of occupations, wage rates, and working conditions available in the community. The nearest thing to an information center is the local office of the state employment service, which can provide information about vacant jobs registered by employers. Since employers are not required to register vacancies, however, and since many of them prefer to recruit labor directly, this gives an incomplete picture of the opportunities available. In many cities, the chamber of commerce or some other employers' organization collects periodic information on wage rates, and in some cases also on fringe benefits and other aspects of personnel policy. This information is compiled for the use of employers, however, and is not open to others in the community.

It would seem desirable that somewhere in the community, possibly at the local employment service office, there should be a roster, not simply of the jobs which happen to be vacant at the moment, but of the principal types of work offered by each employer in the community. This should include the wage rates paid, qualifications required, and other key items of information about each job; and it should be open for inspection at any time by workers interested in a change of employment. This would work some hardship on employers whose jobs are relatively unattractive and whose existence depends partly on the fact that their workers do not know about attractive opportunities elsewhere. Any competitive market penalizes those unable to meet the market price. Employers offering superior wages and conditions, on the other hand, would find it easier to recruit labor than they do at present. From a community point of view, workers would be able to seek jobs in a more informed way, the chances of each job change being in the "right" direction would be greater, and there would be a consequent gain in economic efficiency.

Central to any effort to improve labor market efficiency is the system of public employment offices. This system was established by the Wagner-Peyser Act of 1933. This Act provided that states which established employment service systems and appropriated funds for their support would receive from the federal government an amount equal to that supplied by the states. In return for this grant of funds, the federal government reserved the right to prescribe minimum standards of personnel and operating procedures, which the state services must meet. Between 1933 and 1937, employment service systems were established in all the states and the District of Columbia. These state employment services were "lent" to the Federal Government during World War II and, as the main operating arm of the War Manpower Commission, exercised extensive influence over the movement of workers into and out of essential industries. Shortly after the end of the war, the employment offices were returned to state control. The federal government, through a small overhead organization known as the United States Employment Service, continues to prescribe minimum operating standards and to share the administrative costs of the state systems.

Most cities of ten thousand or more now have a branch of the state employment service staffed by at least one full-time official, and larger cities have proportionately larger offices. Smaller towns and cities are usually served one or two days a week by a traveling official of the employment service. The function of the public employment offices is to provide a meeting place for buyers and sellers of labor. Any employer with a vacant job may place an order at the employment service, specifying the nature of the work, the qualifications required, the starting wage, and other relevant facts. Any unemployed worker may register for work at the employment service, and workers who have applied for unemployment compensation are required to register. The registration form, usually filled out with the aid of a trained interviewer, contains key facts about the worker and about his last few jobs.

The problem of the employment service official is to match orders and registrations as best he can. When an order is received, he looks through the active file of registrants for workers who appear qualified for the job in question. He makes a tentative selection, talks with the worker to find out whether he is interested in the job, and if he is interested, passes him on to the employer. The employer need not hire workers sent out by the employment service, nor need workers accept the jobs to which they are sent, though there is some pressure on workers drawing unemployment compensation. The employment service checks a few days later to find out whether the man was hired or not. If he was, this is counted as a "placement" by the local office.

The number of placements made by the state employment services in private industry remained low throughout the 'thirties, largely because of the low level of demand for labor. There was a great increase in placements during the war years, due partly to the active demand for labor by employers, and partly to the control regulations which required most placements in essential industries to be made through the employment service. Total placements reached a peak of more than eleven million in 1944. Placements have fallen considerably since the end of the war, but remain well above the prewar level. During 1963, nonagricultural placements were running at a rate of more than six million per year. The volume of placements naturally fluctuates with the level of business activity. The placements made by the public employment offices are also concentrated rather heavily in certain occupational groups—domestic and other personal service; farm labor, construction labor, and unskilled labor in general; and semiskilled factory work. There is relatively little placement of skilled tradesmen or white-collar workers, most of whom prefer to seek work directly.

There is no reliable way of estimating what proportion of all placements in private industry is made by the state employment services, but the proportion is probably in the neighborhood of one-fourth. Why is the employment service not more widely used? The main reason is that employers can usually fill a good vacancy quickly without resorting to the employment service. Word of the vacancy gets passed on to friends and relatives of people already in the plant, the foreman remembers someone who used to work on that job and looks him up, or the union has a suggestion to make. Thus a worker with good contacts can usually locate a job through "the grapevine," and feels little need for the employment service. Where employer and worker are able to locate each other directly, there is no need for the employment service to intervene. It exists to supplement other methods of work-seeking, not to supplant them.

The employment service is hampered somewhat by the inherent complexity of the placement job. It is hard to become familiar enough with all the jobs in an area, and with the idiosyncrasies of each employer, so that one can tell whether a particular worker will be acceptable for a particular job. It is difficult also to gauge accurately the experience and abilities of each registrant. When a man says that he is a toolmaker, is he really a toolmaker or only a Grade B machinist? A failure to judge accurately both the man and the job leads not merely to a lost placement, but also to a loss of prestige with the employer and worker involved.

The employment service is also under a certain amount of pressure to refer workers to vacancies even against its better judgment. Employers keep asking, "Why don't you send me someone?" Workers keep asking, "Why can't you find me a job?" A worker drawing unemployment compensation must be willing to accept work at his usual occupation under reasonable conditions in order to remain eligible for benefits. The only way of testing his willingness to work is by referring him to a job. The fact that the local offices of the employment service have to administer this "willingness to work" requirement has an unfortunate effect on their placement activities. It means that a large proportion of registrants at the employment service are unemployment compensation recipients. This causes many workers to look on the employment service as virtually a relief office, while others regard referral to work as simply a formality which must be gone through to earn eligibility for unemployment compensation. It also leads to employer complaints that the employment service refers many unqualified workers, and that employment service registrants constitute the least desirable segment of the labor force.

This point can be generalized. The employment service is widely regarded as a social welfare agency whose task is to find work for the unfortunate. It is put under pressure to give priority in referrals to disadvantaged groups in the labor force—the long-term unemployed, members of minority groups, people with physical or mental disabilities. But the employment service cannot push people into employment in the face of employers' natural desire to find the most efficient candidate for each job. Ill-conceived efforts to do so may sacrifice the respect and cooperation of employers, on whose job orders the service ultimately depends.

Considering these difficulties, the efficiency of employment service operations in most states is surprisingly high. But the gap between performance and potential remains wide, and there are few areas of labor policy in which diligent effort can yield higher economic returns. There is need for clearer recognition of the service as an *economic* agency rather than a *welfare* agency. Its task is to perfect the labor market mechanism, to serve all members of the labor force rather than merely the hard-to-place, to reflect employer requirements accurately and objectively, to locate the man most suited to a particular job rather than the man who needs work most. It cannot hope to correct the distress resulting from inadequate demand for labor, or from personal handicaps, or from mistaken hiring preferences. It can hope to reduce frictional unemployment, to cut employers' hiring and training costs, and to secure a more efficient matching of individual capacities and job requirements.[5]

---

[5] For an eloquent and well-reasoned statement of this view, see E. Wight Bakke, *A Positive Labor Market Policy* (Columbus, Ohio: Charles E. Merrill Books, Inc., 1963).

Effective performance of these functions calls for educational and entrepreneurial activity by the employment service. Not only the unemployed but young people on the point of leaving school, and people who already have a job but want a better job, should be encouraged to register. The usefulness of the service to employers must be demonstrated in action. This may require changes in internal operating procedures, such as exposure of each vacancy to several workers, and of a well-qualified worker to several vacancies. There is evidence that vigorous action along these lines can increase the service's placement volume and its acceptance in the community.[6]

These efforts will remain largely ineffective, however, unless there is a high level of aggregate demand for labor. Employers will turn to the employment service, as they did in large numbers during World War II, when the labor market gets tight enough so that they have difficulty in locating qualified workers through other channels. The purpose of a vigorous full-employment policy is not simply to add to national output. Full employment eases many other labor market problems: weakness of the individual worker's bargaining position, reluctance of workers to look actively for a better job, employer discrimination against certain categories of labor, unwillingness to use employment service facilities, geographical immobility. A flanking attack on these problems by raising the level of aggregate demand will be more successful than direct attacks unaccompanied by a full-employment policy. Effective monetary-fiscal policy *is* labor market policy as well.

GEOGRAPHICAL MOVEMENT

In a country as large and diversified as the United States, there is bound to be a great deal of movement among different areas of the country. The basic reason is that the places where labor demand is increasing most rapidly are not necessarily the places where the population and labor force are increasing most rapidly. Jobs and workers are brought together partly by new industries locating in areas of plentiful labor supply, but mainly by people migrating to the places where jobs are available.

---

[6] See, for example, the account of a very successful experience in Madison, Wisconsin, in Eaton H. Conant, "Public Employment Service Operations in a Clerical Labor Market," *Proceedings of Fifteenth Annual Meeting of IRRA* (1962), pp. 306-314.

The necessity for geographical movement appears strikingly from Table 9, which compares the 1960 distribution of employment in various regions with the distribution of young people about to enter the labor force.[7] It is clear that many young people will have to move from the southern and mountain states to the northeastern states and the Pacific Coast, even if there were no further shifts in the geographical distribution of employment.

TABLE 9

DIFFERENCES BETWEEN THE DISTRIBUTION OF JOBS AND OF PERSONS
10-14 YEARS OLD BY GEOGRAPHIC DIVISIONS, 1960

Geographic Division	Employed in 1960 (Per Cent) (1)	Persons 10–14 Years in 1960 (Per Cent) (2)	Difference Between Columns (2) and (1)
United States	100.0	100.0	—
New England	6.2	5.5	−0.7
Middle Atlantic	20.2	17.5	−2.7
East North Central	20.6	19.8	−0.8
West North Central	8.6	8.5	−0.1
South Atlantic	14.0	15.4	1.4
East South Central	6.0	7.5	1.5
West South Central	8.8	10.0	1.2
Mountain	3.6	4.1	0.5
Pacific	11.9	11.6	−0.3
Minimum Displacement			4.6

But geographical shifts in economic opportunity are continuing; and so actual migration will have to be substantially larger than this. The dimensions of the movement are suggested by the fact that between 1950 and 1960 California gained 30 per cent in population *through net migration alone*. Nevada gained 54 per cent, Arizona 44 per cent, Delaware 20 per cent, Maryland 14 per cent, Colorado 12 per cent. On the other hand, Arkansas lost 23 per cent of its population through migration in this single decade. West Virginia lost 22 per cent, Mississippi 20 per cent, North Dakota 17 per cent, South Dakota 14 per cent, Kentucky 13 per cent. Similar movements are doubtless to be expected between 1960 and 1970.

[7] The data in Table 9 are reworked from Census Bureau data for 1960.

In good measure these movements represent a massive drift of population from country to city. About 31 per cent of the 1940 farm population, largely in the younger age brackets, had moved to the city by 1950. During the 1950's, about one-third of the 1950 farm population moved to town. The total farm to city movement over these twenty years was about eighteen million people.[8]

One reason for this is relatively high rural birth rates. The net fertility rate of rural areas in the United States is about double that of urban areas. The other main factor is the sharp decline in the amount of labor needed in agriculture. Output per farm worker has risen rapidly because of mechanization and improved farming methods; and the decline in labor required per unit of product has not been offset by a proportionate expansion of agricultural output. In an advanced economy such as that of the United States, most families eventually reach a saturation point in terms of the quantities and variety in their diets; and beyond that point the demand for agricultural output can rise only in rough proportion to the growth of population.

The combination of a high rural birth rate and shrinking farm labor requirements has tended to produce a piling-up of surplus population on the land. During depression years, rural population simply accumulates and there is more and more underemployment in agriculture. During prosperous years, however, the high rate of economic activity in the cities sets up a suction which pulls millions of rural people into the expanding manufacturing, trade, and service industries. Agriculture is dependent on a high level of urban employment both to market its products and to provide for its surplus labor supply.

Several other features of internal migration in the United States deserve brief mention. It is primarily a movement of young people; the bulk of the immigrants are less than 25 years of age. It is a movement which is strongly influenced by fluctuations in general economic activity. City-ward movement is heaviest during boom times, and is checked or reversed during depression. Movement is typically from lower-wage to higher-wage areas. People move from low-paid agricultural work to higher-paid industrial work, from small towns to cities with higher wage levels, from the southeastern states to higher wage areas in the north-central states. This suggests that differences

---

[8] "Migration from Farms and Its Meaning," *Monthly Labor Review* (February 1960), pp. 136-40.

in wage levels help to attract people from one area to another.[9] Differences in employment opportunities are also important. People move from areas of low opportunity to areas where many jobs are available. The places where employment is expanding and many jobs are available can typically afford to pay higher wage rates, so that the two factors reinforce each other.

The process of geographical movement in the United States is doubtless far from ideal. Movement between areas is probably at least as ill-informed as movement within areas. Those who move may not be the best qualified to find work elsewhere, and they may not move to the areas where they are most needed.

Systematic movement of labor to known vacancies is aided by the Interarea Recruitment System operated by the state employment services. Under this System an employer order which cannot be filled within the locality is first cleared with other employment service offices in the state. If it remains unfilled, it is passed on to other states which seem likely to have the kind of labor in question. Employment service headquarters in these states pass the information down to their local offices, until eventually some office pulls out the card of a suitable candidate from its file of registrants. Particular attention is given to orders for professional personnel, for whom the market tends to be regional or national rather than local. There is a special Professional Office Network, which now includes 121 offices strategically located in cities through the United States.

These activities face the usual difficulties of employment service operation, and there are additional obstacles of time and distance. But these may be removed increasingly by teletype hookups and other means of high-speed communication. Over the years 1957-62, about 150,000 people a year were placed through the Interarea Recruitment System. One may hope that this figure will rise considerably in future years.

In some cases an alternative to moving the man to the job is moving the job to the man by inducing industrial expansion in areas of labor surplus. Government influences the location of industry every day, sometimes deliberately, sometimes unconsciously. The devices available include: cash subsidies or tax rebates, frequently offered by local governments to persuade an industry to locate in a

---

[9] For a statistical analysis of this relation, see Larry A. Sjaastad, "The Costs and Returns of Human Migration," *Journal of Political Economy*, LXX (October 1962, Supplement) pp. 80-93.

particular area; federal loans to new industries in labor-surplus areas, for which a substantial amount was appropriated in the Area Redevelopment Act of 1961; decisions about the location of defense plants and atomic energy facilities, in which the federal government has a major voice; decisions about minimum wage rates and other aspects of wage structure, which may give one region a considerable advantage over another in labor costs; power developments, which may encourage location in an area by making cheap energy available; decisions about highway construction, freight rate structures, and other aspects of transportation policy, which can substantially alter the advantages of a particular location; and numerous other things.

Decisions about industrial location naturally depend on many factors other than labor. Where other factors are more or less equal, however, there is much to be said for locating a plant in an area of plentiful labor supply rather than in a tight labor market. This may mean putting the plant in a small town rather than a large city, or putting it in the deep South rather than in the northeastern states. Bringing the job to the man, rather than compelling the man to move to the job, may have several advantages. People can continue living in their home areas, which reduces both the monetary and intangible costs involved in large-scale movement of population. Instead of placing extra strains on housing, schools, and community facilities in already crowded areas, new facilities can be created under less crowded conditions. The industry itself has a wider choice of labor supply and should be able to achieve a higher level of labor efficiency.

MOVEMENT UP THE OCCUPATIONAL LADDER

We come now to what is probably the most important kind of movement, both from the standpoint of those involved in it and of general social efficiency. Geographical movement is apt to be a painful necessity, costly to individuals and the community. Movement from employer to employer may be simply an aimless wandering from one mediocre job to another. Real progress comes only through movement to a new job involving more in the way of skill, responsibility, independence, and income. Conversely, movement down the ladder to a poorer job connotes personal disaster.

Freedom to move up in the occupational scale as far as his talents will carry him is important, first of all, to the individual. To the great bulk of the population who live from wages and salaries, this is the main meaning of a free economy. Freedom of enterprise is of direct concern to only a minority of people. Freedom of occupational movement touches almost everyone.

From the standpoint of general economic efficiency, it is important that jobs requiring special skills and talents be filled by the people best qualified to perform them. This is important also from the standpoint of political stability. A damming-up of talent behind barriers of social stratification creates a widespread feeling of injustice, pervasive discontent, and latent revolt. From every point of view, then, the maintenance of "careers open to talent" is a vital problem of a democratic society.

Occupational movement can be analyzed in short-range or long-range terms. One can examine movement up or down the occupational ladder within an individual's lifetime; or one can examine children's occupations in relation to those of parents, to detect shifts between generations. Both types of analysis are important, and we shall say a word about each.

Lifetime mobility

There is evidence that many people who begin work as unskilled laborers are able to work up to semiskilled or skilled jobs. A study of manual workers in New Haven found that, of those who had started as laborers, almost one-third had worked up to skilled jobs by the time they were interviewed, and another third were in semiskilled jobs. Mobility operates in both directions. Of those who had started as skilled craftsmen, one-third had slipped down to lower occupational levels. On a national basis, Woytinsky has estimated that one quarter of those who are unskilled or semiskilled workers at the age of 25 have become skilled workers by the age of 55.[10]

The amount of movement between manual and nonmanual occupations is considerably smaller. A study of a sample of people at all occupational levels in Oakland found that almost half the manual workers had spent some time in nonmanual jobs.[11] These jobs, however, totaled only about 10 per cent of the workers' employment

[10] W. S. Woytinsky, *Labor in the United States* (Washington: Social Science Research Council, 1938).

[11] Seymour M. Lipset and Reinhard Bendix, "Social Mobility and Occupational Career Patterns," *American Journal of Sociology,* LVII, Nos. 4-5 (January-March 1952).

history, the remaining 90 per cent having been spent in manual work. Among people now engaged in professional, business, sales, and other white-collar activity, 60 per cent had spent some time in manual labor, but manual work had comprised only 20 per cent of their work histories. Thus while there is some interchange between manual and white-collar employment, the two groups are largely self-contained.

The most promising avenue of mobility for the manual worker is to start a small business of his own—a retail store, filling station, repair shop, contracting business, trucking concern, or something of the sort. About 40 per cent of the manual workers in the Oakland study had tried to do this at one time or another and a fair number had succeeded. Indeed, half of the present business owners in the sample had begun life as manual workers. The transition from wage earner to proprietor is not easy, however, and even those who can accumulate the necessary capital often turn out to lack managerial ability. After a short time, during which they use up their accumulated savings, they are forced to drop out. Something like 10 per cent of very small businesses suspend operations each year, several times the failure rate for larger businesses.

The other main outlets for energetic and intelligent workers are sales jobs and minor white-collar positions (the Oakland study found that about half of the jobs in these categories were filled by people who had started out in manual labor). Few workers are able to move up any distance in the executive hierarchy or to get into professional and quasi-professional positions. Above a certain level the college man with technical training takes over, and the man who has spent his life as a worker can go no further.

Movement between generations

Occupational movement between generations depends partly on the openness or closedness of the society. If it is traditional for occupations to be passed down from father to son, occupational movement will be hampered. But much depends also on trends in the occupational structure, and on differential birth rates. If the professional and managerial occupations are expanding rapidly, there will not be enough high-status sons to go 'round, and sons from lower occupational levels will have to move up. The same effect follows if the upper occupational groups have birth rates too low to reproduce their own numbers.

Both these tendencies have operated in Western industrial societies over the past century. The higher occupations have been expanding rapidly as a proportion of total employment; and the higher occupational groups have had relatively low birth rates. The result has been a powerful updraft, which has permitted a substantial percentage in each generation to rise above their parents' occupational level.

There have been numerous studies of this phenomenon in countries as different as France, Germany, Britain, the United States, and Japan.[12] The results from various countries are surprisingly similar. Typically about one-third of the sons of manual workers have been able to move up to nonmanual occupations. This definition of "up" may seem questionable, because many manual jobs now pay more than many clerical jobs; but the white-collar occupations as a group still carry superior income, prestige, and sense of middle-class status. At the same time a certain proportion, usually 15 to 25 per cent, of the sons of nonmanual workers have entered manual occupations. There has been substantial movement both upward and downward, with the updrift predominating. The fact that the American figures look so similar to those from other countries runs counter to the popular belief that the United States is in some special sense a "land of opportunity." All rapidly expanding industrial economies seem in fact to be lands of opportunity. While data for the U.S.S.R. in recent decades are not available, it would not be surprising to find them also looking similar to those for the Western countries.

While there is substantial opportunity to move up into some kind of white-collar employment, there is only limited opportunity to move into the "elite groups" of the economy—the professions, politics and the civil service, and business management. Here there are interesting differences among countries, reflecting differences in social traditions and educational opportunities. Lipset and Bendix report that:

. . . French, German, Dutch, British, and Swedish civil servants come from families of higher social status than their American peers, a finding that probably reflects national variation in the status of civil-service positions. In much of Europe, high civil-service positions are considered appropriate and even desirable for men coming from families with elite backgrounds, whereas in the United States this has been generally true only for the diplomatic service. Conversely, studies of members of legislatures and cabinets suggests that American politicians as a group come

[12] For a thorough review and comparison of these studies, see Seymour M. Lipset and Reinhard Bendix, *Social Mobility in Industrial Society* (Berkeley and Los Angeles: University of California Press, 1963), chap. 2.

from families of higher status than do Europeans. . . . In Europe more workers are motivated to enter politics and there is more opportunity for them to do so than in the United States.[13]

There is some evidence that a larger proportion of American than of European professional men come from working-class families. This is reasonable in view of the fact that these occupations require higher education, which is more widely available in the United States than in most other countries. But the percentage of American professional men from manual-working families is still low, since most college students come from business and professional families.

In all countries business executives seem to be predominantly sons of business men. Several studies in the United States suggest that about 60 per cent of business executives have business fathers.[14] Most of the remainder come from professional or other white-collar families, and only 10 to 15 per cent are sons of farmers or manual workers. Moreover, these proportions have changed little over the past century, except for a decline in the number of farmers' sons, which reflects the shrinkage of the agricultural population. Access to top business positions does not seem to be getting harder over the course of time, but neither is it getting appreciably easier.

The key importance of education

At several points we have noted the influence of education on occupational movement. The key propositions are, first, that children whose fathers are in high-income occupations are much more likely to get college training than are children from poorer families; and second, that those who get college training are themselves much more likely to end up in high-income positions. We proceed to document these propositions.[15]

On the first point we may cite a sample survey of 10,000 high school seniors concerning their future educational plans. Two-thirds of the children of professional and executive families, and 40 per cent of the children of other white-collar people, reported that they had already been admitted to college. But the proportion going to college drops to 21 per cent for children of farmers, 20 per cent for service-trade workers, and 16 per cent for factory and other

---

[13] *Op. cit.*, p. 39.

[14] Summarized in Lipset and Bendix, *op. cit.*, chap. 4.

[15] Again we draw heavily on the thorough review of the relevant literature by Lipset and Bendix, *op. cit.*, especially chaps. 3, 7, and 9.

workers. Another sample survey of male adults classified their educational achievement by their father's occupation. About 40 per cent of those whose fathers were business men, professional men, or white-collar workers reported that they had had some college training; but only 14 per cent of sons of skilled and semiskilled workers, and 12 per cent of sons of laborers, had attended college.

The child's intelligence and motivation also influences decisions about college; and there have been studies which enable one to weigh both the effect of innate capacity and parental background. One such study of several thousand Boston high school seniors is reproduced here as Table 10.[16] Looking across the Table, one notes a strong positive relation between intelligence and plans to attend college. But looking down the Table, the strong effect of parental background is also evident. Among the lowest 20 per cent in intelligence, more than half of those from high-income families were nevertheless planning to go to college. In the opposite corner of the Table we note that, among the 20 per cent of most-intelligent children, the proportion planning to go to college was 89 per cent in the highest-income families, but only 29 per cent among children of low-skilled manual workers. Much talent is still wasted in the American economy through failure of able children to go on to higher education.

TABLE 10

PERCENTAGE OF BOYS WHO EXPECTED TO GO TO COLLEGE
(3,348 second- and third-year male students in Boston area high schools, 1950)

Father's occupation	I. Q. Quintile					
	1 (Low)	2	3	4	5 (High)	All quintiles
Major white-collar	56	72	79	82	89	80
Middle white-collar	28	36	47	53	76	52
Minor white-collar	12	20	22	29	55	26
Skilled labor and service	4	15	19	22	40	19
Other labor and service	9	6	10	14	29	12
All occupations	11	17	24	30	52	27

[16] Joseph A. Kahl, "Educational and Occupational Aspirations of 'Common Man' Boys," *Harvard Educational Review* (1953), p. 188. Cited in Lipset and Bendix, *op. cit.*, p. 228.

Children from higher occupational levels, then, are able to get more education than others; and young people with more education are able to get better jobs. A national survey conducted in 1960 by the Survey Research Center of the University of Michigan found that, among members of the sample with college degrees, 81 per cent had gone directly into professional employment or into other white-collar jobs. Among those who had attended college without graduating, 57 per cent started out in white-collar work. For high school graduates, the proportion entering white-collar employments drops to 33 per cent, and for those with an eighth-grade education or less, it falls to 6 per cent.[17]

Similarly, a 1950 Census tabulation of all male manual workers in the United States showed that 70 per cent of professional and technical workers had had college training. Among other white-collar workers, 50 to 60 per cent were high school graduates and a quarter had been to college. Among manual workers, however, only about 20 per cent were high school graduates and less than 5 per cent had attended college.

While the level at which young people enter the labor market is heavily dependent on education, it is influenced also by family background. When one compares people with the same level of education, but with different family backgrounds, one finds that a substantially higher proportion of children of nonmanual workers are able to find their way into nonmanual occupations. In general, only college graduation enables children of manual workers to enter the labor force in a middle-class occupation.

Lipset and Bendix summarize the situation as follows:

If an individual comes from a working-class family, he will typically receive little education or vocational advice; while he attends school his job plans for the future will be vague and when he leaves school he is likely to take the first available job which he can find. Thus, the poverty, lack of education, absence of personal "contacts," lack of planning, and failure to explore fully the available job opportunities that characterize the working-class family are handed down from generation to generation. The same cumulation of factors, which in the working class creates a series of mounting disadvantages, works to the advantage of a child coming from a well-to-do family. . . .[18]

---

[17] James N. Morgan, Martin H. David, Wilbur J. Cohen, and Harvey E. Brazer, *Income and Welfare in the United States* (New York: McGraw-Hill Book Company, Inc., 1962), p. 350.
[18] *Op. cit.*, pp. 197-98.

The problem of equal opportunity

These natural tendencies can doubtless not be eradicated in any society. In the U.S.S.R., despite ideological professions of equality, high government officials, army officers, and industrial managers are reported to seek preferential treatment for their children in college admissions. Parents naturally feel that their children should at least remain on their own educational and occupational level. Even if educational and job opportunities are formally equal, high-status families are likely to take greatest advantage of them.

But this does not argue against striving for greater equality of opportunity. It is clear in principle that young people of equal ability, regardless of parentage, should have equal access to educational facilities and job opportunities. They should be given an equal start in the competitive race. Each should then be allowed to advance as fast and as far as his talents will carry him, to the end that the most exacting jobs will be filled by the ablest people. This seems economically efficient as well as socially just.

As regards manual and routine clerical occupations, it is not difficult to spell out the steps necessary to achieve this objective: free public education through the high school level; adequate vocational guidance along the lines described earlier in this chapter; employer hiring policies and union membership policies which do not discriminate among workers on the basis of race, religion, or other characteristics unrelated to productive efficiency; absence of legal restrictions on entrance to particular occupations; and promotion to better jobs primarily on the basis of ability and performance.

It is more difficult to ensure that capable young people shall have equal opportunity to reach the professional and administrative occupations. The basic problem is that these occupations now require a college degree and often several years of post-graduate study. Students who go from college through a graduate school of business administration may take six years to reach the labor market; lawyers typically require seven years, and doctors may have nine or ten years' training. In many of the private colleges and universities, the cost of a year's education is now approaching three thousand dollars, and nowhere is it less than half this amount. The student and his parents may thus have to invest something between ten and twenty thousand dollars in order for him to become eligible for one of the higher occupations. This is a formidable obstacle. Millions of families cannot even consider such an outlay and able youngsters from these families are simply ruled out of the market, unless by unusual effort they are able to work their own way through college. The situation is improved somewhat by the growing number of scholarships for able students; but the amount of assistance still falls far short of meeting the need.

Two separate problems are involved here, which should not be confused. One is *how many* students should be trained for each of the professional and administrative occupations; the other is *which* young people should be admitted to the limited number of training positions available. Economic reasoning suggests that the first problem should be left to the free and informed choice of individuals. More doctors should be trained so long as there are young people who feel that the financial and other rewards of the profession are more than sufficient to repay the cost and effort of training for it. Under conditions of free and informed choice, earnings in each occupation would eventually achieve an equilibrium level, i.e., a level at which demand for the occupation would just balance the number of people willing to engage in it.

Earnings in many of the higher occupations appear to be well above the equilibrium level, i.e., many more people would like to enter the occupation at the current earnings level if they could gain admission. The existence of such a situation can be diagnosed roughly by comparing the total cost of training for a particular occupation with the additional lifetime income which this training makes possible.[19] Any difference between these two figures may be regarded as a profit (or loss) to be gained by entering the occupation. If a profit exists, one can say that too few people are entering the occupation and that earnings are above their equilibrium level. On this basis, Samuelson once calculated that a dental degree yielded a profit of $53,000, an engineering degree $59,000, and a medical or legal degree $65,000.[20]

---

[19] That is, how much the individual can earn over and above what he could have earned without undergoing the specialized training. One must deduct from the estimated lifetime income of a lawyer or doctor the lifetime income of an average high school graduate, which would have been available without any educational expense. Both cost and return should also, of course, be discounted back to the beginning of the process—say, the date of high school graduation.

[20] P. A. Samuelson, *Economics*, 2nd ed. (New York: McGraw-Hill Book Company, Inc., 1951), p. 105.

How can such a situation continue? Part of the explanation is doubtless ignorance on the part of young people and their parents. Information on earnings in various occupations is not generally available, and most people do not make careful calculations. Another important consideration is that many families cannot afford to make the necessary educational investment, even though they may be aware of the advantages of professional training. Still another factor is that training centers for some professions, notably medicine, are very expensive to build. Neither private philanthropists nor government agencies have been willing to invest in medical schools on an adequate scale, so that the existing schools can no longer accommodate even the number of students who are able to pay the tuition costs. To train an optimum number of people for each of the higher occupations would thus require a combination of improved vocational guidance, more adequate scholarship funds, and heavier investment in buildings, laboratories, and other educational facilities.

The second problem is *which* young people should be admitted to training for each occupation. Assuming that ten thousand students are to enter medical school each year, how should the limited number of places be distributed? Ideally, on the basis of ability, as demonstrated by college records, results of special entrance examinations, and other tests. This raises the financial problem once more. Suppose that half of those who rank highest in terms of ability are not able to pay the cost of an additional four or five years of education. What can be done to overcome this obstacle?

One possibility is outright scholarship grants from state and federal funds. This could be justified as a wise investment in developing the best potential talent in the coming generation. It is also a type of subsidy to education which involves little danger of political interference in the educational process. The scholarship programs for veterans of World War II and the Korean war seem, on the whole, to have operated with marked success. A strong case could be made for continuing this sort of program in peacetime on a more modest basis, limiting it to students of high ability and demonstrated financial need who have been accepted for advanced training by an educational institution.

A more conservative proposal would be to establish a system of loan funds. It can be argued that, since the financial benefit from professional training will come back to the individual in higher income, he should eventually repay the cost of this training rather than take it as an outright gift from society. If Samuelson's calculations are correct, a prospective lawyer or doctor could repay the full cost of his education and still be $65,000 ahead. One could set up a federal Educational Finance Authority, with a substantial revolving fund available for loan to students. Any student able to meet prescribed standards of scholastic ability and character could be allowed to borrow up to some maximum limit and to repay the loan over a period of years after graduation. Universities which have loan funds of this sort have found that most students are good credit risks and that losses through nonpayment are very small. We already have federal lending institutions to provide credit for farmers, small business men, and even large businesses. Educational loans would seem to promise unusually high returns in both economic efficiency and personal satisfaction.

Federal programs of this sort now exist for students in certain areas. Graduate students in science and mathematics receive substantial fellowship support from the National Science Foundation, the National Institute of Health, and other federal agencies. The Health Professions Educational Assistance Act of 1963, in addition to appropriating $175 million for construction of additional teaching facilities, also provided student loan funds for prospective physicians, dentists, and optometrists. These are administered by individual universities, which must put into the fund at least $1 for every $9 of federal funds received. Loans may not exceed $2,000 per student per academic year; but there is no limit on the total amount a student may borrow. Interest is charged at the prevailing federal rate, currently 4 per cent, with a minimum of 3 per cent. Loans are repayable over a 10-year period beginning three years after the student completes his full-time study. Death or permanent disability cancels the obligation.

The status of nonwhite workers

The most glaring opportunity gap in the American economy is that between white and nonwhite workers. Table 11 [21] indicates that there has been some progress on this front since World War II, and if one went back to 1940 or 1930 the progress would appear even greater. But there is still a striking disparity in the occupational distribution of the two groups. Only 17 per cent of nonwhite workers

---

[21] Data for Table 11 are from the *Monthly Labor Review* (July 1963).

are in white-collar occupations, compared with 47 per cent of the white workers; and about half of them are crowded into the laboring and service occupations at the bottom of the skill ladder. This adverse occupational distribution largely accounts for the lower in-

TABLE 11

EMPLOYED PERSONS, BY OCCUPATION GROUP AND COLOR

(Per cent Distribution)

Occupation Group	Nonwhite 1948		Nonwhite 1962		White 1962	
White-collar workers:	9.0		16.7		47.3	
Professional and technical		2.4		5.3		12.6
Managers, proprietors, and officials		2.3		2.6		11.9
Clerical		3.3		7.2		15.8
Sales		1.1		1.6		7.0
Blue-collar workers:	39.7		39.5		35.4	
Craftsmen and foremen		5.3		6.0		13.6
Operatives		20.1		19.9		17.5
Laborers, exc. farm		14.3		13.6		4.3
Service workers:	30.3		32.8		10.6	
Private household		15.1		14.7		2.1
Other		14.7		18.1		8.5
Farm workers:	21.0		11.0		6.8	
Farm owners and managers		8.5		2.7		4.0
Laborers and foremen		12.5		8.3		2.8
Total		100.0		100.0		100.0

come levels of nonwhite families—an average of $3,191 per family in 1961, compared with $5,981 for white families. It also helps to account for the fact that the full-time unemployment rate of non-white workers is more than double that of white workers—11.0 per cent and 4.9 per cent respectively in 1962. The nonwhite group contains a large component of unskilled and low-skilled workers, who are the first to be laid off in recession and the last to be rehired in prosperity.

Why is the occupational distribution so adverse? Part of the answer lies in educational inequality. As recently as 1930 only about 10 per cent of Negro children aged 15 to 18 in Southern and border states were enrolled in public high schools, compared with 34 per cent of white children. This gap has since been substantially closed. In 1961, 95 per cent of Negro children in the United States aged 14 and 15, and 77 per cent of those 16 and 17, were enrolled in school, compared with 98 and 85 per cent of white children in these age groups. Thus among people in their twenties, there is little difference in average years of schooling completed—11 years for the nonwhites, 12½ years for the whites in 1962.

The frontier of educational opportunity has now moved on to the college level. The number of Negro students in colleges and professional schools is growing rapidly, having doubled between 1947 and 1962, but it is still disproportionately small. Negroes formed only about 6 per cent of all college students in 1962, though they were almost 11 per cent of the American population. In addition, there is a wide gap in the *quality* of training received by Negro and white students.

The fact that the economic problem of the Negro is partly an educational problem is suggested by Table 12,[22] which relates 1961 family income to the schooling of the family head. Note that income rises even more rapidly with education for nonwhites than for whites, and that at the level of college graduates the difference between the two groups is not large.

TABLE 12

AVERAGE ANNUAL MONEY INCOME BY COLOR AND EDUCATION OF FAMILY HEAD, 1961

Years of School Completed	White	Nonwhite	Nonwhite as per cent of white
Elementary: 0-7	$3,656	$2,294	62.7
8	4,911	3,338	68.0
High school: 1-3	5,882	3,449	58.6
4	6,390	4,559	71.3
College: 1-3	7,344	5,525	75.2
4 or more	9,315	7,875	84.5

One way of raising the Negro's economic status, then, lies through the educational system. If educational opportunities can be equalized, as regards both quality and numbers enrolled, we shall see much less difference in the occupational distribution of whites and non-

[22] Source: *Monthly Labor Review* (July 1963).

whites several decades from now. But there is need also for direct effort on the employment front, to erode irrational hiring preferences and to ensure hiring on the basis of ability.

Twenty-two of the states now have fair employment practice agencies, among which the New York State Commission Against Discrimination is especially active. There is also a President's Committee on Equal Employment Opportunity which deals with federal contractors. While the formal mission of these agencies is to investigate complaints of discrimination in employment and to take action against offenders, complaints are rare and prosecutions almost unheard of. The more effective agencies, such as the SCAD and the CEEO, regard their function as basically informational and educational—to learn more about existing racial policies in hiring, to explore the rationale of these policies, and to persuade employers that present practices can be modified with a gain in justice and no loss in efficiency.[23]

One must emphasize again the importance of full employment. Negro workers advanced rapidly during both World Wars, not because employers had suddenly become different people, but because they needed labor. An acute shortage of labor can do more than any amount of discussion in modifying hiring standards. In recent years Negroes have borne the brunt of the general sluggishness of the economy; and they have more to gain than any other group in the labor force from a vigorous full-employment policy.

Discussion questions

1. Suppose you have a table showing monthly turnover rates in manufacturing for the past twenty years. Explain how from this table you could pick out periods of business upswing and downswing.

2. (a) What would an ideal local labor market look like? (b) What are some of the main difficulties in the way of establishing such a market?

3. How do the state employment services contribute to better operation of the labor market? What additional steps might be taken to increase their effectiveness?

4. A prominent feature of the past decade is the existence of "depressed areas," with unemployment rates which have remained well above the national average. Compare the advantages of meeting this problem by moving in industries as against moving out people, and indicate what concrete steps you would advise on either or both of these fronts.

[23] See Paul H. Norgren, "Governmental Fair Employment Agencies," in *Proceedings of the Fourteenth Annual Meeting of IRRA* (1961), pp. 120-138.

5. On the basis of your general knowledge, would you expect opportunities for upward occupational movement to be greater in the U.S.A. than in the U.S.S.R.? Why, or why not? What kinds of data would you need to test your hypothesis?

6. In what ways does the United States fall short of the traditional ideal of a "land of opportunity"? How might actual job opportunities be made more nearly equal?

7. What methods would you suggest for determining *how many* young people and *which* young people should be admitted to training for various professional fields?

8. "It is all very well to advocate improved educational opportunities for Negroes. But to get anywhere by this route will take a long time. What is needed is equal job opportunities *now*." Comment.

Selected reading

Bakke, E. Wight, *A Positive Labor Market Policy.* Columbus: Charles E. Merrill Books, 1963.

Edelman, Murray, *Channels of Employment.* Urbana: University of Illinois, 1952.

Friedman, M., and S. Kuznets, *Incomes from Independent Professional Practice.* New York: National Bureau of Economic Research, 1945.

Journal of Political Economy, Vol. LXX, No. 5, Part 2, October 1962, on *Investment in Human Beings.*

Labor Mobility and Economic Opportunity. Cambridge, Mass.: The Technology Press of Massachusetts Institute of Technology and New York: John Wiley & Sons, Inc., 1954.

Lipset, Seymour M., and Reinhard Bendix, *Social Mobility in Industrial Society.* Berkeley and Los Angeles: University of California Press, 1963.

Myers, Charles A., and George P. Shultz, *The Dynamics of a Labor Market.* Englewood Cliffs, N.J.: Prentice-Hall, Inc., 1951.

Palmer, Gladys L., *Labor Mobility in Six Cities.* New York: Social Science Research Council, 1954.

Parnes, H. S., *Research on Labor Mobility.* New York: Social Science Research Council, 1954.

Reynolds, Lloyd G., *The Structure of Labor Markets.* New York: Harper & Row, Publishers, 1951 (Yale Labor and Management Center Series).

U.S. Department of Labor, *Monthly Labor Review*, "A Century of Change: Negroes in the U.S. Economy, 1860-1960" (December 1962); and "Economic Status of Nonwhite Workers, 1955-1962" (July 1963).

Woytinsky, W. S., *Three Aspects of Labor Dynamics.* Washington: Social Science Research Council, 1942.

16

Money Wages And
The Price Level

Why does John Doe, a milling machine operator in the Do-It-Yourself Machine Tool Company of Bridgeport, Connecticut, get $2.50 per hour for his work? Why not $1.00 an hour, or $5.00 an hour? Doe's earnings are influenced by the general level of money wage rates prevailing in the United States. This level has quadrupled over the past generation. A job which paid $0.75 per hour in 1939 would pay something like $3.00 at present.

More important than the dollar amount of Doe's paycheck, however, is how much he can buy with it at the store. The purchasing power of Doe's wage—his "real wage"—has almost doubled since 1939, because money wages have risen much more than prices of consumer goods. Doe's real wage is also a good deal higher than that of men doing similar work in other countries, due to the generally higher productivity of American industry.

Doe's wage level is influenced by the *city*, the *industry*, and the *occupation* in which he is working. Bridgeport is a medium-wage city, not as high as Detroit or San Francisco, not as low as Atlanta or New Orleans. The machine tool industry is a high-wage industry. Doe's job lies toward the upper end of the semiskilled range and his wage is consequently above the plant average.

Finally, his earnings will be influenced by special circumstances within the company. The wage level of the Do-It-Yourself Company may be somewhat above or below that of similar companies in the area, depending on its efficiency and profitability, past custom, management wage policies, degree of union pressure, and a variety of other factors. The precise rating of Doe's job relative to other jobs in the plant will have been determined by management judgment or union-management negotiation. His earnings will depend somewhat on whether he is paid by the hour or on a piecework basis. Company practice will also determine the size of "fringe" or supplementary payments over and above the base rate.

A full understanding of Doe's earnings thus requires an analysis of the money wage level in the economy (Chapter 16), the real wage level and the factors underlying it (Chapter 17), the pattern of relative wage rates for different regions, industries, and occupations in the country (Chapter 18), and the decisions which have to be made about wages and related matters at the plant level (Chapter 19). We shall work through these problems systematically in the next four chapters, starting with broad issues involving the economy as a whole, then narrowing down to sectors of the economy, and focusing finally on the individual plant and job.

First, however, we must say something about the many meanings of the term "wages." This term is not as simple as it appears, and some of the disagreement that arises in discussing wages is due to the fact that people are talking about different things.

THE MEANING OF WAGES

The term "wages" has different connotations to the union leader, the management official, and the worker in the plant. The union leader is apt to think of wages as "that which can be bargained about with the employer," which means principally the schedule of hourly rates of pay for different jobs in the plant. The worker, however, may be more concerned with his "weekly take-home pay," or with how much his weekly paycheck will buy at the store. Management is interested basically in labor cost per unit of output, which depends on the amount produced by workers in the plant as well as on how much they are paid. These differing meanings of wages must be explained before the statistics to be presented later can be fully understood.

"Rates" and "earnings"

Most wage earners have an hourly rate of pay, usually referred to as the "base rate," but this is not necessarily the amount which the worker actually receives. Many men work on a piecework or incentive basis, under which the amount they receive depends on how much they produce. Under an incentive system a worker is expected to earn a good deal more than his base rate—indeed, it is this expectation which gives him the incentive to maintain a high rate of output. An incentive worker's earnings will also fluctuate over the course of time, as he produces more or less on a particular day. Even a worker who is paid on a time basis may receive more per hour than his base rate. He may work overtime and receive extra compensation for this. He may work on a night shift and receive a night shift premium. Various other bonuses and supplementary payments may cause his hourly earnings to be considerably above his base rate of pay.

The distinction between base rates and hourly earnings is even more important for a plant as a whole. There are many reasons why average hourly earnings in a plant may fluctuate without any change in base rates. During the war years 1942-45, for example, there was a large amount of overtime work in most industries, and this work was normally paid for at time-and-one-half. In an effort to attract and hold workers, promotions and individual merit increases were granted much more freely than they normally would have been. Piece rates under incentive systems were unusually liberal. For these and other reasons, during the war years hourly earnings in most plants rose much more than base rates.

One reason for emphasizing this distinction is that almost all published wage statistics relate to average hourly earnings rather than base rates. The main source of wage statistics is the Bureau of Labor Statistics of the Department of Labor. Each month the BLS publishes figures of average weekly earnings, weekly hours worked, and average hourly earnings for a large number of industries in the United States. These figures are compiled by asking a representative group of employers in each industry to report to the Bureau their total plant payroll, number of employees on the payroll, and man-hours worked during a certain week of the month. From these reports it is possible to calculate the hours worked per man, and the average hourly and weekly earnings per man, during the week in question.

During periods of stable employment, changes in base rates are the main reason for changes in hourly and weekly earnings, and the three figures move very closely together. A marked change in the general level of employment, however, is likely to cause considerable discrepancy between the movement of base rates and earnings.

"Take-home pay"

The worker himself is probably most interested in his weekly earnings, frequently referred to as his "take-home pay." One should distinguish here between gross weekly earnings and net earnings after deductions for income taxes, social security, and other purposes. It is net earnings which the worker finds in his pay envelope, and he is apt to regard this as his real rate of pay. The worker's wife is also interested mainly in net weekly take-home. She becomes accustomed to allocating a certain number of dollars per week over the items in the family budget. A decrease in weekly take-home produces an almost immediate deterioration in the family's scale of living, while an increase provides an additional margin for saving or for the purchase of new goods which the family could not previously afford.

The weekly earnings of most workers fluctuate considerably, quite apart from any change in hourly wage rates. During good times, many workers can secure overtime work if they want it, and people with heavy family responsibilities are likely to take advantage of this opportunity. During depression periods, many workers get less than a full week's work, and their weekly take-home shrinks even without any reduction in base rates. This shrinkage of weekly take-home is regarded as a "wage cut" by most workers.

In some types of industry even weekly earnings are not a fair measure of employee welfare, because seasonal and irregular fluctuations in the demand for labor cause workers to lose a great deal of time during the year. One cannot take the full-time weekly earnings of a bituminous coal miner, a bricklayer, a garment cutter, a fruit picker, a lumber worker, or a longshoreman, and multiply by fifty-two to secure his annual earnings. In these and other seasonal industries, the pattern of production is such that the average worker may get only thirty or thirty-five weeks' work during the year. Moreover, the work is usually distributed quite unequally among the available workers. A table of annual earnings for workers in almost any industry will show figures ranging from zero up to several thousand dollars. Tables of this kind are prepared by the Social Security Board for workers in industries covered by the social security system. The variation in the annual earnings of workers in the same industry is striking.[1] Even in supposedly regular industries, many workers work much less than a full year and have correspondingly low earnings.

Money wages and real wages

The worker's welfare depends, not on how much money income he receives, but on the purchasing power of this income—the amount of goods and services which he can buy with it. In this connection economists have coined the term "real wages," which means how much the money wage will buy in goods and services. The object of statistical calculations of real wages is usually to discover whether the real wage level has been rising or falling over some period of time. One may want to find out, for example, whether a certain increase in money wage rates has been accompanied by an increase in real wages, or whether the money wage increase has been canceled out by a rise in the cost of the goods which workers buy. An increase in workers' average hourly earnings from $2.00 to $2.40 with no change in the retail price level is clearly quite different from a 20 per cent wage increase accompanied by a 20 per cent increase in retail prices. In the former case, the workers have benefited to the full extent of the increase in money wages; in the latter case they have not benefited at all.

In order to make this kind of calculation, one needs a good measure of the prices of goods and services purchased by wage earners. No completely satisfactory measure of retail price exists at the present time; indeed, it is not possible to have a perfect measure, for reasons shortly to be explained. The nearest thing to a satisfactory measure is the index of retail prices of goods purchased by moderate-income families in large cities, which is compiled and issued monthly by the Bureau of Labor Statistics.

This index, known officially as the Consumers' Price Index, measures the average change in prices of goods and services purchased by

---

[1] This kind of evidence is not conclusive, of course, since a worker may work in more than one industry during the year. What is required is a tabulation of workers' total annual earnings in *all industries*. This tabulation cannot be obtained at present, partly because only certain industries are covered by the Social Security system.

urban wage-earner and salaried clerical-worker families. It is prepared in the following way. The Bureau starts from a list of goods
and services normally purchased by moderate-income families. This
list is based on a study of actual purchases by single persons and
families of middle-income wage earners and clerical workers during
1960-61. The study shows what goods were bought by these families
and what proportion of the family income was spent on each kind
of goods. About 300 items were selected for inclusion in the cost-of-
living index which themselves represent the greater part of family
spending. This typical "market basket" is used to measure the average price change for all the items typically consumed by wage-earner
and clerical-worker families.

Prices of items are collected by representatives of the BLS at
intervals ranging from a month to four months in 50 cities of all
sizes. Each price is then reduced to a percentage of the average price
for that item during the years 1957-59, which is referred to as the
"base period." The indexes for the 300 items are then averaged
together to obtain a single index for retail prices. It is a weighted
index which reflects the relative importance of the different commodities in the consumption of those families surveyed in 1960-61.
In addition to a retail price index for the U.S. as a whole, the Bureau
prepares separate indexes for about 20 of the largest cities. Different
cities vary considerably in their price levels, mainly as a result of
differing costs of rent, heating, and utilities.[2]

Limitations of the consumers' price index

There are three main reasons why even this carefully prepared
index does not provide a perfectly satisfactory measure of changes
in living costs. First, it measures only the cost of living *in a certain
way*—the way in which certain families lived during 1960-61. As
people's incomes rise, however, there is also an increase in their
standard of living, i.e., their idea of the way in which they *should*
live. During a period of rising incomes and living standards, it always
seems that the cost of living has risen. This rise, however, may be
due solely to the fact that people are buying more commodities,
rather than to the fact that commodity prices have risen; it naturally

---

[2] For an explanation of the methods currently used in computing the CPI,
see *Monthly Labor Review* (July 1963).

costs more to live on a higher level than before. The term "cost of living" is thus rather ambiguous, and it has been dropped entirely by the BLS in recent years. Another difficulty is that, as people's living standards change, the list of items used in making up the index and the relative weight given to each should also be changed. It is not practicable, however, to make fresh budget studies every year. The list thus gets more and more out of date with the passage of time. The index gradually becomes a measure of the cost of living in the way in which people lived some time in the past, rather than the cost of living according to present standards.

The second limitation of the index is that it measures the change in living costs for people *at one income level*. It is true that the income group used in making up the retail price index is an important one, including about two-thirds of all people living in urban places. But what of the remaining one-third? The average change in the index would probably not be applicable either to elderly couples or unusually large families, not to very low- or relatively high-income families. The living standards of these groups are quite different, and the cost of the items they buy will certainly not change by the same percentage from year to year.

A third limitation of the retail price index is that it does not include changes in the *quality* of items on the budget list. If an article improves in quality without any increase in its price, this improvement benefits the consumer just as surely as a price reduction. The improvement in quality, however, will not appear in the retail price index. It is probable that most goods do improve gradually in quality over the course of time. But no way has yet been found to make a precise quantitative adjustment for these quality changes.

The accepted procedure for measuring changes in "real wages" is to adjust the change in money wages over the period in question to take account of the change in retail prices during the same period. Between 1939 and 1962, for example, average hourly earnings in manufacturing increased by 279 per cent, while the consumer price index rose by 117 per cent. Dividing 379 by 217, one finds that real hourly earnings in 1962 were 1.75 times what they were in 1939, i.e., they had increased by 75 per cent over these years. This kind of reasoning is useful, provided one does not take it too seriously. The limitations of the retail price index mean that the measurements have a considerable margin of error. An apparent change of a few per cent in real wages is of doubtful significance. An increase of 25 or 50 per cent in real wages, however, clearly indicates a higher level of consumption.

Wages as a cost of production

Turning to the employer, we find that wages are important primarily as an element in production costs. The employer is interested in two things: how much it costs him to hire a man-hour of labor, and how much output he is able to obtain from this man-hour. It is not wages as such which matter, but wages in relation to productivity.

Published statistics of productivity relate almost entirely to average gross physical productivity. They are obtained by measuring the physical output of a plant or industry over a period of time, measuring the change in man-hours worked over the same period, and dividing the man-hour index into the output index to get an index of productivity. The procedure is comparable to that used in computing real wages. If, for example, the output of a plant has increased from 100 to 300 over a five-year period, while man-hours worked have increased only from 100 to 200, then (average gross physical) productivity has increased by 50 per cent.

Such measures are often termed "the productivity of *labor*," but this is a rather misleading usage. It is quite unlikely that such a large increase in output could have come about solely through increased effort or skill on the part of the workers. It is more likely to have resulted from engineering and managerial improvements, possibly involving the installation of new mechanical equipment. Since these changes involved certain costs to the company, the increase in net productivity was probably a good deal smaller than that in gross productivity. It is wrong to regard the gross productivity increase as a net gain which can be passed on to labor in its entirety. This point will be discussed more fully in a later chapter.

The accounting systems generally used in business are constructed to yield measures of unit production cost—a reciprocal of productivity—rather than measures of productivity itself. The figure which management usually watches is direct labor cost per unit of output. This figure can be obtained by dividing the average hourly cost of labor by average gross physical output per man-hour, or more simply by dividing gross physical output into total factory payroll. An increase in output per man-hour with no change in wage rates will reduce unit labor costs, while a drop in productivity will raise unit costs.

An increase in basic wage rates, with no change in productivity, will of course raise unit labor cost; but an increase in workers' hourly *earnings* does not necessarily do so. Under a straight piece-rate system, for example, the unit labor cost to the employer remain constant no matter how much workers' earnings may increase. Under incentive systems in which workers' earnings rise less than proportionately as their output increases, any increase in workers' output and earnings means a *reduction* in unit labor cost to the employer. In discussing the relation of changes in wage rates and earnings to production costs, therefore, it is necessary always to specify whether one is assuming wages to be paid on a time basis or an output basis. The importance of this point will appear frequently in later chapters.

A CENTURY OF RISING WAGES

The most obvious characteristic of money wages is that they rise over the long run. Phelps Brown and Hopkins have made estimates for the United States and four other countries for the eighty years 1860-1939.[3] Over this period the money wage level tripled in Germany and Britain, rose sixfold in the United States, tenfold in Sweden, and twenty-four times in France. Prices rose also, but less rapidly than wages, so that workers' real purchasing power rose substantially in all the countries. There was little relation, however, between the rate of increase in money and real wages, either as between countries or between different time periods in the same country.

Wage movements in the United States over the past century are summarized in Table 13, and year-to-year changes since 1929 are shown in Figure 9. The trend of money wage rates is strongly upward. This is no recent development, but goes back as far as our records exist. The rise was most rapid during the three war periods covered in Table 13; but a rising wage level is normal in peacetime also. From 1880 to 1914, a long period of peacetime industrial expansion,

---

[3] E. H. Phelps Brown and Sheila V. Hopkins, "The Course of Wage Rates in Five Countries, 1860-1939," *Oxford Economic Papers*, New Series (June 1950), pp. 226-296. The basis for the estimates, which are necessarily rough, is explained in detail in this paper.

money wages rose by about 70 per cent. On a year-to-year basis, wage rates rose in twenty-five years of the period, remained stable in five years, and fell in only four. Since 1948, which may be taken as the end of the World War II inflation, money wages have risen every year and the cumulative rise to 1963 was about 80 per cent.

The price level took a dramatic turn at the beginning of this century. From 1873 to 1900, prices had drifted gradually downward, so that modest money wage increases yielded substantial gains in real wages. Since 1900, however, the price level has tended strongly upward. The only periods of appreciable price decline have been during the post-World War I recession of 1920-21 and the Great Depression of 1929-33. The level of consumer prices today is more than three times as high as it was in 1900.

Movements of real wages are shown in the final column of Table 13. Note that there are no minus signs in this column. There has been no period in which real wages have failed to advance; but the

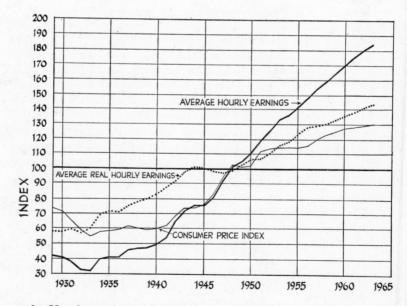

FIG. 9 *Hourly earnings, cost of living, and real hourly earnings in manufacturing, 1929-1963 (1947-49 = 100).*

TABLE 13

MONEY WAGES, CONSUMER PRICES, AND REAL WAGES IN MANUFACTURING,
UNITED STATES, 1860-1963.

	Percentage Change in		
	Money Hourly Wages	Consumer Prices	Real Hourly Wages
1860-70	+53	+41	+ 8
1870-80	−10	−22	+11
1880-90	+18	−11	+32
1890-1900	+ 3	− 8	+12
1900-10	+29	+16	+14
1910-22	+141	+78	+37
1922-30	+12	0	+13
1930-40	+26	−16	+50
1940-50	+131	+72	+34
1950-57	+46	+18	+24
1957-63	+22	+ 8	+13

Sources: 1860-1929, Clarence D. Long, "The Illusion of Wage Rigidity: Long and Short Cycles in Wages and Labor," *Review of Economics and Statistics* (May 1960); which in turn draws on basic research by the author and by Albert Rees at the National Bureau of Economic Research.

1929-1957, Albert Rees, *New Measures of Wage Earner Compensation in Manufacturing, 1914-57.* (New York: National Bureau of Economic Research, Occasional Paper 75, 1960).

1957-63, standard BLS series, computations by the writer.

pace of advance has been variable. There is no visible relation between the rate of increase in real wages and money wages. Real wages rose rapidly in two periods, 1880-90 and 1930-40, when money increases were moderate. The explanation is that the price level was falling. But real wages have also risen sharply in periods such as 1914-20 and 1940-50, when prices were rising rapidly but money wages raced ahead even faster.

It is clear that real wages have risen faster since 1914 than before; and they have risen especially fast since 1930. This is related to an acceleration of productivity in the American economy, which we shall try to account for in Chapter 17. The rate of real wage increase, however, seems to have slowed somewhat in recent years. From 1940 to 1957, real wages in manufacturing were rising at about 3 per cent a year. From 1957 to 1963, this slowed down to about 2 per cent, reflecting a lower growth rate of the economy after 1957.[4]

Explaining the money wage level

Until recently, economists were not much interested in explaining the money wage level. The important thing was the real wage level, on which money wages seem to have little influence. Abnormal fluctuations in prices and money wages would cancel each other out, leaving the real relationships in the economy unchanged. Moreover, such fluctuations were thought always to be set off from the demand side. In the simplest theories, a doubling, say, of the quantity of money would produce a doubling of the price level; and money wages would be pulled along behind. The money wage level had no life of its own.

The combination of strong unionism and high levels of demand in many countries since World War II, however, has caused a shift of outlook. It has been observed that wages are no longer reduced in recession. Unions typically demand and receive wage increases even in recession years; and a combination of rising prices and wages with substantial unemployment is not unusual. Prices have crept up almost continuously. The rate of increase in the United States has been lower than in most other countries; but this may be only because our economy has been operating farther below capacity. Many economists have concluded that the wage level does have a life of its own, that prices can be pushed up from the cost side as well as pulled up from the demand side, and that collective bargaining strengthens the tendency of our economy toward a built-in rise in the price level over the long run. This tendency is often termed "secular inflation."

This has led to intensified study of what determines the rate of increase in money wages. Even under collective bargaining, economic

---

[4] The data in Table 13 relate only to hourly earnings *in manufacturing*. We are probably safe in taking wage trends in manufacturing as reasonably representative of other sectors; but the data for most of these sectors have not yet been thoroughly explored.

Our knowledge of wage and price developments in the period 1860-1914 has been enlarged substantially by two recent monographs: Clarence D. Long, *Wages and Earnings in the United States* (Princeton: Princeton University Press, 1960); and Albert Rees, *Real Wages in Manufacturing, 1890-1914* (Princeton: Princeton University Press, 1961). These new estimates of money and real wages differ considerably from earlier estimates. Thus in accepting them as the basis for Table 13, we come out with figures which differ substantially from those shown in the Third Edition of this text (Table 10, p. 429).

circumstances presumably continue to shape the bargaining positions of the parties. The level of unemployment is important, both through its direct influence in the labor market and because it reflects the degree of idle capacity in the economy. Phillips, on the basis of British data from 1861 to 1957, concluded that there is a strong inverse relation between the rate of money wage increase and the unemployment rate; that the relationship derived for the years 1861-1913 fits about as well for 1913-48 and 1948-57; that 5 per cent unemployment is required in Britain to hold money wages constant; and that with 2½ per cent unemployment, wage increases would be held within the bounds of the 2 to 3 per cent annual increase in productivity.[5]

Samuelson and Solow have made a similar analysis of U. S. data for 1929-59, from which they derive the "modified Phillips curve" shown by the solid line in Figure 10.[6] Since it is the price level in which we are really interested, the vertical axis is calibrated in price units rather than wage units. The point of zero price increase corresponds to a 2½ per cent a year rise in money wages, which is considered to be within the bounds of productivity increase. The authors make an admittedly rough estimate that, with 5 to 6 per cent unemployment, the price level will remain stable. If, on the other hand, unemployment were reduced to 3 per cent, prices might rise 4 to 5 per cent a year. The fact that price stability apparently requires a higher unemployment rate in the United States that in Britain must reflect structural differences in the two economies, but the nature of these is not clear.

While these calculations are intriguing, they should not be taken for more than they are worth. A scatter diagram relating wage increases on the vertical axis to unemployment rates on the horizontal axis does show a downward drift to the right, and one can fit a curve to these observations; but the variance about the curve is quite large. For the postwar years in Great Britain, Phillips' diagrams show that unemployment of 1 to 2 per cent has been associated with wage increases of anything from 2 to 8 per cent a year (excluding an abnormal Korean War increase of 10½ per cent in 1950). The

---

[5] A. W. Phillips, "The Relation Between Unemployment and the Rate of Change of Money Wage Rates in the United Kingdom, 1861-1967," *Economica* (November 1958), pp. 283-299.

[6] Paul Samuelson and Robert Solow, "Analytical Aspects of Anti-Inflation Policy," A.E.A. *Papers and Proceedings* (May 1960), pp. 177-194.

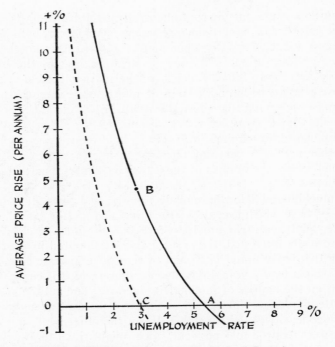

FIG. 10   *A Modified Phillips Curve for the United States.*

Samuelson-Solow scatter diagram, not reproduced here, suggests that unemployment in the neighborhood of 5 per cent has been accompanied by everything from a slight wage decline in one year to a 6 per cent increase in another. So it may not be very meaningful to say that 5 per cent unemployment will *on the average* give us a 2½ per cent rate of increase in money wages. It may give a good deal more than that in some years, a good deal less in others, depending on additional circumstances.

Several economists have experimented with additional variables which might help to explain the looseness of the simple wage-unemployment relation. Bowen, after analyzing the American data from 1947 through 1959, concludes that the direction of change in unemployment is important. "At a given average level of unemployment, wages rise much less rapidly when unemployment is increasing than when unemployment is decreasing. In the postwar period the upward march of wages has been restrained most noticeably in the contraction phase of the three postwar recessions, when unemployment was above 4.3 per cent *and* increasing steadily."[7] Long, after surveying the whole period 1860-1960, concludes also that "wages have been much more responsive to economic downturns than has been recognized."[8] Not only do employers put up stronger resistance to increases in base rates during a recession, but there is a shrinkage of overtime payments and a downgrading of the labor force by making fewer promotions and replacing departing workers by new people in the lower-wage categories.

Eckstein and Wilson, whose analysis is couched in terms of "wage rounds" in the American economy from 1948-60, find that variance in the rate of wage increase can be explained satisfactorily by using two variables: profits, which reflect the state of product markets and the pressures bearing on employers, and the unemployment rate, which affects both union bargaining power and wage setting in non-union labor markets.[9] Bowen's study also found profits to be a significant variable. Klein and Ball have developed a model for postwar changes in the British wage level which relies on recent changes in the consumer price index as well as on the unemployment rate.[10] They find that wage adjustments have "in effect roughly compensated for the effects of price increases between the times at which increases in wage rates have been obtained." But wage increases beyond this are strongly influenced by the unemployment rate.

These statistical relations still give no real explanation of why wage and price increases occur. They are compatible either with the hypothesis that low levels of unemployment reflects excess aggregate demand in the economy, which forces up the price level, which in turn pulls up wages (the "demand inflation" hypothesis); or, that at low levels of unemployment, the labor market is so tight that outsize wage increases are demanded and granted, which raise unit labor costs and force up the price level (the "cost inflation" hypothesis). How can one choose between these hypothesis? Once an inflationary movement is under way, how can one tell whether the initial push

---

[7] William G. Bowen, *Wage Behavior in the Postwar Period.* (Princeton: Industrial Relations Section, Princeton University, 1960), p. 86.

[8] Clarence D. Long, "The Illusion of Wage Rigidity: Long and Short Cycles in Wages and Labor," *Review of Economics and Statistics* (May 1960), pp. 140-151.

[9] Otto Eckstein and Thomas A. Wilson, "Determination of Money Wages in American Industry," *Quarterly Journal of Economics* (October 1962), pp. 379-414.

[10] L. R. Klein and R. J. Ball, "Some Econometrics of the Determination of Absolute Prices and Wages," *Economic Journal* (September 1959), pp. 465-482.

came from the cost side or the demand side? There is no agreed answer at present; but at least we can explore the nature of the problem.

MONEY WAGES AND THE PRICE LEVEL

The commonest situation in actuality is one in which the price level is rising moderately while the wage level is rising faster. This tended to be true even in the "good old days." It was true, for example, of every year from 1898 to 1914 except the recession year 1908. It was true also of almost every year from 1938 to 1963. This situation invariably gives rise to a welter of charges and countercharges. What is causing the price inflation? Employers argue that they are forced to raise prices to cover the excessive wage increases demanded by the unions. Union leaders argue with equal sincerity that they are simply trying to catch up with previous price increases. What is the role of wages? Are they cause, or consequence, or both?

It is difficult if not impossible to answer this question by statistical analysis. One can, however, draw a logical distinction between two types of situation, which are commonly designated as "demand inflation" and "cost inflation." They might also be termed "old-fashioned" and "new-style" inflation.

Wages and demand inflation

Old-fashioned or demand inflation is a familiar topic in economic analysis, and there is no need to repeat the analysis here. It is a situation in which aggregate money demand exceeds capacity output of the economy at current prices. Consumers, business, and government are trying to buy more goods than there are goods available, and something has to give. In principle, one cannot blame one kind of spending more than another for being excessive. It is simply total spending which is excessive. In practice, however, demand inflation is typically associated with marked increases in government spending for war and defense purposes, or in business spending on plant, equipment, and inventories during business cycle upswings.

The appropriate remedy for demand inflation is to cut down the demand of one or more groups in the economy. Government may cut consumer demand by tax increases, or reduce its own expenditures, or attempt to reduce business investment through monetary controls or other methods. Unless adequate action is taken there will be a rise in prices, one result of which will be a more than proportionate increase in business profits. This will stimulate large wage demands, and a cumulative inflationary process will be under way.

Although wages cannot be accused of having set off this process, the speed and intensity of wage reactions will have an important bearing on the subsequent development of the inflation. To take an extreme case, suppose that while prices rise all wage and salary incomes remain unchanged. The purchasing power of wage and salary earners would obviously fall and this would act as a braking factor on the inflation. Conversely, if wages and other consumer incomes adjust rapidly and completely to price changes, this will add to the momentum of the inflation. The shorter the wage lag, the steeper the inflationary spiral.

It is often assumed that collective bargaining shortens the wage lag and thus makes inflations steeper than they would be otherwise. Escalator clauses with wage adjustments every three months based on the consumer price index certainly have this effect. Fixing wages for a year, however, which is still the general rule, may sometimes produce a longer wage lag than would exist without unionism. The net effect of collective bargaining is unclear, and it seems unlikely that it has any major effect on demand inflations.

It is in any case not very plausible to advocate wage freezing or a long wage lag as a remedy for demand inflation. This would be a very unpalatable remedy from the workers' standpoint, for it would mean taking a cut in consumption while tolerating high profits, much of which might go into business investment but some of which would go into high-bracket consumption. One cannot expect union leaders to drag their heels on wage demands when prices are advancing rapidly. For a government to urge them to so is unreasonable as well as ineffectual, and resort should be had to the more direct measures noted above.

Wages and cost inflation

What now of the possibility that wage increases may initiate the process and that the price level may be forced up from the cost side?

This obviously can happen within particular industries. Can it and does it happen in the economy as a whole?

Those who fear "cost inflation" tend to reason in the following way:

1. There is something in the dynamics of the labor movement which will cause unions year in and year out to demand wage increases greater than the tolerable level. This could happen, for example, if unions in the more prosperous sectors of the economy—industries where demand is rising rapidly or productivity is rising unusually fast—took the lead in demanding and securing outsize wage increases; and if rivaly among unions and union leaders then produced pressure on other industries to grant comparable increases. It is assumed also that this wage pressure will continue through good years and bad, so that the advance of wages will no longer be checked by recession as it sometimes has been in the past.

2. Employers will not oppose these wage demands very strongly because of a feeling that higher labor costs can be passed on to customers through higher product prices. This is especially likely to be true where the union enforces the same wage increases on everyone in the industry, and where oligopoly with administered prices makes uniform price adjustments easy. Concretely, it is argued that unions and employers in steel, automobiles, and other durable goods industries will accustom themselves to a rising wage and price level and that the remainder of the economy will be pulled along in their wake.

3. Buyers must, of course, be able to pay these higher prices. Any inflation is a demand inflation in the sense that adequate money demand is essential. It is argued, however, that in a modern economy pledged to full employment the monetary authorities will be forced to adapt themselves to the new wage and price level. If there is any danger of insufficient money demand, the Federal Reserve System and the Treasury will simply pump additional funds into the economy rather than be held responsible for bringing on a recession. The higher price level will be matched by adequate purchasing power, and the economy is then set for the next round of wage and price increases. This is what Hicks and others mean by saying that our monetary system now operates on a "labor standard" rather

than a gold standard, and that the money wage level determines the monetary circulation rather than vice versa.[11]

There is little doubt that something like this could happen in actuality. At the same time, there are a number of factors operating in the other direction:

1. Union wage policies, as was noted in Chapter 10, are not entirely "political" and uninfluenced by the economic environment. Unions will not push as hard for wage increases in a recession year as in a prosperous year, and they will not be as aggressive in a stationary as in an expanding industry. Wage "patterns" established by key unions in a particular year are not transmitted with full force to other sectors of the economy. On the contrary, an examination of wage increases industry by industry in a particular year reveals great unevenness—probably as much as existed thirty or forty years ago.

2. Employer resistance to wage increases cannot be written off as obsolete. Where profits are low or falling, either because of general recession or the economic situation of a particular industry, employers may be expected to fight vigorously and in good measure successfully against large wage increases.

3. In the United States, at least, one cannot say that the monetary authorities give overwhelming weight to employment and are oblivious of the price level. In 1957, for example, the Federal Reserve System acted vigorously to check rising prices and its action contributed to bringing on the recession of 1957-58. Credit was relaxed during the recession, but was tightened again in the fall of 1958 as soon as it became apparent that the low point of the recession had been passed. This was done specifically to check further increases in the price level, and it was done at a time when unemployment was still above five million. Whether the Federal Reserve actions were properly timed is not at issue here, but it is apparent that price stability was an important objective of government policy.

4. Despite the advances in monetary economics over the past generation, we are not yet clever enough to prevent occasional recessions even if we were thoroughly committed to doing so. Reces-

---

[11] For a good exposition and critique of this line of argument, see William G. Bowen, *The Wage-Price Issue.* (Princeton: Princeton University Press, 1960).

sions will not prevent wage increases but will reduce their average size. The recession years 1949, 1954, 1958, and 1961 were marked by moderate wage increases which did not pose a serious threat to price stability.

Who is to blame?

Granted that both demand inflation and cost inflation are possible, how can one tell what is actually going on in a particular case? One sees prices rising 2 per cent a year and money wages rising 5 per cent a year. Where is the impetus coming from?

Simple criteria turn out to be illusory. It is futile to examine whether wages rose "before prices" or "after prices." Wage and price changes are continuous and closely intertwined; and effects can easily precede causes in point of time. The observation that money wages are going up faster than physical productivity is of no avail; for this will happen under *either* demand or cost inflation. One cannot even take excessive aggregate spending as conclusive evidence that the inflation is demand-induced. The rise in spending may be coming from the consumer side and may be fed by unduly large wage increases.

It might be possible to get somewhere by more sophisticated types of analysis. One could look, for example, at the behavior of profit margins per unit of output. If product prices are being pulled up by excess demand, one would expect profit margins to be widening. If, on the other hand, wage increases are the active force, one might expect profit margins to be stationary or decreasing. Again, the price of a product may rise either because its demand curve has shifted to the right or because the supply curve has shifted to the left as a result of cost increases. In the first case, output should increase as price rises, while in the second case output should fall. One might look to see whether there is a close association of price and output increases, sector by sector.[12]

Considering the difficulty of diagnosis, it is not surprising that economists disagree as to whether cost inflation is a serious economic threat or only a minor irritant. There is considerable agreement that

---

[12] These and other possibilities are discussed at greater length in the Samuelson-Solow paper and the Bowen volume already cited. See also two papers by the writer: "Wage-Push and All That," A.E.A. *Papers and Proceedings* (May 1960), pp. 195-204; and "Wages and Inflation—An International View," in *Wages, Prices, Profits, and Productivity* (New York: The American Assembly, 1959), pp. 109-136.

an element of cost-push was present in 1956-58, when sizeable wage and price increases were made in basic steel despite excess capacity in the industry and unemployment in the labor force. These increases tended to push up costs and prices in the many steel-using industries. Since 1958 the debate has died down because the economy has been operating well below capacity and there has been little pressure on the price level. The issue at present is speculative rather than factual. Suppose there were a serious effort to raise aggregate demand and to push down the unemployment rate to 5 per cent, or 4 per cent, or even 3 per cent. At what point would one encounter serious upward pressure on the wage-price level? Can anything be done to postpone this point, and to get fuller employment without undue price increases?

How should wages behave?

Before attacking the policy problem, we must spend a little more time in defining objectives. It is unnecessary and unfeasible to require that the money wage level remain constant. There will be upward pressure on the price level only if wages rise "too rapidly." So we must specify more precisely what we mean by "too rapidly." What rate of wage increase is compatible with a stable price level?

The basic reason why the money incomes of workers and other groups in the economy can rise faster than prices is that per capita output is rising year by year. This creates what Erik Lundberg has termed "wage space"—room for wage increases which will not require an upward adjustment in the price level. As a first approximation, one can define a non-inflationary wage movement as one which raises workers' incomes at the same rate that per capita output is rising. For the United States, Kuznets has estimated this at about 16.4 per cent per decade over the period 1894-1954, but the rate of increase since 1940 has been considerably higher than in earlier years.[13]

This figure in some ways overstates, in other ways understates, the feasible rate of increase in basic wage schedules. On the side of overstatement we may note:

1. Part of the increase in national output comes about through the transfer of workers from low-productivity to high-productivity industries, notably from agriculture to manufacturing, over the course of

---

[13] Simon Kuznets, "Quantitative Aspects of the Economic Growth of Nations," *Economic Development and Cultural Change*, V, No. 1 (October 1956), p. 10.

economic development. This increase in output is presumably offset by increased earnings of the transferred workers in their new occupations, and to use it also as a basis for a general increase in wage schedules would involve double counting. Increases in output from this source should be deducted, therefore, in calculating the feasible rate of wage increase.

2. It is the rate of increase in *earnings* which should correspond to the rate of increase in consumable output. Earnings, however, may rise considerably faster than basic wage rates, particularly during a period of sustained high employment. The reasons include promotion and upgrading of individual workers, over-rating of jobs to permit higher wage offers for recruiting purposes, loosening of time standards on piecework so that earnings pull farther and farther above base rates, and straight over-payment of the union scale. This tendency for earnings to diverge farther and farther above official wage schedules, which Swedish economists have termed "wage drift," has been noticeable in most industrial countries during the 'forties and 'fifties.

3. Workers' incomes have also tended recently to rise faster than basic wage rates because of the rapid growth of fringe benefits. These payments form a rising proportion of workers' total compensation and direct wage payments a declining proportion, as was noted in Chapter 10.

Thus if per capita output is rising 3 per cent per year and one wishes to raise workers' incomes at the same rate, this may require that basic wage schedules be raised only 2 per cent per year. These figures are more illustrative than precise, but may not be too far from the actual situation.

To argue now on the opposite side, why should all types of income in the economy move upward in lock step? Perhaps wage earners' incomes can rise faster than per capita output if other people's incomes are rising less rapidly. Perhaps workers may be able to get "more than their share" of a rising national income at the expense of other groups.

There is doubtless something to this line of argument. If one defines "labor" narrowly to include only wage earners, then wages may gain somewhat at the expense of salaries over the long run. Another "squeezable" group includes recipients of rents, fixed interest payments, annuities, and pensions. Some of these incomes are fixed irrevocably, while others rise only sluggishly and are likely to fall behind the pace of wage increase. It is much harder to transfer income from profits to wages, for reasons which will be explained in the next chapter. The quadrupling of wages in the United States since 1939 has failed to produce any reduction in the ratio of pre-tax profits to corporate income produced.

The feasibility of redistributing income through upward pressure on money wages is probably quite limited. The squeezable groups receive only a minor part of national income. Moreover, their squeezability is limited and tends to get used up over the course of time. One cannot, therefore, rely on income redistribution to allow wage earners' incomes to rise *much* faster than per capita national output is rising.

Taking all these things into account, one can define a tolerable or noninflationary rate of wage increase which would not compel an increase in the price level. But there is no ready way of estimating what this rate may be at a particular time, and thus of getting a yardstick by which we could judge that the actual rate of wage increase is "too rapid" or "about right." The figure most commonly cited for yardstick purposes is the rate of increase of output per man-hour in manufacturing. This figure is clearly inappropriate, relating as it does to only about one-quarter of the economy. Even the more comprehensive figure of national output per capita gives only limited guidance, for the reasons just noted. In the United States at present, the noninflationary rate of increase in wage schedules probably lies somewhere between 2 and 3 per cent per year; but this cannot be proven and can be tested only by experience.

The concept of a feasible, or reasonable, or noninflationary rate of increase in the money wage level is obviously useful. But it is also a dangerous concept, because it is apt to be interpreted as meaning that every wage rate in the economy should rise by a certain percentage every year. This never happens, and it would be very unfortunate if it did happen. Wages should rise faster than average in expanding companies, industries, and regions, and less than average in stationary or declining areas and industries, in order to assist the reallocation of the labor force to the growth points of the economy. Apart from this, the wage structure always contains inequities and anomalies which can be corrected only if there is flexibility for different wages to advance at different speeds. It may also be undesirable for the *average* wage level to advance at the same rate from year to year. Subnormal wage increases are natural in recession years, while in boom years the rate of increase may be unusually high. The feasible rate of wage increase over the long run should not be construed as a yardstick which can be applied inflexibly to particular wage decisions.

ISSUES OF WAGE-PRICE POLICY

Two kinds of policy issue need to be distinguished. First, assuming that the Phillips curve looks as shown in Figure 10, what point on this curve should be taken as a policy objective? Is it better to aim at stable prices at the cost of considerable unemployment, or to aim at low unemployment even though this may push up the price level? Second, can we do anything to move the curve downward to the left, so as to reach higher levels of employment with the same rate of price increase? The first is a problem of balancing conflicting objectives under given conditions. The second is a problem of institutional reform aimed at changing the given conditions in a favorable direction.

The trade-off between inflation and unemployment

In the twelve years 1952-63, the consumer price index rose 15 per cent, or a bit over 1 per cent a year. But more than half of this was due to a sharply rising price level for consumer services. Prices of commodities entering the consumer budget rose only 7 per cent over this period, while prices of services rose 33 per cent.

This rise in the price of services is bound to continue, because production of services is usually not capable of the mechanization which permits steady productivity increases in commodity production. If automobile workers' wages rise 10 per cent, this may be offset by greater productivity, permitting car prices to remain unchanged. But if a doctor raises his fees 10 per cent, the price of his services rises by the same 10 per cent. The price is virtually all labor cost, and varies proportionately with it. The technique of hair cutting has not changed much for hundreds of years. As barbers' wages rise, the price of hair cuts rises with them.

Stability of the consumer price index, then, would require forcing down commodity prices year after year at a rate just sufficient to offset the built-in rise in the price of services.

As regards commodities, it is doubtful that the slight price rise since the end of the Korean War is a genuine rise if due account were taken of improvements in product qality. One of the writer's colleagues, Richard Ruggles, has suggested that this could be tested as follows: give a sample of families, $1,000 each to go on a shopping spree. Give them a 1952 Sears Roebuck catalog and a 1964 catalog, and permit them to order from either catalog but not from both. If they choose to order from the 1964 catalog this must mean that in their judgment 1964 prices, adjusted for quality, are *lower* than 1952 prices. He suspects that most families would use the 1964 catalog; but no foundation has yet put up the money for an actual test.

For these reasons the writer does not feel that the price increases since the end of the Korean War are very significant or alarming. But this dodges the issue, because we have not been very aggressive about pursuing full employment either. Suppose we took fiscal measures—say, a substantial reduction of federal tax rates—to increase aggregate demand, and that this finally brought unemployment down to between 3 and 4 per cent. And suppose that under these conditions prices began to move up, not by 1 per cent a year, but by 2 or 3 per cent a year. Would this still be a good bargain?

The damage done by inflation can readily be exaggerated. There is little basis for the argument that creeping inflation leads inevitably to galloping inflation. Creeping inflation in fact leads simply to more creeping inflation. Nor is there much reason to think that moderate inflation weakens business confidence or undermines business investment. It is at least as plausible to argue that the prospect of a rising price level will inspire business optimism and strengthen the propensity to invest. It is hard to lose money on a rising market.

Inflation hurts people whose incomes cannot readily be adjusted to the rising price level. This means mainly older people living on pensions or fixed annuities. But pensions under the federal Social Security system can be, and doubtless will be, adjusted to future price level increases. There are also a growing number of variable annuity programs, under which the insurance company invests the premiums mainly in stocks rather than bonds, and the annuitant's income reflects the (presumably rising) level of dividend payments. The number of people who are *unavoidably* injured by inflation is probably smaller than the number who have suffered from chronic underemployment in recent years.

Inflation which is expected to continue over the long run does interfere with the sale of bonds and other fixed-income securities. If prices are rising 4 per cent a year, anyone who buys a 4 per cent bond is foolish, for his interest income is being eaten away by capital losses. This would create difficulties mainly for the federal, state, and local governments, since private industry no longer depends much on bond financing.

The most serious objection to inflation, or at least to inflation at a faster rate than prevails in the other leading industrial countries, is probably that it raises the relative price of our exports in foreign markets and thus weakens our competitive position. At the same time it encourages the flow of cheaper foreign imports in the United States. This could impair our balance of payments position, lead to gold outflows, and weaken international confidence in the stability of the dollar. Actually United States prices have risen less than in most other countries over the past decade, and we have maintained a large and even growing export surplus. Our balance of payments problem, which is real and is still continuing, arises from our heavy overseas commitments and from other sources unrelated to the price level.

On the other side of the balance stand the losses from operating the economy substantially below capacity: lower national output, lower consumption levels, lower business investment and hence less capacity for the future, the hardships of total or partial unemployment for many workers, disruption of labor markets, and the frustration of labor market policies which depend on reasonably full employment. These disadvantages are self-evident and have been discussed in earlier chapters.

Where should the balance be struck? Where should one try to land on the Phillips curve? This involves value judgments, and so there can be only preferences rather than agreed answers. The writer's view is that over the past decade we have been too concerned about price increases which have turned out to be slight, and not sufficiently concerned about underproduction and unemployment. He would prefer a more venturesome policy aimed at moving up the Phillips curve to the left; but to anyone whose preferences are different, he could offer only political argument rather than scientific proof.

Institutional and behavioral change

What everyone would really like is to have it both ways, to reduce unemployment substantially without stimulating price increases. This amounts to saying that we would like to shift the Phillips curve leftward, say to the position of the dotted line in Figure 10. Then instead of having to choose between points such as A and B, which are unpalatable in opposite ways, one might arrive at a nice point such as C.

One useful line of action is to reduce the hard core of long-term unemployment through the retraining and placement programs discussed in Chapter 15. This increases the effective labor force by making more workers available at the places and with the skills which employers require. It postpones the point at which employers run out of labor and begin an aggressive bidding up of wage rates.

Beyond this, government can try to persuade strong unions and large companies to be reasonable about wage and price increases under full employment conditions. This is useful, because it leads to fuller analysis of the relevant economic data, more systematic discussion of standards of reasonableness, and a firmer foundation for private and public decision making. But it would be unrealistic to expect marked changes in institutional behavior in the short run. This is partly because standards of reasonableness are bound to be *average* standards for the economy; but actual price and wage decisions relate to a particular company or industry. No one decides about, and so no one is in a position to take responsibility for, the general wage or price level. It is always easy for a company or union to find reasons why it deserves more than the average in a particular year; and it may be hard to find clear evidence pointing in the opposite direction.

One way of injecting a national viewpoint, which has been used particularly in the Scandinavian countries, is through an annual union-industry-government conference on the economic outlook. This conference is held before the wage bargaining season begins. Government economists present estimates of economic developments during the coming year, including projected increases in real national output, real personal income, and real wage payments. These estimates are open to criticism by industry and union economists. The outcome is not a firm agreement on price or wage policy; but the discussions probably serve to narrow the range of differences of opinion about what will be feasible in the year ahead.

Should government go beyond persuasion to regulation? It has been suggested that wage and price increases in key industries such as basic steel be made subject to review and possible veto by a public authority. A little reflection suggests difficulties and disadvantages in this proposal. How would one select the industries to be regulated? How would one take account of their interconnection with other industries through product and labor markets, which might lead to "creeping regulations" embracing eventually most of the economy? What workable standards could be devised for wage-price decisions? How much bureaucratic delay and inefficiency would be involved? Could one get effective enforcement against strong unions?

Because of these difficulties many economists are inclined to discuss this proposal out of hand. But this is perhaps too hasty. One way or another, we should aim at a higher level of employment than has prevailed in the recent past. It may be that, through public discussion, private persuasion, and other informal devices, high employment can be made compatible with a not-too-alarming rate of price increase. But suppose that this does not turn out to be true? Suppose the alternative is maintaining reasonable price stability through serious underemployment as against trying to maintain it through formal regulation? In this event the latter alternative would at least deserve serious discussion.

MONEY WAGES AND EMPLOYMENT

In the preceding section we regarded the level of employment as a cause of changes in the money wage level. What now of causal relationships running in the other direction? Will a change in the money wage level alter the volume of employment and, if so, in which direction? In neoclassical economic reasoning, an increase in the (real) wage level was always associated with a decrease in employment on the general principle that raising the price of anything will reduce purchases of that thing. In the Keynesian system, changes in the money wage level are offset by price changes, do not affect real wages, and have little effect on employment one way or the other. Union leaders tend to argue that wage increases will raise production and employment by increasing consumer purchasing power. Where does the truth lie in this matter?

The only general answer which can be given is "It depends." We are able, however, to specify with some confidence the main factors on which the outcome will depend. These may be set forth in a series of questions:

1. What will be the initial impact of the wage increase on businessmen's employment decisions? Will they maintain employment unchanged and find some way of paying higher wage bills, or will employment be cut back? What will be the immediate impact on total wage payments in the economy?

2. If money wage payments are increased, as they probably will be in the short run, where does the money come from? To what extent are higher wage bills financed by reducing profit margins, to what extent by raising prices to consumers? And how rapidly are price increases by primary producers and manufacturers passed on to the retail level?

3. To the extent that higher wages are financed through lower profits, there is a transfer of income to wage earners from dividend recipients or undistributed corporate profits or both. How does this affect the level of spending in the economy? Is wage earners' marginal propensity to spend appreciably larger than the corresponding propensity for recipients of property income?

4. Will the monetary authorities increase the money supply sufficiently to finance the higher wage-price level without an increase in interest rates? If interest rates rise, how will this affect business investment?

5. What other effects may there be on the inducement to invest? If profit margins are reduced, this will presumably be a bearish factor. On the other hand, rising wages and prices may produce expectations of further increases in the future, and thus foster speculative investment in inventories and equipment. Higher labor costs may also stimulate employers to find ways of replacing labor by machinery. What will be the net effect of these conflicting tendencies?

These considerations can readily be reduced to geometric or algebraic form for greater precision. But even without doing this, one can see that the result may be either a higher level of employment, a lower level, or no change. Suppose, for example, that the initial impact on employment is zero, that higher wage bills are financed mainly through transfers from profits, that wage earners' propensity to spend is much higher than that of profit recipients, that interest rates are unaffected, and that the induced effect on investment is positive. It is clear that employment will rise. This is the kind of case which exponents of wage increases as a depression remedy have in the back of their minds, though it is rarely set forth in full detail and with proper qualification.

It is unfortunately just as easy to construct an opposite set of conditions in which a money wage increase will produce a contraction of output and employment. The conditions of the actual economy lie somewhere between the two extremes, but just where is difficult to determine. As a matter of judgment, one can scarcely feel optimistic about the chances of producing increases in employment through general increases in money wage rates. Bronfenbrenner, who has made some rough estimates for the American economy, concludes that the various propensities are such that wage increases probably have a negative effect on employment.

For this instance, then, the classical view is vindicated against both Lord Keynes and Henry Ford. . . . An increase in wages is unfavorable to employment and output and a decrease favorable if the additional labor is available. . . . As Professor Viner has said in quite another connection, "There's life in the old dogmas yet," even though that life is not absolute, but dependent on factual data as filtered through the statistical estimation process.[14]

Tinbergen, who has attempted similar estimates using Netherlands data, concludes that for a self-contained economy the employment effect of a general wage increase will be small—if anything, slightly negative. If the economy is sufficiently dependent on international trade that it has to worry about the relation of its price level to foreign price levels, the employment effect is certain to be negative.[15]

The only American experience with wage increases as a recovery measure was the increase of about 20 per cent in hourly wage rates for workers under NRA codes in the early New Deal period 1933-34. The announced intent of these increases was to raise the level of employment by increasing purchasing power. The actual effect is difficult to determine because of reductions in hours of work, increases in the size of the government deficit, and other developments which occurred at the same time. The most careful study of the episode concluded that the slight rise in industrial output in 1934 could be entirely explained by the sharp increase in federal relief

---

[14] Martin Bronfenbrenner, "A Contribution to the Aggregative Theory of Wages," *Journal of Political Economy*, LXIV (December 1956), pp. 459-469.

[15] Jan Tinbergen, "The Significance of Wage Policy for Employment," *International Economic Papers*, Vol. I (New York: The Macmillan Company, 1951). See also *Econometrics* (Philadelphia: Blakiston Company, 1951), pp. 173-175, 185-188.

expenditures and the federal deficit.[16] The effect of the wage increases appears to have been neutral or slightly negative.

Space permits only brief mention of two other kinds of controversy over general wage increases. When a recession occurs, there is often considerable argument over whether the recession could have been averted by "proper" behavior of the wage level during the previous prosperity period. Union leaders sometimes maintain that the recession occurred because consumer purchasing power—which they identify with the money wage level—did not rise fast enough to absorb the growing output of industry. This is not at all plausible. Minor recessions are dominated by a decline of business investment in inventories, major recessions by a decline of investment in plant and equipment as well as inventories. Fluctuations in business investment are deeply rooted in the structure of a private enterprise economy, and it is unlikely that they could be averted by any conceivable manipulation of the money wage level.

At the outset of a recession there is also apt to be discussion over whether cuts in money wages would cushion the recession or would make it worse. This is mainly an academic argument, since the money wage level does not decline anyway except in very severe depressions. The possible effects of a wage decline could be analyzed in the same way as our previous analysis of wage increases, and with the same inconclusive result. The balance of practical advantage seems to lie with wage stability during recession, any possible employment gain from wage cutting being more than outweighed by the strikes and industrial strife associated with wage reductions in a unionized economy.

All in all, the money wage level does not seem to be a useful tool of economic stabilization—not just because we cannot control it in practice, but also because the employment effect of general wage changes is conjectural and probably minor. It is too extreme to say that wages make no difference; but they make less difference than other factors which are more predictable and more amenable to central control.

Discussion questions

1. Explain clearly the differences between: (a) base rate, (b) average hourly earnings, (c) average weekly earnings, (d) take-home pay, (e) annual earnings.

---

[16] Leverett S. Lyon and associates, *The National Recovery Administration* (Washington: Brookings Institution, 1935).

2. Why is it important to define carefully what you mean by "wages"? In your answer give at least four examples of different ways in which the term has been used.

3. What is meant by "real wages"? Describe and criticize the methods used to calculate changes in real wages in the United States.

4. Does an increase in the general level of *money wages* necessarily mean a rise in workers' *real wages:* (a) in a single industry? (b) in the economy as a whole?

5. A noninflationary wage movement is defined as one which raises workers' income at the same rate that per capita output is rising. In what ways does this definition overstate or understate the feasible rate of increase in basic wage schedules?

6. Explain the difference between the role of wages in demand inflation and in cost inflation.

7. Does cost inflation constitute a serious threat to price stability in the United States at present? Explain.

8. What are the main considerations to be borne in mind in weighing the danger of excessive unemployment against the danger of excessive price increases?

9. Will a general increase in money wage rates at the bottom of a depression be helpful in raising the level of employment?

Selected reading

The major source of current wage information is the Bureau of Labor Statistics of the Department of Labor. Wage data are published regularly in the *Monthly Labor Review*.

Bowen, William G., *The Wage-Price Issue*. Princeton: Princeton University Press, 1960.

————, *Wage Behavior in the Postwar Period*. Princeton: Industrial Relations Section, 1960.

Creamer, Daniel C., *Behavior of Wage Rates During Business Cycles*. National Bureau of Economic Research (New York), Occasional Paper No. 34 (1950).

Eckstein, Otto, and Thomas A. Wilson, "Determination of Money Wages in American Industry," *Quarterly Journal of Economics* (October 1962), pp. 379-414.

Fellner, William J., "Demand Inflation, Cost Inflation, and Collective Bargaining," in Philip D. Bradley, ed., *The Public Stake in Union Power*. Charlottesville, Va.: University of Virginia Press, 1959.

Long, Clarence D., "The Illusion of Wage Rigidity: Long and Short Cycles in Wages and Labor," *Review of Economics and Statistics* (May 1960), pp. 140-151.

Morton, W. H., "Trade Unionism, Full Employment and Inflation," *American Economic Review*, XL (March 1950), pp. 13-39.

Oxford University Institute of Economics, *The Economics of Full Employment*. Oxford: Basil Blackwell, 1944.

Reder, Melvin W., "The General Level of Money Wages," *Proceedings of the Third Annual Meeting of the IRRA* (1950), pp. 186-202.

Rees, Albert W., "Wage Determination and Involuntary Unemployment," *Journal of Political Economy*, LIX (April 1951), pp. 143-153.

The American Assembly, *Wages, Prices, Profits, and Productivity*. New York: American Assembly, 1960. (Includes papers by Duesenberry, Dunlop, Kendrick, Kerr, Myers, Rees, Reynolds, and Slichter.)

Turvey, Ralph, ed., *Wages Policy Under Full Employment*. London: William Hodge and Company, 1952.

Wright, David McCord, ed., *The Impact of the Union*. New York: Harcourt, Brace & World, Inc., 1951.

17

Productivity, Real Wages, And
Labor's Share Of National Income

The level of real wages in the United States has risen continuously for the past century and more. The rate of increase is somewhat uneven from year to year, but the long-run trend is remarkably consistent. Real wages rise in good years and bad, when money wages are rising and when they are falling.

What can account for such a strong and persistent economic trend? Speaking broadly, the real income of wage earners depends on the size of national output and on the share of national output which wage earners receive. Real wages may rise, therefore, either because national output is rising, or because labor's share of output is increasing, or for both reasons together. In the United States over the past century, the increase in real national output has been of overwhelming importance, and changes in labor's share have been minor by comparison. It is appropriate to begin, therefore, by examining the rise in national output and the reasons behind it.

INPUTS, OUTPUT, AND PRODUCTIVITY

Concepts and measurements

For present purposes we may think of the national economy as a single giant producing mechanism. Into the mechanism at one end go certain quantities of inputs—land and natural resources, capital equipment, labor, management—and out the other end comes a stream of output, usually termed Gross National Product or GNP. If the supply of inputs is increasing year by year, as it has been in the United States, total output should also increase. But a 10 per cent increase in output due solely to a 10 per cent increase in inputs does not indicate any gain in the productivity of resources. One can speak of a gain in productivity only if total output is rising faster than total inputs.

There are many alternative concepts and measures of productivity. Partial productivity measures can be obtained by dividing output by a single input, most commonly labor or capital. When capital is used as divisor, the result is the capital: output ratio, which plays such a large part in discussions of economic growth and development policy. Using labor yields measures of output per worker or per man-hour worked. These partial measures are not very satisfactory, however, because changes in them are difficult to interpret. Suppose one finds that output per man-hour rose 2 per cent a year over a certain period. This could have been due to increased skill and effort on the part of the workers. But it could also have been due entirely to the fact that workers were using increasing amounts of capital over the course of time. Or it could have been due to managerial improvements, or to a variety of other factors. The measurement itself provides no explanation.

John Kendrick has devised a more comprehensive productivity measure which incorporates both labor and capital. His technique is to calculate an index of the amount of labor used in production and an index of the real capital stock (including land). These are next combined by weighing each by the respective shares of labor and capital in national income, to yield an index of total factor input. This is then divided into the index of national output to yield a measure of what Kendrick terms "total factor productivity."[1]

Kendrick's measures cover the period 1889-1957 and show a sharp break around the year 1919. In the earlier period 1889-1919, real

---

[1] The basic relations used can be expressed as

$$\frac{Y}{Y_o} = C \left(a \frac{L}{L_o} + b \frac{K}{K_o} \right),$$ where the subscript o indicates base period quantities. a and b are the labor and capital shares of national income, and C is the measure of total factor productivity. See John W. Kendrick, *Productivity Trends in the United States* (Princeton: Princeton University Press, 1961), and the review article by Evsey D. Domar, "On Total Productivity and All That," *Journal of Political Economy* (Dec. 1962), pp. 597-608.

GNP rose at an average annual rate of 3.9 per cent, inputs of labor and capital rose at 2.6 per cent, and factor productivity grew by 1.3 per cent per year. Over the period 1919-1957, real GNP rose somewhat more slowly at 3.2 per cent per year. There was a much greater slow-down, however, in the inputs of labor and capital, which rose at only 1.1 per cent a year over this period. As regards labor, this reflects cessation of mass immigration, a reduced rate of natural increase, and a marked shortening of the workweek and workyear. As regards capital, it reflects the check to capital formation imposed by the Great Depression and by World War II. The amount of capital in use in 1945 was virtually the same as in 1929. Total factor productivity, then, rose by 2.1 per cent a year from 1919 to 1957. The sharp decline in the growth of inputs was almost, though not quite, offset by a marked rise in the rate of productivity increase, yielding a rate of increase in output only moderately below that of the previous thirty years.

For the past forty years, then, only about one-third of the increase in GNP is accounted for by increased amounts of labor and capital used in production. The remaining two-thirds is attributable to the rise in "total factor productivity." But what *is* total factor productivity? It is really little more than a confession of ignorance. It is an unexplained residual, due to "other factors" not included in the input measures.[2] If all the forces affecting the level of output were included in the production equation, then presumably any increase in output would be fully explained, and the productivity factor C could never increase. The fact that C does rise, and so rapidly, means that there are major forces at work which we have not succeeded in measuring.

Explaining the residual

It is possible to identify some of the factors which have contributed to the residual rise in national output, even though we cannot yet measure their relative importance. They include the following.

[2] There have been numerous other attempts to measure and interpret this residual. While the results differ in detail, there is general agreement that the residual is large and that it accounts for most of the rise of national output in modern times. See in particular two papers by Robert M. Solow, "Technological Change and the Aggregate Production Function," *Review of Economics and Statistics* (August 1957); and "Technical Progress, Capital Formation, and Economic Growth," *American Economic Review*, (May 1962); E. F. Denison, *The Sources of Economic Growth in the United States* (New York: Committee for Economic Development, 1962); and B. F. Massell, "A Disaggregated View of Technical Change," *Journal of Political Economy* (December 1961).

1. QUALITATIVE IMPROVEMENTS IN LABOR AND CAPITAL. The man-hours of labor in use today are not the same as those used in 1900. Today's workers are healthier, more vigorous, and longer-lived than their grandfathers. They have substantially larger amounts of education. The average member of the labor force in 1960 had spent two and one-half times as many days in school as his 1910 counterpart. Today's workers have on the average a considerably longer span of work experience in urban occupations. The fact that they work for fewer hours per week and per year than was true in 1900 probably means that they work a good deal more intensively during each hour.

A venturesome effort to quantify the effect of these improvements has been made by Edward Denison.[3] He calculates an index of labor inputs "adjusted for quality change." Over the period 1909-1957 this index rises by 183 per cent, while the index of man-hours worked rises only 82 per cent. The difference is accounted for mainly by the weight which he gives to increased education and to improved quality of a man-hour's work due to shorter hours, though increased experience is also credited with a small contribution to output. If these surmises are anywhere near correct, they would account for a major part of the unexplained residual.

Capital inputs are measured essentially by their real cost. But a new machine which costs the same and looks much the same as an older machine will often produce considerably more output. This means that technical progress is occurring; and one can say that the growth of technical knowledge is the real source of the greater output. Improved knowledge must usually be incorporated in physical capital, however, before it can begin to influence production. In recent decades there seems to have been marked improvements in buildings as well as in machinery and equipment. Because of changes in building design and space utilization, the ratio of output to floor space has risen sharply.

2. INPUTS NOT INCLUDED IN THE PRODUCTION EQUATION. Kendrick's output measure is a measure of net output or value added. It thus

---

[3] *Op. cit.*, chaps. 5-9. Kendrick's measure also takes account of changes in the occupational mix of the labor force. He relies mainly on a weighted index of labor inputs, in which different grades of labor are weighted by their relative wage levels. Thus a shift in the composition of employment toward skilled, technical, and professional occupations would show up as a rise in labor inputs. But employment on the same job, at the same relative wage level, which becomes more productive because of improved health, education, or training of successive generations of workers, would not be detected. It is this pervasive over-all upgrading of the labor force which Denison has tried to measure.

takes no explicit account of raw materials, purchased energy, and other supplies consumed in the course of production. There have been important economies in the use of raw materials over the past half-century. Kendrick estimates that net material product per unit of raw materials input more than doubled over the period 1900-1952;[4] and that this alone would account for about one-sixth of the observed increase in total factor productivity. There has also been a great increase in the amount of nonhuman energy used in production. Horsepower-hours of energy used per man-hour of work done rose from 0.72 in 1890 to 5.19 in 1950. This is related, of course, to growing mechanization of production; but it does not show up in the measures of capital input. Indeed, energy use has risen about three times as fast as capital input over the years since 1890.

Another important input which does not show up in the production equation is management. Labor and capital do not manage themselves. The same plant and labor force may produce more or less, depending on how the work is organized and directed. There is reason to think that the quality of this input has risen markedly over the years. The scientific management movement of the early 1900's was the harbinger of a more systematic approach to management problems. Research on these problems has intensified steadily, leading most recently to a growing use of mathematical methods and computer techniques. University programs in business administration have grown greatly in size and sophistication, and the educational level of business executives today is much higher than in 1900. While one cannot measure the impact of these developments on productive efficiency, it has certainly been substantial.

3. TECHNICAL PROGRESS. If capital accumulation consisted simply of adding more factories and more machines of the same type to produce the same products, national output would not rise nearly as fast as it does. Indeed, on this basis it would have been impossible for the American economy to generate and absorb the quadrupling of the capital stock which has occurred since 1900. With no change in production methods, the marginal productivity of capital, and consequently the returns on capital, would long since have fallen so low as to discourage further saving and investment.

An essential ingredient of economic growth, then, is continuous

---

[4] *Op. cit.*, p. 95. This is partly due, of course, to a higher degree of processing—for example, in the case of food products—rather than to economies in the strict sense.

development of new and improved products, machines, and production methods. Some of this is done by industrial engineers and production executives as part of their day-to-day job. Some major developments come from spontaneous work by individual inventors. To an increasing extent, however, technical progress is planned by allocating part of corporation budgets to research and development activity. A large amount of basic scientific work is carried on also in universities and government laboratories. Total expenditure on research and development activities, which in 1940 was estimated at less than a billion dollars, is now approaching fifteen billion dollars a year and is still increasing. The number of scientists and engineers in the labor force has risen from about 60,000 in 1900 to almost a million today. The results of scientific work are somewhat unpredictable, and one cannot say that a doubling of research activity will double the flow of useful inventions. Such a massive increase of effort, however, must be partly responsible for the apparent acceleration of productivity increase over the last several decades.

4. GROWING SIZE OF THE ECONOMY. Theories of production usually assume constant returns to scale. Increasing size of an industry, or of an entire economy, is not supposed by itself to change the ratio of output to inputs. This assumption is probably incorrect, and the greatly increased size of the American economy today as compared with 1890 has probably had a favorable effect on productivity.

As an economy expands the social overhead costs of transportation and communications networks, power facilities, and public services are spread over a larger volume of production. More and more industries are able to achieve their own optimum scale, which in the case of highly mechanized industries may be very large. A larger market permits greater industrial specialization and a fuller development of supplementary industries providing materials, components, and services. "The division of labor is limited by the size of the market," as Adam Smith observed two centuries ago.

5. INDUSTRY-MIX OF THE ECONOMY. As an economy grows in size and wealth, the relative importance of different industries changes for the reasons noted in Chapter 13. If the productivity of labor and capital were the same in every branch of production, this would make no difference to the over-all productivity level. In fact, however, productivity does vary from one industry to another. The average productivity level in the economy may rise, therefore, through transfer of resources from low-productivity to high-productivity industries. The

outstanding example is agriculture, where output per man-hour is typically a good deal below that in manufacturing and other urban industries. A shift of labor from agriculture to manufacturing will thus raise average man-hour output for the economy as a whole, even though productivity within each sector remains unchanged. This has been an important factor in the United States over the past century. The process can unfortunately work in the other direction as well. Distribution, government service, and personal service have low rates of productivity increase. As these come to bulk larger and larger in a wealthy economy, they may have a retarding effect on productivity growth.

Productivity increase and real wage increase

It is a truism that the rise of real wages over the long run is related to the rise of productivity. It is important to be clear, however, whether one is speaking of particular firms or industries, or whether one is talking about the economy as a whole.

The reason is that productivity trends vary widely from one branch of production to another. For the private economy as a whole, Kendrick's measure of total factor productivity rose at an average rate of 1.7 per cent per year over the period 1899-1953. The rate of increase was 0.7 per cent, however, in anthracite coal mining, 1.1 per cent in farming, 2.0 per cent in manufacturing, 3.2 per cent in transportation, and 5.5 per cent in electric utilities. Within manufacturing, the productivity increase averaged only 1.0 per cent in lumber products, but was 4.1 per cent for rubber products.[5] When one considers that these rates of increase are compounded annually, it is obvious that productivity levels had pulled very far apart by the end of the period. Taking 1899 as 100, the productivity index for anthracite coal had risen by 1953 to only 147, whereas for electric utilities it had risen to 1,764.

It is clear, then, that wage increases cannot correspond to productivity increases industry by industry. Indeed, Kendrick's calculations for 33 industry groups over the period 1899-1953 show no significant relation between rate of increase in total factor productivity and rate of increase in hourly wage payments. The course of events seems rather to be as follows: in industries where productivity is rising unusually fast, unit production costs and prices will be falling relative to those in industries with a slow rate of productivity growth. This

---

[5] *Op. cit.*, pp. 136-37.

rarely means an *absolute* decline in prices, since the whole price level has been moving upward so rapidly since 1900. It means rather that industries with high productivity increases show smaller price increases than industry in general. Partly because of these relatively low prices, sales and output in these industries rises faster than in other industries. There is a marked relation between an industry's rate of productivity increase and its rate of output increase over the long run.[6]

From one standpoint this result is rather encouraging. Mechanization of production, which is usually a prominent feature of productivity increase, seems often to pose an immediate threat of labor displacement and reduced employment. On a long view, however, the relative cheapening of the product which is made possible by productivity improvements seems favorable to an expansion of output and employment.

Turning from individual industries to the economy as a whole, one would expect to find a marked relation between the average rate of productivity increase and the average increase in the real wage level. Figure 11 presents a partial productivity measure—output per man-hour in private nonfarm industries—and compares this with the move-

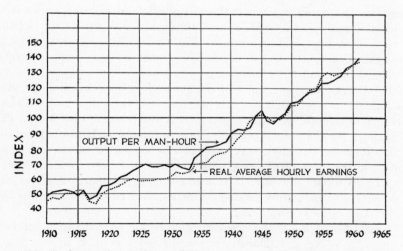

FIG. 11 *Indexes of private nonfarm output per man-hour and private nonfarm real average hourly earnings, 1910-1961 (1947-1949 = 100).*

---

[6] For 33 industries over the years 1899-1953, Kendrick obtained a rank correlation coefficient of 0.64, which is significant at the 1 per cent level. (*op. cit.,* p. 207).

ment of real hourly earnings in the same industries over the years 1909-61.[7] The two indexes move quite closely together over the long run. They could scarcely do otherwise, since labor is much the most important input in production and receives close to 80 per cent of income produced in the economy. This brings us, however, to our next major topic: the forces determining the distribution of national output between the suppliers of labor and capital.

DISTRIBUTION OF NATIONAL OUTPUT

National output is distributed among the population through income payments—money claims entitling the holder to a certain portion of the "heap" of goods and services turned out during the year. Income distribution may be conceived and measured in two main ways. One may sort out income payments according to the type of productive service rendered in return—labor services, use of capital, and so on. This yields a functional or *type distribution* of income. Most economic theorizing has related to distribution in this sense. The classical economists were concerned with distribution of the national product among landlords, capitalists, and laborers, these functional groups coinciding in nineteenth-century England with rather distinct social classes. J. B. Clark and other neoclassical writers developed a more abstract and streamlined scheme in which national output was divided into only two categories—"interest" and "wages," property income and labor income.

One may also sort out individuals or families according to the total amount of income each receives, whether this comes from wages, dividends, or other sources. This yields a *size distribution* of incomes for the country, which is the most useful kind of distribution for many purposes. It reveals both the degree of income inequality and the amount of poverty in the sense of failure to reach some specified money income. It is interesting to compare measures of poverty and inequality among countries, and to examine trends in the same country over time.

Type distributions and size distributions are related in the following way. Wage and salary rates range from very high to very low, and so there is a size distribution of incomes from work. There is

[7] Data for 1909-1956 are from Joint Committee on the Economic Report, *Productivity, Prices, and Incomes* (Washington: Government Printing Office, 1957), p. 48. Subsequent years are from the U.S. *Statistical Abstract*.

also a size distribution of property incomes, ranging from the dividends of a small stockholder to those of a multimillionaire. The over-all size distribution for the economy is a fusion of these two subdistributions. A reduction of inequality may come about by a shift from property incomes to labor incomes. But it may also result from a reduction of inequality *within* the wage and salary sector or *within* the property sector. The gradual reduction of inequality in the United States, as we shall see in Chapter 20, has been due mainly to shifts of the latter sort.

In this chapter we examine only the type distribution of income, the division between "labor" and "capital" shares. The factors determining size distributions, and the problems of inequality and poverty, will be considered in Chapter 20.

Measuring the type distribution of income

Our basic information on type distribution comes from the national income accounts prepared each year by the Department of Commerce. While the figures have a nice air of completeness and precision, a multitude of difficulties lurk just under the surface.

One type of problem relates to classification of incomes. The United States statistics, for example, lump all wage and salary payments together as "compensation of employees." This is unfortunate, because the daily wage of a cleaning woman obviously differs from the salary of the President of General Motors. Lumping the two together makes it impossible to test the important question whether average wages have been rising relative to average salaries over the past several decades.

A second difficulty is that certain groups in the economy—notably farmers, storekeepers, and other small proprietors—have incomes which are a blend of labor and property income. They include payment for the proprietor's labor, his managerial ability, and his capital invested in the enterprise. One can try by heroic assumptions to split these things apart, to say how much of farmers' income should be regarded as wages and how much as interest on land and equipment. Such estimates are highly debatable, however, and it is probably better simply to leave these groups out of account. An analysis of income distribution in corporate enterprises gives a more reliable indication of whether labor has been gaining at the expense of capital or vice versa.

Third, we encounter a problem which we met earlier in productivity analysis—the shifting importance of different industries in the economy. In heavy manufacturing, which employs an unusual amount of capital equipment, interest and profits may absorb 30 per cent of the product and employee compensation only 70 per cent. In government service, on the other hand, the "product" of government is conventionally assumed to be the same as the government payroll, so that employee compensation is 100 per cent of output. If government service increases in importance relative to manufacturing, as has happened over the past generation, this will produce an increase in "labor's share" for the economy as a whole, even though labor's share in manufacturing income may have remained completely unchanged. Any important shift of employment between industries with different ratios of labor to property income will change the average ratios for the economy as a whole.

Fourth, there is a considerable difference between a distribution of income *produced* and of income *received*. On the former basis, the total value product of each industry is divided between employee compensation and property income. Total profits before taxes are considered to belong to the stockholders and, together with interest payments, are allocated to the property share. These measurements provide the best indication of whether the price mechanism itself is redistributing income in one direction or the other—whether, for example, employee compensation is rising faster than value of product so that profit margins are being squeezed.

Income actually received, however, is a different matter. Half of corporate profits are lopped off by taxation. Part of the remainder is retained and reinvested in the business, so that dividend payments are considerably less than post-tax profits. On the other hand, many people receive more than they earn through their current contribution to production. Unemployment compensation payments, old age pensions, other welfare payments, veterans pensions and bonuses, farm price support payments, and other government transfers have a substantial influence on personal incomes. Since government transfers benefit mainly the lower-income groups, one would expect labor's share of income received to be larger than its share of income produced, and this is so in fact.

We shall consider first the distribution of income produced, since this is what most economic theorizing has been about. Income received will be examined briefly at the end of the chapter.

Distribution of income produced: basic determinants

What determines the distribution of income produced between workers and property owners? The nearest thing to a central principle commanding general agreement is the principle of marginal productivity. This principle, however, must be handled with caution. It is often misstated, and much of the argument over it rests on confusion and misunderstanding. We shall try to do as much as can be done in a few pages toward untangling some of the confusion surrounding this subject.

The best approach is to examine the marginal productivity principle as explained by its earliest and clearest exponent, John Bates Clark.[8] What was the problem which Clark had in mind in developing the principle? To what uses did he think it could be put? The key problem which Clark had in mind was this: What forces determine the division of the total physical product of the nation between those who do the work and those who own the property? The return to the former he termed "wages," and the return to the latter "interest." How, then, is total national income divided between wages and interest? In the back of Clark's mind was another problem, the key problem of classical economics during the nineteenth century: How will *changes* in the quantities of labor, capital, and other economic resources over long periods of time alter the distribution of real income among the owners of these resources?

It is important to realize that the problems in mind involved broad tendencies in the economy as a whole over long periods of time. It is on this terrain that marginal productivity analysis works best. It loses its usefulness in direct proportion as one approaches short-run, individual, and dynamic phenomena, i.e., the conditions under which actual business firms operate. It is quite possible to maintain that marginal productivity analysis tells you a good deal about long-run tendencies in the economy, while telling you very little about what will happen in the ABC company during the coming year.

As a method of analyzing these long-run problems, Clark constructed a hypothetical economic system with the following characteristics: (1) Free competition is assumed to prevail throughout the economy, both in the sale of commodities and in the sale of labor

---

[8] John Bates Clark, *The Distribution of Wealth* (New York: The Macmillan Company, 1899).

and other productive services. This implies that prices and wages are not manipulated by collusive agreements or government regulation. (2) The quantity of each productive resource is assumed to be given. Moreover, no changes occur in the tastes of consumers or the state of the industrial arts. The same goods therefore continue to be produced year after year in the same quantities and by the same methods. (3) The *quantity* of capital equipment is regarded as fixed, but it is assumed that the *form* of this equipment can be altered to cooperate most effectively with whatever quantity of labor is available. Although this seems at first glance a queer and unreal assumption, it makes a good deal of sense for long-period problems. Over a period of decades plants *can* be adapted as they wear out and have to be replaced. If labor becomes more plentiful relative to capital, plants and machines can be redesigned so as to use greater quantities of labor. If labor becomes scarcer, equipment can be redesigned to use less labor. (4) Workers are assumed to be interchangeable and of equal efficiency. This assumption means complete absence of occupational specialization. The result is a single wage rate rather than a variety of rates for different occupations. This assumption is not a necessary part of the Clarkian analysis, but is useful for purposes of simplification.

Clark's analysis of the operation of such an economy may be explained by means of a parable. Suppose that all the people in our mythical economy go to sleep some Sunday night, but that on Monday morning only one hundred people wake up and appear for work. These people would probably set to work with spades to dig gardens to keep from starving, and each man would produce very little. Suppose now that another hundred wake up and go to work. This development will doubtless result in more than a doubling of output, for a more effective division of labor will become possible. Now suppose another hundred appear, then another hundred, and so on. Following Clark, we suppose that each time this happens the available capital equipment miraculously changes shape so that it can be most effectively utilized by the number of workers then on hand.

For some time, each additional group of workers will add a more than proportionate amount to the product. As more and more workers are added, however, each man finds himself working with less land and capital equipment than before. A time will come when additional men will add less and less to the total product. The marginal physical product of additional labor will fall steadily.

This process was summarized by Clark in a famous diagram, reproduced here as Figure 12.[9] The line *DE* represents the marginal physical productivity of labor, i.e., the amount added to the national product by the employment of additional workers. Clark showed this curve as falling steadily from the beginning. Actually, it would probably rise for some time, but this point is not of major importance.

OA represents the number of workers available for employment, which we assume to be given and constant. If all these men are employed, the last man added will have a marginal productivity of *AB*. His wage rate cannot be more than *AB*, for then it would not pay to employ him. The wage rate cannot be less than *AB*, for in this event some employer, seeing a chance to make a profit by hiring the worker for less than his marginal productivity, would try to lure him away from his present employer. Competition among employers for labor will insure that the worker receives the full marginal product *AB*, but no more than this.

It follows next that no other worker in the system can receive a wage higher than *AB*. It may seem that the men above the margin —that is, the men to the left of *A* on the diagram—are being cheated by this arrangement. They seem to be producing more than they are getting. Actually, however, under the assumption of perfect interchangeability of workers, no man is more valuable than any other. If a man doing a particular important job were to drop out, a man could be taken from the margin to replace him. Hence one cannot earn more than another. If this were not so, and if each man were paid his specific productivity, nothing would be left over for the other factors of production. As it is, however, the workers as a group receive as wages the area *OABC*, i.e., the number of workers multiplied by the wage rate. The triangular area *BCD* goes to the owners of land and capital.

It should be recalled that the wage axis *OY* is graduated in "real wage" units, not in money wage rates. This is a moneyless economy, or at any rate one in which money is purely a convenience. It is also an economy which does not suffer from cyclical fluctuations in aggregate demand and which has no unemployment problems.

The highly abstract nature of this argument is apparent. Yet it is quite useful for the long-range problems which Clark had in mind. It does help to define the conditions under which an increase in real

---

[9] Clark, *The Distribution of Wealth*, p. 201.

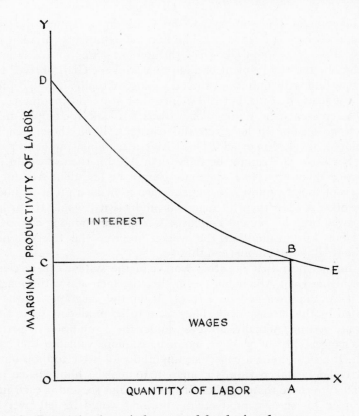

FIG. 12 *Determination of the general level of real wages.*

wage rates is possible. In the Clarkian economy, the level of real wages could rise only if one of the following things happened: (1) A rise in the productivity curve *DE*, the quantity of labor remaining unchanged. This rise might occur because of an increase in the quantity of equipment and natural resources, technical discoveries, increased managerial skill, or increased efficiency of labor. (2) A decrease in the supply of labor, all other factors remaining unchanged, so that one would move to the left on the curve *DE*. (3) An increasing supply of labor which is more than offset by a rising level of productivity. This third situation is the one which has normally existed in the United States.

The opposite sets of circumstances would produce a decline in the level of real wages. It should be pointed out that a decline in the real wage level will not necessarily decrease the *share* of national income going to labor as compared with capital; nor will an increase in the real wage rate necessarily raise the share of national income going to labor. Labor's *share* of national income is shown by the ratio of *OABC* to *OABD*. The way in which this ratio will be affected by a change in the real wage rate, i.e., by an upward or downward movement of *BC*, clearly depends on the slope of the productivity curve *DE*.

The slope of *DE* has a technical significance which is difficult to explain in a few words. Speaking roughly, it indicates the substitutability of labor for capital, i.e., the ease or difficulty with which a given stock of capital equipment can be rearranged to cooperate with increasing quantities of labor in the production process. If the known techniques of production are so rigid that it is difficult to use additional labor in the production process, even allowing long periods of time for readjustment, then *DE* will fall steeply. Under these conditions, a growing labor force with no change in capital or resources would be likely to reduce labor's *share* of national income as well as the wage level itself. If on the other hand labor is highly substitutable for capital, labor's share of national income may be maintained or even increased as the quantity of labor grows.

It should be repeated that we are talking here about the real wage level, not the money wage level, and about broad tendencies in the economy over substantial periods of time. In this context marginal productivity analysis serves the useful purpose of highlighting the importance of factor supplies. It says essentially that the price of a factor of production varies inversely with the supply of that factor. An increase in labor supply, everything else remaining equal, will depress the real wage level while a reduction in labor supply will raise it. In an economy where labor is abundant relative to capital, real wage rates will be low and profit rates high. The sensibleness of these propositions is almost self-evident.

In a growing economy, the supplies of labor and capital will usually be increasing together; but they will probably be increasing at different rates, so that the ratio of capital to labor will be changing. In the United States the capital stock has increased considerably faster than the labor supply. Kendrick estimates that labor inputs in the private domestic economy roughly doubled between 1899 and 1957, while capital inputs increased 3½ times. Thus capital per unit of labor rose on the average about 1 per cent a year over the period.

What should this have done to the earnings of labor and capital? The effect should have been the same as if capital were increasing with the quantity of labor remaining unchanged. In the absence of technical change, this would lower the marginal productivity of capital and thus lower its earnings. In actuality, the earnings of capital have not fallen absolutely, but have fallen sharply relative to wage rates. Kendrick estimates that real income per unit of labor was almost four times as high in 1957 as in 1899. Real income per unit of capital, however, rose only about 15 per cent over this period. Denison's calculations, which on some points differ considerably from Kendrick's, also show real earnings per unit of reproducible capital rising by only about 20 per cent between 1909 and 1957.[10]

Why have the earnings of capital not fallen on an absolute basis? The explanation is mainly that technical progress and the other factors discussed earlier in this chapter have been operating strongly to raise the marginal productivity of both labor and capital. Moreover, technical progress has probably been biased in the direction of labor-saving rather than capital-saving inventions. A labor-saving invention permits the same output to be produced with less labor or, what amounts to the same thing, it permits more capital to be combined with a unit of labor *with no decline in the marginal productivity of capital.* It has the same effect as adding more labor to the economy. These fictitious additions of labor through new inventions have apparently offset the increase in the capital stock to the extent necessary to prevent any absolute decline in the marginal productivity of capital.

Type distribution of income: statistical evidence

How have these price and quantity changes worked themselves out in terms of shares of national income going to labor and capital? The evidence is at first glance somewhat confusing. If one looks at the share of wages and profits in income produced in manufacturing industries, or even in all corporate business, over the last generation there seems to have been little change. For United States corporate business as a whole, profits before taxes were 20.8 per cent of income

---

[10] Kendrick, chap. 5; Denison, chap. 13.

produced in 1929, and averaged 20.4 per cent in 1957-62. Figure 13 shows year to year fluctuations in employee compensation as a percentage of income produced, for manufacturing and for all corporate business, from 1937 to 1962.[11] There is considerable variation in income shares from year to year, due mainly to cyclical fluctuations in business activity. In years of falling output, profits fall disproportionately and labor's share of income tends to rise. This is noticeable in Figure 13 for the years 1938, 1946, 1949, 1954, and 1958. In boom years, on the other hand, profits rise sharply and labor's share of income tends to fall even though the absolute amount of income is increasing. Taking the past generation as a whole, however, labor's share has fluctuated in the range of 70 to 80 per cent of income produced, with no visible trend in either direction.

One possible conclusion from this evidence is that it is hard for wage earners to encroach appreciably on business profits through direct action. Employers can rely on rising productivity as a partial

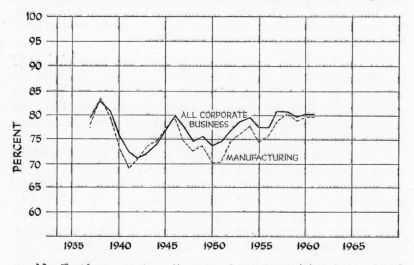

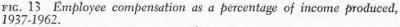

FIG. 13 *Employee compensation as a percentage of income produced, 1937-1962.*

[11] Data are from U.S. Department of Commerce, *National Income by Legal Form of Organization*, and *National Income by Industrial Origin: Manufacturing*, as reported in the *Survey of Current Business*. Employee compensation includes wage and salary disbursements, other employee income, and personal contributions for social insurance.

offset to rising money wages. Moreover, conditions which are favorable to large wage increases also permit employers to pass these on to the buyer in higher prices. Workers can do little, either individually or through union action, to close this escape hatch of price increases. Clark Kerr has put the point in the following parable:

> Each of these types of unionism is engaged in a grand pursuit—a pursuit mainly of the employer. And the employer is always trying, with more or less success, to escape. Now I do not wish to conjure up a picture of poor Eliza being chased across the ice by bloodhounds. Our Eliza is by no means always poor; nor do the bloodhounds always pursue very aggressively (they are often quite gentle creatures). They may even agree to stay a certain distance behind her, or to care for and protect her if she will be nice to them, or they may help arrange for better ice so that both Eliza and they can run faster. However, they may also try to get somebody else to hold Eliza one way or another so that they can catch up with her, which does not, offhand, sound very fair, though it may be quite effective. And, in our little drama Eliza does not always get across the river in time, although she usually does remarkably well and at times even turns around and chases the bloodhounds back again. Beyond that, the bloodhounds sometimes catch somebody else while chasing Eliza. They may even, inadvertently, catch themselves.[12]

Kerr concludes that wage bargaining alone can have little effect on distributive shares. Labor's share can be increased only if the unions are powerful enough to bargain about prices and profits as well as wages, or if the government will agree to "hold Eliza" by price control measures, or if government will rifle Eliza's purse through taxation and distribute the proceeds.

If the picture is broadened, however, to include all sectors of the economy and a longer period of time, there is considerable (though not unanimous) agreement that the share of labor has increased moderately since 1900 or so, while that of capital has fallen. One statistical reason for this is that sectors in which wage payments bulk large, notably government, have been growing in relative importance. This automatically raises the labor share of income produced. But even if government is excluded, the data seem still to show some increase in labor's share.

Three recent studies may be cited. A calculation by Irving Kravis, in which the incomes of independent proprietors are allocated in a

---

[12] Kerr, "Labor's Income Share and the Labor Movement," p. 267.

constant proportion of 65 per cent to labor and 35 per cent to capital, shows the property share of national income falling from 30.6 per cent in 1900-09 to 23.8 per cent in 1949-57.[13] Kendrick's calculations for the private domestic economy show the capital share of national income declining from 30.1 per cent in 1899 to 18.6 per cent in 1957, with the labor share rising from 69.9 per cent to 81.4 per cent.[14] Finally, Denison finds the labor share rising from 69.5 per cent in 1909-13 to 77.3 per cent in 1954-58, with property income declining accordingly.[15] While these studies differ in detailed methodology, they all show property income shrinking from something like 30 per cent at the beginning of the century to something like 20 per cent today.[16]

The increase in labor's share seems to arise partly from the decreased importance of land as an input in production. Denison calculates that returns to land were about 9 per cent of national income in 1909-13 but only 3 per cent in 1954-58. There has also been a relative shrinkage of interest, urban rents, and other fixed property incomes. These payments, being fixed in money terms, tend to be whittled away over the long run by price inflation. Interest payments, for example, fell from 7 per cent of national income in 1929 to about 4 per cent in the early sixties. It may be possible along these lines to reconcile the over-all decline of property income with the fact that corporate profit rates seem to have been quite well maintained.

---

[13] Irving B. Kravis, "Relative Income Shares in Fact and Theory," *American Economic Review* (December 1959), pp. 917-949. The tricky problem of splitting up proprietors' income (which is itself declining in relative importance over time) can of course be solved in several ways. Kravis applies three other methods in addition to the one described. All show the property share declining, but by somewhat different amounts.

[14] Kendrick, *op. cit.*, p. 121.

[15] Denison, *op. cit.*, p. 30.

[16] For other viewpoints on this problem, however, see Simon Kuznets, "Long-Term Changes in the National Income of the U.S.A. since 1870," *Income and Wealth*, Series II (London: Bowes and Bowes, 1952); Edward C. Budd, *Labor's Share of National Income* (unpublished dissertation, University of California, Berkeley, 1954); Clark Kerr, "Labor's Income Share and the Labor Movement," in George W. Taylor and Frank C. Pierson, eds., *New Concepts in Wage Determination* (New York: McGraw-Hill Book Company, Inc., 1957); Paul S. Sultan, "Unionism and Wage-Income Ratios, 1929-51," *Review of Economics and Statistics* (February 1954); and Norman J. Simler, *The Impact of Unionism on Wage-Income Ratios in the Manufacturing Sector of the Economy* (Minneapolis: University of Minnesota Press, 1961).

Distribution of personal income

We noted earlier that income earned through labor and capital services in production is a different thing from income actually received. This is particularly true as regards property income. Profits before taxes are as large today as they were thirty or forty years ago. But corporate profits taxes now take about half of all profits as against only one-sixth in 1925-29. Thus profits *after taxes* have fallen from 19.4 per cent of income produced in 1925-29 to 10.2 per cent in 1957-62.

In addition, there has been a drop in the percentage of profits paid out to stockholders. In 1929 about 70 per cent of corporate profits after taxes were paid out as dividends. This percentage fell drastically during the war years, reached a low of 35 per cent in 1947-48, recovered to about 50 per cent in the early 'fifties, and has been running at about two-thirds in recent years. At the end of 1963, corporate profits before taxes were running at the impressive level of 52 billions a year. But this shrinks to 27 billions after taxes, and only 17 billions actually paid out in dividends.

The result is that property income forms a smaller percentage of income *received* than of income *produced*, while wage and salary incomes form a larger percentage. If one excludes the "mixed incomes" of farmers and other small proprietors and government and business transfer payments, wage and salary incomes formed 84 per cent of the remaining personal income payments in 1962. Rents, interest, and dividend payments formed only 14 per cent. In 1929 the corresponding percentages were 73 per cent for wage-salary income and 27 per cent for property income. Employee compensation bulks considerably larger in actual income receipts than was true a generation ago.

Still more striking results would be obtained if one could calculate wages and salaries as a percentage of *disposable income*, i.e., of personal income after deducting personal income taxes. These taxes take a larger slice of property than of wage-salary incomes, because the former are more heavily concentrated in the upper income brackets. Thus the property share of disposable income is even smaller than that of personal income. The statistics do not permit us to say precisely how much smaller, but property income after all taxes is certainly a minor and decreasing share of the income picture.

There has been something approaching an income revolution since the 1920's, a revolution in which the federal fiscal system has played a central role.

Concluding comment

Throughout the nineteenth century and into the twentieth, "income distribution" in the sense of type distribution was a central issue in economic theory. What determines the share of the "working class" and the "capitalist class" in national output? Is labor exploited by capital? Can the position of labor be improved by forcible appropriation of property income? A great deal of early intellectual support for the labor movement rested on the premise that redistribution of income was desirable and could be accomplished through union organization.

Today these issues seem to have receded into the background. They receive a chapter or two in elementary economics texts and we have given them half a chapter here. But it is difficult to get as excited about them as people did fifty years ago. Why this transformation in the anatomy of economics? There are probably several reasons:

1. In a rapidly growing economy it is obvious that labor's income can be raised faster and farther through growth of national output than through redistribution of national output. No conceivable redistribution of property income in the United States could raise wage and salary incomes by more than 10 or 15 per cent. But the growth of per capita output has doubled real wages in a generation, and there seems no reason why growth cannot continue at the same rate in the future. Interest has thus shifted to the preconditions of rapid economic growth and away from the problem of dividing a static national income.

2. Government has come to the fore as the main agency for redistributing income. While labor has difficulty in capturing property income directly, it can do so indirectly by supporting heavy taxation of profits and personal incomes and large government benefits to wage earners. Controversies over income distribution no longer turn mainly on wage-profit relations, collective bargaining, and so on. They turn rather on the structure of taxation and the allocation of public expenditures.

3. Much of the earlier concern with income distribution had a welfare basis. People were concerned about poverty, and identified the poor with the wage earners. In the United States, at least, poverty is now much reduced compared with even a generation ago. Moreover, such poverty as remains is not mainly a wage problem and cannot be removed simply by raising the wage level. Poverty now exists mainly among people who for one reason or another are not able to earn wages, as will be explained in more detail in Chapter 20.

4. Another contributing factor may be the blurring of the line between worker and capitalist. Most recipients of property income are also in the labor force as salary earners or proprietors. Several million wage and salary earners also own stocks and bonds and receive property income. This point should not be exaggerated. Most wage earners still receive little or no property income, and most property income is still concentrated in relatively few hands. But the long-run tendency is clear, and as it becomes harder to distinguish labor and property incomes as going to different groups of individuals, the analytical distinction between the two types becomes less interesting. The future will probably show a steady increase of interest in the size distribution of income and a continued decline of interest in type distribution.

Discussion questions

1. Explain and assess the significance of Kendrick's concept of total factor productivity.

2. What differences does one notice in the behavior of inputs, output, and total factor productivity from 1919-57 as compared with 1889-1919?

3. What seem to be the main reasons for the rapid rise of factor productivity in recent decades?

4. "Increases in real wages depend basically on the ability of workers and unions to raise man-hour output." Discuss.

5. Explain the difference between, and the relation between, type distributions and size distributions of income.

6. Explain the marginal productivity theory of the determination of labor and capital shares in national income.

7. What has happened since 1900 to (a) the relative *prices* of labor and capital, (b) the relative *shares* of labor and capital in national income? What reasons can one find for the apparent increase in the labor share?

Selected reading

Clark, John Bates, *The Distribution of Wealth*. New York: The Macmillan Company, 1899.

Denison, E. F., "Income Types and Size Distribution," *American Economic Review*, XLIII (May 1954), pp. 254-269.

————, *The Sources of Economic Growth in the United States*. New York: Committee on Economic Development, 1962.

Kendrick, John W., *Productivity Trends in the United States*. Princeton: Princeton University Press, 1961.

Kerr, Clark, "Labor's Income Share and the Labor Movement," in George W. Taylor and Frank C. Pierson, eds., *New Concepts in Wage Determination*. New York: McGraw-Hill Book Company, Inc., 1957.

————, "Productivity and Labor Relations," in *Productivity and Progress*. Sydney, Australia: Angus and Robertson, 1957.

Kravis, Irving B., "Relative Income Shares in Fact and Theory," *American Economic Review* (December 1959), pp. 917-49.

Levinson, Harold M., *Unionism, Wage Trends, and Income Distribution*, Michigan Business Studies, X:4. Ann Arbor: University of Michigan Press, 1951.

Phelps Brown, E. H., *The Economics of Labor*. New Haven: Yale University Press, 1962, chap. 7.

————, and P. E. Hart, "The Share of Wages in National Income," *Economic Journal*, LXII (June 1952), pp. 253-277.

Schuller, George J., "The Secular Trend in Income Distribution by Type, 1869-1948: A Preliminary Estimate," *Review of Economics and Statistics*, XXXV (November 1953), pp. 302-324.

Simler, Norman J., *The Impact of Unionism on Wage-Income Ratios in the Manufacturing Sector of the Economy*. Minneapolis: University of Minnesota Press, 1961.

18

The National Wage Structure

The last two chapters attempted to explain the average level of money wages and real wages for all workers in the economy. This average is a statistical fiction, however, and conceals wide variations in rates of pay on particular jobs. One can still find workers in the United States earning less than a dollar an hour while others earn in excess of five dollars an hour. The judgments which workers, managers, and union officials make about the reasonableness of wages typically turn on a comparison of one wage level with another. Is the wage rate for this job fair relative to rates for other jobs with which it may legitimately be compared? These practical questions lend point to an examination of how great the variation of wages is at present and how it has changed over the course of time.

The factors determining a worker's earnings may be divided into two broad categories. The first is the occupation in which he is employed. A man's occupational level has a major influence on his income, his community standing, and his general way of life. There are traditionally substantial differences between the earnings of laborers, semiskilled workers, and skilled craftsmen. The range of earnings becomes still wider if one goes up the occupational ladder to include salaried managers, proprietors, and professional people.

Occupation, however, is not the only determinant of earning power. In almost any occupation one finds some workers earning twice as much as others. How much a machinist receives is influenced by the plant and industry in which he is employed, by the size of city and region of the country in which he lives, and by a variety of personal factors. Men typically receive more than women for the same kind of work, and (in the United States) white workers receive more than nonwhite workers. We must examine the extent of wage variation on these counts and the reasons for it.

Since we are trying to compare the price of labor at different points in the economy, it would be desirable to use basic wage rates or average hourly earnings as the basis of comparison. Wage rate information is far from complete, however, and is not always classified in a useful way. For some types of comparison, therefore, we are forced to fall back on Census data concerning annual earnings. Since annual earnings are influenced by the amount of time worked during the year, an earnings comparison yields different results from a wage rate comparison. It can be argued that the earnings comparison is superior because a worker's family cannot eat his wage rate—only his annual income. At any rate, the two types of information are different, and this should be borne in mind as we switch back and forth from one to the other.

INFLUENCE OF OCCUPATIONAL LEVEL ON EARNINGS

Major occupational differences

Before considering wage differences within the manual labor force, it will be well to locate manual workers relative to other major occupational groups. We all have a general idea that workers lie toward the bottom of the income scale. A look at the facts will lend precision to our thinking, however, and will produce some surprises. The median annual incomes of employed persons in each major occupational group in 1950 and 1959 are shown in Table 14.[1]

The average incomes revealed by this table look surprisingly low. It is hard to believe that salaried officials in business averaged only about seven thousand dollars in 1959, and salaried professional people only sixty-five hundred. The reason is that the small number of very high salaries in these occupations receive wide publicity, while the hundreds of thousands of people working at modest salaries pass

---

[1] Data are from Carol A. Barry, "White-Collar Employment: Characteristics," *Monthly Labor Review* (February 1961), pp. 139-147.

unnoticed. This optical illusion was pointed out two centuries ago by Adam Smith, who noted that a few large prizes are sufficient to attract people into occupations which on the average yield quite low returns.

TABLE 14

MEDIAN INCOME OF GAINFULLY EMPLOYED MEN, BY OCCUPATION GROUP, 1950 AND 1959.

| | Median Income | | Per cent Increase |
Occupation Group	1950	1959	1950-59
Professional and technical			
Salaried	$3,880	$6,529	68.3
Self-employed	6,188	10,941	76.8
Managers, officials, and proprietors, except farm			
Salaried	4,431	7,080	59.8
Self-employed	3,263	5,299	62.4
Clerical	3,103	4,904	58.0
Sales	3,137	4,892	55.9
Craftsmen	3,293	5,355	62.6
Operatives	2,790	4,281	53.4
Laborers, except farm	1,909	3,150	65.0
Service, except private household	2,303	3,391	47.2

The rank order of incomes shown by these tables is about what one would expect. It is perhaps a little surprising that the independent professional man, not the business executive, stands at the top of the list. The independent professional group as a whole earns about fifty per cent more than the average salaried man in business. The salaried professional group, which is dominated by teachers, stands third in rank but considerably below the independent professionals.

The lowly worker is obviously not always lowly. The average skilled worker in 1959 earned appreciably more than the average man in the sales and clerical group. Rather more surprisingly, he earned more than the average independent business proprietor. The incomes of small business men are always surprisingly low. Proprietors of retail establishments, for example, seem to average about the same as semiskilled factory workers. Yet the highest hope of many wage and salary earners is to own a store, filling station, or other small business.

How can this be? Why do so many people try to enter a field which requires some capital investment, long hours of work, and considerable risk of failure, and which in the end yields less on the average than one could get in paid employment? Desire for independence may be part of the answer. Even if a man knew all the facts, he might count being his own boss as worth some sacrifice of income. But ignorance must also be part of the answer. People expect that their incomes will be higher in self-employment, and many are disappointed. Smith's principle of "large prizes" is applicable here. The fact that some do succeed, and some even succeed in a large way, arouses expectations which are unjustified in the average case.

Within the manual group semiskilled workers earn about one-third more than laborers, and skilled workers earn about two-thirds more. The gap in hourly wage rates is not this wide, as we shall see in a moment. But the skilled workers, in addition to having somewhat higher wage rates, also have more regular employment and this widens their advantage in annual income.

At the bottom of the income pyramid stands the rural population. Farm laborers earn less than half as much as city laborers and have done so consistently over the past fifty years. This presents something of a puzzle which we shall have to explain at a later point.

The last column of Table 14 shows the percentage rise in the average income of each group over the period 1950-59. As background, one should recall that during the war and postwar boom of the 1940's, wage rates for the lower occupational groups rose considerably faster than for the higher. Earnings of manual workers rose faster, in percentage terms, than those of white-collar people; and within the manual group, earnings of laborers rose faster than those of craftsmen. There was a marked equalization of wage-salary incomes.

It is apparent from Table 14 that there was no such tendency during the nineteen fifties. The white-collar groups fully kept up with the manual workers on a percentage basis, and absolute differences in income widened substantially. The largest income gains were scored by professional and technical workers. There are probably two reasons for this. First, professional salaries are sluggish and lagged considerably during the inflation of the 'forties. Their rapid advance in the 'fifties was partly a catching-up reaction. In addition, demand for professional and technical skills has been rising very rapidly, while supply expands only slowly because of the long training required. This should produce a relative rise in the price of professional skills; and it seems in fact to have done so.

It would be interesting to follow the fate of different occupational groups over a long period of time. There is a reasonably well-grounded suspicion, for example, that earnings of manual workers have been rising relative to those of white-collar workers over the long run. McCaffree concluded that the premium for white-collar work has been falling for at least fifty years prior to 1939, mainly because of a rapid increase in the number of high school graduates, most of whom aspire to white-collar work, and the taking over of an increasing proportion of office work by women.[2] In 1939, the annual earnings of white-collar workers were still about 40 per cent above those of all manual workers. This advantage was largely eroded by the sharp inflation of 1940-49, during which manual workers' wage rates rose more rapidly than salaries, and their annual earnings rose even faster because of full employment. Today the skilled workers are well ahead of sales and clerical workers in annual earnings, and even semiskilled workers are getting quite close to the white-collar level.

Wage differences within manual labor

For manual occupations we have information on wage rates over a considerable period in the past. This shows both short-term and long-term movements in the differential between skilled and unskilled wages. The differential appears to narrow in boom periods and to widen again in depression. Differentials narrowed especially fast during 1916-20 and 1940-49, periods of inflation and full employment associated with the two world wars. Inflation and severe labor shortage seem to raise low wage rates faster (percentage-wise) than higher rates and thus reduce the percentage spread between them. After the end of each war boom differentials have tended to widen again, but have not rebounded all the way to the pre-war level. Thus the long-run tendency has been for occupational differentials to decline.

Nor is this tendency characteristic only of the United States. For Britain, Professor Fogarty reports that "skill and responsibility differentials have narrowed markedly since 1913 and especially since 1938, but the process has been stepwise and not continuous. . . . Differentials between skilled and unskilled manual workers narrowed sharply in the first World War, widened a little in the years of deflation

---

[2] K. M. McCaffree, "The Earnings Differential Between White Collar and Manual Occupations," *Review of Economics and Statistics* (February 1953), pp. 20-30.

after it, and stabilized again from 1924 to 1939. There was then another sharp squeeze during the second World War and the years of acute inflation and shortages till 1949. Differentials then once again leveled off, and there has been no further general change till the present."[3]

The American data have been examined in detail by Ober.[4] He calculates that in 1907 the average wage level of skilled workers in manufacturing was roughly double (105 per cent above) that of unskilled workers. The advantage of the skilled workers fell to 75 per cent in 1918-19, 65 per cent in 1937-40, 55 per cent in 1945-47, and something like 45 per cent in the early 'fifties. Similar trends are observable in most other lines of industry. In building construction, for example, union rates for craftsmen were almost exactly double (98 per cent above) those of laborers in 1914. This figure fell to 80 per cent in 1923, 70 per cent in 1938, 54 per cent in 1945, and 38 per cent in 1952. Speaking roughly, one can say that fifty years ago it was normal for craftsmen to receive wage rates twice as high as those for common laborers in the same industry. Today it is normal for them to receive one-third to one-half more than laborers. The gap in *earnings* remains wider than this, however, because of differences in regularity of employment, overtime earnings, and other things.

This summary statement cannot convey the great diversity of occupational differential among plants, industries, and regions in the country. The premium for skilled labor is considerably higher in the South than on the Pacific Coast. In certain industries, too, skilled workers still receive more than double the rates of the unskilled. Women's suits and coats, women's dresses, and precious jewelry have wider occupational differentials than other manufacturing industries, and this can be traced to special skill requirements of the top crafts. Even within the same industry, different plants may have different occupational wage structures because of special production characteristics, management judgments, or union pressures. Looking at the

---

[3]M. P. Fogarty, "Portrait of a Pay Structure," in J. L. Meij, ed., *Internal Wage Structure* (Amsterdam: North-Holland Publishing Co., 1963), pp. 12-13.
[4] Harry Ober, "Occupational Wage Differentials, 1907-1947," *Monthly Labor Review* (August 1948), pp. 127-34. See the review of this and other evidence in Lloyd G. Reynolds and Cynthia H. Taft, *The Evolution of Wage Structure* (New Haven: Yale University Press, 1956), chap. 12; and also Melvin W. Reder, "Wage Differentials: Theory and Measurement," in *Aspects of Labor Economics* (Princeton: Princeton University Press, 1962), pp. 257-311.

economy broadly, however, the trend toward smaller skill premiums is so strong and pervasive as to suggest the operation of powerful economic forces.

This trend toward smaller occupational differentials is characteristic of the mature industrial nations, most of which now have considerably smaller spreads than the United States. In France, skilled workers in manufacturing in 1954 typically earned 25 to 35 per cent more than laborers in the same industry. In Sweden, skilled metalworkers were earning in 1953 about 20 per cent more than unskilled workers, and this is probably typical of a good many manufacturing industries. In Great Britain, skilled workers in many industries in the early 'fifties were earning something like 25 per cent more than laborers in the same industries. In all cases there had been a considerable shrinkage of occupational differentials compared with the years before World War II.

The case of the U.S.S.R. is interesting because of the extent to which wages are controlled by the central planning authorities. Standard wage schedules for each industry and region are promulgated from Moscow; and the total amount which each producing enterprise may spend for labor is specified in its annual plan.

Under the pressure for production and the shortage of qualified workers which prevailed during the 'thirties and 'forties, however, this control structure tended to come apart at the seams. Enterprise managers found ways of paying extra to attract and hold the labor they needed. Low-skilled workers were upgraded arbitrarily to higher job classifications. Incentive standards were allowed to loosen so that incentive workers (about three-fourths of the Soviet industrial labor force at this time) could earn much more than their official wage rates. Length-of-service bonuses and other special premiums were extended to more and more workers. This meant that most plants were exceeding the allowable wage bill specified in their plan; but higher officials seem to have winked at this provided the plant was meeting its production targets.

By 1956 the actual wage structure had departed so far from the official schedules, and had reached such a stage of confusion, that a thoroughgoing wage reform was set in motion. The new wage schedules normally group the jobs in each industry into six occupational grades. The base rate for the highest grade is typically about double the lowest rates; but in some industries of special national importance the top rate is as much as three times the lowest.[5] In general, occupational differentials are wider than in the United States, and much wider than those in the West European countries. This is confirmed by a case study of actual earnings of workers in comparable steel mills in the U.S.S.R., U.S.A., U.K., Germany, Holland, and Italy.[6]

The new wage structure also graduates wages by type of industry, with heavy industry receiving a substantial premium; and by region of the country, with much higher rates for the colder and more remote areas. The wage structure is used mainly as a device for resource allocation, for attracting labor to the places where it is needed in the industrial development program. While the desirability of greater income equality is accepted in principle, it is given lower priority in practice.

EXPLANATION OF OCCUPATIONAL WAGE DIFFERENCES

The principles which would govern relative wage rates in a competitive labor market were sketched out originally by Adam Smith, and his analysis is still accepted as generally valid. Given free choice, Smith argued, each worker would select the job offering maximum net advantage from his point of view. This would not necessarily mean the highest-paying job. The pleasantness or unpleasantness of the work, the time and expense required to learn the occupation, its prestige in the community, the chances of success or failure, regularity and security of employment, and other factors would obviously affect workers' choices. The result would be a system of "equalizing differentials," a wage structure which just equalized the net advantages of different occupations. Jobs with a long learning time, jobs offering only irregular

---

[5] The reform seems to have brought, if anything, a widening of *de facto* occupational differentials: ". . . the basic wage scales promulgated since 1957, although formally narrower than the ones they replaced, in fact provide for wider differentials. This paradox results from the fact that the lower grades in the old scales were nonoperational, whereas it has been one of the objectives of the wage reform to restore grade I as the effective hiring grade. I have tested every available scale and found this to be true: the effective basic wage differential has been widened." (Walter Galenson, "The Soviet Wage Reform," *Proceedings of the Thirteenth Annual Meeting of IRRA* (1960), p. 255). See also Galenson's essay on Soviet wage structure in L. J. Meij, ed., *op. cit.*

[6] See M. Gardner Clark, "Comparative Wage Structures in the Steel Industry of the Soviet Union and Western Countries," *Proceedings of the Thirteenth Annual Meeting of IRRA* (1960), pp. 266-288.

employment, and jobs which are particularly strenuous or unpleasant would have to offer higher wages to offset these disadvantages.

This is what we should call today a supply and demand theory of occupational differences. There will be a demand curve for each type of labor, sloping downward from left to right in the usual way. The higher the wage rate for a particular kind of labor, the less of that kind of labor will be purchased. The rationale of this was explained in Chapter 10 and need not be repeated here.

On the other side of the market, Smith's principles will yield a rising supply curve of labor for each occupation. A few workers may find a particular occupation so interesting and attractive that they will work at it for very low wages. If more workers are required, however, it will be necessary to offer a higher wage to offset the attractions of other occupations; and the more workers needed in a field, the higher the wage which must be offered to attract them. The equilibrium wage for the occupation will be established at the intersection of the supply and demand curves. At this wage the last worker employed— the man at the margin—considers it just worth his while to work in this occupation rather than shift to something else.

The fact that supply and demand conditions *define* a market wage rate for an occupation at a particular time does not mean, of course, that that rate will necessarily be established. It will be established only under the assumed conditions of free and informed occupational choice, operating in a market where wages are not fixed by employer combination, trade unionism, or government. If entrance to an occupation is limited by guild restrictions, licensing systems, or educational barriers, the wage rate for that occupation may remain permanently above the equilibrium level. Wages may also be set above the equilibrium level by collective bargaining or government action. If the wage-fixing body is able to enforce its decrees, the labor market will have to adjust to the situation. Fewer workers will be employed than would have been employed at the (lower) market rate, and there will be a surplus of workers who would have preferred to work in this occupation but must now seek employment somewhere else.

This in brief outline is the "market" or "competitive" theory of occupational wage differences. It can be illustrated by a simple demand and supply diagram of the sort used in Chapter 10.

What of the objection that this abstract reasoning has little to do with wage determination in the real world? Are not actual wage structures shaped by haphazard and irrational worker choices, by company

and union wage policies, by relative bargaining power, by government
intervention in the labor market, and a multitude of other forces
which defy neat classification? Is the demand-supply approach at all
useful in understanding reality?

The answer depends essentially on the kind of question in which
one is interested. One might be interested, for example, in explaining
why a particular semiskilled job in a particular plant pays precisely
eight cents an hour more than the job just beneath it. It would be
foolish to claim that demand-supply analysis gets one very far with
this sort of problem. The mills of the labor market do not grind
this fine. They do not prescribe that a particular differential on a
certain date must be exactly eight cents and no more. An explanation
in terms of discretionary judgment by union and management officials,
worker relations in the shop, and so on, is clearly in order.

But economists are not much interested in this kind of question.
The purpose of economics is to explain the general contours of a
national economy and how these change gradually over decades and
generations. Suppose one is interested in why farm labor rates remain
permanently much below urban labor rates, or why the advantage
of the skilled man over the unskilled has fallen from 100 per cent
to 40 per cent in two generations. For this sort of purpose, one can
get a good deal further with demand-supply analysis than without
it. But, "the proof of the pudding . . . ," and so forth: the only way
to show the usefulness of a conceptual scheme is by using it. Let us
see, therefore, how market reasoning can be used to explore three
of the more striking occupational differences pointed out in the previous section.

Incomes in the professions

The most striking feature of the earnings structure in the United
States is the large premium earned by members of the independent
professions. A doctor earns on the average about three times as much
as the average manual or white-collar worker. Self-employed professionals as a whole earn approximately twice as much. This seems
contradictory to what one would expect under free competition. It
can scarcely be argued that none of the people in the lower 90 per
cent of the occupational scale have the native ability required for
professional occupations. Nor can it be argued that it would not be
worth their while to train for the professions. The extra income earned

by a doctor, a lawyer, or an engineer over his lifetime is sufficient to pay a substantial return on the original educational cost, probably a higher return than can be earned from any other type of investment.

Why, then, do not many more young people train for the profes-sions? The main bottleneck, as was noted in Chapter 15, lies in the educational system. This is partly a matter of personal finance. Students from low-income families can usually not afford the prolonged training required for the professions and increasingly for executive positions in business. But it is also partly a matter of physical in-adequacy of training facilities. There are only so many medical schools in the country, and each can train only so many students a year. The cost of building new schools of high quality is rising so rapidly as to be almost beyond the reach of private philanthropy. Only government funds on a large scale can break this sort of bottleneck, and govern-ment support on an adequate scale is not yet forthcoming.

Artificial restriction of labor supply, in short, is now holding pro-fessional incomes above the equilibrium level. More adequate training facilities, combined with student loan funds and the other measures suggested in Chapter 15, would make possible an increased supply of young people to the professions, and this would gradually reduce the gap between professional incomes and other incomes. Equilibrium would be reached at a point where the extra income yielded by the professions was just sufficient to offset educational costs, including the fact of no income during the training years. (This overlooks con-siderations of prestige and security. It overlooks also the possibility of scarce natural ability in some areas. First-rate surgeons and opera singers will doubtless always command a considerable premium.)

Although this result would be beneficial to those now excluded from the professions and to consumers of professional services, it would be harmful to those already practicing in professional fields. It is quite natural that existing professional societies do not show great enthusiasm for scholarship programs and enlarged training facilities which would flood their occupations with newcomers.

The skilled-unskilled differential

The information presented above on wage rates for skilled and unskilled labor raises at least two questions. First, how could a situa-tion have developed in which skilled men were paid twice as much as laborers? The skilled occupations are more pleasant and attractive on almost every count—regularity of employment, variety and intrinsic interest of the work, community standing, and so on. Why should it ever have been necessary to pay any considerable wage premium for these occupations? Second, why has the skilled-unskilled gap narrowed so greatly in recent decades?

The first question may be rephrased in this way: Why did unskilled wage rates not rise faster before 1914? Why did they not rise fast enough to close the large gap existing between laborers and craftsmen? The answer may be mainly that the supply of unskilled labor was swollen before 1914 from two sources which are now much less important—American farm boys and European immigrants. High rural birth rates, plus a steady decline of labor requirements in agriculture, produced a large surplus of farm population which could be drawn into the urban labor force. European immigrants, who numbered more than a million a year in the twenty years before 1914, also came mainly from a rural background and entered American industry at the unskilled level. Neither group was accustomed to high earnings. They were quite willing to be hired at wages which were low compared with those of skilled craftsmen but considerably better than anything they had known before. The large skill differentials at the turn of the century, then, can be explained not so much in terms of skilled rates having been kept artificially high as in terms of the common labor rate having been depressed by an ample labor supply.

The steady decline of skill differentials over the past fifty years can also be explained reasonably well on a demand-supply basis. The demand for unskilled labor has suffered a relative decline. Urban laborers form only half as large a percentage of the labor force today as they did in 1910, while the percentage of skilled workers has changed very little. This factor alone might have been expected to *widen* skill differentials rather than narrow them. But the significant thing is that the supply of common labor has fallen even faster than the demand, while the supply of skilled workers has increased. European immigration has been virtually cut off since 1914. The influx of low-skilled labor from the farms has become less important with the shrinkage in the relative size of the farm population.

Perhaps most important of all has been the diffusion of educational opportunities throughout the population. At the beginning of this century only a small percentage of young people finished high school. Today a majority of young people in the United States complete the twelfth grade and the proportion is increasing year by year. High school graduates take it for granted that they will enter skilled or white-collar jobs or go on to college. This swells the supply of labor to the higher occupations while depleting the supply of unskilled labor. An increase in manual wages relative to white-collar salaries, and in laborers' wages relative to craftsmen's wages, is a natural consequence.

The sharp inflations of 1916-20 and 1940-49 accelerated the decline of occupational differentials. During rapid inflation it often seems simplest and fairest to raise everyone's wages by the same number of cents per hour. This protects the low-paid worker who is nearest to the margin of subsistence and is hit hardest by rising living costs. In addition, during the 'forties many of the newly-organized industrial unions showed a distinct preference for equal cents-per-hour increases, perhaps because low-skilled workers formed the dominant part of their membership. As a matter of arithmetic, equal cents-per-hour increases necessarily reduce the *percentage* spread between occupational levels. The widespread use of such increases during the 'forties and 'fifties provides a superficial explanation of the decline in occupational differentials. This policy could scarcely have been followed successfully, however, if the underlying demand-supply situation had not also been favorable to a decline in differentials.

How far is this process likely to go in the future? Skill differentials cannot continue to shrink indefinitely, and most of the potential shrinkage has probably already occurred. One might argue on Adam Smithian grounds that laboring jobs are so unattractive that they should actually pay more than skilled jobs, and that the wage structure should be "turned on its head." But it is hard to see how this could happen in practice. Custom and tradition, going back at least to the Middle Ages, demand that the craftsman receive a noticeable premium for his skill. Management finds it expedient to establish wage differences between adjacent skill grades to maintain a promotion ladder in the plant. Unions do not quarrel with this policy. Collective bargaining would be much less fun if wage differentials were not large enough to argue about.

European experience suggests that a premium of 25 per cent for the skilled worker over the laborer may be close to a feasible minimum. One finds few cases in which the gap in actual earnings between the two groups has been reduced below this level. The official wage schedules embodied in union agreements and government decrees sometimes provide a smaller differential, but employers still find ways of paying what they must to recruit skilled workers and keep them

satisfied. Payment over the official scale has been a common phenomenon in Britain, Sweden, and France during the tight labor market of the 'forties and 'fifties, and this has kept differences in actual
earnings wider than they look on paper. In some cases—for example,
in Sweden since 1950—official differentials have been widened in
recognition of the fact that the previous narrowing tendency had gone
too far.

Wages of farm and factory labor

A striking feature of the wage structure in the United States, and
for that matter in many other countries, is the large gap between the
earnings of farm and urban laborers. In the United States the hourly
cash earnings of farm workers, calculated as a percentage of average
hourly earnings in manufacturing, have ranged between a low of 24
per cent in 1934 and a high of 46 per cent in 1945. In no year of
the last several decades have they risen to even half the manufacturing
level. If this is considered an unfair comparison on the ground that
manufacturing work is more highly skilled, it may be pointed out that
farm wage rates have rarely been more than half the rate for common
labor engaged in road building. Farm wages have fluctuated recently
between 40 and 50 per cent of road building rates, a gap which seems
too wide to be explained on any market basis.

Some possible explanations of this differential can be dismissed as
having little validity. It might be that farm laborers are simply less
efficient on the average than factory laborers. Gale Johnson, however,
after a careful analysis of this question, concluded that there is no
evidence of any marked difference in natural ability between the two
groups.[7] It might also be argued that for many decades the rate of
productivity increase was lower in agriculture than in industry. But
this has not been true during the past twenty years, which have seen
a spectacular increase of labor productivity in agriculture. In any
event, as was pointed out in Chapter 17, there is no reason why the
wage level of an industry should move parallel to the rate of productivity change *in that industry alone*.

The true reasons for the large rural-urban differential are rooted
in the structure of the agricultural industry. In an expanding economy,
the demand for farm products—and therefore for farm labor—rises
less rapidly than the demand for manufactures and services. There is

---

[7] D. Gale Johnson, "Comparability of Labor Capacities of Farm and Non-
Farm Labor." *American Economic Review* (June 1953), pp. 296-313.

a physical limit to how much one can eat and, as this limit is approached in a wealthy country, the demand for food cannot rise much faster than population is growing. In the United States, the demand for farm labor has been depressed further by the rapid mechanization of agriculture in recent years—tractors, combine harvesters, cotton pickers, milking machines, and all the rest. To an increasing extent the farm owner-operator can get the work done by himself, without the battery of "hired hands" which was needed in an earlier day. On the supply side, rural birth rates are relatively high and there is a chronic tendency toward accumulation of excess population on the land. This relative plentifulness of farm labor in the face of a declining demand for it helps to explain the low level of farm wage rates.

But why does the large gap between farm and factory wage levels not lead farm laborers to rush to the city in such large numbers that the wage difference would be reduced or eliminated? This is presumably what would happen in a perfectly competitive labor market. The answer is partly that the market is imperfect—country people do not have a clear picture of opportunities elsewhere, they hesitate to face the costs and risks of movement, they are attached to their home communities, and so on. The more important part of the answer, however, is that we are dealing here with a dynamic situation in which *rates of change* are of prime importance. Farm workers do move to the city, but the *rate* at which they move is limited by the level of employment and labor demand in the urban economy. Farm people quite sensibly refuse to exchange even a low farm income for unemployment in the city. Only an obvious abundance of employment opportunities, such as existed during the war booms of 1914-20 and 1939-45, will produce enough migration to raise the relative level of farm wages. During peacetime periods the urban economy typically operates somewhat short of full employment and migration to the city slackens off, so that the farm-city wage gap remains stationary or may even widen. Over the past fifty years as a whole the farm laborer seems to have done no more than hold his own, wartime gains having been offset by peacetime losses.

WAGE DIFFERENCES WITHIN AN OCCUPATION

An explanation of wage differences among occupations carries us only part of the way toward understanding the national wage structure, for there are large differences within the same occupational group. The range of earnings within each occupation is usually a good deal wider than the average difference between it and neighboring occupations. Why is this? Why do some workers enjoy wage rates 50 per cent or more above those of other workers in the same occupational classification?[8] The most important factors are differences in geographical location, type of industry, size and efficiency of plant, and personal characteristics of the worker such as age, sex, and race. The evidence on each of these factors will be reviewed briefly.

Geographic location

The classic example of geographic wage difference in the United States is the "North-South" differential. This is a complicated matter, and the size of the differential is less than one might judge from looking at over-all income statistics. The average annual income of all employed persons in the South is substantially below that in other regions; but this is due partly to the greater importance in the South of agriculture relative to industry, of light industry relative to heavy, of nonwhite workers relative to white workers, and of small towns and cities relative to large cities. The industry mix and labor-force mix would produce lower *average earnings* in the South even though *wage rates* were identical for similar workers in similar occupations.[9]

A proper comparison must rest on relative wage rates for, say, male white workers at the same occupational level in the same kind of industry in cities of the same size, North and South. The limited information of this sort which is available relates mainly to manufacturing. There does seem to be a considerable wage advantage in favor of the North, but this is extremely variable. In some types of industry (furniture, food products, hosiery) the South is 20 to 30 per

---

[8] Miller, *Income of the American People*, Appendix Table C.2.

[9] Fuchs and Perlman calculated that the wages of Southern manufacturing workers in 1954, as a percentage of the national average, were 77.1 per cent for the South Atlantic and 79.1 per cent for the East South Central region. About half of this gap, however, was due to differences in the industry mix. When the data are adjusted for this, the ratio of Southern wages *for similar lines of work* rises to 89.6 per cent in the South Atlantic and 87.4 per cent in the East South Central region. It appears also that the relative position of the South improved somewhat between 1929 and 1954. The 1929 "standardized" wage ratios were 85.2 in the South Atlantic and 78.8 in the East South Central states. See Victor R. Fuchs and Richard Perlman, "Recent Trends in Southern Wage Differentials," *Review of Economics and Statistics* (August 1960), pp. 292-300.

cent below the Northern level; but in other industries (glass, rayon, bituminous coal, basic steel, pulp and paper) there is virtually no difference between the two regions. For manufacturing as a whole, the Southern wage level seems to be 10 to 15 per cent below the North Central states. The Pacific Coast, traditionally the highest-wage area of the country, is perhaps 10 per cent above the North Central region.

It must be recognized, however, that this is a gross simplification of a very complex reality. There is marked variation in wages *within* each of the major regions. If prevailing wage levels were plotted vertically on a map of the United States, yielding what may be termed a "wage contour map," one would find a "height of land" running west from New York through Ohio and Michigan to Chicago. To the south lies a watershed sloping downward to the Gulf Coast. As one goes south through Pennsylvania, Maryland, Virginia, North Carolina, and South Carolina, the prevailing wage level falls gradually but steadily. Again, as one goes north into the New England states, wage levels fall off toward the Canadian border. West of Chicago, wage levels decline until one reaches the mountain states when they begin to rise again and reach a peak on the Pacific Coast. The West Coast, however, has its own "North-South" differential. The highest wage rates are in Washington and Oregon, and the level slopes downward from there through San Francisco and Los Angeles to the Mexican border.

In addition to these regional differences, wages vary significantly by size of community.[10] Even after adjusting for differences in the mix of industries and occupations, there seems to be a difference of 10 to 20 per cent between small-town wages and big-city wages for the same occupational category. These differences are probably somewhat greater than differences in living costs between large and smaller communities, i.e., they are differences in real wages as well as in money wages.

What is the basis for these persistent differences between regions and between communities of different size? The answer lies partly in the fact that net additions to labor supply now come mainly from the rural population. The relatively high birth rates in rural areas lead to an accumulation of population which cannot be absorbed in agriculture, and which is drained off into urban occupations at a rate which

---

[10] Miller, *Income of the American People*, pp. 38-40.

varies with the level of urban employment. The rate of migration to the cities slackens during a depression period such as the 'thirties, and accelerates in boom periods such as the 'forties and 'fifties.

Small towns are in the best position to tap this additional labor supply. A factory located in such a town can easily recruit new employees by spreading word throughout the surrounding countryside. This ready availability of labor means that the small town need not offer as high a wage level as the metropolitan center which must draw its recruits from a wider area. Moreover, lower housing costs and simpler living standards enable small-town workers to feel as well off as city workers even with lower money wages.

A second important factor is the variation of agricultural productivity, and consequently of agricultural incomes, from one region to another. The level of agricultural income in a region provides a sort of base from which the urban wage structure graduates upward. Farm wage rates in the Southeastern states are only about half the level of farm wage rates in New England, and it is consequently not surprising that urban wage rates are lower—particularly wage rates for common labor, which stands in closest competitive relation to agriculture. On the Pacific Coast, on the other hand, farm wage rates are from 50 to 100 per cent above the level of the Northeastern states. This alone would be sufficient to account for higher urban wage rates in the Pacific states. It is interesting, however, that the large geographic differentials which exist in agriculture are "weathered down," as it were, and reflected in more moderate differentials in urban occupations.

Industry wage levels

There are large wage differences among different types of industry. In March 1963, average hourly earnings in some of the high-wage industries were as follows: building construction, $3.22; bituminous coal mining, $3.15; oil refining, $3.31; basic steel, $3.29; rubber tires and tubes, $3.21; flat glass, $3.35; motor vehicles, $3.04. At the lower end of the scale one finds earnings only about half as large: knitting mills, $1.62; cigar manufacture, $1.57; men's and boys' furnishings, $1.44; general merchandise stores, $1.55; cleaning and dyeing plants, $1.32; hotels, $1.23.

The main reason for this is the difference in the kinds of labor employed. Steel and coal mining employ men to do heavy and difficult work involving a considerable degree of skill. In textile manufacturing the labor force is mainly women doing light, mechanical, low-skilled work. This is sufficient to account for a substantial difference in wage levels, but it is not the whole story. If one compares men of the same skill level in the same city, one still finds considerable wage variation based on the industry in which the man is employed. Laborers or truck drivers or maintenance mechanics are paid more in heavy manufacturing than in light manufacturing, and more in manufacturing than in the trade and service industries.

A striking example of this sort has been noted by Dunlop. In July, 1953, the union scale for truck drivers in Boston was as follows:

Type of Service	Hourly Rate
Magazine	$2.49
Newspaper, day	2.39
Oil	2.21
Building construction	2.00
Beer	1.90
Railway express	1.87
Meatpacking	1.83
Grocery, chain store	1.82
Garbage disposal	1.73
General hauling	1.69
Coal	1.65
Movers, piano and household	1.65
Ice	1.56
Linen supply	1.54
Laundry, wholesale	1.28
Scrap, iron and metal	1.27

This is particularly interesting because truck driving is a standardized and interchangeable occupation and because all these rates were set by the same union. Dunlop interprets these differences as stemming mainly from differing competitive conditions and ability to pay in the various industries: ". . . the product market tends to be mirrored in the labor market and to determine the wage structure. The differentials are not transitory; they are not to be dismissed as imperfections. . . . The wage contours and their relative rates reflect the basic nature of product and labor markets."[11] It should be added that by 1962

---

[11] John T. Dunlop, "The Task of Contemporary Wage Theory," in George W. Taylor and Frank E. Pierson, eds., New Concepts in Wage Determination (New York: McGraw-Hill Book Company, Inc., 1957), pp. 135-136.

the union had gone some distance in ironing out these differences; but rates still ranged from $2.14 for wastepaper to $3.24 for magazine delivery.[12]

Though these spreads are unusually large, some differentiation of wage level by type of industry is characteristic of all local labor markets. What is behind this? Why are some industries high-wage and others relatively low-wage? Slichter, Dunlop, Garbarino, and others have suggested that the following conditions make for a high industry wage level:[13]

1. A low ratio of labor costs to total costs, so that wages are not a major factor in management calculations of cost and profit. Oil refining is an outstanding example of this sort.

2. A rapid rate of increase in man-hour output. In a fully competitive economy, as noted in Chapter 16, one might expect all wages to rise at a rate roughly proportionate to the average of man-hour output in the economy as a whole. Productivity changes in a particular industry would not directly affect its wage level. In actuality, however, the specific rate of productivity increase in an industry does have an impact on its wage behavior. Industries with high rates of increase tend to lead the wage parade, while those where productivity is stagnating lag behind.

3. A high ratio of profits to sales. Conditions (2) and (3) are likely to accompany a rapid increase in demand for the industry's products and a rapid expansion of plant capacity. An industry in this situation cannot merely afford to raise wages from a profit standpoint but may be forced to raise wages to attract large numbers of new workers to its expanded plants.

4. A high degree of output concentration in a few companies and "cooperative" pricing arrangements. This prevents the profits of industrial expansion from being eroded by price competition. Behind

---

[12] U.S. Department of Labor, Bureau of Labor Statistics, Bulletin No. 1356 (July 1962).

[13] See in particular Sumner H. Slichter, "Notes on the Structure of Wages," *Review of Economics and Statistics,* XXXII (February 1950), pp. 80-91; John T. Dunlop, "Productivity and the Wage Structure," in *Income, Employment and Public Policy,* Essays in Honor of Alvin H. Hansen (New York: W. W. Norton and Company, 1948); Joseph Garbarino, "A Theory of Interindustry Wage Structure Variation," *Quarterly Journal of Economics,* LXIV (May 1950), pp. 283-305.

the shelter of protected prices, management can decide how the gains of rising productivity are to be distributed among consumers (perhaps in product improvements rather than price reductions), stockholders, and workers. In principle, profits belong to the owners and should go into dividends or be ploughed back into company expansion. But the employees are closer to the seat of power and can usually cause more trouble for management than stockholders can. Management may well decide, therefore, to pay the stockholders customary but not necessarily rising dividends and to use part of profits to maintain a better-than-average wage level. This wins worker goodwill and community prestige, eases recruitment problems, pacifies the union, and makes management's life easier in various ways.

There is evidence, in short, of a good deal of unofficial "profit sharing" by business managers. An industry which can afford to pay high wages is likely to do so as a matter of policy, instead of attempting to get by at the lowest level which the labor market would permit.

Reder points out, however, that the statistical evidence is not entirely conclusive. He emphasizes also the importance of distinguishing clearly between *relative industry wage levels at a point of time* and *relative rates of change in industry wage levels over the course of time.* Cross-section comparisons at a point of time seem to show some influence of industry profit rates, concentration ratios, rates of increase of productivity and employment in the recent past, and so on. If one analyzes changes over fifty or sixty years, however, there is little relation between the rate of wage increase in an industry and rates of increase in employment, capital in use, productivity, or profits. The results are thus close to those of theoretical models of a competitive labor market, where over the long run an industry's relative wage level would change only because of changes in the skill-mix used or in geographical location. It is interesting also that the relative ranking of industries seems to remain rather stable over long periods, and that there is no clear evidence of a decline of inter-industry differentials over time.[14]

Although each industry occupies a certain niche in the national wage structure, this does not mean that every company in the industry will be at precisely the same level. In a few strongly-unionized industries, as was noted in Chapter 10, it has been possible to ap-

---

[14] For an excellent summary of the evidence on these matters, see Melvin Reder's essay in *Aspects of Labor Economics,* cited previously.

proach wage equality for all plants in the industry. This is untypical, however, and diversity rather than equality is the general rule. The earnings of a particular worker, then, in addition to depending on occupation, industry, and geography, will depend on the particular company for which he works. This matter, however, must be left to the next chapter, where we analyze the factors shaping wage decisions at the plant level.

Worker characteristics

In the labor market of economic theory, a unit of labor power is just that. It makes no difference whether the owner of the labor power is white or black, male or female, young or old. In actuality, however, personal characteristics make a substantial difference in earning power. This is not due mainly to wage differences on the same job, but rather to the unequal accessibility of job opportunities to different categories of workers. Adult, male, white workers typically enjoy first claim on the highest-paid and most desirable occupations, while young people, women, and Negro workers are concentrated more heavily in the lower-paid jobs.

In 1960 the median income of male Negro workers was 76 per cent of that of male white workers in the North Central region, 73 per cent in the West, and 37 per cent in the South.[15] This is due mainly to the different occupational distribution of the two groups. In all regions Negro workers are concentrated in the lower manual occupations, and this is particularly true in the South. This means both lower hourly wage rates and less regular employment.

The position of Negro workers as regards employment opportunities and annual earnings has improved materially over the past generation. The high demand for labor during the war and immediate postwar years opened up to Negroes many types of work which had previously been denied them. Between 1940 and 1950 there was a strong movement out of agriculture, common labor, and household service into semiskilled factory jobs—not a long step, but at least a first step up the occupational ladder. While antidiscrimination sentiment and legislation may have had some effect, main credit must be given to the favorable economic environment arising from full employment.

There is little evidence on wage rates of men and women workers

[15] U.S. Department of Labor, *Monthly Labor Review* (December 1962), pp. 1359-1365.

on the same job in the United States. Evidence from other countries suggests that this sort of difference is usually small—perhaps not more than 10 per cent on average. It is not very feasible for an employer to maintain separate rate schedules for men and women workers, and unions typically insist on "equal pay for equal work."

For the most part, however, men and women do different types of work, and jobs which have become identified as "women's work" carry considerably lower wage rates than men's jobs. This is due partly to difference in job content. Manufacturing operations performed by women are typically light and low-skilled, while men do most of the work which is physically exhausting or requires long training. But women receive less partly because they are willing to work for less. Most women workers are either supplementary wage earners in a family or single people without dependents. The paycheck is not as critically important to them as it is to male family head. The supply curve of female labor is thus lower than that of male labor, and employers are able to pay women less than they would have to pay men of the same efficiency to do the same work.

This adverse position of women workers cuts in two directions. From one point of view, it seems unjust that a worker of standard efficiency should receive less simply because she is a woman rather than a man. But from another standpoint the fact that women can be paid less than men gives employers an incentive to hire women wherever possible. Willingness to work for less has been a major factor helping women to penetrate more and more areas of employment. If women were forced to demand the same wage level as men for each type of work, justice might be served but the expansion of employment opportunities for women would be less rapid.

Finally, differences in personal efficiency have an appreciable influence on earning power. Male, white workers of the same age with the same training will not work at the same pace or produce the same amount. Workers differ in intelligence level, muscular coordination, physical endurance, and willingness to exert sustained effort. This fact makes for wider wage differences among plants and industries than would be possible otherwise. It is common in any city to find some plants paying 25 per cent or more above others for the same type of work. The highest-wage plants should be able over the long run to attract, select, and retain workers of superior efficiency, while low-wage plants are forced to accept the leftovers. Thus the high-wage plants will not necessarily have higher labor costs *per unit of output,* and may conceivably have lower costs.

CONCLUDING COMMENTS

The following impressions remain from an examination of the national wage structure:

1. There are wide differences in earning power among manual workers. These differences have three main sources: differences in hourly wage rates on different jobs; differences in regularity of employment on various jobs; and differences in opportunity to get into high-income jobs. Women earn less than men, and Negro workers earn less than white workers partly because their employment opportunities are more restricted. This is a problem of labor mobility and employment practices rather than a wage problem.

2. Differences in hourly wage rates on different jobs in the United States are wider than in most other countries, and wider than one would expect in a static competitive economy. Both in the United States and other countries, however, there has been a tendency toward reduction of wage differences over the past two or three generations. Personal differences between workers on the same type of work in the same plant have been reduced by substitution of standard wage schedules for personal rates. Occupational differences have diminished considerably. Differences among plants in the same industry have diminished in many cases. Geographical and interindustry differences have proven most resistant to change.

3. Full employment is a powerful factor making for reduction of wage differences. A severe shortage of labor, such as existed in the United States during the 'forties, hits the lowest-wage occupations hardest. As they lose labor they are forced to raise wages disproportionately fast in an effort to overtake the higher-wage jobs. Full employment also tends to break down the barriers keeping women, Negroes, and other nonpreferred groups out of the better jobs. When employers find that the types of workers they prefer to hire are insufficient to man the plant, they will adjust their hiring specifica-

tions rather than remain short of labor. These side-effects of full employment provide an additional reason for rating it high on any list of national economic objectives.

4. The other major factor making for equalization of wage (and salary) levels has been the great broadening of educational opportunities over the past two generations. The bottlenecks through which labor is channeled to the more desirable and higher-paid occupations lie in the educational system. Enlargement of these bottlenecks is the most effective and radical remedy for such undesirable inequalities of earning power as still remain in our system.

5. Viewed broadly, the national wage structure is "rational" and understandable in economic terms. The relationship of different wage levels at a particular time, and major shifts in the wage structure over the course of time, can be analyzed quite effectively in terms of demand and supply schedules interacting in a market. This does not mean that the wage structure looks as it might in a perfectly competitive labor market. But even its abnormalities are capable of explanation in largely economic terms.

6. In Chapter 12 it was stated that unionism and collective bargaining have had only a limited effect on the national wage structure. This statement, which may have seemed dogmatic at the time, may now appear more justifiable. Speaking broadly, one can say that the larger the area of comparison the more difficult it becomes to distinguish any effect of collective bargaining. The clearest impact of collective bargaining is on relative wage rates and earnings of different workers in the same plant. There is considerable impact also on relative wage levels of different plants competing in the same product market. But when one looks at the broadest contours of the wage structure—geographical differences, interindustry differences, occupational differences—the specific effects of unionism diminish in importance. They are still visible here and there on the landscape, but they are overshadowed by the effects of economic change and labor mobility.

Discussion questions

1. How are relative wage rates for different occupations determined in a competitive labor market?

2. What are some of the reasons for the decline in differentials between skilled and unskilled workers over the last fifty years?

3. What kind of statistics would you need to discover whether there is a true wage differential between the Northern and Southern states?

4. Why will a comparison of two groups of workers in terms of annual earnings differ from a comparison in terms of hourly wage rates?

5. How can one explain the large wage difference between farm and factory workers?

6. Outline the main reasons for differences in wage rates for similar jobs:
(a) Within a single local area;
(b) Between Northern and Southern states;
(c) Between small cities and large cities;
(d) Between large and small plants.

7. "Legislation should be passed immediately providing that women shall be paid just as much as men would be paid for the same type of work." Discuss.

Selected reading

Garbarino, J. W., "A Theory of Interindustry Wage Variation," *Quarterly Journal of Economics*, LXIV (May 1950), pp. 282-305.

Johnson, D. Gale, "Comparability of Labor Capacities of Farm and Non-farm Labor," *American Economic Review*, XLIII (June 1953), pp. 296-313.

Knowles, K.G.J.C., and D. J. Robertson, "Differences Between the Wages of Skilled and Unskilled Workers, 1880-1950," *Bulletin of Oxford Institute of Statistics* (April 1951), pp. 109-127.

Lester, Richard A., "Southern Wage Differentials: Developments, Analysis, and Implications," *Southern Economic Journal* (April 1947), pp. 386-394.

Meij, J. L., ed., *Internal Wage Structure*. Amsterdam: North-Holland Publishing Co., 1963.

Miller, Herman P., *Income of the American People*. New York: John Wiley & Sons, Inc., 1955.

Ober, Harry, "Occupational Wage Differentials 1907-1947," *Monthly Labor Review*, LXVII (August 1948), pp. 127-133.

Phelps Brown, E. H., and Sheila V. Hopkins, "Seven Centuries of Building Wages," *Economica* (1955), pp. 195-206.

Reder, Melvin W., "Wage Differentials: Theory and Measurement," in *Aspects of Labor Economics*. Princeton: Princeton University Press, 1960.

Reynolds, Lloyd G., and Cynthia H. Taft, *The Evolution of Wage Structure*. New Haven: Yale University Press, 1956, chaps. 1, 12, and 13.

Robertson, D. J., *The Economics of Wages*. New York: St. Martin's Press, 1961.

Ross, Arthur M., and W. Goldner, "The Interindustry Wage Structure," *Quarterly Journal of Economics*, LXIV (May 1950), pp. 254-281.

19

Wage Determination
At The Plant Level

The wage statistics presented in previous chapters were averages for large groups of workers. These averages, while interesting and important, do not relate to decision-making units. No one in the economy is in a position to make decisions about the skilled-unskilled differential or the North-South differential. Primary wage determinations are usually made for a single plant or at most a single company. The only important exceptions are the regional or national collective bargaining agreements found in a number of industries.

In order to understand the detailed behavior of wages, then, one must get down to the grass roots and examine how wage decisions are made at the plant level. To what extent are these decisions shaped by supply and demand pressures in the labor market? How much latitude is there for management discretion, and how is this discretion exercised? Where there is a union in the plant, how is this likely to affect wage rates?

One must distinguish between decisions about the wage level of the plant as a whole and decisions about wage rates for particular jobs. These two types of decision will be examined in turn.

GENERAL WAGE LEVEL OF THE PLANT

In previous chapters we found the supply-demand approach helpful in explaining the national wage structure. We continue to use this approach as a starting point in analyzing wage decisions at the plant level.

The operation of market forces

Consider the following case: Company A is small, relative to the labor market area in which it is located. "Small" means small enough so that it can withdraw labor from other firms without their becoming conscious of this and retaliating by wage increases. The company has a certain plant, machinery, management, and production methods, which are assumed to remain unchanged as wages and employment are varied. We are considering, in other words, short-run rather than long-run adjustments.

We assume workable competition, though not necessarily perfect competition, in the labor market. Workers have adequate job information, they make rational calculations, and at least a certain proportion are willing to change employers in pursuit of economic advantage. Workers are coming into the market continually through layoff and discharge as well as through school leaving and entry to the labor force. So it is reasonable to suppose that Company A can increase its employment simply by offering jobs at the prevailing area wage level. If, on the other hand, it tries to pay less than this, its existing work force will dwindle away through transfer to other employers. If the area wage level for the kind of labor in question is OW, Company A's *labor supply curve* is shown by the horizontal line WW (Figure 14).

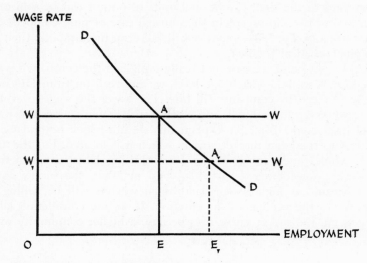

FIG. 14 *Wages and employment in the firm.*

How many workers will Company A be willing to hire at this wage rate? This decision depends on how much the employment of an additional worker adds to the company's revenues. It depends, that is, on the *marginal revenue product* of labor. Company A will expand employment to the point at which *the marginal revenue product* of labor is equal to the wage rate. Why? Because so long as each additional worker's revenue product is greater than his wage, the company gains by employing him. But if things reached a stage at which the worker's revenue product was below his wage, the company would be losing. So it will not go this far, but instead will stop at the point of exact equality.

Suppose that for the wage OW this point is reached with employment of $WA = OE$. And suppose that for a lower wage OW_1 the proper employment level is $W_1A_1 = OE_1$. By making this calculation for all possible wage rates and joining up the A points, we can trace out the curve DD, which is the company's *labor demand curve*.

Why does DD slope downward to the right, i.e., why does labor's marginal revenue product decline as more workers are employed? There are two reasons. First, as more workers are combined with unchanged plant and equipment, each additional worker will add less to the plant's physical output. True, this may not happen for some time, but it is certain to happen eventually. Second, if the company sells its product under conditions of monopoly, oligopoly, or monopolistic competition, its product demand curve will slope downward to the right. Additional units of output can be sold only at a lower price. So except in the unusual case of pure competition, labor's marginal revenue product will fall even more rapidly than its marginal physical product.

Up to this point we have not really explained the company's wage level. Once we know the wage level, we can read off from DD how many workers the company will hire. The lower the wage level, the more workers will be hired, and vice versa. But where does the wage level itself come from? To explain this we must look beyond Company A to the labor market area in which it is located. For the area as a whole, one can assume a forward-rising labor supply curve. If we are considering a particular kind of labor, the supply curve rises because at higher wages additional workers will be willing to transfer to the occupation in question. If we are considering labor in general, the supply curve rises because a higher community wage level will attract some labor from other areas; and even people already in the area may respond to higher wages by entering the labor force in greater numbers, working overtime, and so on.

Now we have already seen that, at a given wage, each firm in the community will have a definite demand for labor. By adding these together we can get the total demand for labor at that wage. And by doing this for all possible wages we can derive a *community demand curve for labor*. The intersection of this with the *community labor supply curve* determines the *community wage level*. Labor supply conditions in the area, each employer's demand curve for labor, and the wage level form an interdependent system.

There are several implications of this analysis. First, in any area at any time there is a prevailing wage level, and each employer must pay this level in order to hold his labor force. He may pay more if he chooses or if the union compels him to pay above the area level. But he must not pay less. The fact that some companies seem able to pay less and still survive over long periods is one of the puzzling features of actual labor markets which we must examine in a moment.

Second, the community wage level is not a static thing. Demand curves for labor are rising over the long run because of capital accumulation and technical progress; and so the course of wage levels is steadily upward. This puts inexorable pressure on the individual employer. Our firm in Figure 14 must be inventive enough to keep its DD curve moving constantly upward to the right. Otherwise it will eventually be swamped by the rising wage tide and will find itself out of business.

Third, market reasoning implies that the employer who is willing to pay the prevailing wage can expand and contract employment at will. The firm's labor supply curve is horizontal at the community wage level. This conclusion seems generally correct, though partly for the extraneous reason that the economy is typically operating below full employment. An expanding employer may be able to get sufficient labor by dipping into the pool of unemployed, including new entrants to the labor market, without needing to attract workers already employed in other firms. It would be necessary to bid up wages to attract labor only if there were full employment, and if the firm in question were large relative to the area. But by the same token aggressive wage bidding by a large firm would invite retaliatory action by other employers, and so is not likely to be undertaken.

The relation is similar to that among oligopolists in product markets, where each firm is free in principle to take independent price action, but is normally deterred from doing so by the certainty of retaliation.[1]

Some complications in actual wage determination

We know that in actuality employers do not just take a thermometer reading of the community wage level and act accordingly. There is scope for judgment in wage setting. Texts on personnel administration give much space to criteria for company wage policy. Companies maintain statistical staffs to collect and analyze wage information and to prepare guide lines for management decision. Top management officials and boards of directors deliberate at length on wage policy. It seems unlikely that management would go to this trouble and expense unless there were real scope for management discretion.

Reality differs in two major respects from the simple model of wage determination outlined above. First, a company does not pay a single rate of wages. It pays a large number of different rates for specialized kinds of labor. Some of these occupations—common laborers, maintenance mechanics, standard clerical occupations—may be in demand by other employers in the area, in which case their wages will be subject to the market pressures just described. But other jobs may be specific to the company in question, and for these jobs there is no "outside market," only an "inside market." The company must still set wage rates for them on one basis or another. The techniques which have been developed for evaluating the worth of a job where no market evaluation exists will be described later in this chapter. Meanwhile, we continue to speak as though the company paid a single wage rate for a single kind of labor, for which there is a community market.

The second difficulty is that the vertical and horizontal axes of Figure 14 do not measure all the variables involved in wage decisions. The price of labor is not just the hourly wage rate. It is the hourly

---

[1] So while there is a rising labor supply curve for an *area*, I am not convinced that the concept of a rising labor supply curve to the *firm* has much explanatory value (except perhaps in the unusual case of a company town where the company *is* the area). The portion of the supposed supply curve *below* the company's existing wage is irrelevant in any event, since wage cutting is not a practical proposition. Looking upward from the existing wage, labor supply will usually be elastic because of underemployment. In any event, a substantial employer will prefer to move up along the community labor supply curve by cooperative action with other employers rather than engage in a "wage war" with uncertain results.

rate, plus the number of hours of work normally available, plus various income supplements, plus a wide variety of nonpecuniary conditions of employment. Similarly for the employment axis. The employer who buys an hour of labor is not buying anything as definite as a ton of coal. What he has bought depends on what he can get out of it. Employers differ in their ability to extract output from labor; and workers differ in their individual capacity to produce.

In a purely formal way, one can get around these difficulties by definition. One can redefine the vertical axis to mean, not hourly wages rates, but total job attractiveness. On the horizontal axis, one can lay out units of labor of standard efficiency, thus getting around differences in management and worker ability. But these logical tricks do not help very much, because now the intersection of the demand and supply curves no longer defines a unique level of money wages.

Let us look a bit further at this second category of complications. On the demand side, economic reasoning usually assumes that the same workers with the same equipment will always produce the same physical output. This amounts to assuming that management is working as hard as possible and is operating the plant with maximum efficiency. But this is not always true. One finds many cases in which a company, faced with union pressure or minimum wage legislation, has found ways of tightening efficiency and saving money so that it could afford a wage higher than it previously thought possible. This "shock effect" may not operate indefinitely, but it can be quite effective the first few times it is applied.

There are substantial differences also in the personal efficiency of labor. If one plant pays 20 per cent more than another, but is able by so doing to recruit workers who are 20 per cent more productive, then its labor cost per unit of output will not be any higher. This doubtless accounts in part for the observed differences in company wage levels in the same labor market. Ideally, it should be possible to apply efficiency tests to the workers being compared and to discover whether the wage differences are offset, in whole or in part, by differences in quality of labor. Little has yet been done in this direction, however, and the issue remains moot.

On the supply side, the employer can change the amount of labor available to him, not only by changing wage rates, but also by changing other terms of employment, altering his hiring preferences, or changing his recruiting efforts.

The hourly wage rate, while important, is only one element influencing the attractiveness of a company's jobs. A low hourly rate may be offset in part by longer hours and overtime pay which increase the weekly take-home. Fringe benefits, tempo of work, physical demands of the job, working conditions, regularity of employment, promotion policies and opportunities, all enter in. A company may have to pay unusually high wages because some of these other conditions are unattractive; and if it wants to attract more labor at the same wage, it may be able to do so by altering nonwage conditions.

Employers typically have hiring preferences based on age, sex, color, education, and other personal characteristics. A company with a wage level which permits it to be choosy may decide to hire only male, white workers, with high school diplomas, within certain height and weight limits, below a certain age ceiling, able to pass certain physical and psychological tests, and so on. Some of these things are related to efficiency, but others simply provide what management considers "a nice bunch of people to work with." But preferences can be adapted to market conditions. If the labor market tightens and the number of applicants who meet the customary standards declines, the company can either raise its wage level or reduce its hiring requirements.

Another possibility is to alter the effort spent in labor recruitment. If plenty of labor is available, the company can sit back and rely on the flow of people to the plant gate. If labor is scarce, the company may have to go out actively into the market, engage in newspaper and radio advertising, make contact with the employment service and private employment agencies, spread the word through its present employees, put on more personnel staff to interview and screen candidates. This costs money; but spending money in this way can shift the labor supply curve.

The employer is thus working with several variables rather than with wages alone. The point has been well put by Hildebrand:

For instance, suppose that the local labor market becomes progressively tighter. To avoid raising wage rates, the employer may intensify his recruiting efforts, perhaps improving non-pecuniary conditions as well. In some cases he may be able to simplify certain jobs, breaking them up into multiples requiring a lower grade of labor. If necessary, he may reduce his standards for hiring and for promotion, deliberately accepting candidates of lower efficiency on the premise that the enforced rise in unit labor costs will be temporary, that poorer workers can later be laid off or demoted. For the same underlying reasons, he may tolerate some rise in costs of turnover, and some fall of efficiency among the already employed, the second expressed by increases in absenteeism, tardiness, and bad work, and possibly by slow-down tactics.

Together, these responses serve as expansion joints for absorbing the shock of a change in market forces, one that enables the employer to put off raising wage rates, mainly by tolerating a decline in labor efficiency and a rise in indirect employment costs. Although unit labor cost will still rise, to some extent its course will be reversible when the market loosens up. By contrast, a rise in wage rates for practical purposes is irreversible.[2]

In speaking of tightening and loosening of the labor market, we have introduced by implication another factor not considered in the simplest theories of wage determination. Wage theory, like micro-economic theory in general, typically starts from the assumption of a stable, fully-employed economy. But companies actually live in a world of cyclical upswings and downswings.

Among other things, this means that severe employer competition for labor is intermittent rather than continuous. At the peak of a boom, when the pool of unemployed has almost vanished and one company can gain workers only at the expense of another, there is strong pressure for each company to keep in step with others on hiring rates. In a serious depression, this pressure largely disappears. A company can now recruit from the unemployed, most of whom will accept any wage which is sufficiently above their unemployment compensation benefits. Within wide limits, each company can go its own way on wages, and the variation of hiring rates tends to increase. The fact that there is considerable unemployment in the American economy at most times permits greater variation of company wage levels than could exist under continuous full employment.

THE NATURE OF WAGE POLICY

The variation of company wage levels for what looks like the same kind of labor is one of the most familiar facts of labor markets. Studies of prevailing rates for selected occupations in many cities of the country were carried out by the Bureau of Labor Statistics for the National War Labor Board during the years 1942-45. The results of these studies have been summarized by Lester.[3] The average spread

---

[2] George H. Hildebrand, "External Influences and the Determination of the Internal Wage Structure," in L. J. Meij, ed., *op. cit.*, pp. 277-278.

[3] Richard A. Lester, "Wage Diversity and Its Theoretical Implications," *Review of Economic Statistics*, XXVIII (August 1946), pp. 152-159.

in straight-time hourly earnings within an area was found to be about 50 per cent of the low rate; that is, if the lowest rate was $1.00 per hour, the highest rate would typically be around $1.50. There were numerous cases, however, in which the highest plant was paying over 50 per cent above the lowest plant.

During the 'fifties the Bureau of Labor Statistics made additional studies of wage rates for key occupations in a large number of cities throughout the country. An analysis of the data for ten northern cities shows considerable variation of rates for the same job in the same city, particularly in the case of low-skilled jobs.[4] For all the skilled occupations studied, the quartile deviation averaged 11.1 per cent, i.e., one-half the rates for the occupation fell within a range of 11.1 per cent on either side of the median. In the case of semiskilled occupations, however, the quartile deviation was 24.3 per cent. The outside limits of the range of rates were considerably wider, of course, and it is not difficult to find cases in which the rate offered by the highest-paying company was double the lowest rate offered in the area.

These studies are difficult to interpret because of a lack of complete comparability in the data. Even though different plants use the same job title, the work may differ a good deal from plant to plant. "Welding" is not the same thing in an aircraft plant and a shipyard; and even "common labor" is not as common as the name implies. Moreover, as we have already noted, workers differ in personal quality, and these differences may be positively correlated with company wage levels. The crude wage differentials would need to be corrected for these factors to obtain a measurement of true wage differentials. Most experienced observers, however, are of the opinion that there are substantial intercompany wage differences even on an adjusted basis.

The typical manager, then, thinks of his company as occupying a certain rank in the wage hierarchy of the area. It "pays the best wages in town," or it is about at the area average, or it is toward the bottom of the area range. Management may simply try to maintain this position, moving up with the area average but not trying to move any faster. Or at times management may conclude that the company could gain by lagging behind or getting ahead of general wage movements, thus changing its relative position. Why do dif-

---

[4] R. L. Raimon, "The Indeterminateness of Wages of Semi-skilled Workers," *Industrial and Labor Relations Reviewer,* VI (January 1953), pp. 180-94.

ferent companies occupy these different positions? And why may a company sometimes decide to change, or be forced to change, its relative ranking? These questions come close to the heart of wage policy as viewed from the operating level.

The company's position in product and labor markets set outside limits, sometimes narrow, sometimes wide, within which management must navigate. There is at any time a maximum and a minimum feasible wage level—a minimum below which it could not hold enough labor to meet production schedules, a maximum above which it could not go for budgetary reasons. If all other items in the estimated budget for the year—sales receipts, raw material costs, and so on—are given, there is some maximum wage bill above which the company would suffer operating losses. The fact that these limits exist does not mean that they are always clearly defined in management's thinking. Management will not work hard to discover their precise position unless it feels that the company is close to one or the other limit and in danger of being pushed beyond it. Management may also work harder to marshal the facts if confronted by union demands than it would under nonunion conditions.

The position of the maximum and minimum points depends on the period of time which is taken into account. The plant may be able to maintain a very low wage level for a few weeks or months, particularly if there is serious unemployment. Over a longer period this wage level would cause it to lose too many workers, and a higher wage level is necessary. Similar considerations apply to the maximum point. Wage rates could be set very high for a short time, since the company could temporarily neglect maintenance and repairs on the plant, pass dividends, and even draw on its cash reserves to meet the wage bill. The firm cannot do these things, however, if it wishes to continue in operation year in and year out. It must at least break even over the long run. If it wishes to expand its operations in future, a positive rate of profit will be necessary, and the wage maximum will be still lower.

The longer the period considered, the lower will be the wage maximum and the higher the wage minimum, and consequently the smaller will be the distance between them. The controversy between "economic" theories of wage determination and "administrative" or "bargaining" theories turns in good measure on this point. Bargaining theorists assert correctly that over short periods the gap between the maximum and minimum points may be so wide that economic theories focused on determination of these points are not very helpful, and one needs some explanation of where the wage rate will settle within the range of discretion. Economic theorists assert, equally correctly, that over longer periods the limits set by economic forces lie closer together and are thus more compelling on the parties. The time factor is also an important reason for differences between union and management positions in collective bargaining. Union officers are apt to lean heavily on what the company could afford to pay in the short run under optimistic assumptions about future sales and profits. Management will usually have a genuinely lower estimate of its wage maximum, partly because it makes conservative estimates of future profits for safety reasons, and partly because it gives greater weight to the long-run expansion needs of the enterprise.

The minimum and maximum wage levels are influenced by quite different sets of forces—the minimum by conditions in the local labor market, the maximum by conditions in markets for the company's products. We are back, in short, to supply and demand in modified form. The wage minimum will be influenced by such things as the rates paid by other companies in the area for comparable work, the level of unemployment in the area, whether other companies' needs for labor are increasing or declining, whether this company plans to increase its employment and how rapidly, and the company's customary wage position in the area. A company which has long been a wage leader in a community is under greater pressure to continue paying high wages than a company which has customarily been near the bottom.

The maximum wage which the company can afford is influenced by industry characteristics such as elasticity of demand for the industry's products, whether product demand is rising or falling, importance of labor costs relative to other costs, and whether pricing is competitive or controlled by tacit agreement. A second important factor is the relative efficiency of the company within its industry. In any industry one usually finds substantial differences in the unit production costs of different companies. An efficient, low-cost company has a higher wage maximum and greater latitude for wage policy than a high-cost company barely able to survive.

The fact that the company's wage minimum and wage maximum are determined by different sets of forces means that there is no necessary connection between them. One finds situations in which the maximum is so far above the minimum that the minimum is of no practical importance. A modern, efficient steel fabricating plant located in a Southern town where it is the sole or leading employer might be in this position. At the other extreme, the minimum and maximum points may virtually coincide, leaving management with very little discretion. A shoe or furniture factory located in Detroit or Pittsburgh might find itself in this position. In practice, industries with low wage-paying ability would avoid these high-wage areas. If a company's wage maximum actually falls below its minimum for any considerable period, it is on its way to extinction.

The more interesting cases are those in which the company's wage maximum is well above the minimum because it is in a profitable and expanding industry, or because it is particularly efficient within its industry, or because it is located in a relatively low-wage area. A company in this happy position will often set a wage level considerably higher than the minimum at which it could just "get by." Slichter has pointed out that "the average hourly earnings of male unskilled labor tends to be high where the net income after taxes is a high percentage of sales. . . . The high correlation between sales margins and the average hourly earnings of common labor . . . reinforces the view that wages, within a considerable range, reflect managerial discretion, that where managements can easily pay high wages they tend to do so, and that where managements are barely breaking even they tend to keep wages down." [5]

Managers of profitable enterprises apparently share some of the profits with employees by setting a higher wage level than is strictly necessary for recruitment purposes. But why should management do this? Is such a policy not treason to the stockholders? Why not maximize profits by paying as little as possible?

A high-wage policy has numerous advantages, some of which even have cash value to the company. It simplifies the recruitment problem. Even though the company might be able to get enough workers at a lower wage level, it can get them faster and with less persuasion at higher wages. This is a particularly important consideration if the company is expanding and wants to be certain of avoiding bottlenecks in labor supply. A high-wage company can also establish strict hiring specifications designed to fill the plant with "a nice class of worker." It can insist on better than average efficiency and perform-

---

[5] Sumner H. Slichter, "Notes on the Structure of Wages," *Review of Economics and Statistics*, XXXII (February 1950), pp. 81-92.

ance on the job, so that higher wages do not cause a proportionate increase in unit labor costs. Most managers doubtless enjoy the good repute which they gain by paying high wages, both with their own employees and in the community generally. A high wage level also has public relations value for the company and helps to ward off criticism and attack. Different managements will evaluate these benefits differently. Some will pay only a little more than they have to, others will pay considerably more. There is considerable scope here for differences of judgment, long-range strategy, and personal preference.

Individual managements are not completely free to make their own judgment of proper wage level. They will usually be under pressure from other companies in the industry not to pay too little, and from other companies in the area not to pay too much. Adam Smith commented that "masters are always and everywhere in a sort of tacit, but constant and uniform combination, not to raise the wages of labor above their actual rate. To violate this combination is everywhere a most unpopular action, and a sort of reproach to a master among his neighbors and equals." An employer who gets too far above the area wage level is accused of "upsetting the market," "pirating labor," and so on. One employer told the writer that if he got more than 15 per cent above the area wage level he was in trouble with other employers, while if he fell more than 15 per cent below the area level he was in trouble over labor supply.

It is also regarded as faintly unethical to fall too far below the wage level of other companies in the same industry. A company which is much below the industry wage level is in a position to undercut others on prices, unless its lower wages are offset by obsolete plant, managerial inefficiency, or other disadvantages. Leaders of the industry, sensitive to this competitive threat, will urge low-wage companies to come up to the industry level and not to engage in "unfair competition."

A company in a high-wage industry but located in a low-wage community is often caught between these two fires. If it conforms to the industry it will be far out of line with the area, and vice versa. Different managements will reach different compromises on this point, depending a good deal on the structure of the industry in question. In oligopolistic industries where each producer is highly visible and cooperation in pricing and other competitive practices is essential, the industry wage level will have dominant influence. Steel, automobile, tire, glass, and petroleum plants are high-wage plants everywhere, and if this puts them above the area level, so much the worse for the area. In small-scale, highly competitive, and relatively anonymous industries, on the other hand, each company may hew closer to the area wage level and gain whatever advantage it can by so doing.

THE IMPACT OF COLLECTIVE BARGAINING

This approach to wage determination leaves room for union pressure as well as management discretion. There is no question that unions have on occasion forced companies to move up closer to their wage maximum than they would have done voluntarily. This is particularly likely to be true of the plant belonging to a high-wage industry but located in a low-wage community. In this case management might prefer to undercut the industry wage level and pay something closer to local standards. Union policy, however, leans in the direction of equalizing the wage levels of companies competing in the same product market. When an industry is organized, therefore, companies which previously enjoyed the advantage of low-wage location are apt to find themselves forced up to a uniform level. Assuming that these companies are as efficient as their competitors, the main effect will be simply a transfer from profits to wages. There may also be some effect on industrial location over the long run, since a company can no longer reduce its wage bill by locating in a low-wage area.

One can also find numerous cases in which a union has enforced greater efficiency via the shock effect, and thus raised the company's wage maximum. The process may involve some reduction in employment, but will not necessarily do so. Many types of waste reduction and methods improvement can be carried out with little effect on employment.

There is probably a tendency, however, for unions to be too optimistic about wage-raising possibilities and to push an occasional employer over the cliff by inadvertence. It has already been pointed out that the wage maximum of the firm is an estimated figure, based on forecasts of future sales, costs, and profits. Union leaders are usually more optimistic than management in their estimate of future profits. They also have considerable faith in management's ability to offset wage increases by improvements in methods. They are unimpressed by management pleas that a proposed wage increase will bankrupt the company and force it to close its doors. They have heard this tale many times before; yet after the wage increase was made, the company usually managed to survive and was often as profitable as before.

This raises a genuine problem of how a union can be convinced that a plant really has reached the limit of its ability to pay. There are times when a wage increase actually would put a company out of operation. How can the union be convinced of this fact? The answer is probably that it can be convinced only if management has previously established such good relations with union leaders that they have confidence in management's word. Another requirement is that management be willing to support its case by giving union officials a full statement of the company's financial position. If management asks the union to forego an otherwise legitimate wage increase solely on the grounds of the company's inability to pay, union leaders are entitled to insist that inability to pay be adequately documented. Unless the leaders have adequate evidence on this point they are in an indefensible position before their members, who are likely to charge that the leaders have "sold out" to management and to strike for higher wages anyway. There are numerous instances in which companies have opened their books to the union for this purpose with very good results.

Where the union is convinced that a company actually has reached its wage maximum and that the maximum cannot be raised further by management effort, it will usually forego demands which would produce a plant shutdown. Union members are likely to favor this course, preferring employment at present wage levels to the hardships and risks of unemployment. National union officials are often reluctant to permit a company to pay wages below the industry level, but in the end they are likely to be guided by membership sentiment. One can find an occasional case in which union wage pressure has put a company out of business, but these are quite exceptional.

The extent of union influence on a company's wage level is difficult to judge. Union influence is presumably to be measured by the wage increases won through collective bargaining *minus* the wage increases which management would have chosen or been forced to make under nonunion conditions. The size of this second quantity is conjectural, and so any conclusion about union influence is bound to be a matter of informed judgment rather than measurement. In many companies, however, both union and management officials would agree that unionism has made some difference.

Looking broadly at the economy as a whole, the writer's judgment would be that the pressures of labor demand and supply are the most important influence on wage decisions. Management policies operating within the range of discretion left by the market probably rank next in importance, with union pressures ranking in third place. Many economists, however, would rank union influence higher than this, and only further study will reveal the truth of the matter.

DETERMINATION OF OCCUPATIONAL WAGE RATES

We proceed now to the second major complication in actual wage determination, the fact that a company usually employs many kinds of labor at many different wage rates. Some kinds of labor may be in general demand throughout the area and hence have an "outside market." This is apt to be true for jobs at the bottom and top of the skill ladder, for unskilled labor on one hand and skilled maintenance craftsmen on the other. It seems also to be true of standard office occupations. Turnover of women in these occupations is quite high, a new crop comes into the market each year through high school graduation, and the new graduates are able to get good information about company salary levels from high school vocational advisers, the public employment service, and shopping around. This puts pressure on each employer to remain within a reasonable distance of prevailing area rates.[6]

But the outside market impinges only at certain points in the company wage structure. There is a great array of semiskilled and skilled production jobs which are specific to a particular industry or even a particular company. Workers are usually not hired into these jobs from the outside, but work up from within the company on a seniority basis. It is not easy for them to transfer to other companies, since the same job may not exist elsewhere, and since other companies also prefer to promote from within. Thus there is an "inside market" for these jobs, but no outside market. The precise

---

[6] For an interesting analysis of competition and salary determination for certain clerical occupations in Boston, see George P. Shultz, "A Nonunion Market for Whitecollar Labor," in *Aspects of Labor Economics*, pp. 107-146.

ranking of jobs, and the determination of proper wage differences between them, becomes a matter for administrative discretion and collective bargaining.

A pattern of job rates develops in the first instance through shop custom. Certain jobs come to be regarded as related to each other on the basis of physical contiguity, sequence of production operations, or a learning sequence in which workers progress from lower to higher rank in a work team. Workers and foremen develop ideas about how much more one of these jobs should pay than another. Once established, these wage relationships tend to persist through custom. When asked to explain why their wage schedule looks as it does, most plant managers will say, "We have always done it that way," or, "It just grew up that way."

Reliance on custom alone, however, is not always satisfactory. It is particularly unsatisfactory as an answer to workers or union officials who contend that a particular rate is too low and should be raised. During the past twenty years or so, therefore, management has turned increasingly to systems of "job rating" or "job evaluation" which purport to provide a scientific basis for determining the relative worth of different jobs. There are several reasons for the popularity of these systems. Some managers believe that they provide an absolutely fair and incontrovertible basis for determining relative wage rates. Even those who recognize that no wage scale can presume to absolute justice seek the definite standards provided by job evaluation because they make for administrative uniformity and simplicity in handling wage matters. Job evaluation provides a yardstick by which management can judge the merit of complaints by workers or the union; at least, it enables management to answer these complaints and to provide a rational explanation of its wage decisions.

Job evaluation procedures

Job evaluation procedures cannot be discussed in any detail here and the student interested in them should consult the standard works on the subject.[7] In general, however, the procedure is as follows:

---

[7] See, for example, J. W. Riegel, *Wage Determination* (Ann Arbor: University of Michigan Press, 1937); Z. C. Dickinson, *Compensating Industrial Effort* (New York: Ronald Press, 1937), chap. 11; C. W. Lytle, *Job Evaluation Methods* (New York: Ronald Press, 1946); F. H. Johnson, R. W. Boise, Jr., and Dudley Pratt, *Job Evaluation* (New York: John H. Wiley and Sons, Inc., 1946).

One must first select a set of "factors" or criteria to be used in rating jobs, and set a maximum point score for each factor. An example is the widely used rating scale of the National Metal Trades Association. The factors used and the maximum possible score for each are as follows: education (70), experience (110), initiative and ingenuity (70), physical effort (50), mental and visual effort (25), responsibility for equipment and processes (25), responsibility for material or product (25), responsibility for safety of others (25), responsibility for work of others (25), working conditions (50), and work hazards (25). More briefly, these factors may be summarized as: education, experience and skill (250), responsibility (100), effort (75), and working conditions (75). This relatively heavy weighting of skill and light weighting of effort is characteristic of most of the other rating scales in current use.

The next step is to make a careful description of each job in the plant, and to rate each job in terms of the selected factors. The rating applies to *the job itself,* not to the workers who happen to be doing the job at the time. The result is a total point score for each job, which enables one to rank all jobs in the plant in order of importance. The next step is usually to group the different jobs into a limited number of brackets or "labor grades." Thus, jobs with a score of 450 to 500 may be put in labor grade 1, jobs with a score of 400 to 450 in labor grade 2, and so on down. In some systems the numbering is the other way round, so that the *lowest* jobs are in labor grade 1.

The actual work of job rating is more complex and controversial than this simple outline would suggest. Many different people have an interest and a voice in the evaluation of each job—the workers on the job, their foremen, the shop steward (in unionized plants), the plant superintendent, the industrial engineers making the survey, personnel officials, and others. There may be marked differences of opinion among these people. If the rating of a job comes out very much above or below its present position in the plant wage structure, there is likely to be criticism and argument. If the rating of a job puts it on the borderline between two labor grades, which may mean a difference of several cents an hour in pay, the workers and even the foreman will try to add a few points on somewhere to push it over the line into the higher grade. The final rating of each job is not a mathematical measurement, but a practical compromise among the judgments of the different people concerned.

It is necessary next to decide what shall be the highest and lowest wage rates in the plant.[8] What rate shall be paid for, say, class 1 toolmakers, and what shall be paid for sweepers, laborers, and janitors? In a nonunion plant, this decision is usually made on a comparative basis, i.e., by surveying the rates currently paid for class 1 toolmakers and laborers by other plants in the area or industry. Under trade unionism, of course, determination of the high and low rates becomes a matter of bargaining, though rates in other plants will probably still be used as data for bargaining purposes.

It must be decided, finally, how rapidly the rates for intermediate labor grades shall rise, i.e., what shall be the shape of the "rate curve." Two quite different rate curves are shown in Figure 15. Employers tend to favor a schedule similar to Curve B, under which rates rise rather slowly for the first few labor grades in which the bulk of the labor force is concentrated, and then more rapidly in the higher labor grades where there are few workers.

As a practical matter, the decision will be influenced a good deal by the shape of the existing wage schedule of the plant. At some stage in the procedure, it is usual to take the existing rate for each job, chart it against the point score for the job, and fit a curve to the scatter diagram thus obtained. The rate curve finally adopted under the job evaluation system will not necessarily have just the same shape as this empirical curve, but is likely to resemble it rather closely. Custom and established wage relationships provide a powerful argument; and if the present wage structure of the plant resembles Curve B, management is unlikely to agree to a new schedule resembling Curve A.

Whatever the shape of the new rate curve, it will turn out that some jobs are currently receiving less than they are entitled to under the new schedule, while other jobs are being paid more than they should be. The accepted way of adjusting existing job rates to the new schedule is as follows: workers on jobs which are currently underpaid are raised immediately to the rate provided for the job in the new schedule; the rates of workers now on overpaid jobs are left unchanged, but new workers on these jobs must be hired at the

<hr>

[8] The company may also select several intermediate jobs which exist in other plants in the area, so that there is an "outside market" for them. A survey is made of the wage rates being paid by other companies for these jobs, and the average wage for each job determined. These averages, or "peg points," can then be used as a guide in determining the company's own rate structure.

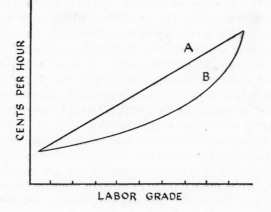

FIG. 15   *Occupational rate curves for a plant.*

lower rates provided in the new schedule. As the old workers leave, retire, or are transferred to higher-rated jobs, the earnings of all workers in the plant are gradually brought into alignment with the new wage schedule.

It is clear from this brief description that rate-setting based on job evaluation is not "scientific" in the sense of mathematical precision. Judgment must be exercised at each step in the procedure—the choice of rating factors, the assignment of the point weights to each factor, the actual description and rating of jobs, the determination of the top and bottom of the wage structure, and the determination of the shape of the rate curve between these points. The judgments of different individuals on each point are bound to differ somewhat, and the final outcome is a working compromise. Job evaluation does, however, make the exercise of judgment more deliberate and systematic than it might be without definite rules of procedure.

Some of the most interesting problems of job evaluation arise in the course of administering an evaluated wage structure after it has been installed. A particular kind of worker becomes scarce, and the market rate for this job rises above the rate provided by the evaluated system. Shall the company continue to adhere to the evaluated rate, or shall it pay whatever is necessary to get workers? Again, a key worker threatens to leave the company unless his rate is raised, which can be done only by reclassifying his job into a higher labor grade. Shall this be done, in violation of job evaluation standards, or shall the company adhere to principle and lose the worker? The industrial engineers in charge of installing and managing the job evaluation system will usually urge that the evaluated rates be adhered to at all costs. Unless the purity of the system is maintained, they argue, it will soon become riddled with exceptions and its original advantages will be lost. Production officials, however, are inclined to regard this argument as "theoretical" and to pay whatever rates are necessary to attract and retain workers.

Another difficulty in the day-to-day administration of job evaluation is the fact that the characteristics of jobs in the plant are continually changing. This makes it necessary to rerate certain jobs from time to time. Since the tendency of modern industry is to make most jobs simpler and easier with the passage of time, usually more jobs are rerated downwards than upwards. The workers on the jobs which are to be down-graded naturally resent such action and resist it to the best of their ability, and management sometimes takes the easy course of overlooking the new ratings and leaving the previous wage rates intact. The result is a gradual accumulation of exceptions to the system.

Unions have been skeptical of job evaluation for reasons noted in Chapter 10. They feel that it tends to freeze the wage structure too rigidly, to reduce the role of collective bargaining, and to restore the setting of job rates to unilateral management control. Unions typically resist the introduction of new job evaluation plans. Where a plan already exists, however, they will usually work under it while at the same time insisting on their right to bargain over the structure of the system and the rating of specific jobs. In a few cases the union has cooperated actively with management in designing a new evaluation program. The outstanding example is the rationalization of wage rates in basic steel, carried out jointly by the United Steelworkers and the major steel companies during the late 'forties.[9] Here the union secured reduction of an unmanageable load of grievances over wage inequities, some over-all increase in earnings for its members, a standard wage structure applicable throughout the industry, and a gradual phasing out of regional wage differences.

---

[9] For a detailed analysis of this case, see Jack Stieber, *The Steel Industry Wage Structure* (Cambridge: Harvard University Press, 1959).

Discussion questions

1. "The price which a company will pay for labor is determined, like any other price, by the interplay of supply and demand forces in the market." Appraise the validity of this statement under nonunion conditions.

2. Statistical surveys show considerable variation in company wage levels for the same type of work in the same locality. How would you explain these findings?

3. Why will the maximum and minimum possible wage levels for a company lie closer together in the long run than the short run?

4. Give several examples of situations in which you would expect that:

(a) the company's maximum and minimum wage levels would lie very close together;

(b) there would be a large gap between the maximum and minimum levels.

5. What considerations are likely to have greatest weight in a management's thinking about wage policy?

Selected reading

Baker, Helen, and John M. True, *The Operation of Job Evaluation Plans.* Princeton: Princeton University Press, 1947.

Gomberg, William A., *A Trade Union Analysis of Time Study*, 2nd ed. Englewood Cliffs, N.J.: Prentice-Hall, Inc., 1955.

Lester, Richard A., *Company Wage Policies*. Princeton: Princeton University Industrial Relations Section, 1948.

————, *Hiring Practices and Labor Competition*. Princeton: Princeton University Industrial Relations Section, 1954.

Nadworny, Milton J., *Scientific Management and the Unions.* Cambridge: Harvard University Press, 1955.

Reynolds, Lloyd G., *The Structure of Labor Markets*. New York: Harper & Row, Publishers, 1951.

Slichter, S. H., J. J. Healy, and E. R. Livernash, *The Impact of Collective Bargaining on Management*. Washington: Brookings Institution, 1960.

Stieber, Jack, *The Steel Industry Wage Structure*. Cambridge: Harvard University Press, 1959.

Taylor, George W., and Frank C. Pierson, eds., *New Concepts in Wage Determination.* New York: McGraw-Hill Book Company, Inc., 1957.

See also the references following Chapter 18.

20

Family Income, Inequality,
And Poverty

The last three chapters have dealt with the factors determining the general level of real wages and the elaborate structure of wage rates for particular occupations. From the standpoint of allocation and use of labor resources, it is wage *rates* which are important. From the standpoint of human welfare, however, it is monthly and annual *family* income which really matters.

The income of a *family* unit is quite a different matter from the wage rate paid to an individual. If the head of a family unit has a high wage rate, this is likely to make for high family income. If the wage earner is employed only irregularly, however, annual income may be quite low. Many family units have no wage earner because of death, disability, or other reasons. Most families have one wage earner; but some have two, three, or even more, which of course swells the size of the family income. Another important consideration is that the number of people who have to be supported out of the family income varies from one to a dozen or more. An income which is adequate for two or three people will be quite inadequate for ten or twelve.

The upshot is that one cannot tell much about the adequacy of family incomes in the United States by looking at the wage structure. It is necessary to make a direct approach to the problem. In this chapter we shall examine the available information on family incomes with a number of questions in mind. How equal or unequal is the distribution of family incomes in the United States at present? Has inequality been increasing or diminishing in recent decades, and why? Does income inequality still constitute a serious problem and, if so, what might be done about it? How many families in the country are still below a decent minimum standard of living? Who are these families and where are they? What could be done to improve their situation?

DISTRIBUTION OF FAMILY INCOMES

The Census Bureau and the Federal Reserve Board make frequent sample surveys of household incomes from which estimates can be made for the population as a whole. In 1961, families living together had a median income of about $6,500. In addition, however, there were about eleven million individuals not living with relatives, and these people had a median income of less than $2,000. The average for this group is low because many of them are young people just entering the labor market at low starting rates, or older people with little earning power and dependent on pensions and social security payments. It is best for most purposes to concentrate on the family units, which include the great majority of those with normal earning power and almost 95 per cent of the total population.

The distribution of family incomes in 1961 is shown in Table 15. There are still a great many families in the lower income brackets. Ten million families, or more than one-fifth of the total, had incomes below $4,000 in 1961; but this group received only about 7 per cent of total personal income. At the upper end of the scale, 8 per cent of all families had incomes of $15,000 or more, and this top group received about one-quarter of all personal income. These figures, to be sure, refer to income before taxes. The incomes of the higher brackets are weathered down considerably by the federal income tax.

This inequality of family incomes is a persistent fact of our economy. The reasons for it are well known, though it is difficult to estimate their relative importance. One reason is the marked inequality in the distribution of income-yielding property. Although many millions of Americans own stocks and bonds, the great majority of these people have very small holdings. Most of the stocks, bonds, and other income-yielding property is held by a small minority of the population. The top 5 per cent of income recipients in the United States receive more than two-thirds of the dividend payments and close to half of all property income. The concentration of property incomes is much greater than that of incomes from work. The top 5 per cent of income recipients get only a little more than 10 per cent of total wage and salary payments.

It would be wrong, however, to think of the upper income brackets as filled with idle coupon clippers. In the American business culture it is unfashionable for an adult male to live on property income alone. Only about 2 per cent of those with incomes above $15,000 live solely on property income. About two-thirds of the group hold a salaried job, while almost all the remainder are self-employed. The high-income individual usually combines substantial income from work with a larger or smaller amount of property income. Property income, indeed, forms only about one-fifth of the total income of the top 5 per cent group. Salary receipts form almost half the total, while the balance is income from self-employment.

More important than the concentration of property incomes is the wide difference in wage and salary levels for people in different occupations. It will be recalled from Chapter 18 that the average earnings of an independent professional man are more than three times those of an unskilled laborer. There are also wide income differences even for families on the same occupational level. There are substantial differences in wage and salary rates within each occupational group, and there are also differences in the amount of work secured during the year. Detailed occupational analysis has shown that the typical coefficient of dispersion (range within which one-half of the incomes fall, divided by the median income) is in the neighborhood of .50. This means that, if the median income in an occupation is $6,000 per year, only half the people in the occupation will fall within a range of (say) $4,500 to $7,500. The other half will fall above or below this range. For some unusually unstable occupations—musicians, dancers, messengers, newsboys, fishermen, lumbermen, construction laborers—the coefficient of dispersion rises to .80 or more.[1]

The number of income earners in a family has an important bearing on its income level. Almost half the families in the country now have more than one earner. A second or third earner in the family may lift it well above the bracket corresponding to the earnings of the husband

---

[1] Herman P. Miller, *Income of the American People* (New York: John Wiley and Sons, Inc., 1955), p. 60.

The figures of $4,500 and $7,500 are illustrative only. There is no reason why the first and third quartiles need be the same distance from the median.

alone. This factor is increasing in importance with the growing proportion of married women in the labor force.

Loss or lack of earning power is a major factor at the bottom of the income scale. Most of the poorest families, as we shall see in a moment, are families in which the head is aged or disabled, or in which death or desertion of the husband has left a wife with small children which makes it impossible for her to work. Marginal farm families on unproductive land are another important part of this group.

TABLE 15

DISTRIBUTION OF FAMILIES AND THEIR INCOME BY FAMILY INCOME LEVEL, 1961

Family Personal Income Before Taxes	Families		Aggregate Personal Income	
	Number (thousands)	Per Cent	Amount (millions)	Per Cent
Under $2,000	3,232	7.0	3,934	1.1
$2,000 to 2,999	3,024	6.6	7,634	2.1
$3,000 to 3,999	4,136	9.0	14,551	4.0
$4,000 to 4,999	4,964	10.7	22,364	6.2
$5,000 to 5,999	5,358	11.6	29,466	8.2
$6,000 to 7,499	7,674	16.6	51,621	14.4
$7,500 to 9,999	8,134	17.6	69,888	19.4
$10,000 to 14,999	6,117	13.2	73,178	20.4
$15,000 and over	3,551	7.7	86,796	24.2
Total	46,190	100.0	359,432	100.0

Source: J. M. Fitzwilliams, "Size Distribution of Incomes," *Survey of Current Business* (April 1963).

TRENDS IN INEQUALITY

The unequal distribution of incomes described in the previous section has long been a source of concern both to scholars and social reformers. In what sense does income inequality constitute a problem? To the extent that it is a problem, what might be done about it?

It will be useful first to look briefly at the history of income inequality in recent decades. Between 1935 and 1950 there was apparently a marked reduction in the inequality of pre-tax incomes (Table 16). In addition, the sharp income tax increases imposed

during World War II, which were only slightly reduced after the
War, produced a still more equal distribution of post-tax or disposable
incomes. Since 1950, on the other hand, there has been little change
in the inequality of pre-tax incomes. Whatever tendencies were
operative between 1935 and 1950 have apparently been arrested
(Table 17). Both these points deserve brief comment.

The equalization of incomes between 1935 and 1950 is quite
striking. The average income of the poorest 20 per cent of families

TABLE 16

DISTRIBUTION OF FAMILY PERSONAL INCOME, BEFORE
FEDERAL INCOME TAXES, 1935-36 AND 1950

		Income before Taxes			
Quintiles (20-per-cent groups)	Mean Income 1935-36 (1950 dollars)	Mean Income 1950 (1950 dollars)	Increase 1935-36 to 1950 (per cent)	Share of all family income 1935-36 (per cent)	1950 (per cent)
Lowest	$ 672	$ 1,514	125	4.2	6.1
Second	1,496	2,972	99	9.3	11.9
Third	2,281	4,063	78	14.2	16.3
Fourth	3,345	5,417	62	20.8	21.8
Highest	8,263	10,941	32	51.5	43.9
Total	3,212	4,981	55	100.0	100.0

rose by 125 per cent during this period, in dollars of constant
purchasing power. The highest 20 per cent, on the other hand, experienced an increase of only 32 per cent. In consequence, the share
of total income received by the top group fell substantially, while
the shares of the two bottom groups rose markedly.[2] A similar tendency is evident in other countries. In Great Britain, for example, the
share of the top 5 per cent of families has fallen from 43 per cent in
1913 to 33 per cent in 1929 and 24 per cent in 1947.[3]

What produced this marked shift toward greater equality? In the
United States, the main forces at work seem to have been . . .

_____

[2] Table 16 is adapted from Selma Goldsmith, George Jaszi, Hyman Kaltz,
and Maurice Liebenberg, "Size Distribution of Income since the Mid-thirties,"
Review of Economics and Statistics (February 1954), pp. 1-32. Table 19 was
computed by the writer, using data from U. S. Bureau of the Census, *Statistical
Abstract of the United States,* 1963, p. 337.

[3] Simon Kuznets, "Economic Growth and Income Inequality," *American
Economic Review,* XLV (March 1955), pp. 1-28.

1. The shift from deep depression in the 'thirties to virtually full employment in the 'forties and 'fifties. The large number of low incomes in the mid-'thirties reflects partly the heavy unemployment prevailing at that time. As these people were reabsorbed into employment during the 'forties, their average incomes and their share of all personal income increased substantially.

2. The marked reduction of wage and salary differentials between occupational levels. Wage rates for laborers rose faster than those for skilled craftsmen, and the earnings of all manual workers rose faster than those of white-collar workers. Within the executive group, top executives with highest salaries lost ground relative to middle and lower management. The reasons for this squeezing together of the wage-salary structure were reviewed in Chapter 18.

3. An improvement in the relative income position, and a reduction in the relative size, of the farm population. Many of the poorest families in the country are rural families, and this was particularly true during the severe agricultural depression of the 'thirties. World War II brought a sharp increase in farm prices and incomes. As the average income of the farm population rose closer to the urban level, and as the proportion of farmers in the total population continued to fall, the result was to reduce over-all inequality of income distribution.

4. A marked increase in government transfer payments to low-income groups in the population—social security payments, old age assistance, unemployment compensation, veterans benefits, farm subsidy payments, and so on.

5. A marked reduction of the share of property income in total personal income. The reduction in the relative importance of interest and rental payments, due partly to inflation, was noted in Chapter 17. While business profits have not fallen as a percentage of national income produced, the percentage of profits *paid out as dividends* has dropped sharply because of corporate income taxation and a larger share of profits retained by corporations to finance plant expansion. Thus rents, interest, and dividends combined, which formed 22 per cent of family incomes in 1929, had fallen to 12 per cent by 1950. Since these types of income accrue mainly to the top 10 per cent or so of income recipients, the effect has been to pull down upper-bracket incomes and bring them closer to the national average.

6. There is also evidence that the upper brackets are now getting a smaller share of this reduced property income. Kuznets' calculations show that during the 1920's the top 5 per cent of income recipients

got more than 80 per cent of all dividend payments, about 45 per cent of all interest payments, 35 per cent of rents, and better than 55 per cent of property income as a whole. By the late 'forties, however, they were getting only 70 per cent of the dividends, 30 per cent of the interest, 20 per cent of the rents, and a bit over 40 per cent of total property income. This suggests that income-yielding property, particularly rental property, is becoming more widely dispersed among the population that it was a generation ago.[4]

When one comes to the 'fifties and 'sixties, however, most of the tendencies which operated from 1935-50 seem to have leveled off. The elimination of the mass unemployment of the 'thirties was a once-for-all change, which could not be repeated. The shrinkage of wage and salary differentials which characterized the 'forties seems also to have ceased for the time being. The farm labor force has now become such a small part of the total labor force that further farm-to-city shifts cannot have a marked effect on income distribution. The position of the low-income groups continues to be buttressed by government transfer payments; but apart from old age pension payments, these benefits seem no more ample than they were in 1950.

In view of all this, it is not surprising that there has been little change in the distribution of pre-tax incomes since 1950. Table 17 is not directly comparable with earlier tables because it includes both families and unattached individuals; but the 1950 and 1961 data in Table 17 are comparable with each other. Note that the percentage increase in average annual income from 1950 to 1961 was very nearly the same for people at all income levels; and that the proportion of total income received by each quintile group was virtually the same in the two years. Nor does there seem any reason to expect substantial changes in the near future. Any changes which do occur, however, are more likely to be toward equality than away from it. As the educational system catches up with the rising demand for white-collar workers, we may see a further reduction of the gap between white-collar and blue-collar incomes. Social security and other transfer payments are likely to be liberalized. Property income may gradually become more evenly distributed throughout the population, though this is a rather puzzling phenomenon. The fact that most saving is

---

TABLE 17

DISTRIBUTION OF INCOME RECEIVED BY FAMILIES AND UNATTACHED
INDIVIDUALS, BEFORE FEDERAL INCOME TAXES, 1950 AND 1961

Quintiles (20-per-cent groups)	*Income before Taxes*				
	Mean Income 1950 (1950 dollars)	*Mean Income 1961 (1950 dollars)*	*Increase 1950 to 1961 (per cent)*	*Share of all income*	
				1950 (per cent)	*1961*
Lowest	1,056	1,294	23	4.8	4.6
Second	2,418	3,071	27	10.9	11.0
Third	3,579	4,572	28	16.1	16.4
Fourth	4,911	6,319	29	22.1	22.6
Highest	10,254	12,654	23	46.1	45.4
Total	4,444	5,582	26	100.0	100.0

done by the highest income groups should mean an increasing concentration of wealth at the top. The rich *should* get richer. Why don't
they? One can think of several possible explanations—estate taxes,
splitting up of estates among several heirs, improvidence and low
ability among children and grandchildren, and the fact that taxation
makes it difficult to build up new fortunes as rapidly as older ones are
being dissipated. But we do not actually know the relative importance
of these and other factors in the situation.

Is inequality still a problem?

It is important to distinguish between *inequality* and *poverty*.
It is clear that there is still a problem of poverty in the sense that
many families do not have enough income to attain a decent minimum standard of living. There would be widespread agreement that
families below some minimum level should be brought up to that
level. An effective attack on poverty does not consist simply of taking
income from the rich and giving it to the poor, as will be explained
in the next section. But it does involve some increase in government
assistance payments, some increase in tax levies on those able to pay
them, and thus some further reduction of income inequality.

Suppose now that this has been done. All families below $4,000 a year or some other figure have been brought up to that level. Is there any reason to worry about the distribution of incomes *above* this basic minimum? If the poorest families can live decently, does it matter whether some moving picture stars and corporation executives earn (before taxes!) a half-million dollars a year? Should we be concerned about inequality *per se?*

The standard arguments on this issue are well known. On the egalitarian side, it is usually argued that a dollar brings less satisfaction to the $50,000-a-year man than to the $5,000-a-year man. Thus a transfer of income from higher to lower income brackets is likely to increase total consumer satisfaction. (This is stoutly denied by others, however, who maintain that one's capacity to get enjoyment from spending money increases with practice!) It is argued also that the envy engendered by wide differences in living standards involves a loss in community satisfaction. I may be content with my $5,000 a year if no one else around me has more than double that amount, but quite unhappy if others in the community have ten or twenty times as much.

Against egalitarianism it is argued that envy and the desire to climb to a higher income bracket perform an indispensable economic function. If incomes are too equal, no one will have an incentive to train for the higher occupations and perform efficiently in them. The fact that most of the personal saving is done by the top income groups is used as an argument for inequality by those who believe our economy suffers from a shortage of capital and as an argument for equality by those who believe that oversaving threatens us with depression. And so it goes.

One could probably get widespread agreement on the desirability of establishing equal *opportunity* for young people to train for professional and managerial occupations within the limits of their native ability. This would accelerate the reduction of wage and salary differentials and close a good deal of the gap between the laborer and the surgeon or corporation president. If we could establish equality of occupational opportunity and could eliminate poverty, the writer would be content to let upper bracket incomes fall where they may. But he would not undertake to convince other people that they should rest content. The question of how far equality should be pursued as an end in itself is a political issue which has divided men for centuries. In modern times, this has turned increasingly into an argument over the tax system. Egalitarians favor steeply progressive income taxes and heavy reliance on federal spending, which is financed mainly from income taxation. Those who believe income equalization has gone too far, or is in danger of going too far, favor state and local spending, excise and sales taxes, and a less steeply graduated income tax than we now have. These are political issues of the purest sort. The economist can say little about them as economist, however strongly he may feel as citizen.

THE EXTENT OF POVERTY

What does the present income distribution mean in terms of the living standards of the population? How many families and individuals can be classified as "poor"? No precise answer can be given to this question, and for several reasons. First, how is one to define "poverty"? The usual approach is to set up an annual budget of goods and services which is regarded as a minimum for a family of specified size. The difficulty is that when one gets above the minimum of food, clothing, and shelter necessary for physical survival, the consumption level which is regarded as "adequate'" becomes a matter of judgment. Lower living standards shade into higher standards by imperceptible degrees, and where one sets the poverty line depends on one's beliefs about how people should be entitled to live. Moreover, conceptions of an adequate living standard change over the course of time. Conditions which were generally prevalent and accepted at one time may be regarded as completely unacceptable fifty years later.

The Bureau of Labor Statistics has prepared a "city worker's family budget," which is estimated to provide a modest but adequate level of living for a family of husband, wife, and two children aged eight to thirteen. It is not a bare subsistence level, but it is far below the "American standard of living" portrayed in moving pictures and magazine advertisements.[5] The cost of this budget in 1960 ranged

---

[5] The components of this budget are described in the *Monthly Labor Review*, LXXXIII (August 1960). It includes, for example, telephone and television, a ratio of seven automobiles to ten families in small and medium-sized cities, and four autos to ten families in the largest cities, four doctor's calls a year for each member of the family, and a serious illness about once in four years; an overcoat for the husband every seven years, and a coat for the wife once in four years; the wife does all cooking, cleaning, and laundry, and is provided with refrigerator, gas or electric stove, and washing machine; one newspaper, one monthly magazine, tobacco and liquor; a small amount for recreation, gifts, and contributions; life insurance but no other provision for saving.

from about $4,600 in Houston to $5,600 in Chicago. It is obvious from Table 17 that a large percentage of families are below this income level, but it is hard to say what one should conclude from this. Are there really this many "poor" families in the country? Or is the budget itself unrealistic?

Assuming that one could agree on the items which should go into the minimum budget, one's troubles have only begun. One cannot simply take the existing distribution of family incomes, set it against the cost of the minimum budget, and then calculate what percentage of families fall below the poverty line. The situation is not so simple as this. Consider a family in which the husband's income alone is insufficient to support the family at a minimum level. The wife therefore works, though unwillingly, and her earnings are sufficient to bring total family income above the poverty line. No one knows how many of the ten million families in which the wife works are in this situation. In business and professional families, the wife frequently prefers to continue working as a "career woman." It seems likely, however, that in wage-earning families the majority of working wives do so out of economic necessity. What weight should be given to this factor? If one says that the family just described is not impoverished, that its living standard is adequate, this amounts to saying that the wife *should* work as well as the husband in order to support the family. This involves a value judgment which is certainly debatable.

Another serious difficulty arises from variation in the size of families. Most standard budgets are computed for a family of four people. But actual families range from two people to ten or more. An income of $4,000 per year might be adequate for a family of two, but seriously inadequate for a family of six or eight. One really needs, therefore, a cross-tabulation of families by size of income, number of people contributing to this income, and number of people dependent upon it for support.

Still another difficulty arises from the fact that family incomes fluctuate considerably from year to year. A period of illness or unemployment for the chief wage earner may plunge the family much below its normal income bracket. Next year some families will be up in the income scale and others down. The number of families below a specified income level in a given year is thus not a safe guide to the number who are *permanently* in a low-income position. The amount of continuing poverty is substantially less than one might judge from income distributions for a single year.

In view of these difficulties it is perhaps unwise to make any quantitative estimate of the extent of poverty. Those who have worked most on the problem, however, estimate that perhaps one-fifth of the American population has seriously substandard incomes on a continuing basis.[6] It seems clear that poverty is still with us on a substantial scale. While we may be nearing the oft-proclaimed "era of plenty," we have not yet reached it.

We know more today than ever before about who the low-income families are and where they are. The characteristics of families at various income levels in 1954 were analyzed in great detail in the Joint Committee study just cited. In 1954, 8.3 million of the 41.9 million families in the United States had money incomes below $2,000. This group of the poorest families was made up as follows:

Farm families (of which 1.6 million were in the South)	2.6 million
Families in which the head was not in the labor force (and 1.6 million of these had family heads over 65)	2.8 million
Families in which the head was unemployed	0.4 million
Families headed by laborers, service workers, and semi-skilled workers	1.5 million
All others	1.0 million
	8.3 million

There has been a more recent analysis by a group of scholars at the Survey Research Center of the University of Michigan.[7] From a national sample of families they secured information on 1959 income and on a wide variety of family characteristics which might be associated with income. The results were then expanded to provide estimates for all families in the United States. While the object was to explain family income in general, they made a special analysis of the lowest income groups.

As an aid in defining the poverty line, they chose a budget prepared by the Community Council of Greater New York, which can be adjusted to families of any size. For a family of four, this budget would have cost $4,330 in New York City in 1959. It is thus leaner than the B.L.S. budget already described. It is virtually a relief

---

[6] See particularly Joint Committee on the Economic Report, "Characteristics of the Low-income Population and Related Federal Programs," 84th Congress, 1st Session (1955).

[7] James N. Morgan, Martin H. David, Wilbur J. Cohen, and Harvey E. Brazer, *Income and Welfare in the United States* (New York: McGraw-Hill Book Company, Inc., 1962).

budget, since it is used by private welfare agencies in New York City to determine eligibility for assistance and free medical care. A family was defined as "poor" if its 1959 income was less than nine-tenths of the cost of this basic budget, adjusted to the size of the family in question. Why only nine-tenths? Partly to err on the side of conservatism, partly to take account of the fact that living costs in most smaller communities are lower than in New York.

On the basis of this yardstick, 20 per cent of the families in the sample were living in poverty. For the nation as a whole, this would come to about ten million families. What were the characteristics of these families? An initial difficulty is that poverty may arise from a half-dozen sources. A particular family may have two, or three, or more of these characteristics. So what is the "cause" of its poverty? To meet this problem the authors developed a sequential analysis, starting with factors which would be sufficient by themselves to explain poverty. If the household head is aged, one need look no further. Similarly if he has grave physical or mental disabilities. Again, a woman with no husband present who has children to support is very likely to fall in the poverty group.

The results of this analysis are shown in Table 18. The number of families for whom a certain characteristic can be ascribed as the prime source of poverty appear along the *diagonal* of the Table. Thus the estimated total of disabled family heads is 1.7 million; but of these 0.9 million are also aged, which would by itself explain their low incomes. So we say that only the remaining 0.8 million are poor because of disability. Again, there are an estimated 2.9 nonwhite families. But about half of these are aged, or disabled, or have other clear sources of poverty. The number who have no visible handicap except being nonwhite reduces to 1.4 million.

The results suggest that more than half the families (5.6 million out of 10.4 million) were poor because of inability to work and earn income. In addition to the aged and disabled, this includes 1.1 million women with children and no husband, and 0.9 million who reported that they are usually employed but worked less than 49 weeks in 1959. Many of these are probably marginal workers or people stranded in depressed areas and occupations.

The remaining 4.8 million family heads were presumably able to earn income, but their families were still poor. Why? Some 1.4 million were Negroes who are found in disproportionate numbers in the lowest occupational groups, where they suffer from low wage rates and irregular employment. Another 1.0 million were self-employed businessmen or farmers, probably mainly farmers. There remains a residual group of 2.4 million families, for whose poverty there is no clear statistical explanation. The authors suggest that "the heads of many of these families are unskilled seasonal workers, for whom yearly unemployment is usual. Others are widows or single females under sixty-five with no work experience, students, and a small number of housekeepers or servants who live in their employers' household and work for room and board." [8]

The protean character of the poverty problem is apparent from these figures. Low wage rates in some areas and occupations are part, but only a minor part, of the total problem. Higher aggregate demand for labor would help the less-skilled groups and the long-term unemployed. But much of the problem lies outside the reach of the market economy. Most families are poor because employment of the family head is unfeasible. The question is at what level these families are to be supported by society, and who is to bear the cost.

The total cost, incidentally, is no longer staggeringly large. Morgan and his associates estimate that it would cost about $10 billion a year to bring every poor family and individual in the economy above the poverty line. This is less than 2 per cent of GNP, and not much more than we are presently spending in the effort to land on the moon.

STRATEGY OF AN ATTACK ON POVERTY

Because poverty has complex roots, it must be attacked simultaneously on many fronts. We cannot assume that a steady rise in the real wage level will automatically eliminate the problem over the course of time. Rising wages have already come close to eliminating poverty for those able to work year in and year out. But a high wage at which not to work is little help; and the main causes of present-day poverty have no direct relation to the wage level.

Some lines of attack on poverty—drawing low-income farm families off the land or raising their productivity on the land, reducing the severity of general depressions, broadening opportunities for education and vocational training, special measures to cope with the "de-

---

[8] *Ibid.*, p. 191.

TABLE 18

PROPORTIONS AND AGGREGATE ESTIMATES OF HEADS OF POOR FAMILIES HAVING CHARACTERISTICS RELATED TO POVERTY WITHIN LIKELY CAUSES OF POVERTY

Likely causes of poverty	Aged	Disabled	Single and has children	Usually employed, unemployed in 1959	Nonwhite	Self-employed businessman or farmer	None of these
1. Aged	100% 2.8 mil.	32% .9 mil.	1% .04 mil.	2% .04 mil.	22% .6 mil.	8% .2 mil.	0%
2. Disabled (not 1)		100% .8 mil.	15% .1 mil.	4% .03 mil.	26% .2 mil.	17% .1 mil.	0%
3. Single and has children (not 1-2)			100% 1.1 mil.	14% .1 mil.	43% .5 mil.	3% .01 mil.	0%
4. Usually employed, worked less than 49 weeks in 1959 (not 1-3)				100% .9 mil.	29% .2 mil.	0%	0%
5. Nonwhite (not 1-4)					100% 1.4 mil.	14% 0.4 mil.	0%
6. Self-employed businessman or farmer (not 1-5)						100% 1.0 mil.	0%
7. Not 1-6							100% 2.4 mil.
All	2.8 mil.	1.7 mil.	1.2 mil.	1.1 mil.	2.9 mil.	1.7 mil.	2.4 mil.

Source: Morgan and others, *op. cit.,* p. 195.

pressed area" problem—have been discussed in earlier chapters. The remaining measures that might be adopted fall into three categories.

1. Setting a floor under the wage level through minimum wage legislation. This is not a major line of attack—most wages are already adequate and those which are not can be raised only a limited distance by legislation—but it is important enough to deserve some discussion.

2. Efforts to offset losses of income resulting from unemployment, old age, illness, disability, and other causes. This is the area of activity generally termed "social security," though it includes also individual, employer-sponsored, or collectively bargained insurance and pension plans. Social security systems are financed to some extent by levies on consumers and taxpayers, and thus involve some redistribution of income from higher to lower income groups. In large measure, however, they simply effect a transfer of income *within* the wage-earning group as between times of earning and not earning.

3. Direct government subsidies to consumption, either in cash or kind.

These various lines of attack will be examined briefly in the remaining sections of the chapter.

ELIMINATING SUBSTANDARD WAGES: MINIMUM WAGE LEGISLATION

The justification for minimum-wage legislation is, first, that not all workers in the economy are protected by collective bargaining; and second, that imperfections in the nonunion labor market make it possible for particular groups of workers to be hired at rates far below those prevailing elsewhere for comparable work. This fact debases the living standards of these workers, encourages inefficient management of the low-wage plants, and poses a competitive threat to establishments with higher wage rates. For these reasons, most industrialized countries have had minimum-wage legislation on their statute books for many years. The United States, the last major country to enact this sort of legislation, has had a federal minimum-wage law since 1938.

The minimum-wage laws of different countries, while similar in intent, differ considerably in their detailed application. Some provide a single minimum wage for all types of employment, while others provide separate minima for different industries. It is frequently provided that the minimum for each industry shall be determined by an industry board or commission, usually including union and management representatives as well as government officials. The minimum wage is usually set at such a level that only a small minority—perhaps 5 to 10 per cent—of the workers in the economy are currently being paid less than this amount. This practice accomplishes the objective of preventing extremely low wage rates without unduly disturbing the general wage level and price level of the country.

The immediate effect of a minimum wage is to raise the labor costs of companies which had workers receiving less than the new minimum. The increase in labor costs will be more than might appear at first glance, for the employer will usually have to raise rates above the minimum as well as those below it. To take a simple case, suppose that Company A has skilled, semiskilled, and unskilled workers, and that these are being paid respectively $1.00, $0.80, and $0.60 per hour. Suppose now that a minimum wage of $0.80 per hour is set for the industry. It will not be feasible for the employer simply to raise the unskilled men to $0.80 and leave other rates unchanged; for this would leave the semiskilled workers on the same level as the unskilled, and would leave the skilled men only $0.20 per hour above the unskilled, instead of $0.40 per hour as before. In order to maintain peace in the plant, the employer may have to raise the rates of the semiskilled and skilled workers to—say—$0.95 and $1.10, respectively. The increase in his payroll, then, will be considerably greater than the cost of bringing the lowest-paid workers up to the minimum.

The possible ways in which such an increase in labor costs may be met were discussed in Chapter 10. It may be met from a reduction of profits, if these have been abnormally large; from an increase in the efficiency of labor, management, or plant and equipment; or from an increase in the price of the product. A rise in the price of the product will normally mean some decline in employment in the industry. Moreover, to the extent that the higher wages are met through higher prices, the gains of the workers whose wages have been raised are made at the expense of other workers and of consumers generally. This situation may be quite legitimate; the price paid by consumers should include a reasonable wage to workers in the industry. It is necessary to realize, however, that the gains secured by workers under minimum-wage legislation are not always costless.

The few studies which have been made of the effect of minimum-wage legislation on specific industries suggest that the second avenue of adjustment noted above—increases in the efficiency of workers, management, and equipment—is probably the most important in practice. Indeed, it was mainly the effects of minimum-wage legislation which caused economists to realize that higher wages need not mean higher costs and prices, but might mean increased efficiency instead. Before the enactment of minimum-wage legislation there have usually been dire predictions of ruin by employers in low-wage industries, prophecies of closed plants and mass unemployment. These predictions seem never to be realized; one comes along a few years later and finds these industries flourishing as well as before. Investigation usually reveals that the answer is a general overhaul of equipment and methods which enable employers to carry on profitably at the higher wage levels.

A less fortunate consequence of minimum-wage laws remains to be mentioned, viz., their tendency to increase the number of unemployable people in the population. There are always certain people who, because of age, accidents, or physical and mental defects, are unable to work at anything approaching the normal rate. Where there is no minimum wage, employers can hire these people and pay them a low wage rate proportionate to their productivity. Where there is a minimum wage, this is no longer possible; the employer cannot afford to keep on his payroll anyone who cannot produce enough to be worth the minimum wage. The result is that workers of very low productivity are discharged and become dependent on private or public support. Minimum wages tend to set a higher standard of employability, to draw a sharper line between the employable and the unemployable, and to increase the number in the latter group.

This effect is mitigated, however, in two ways. First, minimum-wage legislation rarely applies to all industries in the economy. Some of the less employable people who are squeezed out of the industries covered by minimum wages may be able to find employment in agriculture, domestic service, nonprofit institutions, and other uncovered industries. It may not be true that any moron can be a domestic servant, but many have tried. Second, minimum-wage laws frequently permit employers, on proper application and approval, to pay wages below the minimum to learners, old people, and other handicapped workers. Such a provision, while desirable in principle, opens loopholes for evasion of the law and makes the ever-present problem of enforcement still more difficult. Where such a provision exists, the work force of some plants comes to consist mainly of "handicapped" people, while the "learners" employed never seem to learn enough to be raised to the standard rate of pay.

After these preliminary remarks, let us examine briefly the status of minimum-wage legislation in the United States. Early legislative efforts in this field were largely nullified by adverse court decisions. Not until 1937, when the Supreme Court in a five-to-four decision held the minimum-wage law of the state of Washington to be constitutional,[9] was the way open for permanent wage regulation. This decision was followed by enactment of the Fair Labor Standards Act of 1938, commonly known as the Wage-Hour Act. This Act set a minimum wage for workers in industries engaged in interstate commerce, exclusive of agriculture and a few other types of industry, starting at 25 cents an hour in October 1938, rising to 30 cents an hour in October 1939, and to 40 cents an hour in October 1945. It provided also that the minimum wage in a particular industry might be raised as high as 40 cents before 1945 by order of the Wage and Hour Administrator, acting on the recommendation of an industry committee composed of labor, employer, and public representatives. The standard workweek was set at forty hours after October 1940, with limited exceptions for certain seasonal industries. Employers were required to pay time and a half for work beyond this limit.

The original minimum wage levels rapidly became obsolete because of the rapid rise of money wages during the 'forties and 'fifties. The Fair Labor Standards Act was accordingly amended in 1949 to require a minimum wage of 75 cents per hour effective in 1950, in 1955 to provide a $1.00 minimum wage effective in 1956, and in 1961 to require a minimum of $1.25 by 1963. The 1956 increase has been quite thoroughly studied, and seems to have had a substantial impact on such low-wage industries as cigars, fertilizers, sawmills, seamless hosiery, men's and boys' shirts, footwear, and canning. The impact was felt particularly in the Southern states. Many Southern plants

---

[9] *West Coast Hotel Co.* v. *Parrish,* 300 U.S. 379.

in these industries had half or more of their workers below $1.00 an hour at the time the new minimum was imposed. The minimum brought these people up to the $1.00 level, and after some lag also produced increases of varying amount for workers above the minimum. Plant-wide average hourly earnings seem to have risen typically by 10 to 20 per cent. Employment in five industries analyzed by the Bureau of Labor Statistics fell by 8 per cent during the year following the increase in the minimum.[10] It is impossible to separate the impact of the minimum wage from other reasons for short-term fluctuations in employment. There is reason to think, however, that part of the drop in employment may have been due to the higher wage level.

The main problem under the Fair Labor Standards Act has been the pedestrian but important matter of enforcement. In the early years of the Act's operation, there was widespread evasion of it in the low-wage industries. The wages provisions were violated by simply not paying the prescribed minimum, or by paying it and then requiring a "kickback" from the workers. The overtime provisions were frequently violated by requiring workers to "punch out" on the time clock at the end of eight hours, and then return to work unofficially for an extra hour or two. Under nonunion conditions these practices are difficult to detect, since few workers have the knowledge and the courage to lodge a complaint against their employer. The limited staff of the Wage and Hour Division has never allowed it to do more than spot check a small sample of companies each year. In spite of these limitations, however, thousands of violations have been discovered and rectified, and many millions of dollars have been restored to workers in back pay.

Twenty-six states (including all the major industrial states) and the District of Columbia currently have minimum wage laws applying to such intrastate industries as retail trade, laundering and dry-cleaning, hotels and restaurants, hospitals, beauty parlors, and other service establishments. Although a few of the state acts apply to men, the great majority cover only women and minors. The minimum wage is usually not specified in the Act, but is left for administrative determination on the basis of recommendations by industry wage boards or committees. Whatever the nominal principles laid down for the guid-

---

[10] "Effects of the $1 Minimum Wage in Five Industries," *Monthly Labor Review* (May 1958), pp. 492-501.

ance of these committees, the most important factor in practice is the existing wage structure of the industry. The minimum is usually set so as to bring up a minority of employers at the bottom of the wage structure without disturbing the general wage level of the industry unduly. In states and industries where the prevailing wage level is low, the minimum wages are correspondingly low. The state minima are generally below, and sometimes substantially below, the federal minimum.

There is a substantial wage gap between interstate industries subject to the FLSA and local industries not so subject. The latter group includes hotels and restaurants, schools and hospitals, most retailing, local transit, and local service industries. In 1960, when the federal minimum wage was still at $1.00, a B.L.S. survey of nonmetropolitan areas in the South and North Central regions showed the following percentages of workers earning less than $1.00 an hour.

	South	*North Central*
Subject to FLSA	1.5	0.5
Not subject to FLSA	52.1	37.5

In the Southern region, 31.6 per cent of the workers in nonsubject industries were earning less than 75 cents an hour.[11]

This must be reflected in the quality of labor attracted to the two groups of industries. The wage superiority of the interstate industries should permit them to skim the cream of the labor force, while less desirable workers are relegated to local industries at lower wage rates.

It should be emphasized in conclusion that inadequate wage rates cannot be eliminated primarily through legislation. Minimum wage laws can help to tidy up the ragged lower edge of the wage structure. Progress mainly depends, however, on (1) the slow but steady advance of productivity, which gradually lifts the general level of real wages over the course of time, and (2) maintenance of a high level of employment, which gives workers an opportunity to move from low-wage to high-wage jobs and forces employers to compete actively for labor. The high labor demand of the 'forties and early 'fifties, which permitted millions of people to move out of agriculture, domestic service, and other low-wage occupations, did more to eliminate substandard wages than could possibly have been done through legislation.

---

[11] "Wages in Nonmetropolitan Areas, Southern and North Central Regions," *Monthly Labor Review* (Sept. 1963), pp. 1033-39.

INCOME SECURITY: ROLE OF SOCIAL INSURANCE SYSTEMS

A large proportion of the poverty in our society arises, not because wage rates are inadequate, but because the family unit contains no wage-earning member or because the wage earner is not able to work steadily throughout the year. Loss of income resulting from unemployment was discussed in Chapter 14. There are numerous other reasons for loss of income. All who live long enough must face the prospect of becoming too old to work. The worker may be disabled by accident or disease before reaching old age. His earnings may be interrupted by illness, which also involves additional costs for medical care. Premature death of a wage earner may leave his wife and children with no means of support. Some people are unable to work at all because of congenital physical or mental defects.

Most of these things are risks in the actuarial sense. One cannot tell in advance *which* individuals will suffer a certain type of income loss in a particular year, but one can predict roughly *how many* people in the population will be affected and how much money will be necessary to replace their loss of income. This is true of unemployment, old age, work accidents, partial or total disability, illness, and dependency due to the death of a wage earner. As we saw in Chapter 14, any risk whose magnitude is predictable is also insurable. As this has become increasingly recognized, there has been a growing public demand for insurance protection against these risks. Over the past hundred years, every industrial country of the world has set up systems of social insurance. In some countries, including Great Britain, almost every possible type of income loss is provided for through a comprehensive social insurance system.

Social insurance was virtually nonexistent in the United States until the 1930's. Many states had workmen's compensation laws which provided at least partial compensation for loss of income through industrial accidents. Destitution arising from any other source, however, was left to local relief—generally conceded to be the least satisfactory method of meeting economic distress. A long step forward was taken with the Social Security Act of 1935, which (1) stimulated the creation of the state unemployment compensation systems described in Chapter 14; (2) set up a federal system of retirement pensions, the OASI (Old Age and Survivors' Insurance) system; and (3) provided for joint federal-state assistance to blind persons, orphans, and other dependent children, and people beyond the age of sixty-five not qualified for pensions under the OASI system. Since then the United States has moved in the direction of specialized provision for special types of need, making greater use of the insurance principle, and removing more and more types of want from the relief category. Much remains to be done, however, and far too many people are still dependent on the haphazard method of local relief.

The money cost of a comprehensive social security program is impressively high. The British program is estimated to cost something like 12½ per cent of national income. It has been calculated that to apply the same program in Canada would also cost about 12½ per cent of Canadian national income. The New Zealand program, which stands next to that of Great Britain in completeness, was costing only 10 per cent of national income just before World War II, but some of the benefits provided were quite low.[12] It seems likely, therefore, that a comprehensive social security program in the United States would cost something between 10 and 15 per cent of national income. It would probably require a payroll tax of not less than 10 per cent, distributed between employer and worker, plus a supplement from general tax revenues.

It should be pointed out, however, that this cost would not necessarily be *additional* cost. We are already providing through social insurance for loss of income resulting from unemployment, retirement, and premature death. Loss of income through illness, disability, and other causes not covered by social insurance is now borne by the people immediately affected, by their relatives and creditors, or by general relief. But the burden is assessed against individuals in a haphazard way, usually after the emergency has arisen, and without much regard for ability to pay.

A comprehensive social security system cannot be said to "cost more" than absence of such a system unless (1) it increases the *size* of the various risks—the amount of unemployment, the number of disabling accidents, the amount of sickness, the length of time which pensioners live before death, and so on; or (2) it enables the people whose income is cut off in one of these ways to consume more goods and services than they would otherwise consume. There is little evi-

---

[12] These estimates are taken from L. C. Marsh, *Report on Social Security for Canada*, report presented to the Special Committee on Social Security on March 16, 1943 (Ottawa: King's Printer, 1943), p. 16.

dence that social security has the first of these effects; the size of the various risks seems to remain about the same as before. It doubtless does have the second effect. If adequate benefit scales are provided, people cut off from wages or salaries are enabled to live at least at a subsistence level, whereas without social insurance they must exhaust their personal resources, accumulate debts, beg from friends and relatives, and still live at a subhuman level in many cases. A social security system which accomplishes its purpose is bound to be more "expensive" in the sense of diverting a larger flow of goods and services to the maintenance of people in distress. This is surely no objection to the system. On the contrary, this is the whole point of social security—to prevent people from being forced into subhuman living conditions through circumstances beyond their control.

The main effect of social security, however, is not an increase in costs. It is rather a redistribution and systematic budgeting of costs which are already being met in a haphazard and inequitable way. The use of general government revenues, drawn partly from income taxes, makes it possible to assess a larger share of the total cost against the income groups best able to bear it. More important, there is a drastic redistribution of costs within the wage-earning population. Costs are assessed regularly and proportionately over the population as a whole, instead of falling only on those who happen to suffer illness or other incapacity in a particular year. From the standpoint of the individual family budget, costs are distributed evenly over time instead of appearing irregularly and unexpectedly.

There seems no justification for the belief that comprehensive social security is beyond the economic capacity of the United States, particularly when it already exists in many countries whose economic resources and per capita production are much smaller than our own. Our productive capacity, if fully utilized, is easily adequate to guarantee a subsistence minimum to all our citizens under all circumstances. The qualification "if fully used" is important. Severe depression and mass unemployment have a disorganizing effect on a social security system. The revenues of the system fall off because of the decline of payrolls, and the insurance principle itself tends to be undermined. Efforts are made to stretch unemployment compensation to meet the distress resulting from long-term unemployment, and this attempt undermines the actuarial basis of the system. Moreover, receipt of unemployment compensation, compensation for partial disability, and general relief should rightly be conditioned on willingness to work.

Severe depression makes it impossible to test people's willingness to work in the only feasible way—by offering them jobs.

If a comprehensive social security system is feasible, is it also desirable? On the positive side, there seems no doubt that such a system lifts an enormous burden of worry and uncertainty from the shoulders of everyone. All who work and contribute to the insurance fund can now be sure of protection against the worst forms of physical privation. Moreover, social security benefits are paid regardless of the savings or other private resources of the individual. People thus still have an incentive to save in order to live above the bare minimum, which is all that social security can provide. Another favorable aspect of social security, as compared with general relief, is that it is based on contributions by the individual. It is an earned right, not a government handout. It does not, therefore, impair the independence and self-respect of the individual as charity inevitably does.

Will not the availability of income from social security, however, decrease the desire of people to work for an income? Will it not lead them to draw social security benefits whenever possible and for as long as possible, and to avoid work whenever they can? Whether this becomes a serious problem depends largely on how the social security system is constructed and administered. One important factor is the level of benefit payments under social security. The objective is to meet minimum consumption needs of an individual or family during absence of income from regular employment; but "minimum needs" are difficult to define, and reasonable people may well differ on just how much should be allowed to cover them. People of humanitarian bent will be inclined to set the scale high in order to minimize personal hardship. If the scale is set so high that it approaches what the worker could earn on a job, many people will not think it worthwhile to work for a small addition to their income.

It is necessary, therefore, to keep a considerable gap between the scale of social security benefits and the level of wages and salaries. The benefit scales in our present social security laws certainly do not err in the direction of undue generosity. There is little evidence that present unemployment compensation scales deter people from taking jobs when jobs are available. The problem is difficult only for very low-paid workers, who live near the subsistence level even when fully employed. In these cases even a low level of social security benefits may be too close for comfort to the worker's regular wage. This problem will gradually become less acute in the future, however, as the general wage level continues to rise and fewer people are forced to work near the subsistence level.

The other problems are mainly matters of practical administration. There is a problem, for example, of obtaining clear proof of eligibility—that the worker is really unemployed, really sick, really disabled, and so on. Another problem is to insure a strict but fair application of the willingness-to-work rule, so that people who refuse suitable work are barred from benefit payments. It is not difficult to set up proper procedures on these matters; but it is difficult to prevent the administration of these procedures from being warped in one direction or another by political pressures.

Social security in the United States is still an experiment, and there is much to learn before it will operate in a fully satisfactory way. The existence of unsolved problems, however, should not deter us from pushing on toward abolishing the fear of want—surely one of the most challenging goals which a democratic community can set itself.

LOW-COST PROVISION OF SOCIAL NECESSITIES

Most modern states provide an increasing array of goods and services to their citizens, either free or at subsidized prices. Education is usually provided either free or at nominal cost. Certain health services, and in some countries virtually every type of medical and hospital care, are provided without fees. Many countries subsidize housing construction, so that the lower income groups can rent adequate homes for less than they would otherwise pay. Some governments provide school children with free milk, citrus juices, and other requirements for adequate nutrition. The cost of these things is met partly from income and inheritance taxes, which means that the standard of living of the poor is being raised at the expense of the well-to-do.

Direct subsidies to consumption, i.e., government provision of goods and services either free or at prices below full cost, raise certain questions of principle. On the one hand, it may be argued that this interference is an unwise infringement by government on consumers' freedom of choice. If government wishes to raise the living standards of the poor, why not simply give them more cash and leave them to spend it as they please? Why influence them to consume more of those products which some government official thinks they should have? Is it not reasonable to suppose that consumers will get greatest satisfaction by purchasing the goods they individually want? If they choose to buy beer rather than housing, whose business is it but their own?

A strong case can be made along these lines that the great bulk of consumption should continue to be guided, as it now is in the United States, by the free choices of individual consumers. A case can also be made, however, that there should be exceptions to this general rule and that some lines of consumption should be stimulated by government action. It sounds dangerously authoritarian to assert that consumers do not know their own minds. Yet there is good evidence that people do underbuy on certain types of commodity because of shortcomings of information or foresight. Most people tend, for example, to underbuy on education and preventive medical care. The consequences of their underconsumption of these things fall on others in the community as well as themselves, and also fall to a considerable extent on the next generation. It may be argued that government stimulation of these types of consumption is necessary to protect the long-run interests of the community.

There is also evidence that, with respect to certain types of consumption, the choices of individual consumers may be inadequate to produce the desired results. It is doubtful, for example, that the desire of people for better housing—even if supported by adequate incomes —can by itself bring about the abolition of slums and the construction of new housing in such a way as to prevent the development of future slums. In cases of this sort, where the market mechanism does not seem to operate rapidly or efficiently, it may be argued that consumers are entitled to make their preferences effective through their elected representatives in government. In a democratic country, government activities are presumably directed toward purposes which a large body of the citizens favor. It seems arbitrary to assert that such purposes may not include the stimulation of certain lines of consumption.

Government subsidies to consumption, properly limited and controlled, are a useful flanking maneuver against the problem of want. This problem is so complex that it requires a coordinated use of all the weapons in the arsenal of modern social legislation—antidepression measures, social insurance, family-allowance systems, minimum-wage legislation, a progressive tax structure, and direct subsidies of consumption at those points where consumer choice seems seriously inadequate.

Discussion questions

1. "Inequality of personal and family incomes is a persistent fact of our economy." Explain the main reasons for the present inequality of family incomes in the United States.

2. What are the main factors accounting for the decline of income inequality between 1935 and 1950? Which of these would you expect to be of continuing importance in the future?

3. Do you think the government should take steps toward further equalization of incomes? Why, or why not? If steps should be taken, what specific measures would you advocate?

4. What are the main problems encountered in trying to measure the amount of poverty in the United States?

5. What are the most important sources of poverty at the present time?

6. Discuss some of the problems encountered in trying to draft a good minimum wage law.

7. What main kinds of income loss are not yet covered by the American social security system? Should they be covered, and how might this be done?

8. "It is not a good idea for government to provide poor families with food, housing, medical care, or what not, at cut-rate prices. Where subsidies are desirable, it is better to give a cash subsidy and let people spend it as they prefer." Discuss.

Selected reading

Beveridge, Sir William, *Social Insurance and Allied Services.* New York: The Macmillan Company, 1942.

Burns, Eveline M., *Social Security and Public Policy.* New York: McGraw-Hill Book Company, Inc., 1956.

Morgan, James N., "The Anatomy of Income Distribution," *Review of Economics and Statistics* (August 1962), pp. 270-283.

Morgan, James N., Martin H. David, Wilbur J. Cohen, and Harvey E. Brazer, *Income and Welfare in the United States.* New York: McGraw-Hill Book Company, Inc., 1962.

United States Congress, Joint Committee on the Economic Report, Subcommittee on Low Income Families, *Low Income Families.* 84th Congress, 1st Session (1955).

EPILOGUE

21

Issues for This Generation

Scholars are usually behind the march of history. It is easier to analyze past controversies than to detect the emerging issues of the future. Moreover, the older issues are never entirely solved. We are still concerned with averting depression and maintaining minimum levels of wages and social insurance, which were major problems of the nineteen-thirties; with developing workable collective bargaining procedures and maintaining continuity of production in essential industries, issues which emerged clearly in the 'forties; with restraining abuses of union power, attaining a higher rate of economic growth, and coping with cost inflation, which aroused concern during the 'fifties. Some of these problems are doubtless incapable of final solution; and we continue to worry about them with the affection of a dog for a well-chewed bone.

But priorities change with time; and it is useful to shake oneself free of the incubus of history, and to ask what will appear as important issues over the next generation. This runs the risk of missing the mark and of emphasizing things which turn out to be ephemeral. But one man's guesses may at least serve to stimulate discussion and disagreement.

I have tried to single out issues which are intrinsically important and which are also susceptible to public action, issues which require new measures of social engineering. This means leaving out areas in which progress has now become routine. For example, one can take it for granted that real wage levels will continue to rise and that legal minimum wages and social insurance benefits will rise with them.

541

I also omit areas in which direct government intervention does not seem appropriate. Does automation, for example, constitute "a problem"? Not in the sense that we would want to penalize introduction of more efficient equipment. Technical change should probably be speeded up rather than retarded. But retraining and re-employment of workers displaced by mechanization does constitute a problem.

Within these ground rules, my priority list reduces to six items: maintaining high aggregate demand for labor; improving the marketing of labor; establishing equal educational opportunity; establishing equal job opportunities for Negro workers; eliminating pockets of poverty; and improving the framework of collective bargaining. These things have all been discussed in earlier chapters. But by re-emphasizing them we may bring out certain highlights and lend perspective to the book as a whole.

A HIGH LEVEL OF EMPLOYMENT

Since the mid-'fifties the American economy has operated well below capacity. How far below, no one can say with certainty; but on an average of good and bad years, unused capacity may have been of the order of 10 per cent. In addition to an excessive number of full-time unemployed, there are millions of partially or disguisedly unemployed: part-time workers who would prefer longer hours, marginal farmers who would move to town if jobs were available, low-skilled workers who could be upgraded to higher jobs.

Raising the economy toward full employment would not only provide jobs and add to national output; it would also be a long step toward solving a variety of other problems. Why do surplus people accumulate in agriculture and remain there at low income levels? Why are workers with limited education, or with physical or mental handicaps, ruled out as unemployable instead of being set to tasks they could do? Why do workers hesitate to change jobs freely, and resist displacement by mechanization? Why does retraining of the unemployed for new jobs often seem academic? The answer in each case is inadequate demand for labor. Many of the measures suggested in later sections make sense only if there are enough jobs for all who want them.

What can be done to keep the economy operating closer to capacity? We start from the proposition that, at full-employment income levels, households and businesses will choose to save a certain percentage of their incomes; that this level of saving must be matched by investment if full employment is to continue; and that in our kind of economy most of this must be private investment. So one basic problem is what can be done to hold private investment at a sustained high level. High investment, apart from its immediate effect on employment, means more productive capacity and more output in future years.

Part of the answer doubtless lies in the tax structure. The present federal tax structure has developed haphazardly over the years. It professes to prevent anyone from getting too rich, but doesn't succeed very well. Numerous loopholes yield profit windfalls to certain groups. Yet over-all we penalize profits and new investment more heavily than most other capitalist countries. There is need for a complete re-thinking of the tax system, giving high priority to investment and rapid economic growth.

A meaningful government commitment to full employment has also proven stimulating to private investment in France, Sweden, Japan, and a number of other countries. In these countries industrial and government leaders consult in advance on what rate of increase in GNP can reasonably be attained in the year ahead. There are detailed calculations of what this will mean for demand in each industry, and how much new productive capacity will be required to meet these demands. Government puts its own investment plans on the table, and these are combined with the investment plans of private industry. If it appears that total investment plus expected consumer spending will exceed the capacity of the economy, government may decide to cut back its investment program or raise tax rates. If on the other hand it appears that total investment will be too low to attain full employment, government may urge private industries to raise their investment targets or may alter its own budget plans. The outcome is a program which will balance out at full employment, which is internally consistent, and which is accepted by the business community as a "best guess" about what will actually happen.

After participating in this exercise for some years and observing that actual GNP comes out close to the plan targets, businessmen eventually become convinced that they can safely take these targets as a guide in their own investment planning. A company will invest more heavily and more regularly if it believes that GNP is going to rise 5 per cent every year than if it regards the future as largely unpredictable. With enough companies doing this simultaneously, and with the government budget playing its proper role, the expected increase in GNP will actually occur. This concerted envisaging of the future, far from constituting "meddlesome government intervention," is practical and helpful from a strictly business viewpoint.

It would be useful also to increase the rate of technical change. The faster new products and production processes are developed, the more rapidly will existing equipment become obsolete and new investment become necessary. But it is hard to say just how this can be done. A larger output of scientists and engineers seems desirable. But there are difficult questions of how effort should be divided between pure and applied research, and of what organization and financing of scientific work is most conducive to rapid progress.

A high level of private investment should be accompanied by adequate programs of public investment. The continuing needs in this area are very large. They include public schools, colleges, professional schools, hospitals, and other educational and health facilities; highways, waterways, and urban and commuter transportation; urban redevelopment programs; low-cost housing; parks, forests, and recreational facilities; atomic energy and space installations; and many other things. We have probably done less in these directions over the past decade than would have been desirable. Long-range programs whose economic yield has been carefully evaluated are preferable to "emergency public works" improvised hastily after unemployment has already developed.

In accounting for the cost of government investment, it would be wise to separate current and capital budgets as is now done in most other countries. The current budget includes the civil service payroll, the military payroll, the cost of purchased goods and materials, interest on the public debt, and other transfer payments. This budget is normally covered out of current revenue. Investment expenditures, on the other hand, are listed in a separate capital budget. Part of this budget may also be covered from current income; but most countries consider it legitimate for government to borrow to meet investment costs. Borrowing for this purpose is not thought of as involving a "government deficit." Our federal budget, which treats government investment as a current item to be fully offset by current revenue, any failure to do this constituting a "deficit," may have been satisfactory when federal expenditures were very small. But today this procedure is misleading and interferes with sensible fiscal management.

A word on the revenue side of the budget in relation to full employment. The accepted principle is that taxes should be set at such a level that business investment, plus government purchases of goods and services, plus household spending, plus the excess of exports over imports, will equal the economy's productive capacity at full employment. If total demand is too low, taxes should be cut to release more private spending. If demand is too high, taxes should be raised to drain off the excess demand. Budget policy should aim to balance total demand and supply in the economy rather than to balance government income and outgo. This view has been taught by economists for several decades, and is widely and successfully practiced in other countries. Almost the only unconvinced groups in the world seem to be certain segments of opinion in the United States. It would be amusing, if it were not so serious, to hear Senators arguing that the finances of the United States should be managed like those of a corner grocery store; and to hear business leaders opposing tax reductions which would benefit both business and the economy.

The view that the most effective attack on underemployment lies through the fiscal system implies that some other favorite remedies are inappropriate, including some which are dear to the hearts of union leaders. AFL-CIO conventions continue to pass resolutions endorsing a cut in the workweek and a more rapid rise of money wage rates as solutions for unemployment. A cut in the workweek, as we noted in Chapter 9, does not create additional employment, but simply spreads the existing work over more people. It sets a lower ceiling on national output and on workers' real incomes. If a large proportion of workers feel that the 40-hour week is beyond their personal optimum, and want to trade income for additional leisure, a cut in the workweek would be justifiable. But there is little indication that this is the case.

The argument for outsize money wage increases is that they will transfer income from profit recipients to wage earners with a higher marginal propensity to consume, which will reduce the national savings rate and hence allow full employment with a lower level of investment. The defect of this argument is in the first step. We noted in Chapter 16 that the money wage level has little effect on real wages or on the distribution of income between wages and profits.

IMPROVED LABOR MARKETING

Assuming that underemployment has been eliminated and that there are enough jobs to go around, the next requirement is to help workers adapt to the rapidly shifting pattern of labor demand. This should not, of course, entail any infringement on free choice of employment. We should aim rather to create institutional conditions which will make personal preferences truly effective.

The lines of action required were outlined in Chapter 15. The prime need is for an improved network of employment service offices. The public image of the employment service needs to be reshaped, and the historic connection with unemployment compensation loosened if not broken. The mission of the employment service is not to test people's willingness to work, or to find jobs for the least employable groups in the population, or for those in greatest financial need. Its function is to improve the market mechanism, to create an effective labor exchange, to match the characteristics of vacant jobs with the preferences and qualifications of available workers. This is a technical, skilled, and essentially neutral job, from which employers should benefit at least as much as employees. The employment service can grow to maximum usefulness only if it can be transformed from a "labor agency" with a faint relief odor into an economic agency serving the whole community.

A second essential activity is forecasting of labor demands by occupation, industry, and region. This can be especially helpful to people still in high school or college. There is no reason why young people choosing careers should have to "fly blind" to the extent that they have done in the past. Demand forecasts are needed also as a guide to retraining programs for adult workers.

The occupational forecasting work of the U.S. Bureau of Labor Statistics dates only from the late 'forties, but has already achieved considerable success and influence. A recent appraisal compares the actual 1950-60 employment changes in 108 occupations with those forecast by the first B.L.S. *Occupational Outlook Handbook* issued in 1949. The author reports that "it was successful in about 3 out of 4 cases in projecting the direction and relative magnitude of all changes in employment by occupation and by industry, both increases and decreases."[1] It was particularly successful in identifying declining industries and occupations. On the whole, these early forecasts had a conservative bias. There were 41 understatements of future growth of demand, only 10 overstatements. This seems to have been due partly to the depression psychology still prevailing in the late 'forties, and partly to a serious underestimate of future population growth.

If all the above steps have been taken, there is adequate over-all demand for labor. There are forecasts of the detailed pattern of jobs by area, occupation, and industry. There is a placement mechanism, the employment service, for referring candidates to these jobs as they become available. The remaining needs are good vocational training and vocational advice for young people, and a massive retraining program for adult workers. Even in the underemployed economy of the early 'sixties there were labor shortages in many skilled, technical, and white-collar occupations. At the same time there were many workers without job skills or with skills for which demand is declining. This will continue to be a problem in the years ahead. The structure of labor demand will probably shift even more rapidly in future decades, creating simultaneously shortage points and pools of obsolete skills, which even the best forecasting cannot prevent. Adult vocational training schemes can thus make a direct contribution to reducing frictional unemployment and raising national output.

Any unemployed worker who lacks work skills, or whose skills are unlikely to be in demand within the visible future, should be able to apply for vocational training, and should be supported at an unemployment compensation level during the training period. The courses offered should be based on realistic forecasts of future demand trends. There should be close cooperation between training authorities and the employment service, so that workers completing training are fed into the labor market effectively. There should be aids to inter-area movement where necessary. Promising steps in this direction have been taken under the Manpower Development and Training Act of 1962; but the number of people being trained under this Act is still only a small fraction of those who need retraining. This may be due partly to a nagging suspicion that too few jobs will be available in the end, in which event training becomes demoralizing and futile. This is why we have emphasized so strongly the need for full employment as an underpinning of all other labor market programs.

[1] Harold Goldstein, "B.L.S. Occupational Trend Projections: an Appraisal," *Monthly Labor Review* (October 1963), pp. 1135-38.

EQUAL JOB OPPORTUNITIES THROUGH EDUCATION

In a market economy, equality means an equal start in the occupational race. It means opportunity to compete for work in any occupation within limits set only by personal preference and ability. From another standpoint it involves *equal opportunity to earn income.* This does not mean that earned incomes actually will be equal. But they will be more nearly equal with free occupational competition than without it; and the remaining inequality can be rationalized on economic grounds.

In a complex industrial economy, where an increasing proportion of jobs require long training periods, young people are channeled into occupations through the educational system. Equal job opportunity, therefore, requires that young people be selected for advanced training on the basis of personal ability and preference, without biases arising from parentage or family income level. We noted in Chapter 15 that this is far from being the case at present.

The high school years are crucial. This is the point at which educational and career plans are still flexible, all avenues are open, nothing has yet been committed. Parental influence will not necessarily lead to correct decisions at this stage. Many parents, particularly in the lower occupational levels, have only a hazy idea of professional and managerial opportunities and of the returns from investment in higher education. This, plus the fact that they have limited funds for investment, may lead them to discourage even very able children from going on to college. There is need for active effort by high school teachers and vocational advisers to identify students who have the ability to do college work, to encourage them to plan for college admission, and to acquaint them with possible sources of financing. This could do much to check the large waste of talent which occurs at present.

The majority of students who will not go on to college should be given a realistic basis for judging both the attractiveness of various occupations and their own capacities. During their last year or two in high school they should become familiar with the occupational structure of the economy, prospective earnings in various occupations, the nature of the work and other nonwage characteristics, the amount and type of specialized training required, the trend of demand and the chances of securing employment, employers' hiring methods and requirements, and the operation of the employment service and other placement agencies. This might be done through regular classroom courses, supplemented by class visits to stores, offices, factories, and other places of employment, and perhaps by guest lectures by people especially familiar with particular fields. Some high schools, in cooperation with the employment service, are already doing a good job of counseling and placement, particularly for girls interested in office occupations. But in most schools these possibilities are not fully exploited.

As regards high school curriculum, students with little aptitude for academic subjects can probably benefit from spending much of their time on vocational instruction. It is important, however, that instruction be related realistically to employment possibilities, which is typically not true at present. We are presently spending about a quarter of a billion dollars a year on vocational education, of which about one-fifth comes from federal grants and the remainder from the states and localities. Close to two million high school students are enrolled in vocational courses. But because of Congressional restrictions and institutional inertia, about half of these are studying home economics, which is mainly a preparation for homemaking rather than employment; and another quarter are studying agriculture, where employment opportunities are shrinking rapidly. Only one-sixth are classified as studying "trades and industries," where the expanding opportunities mainly lie; and only one high school out of ten offers any instruction in these subjects.[2] This maladjustment between the direction of vocational training and the pattern of labor demand calls for remedial measures.

The percentage of high school graduates going on to college will undoubtedly continue to rise. Higher education is a consumer good as well as an investment good, and it has a high income elasticity of demand. As more families reach an income level at which they can readily afford college expenses, more young people will proceed to college almost automatically. If steps are also taken to encourage and assist children from low-income families to go to college, this will further increase the rate of college attendance. Considering that high school classes are increasing steadily in size because of the postwar baby boom, the prospective increase in college enrollment between

---

[2] "Vocational Education in 1961," *Monthly Labor Review* (October 1963), pp. 1162-65.

1965 and 1975 is staggering. Among other things, it will mean a sharp rise in the percentage of college students enrolled in public institutions. Private institutions, even if they wished to expand at this rate, do not have the neecssary resources; and so most of the enrollment pressure will fall on the state colleges and universities.

This prospect raises several issues, which had best be put as questions since there is little agreement on the answers.

First, who is to bear the cost of building new classrooms, libraries, laboratories, dormitories, and other educational facilities? For the speed and scale of expansion required, federal participation seems necessary and is in fact already underway. But what proportion of the cost should come from federal funds—one-third, one-half, two-thirds? This will affect the distribution of costs among the states. Federal revenues come largely from progressive income taxation, and hence come disproportionately from the states with higher per capita incomes. The larger the federal participation in any expenditure program, the larger the income transfers from the wealthier states to the poorer ones.

Second, where are the teachers to come from? The output of college teachers from our graduate schools has increased only moderately over the past decade, and is falling far behind the rate of increase in college enrollments. Except for federal programs in the sciences, and such private ventures as the Woodrow Wilson fellowships, there has been little effort to repair this deficiency. Instead, the federal government and the private foundations have been depleting the teaching ranks by recruiting scientists, engineers, economists, and others into research and administrative activities, where one suspects their social productivity is often lower than it would be in the classroom. We have been living on our intellectual capital in a quite shortsighted way. Since it takes close to ten years to turn out a qualified college teacher, it is already too late to do much about this during the 'sixties, and the average quality of college teaching is certain to deteriorate for some time to come.[3] But an intensive effort to raise the annual output of teachers by fifty to one hundred per cent could begin to bear fruit in the 'seventies. Market forces are working in this direction. Salaries and perquisites of college teachers have been rising quite rapidly, and are increasingly competitive with opportunities in industry and

---

[3] The writer doubts that teaching machines, closed-circuit television, and other mechanical aids are a fully satisfactory substitute for personal discussion. But this may be only the jaundiced view of a craftsman threatened with technological displacement!

government. But supply reactions are sluggish, and the market could do with a little help.

Third, how should teachers' salaries and other current educational expenses be financed? The public colleges and universities have traditionally followed a low-tuition policy, and costs have been covered largely from tax revenues. But this policy is beginning to bend under the pressure of rapidly rising costs, and some states have raised tuition charges substantially. This can be justified on the ground that higher education has cash value to the student in terms of future income, and that he should, therefore, pay a price for it. On the other hand, the higher the tuition, the more people from low-income families will be deterred from entering college unless scholarship or loan funds are increased simultaneously.

Fourth, how can qualified young people whose parents are unable to pay for their college expenses secure the necessary financing? This question is interlocked with the previous one. The higher the level of tuition charges imposed, the more serious is the personal financial problem of the needy student. However the two questions are resolved, the outcome should be that no able young person is barred from college for financial reasons. The funds will have to come mainly from public sources; but they can be loan funds rather than outright grants. The National Defense Education Act now provides $90 million of federal funds per year for loans to undergraduates specializing in science, mathematics, and modern foreign languages. The funds are administered through colleges and universities, which must provide $1 of their own funds for each $9 of federal funds received. Over the first five years of the program, some 490,000 students received loans under the Act. The average loan was about $500 per year, obviously only a part of total college expenses, but often the vital margin which made college possible at all. Over the same period, some 7,000 graduate students in these areas received outright scholarships at a total cost of $80 million.

This program has worked well. But why should it apply only to students in these areas? Can one safely assert that studying German or chemistry is important to the nation, while studying economics or history is not? Why should not the program be extended to qualified students in any area? This would require a considerably larger revolving fund than that now provided under NDEA; but since the money is repayable with interest, there is no cost to government beyond administrative expenses and a risk of loan default which thus far has turned out to be negligible.

EQUAL OPPORTUNITIES FOR NEGRO WORKERS

The status of the Negro in American society is far more than an economic problem. It is a social and political problem, with deep roots in the past. But it has an important economic aspect. Americans are often accused of living by the dollar sign. While this may be deplorable in some respects, it has one beneficial effect. People who have money and who can buy the outward symbols of affluence tend to be respected, regardless of their personal characteristics. If Negroes were distributed in the same proportions as whites throughout the occupational structure, if they enjoyed the same average family income, their present difficulties would be lessened. Equal opportunity to qualify for any occupation on the basis of merit would contribute toward this end.

Equal occupational opportunity, in addition to being a matter of justice, is a requirement for economic efficiency. If a person is utilized below his inherent capacity, if he is barred arbitrarily from higher tasks for which he is qualified or could qualify, national output is reduced.

The measures suggested in earlier sections would be even more beneficial to Negroes than to white workers. Adequate total demand for labor would cut into the high percentage of Negro unemployed, and would stimulate the upgrading of Negroes to better jobs. A large proportion of Negro workers lack job skills, and so adult retraining programs would be particularly helpful to them. Measures to raise the quality of education throughout the country, and to enable qualified youngsters to get money for college expenses, would be especially beneficial to Negro families since such a large percentage of them fall in the low-income brackets.

If these lines of activity were pushed vigorously enough, we should eventually reach a stage at which special programs for Negroes would not be necessary. But this is a dream of the future. Special efforts will be necessary for a long time to come. There is need to raise the quality of Negro colleges and universities, while at the same time working toward equality of treatment in college admissions generally. The retraining problems of low-skilled Negro workers require special attention. There is need for continued effort to reduce discrimination in hiring and promotion. Progress is being made on this front. In the past, many industrial plants have maintained separate seniority rosters and promotion ladders for Negro and white workers, which halted the Negro worker in a dead-end job at a low wage level. More and more companies are now integrating these rosters so that a Negro can progress to the highest skill and pay levels on a merit basis. The building construction unions and employers, with a certain amount of federal prodding, are moving toward selection of young people for apprentice training on a merit basis.

Eroding discriminatory hiring practices will still be a long, slow process. The main difficulty is often not employer resistance to equal treatment, but resistance by white workers who regard the Negroes as potential competitors for the better jobs. Full employment would ease these issues of economic competition, though it would not entirely remove them.

ELIMINATING POCKETS OF POVERTY

Discussions of poverty are beset by the notion that, if people are poor, it must be because they are unwilling to work; and that if they are enabled to subsist without working, their incentive to work will be further reduced. This misses the heart of the problem. The population does contain some ne'er-do-wells who are quite capable of working but prefer not to. But most people are poor because they cannot work regularly on account of age or other disabilities.

This is why poverty does not cure itself automatically as the wage level rises. The increase in real wages over the past century has virtually eliminated poverty among regularly employed members of the labor force. But the tide of affluence bypasses certain groups which, because they are not attached to any payroll, fail to participate in the general advance.

The most effective antipoverty measure of modern times is the Social Security Act of 1935, as amended and improved since that time. The central purpose of this Act is to enable regularly employed workers, through payroll taxes levied on them and their employers, to build an insurance fund from which they can draw monthly benefit payments after reaching retirement age (normally 65, though a covered worker can now retire with reduced benefits at age 62). In the late 'fifties the Act was extended to provide for permanent disability. A covered worker who becomes permanently disabled before age 65 is treated as though he had reached 65, and begins to draw benefits at the regular scale.

More than 90 per cent of all workers in paid employment are now covered by the social security system. In 1963 about 17 million people, roughly two-thirds of all men and women 65 and over, were drawing benefit payments, and total payments were running at the rate of $15 billion a year. Benefit amounts are related to previous earnings, with a maximum of $127 per month. The wife of a pensioned worker may receive up to half this amount, and further allowances are provided for dependent children, but total family benefits cannot exceed $254 per month. If the worker lives in a city and has no other resources, these amounts would not lift him above the poverty line. But the Act has greatly reduced the amount of hardship arising from disability and old age.

The Social Security Act also provides assistance payments to certain specialized groups: aged or disabled people who for one reason or another have not managed to qualify for regular pensions; needy blind persons; and dependent children who have been deprived of support by the parent's death, disability, unemployment, or absence from home. Each state determines what is a reasonable standard of living, measures the applicant's resources against it, and determines how much assistance he should receive; but the federal government provides three-quarters of the cost, provided the state program meets certain minimum standards.

But some people still fall through these safety nets. A worker suffering from long-term unemployment, for example, may have exhausted his unemployment compensation rights, be too young for old age pensions, and free of any other disabilities which would bring him within the terms of the Social Security Act. Where is he to go? The utlimate resort for such people is general relief. Since this is financed from local tax sources, it is usually niggardly in amount and demeaning in administration.

Why should we not specify that any destitute member of the American community is entitled to live at a decent minimum level? To the extent that state and local funds are not adequate for this purpose, they could be supplemented by federal grants-in-aid as is done now for the special groups covered by the Social Security Act. Morgan and others have estimated the cost of doing this at less than 2 per cent of our GNP. Would it not be worth this amount to announce to ourselves and to the world that poverty no longer exists in the United States?

At this point one comes up against the bogey of willingness to work. It is certainly reasonable to provide that anyone capable of working be required to accept employment under suitable terms and conditions. Anyone who refuses such employment might well be left to private charity and his own devices. But if we want to compel employable relief clients to take jobs, the jobs must be available. The difficulty with applying a willingness-to-work test at present is that the labor market is too loose to make the test realistic.

One virtue of the approach suggested here is that it might generate pressure for a vigorous full-employment policy. If we undertook to support all the needy at a decent level, some of these would turn out to be able-bodied unemployed. The sight of these people sitting on the relief rolls might stimulate action to make more jobs available; and if this were done, the test of willingness to work could become effective. But if we must err in one direction or the other, it seems better to support some work-shy people in idleness than to let genuinely deserving and unemployable people suffer want in the midst of plenty.

IMPROVING THE FRAMEWORK OF COLLECTIVE BARGAINING

We shall not re-argue the pros and cons of collective bargaining. Our reasons for considering it a useful institution were explained in Chapter 12. But there is no real consensus on this matter in the United States. Many employers, and many of the general public, continue to regard collective bargaining as useless or pernicious.

There would be more consensus on the proposition that workers should have the right to choose between a union and no union. Whatever choice they make may be mistaken. But a democratic society confers the right to make this sort of mistake. Representation elections under the auspices of the National Labor Relations Board, and protection of the voters against unfair pressure from either union or employer, serve a useful purpose.

The union undertakes to protect workers against unfair discipline or other arbitrary actions by the employer. But what about protection against the union organization itself? There is a good case for legislation guaranteeing certain basic rights: admission to membership on a nondiscriminatory basis, equal participation in union affairs, and protection against expulsion or other discipline without due process of law.

Apart from guaranteeing these rights and establishing normal standards of financial accountability, it is doubtful that government should intervene in union elections or other internal affairs. It is illusory to think that unions can ever be made "democratic" in a town-meeting sense. Direct control of policy by the membership is not in the nature of any large voluntary organization, whether this be the Republican Party, the American Medical Association, or the stockholders of General Motors. Control gravitates to an active minority, whose self-interest is heavily involved, and for whom the politics of the organization becomes a major preoccupation. It is not feasible to require unions to behave differently. If one can protect the right of dissenting members to stay in the union and speak their mind, they will be able to exert influence on policy and on the choice of leaders; and this is the most one can reasonably expect.

In addition to protecting the individual worker against inequitable treatment from any quarter, it may be desirable to restrict the tactics which union and management organizations can use against each other—for example, secondary boycotts and similar billiard-shot tactics by unions, or refusal to deal with the union by employers. But the list of proscribed practices should be kept very short, otherwise government will be drawn into every facet of individual relations.

Over the past generation, unfortunately, our labor law has spread out far beyond the really essential objectives. Whenever unions or managements were doing anything which the other side disliked, there has been an outcry of "let's pass a law." Legislation has grown more complex and technical, the jurisdiction of the NLRB and the courts has been steadily extended, and the whole process of industrial relations has been infected by a creeping legalism.

The present need is to minimize government intervention in labor relations rather than increase it. Ideally, the whole body of federal legislation should be redrafted and streamlined to focus directly on the few objectives outlined above.

While in general we need less government intervention in collective bargaining, there is at least one problem which may call for new regulatory measures. This involves peaceable adjustment of disputes in transportation, public utilities, and other industries whose continuous operation is essential to public safety and convenience. Work stoppages in these industries inflict economic damage and also reduce public esteem for collective bargaining.

Work stoppages in essential industries are in fact usually avoided or settled after a brief period. But they are settled by extra-legal improvisation at the last moment, rather than by an orderly and accepted procedure. The most dramatic recent example is the dispute over railroad work rules, which has dragged on for years and is still unsettled at this writing. It is predictable that before long we shall have another threatened national rail strike and another round of hurried improvisation.

It is not surprising that the public becomes impatient with proce dures which seem so hazardous and inconclusive. Anyone who could devise an equitable and enforceable method of handling these dis- putes would deserve a Nobel prize for industrial peace. He would also have done much to restore the good repute of collective bargaining in the American community.

Index

AARON, BENJAMIN, 99, 106, 125, 130, 133, 140, 294
Abbeglen, James C., 151
AFL: *see* American Federation of Labor
AFL-CIO:
  anti-communist measures, 57-60
  in elections, 71-72
  formation of, 31, 40-45
Agency shop, 194
Agricultural labor, 3-7, 331, 334, 339, 388-89, 465, 475-76, 479, 515, 523
American Arbitration Association, 180
American Federation of Labor:
  formation of, 28, 31, 35-38
  growth of membership, 40-41
  merger with CIO, 40-45
  political activities, 71-72
Anderson, George, 282
Anderson, H. D., 376
Anti-racketeering laws, 90-93
Apprenticeship, 189-90
Arbitration, 179-82, 280-83, 288-89
Area Redevelopment Act, 390
Argentina, 19
Armour Company, 175
Atomic Energy Labor-Management Relations Panel, 288
Australia, 3, 19, 60, 62, 270, 282
Automation, 230-34, 337-38
Automobile Workers, United, 45, 97, 166, 171, 180, 222, 223, 250, 262, 368

BAKER, HELEN, 157, 509
Bakery Workers, 98
Bakke, E. Wight, 28, 52, 63, 78, 94, 149, 157, 385, 404
Bakunin, M., 56
Baldwin, George B., 337
Ball, R. J., 419
Bancroft, Gertrude, 344
Barbash, Jack, 82, 84, 107
Barbers' Union, 70, 164

Barcus, Norman, 368
Bargaining unit, 160-62
Barkin, S., 52
Barnett, George, 236
Barry, Carol A., 463
Beck, Dave, 89, 90
Becker, Joseph M., 361
Bedaux system, 223
Belgium, 3, 60
Bendix, Reinhard, 391, 393, 394, 395, 404
Bergson, Abram, 22
Bernstein, Irving, 52, 140, 287, 288, 291, 293, 294
Berry, George, 94
Bethlehem Steel Corporation, 40
Beveridge, William H., 370, 537
Board of inquiry, 287-88
"Bogus" rule of ITU, 226-27
Boilermakers' Union, 189
Boise, R. W., Jr., 504
Booth, Philip, 368
Boulwarism, 152
Bowen, William G., 419, 423, 424, 436
Boycott, 114, 122, 124, 127, 128, 133, 137, 273, 277
Braun, Kurt, 282
Brazer, Harvey E., 396, 521, 537
Brewster, Frank, 89
Brindell, Robert P., 91
Bronfenbrenner, Martin, 434
Brooks, George, 215
Brown, Douglass V., 125
Brown, E. C., 120, 140
Budd, Edward C., 457
Building Service Employees Union, 48
Building Trades unions, 44, 65, 91, 226
Bureau of Labor Statistics, U.S., 45, 249, 263, 333, 346, 407, 409, 495, 496, 519, 529, 546
Burns, Eveline M., 357, 370, 537
Business cycles (*see also* Depression; Recession):

Business cycles (*cont.*)
income fluctuations in, 455
strikes and, 269
unemployment and, 203, 229, 346,
349-51
union growth and, 28-31
wage movements in, 423

CALKINS, FAY, 78
Canada, 3, 19, 61, 270, 341, 532
Carpenters' unions, 25, 41, 91, 94
Census Bureau, 320, 332, 340, 342,
387, 511
Chamber of Commerce, U.S., 263
Chamberlain, Neil W., 63, 64, 78,
184, 186
Checkoff, 122, 127, 197-98
Cheit, Earl F., 370
Chinoy, Eli, 86
Christenson, C. L., 164, 230, 236
Chrysler Corporation, 40
Cigar Makers' Union, 36
CIO: *see* Congress of Industrial
Organizations
Civil Service: *see* Government
employees
Clark, Colin, 331
Clark, John Bates, 446, 449, 451, 461
Clark, M. Gardner, 469
Clayton Act, 116-17
Closed shop, 126, 190-94
Clothing industry, 41, 69, 86, 124,
167, 193, 200, 201, 242, 245, 346
Clothing Workers, Amalgamated, 39,
90, 252
Coal industry (*see also* Mine Workers,
United), 65, 86, 123, 167
Cohen, W. J., 357, 396, 521, 537
Cole, David L., 175
Coleman, J. S., 96
Collective bargaining:
arbitration in, 179-82, 280-83, 288-
89
Clayton Act, 116-17
compulsory arbitration versus, 280-83
foreman's role, 308-10
improving framework of, 555-57
injunction in, 114-16, 286
issues in: hours of work, 210-16
issues in: production methods,
211-36
issues in: wages, 238-65, 501-3

judicial regulation of, 110-17
Landrum-Griffin Act, 124-25
management and, 141-58
multiemployer agreements, 162-67
Norris-LaGuardia Act, 117-19
objectives of, 65-68
personnel policies and, 310
procedures, 167-76
scope of, 132
strikes and, 114-17, 122, 128, 173,
280-83
Taft-Hartley Act, 122-39
unfair practices, employer, 129-33
unfair practices, union, 133-34
union tactics, 159-85
Wagner Act, 119-22
Committee on Economic Security, 363
Committee on Equal Employment
Opportunity, 403
Commons, John R., 28, 52, 112
Commonwealth v. Hunt, 113
Communism, 57-60, 104, 124
Compulsory arbitration, 280-83, 288-89
Conant, Eaton H., 386
Conciliation, 283-85
Congress of Industrial Organizations:
expulsion of communists, 41
merger with AFL, 40-45
under NLRB, 161-62
organization of, 30, 39-40
political activities, 71-72
Connerton, Robert J., 105
Conspiracy doctrine, 113-14
Construction industry (*see also* Build-
ing Trades unions), 44, 65, 86, 91,
124, 163-64, 193, 194, 200, 201,
225, 467
Consumer's Price Index, 250, 409-12
Continuous negotiation, 174-76
Contract, union:
compensation under, 187-88
complexity of, 5
function of, 37-38
job security in, 187, 198-209
negotiation of, 160, 249
provisions of, 68, 160, 187-88
work schedules in, 187, 212-13
Cordwainers' Union, 25
Courts: *see* Judicial control
Cox, Archibald, 291, 293
Craft unionism, 39-40
Creamer, Daniel C., 436
Crime: *see* Racketeering; Violence

Curran, Joseph, 58
Cushman, E. L., 231, 237

DAVEY, H. W., 186
David, Martin H., 396, 521, 537
Davidson, P. E., 376
Debs, Eugene V., 61
Denison, E. F., 440, 441, 457, 461
Denmark, 60, 61
Department Store Employees' Union,
    48
Depression, 28, 29, 33, 66, 202, 269,
    297, 388, 408, 440, 523, 533
Derber, Milton, 158
Dickenson, Z. C., 504
Director, Aaron, 349
Discharge, 207-9, 308
Discipline, 207-9
Discrimination, 120, 134, 194, 274,
    403, 483, 553
Domar, Evsey D., 439
Douglas, Paul H., 339, 349
Dubin, Robert, 107, 177, 184, 269
Dubinsky, David, 40
Dunlop, John T., 22, 125, 175, 184,
    186, 244, 264, 480, 481
Durand, John D., 320, 344

EARNINGS (see also Wages):
    determinants of earning power,
        462-63
    hours of work and, 407
    median incomes by occupation
        groups, 464 (table)
    occupational differences, 463-76
    occupational rate curves, 507 (fig.)
Eckstein, Otto, 419, 436
Economic stabilization, 432-36
Edelman, Murray, 404
Education:
    importance of, 394-97
    job opportunities through, 548-51
    loan funds for, 399-400
    percentage expected to go to college,
        395 (table)
    scholarship grants, 399
    vocational, 548-51
Electrical, Radio and Machine
        Workers, United, 41, 166, 189
Electrical Workers (IBEW), 48, 226
Employees, dependent status of, 4-5

Employment (see also Labor market;
        Unemployment):
    changing patterns of, 331-38
    civilian labor force, 329 (fig.)
    high level of, 542-45
    levels of, 328-30
    money wages and, 432-35
    public employment services, 347,
        381-86, 547
    wage policies and, 432-35
    worker characteristics, 483-85
Employment Security Act, 367
Enarson, Harold L., 287, 288, 291,
    293, 294
Engels, F., 56
England: see Great Britain
Equal opportunity, 397-400
Escalator clauses, 250, 421
Essential industries disputes, 285-93,
    556-57
Ethical Practices Committee, 98
Evans, H., 140
Experience rating, 359-60

FAIR LABOR STANDARDS ACT, 211, 212,
    528, 529
Family incomes: see Income, personal
Featherbedding, 136, 227, 273
Federal Mediation and Conciliation
        Service, 180, 283, 284
Feldman, Arnold S., 22
Feldman, Herman, 349, 359
Fellner, William J., 436
Finances, union, 83-84, 89-90
Financial malfeasance, 89-90, 105
Firestone Tire and Rubber Company,
    40
Fisher, Llyod H., 107, 163
Fleming, Robben W., 133, 287, 288,
    291, 293, 294
Florence, P. Sargant, 236, 344
Foenander, O. de R., 282
Fogarty, M. P., 467
Ford Motor Company, 40, 166, 180,
    264
Foremen, 308-10
France, 3, 19, 56, 59, 60, 76, 270, 341,
    393, 413, 468, 475, 543
France, R. R., 290
Franke, Walter H., 348
Frankfurter, Felix, 115, 140

Friedman, M., 404
Fringe benefits, 199, 260-64, 305-8
Fuchs, Victor R., 477
Full employment, 214, 299, 348, 355, 386, 485-86, 545, 547, 555
Fuller, S. H., 185, 264

GALENSON, WALTER, 22, 55, 62, 78, 107, 469
Garbarino, Joseph W., 251, 264, 481, 487
Gardner, Burleigh B., 158
Garment Workers, Ladies', 39, 41, 90, 181, 223, 242
General Electric Corporation, 40, 152, 166
General Motors Corporation, 40, 141, 166, 180, 250
Germany, 3, 19, 56, 59, 60, 61, 182, 270, 331, 341, 393, 413, 469
Ginzberg, Eli, 82, 107
Goldberg, Arthur J., 53, 285
Golden, C. S., 184
Goldner, W., 487
Goldsmith, Selma, 514
Goldstein, Harold, 547
Gomberg, William A., 236, 509
Gompers, Samuel, 36-38, 70, 116
Goodrich, B.F., Company, 40
Goodyear Tire and Rubber Company, 40
Gouldner, A. W., 86
Government employees' unions, 48, 51
Government, role of, in labor relations, 20, 556-57
Great Britain, 3, 19, 25, 56, 59, 60, 62, 76, 112, 125, 182, 192, 270, 312, 331, 340, 341, 393, 413, 417, 468, 469, 475, 514, 531-32
Great Northern Paper Company, 166
Green, William, 43
Greene, Nathan, 115, 140
Gregory, C. O., 112, 113, 140, 272
Grievance machinery, 126, 176-82, 309
Grodin, Joseph R., 99
Gross National Product (*see also* Productivity), 355-56, 439-40, 543-44
    marginal productivity of labor, 451-54
Grundy, J. R., 73

HABER, WILLIAM, 226, 333, 357
Hansen, Alvin H., 481
Hansen, W. L., 327
Harbison, Frederick H., 22, 184
Hardman, J. B. S., 37, 94
Hart, P. E., 461
Hartman, Paul J., 270, 294
Hatters' Union, 242
Health Professions Educational Assistance Act, 400
Health and welfare plans, 132, 262, 306, 535-37
Healy, James J., 156, 158, 177, 185, 186, 189, 199, 209, 229, 237, 265, 509
Herberg, Will, 93
Hildebrand, George H., 495
Hill, Lee H., 158
Hillman, Sidney, 40, 96, 245
Hiring, control of, 66-67, 188-94
Hiring halls, 201, 350
Hod Carriers, 103
Hoffa, James, 90
Hohman, E. P., 201
Holidays, 216, 261
Hook, Charles R., Jr., 158
Hopkins, Sheila, 413, 487
Hosiery Workers, 252
Hours of work, 210-16
    annual, 216
    averages in manufacturing, 212 (fig.)
    earnings and, 407
    Fair Labor Standards Act, 211, 212
    union influence on, 211-13, 305, 306
    wages and, 408-9
    workweek, 210-16, 306-7, 545
Hoxie, R. F., 33, 55
Human Relations Research Committee, 174
Hutcheson, William, 94

INCENTIVE SYSTEMS, 12, 217-24
Income, personal (*see also* National income):
    distribution of, 458-59
    equal opportunity to earn, 548
    family income distribution, 514 (*table*), 517 (*table*)
    family incomes, 510-13 (*table*)
    inequality in, 513-19
    median incomes by occupation groups, 464 (*table*)

Income, personal (*cont.*)
  professions, 471-72
  security, 531-35
India, 19, 270
Industrial relations, organization for, 153-57
Industrial Relations Research Association, 344
Industrial Union Department of AFL-CIO, 44
Industrial unionism, 39-40
Industrial Workers of the World, 38
Industrialization, 3-15
Inflation, 419, 420-24, 428-30, 457, 474
Injunction, 111, 114-16, 286
Input:
  land as input in production, 457
  output, productivity, and, 438-46
Interarea Recruitment System, 389
Interstate Commerce Commission Act, 167
Italy, 19, 59, 60, 76, 270, 341, 469

JAFFE, A. J., 320, 344
Japan, 3, 4, 19, 341, 393, 543
Jaszi, George, 514
Jensen, Vernon H., 351
Job choices and labor mobility, 296-97
Job evaluation, 259, 504-8
Job opportunities:
  control of, by union, 66-67, 188-94
  through education, 548-51
Job tenure and security, 186-209
Johnson, D. Gale, 475, 487
Johnson, F. H., 504
Joint Committee on Economic Report, 446, 521, 537
Joseph, Myron L., 173
Judicial control of unions (*see also* Boycott; Injunction; Picketing; Strikes), 110-17
Jurisdictional disputes, 127, 273, 277

KAHL, JOSEPH A., 395
Kahn, Robert L., 108
Kaiser Steel Company, 175, 232
Kaltz, Hyman, 514
Karsch, Bernard, 86
Kaufman, Jacob J., 294
Kendrick, John W., 439, 441, 445, 454, 457, 461

Kennedy, Thomas, 254, 265
Kennedy, Van Dusen, 177, 178, 236, 265
Kerr, Clark, 12, 19, 22, 28, 52, 94, 108, 138, 149, 163, 175, 269, 312, 456, 457, 461
Key, V. O., Jr., 70, 73, 78
Kidd, C. V., 359
Killingsworth, C. C., 121, 140, 231, 344
Klein, L. R., 419
Knights of Labor, 32, 35, 36, 37
Knowles, K. G. J. C., 294, 487
Korean War, 30, 250, 429
Kornhauser, Arthur, 78, 107, 177, 184, 269
Kovner, Joseph, 93
Kravis, Irving B., 457, 461
Kuhn, James W., 185
Kuznets, Simon, 331, 404, 425, 457, 514, 516

LABOR EXCHANGES: *see* Public Employment Services
Labor Force:
  civilian labor force, 329 (*fig.*)
  definition and measurement, 320-21
  industrial composition of, 333-34 (*tables*)
  occupational composition of, 335 (*table*)
  participation in, 320-28
  participation rates by age and sex, 323 (*table*)
  population by work status, 322 (*fig.*)
  women in, 325-27, 335, 484, 485
Labor law, development of, 109-39, 556
Labor-Management Relations Act: *see* Taft-Hartley Act
Labor-Management Reporting and Disclosure Act: *see* Landrum-Griffin Act
Labor market:
  controlling labor supply, 191 (*fig.*)
  development of, 10-18
  improvement of, 380-86, 546-47
  labor force defined, 320-21
  labor supply in, 318-20
  mobility in, 371-404
  pervasiveness of, 6-7
  public employment services, 381-86, 547

Labor market: (*cont.*)
    rural labor in, 475-76
    structure of, 238-43, 296-99
    trade unions and, 296-99
    turnover rates, 372 (fig.)
    wage policies and, 488-501
Labor Relations acts: *see* Clayton Act;
    Landrum-Griffin Act; Norris-La-
    Guardia Act; State Labor legisla-
    tion; Taft-Hartley Act; Wagner
    Act
Landrum-Griffin Act, 49, 84, 100-107,
    124-25
Latin America, 3, 60
Layoffs, 202-3, 206, 207, 308
Lea Act, 227
Leiserson, William, 108
Lenin, V. I., 56
Lester, Richard A., 78, 163, 185, 254,
    257, 290, 359, 362, 368, 370, 487,
    509
Letter Carriers' Union, 48
Levinson, Harold M., 226, 461
Lewis, H. Gregg, 252, 265
Lewis, John L., 40, 43, 94, 96, 245
Liebenberg, Maurice, 514
Lipset, Seymour M., 96, 391, 393,
    394, 395, 404
Livernash, E. Robert, 156, 158, 177,
    185, 189, 199, 209, 229, 237, 265,
    509
Lobbying, 70, 72-74
Local unions, 85-88
London, Jack, 86
Long, Clarence D., 320, 321, 324, 325,
    326, 327, 344, 416, 419, 436
Longshoremen's unions, 92, 98, 181,
    228, 350-51
Lorwin, Lewis L., 53
Lundberg, Erik, 425
Lyon, Leverett S., 435
Lytle, C. W., 504

MacDonald, Lois, 290
Machinists, International Association
    of, 41, 166, 189, 223
Maclaurin, W. R., 282, 376
Madison, C. A., 82
Mahon, William, 94
Maintenance of Membership, 194, 198
Make-work rules, 225-30
Malisoff, Harry, 365, 368

Management, attitudes and problems,
    141-58, 309
Mann, J. Keith, 288
Manpower Development and Training
    Act, 352, 547
Maritime Union, National, 44, 58
Market forces, 238-43, 489-92
Marsh, L. C., 532
Marx, Karl, 56, 60
Massachusetts Choice-of-Procedures
    Law, 291-93
Massell, B. F., 440
Mathewson, Stanley B., 236
Mayer, Albert J., 78
McCabe, D. A., 254
McCaffree, K. M., 466
McClellan Committee, 89, 90, 100
McConnell, J. W., 107
Meany, George, 43
Mechanization: *see* Automation
Mediation, 179-82, 283-85
Meij, J. L., 467, 487
Metal Trades, 44
Mexico, 19
Migration of labor, 257, 386-90
Miller, Ann R., 333
Miller, Herman P., 477, 478, 487, 512
Millis, H. A., 120, 140
Mills, C. Wright, 93, 94, 108
Mincer, Jacob, 326
Mine Workers, United, 39, 41, 69, 82,
    103, 124, 230, 252
Minimum wage legislation, 70, 525-30
Mobility of labor:
    geographic distribution, 387 (*table*)
    geographical, 353, 386-90
    job choices and, 296-97
    job security and, 6
    labor market policy and, 371-404
    lifetime, 391-92
    movement between generations,
        392-94
    obstacles to, 376-78
    occupational, 390-403
    seniority and, 205-6
    within an area, 374-86
    worker attitudes, 378-80
Moonlighting, 215
Moore, David G., 158
Moore, Wilbert E., 22
Morgan, James N., 396, 521, 537
Morton, W. H., 437
Moses, L., 215

Motion Picture Projectors' Union, 227
Multi-unit bargaining, 162-67
Murray, Philip, 43
Musicians, American Federation of, 48, 83, 227
Myers, Charles A., 22, 125, 158, 374, 376, 404
Myers, Frederic, 195

NADWORNY, MILTON J., 509
National Association of Manufacturers, 70
National Defense Education Act, 551
National emergency disputes, 128, 136, 286, 556-57
National income:
   distribution, 446-60
   employee compensation per cent of, 455 (*fig.*)
   employee share, 454-57
   family incomes, 512-13
   government role, 456, 459
   inequalities, 513-19
   labor's share of, 438-61
   measurement of, 447-48
   productivity and, 438-46
   profit percentage of, 454-56, 515
   real wages and, 300-303
National Industrial Recovery Act, 118
National Institute of Health, 400
National Labor Relations Act: see Wagner Act
National Labor Relations Board, 40, 44, 75, 110, 120, 129-36, 160-61, 555
National Labor Union, 32, 211
National Mediation Board, 286
National Recovery Administration, 211, 434
National Science Foundation, 400
National War Labor Board, 122, 280, 283, 290, 495
Naumkeag Steam Cotton Company, 267
Negro workers, 342, 400-403, 483, 485
   equal opportunities for, 552-53
Netherlands, 19, 393, 434, 469
New York City Labor Relations Division, 285
New York State Commission Against Discrimination, 403
New York State Crime Commission, 92

New York Waterfront Commission, 350
New Zealand, 3, 60, 532
Newcomer, Mabel, 151
Newspaper and Mail Deliverers Union of N. Y., 191
Nonwhite workers (*see also* Negro workers), 400-403
   annual income, 402 (*table*)
   employed persons, 401 (*table*)
Norgren, Paul H., 403
Norris-LaGuardia Act, 117-19
Northrup, Herbert R., 288
Norway, 19, 59, 60, 62, 270
Nyman, R. C., 268

OBER, HARRY, 467, 487
Occupational Outlook Handbook, 546
Oi, W., 215
Okun, Arthur M., 355
Old Age and Survivors' Insurance (OASI), 531
Open shop, 197
Operating Engineers, 103, 227
Output (*see also* Productivity), 213-14
   distribution of national output, 446-60
   hourly earnings and, 445 (*fig.*)
   level of, 4
   limitation of, 225-26
   productivity and, 438-46
   wage levels and, 425-26
Overtime, 87, 212, 215

PALMER, GLADYS L., 237, 333, 374, 376, 404
Parker, V. D., 184
Parnes, H. S., 404
Pattern bargaining, 165-67
Pension plans, 132, 262
Perlman, Richard, 477
Perlman, Selig, 53, 55, 67, 78, 198
Permit card system, 192
Personnel management (*see also* Industrial relations), 210, 310
Peterson, Florence, 82
Petrillo, James Caesar, 96
Phelps Brown, E. H., 22, 265, 413, 461, 487
Phelps, Orme W., 208, 209
Phillips, A. W., 417

Physical working conditions, 234-36
Picketing (*see also* Strikes), 122, 124, 137, 275-78
Piecework, 12, 87, 217-21
Pierson, Frank, 287, 457, 461, 480
Pigors, Paul, 158
Plant seizure, 290-91
Plumbers' Union, 48, 189, 225
Political Education Committee, AFL-CIO, 71
Poverty, 460, 519-25
    characteristics related to, 524 (*table*)
    eliminating, 553-55
Pratt, Dudley, 504
Preferential hiring, 126, 134, 193
Presgrave, Ralph, 237
Previant, David, 105
Price level and money wages, 247, 299-300, 420-32
Printing and publishing (*see also* Typographical Union, International), 65, 86, 193, 200
Product markets, competition in, 298-99
Productivity (*see also* Output):
    increase and real wages, 444-46
    inputs, output, and, 438-46
    labor's share of national income, 438-61
    make-work rules and, 225-30
    marginal productivity of labor, 451-54
    national income and, 438-46
    output and hourly earnings, 445 (*fig.*)
    wages and, 412-13, 444-46
Professional incomes, 471-72
Professional Office Network, 389
Professional unions, 51
Profits, 144-47, 247, 448, 454-56, 515
Promotions, 204-5, 206, 207
Public employment services, 347, 381-86, 547
Pulp, Sulphate, and Paper Mill Workers, 166

QUILL, MICHAEL, 58

RACKETEERING, 90-93

Railroad industry, 44, 65, 69, 123, 167, 194, 202, 224, 227-28, 289, 557
Railway Labor Act, 69, 128, 167, 286, 287, 289
Raimon, R. L., 496
Real wages, 300-303, 409-10, 452 (*fig.*)
Recession, 248, 423-24, 435
Reder, Melvin W., 215, 437, 467, 482, 487
Rees, Albert, 84, 191, 209, 244, 252, 265, 269, 416, 437
Referendum, in union elections, 81
Rehiring, 203, 207
Republic Steel Corporation, 40
Retail Clerks' Union, 48
Reuther, Walter, 43, 44, 58, 299
Reynolds, Lloyd G., 255, 265, 374, 376, 404, 467, 487, 509
Riegel, J. W., 504
Right-to-work laws, 137, 195
Roberts, B. C., 51
Robertson, D. J., 487
Robertson, David B., 94
Robie, E. A., 254
Ross, Arthur M., 74, 107, 177, 183, 184, 244, 265, 266, 269, 270, 294, 297, 487
Ruggles, Richard, 429
Russia, 3, 4, 11, 15, 19, 56, 58, 393, 397, 468, 469

SAMUELSON, P. A., 398, 417, 424
Saposs, David, 78
Sayles, Leonard, 85, 86, 108
Schuller, George J., 461
Seamen's unions (*see also* Maritime Union, National), 69, 201
Seidman, Harold, 91
Seidman, Joel, 86, 93
Selekman, B. M., 185, 264, 309
Selekman, S. K., 185, 264
Seltzer, George, 166
Seniority, 199-207, 308
Shape-up, 92, 350-51
Sharp, Ian G., 294
Sheppard, Harold L., 78
Shister, Joseph, 99, 125, 130, 133, 140, 163, 294, 376
Shoemakers' union, 25, 31
Shop steward, 179
Shultz, George P., 265, 291, 294, 337, 338, 374, 404, 503

Siegel, Abraham, 12, 19, 269
Simler, Norman J., 265, 457, 461
Sjaastad, Larry A., 389
Slavick, Fred, 368
Slichter Law, 306-7
Slichter, Sumner H., 140, 156, 158,
    177, 185, 189, 196, 199, 207,
    209, 229, 230, 237, 265, 287,
    306, 376, 481, 499, 509
Smith, Adam, 443, 469
Smith, D. M., 359
Smith, Russell A., 133
Sobel, Irvin, 328
Social insurance, 531-35
Social legislation, 312, 536-37
Social Security:
    federal, 261, 262, 357-58, 366, 429,
        525, 531-35, 553-54
    private plans, 261, 306, 368-69
Socialism, 60-62
Solow, Robert, 417, 424, 440
Somers, G. G., 231, 237
Sorel, G., 56
South Africa, 3
Southern Pacific Company v. *Arizona*,
    228
State labor legislation, 120-22, 137,
    194-95, 276, 290, 529
Steelworkers of America, United, 45,
    165, 166, 171, 181, 260, 368,
    508
Stevens, Carl, 173
Stewart, Charles D., 320, 344
Stieber, Jack, 265, 508, 509
Strauss, George, 85, 86, 108
Street Railway Workers, 94, 252
Strikes, 27, 114-17, 122, 123, 128,
    137, 173, 174, 175, 181-82, 232,
    266-94
    in selected countries, 271 (*table*)
Sultan, Paul, 209, 457
Summers, C. W., 99, 125, 130, 133,
    140, 294
Super-seniority, 204
Supplementary Unemployment Bene-
    fits (SUB), 262, 368-69
Sweden, 3, 4, 19, 59, 60, 62, 182,
    270, 331, 341, 353, 393, 413,
    468, 475, 543

TAFT, CYNTHIA H., 255, 467, 487

Taft-Hartley Act, 43, 49, 71, 122-39,
    160-61
    closed shop ban, 193
    strikes and, 274-78, 290
Taft, Philip, 53, 83, 84, 87, 88, 91,
    93, 108
Tannenbaum, Arnold S., 108
Tannenbaum, Frank, 54, 78
Tannenhaus, J., 276
Taylor, George, W., 140, 175, 185,
    283, 294, 457, 461, 480, 509
Teamsters' Union, 45, 48, 82, 89, 98,
    103, 164, 228
Technical change: see Automation
Technical unions, 51
Textile industry, 222, 243, 246
Textile Workers' Union, 69, 81, 252
Thornhill v. *Alabama*, 276
Time-study procedures, 217-19
Timework, 221-23
Tinbergen, Jan, 434
Tobin, Daniel, 94, 96
Trade unions (*see also* Unionism):
    bargaining tactics, 159-85
    democracy of, 96-97, 556
    finances, 83-84, 89-90
    impact on management organization,
        148-53, 155-57
    labor market and, 296-99
    leadership domination, 93-96
    local unions, 85-88
    national unions, 79-88
    Negro membership in, 100, 102,
        194
    price fixing arrangements, 164
    regulation of, 97-107
    under Taft-Hartley Act, 122-39
    wage policies, 238-65, 297-98, 304-5,
        501-3
Training and retraining programs, 188-
    90, 352-54, 547
Transfers, 204-5
Transport Workers' Union, 58, 92
Trow, M., 96
Troy, Leo, 48
Trucking industry (*see also* Teamsters'
    Union), 86, 91, 92, 131, 167, 480
True, John M., 509
Truman, David B., 78
Turnbull, John G., 370
Turvey, Ralph, 437
Typographical Union, International,
    31, 93, 189, 226, 228

ULMAN, LLOYD, 53
Unemployment (*see also* Employment;
   Labor Market):
   characteristics of, 338-43
   civilian labor force, 329 (*fig.*)
   cyclical, 203
   demand, 348-49, 354-56
   financing unavoidable, 356-64
   frictional, 346-47, 351-54, 547
   lines of action, 349-56
   per cent of labor force, 340 (*fig.*)
   seasonal and casual, 229, 346, 349-
      51
   sources of, 345-49
   suggested solutions, 545
   volume of, 338-43
Unemployment compensation, 356-69,
   533
   benefits, 262-64, 360-66
   costs, 359, 366-68
   coverage, 358-59
   experience rating, 359-60
   private plans, 368-69
Unfair practices, employers, 119-20,
   129-33, 274
Unfair practices, unions, 126, 133-34,
   277
Union Label Trades, 44
Union security, 186-209
Union shop, 126, 194-98
Unionism (*see also* Trade unions):
   AFL-CIO rivalry, 40-45
   in administrative process, 74-75
   communism and, 57-60, 104
   craft unionism, 39-40
   in elections, 70-72
   federations, 35-38
   history of, 25-53
   hours of work, influence on, 211-13,
      305, 306
   industrial unionism, 39-40
   in legislative process, 72-74
   local unions, 85-88
   management, participation in, 62-65
   membership, 29 (*fig.*), 30 (*table*),
      42 (*table*), 46 (*table*)
   membership, future outlook, 48-51
   membership, growth of, 28-31, 119,
      121
   national unions, 32-35
   objectives of, 65-77
   political tactics, 68-75
   radical politics and, 55-62

   regional differences, 47-48
   social changes and, 76
   socialism and, 60-62
   status of individual worker, 310-12
   structure of, 44-45
   welfare state and, 76
   white-collar unionism, 50-51
United States Steel Corporation, 40,
   165, 180, 231

VACATIONS, 216, 261
Violence, 92, 277-78
Vocational education, 548-51

WAGE-HOUR Act: *see* Fair Labor
   Standards Act
Wages (*see also* Earnings; Real wages):
   annual wage plans, 262
   collective bargaining, impact on,
      238-65, 501-3
   as a cost of production, 412-13
   deferred wage increase, 250
   defined, 406-13
   determinants of earning power, 462-
      63
   differentials, geographic, 477-79,
      485
   differentials, inter-firm, 254-58
   differentials, inter-industry, 479-83,
      485
   differentials, North-South, 256-57
   differentials, occupational, 469-76,
      485, 503-8, 515
   differentials, rural-urban, 475-76
   differentials, skilled-unskilled, 489-75
   differentials within an occupation,
      476-85
   earnings and cost of living, 414
      (*fig.*)
   eliminating substandard wages, 525-
      30
   employee compensation, per cent of
      national income, 455 (*fig.*)
   employment and, 432-35
   employment in the firm, 489 (*fig.*)
   escalator clauses, 250, 421
   family incomes, 510-13
   hours of work and, 408-9
   incentive systems, 217-24
   median incomes by occupation
      group, 464 (*table*)

Wages: (*cont.*)
  minimum wage legislation, 70, 525-30
  money wage level, 416-20
  movements of wage level, 413-20
  nature of wage policy, 495-501
  occupational rate curves, 507 (*fig.*)
  output and hourly earnings, 445 (*fig.*)
  at the plant level, 488-95
  poverty and, 519-25
  price level and, 247, 299-300, 420-32
  productivity and, 412-13, 444-46
  professional incomes and, 471-72
  reopening clauses, 249
  structure of, 254-60, 462-87
  take-home pay, 408-9
  union influence on, 240 (*fig.*)
Wagner Act, 119-22
Wagner-Peyser Act, 382
Walker, Kenneth, 294
War Manpower Commission, 383
Warner, W. Lloyd, 151
Waterfront Commission of N. Y. and N. J., 92, 98
Waterfront labor market, 350-51
Webb, Sidney, and Beatrice, 25, 53, 56, 67, 78, 254
Weber, Peter, 89-90
Weinberg, N., 231, 237
Welfare and Pension Plans Disclosure Act, 262

Welfare plans, 132, 262, 306, 535-37
West Coast Hotel Co. v. *Parrish*, 528
Westinghouse Corporation, 40, 166
White-collar workers, 50-51, 333-34
Whyte, William F., 158
Wilber, Arnold, 338
Wilcock, Richard C., 158, 328, 348
Williams, C. Arthur, Jr., 370
Williams, Constance, 376
Wilson, Thomas A., 419, 436
Wirtz, Willard, 285
Witte, Edwin E., 112, 140, 294
Wollett, Donald H., 133
Women in labor force, 325-27, 335, 484, 485
Work-sharing rules, 200-204
Work speeds, 216-24
Workweek, 210-16, 306-7, 545
World War I, 29, 211
World War II, 30, 59, 183, 213, 252, 280, 290, 328, 347, 383, 407, 416, 440, 515
Woytinsky, W. S., 321, 344, 370, 376, 391, 404
Wright, David McC., 265, 437

Yellow-dog contracts, 118
Young, Edwin, 158
Youngstown Sheet and Tube Company, 40